Classic Readings in Organizational Behavior

Classic Readings in Organizational Behavior

J. Steven Ott
University of Maine

Brooks/Cole Publishing Company
Pacific Grove, California

Brooks/Cole Publishing Company
A Division of Wadsworth, Inc.

Printed in the United States of America

10 9 8 7 6 5 4 3 2 1

Library of Congress Cataloging in Publication Data
Classic readings in organizational behavior / J. Steven Ott, editor.
    p.   cm.
  Includes bibliographies.
  ISBN 0-534-11073-8
   1. Organizational behavior. I. Ott, J. Steven.
HD58.7.C52   1989
658.3—dc19   88-7779
                        CIP

Preface

Classic Readings in Organizational Behavior has been designed to meet several purposes: (1) to be a stand-alone collection of the most important writings about organizational behavior, (2) to supplement any of several excellent college and graduate-level texts on the subject,[1] and (3) to fill a gap that was intentionally left in Shafritz and Ott's 2nd edition of *Classics of Organization Theory* (1987). As Shafritz and Ott explain in their *Introduction*, "[we] were faced with one particularly difficult decision: whether or not to include the human relations school of organization theory or, as it is often labeled, the field of organizational behavior." Our decision was made mostly on pragmatic grounds. The field of organizational behavior simply is too large to squeeze its most important works into a volume that incorporates pieces from all walks of organization theory. The decision to omit organizational behavior from *Classics of Organization Theory* was painful but necessary. We made a calculated decision to limit that volume to the macroperspective of organization theory—*how and why organizations behave as they do,* and to hold the microperspective of organizational behavior—*the way individuals behave in organizations,* for this volume.

Although the decision may have been painful at the time, it made decisions about this volume much easier. The unequivocal separation between the coverage of the two books eliminated all temptation to include favorite articles in both volumes, so there is no duplication. Second, there is no need to do more than this *Preface*'s very quick review of the other "schools" or "perspectives" of organization theory that have struggled through ascendancy, dominance, challenge by other schools, and gone into reluctant decline—the schools that intellectually and emotionally paved the way for and have followed organizational behavior. The reader is referred to Shafritz and Ott (1987) for more complete discussions and selected readings.

As the title, *Classic Readings in Organizational Behavior* implies, this book is a collection of *classics*. Although some important recent articles are included, no

---

[1]To cite just a few: Cohen, A. R., Fink, S. L., Gadon, H., & Willits, R. D. (1988). *Effective behavior in organizations* (4th ed.). Homewood, IL: Richard D. Irwin. Dunham, R. B. (1984). *Organizational behavior.* Homewood, IL: Richard D. Irwin. Hampton, D. R., Summer, C. E., & Webber, R. A. (1987). *Organizational behavior and the practice of management* (5th ed.). Glenview, IL: Scott, Foresman and Company. Organ, D. W., & Bateman, T. (1986). *Organizational behavior: An applied psychological approach* (3rd ed.). Plano, TX: Business Publications, Inc. Reitz, H. J. (1987). *Behavior in organizations* (3rd ed.). Homewood, IL: Richard D. Irwin.

attempt has been made to incorporate selections that reflect all of the recent trends and developments in the field. Current trends are not the purpose of this book. Rather, this collection presents the most enduring themes and works of organizational behavior, organized in a way that is conceptually sound, useful in practice, and allows the reader to track the historical development of the most important topics.

The older works have not been included simply because they are interesting relics—reminders of quaint but outdated thinking. Although organizational behavior has experienced marked growth and maturation over the decades, many of the *basics* remain the same. In fact, this is a field in which it sometimes feels as though the more we learn about the important things, the less we truly know. (For a good example, see Warren Bennis' lamentful 1976 piece which is reprinted in Chapter III, "Mortal Stakes: Where Have All the Leaders Gone?".) The laws of physics and gravity do not change with intellectual fashions or technological advances, nor do the basic psychological, cultural, or social characteristics of people. Just as those who would build spaceships have to start by studying Newton, those who would work with people in organizations must start with 1930s writers such as Mary Parker Follett and Chester I. Barnard. The future will always build upon what is enduring from the past. That is the rationale for this book—to provide those who seek to understand and/or to advance organization theory with a convenient place to find the essentials, indeed the classics, of organizational behavior's past. Once-dominant ideas and perspectives on organizations may lose the center stage, but they do not die. Their thinking influences subsequent writers, even those who may reject their basic assumptions and tenets. However old some of the articles may be, they are not dated. A classic *is* a classic because it continues to be of value to each new generation of students and practitioners.

Inherently, organizations are part of the society and the culture in which they are situated and operate. Human behavior—and thus organizational behavior—is heavily influenced by culturally rooted beliefs, values, assumptions, and behavioral norms affecting all aspects of organizational life. For this reason, a society's ways of thinking about how people behave in organizations do not develop in a vacuum. They reflect what is going on in the contemporary world of the time. Thus, contributions to organizational behavior vary by what was happening when and where, and in different cultures and subcultures. The advent of World War II, the American P.O.W.s who defected following the Korean war, the "flower child"/antiestablishment/self-development era of the 1960s, and the computer/information society of the 1970s, all substantially influenced the evolution of our thinking, our theories, and our research about people in organizations. In order to truly understand organizational behavior as it exists today, one must appreciate the historical contexts through which it developed and the cultural milieux during and in which important contributions were made to its body of knowledge. In order to help readers place writings in their historical contexts, A *Chronology of the Theoretical Developments in Organizational Behavior,* a review of the most important events and publications in the field, follows the *Introduction.*

CRITERIA FOR SELECTION

Several criteria were used to select these particular classics of organizational behavior for inclusion. The first was the answer to the question: "Should the serious student of organizational behavior be expected to be able to identify this author and his or her basic themes?" If the answer was yes, then it was so because such a contribution has long been, or is increasingly being recognized as, an important theme by a significant writer. While I expect to be criticized for excluding other articles and writers, it will be more difficult to honestly criticize my inclusions. The writers and pieces chosen are among the most widely quoted and reprinted by students and theorists in the field of organizational behavior. Some of the recent pieces had to be exceptions. I felt that it was important to include a light sprinkling of *potentially important* current articles along with the time-tested classics. Obviously, these newer articles have not been cited as extensively as those written twenty or thirty years earlier. Thus, more subjective judgments were required about their inclusion.

The second criterion is related to the first: Each article or chapter from a book had to make a basic statement that has been consistently echoed or attacked over the years. The selection had to be acknowledged as important—significant—in the sense that it must have been (or will become) an integral part of the foundation for the subsequent building of the field of organizational behavior.

The third criterion was that articles had to be readable. Fortunately, this was a relatively easy criterion to meet. Much of the literature on organizational behavior is easily understandable and interesting. However, some of the truly great works are of a length which, in my judgment, detracts from their major themes. Consequently, some articles have been shortened for this book, but the only editing has been "editing out": No sentences have been changed or added to the original.

ORGANIZATION OF THE BOOK

This book is structured around the most important topics in the field of organizational behavior. Then the readings within each topical chapter are organized chronologically. An author's choice of major topics and the sequence of their presentation reflects his or her conceptual framework of a field. Thus, the structure of a book in and of itself communicates the author's implicit perspective of the field, and this is no exception. The readings are grouped in six chapters that reflect the most pervasive themes in the literature of organizational behavior:

- Motivation;
- Group and intergroup relations;
- Leadership;
- The person-organization interface (the context of organizational behavior);
- Power and dependence; and
- Processes for creating organizational change (including the subfield of organization development [O.D.]).

The development of behavioral science theory tends to be cumulative, but almost never in a straight line. Sometimes the cumulative building of theory is accomplished through adoption of prior theorists' logic and research findings. In other instances, it is by trying unsuccessfully to use prior theorists' works, rejecting them, and veering off in a new exploratory direction. The chronological sequencing of readings within topics should allow the reader to track some of the important ebbs and flows of theory development over the decades. For those who are interested in a quick overview of the historical evolution of organizational behavior, a *Chronology* follows the *Introduction.*

ACKNOWLEDGMENTS

Many people have contributed valuable insights and assistance that have helped me write and assemble this book. I am always reluctant to list names in an acknowledgment, for any listing is bound to overlook some people who should be recognized, and a mere listing of names is entirely inadequate thanks. Nevertheless, there are some individuals who simply must be acknowledged. First and foremost is Jay Shafritz from the University of Pittsburgh, who is a part of this book in so many ways. Sam Overman and Dail Neugarten at the University of Colorado-Denver provided numerous ideas; G. Thomas Taylor at the University of Maine made resources available that truly helped in preparing the manuscript; Al Hyde, who recently moved from San Francisco State University to the University of Pittsburgh, provided inspiration and motivation; David Sullivan organized and wrote most of the introduction to the chapter on leadership; Alice Kaiser researched and wrote the *Chronology.* Those individuals kind enough to review this book include: Bruce H. Johnson, Gustavus Adolphus College; Carl J. Bellone, California State University, Hayward; Edward J. Conlon, University of Iowa; Andrew McNitt, Eastern Illinois University; and Susan J. B. Cox, University of North Carolina–Greensboro. Thanks also to Gregg Scott for his astute proofreading; and to Eva McLaughlin, Margaret Colman, and Kim Pelletier, who were almost magicians in managing the manuscript production.

J. Steven Ott

Contents

Chapter I
Motivation, 27

Chapter IV
People in Organizations: The Context, 356

Chapter V
Power and Influence, 420

Chapter VI
Organizational Change and Development, 510

Introduction

DEFINING ORGANIZATIONAL BEHAVIOR

Organizational behavior seeks to understand human behavior in organizational contexts. It examines the ways people cope with the problems and opportunities of organizational life. It asks questions such as:

- Why do people behave the way they do when they are in organizations?
- Under what circumstances will peoples' behavior in organizations change?
- What impacts do organizations have on the behavior of individuals, formal groups (such as departments), and informal groups (such as people from several departments who meet regularly in the company lunchroom)?
- Why do different groups in the same organization develop different behavioral norms?

Organizational behavior results from the many complex interactions that occur daily between humans, groups of humans, and the organizational environment in which they spend their workday. Therefore, in order to understand these interactions, it is first necessary to know something about:

- The behavior of people and groups in general;
- Organizations and organizational environments; and
- The behavior of people and groups when they are in organizations.

Organizational behavior has at least two very different meanings, and these differences are important. First, organizational behavior (or "OB") is the actual behavior of individuals and groups in and around purposeful organizations. It is the application of the theories, methods, and research findings of the behavioral sciences—particularly of psychology, social psychology, sociology, cultural anthropology, and to a lesser degree of economics and political science—to understanding the behavior of humans in organizations. However, understanding is not the sole goal of organizational behavior. OB practitioners apply knowledge, understanding, and techniques from the behavioral sciences in attempts to improve the functioning of organizations and to improve the fit between organizations' and their members' needs and wants.

Although behavioral scientists are interested in human behavior in any organization setting, their primary focus always has been on behavior in the work-

1

place—on employment-related organizational behavior. Organizational behavior is mostly about behavior in settings where there tend to be constraints on people; where there is an economic relationship between individuals and their organizations. People are not as free to establish and terminate employment relationships as they are other types of relationships with organizations. Usually there is a structured set of roles, a hierarchy of relations, and ongoing goal-related activities (although the goals may or may not be organizationally sanctioned).

Second, organizational behavior is one of several frameworks or *perspectives* on what makes an organization work. A perspective defines the organizational variables that are important enough to warrant the attention of managers and students of organizations. Perspectives identify what a person sees when looking at an organization and, therefore, almost prescribes what *levers* to use when trying to change or stabilize an organization. But, a perspective is more than a way of seeing and approaching an organization. It is also a set of bedrock beliefs and values about, for example, the basic purposes for organizations, their fundamental right to existence, the nature of their links to the surrounding environment, and—most important for organizational behavior—the whole of their relationships with the people who work in them.

Students and practitioners of management have always been interested in and concerned with the behavior of people in organizations. But, fundamental assumptions about the behavior of people at work did not change dramatically from the beginnings of humankind's attempts to organize until only a few decades ago. Using the traditional "the boss knows best" mind-set (set of assumptions), Hugo Münsterberg (1863–1916), the German-born psychologist whose later work at Harvard would earn him the title of "father" of industrial or applied psychology, pioneered the application of psychological findings from laboratory experiments to practical matters. He sought to match the abilities of new hires with a company's work demands, to positively influence employee attitudes toward their work and their company, and to understand the impact of psychological conditions on employee productivity (H. Münsterberg, 1913; M. Münsterberg, 1922). Münsterberg's approach characterized how the behavioral sciences tended to be applied in organizations well into the 1950s. During and following World War II, the armed services were particularly active in conducting and sponsoring research into how the military could best *find and shape people to fit its needs.* This theme or quest became known as *Industrial Psychology* and more recently as *industrial/organizational psychology* or *I/O psychology.*

In contrast to the Hugo Münsterberg-type perspective on organizational behavior, the 1960s and 1970s "modern breed" of applied behavioral scientists have focused their attention on seeking to answer questions such as how organizations could and should allow and encourage their people to grow and develop. From this perspective, it was *assumed* that organizational creativity, flexibility, and prosperity would flow naturally from employee growth and development. The essence of the relationship between organization and people was redefined from dependence to codependence. People were considered to be as or more important than the organization itself. The organizational behavior methods and techniques of the 1960s and 1970s could not have been used in Münsterberg's days, *because we didn't believe (assume) that codependence was the "right" relationship between an organization and its employees.* All of this is what is meant by a *perspective.*

Although practitioners and researchers have been interested in the behavior of people inside organizations for a very long time, it has only been since about 1957—when our basic assumptions about the relationship between organizations and people truly began to change—that the *organizational behavior perspective* came into being. Those who *see* organizations through the *lenses* of the organizational behavior perspective focus on people, groups, and relationships among them and the organizational environment. For example, when organizational behaviorists contemplate the introduction of a new technology, they will immediately start thinking about and planning:

- How to minimize fear of change by involving people at all levels in designing the introduction of the changes;
- How to minimize the negative impacts of the change on groups of workers (such as older, less-skilled, or younger);
- How to coopt informal leaders, especially those who might become antagonistic; and
- Alternatives for employees who do not see the changes being consistent with their personal goals.

Because the organizational behavior perspective places a very high value on humans as individuals, things typically are done very openly and honestly, providing employees with maximum amounts of accurate information, so they can make informed decisions with free will about their future (Argyris, 1970).

But there are other perspectives as well, each with its own assumptions, values, and *levers*—ways of approaching issues such as organizational change and stabilization (Shafritz & Ott, 1987). The systems perspective focuses on things such as an organization's information systems and its decision processes (Kast & Rosenzweig, 1970; Thompson, 1967); the structural perspective emphasizes things like the structural arrangement of the organization, the organization of work within the structure, and the procedures and rules that maintain order (Blau & Scott, 1962; Burns & Stalker, 1961; Mintzberg, 1979); and, the power perspective looks mostly at managing conflict, building, maintaining, and using coalitions, and the nature of real and perceived power relationships (Kotter, 1985; Pfeffer, 1981; Salancik & Pfeffer, 1977).

Thus, as a perspective of organization theory, organizational behavior is one of several ways of looking at and thinking about organizations (and people) which is defined by a set of basic assumptions about people, organizations, and the relationships, dynamics, and tensions between and among them. It is common to refer to this second use of the phrase, *organizational behavior* as the *human relations* or *human resources school, perspective,* or *frame* of organization theory. In order to distinguish clearly between the two meanings and thus to avoid confusion, the phrase, *organizational behavior* is used throughout this book to mean *the behavior of individuals and groups in and around purposeful organizations.* To differentiate, the phrase *organizational behavior perspective,* or *human relations perspective,* refers to the school or perspective of organization theory that reflects basic managerial assumptions about employees similar to those of Theory X and Theory Y, as articulated by Douglas McGregor. (See Chapter I, *Motivation.*)

Organizational behavior is solidly grounded in theory and in empirical research. It uses applications of theory, methods, and findings about the behavior of people and groups in general, about social organizations, and about people in purposeful social organizations, adapted from long-established behavioral science disciplines. No other perspective of organizations has ever had such a wealth of research findings and methods at its disposal.

It is difficult to draw a clear distinction between what behavior is and is not *organizational,* since out-of-organizational behavior lives affect behavior in organizations and vice versa. In general, however, behavior is considered organizational if something associated with the organization causes or enhances the behavior, the behavior results from an organizational activity or function, or organizational meaning is attached to the behavior.

Assumptions about human behavior are crucial for understanding how managers and workers interact in organizations. Each perspective on organizations has its own fundamental tenets or assumptions which are very different. The tenets of the "modern" structural perspective and the organizational behavior perspective (as they are articulated by Bolman and Deal, 1984[1]) are presented side-by-side in Table 1—to emphasize the differences and to highlight how the differences cause these two schools to differ with respect to almost everything!

Assumptions are more than beliefs or values: They are givens or truths that are held so strongly that they are no longer questioned nor even consciously thought about. They are the foundation and the justification (Sathe, 1985) for the perspective's beliefs, truths, values, and ways of doing things.

The assumptions of the Münsterberg-early I/O psychology perspective continued well into the 1950s. It was assumed that people should be fit to the organization: The organization had set needs to be filled. Thus, during the "classical era" of organization theory—from the late 1800s through the 1940s—the organizational role of the applied behavioral sciences largely consisted of helping organizations find and shape people to serve as *replacement parts* for *organizational machines.* The dominant theorists of organizations during these years were people such as Frederick Winslow Taylor (1911) and his disciples in *scientific management,* and Max Weber (1922), the brilliant theorist of *bureaucracy* (Shafritz & Ott, 1987).

Although the Münsterberg-I/O psychology theme provided important early background for organizational behavior, its more important direct genealogy lies in social psychology. The one most significant set of events that led to a conscious field of organizational behavior was the multiyear work done by the Elton Mayo team at the Hawthorne plant of the Western Electric Company beginning in 1927 (Mayo, 1933; Roethlisberger & Dixon, 1939). Three other significant threads or

TABLE 1 • TENETS OF THE "MODERN" STRUCTURAL PERSPECTIVE AND THE ORGANIZATIONAL BEHAVIOR PERSPECTIVE SIDE-BY-SIDE FOR COMPARISON

"Modern" Structural School	Organizational Behavior Perspective
1. Organizations are rational institutions whose primary purpose is to accomplish established objectives; rational organizational behavior is achieved best through systems of defined rules and formal authority. Organizational control and coordination are key to maintaining organizational rationality.	1. Organizations exist to serve human needs. Humans do not exist to serve organizational needs.
2. There is a "best" structure for any organization in light of its given objectives, the environmental conditions surrounding it, the nature of its products and/or services, and the technology of the production processes.	2. Organizations and people need each other. Organizations need the ideas, energy, and talent that people provide, while people need the careers, salaries, and work opportunities that organizations provide.
3. Specialization and the division of labor increase the quality and quantity of production—particularly in highly skilled operations and professions.	3. When the fit between the individual and the organization is poor, one or both will suffer. The individual will be exploited or will seek to exploit the organization or both.
4. Most problems in an organization result from structural flaws and can be solved by changing the structure (pp. 31–32)	4. When the fit is good between the individual and the organization, both benefit. Humans are able to do meaningful and satisfying work while providing the resources the organization needs to accomplish its mission (p. 65).

Adapted from: Lee G. Bolman and Terrence E. Deal (1984). *Modern Approaches to Understanding and Managing Organizations.* San Francisco: Jossey-Bass.

forces also accounted for a great deal of the direction of industrial social psychology research and practice into the 1950s (Haire, 1954):

1. The late 1930s contributions by Kurt Lewin in group dynamics, with important contributions by Lippitt and White (group climate and leadership) and Bavelas (leadership as a group problem);

2. Jacob Moreno's work on sociometry (the network of relations among people in a group) and sociodrama (role playing); and

3. The rapid rise of industry and government willingness to ask social psychologists for help during World War II. This trend was a start toward establishing a role for social scientist *(process)* consultants that differed substantially from *content consultants.*

During these early years, industrial social psychology differed quite markedly from I/O psychology in its interests and premises. Whereas I/O psychology was busily engaged in trying to solve organizational problems (for example, selecting people to fit into positions), industrial social psychology developed an early concern for creating a psychological—rather than an institutional or technical—definition of the work setting. In this arena, the Hawthorne studies of Mayo and his collaborators were extraordinary contributions.

Once again, the difference between the I/O psychology approach and the work of Mayo, Roethlisberger, and their associates at the Hawthorne plant, lay in their *assumptions*. The I/O psychologists adopted the assumptions of classical organization theory and shaped their field to fit its tenets. Those assumptions are:

1. Organizations exist to accomplish production-related and economic goals.
2. There is one best way to organize for production, and that way can be found through systematic, scientific inquiry. (In this instance, systematic, scientific, *psychological* inquiry.)
3. Production is maximized through specialization and division of labor.
4. People and organizations act in accordance with rational economic principles.

It is important to note that the Mayo team—like the I/O psychology groups—began its work trying to fit into the mold of classical organization theory thinking. The team phrased its questions in the language and concepts industry was accustomed to using, to see and explain problems such as: productivity in relationship to such factors as the amount of light, the rate of flow of materials, and alternative wage payment plans. The Mayo team succeeded in making significant breakthroughs in understanding only after it redefined the Hawthorne problems as social psychological problems—problems conceptualized in such terms as interpersonal relations in groups, group norms, control over one's own environment, and personal recognition. It was only after the Mayo team achieved this breakthrough that it became the "grandfather"—the direct precursor—of the field of organizational behavior and of the human relations perspective of organization theory. The Hawthorne studies laid the foundation for a set of assumptions that would be fully articulated and would displace the assumptions of classical organization theory 20 years later.

Despite their later start, the industrial social psychologists were years ahead of the industrial psychologists in understanding that behavior in organizations could not be understood nor controlled by viewing behavior solely as an organizational phenomenon or solely from an organizational vantage point. The organization is not the independent variable to be manipulated in order to change behavior (as a dependent variable)—even though organizations pay employees to help them achieve organizational goals. Instead, the organization must be seen as the context in which behavior occurs. It is both an independent and a dependent variable. The organization influences human behavior just as behavior shapes the organization. The interactions shape conceptualizations of jobs, human communication and interaction in work groups, the impacts of participation in decisions about one's own work, roles (in general), and the roles of leaders.

Between 1957 and 1960, the organizational behavior perspective literally exploded onto the organization scene. On April 9, 1957, Douglas M. McGregor delivered the Fifth Anniversary Convocation address to the School of Industrial Management at the Massachusetts Institute of Technology. He titled his address, "The Human Side of Enterprise." Three years later, McGregor expanded his talk into what has become one of the most influential books on organizational behavior and organization theory. In *The Human Side of Enterprise,* McGregor articulated how managerial assumptions about employees become self-fulfilling prophesies. He labeled his two sets of contrasting assumptions *Theory X* and *Theory Y,* but they are more than just theories. McGregor had articulated the basic assumptions of the organizational behavior perspective.

The organizational behavior perspective is the most optimistic of all perspectives of organization. Building from Douglas McGregor's Theory X and Theory Y assumptions, organizational behavior has assumed that under the right circumstances, people and organizations will grow and prosper together. The ultimate worth of people is an overarching value of the human relations movement—a worthy end in-and-of-itself—not simply a means or process for achieving a higher-order organizational end. Individuals and organizations are not necessarily antagonists. Managers can learn to unleash previously stifled energies and creativities. The beliefs, values, and tenets of organizational behavior are noble, uplifting, and exciting. They hold a promise for humankind, especially those who will spend their lifetime working in organizations.

As one would expect of a very optimistic and humanistic set of assumptions and values, they (and the strategies of organizational behavior) became strongly normative (prescriptive). For many organizational behavior practitioners of the 1960s and 1970s, the perspective's assumptions and methods became a cause. Hopefully, through the choice of articles and the introductions to each chapter, this volume communicates these optimistic tenets and values, and articulates the logical and emotional reasons why the organizational behavior perspective developed into a virtual movement. This is the true essence of *organizational behavior.*

CHAPTER NOTE

1. Bolman and Deal (1984) use the labels, "Human Resources Frame" and "Systems and Structural Frame."

REFERENCES

Allport, G. W. (1954). The historical background of modern social psychology. In, G. Lindzey (Ed.), *Handbook of social psychology: Volume II: Special fields and applications* (pp. 3–56). Reading, MA: Addison-Wesley Publishing Co.

Argyris, C. (1970). *Intervention theory and method.* Reading, MA: Addison-Wesley Publishing Co.

Bell, D. (1956). *Work and its discontents.* Boston: Beacon Press.

Bennis, W. G. (1976). *The unconscious conspiracy: Why leaders can't lead.* New York: AMACOM.

Berelson, B., & Steiner, G. A. (1964). *Human behavior: An inventory of scientific findings.* New York: Harcourt, Brace & World.

Blau, P. M., & Scott, W. R. (1962). *Formal organizations: A comparative approach.* San Francisco: Chandler Publishing.

Bolman, L. G., & Deal, T. E. (1984). *Modern approaches to understanding and managing organizations.* San Francisco: Jossey-Bass.

Burns, T., & Stalker, G. M. (1961). *The management of innovation.* London, UK: Tavistock Publications.

Cohen, A. R., Fink, S. L., Gadon, H., & Willits, R. D. (1984). *Effective behavior in organizations* (3d ed.). Homewood, IL: Richard D. Irwin.

Dunham, R. B. (1984). *Organizational behavior.* Homewood, IL: Richard D. Irwin.

Gantt, H. L. (1908). Training workmen in habits of industry and cooperation. Paper presented to the American Society of Mechanical Engineers.

George, C. S., Jr. (1972). *The history of management thought* (2d ed.). Englewood Cliffs, NJ: Prentice-Hall, Inc.

Haire, M. (1954). Industrial social psychology. In, G. Lindzey (Ed.), *Handbook of social psychology: Volume II: Special fields and applications* (pp. 1104–1123). Reading, MA: Addison-Wesley Publishing Company.

Hampton, D. R., Summer, C. E., & Webber, R. A. (1987). *Organizational behavior and the practice of management* (5th ed.). Glenview, IL: Scott, Foresman and Company.

Hersey, P., & Blanchard, K. H. (1982). *Management of organizational behavior: Utilizing human resources* (4th ed.). Englewood Cliffs, NJ: Prentice-Hall.

Kast, F. E., & Rosenzweig, J. E. (1970). *Organization and management: A systems approach.* New York: McGraw-Hill.

Kotter, J. P. (1985). *Power and influence: Beyond formal authority.* New York: Free Press.

Kuhn, T. S. (1970). *The structure of scientific revolutions* (2d ed., enlarged). Chicago: University of Chicago Press.

Lewin, K. (1947). Frontiers in group dynamics: Concept, method and reality in social science: Social equilibrium and social change. *Human Relations, 1,* 5–41.

Lewin, K. (1948). *Resolving social conflicts.* New York: Harper.

Luthans, F. (1972). *Contemporary readings in organizational behavior.* New York: McGraw-Hill.

Mayo, G. E. (1933). *The human problems of an industrial civilization.* Boston, MA: Harvard Business School, Division of Research.

McGregor, D. M. (1957, April). The human side of enterprise. Address to the Fifth Anniversary Convocation of the School of Industrial Management, Massachusetts Institute of Technology. In, *Adventure in thought and action.* Cambridge, Mass.: M.I.T. School of Industrial Management, 1957. Reprinted in W. G. Bennis, E. H. Schein, & C. McGregor (eds.), *Leadership and motivation: Essays of Douglas McGregor* (pp. 3–20). Cambridge, MA: The M.I.T. Press.

McGregor, D. M. (1960). *The human side of enterprise.* New York: McGraw-Hill.

Mintzberg, H. (1979). *The Structuring of Organizations.* Englewood Cliffs, NJ: Prentice-Hall.

Münsterberg, H. (1913). *Psychology and industrial efficiency.* Boston: Houghton Mifflin Company.

Münsterberg, M. (1922). *Hugo Münsterberg, his life and work.* New York: D. Appleton and Company.

Organ, D. W., & Bateman, T. (1986). *Organizational behavior: An applied psychological approach* (3d ed.). Plano, TX: Business Publications, Inc.

Pfeffer, J. (1981). *Power in organizations.* Boston: Pitman Publishing.

Reitz, H. J. (1987). *Behavior in organizations* (3d ed.). Homewood, IL: Richard D. Irwin.

Roethlisberger, F. J., & Dixon, W. J. (1939). *Management and the worker.* Cambridge, MA: Harvard University Press.

Salancik, G. R., & Pfeffer, J. (1977). Who gets power—and how they hold on to it: A strategic-contingency model of power. *Organizational Dynamics, 5,* 2–21.

Sathe, V. (1985). *Culture and related corporate realities.* Homewood, IL: Richard D. Irwin.

Shafritz, J.M., & Ott, J. S. (1987). *Classics of organization theory* (2d ed., revised and expanded). Chicago: The Dorsey Press.

Taylor, F. W. (1911). *The principles of scientific management.* New York: W. W. Norton.

Thompson, J. D. (1967). *Organizations in action.* New York: McGraw-Hill.

Weber, M. (1922). Bureaucracy. In H. Gerth & C. W. Mills (Eds.), *Max Weber: Essays in sociology.* Oxford, UK: Oxford University Press.

Wilson, J. A. (1951). *The culture of ancient Egypt.* Chicago: University of Chicago Press.

Wren, D. A. (1972). *The evolution of management thought.* New York: Ronald Press.

A CHRONOLOGY OF THE THEORETICAL DEVELOPMENTS
IN ORGANIZATIONAL BEHAVIOR*

2100 B.C.   Hammurabi, King of Babylon, establishes a written code of 282 laws which control every aspect of Babylonian life including individual behavior, interpersonal relations, and other societal matters. This may have been the first employee policy handbook.

1750 B.C.   Ancient Egyptians assign ten workers to each supervisor while building the pyramids. This may have been the earliest recorded use of the span of control concept.

1491 B.C.   During the exodus from Egypt, Jethro, the father-in-law of Moses, urges Moses to delegate authority over the tribes of Israel along hierarchical lines.

525 B.C.   Confucius writes that obedience to the organization (government) is the most "respectable goal of citizenship." This becomes the basic justification for authority systems.

425 B.C.   Socrates suggests that organizations as entities are basically alike, though their purposes and functions might vary. In his explanation to Nicomachides, he hints at "generic management" principles.

370 B.C.   In his description of an ancient Greek shoe factory, Xenophon explains the benefits of division of labor: "He who devotes himself to a very highly specialized line of work is bound to do it in the best possible manner."

350 B.C.   In *Politics,* Aristotle develops foundations for many modern management concepts, including specialization of labor, delegation of authority, departmentalization, decentralization, and leadership selection.

1200   Medieval European guilds function as quality circles to ensure fine craftsmanship.

1450   Johann Gutenburg's invention of movable type begins the "information explosion" by making dissemination of information quicker, more accurate, and less expensive.

1490   John Calvin, Protestant religious reformer, promotes the merit system by promising a reward "of eternal life in His (God's) kingdom to the faithful who do God's work."

The Puritan movement champions the concepts of time management, duty to work, and motivation theories; wasting time is considered the "deadliest of sins."

*By Alice E. Kaiser, Graduate School of Public and International Affairs, University of Pittsburgh.

1527 Machiavelli's *The Prince* offers managers practical advice for developing authoritarian structures within organizations. His justification is that "all men are bad and ever ready to display their vicious nature."

1651 In his essay, *Leviathan,* Thomas Hobbes advocates strong centralized leadership as a means of bringing "order to the chaos created by man." He provides a justification for autocratic rule, thereby establishing the pattern for organizations through the nineteenth century.

1690 In his *Two Treatises of Government,* John Locke provides the philosophical framework for the justification of the U.S. Declaration of Independence. In effect, John Locke advocates participatory management when he argues that leadership is granted by the governed.

1762 Jean Jacques Rousseau in *The Social Contract* postulates that governments work best when they are chosen and controlled by the governed. This concept furthers the idea of participatory management.

1776 Adam Smith in *The Wealth of Nations* revolutionizes economic and organizational thought by suggesting the use of centralization of labor and equipment in factories, division of specialized labor, and management of specialization in factories.

1800 In Britain, the Roebuck and Garrett Company seeks to maintain organizational harmony by putting factories only in locations where workers are perceived to be "reliable, loyal, and controllable."

1811 The Luddites, workers in English textile mills, seek to destroy new textile machinery that is displacing them. This is an early example of management's need to plan for organizational change.

1813 In his "Address to the Superintendents of Manufactures," Robert Owens encourages managers to provide their *vital machines* (employees) with as much attention as they do their *inanimate machines.*

1832 In the first managerial textbooks, *The Carding and Spinning of Masters' Assistant* and *The Cotton Spinners' Manual,* James Montgomery promotes the control function of management: Managers must be "just and impartial, firm and decisive, and always alert to prevent rather than check employee faults."

1881 Joseph Wharton donates $100,000 to the University of Pennsylvania to begin the first school of professional management in the United States; the school was called the Wharton School.

1883 Frederick W. Taylor begins experiments in Midvale and Bethlehem Steel plants which eventually lead to his concepts of *scientific management.*

1902 Vilfredo Pareto becomes the "father" of the concept of *social systems*; his societal notions would later be applied by Elton Mayo and the human relationists in an organizational context.

1903   In Frederick W. Taylor's book, *Shop Management,* he explains the role of management in motivating workers to avoid "natural soldiering," the natural tendency of people to "take it easy."

1909   Hugo Münsterberg, considered the "father of organizational psychology," writes "The Market and Psychology," in which he cautions managers to be concerned with "all the questions of the mind . . . like fatigue, monotony, interest, learning, work satisfaction, and rewards." He is the first to encourage government funded research in the area of industrial psychology.

1911   Frederick W. Taylor's book, *The Principles of Scientific Management,* investigates the influence of salary, mechanical design, and work layout on individual job performance to discover the "one best way" of accomplishing a given task.

Walter D. Scott's series of articles, "The Psychology of Business," published in *System Magazine* are some of the first to apply principles of psychology to motivation and productivity in the workplace.

1912   Edward Cadbury, using his chocolate factories as a laboratory, pioneers the field of industrial psychology with his book, *Experiments in Industrial Organization.*

1913   Hugo Münsterberg's book, *Psychology and Industrial Efficiency,* addresses personnel selection, equipment design, product packaging, and other concerns in an attempt to match the "best man" with the "best work" in order to get the "best possible effect."

Lillian M. Gilbreth's "The Psychology of Management," published in *Industrial Engineering Magazine,* becomes one of the earliest contributions to the understanding of human behavior in the industrial setting.

1914   *Political Parties,* the result of Robert Michels's study of labor unions in prewar Europe, formulates his iron law of oligarchy: "Who says organization, says oligarchy."

1918   *Hiring The Worker* by Roy Kelley is the first book to discuss job descriptions; application forms; job specification; interviews; use of medical examinations in hiring; and procedures for training, placement, transfers, promotions, and discharges.

1920   At Columbia University, Ordway Tead teaches the first personnel administration course in the United States.

1924   As a joint project, the National Research Council, Massachusetts Institute of Technology (MIT), and Harvard University begin their investigations of group behavior and worker sentiments at the Hawthorne works of the Western Electric Company in Chicago.

Elton Mayo explains in "The Basis of Industrial Psychology," published by the *Bulletin of the Taylor Society,* that short work breaks improve worker motivation and decrease employee turnover rates; this notion supports the importance of *social environment* in the workplace.

1926 Mary Parker Follett's chapter, "The Giving of Orders," is one of the very first calls for the use of a participatory leadership style, in which employees and employers cooperate to assess the situation and collaboratively decide what should be done.

1933 Elton Mayo makes the first significant call for the human relations movement in his Hawthorne studies interim report entitled, *The Human Problems of an Industrial Civilization.*

1937 The American Association for Applied Psychology is organized to study industrial and organizational psychology.

Luther Gulick's "Notes on the Theory of Organization" summarizes the seven functional elements of the work of an executive in his mnemonic expression, POSDCORB; these include planning, organizing, staffing, directing, coordinating, reporting, and budgeting.

Walter C. Langer publishes his book, *Psychology and Human Living,* in which he provides the first significant discussion of human needs, repression, and integration of personality, and their application to the workplace.

1938 *Functions of the Executive,* by Chester I. Barnard, suggests that the purpose of a manager is to balance organizational and workers' needs. This encourages and foreshadows the postwar revolution in thinking about organizational behavior.

1939 Kurt Lewin, Ronald Lippett, and Ralph K. White's article, "Patterns of Aggressive Behavior in Experimentally Created Social Climates," published in the *Journal of Social Psychology,* is the first empirical study of the effects of various leadership styles. Their work becomes the basis of the popularity of participative management techniques.

F. J. Roethlisberger and W. J. Dickson publish *Management and the Worker,* the definitive account of the Hawthorne studies.

1940 Robert K. Merton's *Social Forces* article, "Bureaucratic Structure and Personality," explains how bureaucratic structures exert pressures on people to conform to patterns of obligations, and eventually cause people to adhere to rules as a matter of blind conformance.

1942 Carl Rogers's *Counseling and Psychotherapy* offers human relations training as a method to overcome communication barriers and enhance interpersonal skills. These techniques lead to "control through leadership rather than force."

1943 Abraham Maslow's *needs hierarchy* first appears in his *Psychological Review* article, "A Theory of Human Motivation."

1945 Kurt Lewin forms the Research Center for Group Dynamics at MIT to perform experiments in group behavior. In 1948, Lewin's research center moves to the University of Michigan and becomes a branch of the Institute for Social Research.

1946 Rensis Likert develops the Institute for Social Research at the University of Michigan to conduct studies in the social sciences.

1947 The National Training Laboratory for Group Development, the predecessor to the National Training Laboratory Institute for Applied Behavioral Science, is established in Bethel, Maine, to conduct experimentation and training in group behavior.

1948 In their *Human Relations* article, "Overcoming Resistance to Change," Lester Coch and John R. P. French, Jr., note that employees resist change less when the need for it is effectively communicated to them and when the workers are involved in planning the changes.

Kenneth D. Benne and Paul Sheats's article, "Functional Role of Group Members," published in *Journal of Social Issues*, identifies three group role categories: *group task; group building and maintenance;* and *nonparticipatory.* These become the basis for future leadership research and training programs.

1949 In his *Public Administration Review* article, "Power and Administration," Norton E. Long finds that power is the lifeblood of administration, and that managers have to do more than simply apply the scientific method to problems—they have to attain, maintain, and increase their power, or risk failing in their mission.

The term *behavioral sciences* is first put into use by the Ford Foundation to describe its funding for interdisciplinary research in the social sciences; and is later adopted by a group of University of Chicago scientists seeking such funding.

1950 Ralph M. Stogdill in his *Psychological Bulletin* article, "Leadership, Membership, and Organization," identifies the importance of the leader's role in influencing group efforts toward goal setting and goal achievement. His ideas become the basis for modern leadership research.

1951 Alex Bavelas and Dermot Barrett's article, "An Experimental Approach to Organizational Communication," appearing in *Personnel*, recognizes that the effectiveness of an organization is based on the availability of information and that communication is "the basic process out of which all other functions derive."

Eric L. Trist and K. W. Bamforth's pioneering sociotechnical systems study of British miners, "Some Social and Psychological Consequences of the Longwall Method of Coal-getting," demonstrates that the introduction of new structural and technological systems can destroy important social systems.

"Effects of Group Pressure upon the Modification and Distortion of Judgments," by Solomon Asch, describes his experiments showing that a sizable minority of subjects alter their judgment to match that of the majority, even when the facts clearly demonstrate the majority is wrong.

Kurt Lewin proposes a general model of change consisting of three phases, *unfreezing, change,* and *refreezing,* in his *Field Theory in Social Science.* This model becomes the conceptual frame for organization development.

Ludwig von Bertalanffy's article, "General Systems Theory: A New Approach to the Utility of Science," is published in *Human Biology.* This becomes the intellectual foundation for the systems approach to organizational thinking.

1953 Dorwin Cartwright's address to the Society for the Psychological Study of Social Issues, titled "Power: A Neglected Variable in Social Psychology," identifies leadership and social roles, public opinion, rumor, propaganda, prejudice, attitude change, morale, communications, race relations, and conflicts of value, as leading social issues which cannot be understood except through the concept of power.

1954 *The Practice of Management,* written by Peter F. Drucker, outlines his famous *management by objectives* (MBO) approach; a way that management might give "full scope to individual strength and responsibility, and at the same time give direction of vision and effort, establish teamwork, and harmonize the goals of the individual."

Bernard M. Bass's *Psychological Bulletin* article, "The Leaderless Group Discussion," identifies a leadership training program in which a leader is not selected but rather emerges from the group's task.

In their *American Sociological Review* article, "Some Findings Relevant to the Great Man Theory of Leadership," Edgar F. Borgatta, Robert F. Bales, and Authur S. Couch promote the concept of leader assessment centers as a way to recognize individual leadership ability.

John C. Flanagan's work, "The Critical Incident Technique," published in *Psychological Bulletin,* seeks to evaluate job performance against a predetermined list of incidents recognized as essential to satisfactorily doing the task.

1955 Arthur H. Brayfield and Walter H. Crockett's *Psychological Bulletin* article,

"Employee Attitudes and Employee Performance," claims that there is no direct influence of job satisfaction on worker performance; in other words, a happy worker is not necessarily a better worker.

The Organization Man by William H. Whyte, Jr., describes empirical findings about individuals who accept organizational values and find harmony in conforming to all policies.

In the premier issue of *Administrative Science Quarterly*, Talcott Parsons's article, "Suggestions for a Sociological Approach to the Theory of Organizations," defines an organization as a social system that focuses on the attainment of specific goals and contributes, in turn, to the accomplishment of goals of the larger organization or society itself.

1957   Chris Argyris asserts in his first major book, *Personality and Organization*, that there is an inherent conflict between the personality of a mature adult and the needs of modern organizations.

Keith Davis's work, *Human Relations In Business*, offers human relations skills as a means to motivate people to work together "productively, cooperatively, and with economic, psychological, and social satisfaction."

Philip Selznick in *Leadership in Administration* anticipates many of the 1980s notions of *transformational leadership* when he asserts that the function of an institutional leader is to help shape the environment in which the institution operates and to define new institutional directions through recruitment, training, and bargaining.

The first organization development (OD) program is designed by Herbert Shepard and Robert Blake, and is implemented at (Esso) Standard Oil Company.

On April 9, Douglas M. McGregor delivers the Fifth Anniversary Convocation address to the School of Industrial Management at the Massachusetts Institute of Technology. His address, "The Human Side of Enterprise," was expanded into a book by the same title in 1960.

Leon Festinger's *A Theory of Cognitive Dissonance* suggests that dissonance is a motivator of human behavior.

Alvin W. Gouldner's *Administrative Science Quarterly* study, "Cosmopolitans and Locals: Toward an Analysis of Latent Social Roles," finds that people with different role orientations differ in their degree of influenceability, level of participation in the organization, willingness to accept organizational rules, and informal relations at work.

1958   Robert Tannenbaum and Warren H. Schmidt's *Harvard Business Review* article, "How to Choose a Leadership Pattern," describes "democratic management" and devises a leadership continuum ranging from authoritarian to democratic.

Organizations by James G. March and Herbert Simon provides an overview of the behavioral sciences' influence in organization theory.

Leon Festinger, the father of cognitive dissonance theory, writes "The Motivating Effect of Cognitive Dissonance," which becomes the theoretical foundation for the "inequity theories of motivation."

1959   John R. P. French and Bertram Raven identify five bases of power (expert, referent, reward, legitimate, and coercive) in their article, "The Bases of Social Power." They argue that managers should not rely on coercive and expert power bases, since they are least effective.

Herzberg, Mausner, and Snyderman's *The Motivation to Work* puts forth the motivation-hygiene theory of worker motivation.

Robert Gordon and James Howell in their book, *Higher Education In Business,* emphasize the importance of the behavioral sciences when they call for more behavioral science courses in business school curricula.

In *Modern Organizational Theory,* Cyert and March prepare a chapter, "A Behavioral Theory of Organizational Objectives," which postulates that power and politics impact on the formation of organizational goals. Their work is an early precursor of the power and politics school.

1960   Herbert Kaufman's *The Forest Ranger* describes how employee conformity can be increased through organizational and professional socialization efforts.

Donald F. Roy's *Human Organization* study, "Banana Time: Job Satisfaction and Informal Interaction," finds that workers in monotonous jobs survive psychologically through informal interaction; they keep from "going nuts" by talking and fooling around in a nonstop, highly stylized, and ritualistic manner.

Douglas M. McGregor's book, *The Human Side of Enterprise,* articulates the basic assumptions of the organizational behavior perspective and becomes perhaps the single most influential work in organizational behavior and organizational theory.

1961   Harold Koontz explains in his *Academy of Management Journal* article, "The Management Theory Jungle," that the major schools of management thought are "semantic jungles" filled with jargon.

Victor A. Thompson's *Modern Organizations* indicates that bureaucratic dysfunction is a result of "an imbalance between ability and authority."

Burns and Stalker's *The Management of Innovation* advocates a contingency model of leadership when it articulates the need for different types of management systems (organic and mechanistic) under differing circumstances.

Rensis Likert's *New Patterns of Management* offers an empirically based defense of participatory management and organization development techniques.

According to Amatai Etzioni's *A Comparative Analysis of Complex Organizations*, an organization is more effective when its goal and compliance structures are compatible.

1962 In his *Administrative Science Quarterly* article, "Control In Organizations: Individual Adjustment and Organizational Performance," Arnold S. Tannenbaum explains that distributing control more broadly within the organization helps to encourage involvement and adherence to the group norms by its members.

Robert Kahn and Daniel Katz report their findings on the supervisor's role, the closeness of supervision, the quality of supportiveness, and the amount of group cohesiveness on the productivity and level of morale of organizational groups, in "Leadership Practices in Relation to Productivity and Morale."

In "The Concept of Power and the Concept of Man," Mason Haire traces the change in the ultimate sources of organizational authority from the state to organizational ownership, and forecasts an eventual shift to the authority of the work group.

Robert Presthus's work, *The Organizational Society*, presents his threefold classification of patterns of organizational accommodations: *upward-mobiles*, those who accept goals and values of the organization as their own; *indifferents*, those who reject organizational values and seek personal satisfaction off the job; and *ambivalents*, those unable to cope with organizational demands but still desire its rewards.

Blau and Scott write *Formal Organizations: A Comparative Approach*, in which they argue that all organizations have both an informal and formal structure, and that one cannot understand formal structure without first understanding the informal workings of an organization.

1963 March and Cyert's *A Behavioral Theory of the Firm* asserts that most decisions within organizations are multi-individual (organizational) decisions rather than "entrepreneurial."

1964 Herbert Simon's *Administrative Science Quarterly* article, "On The Concept of Organizational Goals," suggests that individual organizational goals may not necessarily be the determiner of organizational decision making; rather, organizational goals are the "actions that satisfy a whole set of constraints."

Considered the father of Transactional Analysis (TA), Eric Berne in his book, *Games People Play: The Psychology of Human Relationships* identifies three *ego states:* the *parent,* the *adult,* and the *child;* he further suggests that successful managers should strive for adult-adult relationships.

The Managerial Grid: Key Orientations for Achieving Production Through People, by Robert Blake and Jane Mouton, is a diagnostic device for leadership development programs which provides a *grid* of leadership style possibilities based on managerial assumptions about people and production.

1965 Robert L. Kahn's *Organizational Stress* is the first major study of the mental health consequences of organizational role conflict and ambiguity.

James G. March prepares *Handbook of Organizations,* a series of essays which attempts to consolidate all scientific knowledge about organizations and organizational behavior.

1966 *Think Magazine* publishes David C. McClelland's article, "That Urge to Achieve," in which he identifies two groups of people: the majority of whom aren't concerned about achieving, the minority who are challenged by the opportunity to achieve. This notion becomes a premise for future motivation studies.

The Social Psychology of Organizations by Daniel Katz and Robert L. Kahn seeks to unify the findings of behavioral science on organizational behavior through open systems theory.

Fred Fiedler, in "The Contingency Model: A Theory of Leadership Effectiveness," argues that organizations should not try to change leaders to fit them, but instead should change their situations to mesh with the style of their leaders.

In "Applying Behavioral Sciences to Planned Organizational Change," a chapter from his book, *Changing Organizations,* Warren Bennis describes planned change as a link between theory and practice and as a deliberate and collaborative process involving change agents and client-systems who are brought together to solve a problem.

1967 The *Personnel Administration* article, "Organizations of the Future," by Warren Bennis states that bureaucracy will disappear due to rapid and unexpected change, unprecedented growth in organizational size, increasing complexity in modern technology, and philosophical changes in managerial controls and behaviors.

In "Patterns of Organization Change," appearing in *Harvard Business Review,* Larry E. Greiner calls for organizational changes to be less based on management intuition and more frequently determined by empirical studies.

In their *Personnel Administration* article, "Grid Organization Development," Robert A. Blake and Jane S. Mouton explain that organizational goals determine managers' actions; they offer an innovative, systematic approach to "organizational development."

Fred E. Fiedler publishes his work, *A Theory of Leadership Effectiveness,* which proposes that leadership style must fit the circumstances; there is no one best way to perform leadership tasks.

Norman Maier in his *Psychological Review* article, "Assets and Liabilities in Group Problem-Solving," explains that the benefits of group versus individual problem-solving depends on the "nature of the problem, the goals to be achieved, and the skill of the discussion leader."

Anthony Downs's *Inside Bureaucracy* seeks to develop laws and propositions that would aid in predicting the behavior of bureaus and bureaucrats.

William G. Scott's *Organization Theory: A Behavioral Analysis for Management* suggests that an "individual's opportunity for self-realization at work" can be actualized by applying "industrial humanism" concepts such as reducing authoritarian tendencies in organizations, encouraging participatory decision making on all levels, and integrating individual and corporate goals.

Anthony Jay's *Management and Machiavelli* applies Machiavelli's political principles (from *The Prince*) to modern organizational management.

1968 In *Group Dynamics,* Dorwin Cartwright and Alvin Zander propose that the systematic study of group dynamics would advance knowledge of the nature of groups; how they are organized; and relationships among individuals, other groups, and larger institutions.

John P. Campbell and M. D. Dunnette's "Effectiveness of T-Group Experiences in Managerial Training and Development," appearing in *Psychological Bulletin,* provides a critical review of T-Group literature. They conclude that "an individual's positive feelings about his T-Group experiences" cannot be scientifically measured, nor should they be based entirely on "existential grounds."

Harold Wilensky's *Organizational Intelligence* presents the pioneering study of the flow and perception of information in organizations.

Frederick Herzberg's *Harvard Business Review* article, "One More Time, How Do You Motivate Employees?", catapults *motivators* or *satisfiers* and *hygiene factors* into the forefront of organizational motivation theory.

1969 In Fred E. Fiedler's *Psychology Today* article, "Style or Circumstance: The Leadership Enigma," three elements of effective leadership are identified: power of the leader; the task at hand; and the leader-member relationships. He determines that jobs should be designed to fit individual leadership styles rather than the reverse.

Paul Hersey and Kenneth R. Blanchard's "Life Cycle Theory of Leadership," appearing in *Training and Development Journal,* asserts that the appropriate leadership style for a given situation depends upon the employee's education and experience levels, achievement motivation, and willingness to accept responsibility by the subordinates.

Wendell French, in his *California Management Review* article, "Organization Development: Objectives, Assumptions, and Strategies," defines organization development as a total system of planned change.

Harold M. F. Rush's *Behavioral Science: Concepts and Management Application* challenges managers to better understand the behavioral sciences so they can more effectively motivate the "new breed of employee," who is better educated, more politically, socially, and economically astute, and more difficult to control.

Richard E. Walton and John M. Dutton's *Administrative Science Quarterly* article, "The Management of Interdepartmental Conflict: A Model and Review," provides a diagnostic model for managers to determine what needs changing in order to prevent or terminate interdepartmental conflicts.

1970   In his book, *Organizational Psychology,* Edgar H. Schein distinguishes between formal and informal groups within organizations and indicates that effective group work is a result of considering the "characteristics of the members and assessing the likelihood of their being able to work with one another and serve one another's needs."

In "Expectancy Theory," John P. Campbell, Marvin D. Dunnette, Edward E. Lawler III, and Karl E. Weick, Jr., articulate the *expectancy theories of motivation.* People are motivated by calculating how much they want something, how much of it they think they will get, how likely it is their actions will cause them to get it, and how much others in similar circumstances have received.

Chris Argyris writes *Intervention Theory and Methods,* which becomes one of the most widely cited and enduring works on organizational consulting for change that is written from the organizational behavior/organization development perspective.

1971   Rensis Likert's *Michigan Business Review* article, "Human Organizational Measurements: Key to Financial Success," emphasizes that assessing human elements of an organization can identify organizational problems before they occur; he argues that implementing human organizational measurements can help ensure an organization's long-term success.

B. F. Skinner, in *Beyond Freedom and Dignity,* demands a change in the contemporary views of people and how they are motivated in an organization; his alternative includes using *behavior modification* strategies by applying operant conditioning principles to improve employee motivation.

In their *Journal of Applied Psychology* article, "Employee Reactions to Job Characteristics," J. Richard Hackman and Edward E. Lawler III identify four core job dimensions, variety, autonomy, task identity, and feedback, which, they claim, relate to job satisfaction, motivation, quality of work, and decreased absenteeism.

Irving Janis's "Groupthink," first published in *Psychology Today,* proposes that group cohesion can lead to the deterioration of effective group decision-making efforts.

1972   *The Future Executive,* Harlan Cleveland's book, asserts that decision making in the future will call for "continuous improvisation on a general sense of direction."

1973   Jay Galbraith's *Designing Complex Organizations* claims that the amount of information an organization needs is a result of the levels of its uncertainty, interdependence of units and functions, and adaptation mechanisms.

1974   Robert J. House and Terrance R. Mitchell's *Journal of Contemporary Business* article, "Path-Goal Theory of Leadership," offers path-goal theory as a useful tool for explaining the effectiveness of certain leadership styles in given situations.

Victor H. Vroom's *Organizational Dynamics* article, "A New Look at Managerial Decision-Making," develops a useful model whereby leaders can perform a diagnosis of a situation to determine which leadership style is most appropriate.

Steven Kerr's *Academy of Management Journal* article, "On the Folly of Rewarding A, While Hoping for B," substantiates that many organizational reward systems are "fouled up"—they pay off for behaviors other than those they are seeking.

1976   Douglas W. Bray's "The Assessment Center Method," part of the *Training and Development Handbook,* promotes the idea of observing individual behaviors in simulated job-related situations (assessment centers) for evaluative purposes.

Michael Maccoby psychoanalytically interviews 250 corporate managers and discovers *The Gamesman,* a manager whose main interest lies in "competitive activity where he can prove himself a winner."

In "Moral Stakes: Where Have All the Leaders Gone?" Warren Bennis coins the phrase *social architects* to describe what he considers to be the most important roles of organizational leaders: understanding the organizational culture, having a sense of vision, and encouraging people to be innovative.

1977   The *American Psychologist* article, "Job Satisfaction Reconsidered," by Walter R. Nord explains that a revision of accepted economic and political ideologies is necessary if distribution of power in organizations is to be altered.

Gerald Salancik and Jeffrey Pfeffer's *Organizational Dynamics* article "Who Gets Power—And How They Hold on to It: A Strategic-contingency Model of Power," views the use of power by subunits as an important means by which organizations align themselves with their critical needs; thus, suppression of the use of power reduces organizational adaptability.

John P. Kotter's *Harvard Business Review* article, "Power, Dependence, and Effective Management," describes how successful managers build their power by creating a sense of obligation in others, creating images, fostering unconscious identification with these images, and feeding peoples' beliefs that they are dependent upon the images.

1978 Daniel Katz and Robert L. Kahn publish *The Social Psychology of Organizations* in which they coin the term *open system approach*. They advocate creating organizations that are open to change.

William G. Ouchi and Alfred M. Jaeger popularize a third *ideal type organization* in their *Academy of Management Review* article, "Type Z Organization: Stability In The Midst of Mobility." The three types include: Type A (American); Type J (Japanese); and Type Z (one which combines the best of both types). This article becomes the first of many dealing with Japanese management strategies.

Thomas J. Peter's *Organizational Dynamics* article, "Symbols, Patterns, and Settings: An Optimistic Case for Getting Things Done," is the first major analysis of symbolic management in organizations to gain significant attention in the mainstream literature of organization theory.

Herbert C. Kelman and Donald P. Warwick examine stages in organizational interventions that are likely to surface important ethical issues, in *The Ethics of Social Intervention*.

1979 In his book, *The Structuring of Organizations*, Henry Mintzberg defines "the operating core, strategic apex, middle line, technostructure, and support staff" as the five basic components of an organization. This is his first book in an interactive series on "the Theory of Management Policy."

1981 *Power in Organizations* by Jeffrey Pfeffer proposes that intergroup conflicts are inevitable in organizations because of inherent differences between perspectives and ongoing competition for scarce organizational resources; coalitions are the means through which people muster power for political contests.

In "'Democracy' as Hierarchy and Alienation," Frederick Thayer proposes that employee alienation can be ended by eradicating hierarchy, and alienation cannot be eradicated so long as hierarchy remains.

1982 Barry Staw's chapter, "Motivation in Organizations: Toward Synthesis and Redirection," echoes wide disenchantment with the usefulness of existing theories of motivation and attempts to broaden the conceptualization of motivation through viewing individuals as actors who change the "rules" of traditional motivation theories.

1983 Henry Mintzberg, in *Power in and Around Organizations*, proposes that "everyone exhibits a lust for power" and the dynamic of the organization is based on the struggle between various *influencers* to control the organization.

As a result, he molds the power and politics school of organizational theory into an integrative theory of management policy.

Meryl R. Louis's article, "Organizations as Cultural Bearing Milieux," becomes the first readable, integrative statement of the organizational cultural school's assumptions and positions.

R. E. Quinn and Kim Cameron suggest in their *Management Science* article, "Organizational Life Cycles and Shifting Criteria of Effectiveness: Some Preliminary Evidence," that effectiveness is defined differently throughout an organization's life cycle.

In the *Organizational Dynamics* article, "Some Action Implications of Corporate Culture: A Manager's Guide to Action," Vijay Sathe offers managerial guidelines for changing organizational culture.

Daniel C. Feldman and Hugh J. Arnold's *Managing Individual and Group Behavior in Organizations* concludes that individual motivation is based on the sum of intrinsic and extrinsic motivation sources and not merely upon a manager's ability to motivate.

In *The Change Masters,* Rosabeth Moss Kanter defines *change masters* as architects of organizational change; they are the right people in the right places at the right time.

1984   J. Bernard Keys and Thomas R. Miller in their *Academy of Management Review* article, "The Japanese Management Theory Jungle," outline seven explanations for the success of Japanese management techniques: 1) superior manufacturing practices; 2) increased quality and quantity coupled with reduced cost factors; 3) participatory management practices; 4) employment of statistical quality control techniques; 5) consensus decision making; 6) lifetime job security; and 7) long-term planning. These concepts become the basis for much of management training in the 1980s.

Thomas J. Sergiovanni and John Corbally edit the first notable collection of papers on the organizational culture perspective, *Leadership and Organizational Culture.*

Thomas J. Sergiovanni's "Leadership as Cultural Expression," proposes that organizational leadership is a cultural artifact: The shape and style of leadership results from the unique mixture of organizational culture and the *density* of leadership competence.

Tichy and Ulrich's *Sloan Management Review* article, "The Leadership Challenge—A Call for the Transformational Leader," describes the functions of a transformational leader as those of a cheerleader and a belief model during radical organizational change.

Caren Siehl and Joanne Martin report the findings of the first major quantitative and qualitative empirical study of organizational culture in their "The Role of Symbolic Management: How Can Managers Effectively Transmit Organizational Culture?"

In *Goal Setting: A Motivational Technique That Works*, Edwin A. Locke and Gary P. Latham encourage managers to set goals based on their findings that an individual worker's performance increases as goal difficulty increases (assuming the person is willing and has the ability to do the work).

1985   Edgar Schein writes his comprehensive and integrative statement of the organizational culture school in *Organizational Culture and Leadership*.

In a chapter from *The Politics of Management*, Douglas Yates, Jr. describes the management of political conflict as the process of managing strategic conflict between actors who possess different forms of resources, and reminds managers that using power is costly: It depletes one's reservoir of credible power.

Warren Bennis and Burt Nanus reemphasize the importance of vision, power, and context for establishing leadership in organizations, in *Leaders: The Strategies for Taking Charge*.

Vijay Sathe addresses problems of coping individually with an organizational culture, including organizational entry, getting established and operating, and influencing change, in *Culture and Related Corporate Realities*.

1986   S. G. Harris and R. I. Sutton's *Academy of Management Journal* article, "Functions of Parting Ceremonies in Dying Organizations," focuses on the particular importance of symbolic leadership during periods of organizational decline.

In *The Transformational Leader*, Noel Tichy and Mary Anne Devanna propose a Lewin-type "three-act framework" for transformational leadership—the "leadership of change, innovation, and entrepreneurship."

1987   Research findings by Edward Lawler and Susan Morhrman suggest that in the long term, quality cricles have difficulty coexisting with traditional management approaches. Quality circles require basic management changes, or they will not be effective, and alternative strategies should be used. In the *Organizational Dynamics* piece, "Quality Circles: After the Honeymoon."

A. B. Shani and B. J. Eberhardt describe a quality circle as part of a parallel organization created to address work-related issues to which the formal organization is unable to respond. In their *Group and Organization Studies* article, "Parallel Organization in a Health-Care Institution."

1988   Dov Eden's *JABS* article, "OD and Self-Fulfilling Prophesy: Boosting Productivity by Raising Expectations," explains why the process of raising employees' expectations for organizational effectiveness actually increases the effectiveness of an OD intervention.

Ralph Kilmann and Teresa Joyce Covin publish the first comprehensive collection of research studies and practitioner papers targeting the implementation of transformational change, in *Corporate Transformation*. In *The Leadership Factor*, John Kotter expands upon his prior studies of power and leadership in organizations, to explain why organizations often do not have adequate leadership capacity, and proposes steps to rectify the problems.

CHAPTER I

Motivation

For hundreds of years, the motivation of workers has been the proverbial "pot of gold to be found at the end of the rainbow" for management practitioners and students of organizational behavior. If employees could be motivated to produce just slightly more, the economic rewards to individual organizations and to societies would be immense. Although there always has been consensus about the need for motivated employees, the same cannot be said for beliefs about how to induce higher levels of motivation. Not only have prevailing views (or theories) of motivation changed radically over the course of organizational history, but incompatible theories usually have competed with each other at the same points in time. Some theories of motivation have been developed from empirical research, but most have not. Some theories assume that employees act rationally: Managers simply need to manipulate rewards and punishments rationally, fairly, and consistently. Other theories start from the position that managerial assumptions about employees—which undergird such systems of rewards and punishments—actually stifle employee motivation.

Even today, widely divergent views remain about the essence of motivation in organizations. This chapter attempts to sort, organize, and summarize some of the more important theories that have been proposed over the years. The readings in this chapter are organized chronologically *within* major groups of motivation theories. For purposes of perspective, the chapter starts its analysis back in the 1760s, at the beginning of the Industrial Revolution.

Motivation Theory Prior to the Hawthorne Studies

Even in the early years of the Industrial Revolution (beginning about 1760), *employee discipline* was one of the most vexing problems confronting managers in the factory system of mass production. Motivating employees and strategic use of negative sanctions were integral tactics for maintaining production and discipline. Prior to the Industrial Revolution, most workers worked under craft traditions or were agrarians and had some degree of independence (Wren, 1972, Chapter 3). But, the new style factories needed workers who fit into the factory system's production concept which was driven by the principle of the *division of labor* (Smith, 1776). Workers had to produce on a schedule not of their own choosing. Expensive machines had to be kept busy. Production shifted from labor-intensive to capital-intensive; and society's basic concept of humans at work changed with this shifting economic base (Haire, 1962). Although some early industrialists reportedly threw periodic feasts in attempts to build company loyalty, reduce absenteeism, and thereby keep production high, the backbone of motivational strategy was the incentive piece-rate system of compensation. Workers were paid for production output rather than for hours at work.

The twentieth-century scientific management movement of Frederick Winslow Taylor, Lillian and Frank Gilbreth, Henry Gantt, and others followed naturally from the piece-rate payment system ethic of the industrial revolution/factory system of production. (See Shafritz & Ott, 1987, Chapter 1). Under scientific management principles, motivational methods were rooted in the concept of workers as *rational economic men*. People work for money: Tie compensation to production, and employees produce more (Gantt, 1910). Deal only with individual employees, and try to prevent the formation of groups because they restrict output and lead to unions. Beyond restricting output, Taylor saw productivity limited primarily by workers' ignorance of how to maximize production. To Taylor, scientific study of production processes (what he called *scientific management*) was the answer. It would provide for standardization, for the improvement of practices, and for techniques that would reduce worker fatigue. With better procedures and less fatigue, employee income and company profits would increase (Taylor, 1911).

The Hawthorne Studies

In 1924 a team of researchers under the aegis of the National Academy of Sciences' National Research Council went to the Hawthorne plant of the Western Electric Company, near Chicago, to study ways for improving productivity. The research team began its work from the perspective—the assumptions, precepts, and principles—of scientific management. Scientific investigative procedures (including control groups) were used to find and identify environmental changes which would increase worker productivity. Their investigations focused on room temperature, humidity, and illumination levels (Pennock, 1930). Interestingly, illumination was included as an experimental variable because scientific management studies by Frederick Winslow Taylor (1911) fifteen years earlier had identified illumination as an easily controlled variable for influencing productivity. The early Hawthorne studies caused confusion. Worker output continued to increase even as illumination decreased.

By 1927, the results were so snarled that Western Electric and the National Research Council were ready to abandon the entire endeavor. In that year George Pennock, Western Electric's superintendent of inspection, heard Harvard professor Elton Mayo speak at a meeting and invited him to take a team to Hawthorne. Team members eventually included Fritz Roethlisberger, George Homans, and T. N. Whitehead. The results are legendary. However, it was not until the Mayo-led Hawthorne team discarded its rational economic man/scientific management assumptions about people at work, that the groundwork was laid for what we have been calling in this volume the field of *organizational behavior*—a perspective with its own very different set of assumptions. (See the *Introduction* to this book.) The long-held assumptions of Industrial/Organizational psychology, that people could and should be fit to organizations, had been challenged. The process had begun that would render obsolete scientific management's assumptions about people and how to motivate them.

The Hawthorne experiments were the emotional and intellectual wellspring of the organizational behavior perspective and modern theories of motivation. The Hawthorne experiments showed that complex, interactional variables make the difference in motivating people—things like attention paid to workers as individuals, workers' control over their own work, differences between individuals' needs, management willingness to listen, group norms, and direct feedback.

Fritz J. Roethlisberger, of the Harvard Business School, is the best known chronicler of the Hawthorne studies. Roethlisberger, with William J. Dickson of the Western Electric Company, wrote the most comprehensive account of the Hawthorne studies, *Management and the Worker* (1939). Roethlisberger's chapter, which is reprinted here, "The Hawthorne Experiments," is from his shorter 1941 book, *Management and Morale*.

Need Theories of Motivation

All discussions of *need theories of motivation* start with Abraham Maslow. His *hierarchy of needs* stands alongside the Hawthorne experiments and Douglas Mc-Gregor's *Theory X* and *Theory Y* as *the* departure points for studying motivation in organizations. An overview of Maslow's basic theory of needs is presented here from his 1943 *Psychological Review* article, "A Theory of Human Motivation." Maslow's theoretical premises can be summarized in a few phrases:

- All humans have needs which underlie their motivational structure;
- As lower levels of needs are satisfied, they no longer "drive" behavior;
- Satisfied needs are not motivators; and
- As lower level needs of workers become satisfied, higher order needs take over as the motivating forces.

Maslow's theory has been attacked frequently. Few empirical studies have supported it, and it oversimplifies the complex structure of human needs and motivations (for example, see Wahba & Bridwell, 1973). Several modified needs hierarchies have been proposed over the years which reportedly are better able to withstand empirical testing (for example, Alderfer, 1969). But, despite the criticisms and the continuing advances across the spectrum of applied behavioral sciences, Abraham Maslow's theory continues to occupy a most honored and prominent place in organizational behavior and management textbooks.

Theory X and Theory Y

Douglas McGregor's *The Human Side of Enterprise* is about much more than the motivation of people at work. In its totality, it is a cogent articulation of the basic assumptions of the organizational behavior perspective. Theory X and Theory Y are contrasting basic managerial assumptions about employees which, in McGregor's words, become self-fulfilling prophesies. Managerial assumptions *cause* employee behavior. Theory X and Theory Y are ways of seeing and thinking about people which, in turn, affect their behavior. Thus, "The Human Side of Enterprise" (1957b), which is reprinted in this chapter, is a landmark theory of motivation.

Theory X assumptions represent a restatement of the tenets of the scientific management movement. For example, human beings inherently dislike work and will avoid it if possible. Most people must be coerced, controlled, directed, or threatened with punishment to get them to work toward the achievement of organizational objectives; and, humans prefer to be directed, to avoid responsibility, and will seek security above all else. These assumptions serve as polar opposites to McGregor's Theory Y.

Theory Y assumptions postulate, for example: People do not inherently dislike work; work can be a source of satisfaction. People will exercise self-direction and self-control if they are committed to organizational objectives. People are willing to seek and to accept responsibility; avoidance of responsibility is not natural, it is a consequence of experiences. The intellectual potential of most humans is only partially utilized at work.

Cognitive Dissonance and Inequity Theories of Motivation

When two or more people or things around a person are in a state of disharmony, imbalance, or incongruity, that imbalance causes *dissonance* (or discomfort). According to *cognitive dissonance theory,* people will act—*will do something*—to reduce or eliminate dissonance. For example, I like two people, "A" and "B," but "A" does not like "B." An imbalance exists which causes dissonance, and I will act to eliminate it. The theory of cognitive dissonance cannot predict what I will do, but it says that I will be motivated to do something. I might try to change "A's" feelings toward "B"; or I might change my feelings about either "A" or "B" and then sever my relationship with the out-of-favor person. Similarly, if I believe that wearing a seat belt will not save my life in the event of a car accident, but I fasten my seat belt anyway because state law says I must, dissonance is created by the incongruity between my belief and my behavior. Cognitive dissonance theory predicts that I will be motivated to reduce or eliminate the dissonance. I might stop wearing a seat belt (for example, by convincing myself that the probability of getting caught violating the law is low or the legal penalty is too minimal to worry about) or, as the authors of the state law hope, I could allow my belief to be altered. If my belief does change, I probably will continue to "buckle up" even if the seat belt law is repealed some day.

Cognitive dissonance theory has many practical managerial applications for motivating employees. For example, management can require workers to do certain things in the hope that attitudes or beliefs will follow—just as in the seat belt example. On the other hand, management can attempt to change peoples' attitudes or beliefs (Zimbardo & Ebbesen, 1970) in hope that the resulting cognitive dissonance will motivate a behavior change (Ott, 1989, Chapter 4). In contrast, under cognitive dissonance theories, motivation is *engineered* by intentionally creating dissonance and then not allowing the desired state to change (in the examples used here, beliefs or behavior).

Cognitive dissonance provides the theoretical basis for what are known as *inequity theories of motivation.* Inequity theories postulate that workers are motivated to act (for example, to produce more or less) by their perceptions of inequities in the environment (such as between *their* levels of work and compensation, and *others'* levels of work and compensation) (Adams, 1963). The theory of cognitive dissonance assumes that a worker performing the same work as another but being paid significantly less will do something to relieve this dissonance. Among the worker's options are asking for a raise, restricting output, or seeking another job.

The 1958 article, "The Motivating Effect of Cognitive Dissonance," by Leon Festinger, the "father" of cognitive dissonance theory, is reprinted in this chapter.

More Need Theories

David McClelland and Frederick Herzberg are two of the most widely cited of the numerous students and theorists who studied and wrote about motivation in organizations during the 1960s. Herzberg and McClelland began the construction of their motivation theories with Abraham Maslow's need theory, and both were also influenced substantially by the Theory X and Theory Y assumptions of Douglas McGregor.

David McClelland postulates that people have three basic needs (or drives) which vary in intensity under different circumstances: *achievement, power,* and *affiliation.* In his 1966 article, "That Urge to Achieve," which is included in this chapter, McClelland focuses on people with a high need to achieve, which he calls *achievement motivation.* Even though all people have some need to achieve, McClelland asserts that "most people in this world . . . can be divided into two broad groups. There is that minority which is challenged by opportunity and willing to work hard to achieve something, and the majority which really does not care all that much" (p. 82)—people with high and low achievement motivation respectively. Business executives, particularly if they are in positions of real responsibility or if they are salesmen, tend to score high in achievement need. McClelland's article describes techniques he and his associates have used to develop achievement needs in people, and their failures in trying to develop high achievement attitudes among low income groups. It isn't enough to change a person's motivation if the environment in which he or she lives doesn't support the new efforts—at least to some degree. In balance, however, McClelland contends that achievement motivation can be raised through training.

Frederick Herzberg's theory of motivation evolved from extensive empirical research. Herzberg and his collaborating researchers would ask people to identify situations when they felt particularly satisfied and dissatisfied with their job (Herzberg, Mausner & Snyderman, 1959). From thousands of responses, Herzberg developed the motivation-hygiene theory which holds:

- *Motivators* or *satisfiers* are variables centered in the work (or work content) which satisfy self-actualization-type needs (Maslow, 1943) and lead to higher motivation. Examples of Herzberg's motivators include achievement, recognition for achievement, and opportunities for self-development.
- In contrast, *hygiene factors* are maintainers—preventers of dissatisfaction. A few examples of hygiene factors are supervision, administrative practices, and (in most respects) pay.

According to Herzberg's theory, which is described here in his 1968 article, "One More Time: How Do You Motivate Employees?", motivators and hygiene factors are on different dimensions or planes. They are not extreme points on a single scalar continuum. The presence of hygiene factors does not motivate, it only prevents dissatisfaction; and the absence of motivators does not cause employees to be dissatisfied, it only yields nonmotivated employees. If managers want satisfied employees, they should pay attention to hygiene factors, like pay and working conditions. However,

hygiene factors do not "turn employees on": They only neutralize negative sentiments. In order to increase motivation, managers must work with motivators.

Herzberg's work has been attacked with great vigor on two fronts. First, numerous behavioral researchers have tried unsuccessfully to replicate his findings, which
has raised serious questions about the validity of his research methods (Vroom,
1964). The second line of criticism directed at Herzberg has essentially been an
argument against any and all simplistic, static, one- or two-dimensional theories of
motivation, and for more complex, contingency-type theories (Behling, Labovitz,
& Kosmo, 1968; Schein, 1980). Despite the sometimes bitter criticisms of motivation-hygiene theory, its popularity continues among management practitioners
and trainers. Its greatest weakness—simplicity—also gives it credibility.

Expectancy Theory of Motivation

Expectancy theory holds that people are motivated by two dynamics: How much they
want certain rewards (or to avoid negative sanctions) and the expectancy (probability)
that their actions will garner the rewards. Victor Vroom (1969), the most respected
expectancy theorist, identifies four classes of variables that comprise expectancy theory:

1. The amounts of particular classes of outcomes such as pay, status, accep-
    tance, and influence, attained by the person.
2. The strength of the person's desire or aversion for outcomes.
3. The amounts of these outcomes believed by the person to be received by
    comparable others.
4. The amounts of these outcomes which the person expected to receive or
    has received at earlier points in time (p. 207).

Very simply, expectancy theory claims that people are motivated by calculating
how much they want something, how much of it they think they will get, how
likely it is their actions will cause them to get it, and how much others in similar
circumstances have received. (Notice how this last calculation resembles *inequity
theories* from a few pages back.) "Expectancy Theory," by John Campbell, Marvin
Dunnette, Edward Lawler III, and Karl Weick, Jr. (reprinted in this chapter), presents a very clear and concise statement of the theory's elements.

Reinforcement Theory: Reward Systems

Virtually all organizations attempt to motivate employees through combinations of rewards and punishments. Reinforcement theories of motivation assume that people at
work seek rewards and try to avoid punishments. By rewarding activities the organization wants done and punishing counterproductive behavior, managers *engineer* the accomplishment of organizational goals. "Whether dealing with monkeys, rats, or human
beings, . . . most organisms seek information concerning what activities are rewarded, and then seek to do (or at least pretend to do) those things. . . . Nevertheless, numerous examples exist of reward systems that are fouled up in that behaviors which are rewarded are those which the rewarder is trying to *discourage*"
(Kerr, 1975, p. 769). Reinforcement theories of motivation focus on the behavioral
effects of rewards and punishments. In "On the Folly of Rewarding A, While Hop-

ing for B," which is included in this chapter, Steven Kerr reports on his observations and research findings from organizations engaged in manufacturing, medicine, rehabilitation, higher education, and insurance that support his assertion. Kerr attributes the prevalence of "fouled up" reward systems to management's:

- Fascination with "objective" (quantifiable) performance criteria which tend to cause goal displacement;
- Overemphasis on visible, easily measured behaviors;
- Hypocrisy—rewarding desired behavior but claiming the behavior was not desired; and
- Emphasizing morality or equity rather than efficiency.

Kerr concludes that managers should consider the possibility that they have "installed reward systems which are paying off for behaviors other than those they are seeking" (p. 781).

Motivation Theories: A Synthesis

This chapter tries to present a balanced sampling of the more important theories of motivation both in this *Introduction* and in the nine selected readings. If the result is confusing and inconclusive, I apologize. However, in many ways, motivation *is* "the proverbial pot of gold at the end of the rainbow." We may never totally unlock its mysteries. Humans are complicated, ever-changing beings. Organizations are complex social systems. Understanding and predicting either is extremely difficult (Schein, 1980, Chapters 6 and 11). Discovering universal truths about what motivates people in the context of organizations may be an unrealistic "pot of gold" to seek. On the other hand, much has been learned about what does and does not cause people to "turn on" or "tune out" at work.

With this background, the introduction to motivation concludes with Barry Staw's 1982 chapter, "Motivation in Organizations: Toward Synthesis and Redirection." Staw undertakes two monumental tasks: (1) synthesizing the major theories of motivation or, to use different words, pulling together a lot of information on "ways by which individuals come to grips with their social worlds" (p. 89); and (2), being "an impetus toward a broadening of our conceptualization of motivation and a reconsideration of established theory in the area" (p. 89). Staw's synthesis and redirection brings this chapter's overview of motivation theory up into the 1980s. Appropriately, it concludes the chapter with a challenge for the future study of motivation in organizations. In so doing, Staw views individuals in organizations as actors who can and do change the "rules" of traditional motivation theories.

REFERENCES

Adams, J. S. (1963). Toward an understanding of inequity. *Journal of Abnormal Social Psychology*, 67, 422–436.

Alderfer, J. S. (1969). An empirical test of a new theory of human needs. *Organizational Behavior and Human Performance*, 4, 142–175.

Atkinson, J. W., & Raynor, J. O. (1974). *Motivation and achievement*. New York: John Wiley.

Behling, O., Labovitz, G., & Kosmo, R. (1968). The Herzberg controversy: A critical reappraisal. *Academy of Management Journal, 11*(1), 99–108.

Behling, O., & Starke, F. (1973). The postulates of expectancy theory. *Academy of Management Journal, 16*, 373–388.

Campbell, J. P., Dunnette, M. D., Lawler, E. E. III, & Weick, K. E., Jr. (1970). Expectancy theory. In, J. P. Campbell, M. D. Dunnette, E. E. Lawler, III, & K. E. Weick, Jr. (Eds.), *Managerial behavior, performance and effectiveness* (pp. 343–348). New York: McGraw-Hill.

Cohen, A. R., Fink, S. L., Gadon, H., & Willits, R. D. (1988). *Effective behavior in organizations* (4th ed.). Homewood, IL: Richard D. Irwin.

Deci, E. L. (1971). The effects of externally mediated rewards on intrinsic motivation. *Journal of Personality and Social Psychology, 18*, 105–115.

Festinger, L. (1954). Motivations leading to social behavior. In, M. R. Jones (Ed.), *Nebraska symposium on motivation*. Lincoln, NE: Univeristy of Nebraska Press.

Festinger, L. (1957). *A theory of cognitive dissonance*. Stanford, CA: Stanford University Press.

Festinger, L. (1958). The motivating effect of cognitive dissonance. In, G. Lindzey (Ed.), *Assessment of human motives* (pp. 69–86). New York: Holt, Rinehart & Co.

Gantt, H. L. (1910). *Work, wages, and profit*. New York: Engineering Magazine Company.

Hackman, J. R., & Oldham, G. R. (1976). Motivation through the design of work. *Organizational Behavior and Human Performance, 16*, 250–279.

Haire, M. (1962). The concept of power and the concept of man. In, G. B. Strother (Ed.), *Social science approaches to business behavior* (pp. 163–183). Homewood, IL: Richard D. Irwin.

Herzberg, F. (January/February 1968). One more time: How do you motivate employees?". *Harvard Business Review, 46* (1).

Herzberg, F., Mausner, B., & Snyderman, B. B. (1959). *The motivation to work*. New York: John Wiley & Sons.

Kerr, S. (December, 1975). On the folly of rewarding A, while hoping for B. *Academy of Management Journal, 18*(4), 769–782.

Lawler, E. E., III, & Porter, L. W. (1963). Perceptions regarding management compensation. *Industrial Relations, 3*, 41–49.

Litwin, G. H., & Stringer, R. A., Jr. (1968). *Motivation and organizational climate*. Boston: Harvard University Press.

Maslow, A. H. (1943). A theory of human motivation. *Psychological Review, 50*.

Mayo, E. (1933). *The human problems of an industrial civilization*. New York: MacMillan.

McClelland, D. C. (1961). *The achieving society*. Princeton, NJ: Van Nostrand.

McClelland, D. C. (1966). That urge to achieve. *Think* (published by International Business Machines Corporation), 82–89.

McGregor, D. M. (April 1957a). The human side of enterprise. Address to the Fifth Anniversary Convocation of the School of Industrial Management, Massachusetts Institute of Technology. In, *Adventure in thought and action*. Cambridge, MA: M.I.T. School of Industrial Management, 1957. Reprinted in W. G. Bennis, E. H. Schein, & C. McGregor (Eds.), *Leadership and motivation: Essays of Douglas McGregor* (pp. 3–20). Cambridge, MA: The M.I.T. Press, 1966.

McGregor, D. M. (November 1957b). The human side of enterprise. *Management Review, 22–28, 88–92*.

McGregor, D. M. (1960). *The human side of enterprise.* New York: McGraw-Hill.

Organ, D. W., & Bateman, T. (1986). *Organizational behavior: An applied psychological approach* (3rd ed.). Plano, TX: Business Publications, Inc.

Ott, J. S. (1989). *The organizational culture perspective.* Chicago: The Dorsey Press.

Pennock, G. (1930). Industrial research at Hawthorne. *The Personnel Journal, 8,* 296.

Roethlisberger, F. I. (1941). *Management and morale.* Cambridge, MA: Harvard University Press.

Roethlisberger, F. J., & Dickson, W. J. (1939). *Management and the worker.* Cambridge, MA: Harvard University Press.

Ross, I. C., & Zander, A. (1957). Need satisfactions and employee turnover. *Personnel Psychology, 10,* 327–338.

Schein, E. H. (1980). *Organizational psychology* (3rd ed.). Englewood Cliffs, NJ: Prentice-Hall.

Shafritz, J. M., & Ott, J. S. (1987). *Classics of organization theory* (2d ed., revised and expanded). Chicago: The Dorsey Press.

Smith, A. (1776). Of the division of labor. In, A. Smith, *The wealth of nations* (Chapter 1).

Staw, B. M. (1982). Motivation in organizations: Toward synthesis and redirection. In, B. M. Staw & G. R. Salancik (Eds.), *New directions in organizational behavior* (pp. 55–95). Malabar, FL: Robert E. Krieger Publishing Company.

Taylor, F. W. (1903). *Shop management.* New York: Harper & Row.

Taylor, F. W. (1911). *The principles of scientific management.* New York: Harper & Row.

Urwick, L. (Ed.). (1956). *The golden book of management.* London, UK: Newman Neame.

Vroom, V. H. (1964). *Work and motivation.* New York: John Wiley & Sons.

Vroom, V. H. (1969). Industrial social psychology. In, G. Lindzey & E. Aronson (Eds.) *The handbook of social psychology* (Vol. 5) (2d ed.) (pp. 200–208). Reading, MA: Addison-Wesley Publishing Co.

Vroom, V. H., & Deci, E. L. (Eds.). (1970). *Management and motivation.* Harmondsworth, UK: Penguin Books.

Wahba, M. A., & Bridwell, L. G. (1973). Maslow reconsidered: A review of research on the need hierarchy theory. Boston: *Proceedings of the 1973 meetings of the Academy of Management.*

Wren, D. A. (1972). *The evolution of management thought.* New York: The Ronald Press.

Zaleznik, A., Christensen, C. R., & Roethlisberger, F. J. (1958). *The motivation, productivity and satisfaction of workers: A prediction study.* Cambridge, MA: Harvard University, Graduate School of Business Administration.

Zimbardo, P., & Ebbesen, E. B. (1970). *Influencing attitudes and changing behavior* (rev. printing). Reading, MA: Addison-Wesley Publishing Co.

1

The Hawthorne Experiments

Frederick J. Roethlisberger

At a recent meeting the researches in personnel at the Hawthorne plant of the Western Electric Company were mentioned by both a management man and a union man. There seemed to be no difference of opinion between the two regarding the importance or relevance of these research findings for effective management-employee relations. This seemed to me interesting because it suggested that the labor situation can be discussed at a level where both sides can roughly agree. The question of what this level is can be answered only after closer examination of these studies.

In the February, 1941, issue of the *Reader's Digest* there appeared a summary statement of these researches by Stuart Chase, under the title, "What Makes the Worker Like to Work?" At the conclusion of his article, Stuart Chase said, "There is an idea here so big that it leaves one gasping." Just what Mr. Chase meant by this statement is not explained, but to find out one can go back to the actual studies and see what was learned from them. In my opinion, the results were very simple and obvious—as Sherlock Holmes used to say to Dr. Watson, "Elementary, my dear Watson." Now this is what may have left Stuart Chase "gasping"—the systematic exploitation of the simple and the obvious which these studies represent.

There seems to be an assumption to-day that we need a complex set of ideas to handle the complex problems of this complex world in which we live. We assume that a big problem needs a big idea; a complex problem needs a complex idea for its solution. As a result, our thinking tends to become more and more tortuous and muddled. Nowhere is this more true than in matters of human behavior. It seems to me that the road back to sanity—and here is where my title comes in—lies

1. In having a few simple and clear ideas about the world in which we live.

2. In complicating our ideas, not in a vacuum, but only in reference to things we can observe, see, feel, hear, and touch. Let us not generalize from verbal definitions; let us know in fact what we are talking about.

3. In having a very simple method by means of which we can explore our complex world. We need a tool which will allow us to get the data from which our generalizations are to be drawn. We need a simple skill to keep us in touch with what is sometimes referred to as "reality."

4. In being "tough-minded," i.e., in not letting ourselves be too disappointed because the complex world never quite fulfills our most cherished expectations of it. Let

Source: Reprinted by permission of the publishers from *Management and Morale* by F. J. Roethlisberger, Cambridge, Massachusetts: Harvard University Press, Copyright © 1941 by the President and Fellows of Harvard College; © 1969 by F. J. Roethlisberger.

us remember that the concrete phenomena will always elude any set of abstractions that we can make of them.

5. In knowing very clearly the class of phenomena to which our ideas and methods relate. Now, this is merely a way of saying, "Do not use a saw as a hammer." A saw is a useful tool precisely because it is limited and designed for a certain purpose. Do not criticize the usefulness of a saw because it does not make a good hammer.

Although this last statement is obvious with regard to such things as "saws" and "hammers," it is less well understood in the area of human relations. Too often we try to solve human problems with nonhuman tools and, what is still more extraordinary, in terms of nonhuman data. We take data from which all human meaning has been deleted and then are surprised to find that we reach conclusions which have no human significance.

It is my simple thesis that a human problem requires a human solution. First, we have to learn to recognize a human problem when we see one; and, second, upon recognizing it, we have to learn to deal with it as such and not as if it were something else. Too often at the verbal level we talk glibly about the importance of the human factor; and too seldom at the concrete level of behavior do we recognize a human problem for what it is and deal with it as such. *A human problem to be brought to a human solution requires human data and human tools.* It is my purpose to use the Western Electric researches as an illustration of what I mean by this statement, because, if they deserve the publicity and acclaim which they have received, it is because, in my opinion, they have so conclusively demonstrated

this point. In this sense they are the road back to sanity in management-employee relations.

EXPERIMENTS IN ILLUMINATION

The Western Electric researches started about sixteen years ago, in the Hawthorne plant, with a series of experiments on illumination. The purpose was to find out the relation of the quality and quantity of illumination to the efficiency of industrial workers. These studies lasted several years, and I shall not describe them in detail. It will suffice to point out that the results were quite different from what had been expected.

In one experiment the workers were divided into two groups. One group, called the "test group," was to work under different illumination intensities. The other group, called the "control group," was to work under an intensity of illumination as nearly constant as possible. During the first experiment, the test group was submitted to three different intensities of illumination of increasing magnitude, 24, 46, and 70 foot candles. What were the results of this early experiment? Production increased in both rooms—in both the test group and the control group—and the rise in output was roughly of the same magnitude in both cases.

In another experiment, the light under which the test group worked was decreased from 10 to 3 foot candles, while the control group worked, as before, under a constant level of illumination intensity. In this case the output rate in the test group went up instead of down. It also went up in the control group.

In still another experiment, the workers were allowed to believe that the illumination was being increased, although, in fact, no change in intensity was made. The workers commented favorably on the improved lighting condition, but there was no appreciable change in output. At another time, the workers were allowed to believe that the intensity of illumination was being decreased, although again, in fact, no actual change was made. The workers complained somewhat about the poorer lighting, but again there was no appreciable effect on output.

And finally, in another experiment, the intensity of illumination was decreased to .06 of a foot candle, which is the intensity of illumination approximately equivalent to that of ordinary moonlight. Not until this point was reached was there any appreciable decline in the output rate.

What did the experimenters learn? Obviously, as Stuart Chase said, there was something "screwy," but the experimenters were not quite sure who or what was screwy—they themselves, the subjects, or the results. One thing was clear: the results were negative. Nothing of a positive nature had been learned about the relation of illumination to industrial efficiency. If the results were to be taken at their face value, it would appear that there was no relation between illumination and industrial efficiency. However, the investigators were not yet quite willing to draw this conclusion. They realized the difficulty of testing for the effect of a single variable in a situation where there were many uncontrolled variables. It was thought therefore that another experiment should be devised in which other variables affecting the output of workers could be better controlled.

A few of the tough-minded experimenters already were beginning to suspect their basic ideas and assumptions with regard to human motivation. It occurred to them that the trouble was not so much with the results or with the subjects as it was with their notion regarding the way their subjects were supposed to behave—the notion of a simple cause-and-effect, direct relationship between certain physical changes in the workers' environment and the responses of the workers to these changes. Such a notion completely ignored the human meaning of these changes to the people who were subjected to them.

In the illumination experiments, therefore, we have a classic example of trying to deal with a human situation in nonhuman terms. The experimenters had obtained no human data; they had been handling electric-light bulbs and plotting average output curves. Hence their results had no human significance. That is why they seemed screwy. Let me suggest here, however, that the results were not screwy, but the experimenters were—a "screwy" person being by definition one who is not acting in accordance with the customary human values of the situation in which he finds himself.

THE RELAY ASSEMBLY TEST ROOM

Another experiment was framed, in which it was planned to submit a segregated group of workers to different kinds of working conditions. The idea was very simple: A group of five girls were placed in a separate room where their conditions of work could be carefully controlled, where their output could be measured, and where they could be closely observed. It was decided to introduce at specified intervals different changes in working conditions and to see what effect these innovations had on output. Also, records were kept, such as the temperature and humidity of the room, the number of hours each girl slept at night, the kind and amount of food she ate for breakfast, lunch, and dinner. Output was carefully measured, the time it took each girl to assemble a telephone relay of approximately forty parts (roughly a minute) being automatically recorded each time; quality records were kept; each girl had a physical examination at regular intervals. Under these conditions of close observation the girls were studied for a period of five years. Literally tons of material were collected. Probably nowhere in the world has so much material been collected about a small group of workers for such a long period of time.

But what about the results? They can be stated very briefly. When all is said and done, they amount roughly to this: A skillful statistician spent several years trying to relate variations in output with variations in the physical circumstances of these five operators. For example, he correlated the hours that each girl spent in bed the night before with variations in output the following day. Inasmuch as some people said that the effect of being out late one night was not felt the following day but the day after that, he correlated variations in output with the amount of rest the operators had had two nights before. I mention this just to point out the fact that he missed no obvious tricks and that he did a careful job and a thorough one, and it took him many years to do it. The attempt to relate changes in physical circumstances to variations in output resulted in not a single correlation of enough statistical significance to be recognized by any competent statistician as having any meaning.

Now, of course, it would be misleading to say that this negative result was the only conclusion reached. There were positive conclusions, and it did not take the experimenters more than two years to find out that they had missed the boat. After two years of work, certain things happened which

made them sit up and take notice. Different experimental conditions of work, in the nature of changes in the number and duration of rest pauses and differences in the length of the working day and week, had been introduced in this Relay Assembly Test Room. For example, the investigators first introduced two five-minute rests, one in the morning and one in the afternoon. Then they increased the length of these rests, and after that they introduced the rests at different times of the day. During one experimental period they served the operators a specially prepared lunch during the rest. In the later periods, they decreased the length of the working day by one-half hour and then by one hour. They gave the operators Saturday morning off for a while. Altogether, thirteen such periods of different working conditions were introduced in the first two years.

During the first year and a half of the experiment, everybody was happy, both the investigators and the operators. The investigators were happy because as conditions of work improved the output rate rose steadily. Here, it appeared, was strong evidence in favor of their preconceived hypothesis that fatigue was the major factor limiting output. The operators were happy because their conditions of work were being improved, they were earning more money, and they were objects of considerable attention from top management. But then one investigator—one of those tough-minded fellows—suggested that they restore the original conditions of work, that is, go back to a full forty-eight-hour week without rests, lunches and what not. This was Period XII. Then the happy state of affairs, when everything was going along as it theoretically should, went sour. Output, instead of taking the expected nose dive, maintained its high level.

Again the investigators were forcibly reminded that human situations are likely to be complex. In any human situation, whenever a simple change is introduced—a rest pause, for example—other changes, unwanted and unanticipated, may also be brought about. What I am saying here is very simple. If one experiments on a stone, the stone does not know it is being experimented upon—all of which makes it simple for people experimenting on stones. But if a human being is being experimented upon, he is likely to know it. Therefore, his attitudes toward the experiment and toward the experimenters become very important factors in determining his responses to the situation.

Now that is what happened in the Relay Assembly Test Room. To the investigators, it was essential that the workers give their full and whole-hearted coöperation to the experiment. They did not want the operators to work harder or easier depending upon their attitude toward the conditions that were imposed. They wanted them to work as they felt, so that they could be sure that the different physical conditions of work were solely responsible for the variations in output. For each of the experimental changes, they wanted subjects whose responses would be uninfluenced by so-called "psychological factors."

In order to bring this about, the investigators did everything in their power to secure the complete coöperation of their subjects, with the result that almost all the practices common to the shop were altered. The operators were consulted about the changes to be made, and, indeed, several plans were abandoned because they met with the disapproval of the girls. They were questioned sympathetically about their reactions to the conditions imposed, and

many of these conferences took place in the office of the superintendent. The girls were allowed to talk at work; their "bogey" was eliminated. Their physical health and well-being became matters of great concern. Their opinions, hopes, and fears were eagerly sought. What happened was that in the very process of setting the conditions for the test—a so-called "controlled" experiment—the experimenters had completely altered the social situation of the room. Inadvertently a change had been introduced which was far more important than the planned experimental innovations: the customary supervision in the room had been revolutionized. This accounted for the better attitudes of the girls and their improved rate of work.

THE DEVELOPMENT OF A NEW AND MORE FRUITFUL POINT OF VIEW

After Period XII in the Relay Assembly Test Room, the investigators decided to change their ideas radically. What all their experiments had dramatically and conclusively demonstrated was the importance of employee attitudes and sentiments. It was clear that the responses of workers to what was happening about them were dependent upon the significance these events had for them. In most work situations the meaning of a change is likely to be as important, if not more so, than the change itself. This was the great *éclaircissement*, the new illumination, that came from the research. It was an illumination quite different from what they had expected from the illumination studies. Curiously enough, this discovery is nothing very new or startling. It is something which anyone who has had some concrete experience in handling other people intuitively recognizes and practices.

Whether or not a person is going to give his services whole-heartedly to a group depends, in good part, on the way he feels about his job, his fellow workers, and supervisors—the meaning for him of what is happening about him.

However, when the experimenters began to tackle the problem of employee attitudes and the factors determining such attitudes—when they began to tackle the problem of "meaning"—they entered a sort of twilight zone where things are never quite what they seem. Moreover, overnight, as it were, they were robbed of all the tools they had so carefully forged; for all their previous tools were nonhuman tools concerned with the measurement of output, temperature, humidity, etc., and these were no longer useful for the human data that they now wanted to obtain. What the experimenters now wanted to know was how a person felt, what his intimate thinking, reflections, and preoccupations were, and what he liked and disliked about his work environment. In short, what did the whole blooming business—his job, his supervision, his working conditions—mean to him? Now this was human stuff, and there were no tools, or at least the experimenters knew of none, for obtaining and evaluating this kind of material.

Fortunately, there were a few courageous souls among the experimenters. These men were not metaphysicians, psychologists, academicians, professors, intellectuals, or what have you. They were men of common sense and of practical affairs. They were not driven by any great heroic desire to change the world. They were true experimenters, that is, men compelled to follow the implications of their own monkey business. All the evidence of their studies was pointing in one direction. Would they take the jump? They did.

EXPERIMENTS IN INTERVIEWING WORKERS

A few tough-minded experimenters decided to go into the shops and—completely disarmed and denuded of their elaborate logical equipment and in all humility—to see if they could learn how to get the workers to talk about things that were important to them and could learn to understand what the workers were trying to tell them. This was a revolutionary idea in the year 1928, when this interviewing program started—the idea of getting a worker to talk to you and to listen sympathetically, but intelligently, to what he had to say. In that year a new era of personnel relations began. It was the first real attempt to get human data and to forge human tools to get them. In that year a novel idea was born; dimly the experimenters perceived a new method of human control. In that year the Rubicon was crossed from which there could be no return to the "good old days." Not that the experimenters ever wanted to return, because they now entered a world so exciting, so intriguing, and so full of promise that it made the "good old days" seem like the prattle and play of children.

When these experimenters decided to enter the world of "meaning," with very few tools, but with a strong sense of curiosity and a willingness to learn, they had many interesting adventures. It would be too long a story to tell all of them, or even a small part of them. They made plenty of mistakes, but they were not afraid to learn.

At first, they found it difficult to learn to give full and complete attention to what a person had to say without interrupting him before he was through. They found it difficult to learn not to give advice, not to make or imply moral judgments about the speaker, not to argue, not to be too clever, not to dominate the conversation, not to ask leading questions. They found it difficult to get the person to talk about matters which were important to him and not to the interviewer. But, most important of all, they found it difficult to learn that perhaps the thing most significant to a person was not something in his immediate work situation.

Gradually, however, they learned these things. They discovered that sooner or later a person tends to talk about what is uppermost in his mind to a sympathetic and skillful listener, and they became more proficient in interpreting what a person is saying or trying to say. Of course they protected the confidences given to them and made absolutely sure that nothing an employee said could ever be used against him. Slowly they began to forge a simple human tool—imperfect, to be sure—to get the kind of data they wanted. They called this method "interviewing." I would hesitate to say the number of manhours of labor which went into the forging of this tool. There followed from studies made through its use a gradually changing conception of the worker and his behavior.

A NEW WAY OF VIEWING EMPLOYEE SATISFACTION AND DISSATISFACTION

When the experimenters started to study employee likes and dislikes, they assumed, at first, that they would find a simple and logical relation between a person's likes or dislikes and certain items and events in his immediate work situation. They expected to find a simple connection, for example, between a person's complaint and the object about which he was complaining. Hence, the solution would be easy: Correct the ob-

ject of the complaint, if possible, and presto! the complaint would disappear. Unfortunately, however, the world of human behavior is not so simple as this conception of it; and it took the investigators several arduous and painful years to find this out. I will mention only a few interesting experiences they had.

Several times they changed the objects of the complaint only to find that the attitudes of the complainants remained unchanged. In these cases, correcting the object of the complaint did not remedy the complaint or the attitude of the person expressing it. A certain complaint might disappear, to be sure, only to have another one arise. Here the investigators were running into so-called "chronic kickers," people whose dissatisfactions were more deeply rooted in factors relating to their personal histories. For such people the simple remedy of changing the object of the complaint was not enough.

Several times they did absolutely nothing about the object of the complaint, but after the interview, curiously enough, the complaint disappeared. A typical example of this was that of a woman who complained at great length and with considerable feeling about the poor food being served in the company restaurant. When, a few days later, she chanced to meet the interviewer, she commented with great enthusiasm upon the improved food and thanked the interviewer for communicating her grievance to management and for securing such prompt action. Here no change had been made in the thing criticized; yet the employee felt that something had been done.

Many times they found that people did not really want anything done about the things of which they were complaining. What they did want was an opportunity to talk about their troubles to a sympathetic listener. It was astonishing to find the number of instances in which workers complained about things which had happened many, many years ago, but which they described as vividly as if they had happened just a day before.

Here again, something was "screwy," but this time the experimenters realized that it was their assumptions which were screwy. They were assuming that the meanings which people assign to their experience are essentially logical. They were carrying in their heads the notion of the "economic man," a man primarily motivated by economic interest, whose logical capacities were being used in the service of this self-interest.

Gradually and painfully in the light of the evidence, which was overwhelming, the experimenters had been forced to abandon this conception of the worker and his behavior. Only with a new working hypothesis could they make sense of the data they had collected. The conception of the worker which they developed is actually nothing very new or startling; it is one which any effective administrator intuitively recognizes and practices in handling human beings.

First, they found that the behavior of workers could not be understood apart from their feelings or sentiments. I shall use the word "sentiment" hereafter to refer not only to such things as feelings and emotions, but also to a much wider range of phenomena which may not be expressed in violent feelings or emotions—phenomena that are referred to by such words as "loyalty," "integrity," "solidarity."

Secondly, they found that sentiments are easily disguised, and hence are difficult to recognize and to study. Manifestations of sentiment take a number of different forms. Feelings of personal integrity, for example, can be expressed

by a handshake; they can also be expressed, when violated, by a sitdown strike. Moreover, people like to rationalize their sentiments and to objectify them. We are not so likely to say "I feel bad," as to say "The world is bad." In other words, we like to endow the world with those attributes and qualities which will justify and account for the feelings and sentiments we have toward it; we tend to project our sentiments on the outside world.

Thirdly, they found that manifestations of sentiment could not be understood as things in and by themselves, but only in terms of the total situation of the person. To comprehend why a person felt the way he did, a wider range of phenomena had to be explored. The following three diagrams illustrate roughly the development of this point of view.

It will be remembered that at first the investigators assumed a simple and direct relation between certain physical changes in the worker's environment and his responses to them. This simple state of mind is illustrated in diagram I. But

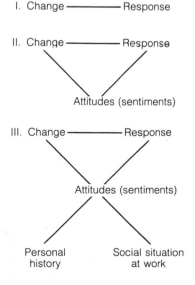

I. Change ———————— Response

II. Change ———————— Response
Attitudes (sentiments)

III. Change ———————— Response
Attitudes (sentiments)
Personal history   Social situation at work

all the evidence of the early experiments showed that the responses of employees to changes in their immediate working environment can be understood only in terms of their attitudes—the "meaning" these changes have for them. This point of view is represented in diagram II. However, the "meaning" which these changes have for the worker is not strictly and primarily logical, for they are fraught with human feelings and values. The "meaning," therefore, which any individual worker assigns to a particular change depends upon (I) his social "conditioning," or what sentiments (values, hopes, fears, expectations, etc.) he is bringing to the work situation because of his previous family and group associations, and hence the relation of the change to these sentiments; and (2) the kind of human satisfaction he is deriving from his social participation with other workers and supervisors in the immediate work group of which he is a member, and hence the effect of the change on his customary interpersonal realtions. This way of regarding the responses of workers (both verbal and overt) is represented in diagram III. It says briefly: Sentiments do not appear in a vacuum; they do not come out of the blue; they appear in a social context. They have to be considered in terms of that context, and apart from it they are likely to be misunderstood.

One further point should be made about that aspect of the worker's environment designated "Social Situation at Work" in diagram III. What is meant is that the worker is not an isolated, atomic individual; he is a member of a group, or of groups. Within each of these groups the individuals have feelings and sentiments toward each other, which bind them together in collaborative effort. Moreover, these collective sentiments can, and do, become attached to every item and object in the industrial environment—even to output. Material goods, output, wages, hours of work, and so on, cannot be treated as things in themselves. Instead, they must be interpreted as carriers of social value.

OUTPUT AS A FORM OF SOCIAL BEHAVIOR

That output is a form of social behavior was well illustrated in a study made by the Hawthorne experimenters, called the Bank Wiring Observation Room. This room contained fourteen workmen representing three occupational groups—wiremen, soldermen, and inspectors. These men were on group piecework, where the more they turned out the more they earned. In such a situation one might have expected that they would have been interested in maintaining total output and that the faster workers would have put pressure on the slower workers to improve their efficiency. But this was not the case. Operating within this group were four basic sentiments, which can be expressed briefly as follows: (I) You should not turn out too much work; if you do, you are a "rate buster." (2) You should not turn out too little work; if you do, you are a "chiseler." (3) You should not say anything to a supervisor which would react to the detriment of one of your associates; if you do, you are a "squealer." (4) You should not be too officious; that is, if you are an inspector you should not act like one.

To be an accepted member of the group a man had to act in accordance with these social standards. One man in this group exceeded the group standard of what constituted a fair day's work. Social pressure was put on him to conform, but without avail, since he enjoyed doing things the others disliked.

The best-liked person in the group was the one who kept his output exactly where the group agreed it should be.

Inasmuch as the operators were agreed as to what constituted a day's work, one might have expected rate of output to be about the same for each member of the group. This was by no means the case; there were marked differences. At first the experimenters thought that the differences in individual performance were related to differences in ability, so they compared each worker's relative rank in output with his relative rank in intelligence and dexterity as measured by certain tests. The results were interesting: The lowest producer in the room ranked first in intelligence and third in dexterity; the highest producer in the room was seventh in dexterity and lowest in intelligence. Here surely was a situation in which the native capacities of the men were not finding expression. From the viewpoint of logical, economic behavior, this room did not make sense. Only in terms of powerful sentiments could these individual differences in output level be explained. Each worker's level of output reflected his position in the informal organization of the group.

WHAT MAKES THE WORKER NOT WANT TO COÖPERATE

As a result of the Bank Wiring Observation Room, the Hawthorne researchers became more and more interested in the informal employee groups which tend to form within the formal organization of the company, and which are not likely to be represented in the organization chart. They became interested in the beliefs and creeds which have the effect of making each individual feel an integral part of the group and which make the group appear as a single unit, in the social codes and norms of behavior by means of which employees automatically work together in a group without any conscious choice as to whether they will or will not coöperate. They studied the important social functions these groups perform for their members, the histories of these informal work groups, how they spontaneously appear, how they tend to perpetuate themselves, multiply, and disappear, how they are in constant jeopardy from technical change, and hence how they tend to resist innovation. In particular, they became interested in those groups whose norms and codes of behavior are at variance with the technical and economic objectives of the company as a whole. They examined the social conditions under which it is more likely for the employee group to separate itself out in opposition to the remainder of the groups which make up the total organization. In such phenomena they felt that they had at last arrived at the heart of the problem of effective collaboration. They obtained a new enlightenment of the present industrial scene; from this point of view, many perplexing problems became more intelligible.

Some people claim, for example, that the size of the pay envelope is the major demand which the employee is making of his job. All the worker wants is to be told what to do and to get paid for doing it. If we look at him and his job in terms of sentiments, this is far from being as generally true as we would like to believe. Most of us want the satisfaction that comes from being accepted and recognized as people of worth by our friends and work associates. Money is only a small part of this social recognition. The way we are greeted by our boss, being asked to help a newcomer, being asked to keep an eye on a difficult operation, being given a job requiring special skill—all of these are acts of social recognition. They tell us how we stand in our work group. We all want tangible evidence of our social importance. We want to have a skill that is socially recognized as useful. We want the feeling of security that comes not so much from the amount of money we have in the bank as from being an accepted member of a group. A man whose job is without social function is like a man without a country; the activity to which he has to give the major portion of his life is robbed of all human meaning and significance.

If this is true—and all the evidence of the Western Electric researches points in this direction—have we not a clue as to the possible basis for labor unrest and disputes? Granted that these disputes are often stated in terms of wages, hours of work, and physical conditions of work, is it not possible that these demands are disguising, or in part are the symptomatic expression of, much more deeply rooted human situations which we have not as yet learned to recognize, to understand, or to control? It has been said there is an irresistible urge on the part of workers to tell the boss off, to tell the boss to go to hell. For some workers this generalization may hold, and I have no reason to believe it does not. But, in those situations where it does, it is telling us something very important about these particular workers and their work situations. Workers who want to tell their boss to go to hell sound to me like people whose feelings of personal integrity have been seriously injured. What in their work situations has shattered their feelings of personal integrity? Until we understand better the answer to this question, we cannot handle effectively people who manifest such sentiments. Without such understanding we are dealing only with words and not with human situations—as I fear our overlo-

gicized machinery for handling employee grievances sometimes does.

The matters of importance to workers which the Hawthorne researches disclosed are not settled primarily by negotiating contracts. If industry today is filled with people living in a social void and without social function, a labor contract can do little to make coöperation possible. If, on the other hand, the workers are an integral part of the social situations in which they work, a legal contract is not of the first importance. Too many of us are more interested in getting our words legally straight than in getting our situations humanly straight.

In summary, therefore, the Western Electric researches seem to me like a beginning on the road back to sanity in employee relations because (1) they offer a fruitful working hypothesis, a few simple and relatively clear ideas for the study and understanding of human situations in business; (2) they offer a simple method by means of which we can explore and deal with the complex human problems in a business organization—this method is a human method: it deals with things which are important to people; and (3) they throw a new light on the precondition for effective collaboration. Too often we think of collaboration as something which can be logically or legally contrived. The Western Electric studies indicate that it is far more a matter of sentiment than a matter of logic. Workers are not isolated, unrelated individuals; they are social animals and should be treated as such.

This statement—the worker is a social animal and should be treated as such—is simple, but the systematic and consistent practice of this point of view is not. If it were systematically practiced, it would revolutionize present-day personnel work. Our technological development in the past hundred years has been tremendous. Our methods of handling people are still archaic. If this civilization is to survive, we must obtain a new understanding of human motivation and behavior in business organizations—an understanding which can be simply but effectively practiced. The Western Electric researches contribute a first step in this direction.

2
A Theory of Human Motivation
Abraham H. Maslow

I. INTRODUCTION

In a previous paper (13) various propositions were presented which would have to be included in any theory of human motivation that could lay claim to being definitive. These conclusions may be briefly summarized as follows:

1. The integrated wholeness of the organism must be one of the foundation stones of motivation theory.

2. The hunger drive (or any other physiological drive) was rejected as a centering point or model for a definitive theory of motivation. Any drive that is somatically based and localizable was shown to be atypical rather than typical in human motivation.

3. Such a theory should stress and center itself upon ultimate or basic goals rather than partial or superficial ones, upon ends rather than means to these ends. Such a stress would imply a more central place for unconscious than for conscious motivations.

4. There are usually available various cultural paths to the same goal. Therefore conscious, specific, local-cultural desires are not as fundamental in motivation theory as the more basic, unconscious goals.

5. Any motivated behavior, either preparatory or consummatory, must be understood to be a channel through which many basic needs may be simultaneously expressed or satisfied. Typically an act has *more* than one motivation.

6. Practically all organismic states are to be understood as motivated and as motivating.

7. Human needs arrange themselves in hierarchies of prepotency. That is to say, the appearance of one need usually rests on the prior satisfaction of another, more prepotent need. Man is a perpetually wanting animal. Also no need or drive can be treated as if it were isolated or discrete; every drive is related to the state of satisfaction or dissatisfaction of other drives.

8. *Lists* of drives will get us nowhere for various theoretical and practical reasons. Furthermore any classification of motivations must deal with the problem of levels of specificity or generalization of the motives to be classified.

9. Classifications of motivations must be based upon goals rather

Source: From "A Theory of Human Motivation," by Abraham H. Maslow, *Psychological Review,* 50. Copyright 1943 by the American Psychological Association. Reprinted by permission.

than upon instigating drives or motivated behavior.

10. Motivation theory should be human-centered rather than animal-centered.

11. The situation or the field in which the organism reacts must be taken into account but the field alone can rarely serve as an exclusive explanation for behavior. Furthermore the field itself must be interpreted in terms of the organism. Field theory cannot be a substitute for motivation theory.

12. Not only the integration of the organism must be taken into account, but also the possibility of isolated, specific, partial or segmental reactions.

It has since become necessary to add to these another affirmation.

13. Motivation theory is not synonymous with behavior theory. The motivations are only one class of determinants of behavior. While behavior is almost always motivated, it is also almost always biologically, culturally and situationally determined as well.

The present paper is an attempt to formulate a positive theory of motivation which will satisfy these theoretical demands and at the same time conform to the known facts, clinical and observational as well as experimental. It derives most directly, however, from clinical experience. This theory is, I think, in the functionalist tradition of James and Dewey, and is fused with the holism of Wertheimer (19), Goldstein (6), and Gestalt Psychology, and with the dynamicism of Freud (4) and Adler (1). This fusion or synthesis may arbitrarily be called a 'general-dynamic' theory.

It is far easier to perceive and to criticize the aspects in motivation theory than to remedy them. Mostly this is because of the very serious lack of sound data in this area. I conceive this lack of sound facts to be due primarily to the absence of a valid theory of motivation. The present theory then must be considered to be a suggested program or framework for future research and must stand or fall, not so much on facts available or evidence presented, as upon researches yet to be done, researches suggested perhaps, by the questions raised in this paper.

II. THE BASIC NEEDS

The 'physiological' needs. The needs that are usually taken as the starting point for motivation theory are the so-called physiological drives. Two recent lines of research make it necessary to revise our customary notions about these needs, first, the development of the concept of homeostasis, and second, the finding that appetites (preferential choices among foods) are a fairly efficient indication of actual needs or lacks in the body.

Homeostasis refers to the body's automatic efforts to maintain a constant, normal state of the blood stream. Cannon (2) has described this process for (1) the water content of the blood, (2) salt content, (3) sugar content, (4) protein content, (5) fat content, (6) calcium content, (7) oxygen content, (8) constant hydrogen-ion level (acid-base balance) and (9) constant temperature of the blood. Obviously this list can be extended to include other minerals, the hormones, vitamins, etc.

Young in a recent article (21) has summarized the work on appetite in its relation to body needs. If the body lacks some chemical, the individual will tend to develop a specific appetite or partial hunger for that food element.

Thus it seems impossible as well as useless to make any list of fundamental physiological needs for they can come to almost any number one might wish, depending on the degree of specificity of description. We can not identify all physiological needs as homeostatic. That sexual desire, sleepiness, sheer activity and maternal behavior in animals, are homeostatic, has not yet been demonstrated. Furthermore, this list would not include the various sensory pleasures (tastes, smells, tickling, stroking) which are probably physiological and which may become the goals of motivated behavior.

In a previous paper (13) it has been pointed out that these physiological drives or needs are to be considered unusual rather than typical because they are isolable, and because they are localizable somatically. That is to say, they are relatively independent of each other, of other motivations and of the organism as a whole, and secondly, in many cases, it is possible to demonstrate a localized, underlying somatic base for the drive. This is true less generally than has been thought (exceptions are fatigue, sleepiness, maternal responses) but it is still true in the classic instance of hunger, sex, and thirst.

It should be pointed out again that any of the physiological needs and the consummatory behavior involved with them serve as channels for all sorts of other needs as well. That is to say, the person who thinks he is hungry may actually be seeking more for comfort, or dependence, than for vitamins or proteins. Conversely, it is possible to satisfy the hunger need in part by other activities such as drinking water or smoking cigarettes. In other words, relatively isolable as these physiological needs are, they are not completely so.

Undoubtedly these physiological needs are the most prepotent of all needs. What this means specifically is, that in the human being who is missing everything in life in an extreme fashion, it is most likely that the major motivation would be the physiological needs rather than any others. A person who is lacking food, safety, love, and esteem would most probably hunger for food more strongly than for anything else.

If all the needs are unsatisfied, and the organism is then dominated by the physiological needs, all other needs may become simply nonexistent or be pushed into the background. It is then fair to characterize the whole organism by saying simply that it is hungry, for consciousness is almost completely preempted by hunger. All capacities are put into the service of hunger-satisfaction, and the organization of these capacities is almost entirely determined by the one purpose of satisfying hunger. The receptors and effectors, the intelligence, memory, habits, all may now be defined simply as hunger-gratifying tools. Capacities that are not useful for this purpose lie dormant, or are pushed into the background. The urge to write poetry, the desire to acquire an automobile, the interest in American history, the desire for a new pair of shoes are, in the extreme case, forgotten or become of secondary importance. For the man who is extremely and dangerously hungry, no other interests exist but food. He dreams food, he remembers food, he thinks about food, he emotes only about food, he perceives only food and he wants only food. The more subtle determinants that ordinarily fuse with the physiological drives in organizing even feeding, drinking or sexual behavior, may now be so completely overwhelmed as to allow us to speak at this time (but *only* at this time) of pure hunger drive and behavior, with the one unqualified aim of relief.

Another peculiar characteristic of the human organism when it is dominated by a certain need is that the whole philosophy of the future tends also to change. For our chronically and extremely hungry man, Utopia can be defined very simply as a place where there is plenty of food. He tends to think that, if only he is guaranteed food for the rest of his life, he will be perfectly happy and will never want anything more. Life itself tends to be defined in terms of eating. Anything else will be defined as unimportant. Freedom, love, community feeling, respect, philosophy, may all be waved aside as fripperies which are useless since they fail to fill the stomach. Such a man may fairly be said to live by bread alone.

It cannot possibly be denied that such things are true but their *generality* can be denied. Emergency conditions are, almost by definition, rare in the normally functioning peaceful society. That this truism can be forgotten is due mainly to two reasons. First, rats have few motivations other than physiological ones, and since so much of the research upon motivation has been made with these animals, it is easy to carry the rat-picture over to the human being. Secondly, it is too often not realized that culture itself is an adaptive tool, one of whose main functions is to make the physiological emergencies come less and less often. In most of the known societies, chronic extreme hunger of the emergency type is rare, rather than common. In any case, this is still true in the United States. The average American citizen is experiencing appetite rather than hunger when he says "I am hungry." He is apt to experience sheer life-and-death hunger only by accident and then only a few times through his entire life.

Obviously a good way to obscure the 'higher' motivations, and to get a lop-sided view of human capacities and human nature, is to make the organism extremely and chronically hungry or thirsty. Anyone who attempts to make an emergency picture into a typical one, and who will measure all of man's goals and desires by his behavior during extreme physiological deprivation is certainly being blind to many things. It is quite true that man lives by bread alone—when there is no bread. But what happens to man's desires when there *is* plenty of bread and when his belly is chronically filled?

At once other (and 'higher') needs emerge and these, rather than physiological hungers, dominate the organism. And when these in turn are satisfied, again new (and still 'higher') needs emerge and so on. This is what we mean by saying that the basic human needs are organized into a hierarchy of relative prepotency.

One main implication of this phrasing is that gratification becomes as important a concept as deprivation in motivation theory, for it releases the organism from the domination of a relatively more physiological need, permitting thereby the emergence of other more social goals. The physiological needs, along with their partial goals, when chronically gratified cease to exist as active determinants or organizers of behavior. They now exist only in a potential fashion in the sense that they may emerge again to dominate the organism if they are thwarted. But a want that is satisfied is no longer a want. The organism is dominated and its behavior organized only by unsatisifed needs. If hunger is satisfied, it becomes unimportant in the current dynamics of the individual.

This statement is somewhat qualified by a hypothesis to be discussed more fully later, namely that it is precisely those individuals in whom a certain need has always been satisfied who are best equipped to tolerate deprivation of that need in the future, and that furthermore, those who have been deprived in the past will react differently to current satisfactions than the one who has never been deprived.

The safety needs. If the physiological needs are relatively well gratified, there then emerges a new set of needs, which we may categorize roughly as the safety needs. All that has been said of the physiological needs is equally true, although in lesser degree, of these desires. The organism may equally well be wholly dominated by them. They may serve as the almost exclusive organizers of behavior, recruiting all the capacities of the organism in their service, and we may then fairly describe the whole organism as a safety-seeking mechanism. Again we may say of the receptors, the effectors, of the intellect and the other capacities that they are primarily safety-seeking tools. Again, as in the hungry man, we find that the dominating goal is a strong determinant not only of his current world-outlook and philosophy but also of his philosophy of the future. Practically everything looks less important than safety, (even sometimes the physiological needs which being satisfied, are now underestimated). A man, in this state, if it is extreme enough and chronic enough, may be characterized as living almost for safety alone.

Although in this paper we are interested primarily in the needs of the adult, we can approach an understanding of his safety needs perhaps more efficiently by observation of infants and children, in whom these needs are much more simple and obvious. One reason for the clearer appearance of the threat or danger reaction in infants, is that they do not inhibit this reaction at all, whereas adults in our society have been taught to inhibit it at all costs. Thus even when adults do feel their safety to be threatened we may not be able to see this on the surface. Infants

will react in a total fashion and as if they were endangered, if they are disturbed or dropped suddenly, startled by loud noises, flashing light, or other unusual sensory stimulation, by rough handling, by general loss of support in the mother's arms, or by inadequate support.[1]

In infants we can also see a much more direct reaction to bodily illnesses of various kinds. Sometimes these illnesses seem to be immediately and *per se* threatening and seem to make the child feel unsafe. For instance, vomiting, colic, or other sharp pains seem to make the child look at the whole world in a different way. At such a moment of pain, it may be postulated that, for the child, the appearance of the whole world suddenly changes from sunniness to darkness, so to speak, and becomes a place in which anything at all might happen, in which previously stable things have suddenly become unstable. Thus a child who because of some bad food is taken ill may, for a day or two, develop fear, nightmares, and a need for protection and reassurance never seen in him before his illness.

Another indication of the child's need for safety is his preference for some kind of undisrupted routine or rhythm. He seems to want a predictable, orderly world. For instance, injustice, unfairness, or inconsistency in the parents seems to make a child feel anxious and unsafe. This attitude may be not so much because of the injustice *per se* or any particular pains involved, but rather because this treatment threatens

[1]As the child grows up, sheer knowledge and familiarity as well as better motor development make these 'dangers' less and less dangerous and more and more manageable. Throughout life it may be said that one of the main conative functions of education is this neutralizing of apparent dangers through knowledge, *e.g.*, I am not afraid of thunder because I know something about it.

to make the world look unreliable, or unsafe, or unpredictable. Young children seem to thrive better under a system which has at least a skeletal outline of rigidity, in which there is a schedule of a kind, some sort of routine, something that can be counted upon, not only for the present but also far into the future. Perhaps one could express this more accurately by saying that the child needs an organized world rather than an unorganized or unstructured one.

The central role of the parents and the normal family setup are indisputable. Quarreling, physical assault, separation, divorce or death within the family may be particularly terrifying. Also parental outbursts of rage or threats of punishment directed to the child, calling him names, speaking to him harshly, shaking him, handling him roughly, or actual physical punishment sometimes elicit such total panic and terror in the child that we must assume more is involved than the physical pain alone. While it is true that in some children this terror may represent also a fear of loss of parental love, it can also occur in completely rejected children, who seem to cling to the hating parents more for sheer safety and protection than because of hope of love.

Confronting the average child with new, unfamiliar, strange, unmanageable stimuli or situations will too frequently elicit the danger or terror reaction, as for example, getting lost or even being separated from the parents for a short time, being confronted with new faces, new situations or new tasks, the sight of strange, unfamiliar or uncontrollable objects, illness or death. Particularly at such times, the child's frantic clinging to his parents is eloquent testimony to their role as protectors (quite apart from their roles as food-givers and love-givers).

From these and similar observations, we may generalize and say that the average child in our society generally prefers a safe, orderly, predictable, organized world, which he can count on, and in which unexpected, unmanageable or other dangerous things do not happen, and in which, in any case, he has all-powerful parents who protect and shield him from harm.

That these reactions may so easily be observed in children is in a way a proof of the fact that children in our society, feel too unsafe (or, in a word, are badly brought up). Children who are reared in an unthreatening, loving family do *not* ordinarily react as we have described above (17). In such children the danger reactions are apt to come mostly to objects or situations that adults too would consider dangerous.[2]

The healthy, normal, fortunate adult in our culture is largely satisfied in his safety needs. The peaceful, smoothly running, 'good' society ordinarily makes its members feel safe enough from wild animals, extremes of temperature, criminals, assault and murder, tyranny, etc. Therefore, in a very real sense, he no longer has any safety needs as active motivators. Just as a sated man no longer feels hungry, a safe man no longer feels endangered. If we wish to see these needs directly and clearly we must turn to neurotic or near-neurotic individuals, and to the economic and social underdogs. In between these extremes, we can perceive the expressions of safety needs only in such phenomena

[2] A 'test battery' for safety might be confronting the child with a small exploding firecracker, or with a bewhiskered face, having the mother leave the room, putting him upon a high ladder, a hypodermic injection, having a mouse crawl up to him, etc. Of course I cannot seriously recommend the deliberate use of such 'tests' for they might very well harm the child being tested. But these and similar situations come up by the score in the child's ordinary day-to-day living and may be observed. There is no reason why these stimuli should not be used with, for example, young chimpanzees.

as, for instance, the common preference for a job with tenure and protection, the desire for a savings account, and for insurance of various kinds (medical, dental, unemployment, disability, old age).

Other broader aspects of the attempt to seek safety and stability in the world are seen in the very common preference for familiar rather than unfamiliar things, or for the known rather than the unknown. The tendency to have some religion or world-philosophy that organizes the universe and the men in it into some sort of satisfactorily coherent, meaningful whole is also in part motivated by safety-seeking. Here too we may list science and philosophy in general as partially motivated by the safety needs (we shall see later that there are also other motivations to scientific, philosophical or religious endeavor).

Otherwise the need for safety is seen as an active and dominant mobilizer of the organism's resources only in emergencies, *e.g.*, war, disease, natural catastrophes, crime waves, societal disorganization, neurosis, brain injury, chronically bad situation.

Some neurotic adults in our society are, in many ways, like the unsafe child in their desire for safety, although in the former it takes on a somewhat special appearance. Their reaction is often to unknown, psychological dangers in a world that is perceived to be hostile, overwhelming and threatening. Such a person behaves as if a great catastrophe were almost always impending, *i.e.*, he is usually responding as if to an emergency. His safety needs often find specific expression in a search for a protector, or a stronger person on whom he may depend, or perhaps, a Fuehrer.

The neurotic individual may be described in a slightly different way with some usefulness as a grown-up person who retains his childish attitudes toward the world. That is to say, a neurotic adult may be said to behave 'as if' he were actually afraid of a spanking, or of his mother's disapproval, or of being abandoned by his parents, or having his food taken away from him. It is as if his childish attitudes of fear and threat reaction to a dangerous world had gone underground, and untouched by the growing up and learning processes, were now ready to be called out by any stimulus that would make a child feel endangered and threatened.[3]

The neurosis in which the search for safety takes its clearest form is in the compulsive-obsessive neurosis. Compulsive-obsessives try frantically to order and stabilize the world so that no unmanageable, unexpected or unfamiliar dangers will ever appear (14). They hedge themselves about with all sorts of ceremonials, rules and formulas so that every possible contingency may be provided for and so that no new contingencies may appear. They are much like the brain injured cases, described by Goldstein (6), who manage to maintain their equilibrium by avoiding everything unfamiliar and strange and by ordering their restricted world in such a neat, disciplined, orderly fashion that everything in the world can be counted upon. They try to arrange the world so that anything unexpected (dangers) cannot possibly occur. If, through no fault of their own, something unexpected does occur, they go into a panic reaction as if this unexpected occurrence constituted a grave danger. What we can see only as a none-too-strong preference in the healthy person, *e.g.*, preference for the familiar, becomes a life-and-death necessity in abnormal cases.

[3]Not all neurotic individuals feel unsafe. Neurosis may have at its core a thwarting of the affection and esteem needs in a person who is generally safe.

The love needs. If both the physiological and the safety needs are fairly well gratified, then there will emerge the love and affection and belongingness needs, and the whole cycle already described will repeat itself with this new center. Now the person will feel keenly, as never before, the absence of friends, or a sweetheart, or a wife, or children. He will hunger for affectionate relations with people in general, namely, for a place in his group, and he will strive with great intensity to achieve this goal. He will want to attain such a place more than anything else in the world and may even forget that once, when he was hungry, he sneered at love.

In our society the thwarting of these needs is the most commonly found core in cases of maladjustment and more severe psychopathology. Love and affection, as well as their possible expression in sexuality, are generally looked upon with ambivalence and are customarily hedged about with many restrictions and inhibitions. Practically all theorists of psychopathology have stressed thwarting of the love needs as basic in the picture of maladjustment. Many clinical studies have therefore been made of this need and we know more about it perhaps than any of the other needs except the physiological ones (14).

One thing that must be stressed at this point is that love is not synonymous with sex. Sex may be studied as a purely physiological need. Ordinarily sexual behavior is multi-determined, that is to say, determined not only by sexual but also by other needs, chief among which are the love and affection needs. Also not to be overlooked is the fact that the love needs involve both giving *and* receiving love.[4]

The esteem needs. All people in our society (with a few pathological exceptions) have a need or desire for a stable, firmly based, (usually) high evaluation of themselves, for self-respect, or self-esteem, and for the esteem of others. By firmly based self-esteem, we mean that which is soundly based upon real capacity, achievement and respect from others. These needs may be classified into two subsidiary sets. These are, first, the desire for strength, for achievement, for adequacy, for confidence in the face of the world, and for independence and freedom.[5] Secondly, we have what we may call the desire for reputation or prestige (defining it as respect or esteem from other people), recognition, attention, importance or appreciation.[6] These needs have been relatively stressed by Alfred Adler and his followers, and have been relatively neglected by Freud and the psychoanalysts. More and more today however there is appearing widespread appreciation of their central importance.

Satisfaction of the self-esteem need leads to feelings of self-confidence, worth, strength, capability and adequacy of being useful and necessary in

[4]For further details see (12) and (16, Chap. 5).

[5]Whether or not this particular desire is universal we do not know. The crucial question, especially important today, is "Will men who are enslaved and dominated, inevitably feel dissatisfied and rebellious?" We may assume on the basis of commonly known clinical data that a man who has known true freedom (not paid for by giving up safety and security but rather built on the basis of adequate safety and security) will not willingly or easily allow his freedom to be taken away from him. But we do not know that this is true for the person born into slavery. The events of the next decade should give us our answer. See discussion of this problem in (5).

[6]Perhaps the desire for prestige and respect from others is subsidiary to the desire for self-esteem or confidence in oneself. Observation of children seems to indicate that this is so, but clinical data give no clear support for such a conclusion.

the world. But thwarting of these needs produces feelings of inferiority, of weakness and of helplessness. These feelings in turn give rise to either basic discouragement or else compensatory or neurotic trends. An appreciation of the necessity of basic self-confidence and an understanding of how helpless people are without it, can be easily gained from a study of severe traumatic neurosis (8).[7]

The need for self-actualization. Even if all these needs are satisfied, we may still often (if not always) expect that a new discontent and restlessness will soon develop, unless the individual is doing what he is fitted for. A musician must make music, an artist must paint, a poet must write, if he is to be ultimately happy. What a man *can* be, he *must* be. This need we may call self-actualization.

This term, first coined by Kurt Goldstein, is being used in this paper in a much more specific and limited fashion. It refers to the desire for self-fulfillment, namely, to the tendency for him to become actualized in what he is potentially. This tendency might be phrased as the desire to become more and more what one is, to become everything that one is capable of becoming.

The specific form that these needs will take will of course vary greatly from person to person. In one individual it may take the form of the desire to be an ideal mother, in another it may be expressed athletically, and in still another it may be expressed in painting pictures or in inventions. It is not necessarily a creative urge although in people who have any capacities for creation it will take this form.

The clear emergence of these needs

rests upon prior satisfaction of the physiological, safety, love and esteem needs. We shall call people who are satisfied in these needs, basically satisfied people, and it is from these that we may expect the fullest (and healthiest) creativeness.[8] Since, in our society, basically satisfied people are the exception, we do not know much about self-actualization, either experimentally or clinically. It remains a challenging problem for research.

The preconditions for the basic need satisfactions. There are certain conditions which are immediate prerequisites for the basic need satisfactions. Danger to these is reacted to almost as if it were a direct danger to the basic needs themselves. Such conditions as freedom to speak, freedom to do what one wishes so long as no harm is done to others, freedom to express one's self, freedom to investigate and seek for information, freedom to defend one's self, justice, fairness, honesty, orderliness in the group are examples of such preconditions for basic need satisfactions. Thwarting in these freedoms will be reacted to with a threat or emergency response. These conditions are not ends in themselves but they are *almost* so since they are so closely related to the basic needs, which are apparently the only ends in themselves. These con-

---

[7]For more extensive discussion of normal self-esteem, as well as for reports of various researches, see (11).

[8]Clearly creative behavior, like painting, is like any other behavior in having multiple determinants. It may be seen in 'innately creative' people whether they are satisfied or not, happy or unhappy, hungry or sated. Also it is clear that creative activity may be compensatory, ameliorative or purely economic. It is my impression (as yet unconfirmed) that it is possible to distinguish the artistic and intellectual products of basically satisfied people from those of basically unsatisfied people by inspection alone. In any case, here too we must distinguish, in a dynamic fashion, the overt behavior itself from its various motivations or purposes.

ditions are defended because without them the basic satisfactions are quite impossible, or at least, very severely endangered.

If we remember that the cognitive capacities (perceptual, intellectual, learning) are a set of adjustive tools, which have, among other functions, that of satisfaction of our basic needs, then it is clear that any danger to them, any deprivation or blocking of their free use, must also be indirectly threatening to the basic needs themselves. Such a statement is a partial solution of the general problems of curiosity, the search for knowledge, truth and wisdom, and the ever-persistent urge to solve the cosmic mysteries.

We must therefore introduce another hypothesis and speak of degrees of closeness to the basic needs, for we have already pointed out that *any* conscious desires (partial goals) are more or less important as they are more or less close to the basic needs. The same statement may be made for various behavior acts. An act is psychologically important if it contributes directly to satisfaction of basic needs. The less directly it so contributes, or the weaker this contribution is, the less important this act must be conceived to be from the point of view of dynamic psychology. A similar statement may be made for the various defense or coping mechanisms. Some are very directly related to the protection or attainment of the basic needs, others are only weakly and distantly related. Indeed if we wished, we could speak of more basic and less basic defense mechanisms, and then affirm that danger to the more basic defenses (always remembering that this is so only because of their relationship to the basic needs).

The desires to know and to understand. So far, we have mentioned the cognitive needs only in passing. Acquiring knowledge and systematizing the uni-verse have been considered as, in part, techniques for the achievement of basic safety in the world, or, for the intelligent man, expressions of self-actualization. Also freedom of inquiry and expression have been discussed as preconditions of satisfactions of the basic needs. True though these formulations may be, they do not constitute definitive answers to the question as to the motivation role of curiosity, learning, philosophizing, experimenting, etc. They are, at best, no more than partial answers.

This question is especially difficult because we know so little about the facts. Curiosity, exploration, desire for the facts, desire to know may certainly be observed easily enough. The fact that they often are pursued even at great cost to the individual's safety is an earnest of the partial character of our previous discussion. In addition, the writer must admit that, though he has sufficient clinical evidence to postulate the desire to know as a very strong drive in intelligent people, no data are available for unintelligent people. It may then be largely a function of relatively high intelligence. Rather tentatively, then, and largely in the hope of stimulating discussion and research, we shall postulate a basic desire to know, to be aware of reality, to get the facts, to satisfy curiosity, or as Wertheimer phrases it, to see rather than to be blind.

This postulation, however, is not enough. Even after we know, we are impelled to know more and more minutely and microscopically on the one hand, and on the other, more and more extensively in the direction of a world philosophy, religion, etc. The facts that we acquire, if they are isolated or atomistic, inevitably get theorized about, and either analyzed or organized or both. This process has been phrased by some as the search for 'meaning.' We shall then postulate a desire to understand, to systematize, to organize, to analyze, to look for relations and meanings.

Once these desires are accepted for discussion, we see that they too form themselves into a small hierarchy in which the desire to know is prepotent over the desire to understand. All the characteristics of a hierarchy of prepotency that we have described above, seem to hold for this one as well.

We must guard ourselves against the too easy tendency to separate these desires from the basic needs we have discussed above, *i.e.*, to make a sharp dichotomy between 'cognitive' and 'conative' needs. The desire to know and to understand are themselves conative, *i.e.*, have a striving character, and are as much personality needs as the 'basic needs' we have already discussed (19).

III. FURTHER CHARACTERISTICS OF THE BASIC NEEDS

The degree of fixity of the hierarchy of basic needs. We have spoken so far as if this hierarchy were a fixed order but actually it is not nearly as rigid as we may have implied. It is true that most of the people with whom we have worked have seemed to have these basic needs in about the order that has been indicated. However, there have been a number of exceptions.

1. There are some people in whom, for instance, self-esteem seems to be more important than love. This most common reversal in the hierarchy is usually due to the development of the notion that the person who is most likely to be loved is a strong or powerful person, one who inspires respect or fear, and who is self confident or aggressive. Therefore such people who lack love and seek it, may try hard to put on a front of aggressive, confident behavior. But essentially they seek high self-esteem and its behavior expressions more as a means-to-an-end than for its own sake; they seek self-assertion for the sake of love rather than for self-esteem itself.

2. There are other, apparently innately creative people in whom the drive to creativeness seems to be more important than any other counter-determinant. Their creativeness might appear not as self-actualization released by basic satisfaction, but in spite of lack of basic satisfaction.

3. In certain people the level of aspiration may be permanently deadened or lowered. That is to say, the less prepotent goals may simply be lost, and may disappear forever, so that the person who has experienced life at a very low level, *i.e.*, chronic unemployment, may continue to be satisfied for the rest of his life if only he can get enough food.

4. The so-called 'psychopathic personality' is another example of permanent loss of the love needs. These are people who, according to the best data available (9), have been starved for love in the earliest months of their lives and have simply lost forever the desire and the ability to give and to receive affection (as animals lose sucking or pecking reflexes that are not exercised soon enough after birth).

5. Another cause of reversal of the hierarchy is that when a need has been satisfied for a long time, this need may be underevaluated. People who have never experienced chronic hunger are apt to underestimate its effects and to look upon food as a rather unimportant thing. If they are dominated by a higher need, this higher need will seem to be the most important of all. It then be-

comes possible, and indeed does actually happen, that they may, for the sake of this higher need, put themselves into the position of being deprived in a more basic need. We may expect that after a long-time deprivation of the more basic need there will be a tendency to reevaluate both needs so that the more prepotent need will actually become consciously prepotent for the individual who may have given it up very lightly. Thus, a man who has given up his job rather than lose his self-respect, and who then starves for six months or so, may be willing to take his job back even at the price of losing his self-respect.

6. Another partial explanation of *apparent* reversals is seen in the fact that we have been talking about the hierarchy of prepotency in terms of consciously felt wants or desires rather than of behavior. Looking at behavior itself may give us the wrong impression. What we have claimed is that the person will *want* the more basic of two needs when deprived in both. There is no necessary implication here that he will act upon his desires. Let us say again that there are many determinants of behavior other than the needs and desires.

7. Perhaps more important than all these exceptions are the ones that involve ideals, high social standards, high values and the like. With such values people become martyrs; they will give up everything for the sake of a particular ideal, or value. These people may be understood, at least in part, by reference to one basic concept (or hypothesis) which may be called 'increased frustration-tolerance through early gratification.' People who have been satisfied in their basic needs throughout their lives, particularly in their earlier years, seem to develop exceptional power to withstand present or future thwarting of these needs simply because they have strong, healthy character structure as a result of basic satisfaction. They are the 'strong' people who can easily weather disagreement or opposition, who can swim against the stream of public opinion and who can stand up for the truth at great personal cost. It is just the ones who have loved and been well loved, and who have had many deep friendships who can hold out against hatred, rejection or persecution.

I say all this in spite of the fact that there is a certain amount of sheer habituation which is also involved in any full discussion of frustration tolerance. For instance, it is likely that those persons who have been accustomed to relative starvation for a long time, are partially enabled thereby to withstand food deprivation. What sort of balance must be made between these two tendencies, of habituation on the one hand, and of past satisfaction breeding present frustration tolerance on the other hand, remains to be worked out by further research. Meanwhile we may assume that they are both operative, side by side, since they do not contradict each other. In respect to this phenomenon of increased frustration tolerance, it seems probable that the most important gratifications come in the first two years of life. That is to say, people who have been made secure and strong in the earliest years, tend to remain secure and strong thereafter in the face of whatever threatens.

Degrees of relative satisfaction. So far, our theoretical discussion may have given the impression that these five sets of needs are somehow in a step-wise, all-or-none relationships to each other. We have spoken in such terms as the following: "If one need is satisfied, then another emerges." This statement might give the false impression that a need must be satisfied 100 per cent before the next need emerges. In actual fact, most members of our society who are normal, are partially satisfied in all their basic needs and partially unsatisfied in all their basic needs at the same time. A more realistic description of the hierarchy would be in terms of decreasing percentages of satisfaction as we go up the hierarchy of prepotency. For instance, if I may assign arbitrary figures for the sake of illustration, it is as if the average citizen is satisfied perhaps 85 per cent in his physiological needs, 70 per cent in his safety needs, 50 per cent in his love needs, 40 per cent in his self-esteem needs, and 10 per cent in his self-actualization needs.

As for the concept of emergence of a new need after satisfaction of the prepotent need, this emergence is not a sudden, saltatory phenomenon but rather a gradual emergence by slow degrees from nothingness. For instance, if prepotent need A is satisfied only 10 per cent then need B may not be visible at all. However, as this need A becomes satisfied 25 per cent, need B may emerge 5 per cent, as need A becomes satisfied 75 per cent need B may emerge 90 per cent, and so on.

Unconscious character of needs. These needs are neither necessarily conscious nor unconscious. On the whole, however, in the average person, they are more often unconscious rather than conscious. It is not necessary at this point to overhaul the tremendous mass of evidence which indicates the crucial importance of unconscious motivation. It would by now be expected, on a priori grounds alone, that unconscious motivations would on the whole be rather more important than the conscious motivations. What we have called the basic needs are very often largely unconscious although they may, with suitable techniques, and with sophisticated people become conscious.

Cultural specificity and generality of needs. This classification of basic needs makes some attempt to take account of the relative unity behind the superficial differences in specific desires from one culture to another. Certainly in any particular culture an individual's conscious motivational content will usually be extremely different from the conscious motivational content of an individual in another society. However, it is the common experience of anthropologists that people, even in different societies, are much more alike than we would think from our first contact with them, and that as we know them better we seem to find more and more of this commonness. We then recognize the most startling differences to be superficial rather than basic, *e.g.*, differences in style of hairdress, clothes, tastes in food, etc. Our classification of basic needs is in part an attempt to account for this unity behind the apparent diversity from culture to culture. No claim is made that it is ultimate or universal for all cultures. The claim is made only that it is relatively *more* ultimate, more universal, more basic, than the superficial conscious desires from culture to culture, and makes a somewhat closer approach to common-human characteristics. Basic needs are *more* common-human than superficial desires or behaviors.

Multiple motivations of behavior. These needs must be understood *not* to be *exclusive* or single determiners of certain kinds of behavior. An example may be found in any behavior that seems to be physiologically motivated, such as eating, or sexual play or the like. The clinical psychologists have long since found that any behavior may be a channel through which flow various determinants. Or to say it in another way, most behavior is multi-motivated. Within the sphere of motivational determinants any behavior tends to be

maslow

determined by several or *all* of the basic needs simultaneously rather than by only one of them. The latter would be more an exception that the former. Eating may be partially for the sake of filling the stomach, and partially for the sake of comfort and amelioration of other needs. One may make love not only for pure sexual release, but also to convince one's self of one's masculinity, or to make a conquest, to feel powerful, or to win more basic affection. As an illustration, I may point out that it would be possible (theoretically if not practically) to analyze a single act of an individual and see in it the expression of his physiological needs, his safety needs, his love needs, his esteem needs and self-actualization. This contrasts sharply with the more naive brand of trait psychology in which one trait or one motive accounts for a certain kind of act, *i.e.*, an aggressive act is traced soley to a trait of aggressiveness.

Multiple determinants of behavior. Not all behavior is determined by the basic needs. We might even say that not all behavior is motivated. There are many determinants of behavior other than motives.[9] For instance, one other important class of determinants is the so-called 'field' determinants. Theoretically, at least, behavior may be determined completely by the field, or even by specific isolated external stimuli, as in association of ideas, or certain conditioned reflexes. If in response to the stimulus word 'table,' I immediately perceive a memory image of a table, this response certainly has nothing to do with my basic needs.

Secondly, we may call attention again to the concept of 'degree of closeness to the basic needs' or 'degree of motivation.' Some behavior is highly motivated, other behavior is only weakly motivated. Some is not motivated at all (but all behavior is determined).

Another important point[10] is that there is a basic difference between expressive behavior and coping behavior (functional striving, purposive goal seeking). An expressive behavior does not try to do anything; it is simply a reflection of the personality. A stupid man behaves stupidly, not because he wants to, or tries to, or is motivated to, but simply because he *is* what he is. The same is true when I speak in a bass voice rather than tenor or soprano. The random movements of a healthy child, the smile on the face of a happy man even when he is alone, the springiness of the healthy man's walk, and the erectness of his carriage are other examples of expressive, non-functional behavior. Also the *style* in which a man carries out almost all his behavior, motivated as well as unmotivated, is often expressive.

We may then ask, is *all* behavior expressive or reflective of the character structure? The answer is 'No.' Rote, habitual, automatized, or conventional behavior may or may not be expressive. The same is true for most 'stimulus-bound' behaviors.

It is finally necessary to stress that expressiveness of behavior, and goal-directedness of behavior are not mutually exclusive categories. Average behavior is usually both.

Goals as centering principle in motivation theory. It will be observed that the basic principle in our classification has been neither the instigation nor the motivated behavior but rather the functions, effects, purposes, or goals of the behavior. It has been proven sufficiently by various people that this is the most

---

[9] I am aware that many psychologists and psychoanalysts use the term 'motivated' and 'determined' synonymously, *e.g.*, Freud. But I consider this an obfuscating usage. Sharp distinctions are necessary for clarity of thought, and precision in experimentation.

[10] To be discussed fully in a subsequent publication.

suitable point for centering in any motivation theory.[11]

Animal- and human-centering. This theory starts with the human being rather than any lower and presumably 'simpler' animal. Too many of the findings that have been made in animals have been proven to be true for animals but not for the human being. There is no reason whatsoever why we should start with animals in order to study human motivation. The logic or rather illogic behind this general fallacy of 'pseudo-simplicity' has been exposed often enough by philosophers and logicians as well as by scientists in each of the various fields. It is no more necessary to study animals before one can study man than it is to study mathematics before one can study geology or psychology or biology.

We may also reject the old, naive behaviorism which assumed that it was somehow necessary, or at least more 'scientific' to judge human beings by animal standards. One consequence of this belief was that the whole notion of purpose and goal was excluded from motivational psychology simply because one could not ask a white rat about his purposes. Tolman (18) has long since proven in animal studies themselves that this exclusion was not necessary.

Motivation and the theory of psychopathogenesis. The conscious motivational content of everyday life has, according to the foregoing, been conceived to be relatively important or unimportant accordingly as it is more or less closely related to the basic goals. A desire for an ice cream cone might actually be an indirect expression of a desire for love. If it is, then this desire for the ice cream cone becomes extremely

important motivation. If however the ice cream is simply something to cool the mouth with, or a casual appetitive reaction, then the desire is relatively unimportant. Everyday conscious desires are to be regarded as symptoms, as *surface indicators of more basic needs.* If we were to take these superficial desires at their face value we would find ourselves in a state of complete confusion which could never be resolved, since we would be dealing seriously with symptoms rather than with what lay behind the symptoms.

Thwarting of unimportant desires produces no psychopathological results; thwarting of a basically important need does produce such results. Any theory of psychopathogenesis must then be based on a sound theory of motivation. A conflict or a frustration is not necessarily pathogenic. It becomes so only when it threatens or thwarts the basic needs, or partial needs that are closely related to the basic needs (10).

The role of gratified needs. It has been pointed out above several times that our needs usually emerge only when more prepotent needs have been gratified. Thus gratification has an important role in motivation theory. Apart from this, however, needs cease to play an active determining or organizing role as soon as they are gratified.

What this means is that, *e.g.*, a basically satisfied person no longer has the needs for esteem, love, safety, etc. The only sense in which he might be said to have them is in the almost metaphysical sense that a sated man has hunger, or a filled bottle has emptiness. If we are interested in what *actually* motivates us, and not in what has, will, or might motivate us, then a satisfied need is not a motivator. It must be considered for all practical purposes simply not to exist, to have disappeared. This point should be emphasized because it has been either

[11]The interested reader is referred to the very excellent discussion of this point in Murray's *Explorations in Personality* (15).

maslow

overlooked or contradicted in every theory of motivation I know.[12] The perfectly healthy, normal, fortunate man has no sex needs or hunger needs, or needs for safety, or for love, or for prestige, or self-esteem, except in stray moments of quickly passing threat. If we were to say otherwise, we should also have to aver that every man had all the pathological reflexes, *e.g.*, Babinski, etc., because if his nervous system were damaged, these would appear.

It is such considerations as these that suggest the bold postulation that a man who is thwarted in any of his basic needs may fairly be envisaged simply as a sick man. This is a fair parallel to our designation as 'sick' of the man who lacks vitamins or minerals. Who is to say that a lack of love is less important than a lack of vitamins? Since we know the pathogenic effects of love starvation, who is to say that we are invoking value-questions in an unscientific or illegitimate way, any more than the physician does who diagnoses and treats pellagra or scurvy? If I were permitted this usage, I should then say simply that a healthy man is primarily motivated by his needs to develop and actualize his fullest potentialities and capacities. If a man has any other basic needs in any active, chronic sense, then he is simply an unhealthy man. He is as surely sick as if he had suddenly developed a strong salt-hunger or calcium hunger.[13]

If this statement seems unusual or paradoxical the reader may be assured that this is only one among many such paradoxes that will appear as we revise our ways of looking at man's deeper motivations. When we ask what man wants of life, we deal with his very essence.

IV. SUMMARY

1. There are at least five sets of goals, which we may call basic needs. These are briefly physiological, safety, love, esteem, and self-actualization. In addition, we are motivated by the desire to achieve or maintain the various conditions upon which these basic satisfactions rest and by certain more intellectual desires.

2. These basic goals are related to each other, being arranged in a hierarchy of prepotency. This means that the most prepotent goal will monopolize consciousness and will tend of itself to organize the recruitment of the various capacities of the organism. The less prepotent needs are minimized, even forgotten or denied. But when a need is fairly well satisfied, the next prepotent ('higher') need emerges, in turn to dominate the conscious life and to serve as the center of organization of behavior, since gratified needs are not active motivators.

Thus man is a perpetually wanting animal. Ordinarily the satisfaction of these wants is not altogether mutually exclusive, but only tends to be. The average member of our society is most often partially satisfied and partially unsatisfied in all of his wants. The hierarchy principle is usually empirically

[12]Note that acceptance of this theory necessitates basic revision of the Freudian theory.

[13]If we were to use the word 'sick' in this way, we should then also have to face squarely the relations of man to his society. One clear implication of our definition would be that (1) since a man is to be called sick who is basically thwarted, and (2) since such basic thwarting is made possible ultimately only by forces outside the individual, then (3) sickness in the individual must come ultimately from a

sickness in the society. The 'good' or healthy society would then be defined as one that permitted man's highest purposes to emerge by satisfying all his prepotent basic needs.

observed in terms of increasing percentages of non-satisfaction as we go up the hierarchy. Reversals of the average order of the hierarchy are sometimes observed. Also it has been observed that an individual may permanently lose the higher wants in the hierarchy under special conditions. There are not only ordinarily multiple motivations for usual behavior, but in addition many determinants other than motives.

3. Any thwarting or possibility of thwarting of these basic human goals, or danger to the defenses which protect them, or to the conditions upon which they rest, is considered to be a psychological threat. With a few exceptions, all psychopathology may be partially traced to such threats. A basically thwarted man may actually be defined as a 'sick' man, if we wish.

4. It is such basic threats which bring about the general emergency reactions.

5. Certain other basic problems have not been dealt with because of limitations of space. Among these are (*a*) the problem of values in any definitive motivation theory, (*b*) the relation between appetites, desires, needs and what is 'good' for the organism, (*c*) the etiology of the basic needs and their possible derivation in early childhood, (*d*) redefinition of motivational concepts, *i.e.*, drive, desire, wish, need, goal, (*e*) implication of our theory for hedonistic theory, (*f*) the nature of the uncompleted act, of success and failure, and of aspiration-level, (*g*) the role of association, habit and conditioning, (*h*) relation to the theory of inter-personal relations, (*i*) implications for psychotherapy, (*j*) implication for theory of society, (*k*) the theory of selfishness, (*l*) the relation between needs and cultural patterns, (*m*) the relation between this

theory and Allport's theory of functional autonomy. These as well as certain other less important questions must be considered as motivation theory attempts to become definitive.

REFERENCES

1. Adler, A. *Social interest.* London: Faber & Faber, 1938.

2. Cannon, W. B. *Wisdom of the body.* New York: Norton, 1932.

3. Freud, A. *The ego and the mechanisms of defense.* London: Hogarth, 1937.

4. Freud, S. *New introductory lectures on psychoanalysis.* New York: Norton, 1933.

5. Fromm, E. *Escape from freedom.* New York: Farrar and Rinehart, 1941.

6. Goldstein, K. *The organism.* New York: American Book Co., 1939.

7. Horney, K. *The neurotic personality of our time.* New York: Norton, 1937.

8. Kardiner, A. *The traumatic neuroses of war.* New York: Hoeber, 1941.

9. Levy, D. M. Primary affect hunger. *Amer. J. Psychiat.*, 1937, 94, 643–652.

10. Maslow, A. H. Conflict, frustration, and the theory of threat. *J. Abnorm. (soc.) Psychol.*, 1943, 38, 81–86.

11. ———. Dominance, personality and social behavior in women. *J. Soc. Psychol.*, 1939, 10, 3–39.

12. ———. The dynamics of psychological security-insecurity. *Character & Pers.*, 1942, 10, 331–344.

13. ———. A preface to motivation theory. *Psychosomatic Med.*, 1943, 5, 85–92.

14. ———, & Mittelmann, B. *Principles of abnormal psychology.* New York: Harper & Bros., 1941.

15. Murray, H. A., *et al. Explorations in personality.* New York: Oxford University Press, 1938.

16. Plant, J. *Personality and the cultural pattern.* New York: Commonwealth Fund, 1937.

17. Shirley, M. Children's adjustments to a strange situation. *J. Abnorm. (soc.) Psychol.*, 1942, 37, 201–217.

18. Tolman, E. C. *Purposive behavior in animals and men.* New York: Century, 1932.

19. Wertheimer, M. Unpublished lectures at the New School for Social Research.

20. Young, P. T. *Motivation of behavior.* New York: John Wiley & Sons, 1936.

21. ————. The experimental analysis of appetite. *Psychol. Bull.,* 1941, 38, 129–164.

3
The Human Side of Enterprise
Douglas Murray McGregor

It has become trite to say that industry has the fundamental know-how to utilize physical science and technology for the material benefit of mankind, and that we must now learn how to utilize the social sciences to make our human organizations truly effective.

To a degree, the social sciences today are in a position like that of the physical sciences with respect to atomic energy in the thirties. We know that past conceptions of the nature of man are inadequate and, in many ways, incorrect. We are becoming quite certain that, under proper conditions, unimagined resources of creative human energy could become available within the organizational setting.

We cannot tell industrial management how to apply this new knowledge in simple, economic ways. We know it will require years of exploration, much costly development research, and a substantial amount of creative imagination on the part of management to discover how to apply this growing knowledge to the organization of human effort in industry.

MANAGEMENT'S TASK: THE CONVENTIONAL VIEW

The conventional conception of management's task in harnessing human energy to organizational requirements can be stated broadly in terms of three propositions. In order to avoid the complications introduced by a label, let us call this set of propositions "Theory X":

1. Management is responsible for organizing the elements of productive enterprise—money, materials, equipment, people—in the interest of economic ends.

2. With respect to people, this is a process of directing their efforts, motivating them, controlling their actions, modifying their behavior to fit the needs of the organization.

3. Without this active intervention by management, people would be passive—even resistant—to organizational needs. They must therefore be persuaded, rewarded, punished, controlled—their activities must be directed. This is management's task. We often sum it up by saying that management consists of getting things done through other people.

    Behind this conventional theory there are several additional beliefs—less explicit, but widespread:

4. The average man is by nature indolent—he works as little as possible.

Source: Reprinted, by permission of the publisher, from "The Human Side of Enterprise" by Douglas Murray McGregor, 1957, *Management Review*. Copyright 1957 by the American Management Association, New York. All rights reserved.

Note: This article is based on an address by Dr. McGregor before the Fifth Anniversary Convocation of the M.I.T. School of Industrial Management.

5. He lacks ambition, dislikes responsibility, prefers to be led.
6. He is inherently self-centered, indifferent to organizational needs.
7. He is by nature resistant to change.
8. He is gullible, not very bright, the ready dupe of the charlatan and the demagogue.

The human side of economic enterprise today is fashioned from propositions and beliefs such as these. Conventional organization structures and managerial policies, practices, and programs reflect these assumptions.

In accomplishing its task—with these assumptions as guides—management has conceived of a range of possibilities.

At one extreme, management can be "hard" or "strong." The methods for directing behavior involve coercion and threat (usually disguised), close supervision, tight controls over behavior. At the other extreme, management can be "soft" or "weak." The methods for directing behavior involve being permissive, satisfying people's demands, achieving harmony. Then they will be tractable, accept direction.

This range has been fairly completely explored during the past half century, and management has learned some things from the exploration. There are difficulties in the "hard" approach. Force breeds counter-forces: restriction of output, antagonism, militant unionism, subtle but effective sabotage of management objectives. This "hard" approach is especially difficult during times of full employment.

There are also difficulties in the "soft" approach. It leads frequently to the abdication of management—to harmony, perhaps, but to indifferent performance. People take advantage of the soft approach. They continually expect more, but they give less and less.

Currently, the popular theme is "firm but fair." This is an attempt to gain the advantages of both the hard and the soft approaches. It is reminiscent of Teddy Roosevelt's "speak softly and carry a big stick."

IS THE CONVENTIONAL VIEW CORRECT?

The findings which are beginning to emerge from the social sciences challenge this whole set of beliefs about man and human nature and about the task of management. The evidence is far from conclusive, certainly, but it is suggestive. It comes from the laboratory, the clinic, the schoolroom, the home, and even to a limited extent from industry itself.

The social scientist does not deny that human behavior in industrial organization today is approximately what management perceives it to be. He has, in fact, observed it and studied it fairly extensively. But he is pretty sure that this behavior is *not* a consequence of man's inherent nature. It is a consequence rather of the nature of industrial organizations, of management philosophy, policy, and practice. The conventional approach of Theory X is based on mistaken notions of what is cause and what is effect.

Perhaps the best way to indicate why the conventional approach of management is inadequate is to consider the subject of motivation.

PHYSIOLOGICAL NEEDS

Man is a wanting animal—as soon as one of his needs is satisfied, another appears in its place. This process is unending. It continues from birth to death.

Man's needs are organized in a series

of levels—a hierarchy of importance. At the lowest level, but pre-eminent in importance when they are thwarted, are his *physiological needs.* Man lives for bread alone, when there is no bread. Unless the circumstances are unusual, his needs for love, for status, for recognition are inoperative when his stomach has been empty for a while. But when he eats regularly and adequately, hunger ceases to be an important motivation. The same is true of the other physiological needs of man—for rest, exercise, shelter, protection from the elements.

A satisfied need is not a motivator of behavior! This is a fact of profound significance that is regularly ignored in the conventional approach to the management of people. Consider your own need for air: Except as you are deprived of it, it has no appreciable motivating effect upon your behavior.

SAFETY NEEDS

When the physiological needs are reasonably satisfied, needs at the next higher level begin to dominate man's behavior—to motivate him. These are called *safety needs.* They are needs for protection against danger, threat, deprivation. Some people mistakenly refer to these as needs for security. However, unless man is in a dependent relationship where he fears arbitrary deprivation, he does not demand security. The need is for the "fairest possible break." When he is confident of this, he is more than willing to take risks. But when he feels threatened or dependent, his greatest need is for guarantees, for protection, for security.

The fact needs little emphasis that, since every industrial employee is in a dependent relationship, safety needs may assume considerable importance. Arbitrary management actions, behav-ior which arouses uncertainty with respect to continued employment or which reflects favoritism or discrimination, unpredictable administration of policy—these can be powerful motivators of the safety needs in the employment relationship *at every level,* from worker to vice president.

SOCIAL NEEDS

When man's physiological needs are satisfied and he is no longer fearful about his physical welfare, his *social needs* become important motivators of his behavior—needs for belonging, for association, for acceptance by his fellows, for giving and receiving friendship and love.

Management knows today of the existence of these needs, but it often assumes quite wrongly that they represent a threat to the organization. Many studies have demonstrated that the tightly knit, cohesive work group may, under proper conditions, be far more effective than an equal number of separate individuals in achieving organizational goals.

Yet management, fearing group hostility to its own objectives, often goes to considerable lengths to control and direct human efforts in ways that are inimical to the natural "groupiness" of human beings. When man's social needs—and perhaps his safety needs, too—are thus thwarted, he behaves in ways which tend to defeat organizational objectives. He becomes resistant, antagonistic, uncooperative. But this behavior is a consequence, not a cause.

EGO NEEDS

Above the social needs—in the sense that they do not become motivators until lower needs are reasonably satisfied— are the needs of greatest significance to management and to man himself. They are the *egoistic needs*, and they are of two kinds:

1. Those needs that relate to one's self-esteem—needs for self-confidence, for independence, for achievement, for competence, for knowledge.
2. Those needs that relate to one's reputation—needs for status, for recognition, for appreciation, for the deserved respect of one's fellows.

Unlike the lower needs, these are rarely satisfied; man seeks indefinitely for more satisfaction of these needs once they have become important to him. But they do not appear in any significant way until physiological, safety, and social needs are all reasonably satisfied.

The typical industrial organization offers few opportunities for the satisfaction of these egoistic needs to people at lower levels in the hierarchy. The conventional methods of organizing work, particularly in mass-production industries, give little heed to these aspects of human motivation. If the practices of scientific management were deliberately calculated to thwart these needs, they could hardly accomplish this purpose better than they do.

SELF-FULFILLMENT NEEDS

Finally—a capstone, as it were, on the hierarchy of man's needs—there are what we may call the *needs for self-fulfillment*. These are the needs for realizing one's own potentialities, for continued self-development, for being creative in the broadest sense of that term.

It is clear that the conditions of modern life give only limited opportunity for these relatively weak needs to obtain expression. The deprivation most people experience with respect to other lower-level needs diverts their energies into the struggle to satisfy *those* needs, and the needs for self-fulfillment remain dormant.

MANAGEMENT AND MOTIVATION

We recognize readily enough that a man suffering from a severe dietary deficiency is sick. The deprivation of physiological needs has behavioral consequences. The same is true—although less well recognized—of deprivation of higher-level needs. The man whose needs for safety, association, independence, or status are thwarted is sick just as surely as the man who has rickets. And his sickness will have behavioral consequences. We will be mistaken if we attribute his resultant passivity, his hostility, his refusal to accept responsibility to his inherent "human nature." These forms of behavior are *symptoms* of illness—of deprivation of his social and egoistic needs.

The man whose lower-level needs are satisfied is not motivated to satisfy those needs any longer. For practical purposes they exist no longer. Management often asks, "Why aren't people more productive? We pay good wages, provide good working conditions, have excellent fringe benefits and steady employment. Yet people do not seem to be willing to put forth more than minimum effort."

The fact that management has provided for these physiological and safety needs has shifted the motivational emphasis to the social and perhaps to the egoistic needs. Unless there are opportunities *at work* to satisfy these higher-level needs, people will be deprived; and their behavior will reflect this deprivation. Under such conditions, if management continues to focus its attention on physiological needs, its efforts are bound to be ineffective.

People *will* make insistent demands for more money under these conditions. It becomes more important than ever to buy the material goods and services which can provide limited satisfaction of the thwarted needs. Although money has only limited value in satisfying many higher-level needs, it can become the focus of interest if it is the *only* means available.

THE CARROT-AND-STICK APPROACH

The carrot-and-stick theory of motivation (like Newtonian physical theory) works reasonably well under certain circumstances. The *means* for satisfying man's physiological and (within limits) his safety needs can be provided or withheld by management. Employment itself is such a means, and so are wages, working conditions, and benefits. By these means the individual can be controlled so long as he is struggling for subsistence.

But the carrot-and-stick theory does not work at all once man has reached an adequate subsistence level and is motivated primarily by higher needs. Management cannot provide a man with self-respect, or with the respect of his fellows, or with the satisfaction of needs for self-fulfillment. It can create such conditions that he is encouraged and enabled to seek such satisfactions for *himself*, or it can thwart him by failing to create those conditions.

But this creation of conditions is not "control." It is not a good device for directing behavior. And so management finds itself in an odd position. The high standard of living created by our modern technological know-how provides quite adequately for the satisfaction of

physiological and safety needs. The only significant exception is where management practices have not created confidence in a "fair break"—and thus where safety needs are thwarted. But by making possible the satisfaction of low-level needs, management has deprived itself of the ability to use as motivators the devices on which conventional theory has taught it to rely—rewards, promises, incentives, or threats and other coercive devices.

The philosophy of management by direction and control—*regardless of whether it is hard or soft*—is inadequate to motivate because the human needs on which this approach relies are today unimportant motivators of behavior. Direction and control are essentially useless in motivating people whose important needs are social and egoistic. Both the hard and the soft approach fail today because they are simply irrelevant to the situation.

People, deprived of opportunities to satisfy at work the needs which are now important to them, behave exactly as we might predict—with indolence, passivity, resistance to change, lack of responsibility, willingness to follow the demagogue, unreasonable demands for economic benefits. It would seem that we are caught in a web of our own weaving.

A NEW THEORY OF MANAGEMENT

For these and many other reasons, we require a different theory of the task of managing people based on more adequate assumptions about human nature and human motivation. I am going to be so bold as to suggest the broad dimensions of such a theory. Call it "Theory Y," if you will.

1. Management is responsible for

organizing the elements of productive enterprise—money, materials, equipment, people—in the interest of economic ends.

2. People are *not* by nature passive or resistant to organizational needs. They have become so as a result of experience in organizations.

3. The motivation, the potential for development, the capacity for assuming responsibility, the readiness to direct behavior toward organizational goals are all present in people. Management does not put them there. It is a responsibility of management to make it possible for people to recognize and develop these human characteristics for themselves.

4. The essential task of management is to arrange organizational conditions and methods of operation so that people can achieve their own goals *best* by directing *their own* efforts toward organizational objectives.

This is a process primarily of creating opportunities, releasing potential, removing obstacles, encouraging growth, providing guidance. It is what Peter Drucker has called "management by objectives" in contrast to "management by control." It does *not* involve the abdication of management, the absence of leadership, the lowering of standards, or the other characteristics usually associated with the "soft" approach under Theory X.

SOME DIFFICULTIES

It is no more possible to create an organization today which will be a full, effective application of this theory than it was to build an atomic power plant in 1945. There are many formidable obstacles to overcome.

The conditions imposed by conventional organization theory and by the approach of scientific management for the past half century have tied men to limited jobs which do not utilize their capabilities, have discouraged the acceptance of responsibility, have encouraged passivity, have eliminated meaning from work. Man's habits, attitudes, expectations—his whole conception of membership in an industrial organization—have been conditioned by his experience under these circumstances.

People today are accustomed to being directed, manipulated, controlled in industrial organizations and to finding satisfaction for their social, egoistic, and self-fulfillment needs away from the job. This is true of much of management as well as of workers. Genuine "industrial citizenship"—to borrow again a term from Drucker—is a remote and unrealistic idea, the meaning of which has not even been considered by most members of industrial organizations.

Another way of saying this is that Theory X places exclusive reliance upon external control of human behavior, while Theory Y relies heavily on self-control and self-direction. It is worth noting that this difference is the difference between treating people as children and treating them as mature adults. After generations of the former, we cannot expect to shift to the latter overnight.

STEPS IN THE RIGHT DIRECTION

Before we are overwhelmed by the obstacles, let us remember that the application of theory is always slow. Progress is usually achieved in small steps. Some innovative ideas which are entirely consistent with Theory Y are today being applied with some success.

Decentralization and Delegation

These are ways of freeing people from the too-close control of conventional organization, giving them a degree of freedom to direct their own activities, to assume responsibility, and, importantly, to satisfy their egoistic needs. In this connection, the flat organization of Sears, Roebuck and Company provides an interesting example. It forces "management by objectives," since it enlarges the number of people reporting to a manager until he cannot direct and control them in the conventional manner.

Job Enlargement

This concept, pioneered by I.B.M. and Detroit Edison, is quite consistent with Theory Y. It encourages the acceptance of responsibility at the bottom of the organization; it provides opportunities for satisfying social and egoistic needs. In fact, the reorganization of work at the factory level offers one of the more challenging opportunities for innovation consistent with Theory Y.

Participation and Consultative Management

Under proper conditions, participation and consultative management provide encouragement to people to direct their creative energies toward organizational objectives, give them some voice in decisions that affect them, provide significant opportunities for the satisfaction of social and egoistic needs. The Scanlon Plan is the outstanding embodiment of these ideas in practice.

Performance Appraisal

Even a cursory examination of conventional programs of performance appraisal within the ranks of management will reveal how completely consistent they are with Theory X. In fact, most such programs tend to treat the individual as though he were a product under inspection on the assembly line.

A few companies—among them General Mills, Ansul Chemical, and General Electric—have been experimenting with approaches which involve the individual in setting "targets" or objectives *for himself* and in a *self*-evaluation of performance semiannually or annually. Of course, the superior plays an important leadership role in this process—one, in fact, which demands substantially more competence than the conventional approach. The role is, however, considerably more congenial to many managers than the role of "judge" or "inspector" which is usually forced upon them. Above all, the individual is encouraged to take a greater responsibility for planning and appraising his own contribution to organizational objectives; and the accompanying effects on egoistic and self-fulfillment needs are substantial.

APPLYING THE IDEAS

The not infrequent failure of such ideas as these to work as well as expected is often attributable to the fact that a management has "bought the idea" but applied it within the framework of Theory X and its assumptions.

Delegation is not an effective way of exercising management by control. Participation becomes a farce when it is applied as a sales gimmick or a device for kidding people into thinking they are important. Only the management that has confidence in human capacities and is itself directed toward organizational objectives rather than toward the preservation of personal power can grasp the implications of this emerging theory. Such management will find and apply successfully other innovative ideas as we move slowly toward the full implementation of a theory like Y.

THE HUMAN SIDE OF ENTERPRISE

It is quite possible for us to realize substantial improvements in the effectiveness of industrial organizations during the next decade or two. The social sciences can contribute much to such developments; we are only beginning to grasp the implications of the growing body of knowledge in these fields. But if this conviction is to become a reality instead of a pious hope, we will need to view the process of releasing the energy of the atom for constructive human ends—as a slow, costly, sometimes discouraging approach toward a goal which would seem to many to be quite unrealistic.

The ingenuity and the perseverance of industrial management in the pursuit of economic ends have changed many scientific and technological dreams into commonplace realities. It is now becoming clear that the application of these same talents to the human side of enterprise will not only enhance substantially these materialistic achievements, but will bring us one step closer to "the good society."

4

The Motivating Effect of Cognitive Dissonance

Leon Festinger

COGNITIVE DISSONANCE AS A MOTIVATING STATE

I should like to postulate the existence of *cognitive dissonance* as a motivating state in human beings. Since most of you probably never heard of cognitive dissonance, I assume that so far I have been no more informative than if I had said that I wish to postulate X as a motivating state. I will try, then, to provide a conceptual definition of cognitive dissonance.

Definition of Dissonance. The word "dissonance" was not chosen arbitrarily to denote this motivating state. It was chosen because its ordinary meaning in the English language is close to the technical meaning I want to give it. The synonyms which the dictionary gives for the word "dissonant" are "harsh," "jarring," "grating," "unmelodious," "inharmonious," "inconsistent," "contradictory," "disagreeing," "incongruous," "discrepant." The word, in this ordinary meaning, specifies a relation between two things. In connection with musical tones, where it is usually used, the relation between the tones is such that they sound unpleasant together. In general, one might say that a dissonant relation exists between two things which occur together, if, in some way, they do not belong together or fit together.

Cognitive dissonance refers to this kind of relation between cognitions which exist simultaneously for a person. If a person knows two things, for example, something about himself and something about the world in which he lives, which somehow do not fit together, we will speak of this as cognitive dissonance. Thus, for example, a person might know that he is a very intelligent, highly capable person. At the same time, let us imagine, he knows that he meets repeated failure. These two cognitions would be dissonant—they do not fit together. In general, two cognitions are dissonant with each other if, considering these two cognitions alone, the obverse of one follows from the other. Thus, in the example we have given, it follows from the fact that a person is highly capable that he does not continually meet with failure.

The phrase "follows from" that was used in the previous two sentences needs some explaining. Without going into it in too great detail here, I should like to stress that we are concerned with psychological implication and not necessarily logical implication. The psychological implication which one cognition can have for another cognition can arise from a variety of circumstances. There can be psychological implication because of experience and what one has learned. Thus, if a person is out in the rain with no umbrella or raincoat, it follows from this that he will get wet. There can also be psychological implication because of cultural

Source: From: "The Motivating Effect of Cognitive Dissonance" by Leon Festinger, from *Assessment of Human Motives*, edited by Gardner Lindzey (New York: Holt, Rinehart & Winston, 1958), pp. 69–85. Reprinted by permission.

mores and definition. If one is at a highly formal dinner party, it follows from this that one does not pick up the food with one's fingers. I do not have the time to be thorough or exhaustive in my discussion here, but I hope I have sufficiently explained the concept of dissonance so that we can proceed.

How Cognitive Dissonance Resembles Other Need States. Thus far I have said nothing about the motivating aspects of cognitive dissonance. This is the next step. I wish to hypothesize that the existence of cognitive dissonance is comparable to any other need state. Just as hunger is motivating, cognitive dissonance is motivating. Cognitive dissonance will give rise to activity oriented toward reducing or eliminating the dissonance. Successful reduction of dissonance is rewarding in the same sense that eating when one is hungry is rewarding.

In other words, if two cognitions are dissonant with each other there will be some tendency for the person to attempt to change one of them so that they do fit together, thus reducing or eliminating the dissonance. There are also other ways in which dissonance may be reduced but, not having the time to go into a complete discussion of this, I would rather confine myself to this one manifestation of the motivating character of cognitive dissonance.

Data Needed to Demonstrate the Motivating Character of Cognitive Dissonance. Before proceeding, let us consider for a moment the kinds of data one would like to have in order to document the contention that cognitive dissonance is a motivating state. One would like to have at least the following kinds of data:

1. Determination at Time 1 that a state of cognitive dissonance exists. This could be done either by measurement or by experimental manipulation.

2. Determination at Time 2 that the dissonance has been eliminated or reduced in magnitude.

3. Data concerning the behavioral process whereby the person has succeeded in changing some cognition, thus reducing the dissonance.

Actually, the above three items are minimal and would probably not be sufficient to demonstrate cogently the validity of the theory concerning cognitive dissonance. Consider the following example. We have determined for a certain person that at one time he believes that tomatoes are poisonous and also knows that his neighbor eats them continually with apparently no ill effect. A dissonance between these two cognitions certainly exists. We then observe that he talks to people about it, shows evidence of being bothered by it, and at a later time, no longer believes that tomatoes are poisonous. The dissonance has been eliminated. But this example would not be very convincing. There are too many alternative ways of understanding this change in the person's belief about tomatoes. He is simply, someone might say, being responsive to the real world.

The kind of data that would be more convincing concerning the motivating aspects of dissonance would be data concerning instances where the dissonance was reduced in the other direction, such as is exemplified in the old joke about the psychiatrist who had a patient who believed he was dead. After getting agreement from the patient that dead men do not bleed, and being certain that the patient understood this, the psychiatrist made a cut on the patient's arm and, as the blood poured out, leaned back in his chair, smiling. Whereupon the patient, with a look of dismay on his face, said, "Well, what do you know, dead men *do* bleed." This kind of thing, if it occurred actually, would be harder to explain in alternative ways.

In other words, one has to demonstrate the effects of dissonance in circumstances where these effects are not easily explainable on the basis of other existing theories. Indeed, if one cannot do this, then one could well ask what the usefulness was of this new notion that explained nothing that was not already understood. Consequently, in order to persuade you of the validity of cognitive dissonance and its motivating characteristics I will give two examples where dissonance reduction produced results somewhat contrary to what one would expect on the basis of the operation of other human motives.

Some Examples of Unusual Manifestations of Dissonance Reduction.

Example 1: One rather intriguing example comes from a pair of studies of rumors following disasters. Prasad (1950) systematically recorded rumors which were widely current immediately following an especially severe earthquake in India, in 1934. The quake itself, a strong and prolonged one, was felt over a wide geographical area. Actual damage, however, was quite localized and, for a period of days, communication with the damaged area was very poor. The rumors were collected in the area which felt the shock of the earthquake but which did not suffer any damage. We are, then, dealing with communication of rumors among people who felt the shock of the earthquake but who did not see any damage or destruction.

While Prasad reports little concerning the emotional reactions of people to the quake, it is probably plausible to assume that these people who knew little about earthquakes had a strong reaction of fear to the violent and prolonged shaking of the ground. We may also assume that such a strong fear reaction does not vanish immediately but probably persists for some time after the actual shock of the quake is over.

Let us speculate about the content of the cognition of these persons. When the earthquake was over they had this strong, persistent fear reaction but they could see nothing different around them, no destruction, no further threatening things. In short, a situation had been produced where dissonance existed between cognition corresponding to the fear they felt and the knowledge of what they saw around them which, one might say, amounted to the cognition that there was nothing to be afraid of.

The vast majority of the rumors which were widely circulated were rumors which, if believed, provided cognition consonant with being afraid. One might even call them "fear-provoking" rumors, although, if our interpretation is correct, they would more properly be called "fear justifying" rumors. The following are a fair sample of the rumors which Prasad collected:

> There will be a severe cyclone at Patna between January 18 and January 19. (The earthquake occurred on January 15.)

> There will be a severe earthquake on the lunar eclipse day.

> A flood was rushing from the Nepal borders to Madhubani.

> January 23 will be a fatal day. Unforseeable calamities will arise.

Here, then, is an instance where the reduction of dissonance produced results which looked like fear arousal.

If this explanation is correct in accounting for the prevalence of these "fear-justifying" rumors, there is one clear implication, namely, that if rumors had been collected among persons living *in* the area of destruction, few, if any, of such rumors would have been found. Those persons directly in the area of destruction caused by the earthquake were, undoubtedly, also frightened. Indeed, their fear reaction would very likely have been even stronger than that of the persons who merely felt the shock of the quake. But for the people in the area of destruction, no cognitive dissonance would have been created. The things they could see around them, the destruction, the wounded and killed, would produce cognition which would certainly be consonant with feeling afraid. There would be no impulse or desire to acquire additional cognitions which fit with the fear, and fearful rumors of the type so prevalent outside the area of destruction should have been absent.

Unfortunately, Prasad presents no data on rumors which circulated inside the area of destruction following the earthquake. There is, however, another study reported by Sinha (1952) which bears on this. This study reports a careful collection of rumors following a disaster in Darjeeling, India, a disaster which was fully comparable to the earthquake in terms of destruction and loss of life but which, unfortunately for purposes of comparison, did not arise from an earthquake but from a landslide. Nevertheless, it must have produced considerable fear among the people. Sinha directly compares the two when, in describing the landslide disaster, he states:

> There was a feeling of instability and uncertainty similar to that which followed the Great Indian Earthquake of 1934. (p. 200)

There is, however, one important difference between the study reported by Prasad and the one reported by Sinha. While the rumors following the earthquake were collected among per-

sons outside of the area of destruction, the rumors which Sinha reports were collected from persons in Darjeeling who actually were in the area and witnessed the destruction. Since for these people there would have been no dissonance—what they saw and knew was quite consonant with being afraid—we would not expect disaster rumors to arise and spread among them.

Actually, in Sinha's report, there is a complete absence of rumors predicting further disasters or of any type of rumor that might be regarded as supplying cognition consonant with being afraid. The contrast between the rumors reported by Sinha and those reported by Prasad is certainly strong.

Example 2: Another intriguing example of the reduction of dissonance in a startling manner comes from a study I did together with Riecken and Schachter (1956) of a group of people who predicted that, on a given date, a catastrophic flood would overwhelm most of the world. This prediction of the catastrophic flood had been given to the people in direct communications from the gods and was an integral part of their religious beliefs. When the predicted date arrived and passed there was considerable dissonance established in these people. They continued to believe in their gods and in the validity of the communications from them, and at the same time they knew that the prediction of the flood had been wrong. We observed the movement as participants for approximately two months preceding and one month after this unequivocal disproof of part of their belief. The point of the study was, of course, to observe how they would react to the dissonance. Let me give a few of the details of the disproof and how they reacted to it.

For some time it had been clear to the people in the group that those who were chosen were to be picked up by flying saucers before the cataclysm occurred. Some of the believers, these mainly college students, were advised to go home and wait individually for the flying saucer that would arrive for each of them. This was reasonable and plausible, since the data of the cataclysm happened to occur during an academic holiday. Most of the group, including the most central and most heavily committed members, gathered together in the home of the woman who received the messages from the gods to wait together for the arrival of the saucer. For these latter, disproof of the prediction, in the form of evidence that the messages were not valid, began to occur four days before the predicted event was to take place. A message informed them that a saucer would land in the back yard of the house at 4:00 P.M. to pick up the members of the group. With coat in hand they waited, but no saucer came. A later message told them there had been a delay—the saucer would arrive at midnight. Midst absolute secrecy (the neighbors and press must not know), they waited outdoors on a cold and snowy night for over an hour, but still no saucer came. Another message told them to continue waiting, but still no saucer came. At about 3:00 A.M. they gave up, interpreting the events of that night as a test, a drill, and a rehearsal for the real pickup which would still soon take place.

Tensely, they waited for the final orders to come through—for the messages which would tell them the time, place, and procedure for the actual pickup. Finally, on the day before the cataclysm was to strike, the messages came. At midnight a man would come to the door of the house and take them to the place where the flying saucer would be parked. More messages came that day, one after another, instructing them in the passwords that would be necessary in order to board the saucer, in preparatory procedures such as removal of metal from clothing, removal of personal identification, maintaining silence at certain times, and the like. The day was spent by the group in preparation and rehearsal of the necessary procedures and, when midnight came, the group sat waiting in readiness. But no knock came at the door, no one came to lead them to the flying saucer.

From midnight to five o'clock in the morning the group sat there struggling to understand what had happened, struggling to find some explanation that would enable them to recover somewhat from the shattering realization that they would not be picked up by a flying saucer and that consequently the flood itself would not occur as predicted. It is doubtful that anyone alone, without the support of the others, could have withstood the impact of this disproof of the prediction. Indeed, those members of the group who had gone to their homes to wait alone, alone in the sense that they did not have other believers with them, did not withstand it. Almost all of them became skeptics afterward. In other words, without easily obtainable social support to begin reducing the dissonance, the dissonance was sufficient to cause the belief to be discarded in spite of the commitment to it. But the members of the group that had gathered together in the home of the woman who received the messages could, and did, provide social support for one another. They kept reassuring one another of the validity of the messages and that some explanation would be found.

At fifteen minutes before five o'clock that morning an explanation was found that was at least temporarily satisfactory. A message arrived from God which, in effect, said that He had saved

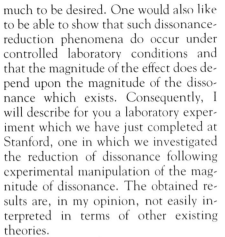

the world and stayed the flood because of this group and the light and strength this group had spread throughout the world that night.

The behavior of these people from that moment onwards presented a revealing contrast to their previous behavior. These people, who had been disinterested in publicity and even avoided it, became avid publicity seekers. For four successive days, finding a new reason each day, they invited the press into the house, gave lengthy interviews, and attempted to attract the public to their ideas. The first day they called all the newspapers and news services, informed them of the fact that the world had been saved and invited them to come and get interviews. The second day, a ban on having photographs taken was lifted, and the newspapers were once more called to inform them of the fact and to invite them to come to the house and take pictures. On the third day they once more called the press to inform them that on the next afternoon they would gather on their front lawn singing and that it was possible a space man would visit them at that time. What is more, the general public was specifically invited to come and watch. And on the fourth day, newspapermen and about two hundred people came to watch the group singing on the front lawn. There were almost no lengths to which these people would not go to attract publicity and potential believers in the validity of the messages. If, indeed, more and more converts could be found, more and more people who believed in the messages and the things the messages said, then the dissonance between their belief and the knowledge that the messages had not been correct could be reduced.

These examples, while they do illustrate attempts to reduce dissonance in rather surprising directions, still leave much to be desired. One would also like to be able to show that such dissonance-reduction phenomena do occur under controlled laboratory conditions and that the magnitude of the effect does depend upon the magnitude of the dissonance which exists. Consequently, I will describe for you a laboratory experiment which we have just completed at Stanford, one in which we investigated the reduction of dissonance following experimental manipulation of the magnitude of dissonance. The obtained results are, in my opinion, not easily interpreted in terms of other existing theories.

An Experimental Investigation. In this experiment, we created dissonance in the subjects by inducing them to say something which was at variance with their private opinion. It is clear that this kind of situation does produce dissonance between what the person believes and what he knows he has said. There are also cognitive consonances for the person. His cognitions concerning the things that induced him to make the public statement are consonant with his knowledge of having done it. The total magnitude of the dissonance between all other relevant cognitions taken together and the knowledge of what he has publicly said will, of course, be a function of the number and importance of the dissonances in relation to the number and importance of the consonances. One could, then, manipulate the total magnitude of dissonance experimentally by holding everything constant and varying the strength of the inducement for the person to state something publicly which was at variance with his private opinion. The *stronger* the inducement to do this, the *less* would be the over-all magnitude of dissonance created.

Let us imagine a concrete situation. Suppose a number of people have had an experience to which they reacted negatively. Each of these persons, then, let us say, is offered a different amount of money to tell someone else that the experience was very pleasant and enjoyable. In each case, let us further imagine, the amount of money offered is at least large enough so that the person accepts the money and engages in the overt behavior required. Certainly, after telling someone that the experience was enjoyable, there is a dissonance between his cognition of what he has said and his own private opinion.

This dissonance could, clearly, be reduced if the person persuades himself that the experience was, indeed, fairly pleasant and enjoyable, that is, if he changes his private opinion so that it corresponds more closely with what he has said. The greater the dissonance, the more frequently should one observe such subsequent attitude change. We would expect, then, that, after the person had told someone else that the experience was pleasant and enjoyable, he would change his private opinions concerning the experience to some extent. We would further expect that the more money he was given to induce him to make the public statement, the smaller would be the subsequent opinion change, because less dissonance had been created initially.

Now for the details of the experiment. I will describe it as it proceeded for the subject, with occasional explanatory comments. Each subject had signed up for a two hour experiment on "measures of performance." The subjects were all students from the Introductory Psychology course at Stanford where they are required to serve a certain number of hours as subjects in experiments. When the student arrived he was met by the experimenter and, with a minimum of explanation, was given a

repetitive motor task to work on. He packed a frame full of little spools, then emptied it, then packed it again, and so on for a half hour. He was then given another task to do in which he turned rows of pegs, each a quarter turn, then turned them all another quarter turn, and so on for another half hour. When he had finished, the experimenter informed him that the experiment was over, thanked him for his participation, and proceeded to explain to him what the experiment was about and what its purpose was.

From our point of view, the purpose of this initial part was to provide for each subject an experience which was rather dull, boring, and somewhat fatiguing. The student, however, believed this to be the whole experiment. The explanation of the experiment given to the student was that the experiment was concerned with the effect of preparatory set on performance. He was told that there were two conditions in the experiment, one of these being the condition he had experienced where the subject was told nothing ahead of time. The other condition, the experimenter explained, was one in which the subject, before working on the tasks, was led to expect that they were very enjoyable, very interesting, and lots of fun. The procedure for subjects in this other condition, the experimenter explained, proceeded in the following manner. A person working for us is introduced to the waiting subject as someone who has just finished the experiment and will tell the prospective subject a little about it. This person who works for us then tells the waiting subject that the experiment is very enjoyable, interesting, and lots of fun. In this way, the subjects in the other condition are given the set we want them to have. This concluded the false explanation of the experiment to the student and, in the control group, nothing more was done at this point.

In the experimental groups, however, the experimenter continued by telling the subject that he had a rather unusual proposal to make. It seems that the next subject is scheduled to be in that condition where he is to be convinced in advance that the experiment is enjoyable and a lot of fun. The person who works for us and usually does this, however, although very reliable, could not do it today. We thought we would take a chance and ask him (the student) to do it for us. We would like, if agreeable to him, to hire him on the same basis that the other person was hired to work for us. We would like to put him on the payroll and pay him a lump sum of money to go tell the waiting subject that the experiment is enjoyable, interesting, and fun; and he was also to be on tap for us in case this kind of emergency arises again.

There were two experimental conditions which we actually conducted. The procedure was absolutely identical in both except for the amount of money that the subjects were paid as "the lump sum." In one condition they were paid one dollar for their immediate and possible future services. In the other condition they were paid twenty dollars. When the student agreed to do this, he was actually given the money and he signed a receipt for it. He was then taken into the room where the next subject was waiting and introduced to her by the experimenter, who said that the student had just been a subject in the experiment and would tell her a bit about it. The experimenter then went out, leaving student and the waiting subject together for two and a half minutes. The waiting subject was actually a girl in our employ. Her instructions were very simple. After the student had told her that the experiment was interesting, enjoyable and lots of fun, she was to say something like, "Oh, a friend of mine who took it yesterday told me it was dull and that if I could I should get out of it." After that she was simply supposed to agree with whatever the student said. If, as almost always happened, the student reaffirmed that the experiment was fun, she was to say that she was glad to hear it. The following is a typical record of this interchange which was recorded on a tape recorder for all subjects.

Student: It's quite a deal.

Girl: Is it?

Student: Yeah—it's kind of fun. You play with pegs and spools. I don't know what it's supposed to test, but it's a lot of fun.

Girl: I'm living over at Moore. I have a friend who took the experiment last week and she wouldn't tell me what she did but she said it was very boring.

Student: I don't know—it's kind of fun when you get going at it.

Girl: Oh, really? Well, I'm relieved to hear you say that in a way. Gosh, I was kind of worried.

Student: It's kind of interesting to play with those things. I can't figure out what they're trying to test but it's kind of fun.

Girl: You sit there trying to figure out what it is, huh?

Student: (laughs) I guess so. It's kind of fun—fun to work on. It's interesting to do something with your hands. Lots of fun. What class you in— sophomore?

Girl: No, senior.

Student: Senior? *(laughs)* Quite a difference.

Girl: Yeah. I wanted to get some Psych in before I graduate. *(few seconds silence)*

Student: Quite a challenge. Yeah. Some of them are fun—some of them don't seem to have much point to them. *(Here the subject talked for a few seconds about other experiments he had taken.)*

When the experimenter returned, after two and a half minutes, he sent the girl into the experimental room, telling her he would be there in a few minutes. He then obtained the student's phone number in order to continue the fiction that the student was to be available for future services of like nature. The experimenter then thanked the subject and made a brief speech in which he said that most subjects found the experimental tasks very interesting and enjoyed them, and that, when he thinks about it, he will probably agree. The purpose of this brief speech is to provide some cognitive material which the subject can use to reduce dissonance, assuming that such dissonance exists. The identical speech is, of course, made to the control subjects, too.

The only remaining problem in the experiment was to obtain a measure of what each subject honestly thought privately about the tasks on which he had worked for an hour. It seemed desirable, naturally, to obtain this measure in a situation where the subject would be inclined to be very frank in his statements. It also seemed desirable to obtain these measures quite independently of the actual experiment. This was done in the following manner. It had previously been announced by the instructor in the Introductory Psychology class that, since students were required to participate in experiments, the Psychology Department was going to do a study to assess the value of the experiences they had. The purpose of this, the instructor had explained, was to help improve the selection of experiments in the future. They were told that a sample of them, after serving in experiments, would be interviewed about them. It would be to their advantage, and to the advantage of future students in the course, for them to be very frank and honest in these interviews.

In our experiment, the student was told that someone from Introductory Psychology probably wanted to interview him. The experimenter confessed ignorance about what this impending interview was about but said he had been told that the subject would know about it. Usually at this point the subject nodded his head or otherwise indicated that he did, indeed, know what it was about. The experimenter then took him to an office where the interviewer was waiting, said good-bye to the subject, and left.

The interview itself was rather brief. Four questions were asked, namely, how interesting and enjoyable the experiment was, how much the subject learned from it, how important he thought it was scientifically, and how much he would like to participate in a similar experiment again. The important question, for us, is the first one concerning how interesting and enjoyable the experiment was, since this was the content area in which dissonance was established for the experimental subjects.

Let us look, then, at what the results show. Figure 1 shows the average rating, for each of the three conditions, for the question concerning how interesting and enjoyable the experiment was. A rating of -5 meant extremely dull and boring, $+5$ meant extremely interesting and enjoyable, and 0 meant neutral.

The subject could, of course, rate his reaction to the experiment anywhere between −5 and +5. The average rating for the control group is represented as a horizontal dotted line across the figure. It is done this way since the data from the control group actually provide a base line. This is how subjects reacted to the experiment after having gone through it and having been told exactly the same things that the experimental subjects were told. They simply were never asked to, and never did, tell the waiting subject that the experiment was interesting, enjoyable, and lots of fun. It turns out that, on the average, the control group rates the experiment −.45 for how enjoyable it was, slightly below neutral. In the One Dollar experimental condition there is a definite increase over the control group. Here the average rating is +1.35, definitely on the positive side of the scale and significantly different from the control group at the 1 per cent level of confidence. In other words, in the One Dollar condition the dissonance between their private opinion of the experiment and their knowledge of what they had said to the waiting subject was reduced significantly by changing their private opinion somewhat, to bring it closer to what they had overtly said.

But now let us turn our attention to the Twenty Dollar condition. Here the magnitude of dissonance experimentally

FIGURE 1 • RELATION BETWEEN MAGNITUDE OF REWARD USED TO ELICIT COMPLIANCE AND SUBSEQUENT RATING OF HOW ENJOYABLE THE EXPERIMENT WAS.

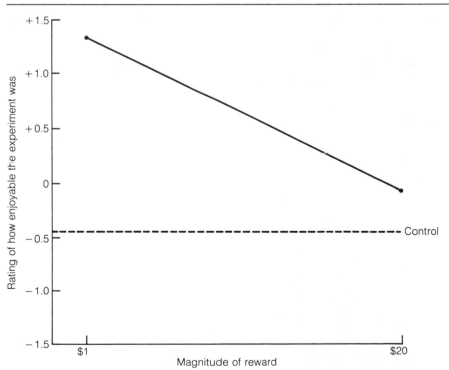

created was less than in the One Dollar condition because of the greater importance of the cognition that was consonant with what they knew they had done. It seems undeniable that twenty dollars is a good deal more important than one dollar. There should hence be less pressure to reduce the dissonance, and indeed, the average rating for the Twenty Dollar condition is − .05, only slightly above the Control condition and significantly different from the One Dollar condition at the 2 per cent level of confidence.

SUMMARY AND CONCLUSIONS

The evidence for the validity and usefulness of conceiving cognitive dissonance as motivating is as follows:

1. Evidence that the existence of cognitive dissonance sometimes leads to behavior that appears very strange indeed when viewed only from the standpoint of commonly accepted motives. Here I have had time only to give two examples illustrating this phenomenon.

2. Evidence that the amount of reduction of dissonance is a direct function of the magnitude of dissonance which exists. I illustrated this by describing a laboratory experiment where, under controlled conditions, the magnitude of dissonance was experimentally manipulated.

REFERENCES

Festinger, Leon. *A theory of cognitive dissonance.* Evanston, Ill.: Row-Peterson, 1957.

———, Riecken, H. W., and Schachter, S. *When prophecy fails.* Minneapolis: University of Minnesota Press, 1956.

Janis, I. L., and King, B. T. The influence of role-playing on opinion change. *J. Abnorm. (soc.) Psychol.*, 1954, 49, 211–218.

King, B. T., and Janis, I. L. Comparison of the effectiveness of improvised versus nonimprovised role-playing in producing opinion changes. *Human Relations*, 1956, 9, 177–186.

Prasad, J. A comparative study of rumors and reports in earthquakes. *Brit. J. Psychol.*, 1950, 41, 129–144.

Sinha, D. Behavior in a catastrophic situation: a psychological study of reports and rumors. *Brit. J. Psychol.*, 1952, 43, 200–209.

5
That Urge to Achieve
David C. McClelland

Most people in this world, psychologically, can be divided into two broad groups. There is that minority which is challenged by opportunity and willing to work hard to achieve something, and the majority which really does not care all that much.

For nearly twenty years now, psychologists have tried to penetrate the mystery of this curious dichotomy. Is the need to achieve (or the absence of it) an accident, is it hereditary, or is it the result of environment? Is it a single, isolatable human motive, or a combination of motives—the desire to accumulate wealth, power, fame? Most important of all, is there some technique that could give this will to achieve to people, even whole societies, who do not now have it?

While we do not yet have complete answers for any of these questions, years of work have given us partial answers to most of them and insights into all of them. There is a distinct human motive, distinguishable from others. It can be found, in fact tested for, in any group.

Let me give you one example. Several years ago, a careful study was made of 450 workers who had been thrown out of work by a plant shutdown in Erie, Pennsylvania. Most of the unemployed workers stayed home for a while and then checked back with the United States Employment Service to see if their old jobs or similar ones were available. But a small minority among them behaved differently; the day they were laid off, they started job-hunting.

They checked both the United States and the Pennsylvania Employment Office; they studied the "Help Wanted" sections of the papers; they checked through their union, their church, and various fraternal organizations; they looked into training courses to learn a new skill; they even left town to look for work, while the majority when questioned said they would not under any circumstances move away from Erie to obtain a job. Obviously the members of that active minority were differently motivated. All the men were more or less in the same situation objectively: they needed work, money, food, shelter, job security. Yet only a minority showed initiative and enterprise in finding what they needed. Why? Psychologists, after years of research, now believe they can answer that question. They have demonstrated that these men possessed in greater degree a specific type of human motivation. For the moment let us refer to this personality characteristic as "Motive A" and review some of the other characteristics of the men who have more of the motive than other men.

Suppose they are confronted by a work situation in which they can set their own goals as to how difficult a task they will undertake. In the psychological laboratory, such a situation is very

Source: Reprinted by permission from *Think* magazine, pp. 82–89, published by IBM. Copyright © 1966 by International Business Machines Corporation.

simply created by asking them to throw rings over a peg from any distance they may choose. Most men throw more or less randomly, standing now close, now far away, but those with Motive A seem to calculate carefully where they are most likely to get a sense of mastery. They stand nearly always at moderate distances, not so close as to make the task ridiculously easy, nor so far away as to make it impossible. They set moderately difficult, but potentially achievable goals for themselves, where they objectively have only about a one-in-three chance of succeeding. In other words, they are always setting challenges for themselves, tasks to make them stretch themselves a little.

But they behave like this only if *they* can influence the outcome by performing the work themselves. They prefer not to gamble at all. Say they are given a choice between rolling dice with one in three chances of winning and working on a problem with a one-in-three chance of solving in the time allotted, they choose to work on the problem even though rolling the dice is obviously less work and the odds of winning are the same. They prefer to work at a problem rather than leave the outcome to chance or to others.

Obviously they are concerned with personal achievement rather than with the rewards of success *per se*, since they stand just as much chance of getting those rewards by throwing the dice. This leads to another characteristic the Motive A men show—namely, a strong preference for work situations in which they get concrete feedback on how well they are doing, as one does, say in playing golf, or in being a salesman, but as one does not in teaching, or in personnel counseling. A golfer always knows his score and can compare how well he is doing with par or with his own performance yesterday or last week. A

teacher has no such concrete feedback on how well he is doing in "getting across" to his students.

THE *n* ACH MEN

But why do certain men behave like this? At one level the reply is simple: because they habitually spend their time thinking about doing things better. In fact, psychologists typically measure the strength of Motive A by taking samples of a man's spontaneous thoughts (such as making up a story about a picture they have been shown) and counting the frequency with which he mentions doing things better. The count is objective and can even be made these days with the help of a computer program for content analysis. It yields what is referred to technically as an individual's *n* Ach score (for "need for Achievement"). It is not difficult to understand why people who think constantly about "doing better" are more apt to do better at job-hunting, to set moderate, achievable goals for themselves, to dislike gambling (because they get no achievement satisfaction from success), and to prefer work situations where they can tell easily whether they are improving or not. But why some people and not others come to think this way is another question. The evidence suggests it is not because of special training they get in the home from parents who set moderately high achievement goals but who are warm, encourging, and non-authoritarian in helping their children reach these goals.

Such detailed knowledge about one motive helps correct a lot of common sense ideas about human motivation. For example, much public policy (and much business policy) is based on the simple-minded notion that people will work harder "if they have to." As a first approximation, the idea isn't totally wrong, but it is only a half-truth. The majority of unemployed workers in Erie "had to" find work as much as those with higher *n* Ach but they certainly didn't work as hard at it. Or again, it is frequently assumed that *any* strong motive will lead to doing things better. Wouldn't it be fair to say that most of the Erie workers were just "unmotivated"? But our detailed knowledge of various human motives shows that each one leads a person to behave in *different* ways. The contrast is not between being "motivated" or "unmotivated" but between being motivated toward A or toward B or C, etc.

A simple experiment makes the point nicely: subjects were told that they could choose as a working partner either a close friend or a stranger who was known to be an expert on the problem to be solved. Those with higher *n* Ach (more "need to achieve") chose the experts over their friends, whereas those with more *n* Aff (the "need to affiliate with others") chose friends over experts. The latter were not "unmotivated;" their desire to be with someone they liked was simply a stronger motive than their desire to excel at the task. Other such needs have been studied by psychologists. For instance, the need for Power is often confused with the need for Achievement because both may lead to "outstanding" activities. There is a distinct difference. People with a strong need for Power want to command attention, get recognition, and control others. They are more active in political life and tend to busy themselves primarily with controlling the channels of communication both up to the top and down to the people so that they are more "in charge." Those with high *n* Power are not as concerned with improving their work performance daily as those with high *n* Ach.

It follows, from what we have been able to learn, that not all "great achievers" score high in *n* Ach. Many generals, outstanding politicians, great research scientists do not, for instance, because their work requires other personality characteristics, other motives. A general or a politician must be more concerned with power relationships, a research scientist must be able to go for long periods without the immediate feedback the person with high *n* Ach requires, etc. On the other hand, business executives, particularly if they are in positions of real responsibility or if they are salesmen, tend to score high in *n* Ach. This is true even in a Communist country like Poland: apparently there, as well as in a private economy, a manager succeeds if he is concerned about improving all the time, setting moderate goals, keeping track of his or the company's performance, etc.

MOTIVATION AND HALF-TRUTHS

Since careful study has shown that common sense notions about motivation are at best half-truths, it also follows that you cannot trust what people tell you about their motives. After all, they often get their ideas about their own motives from common sense. Thus a general may say he is interested in achievement (because he has obviously achieved), or a businessman that he is interested only in making money (because he has made money), or one of the majority of unemployed in Erie that he desperately wants a job (because he knows he needs one); but a careful check of what each one thinks about and how he spends his time may show that each is concerned about quite different things. It requires special measurement techniques to identify the presence of *n* Ach and other such motives. Thus what people say and believe is not very closely related to these "hidden" motives which seem to affect a person's "style of life" more than his political, religious or social attitudes. Thus *n* Ach produces enterprising men among labor leaders or managers, Republicans or Democrats, Catholics or Protestants, capitalists or Communists.

Wherever people begin to think often in *n* Ach terms, things begin to move. Men with high *n* Ach get more raises and are promoted more rapidly, because they keep actively seeking ways to do a better job. Companies with many such men grow faster. In one comparison of two firms in Mexico, it was discovered that all but one of the top executives of a fast growing firm had higher *n* Ach scores than the highest scoring executive in an equally large but slow-growing firm. Countries with many such rapidly growing firms tend to show above average rates of national economic growth. This appears to be the reason why correlations have regularly been found between the *n* Ach content in popular literature (such as popular songs or stories in children's textbooks) and subsequent rates of national economic growth. A nation which is thinking about doing better all the time (as shown in its popular literature) actually does do better economically speaking. Careful quantitative studies have shown this to be true in Ancient Greece, in Spain in the Middle Ages, in England from 1400–1800, as well as among contemporary nations, whether capitalist or Communist, developed or underdeveloped.

Contrast these two stories for example. Which one contains more *n* Ach? Which one reflects a state of mind which ought to lead to harder striving to improve the way things are?

Excerpt from story A (4th grade reader): "Don't Ever Owe a Man—The world is an illusion. Wife, children, horses, and cows are all just ties of fate. They are ephemeral. Each after fulfilling his part in life disappears. So we should not clamour after riches which are not permanent. As long as we live it is wise not to have any attachments and just think of God. We have to spend our lives without trouble, for is it not time that there is an end to grievances? So it is better to live knowing the real state of affairs. Don't get entangled in the meshes of family life."

Excerpt from story B (4th grade reader): "How I Do Like to Learn—I was sent to an accelerated technical high school. I was so happy I cried. Learning is not very easy. In the beginning I couldn't understand what the teacher taught us. I always got a red cross mark on my papers. The boy sitting next to me was very enthusiastic and also an outstanding student. When he found I couldn't do the problems he offered to show me how he had done them. I could not copy his work. I must learn through my own reasoning. I gave his paper back and explained I had to do it myself. Sometimes I worked on a problem until midnight. If I couldn't finish, I started early in the morning. The red cross marks on my work were getting less common. I conquered my difficulties. My marks rose. I graduated and went on to college."

Most readers would agree, without any special knowledge of the *n* Ach coding system, that the second story shows more concern with improvement than the first, which comes from a contemporary reader used in Indian public schools. In fact the latter has a certain Horatio Alger quality that is reminiscent of our own McGuffey readers of several generations ago. It appears today in the textbooks of Communist China. It should not, therefore, come as a surprise if a nation like Communist China, obsessed as it is with improvement, tended in the long run to outproduce a nation like India, which appears to be more fatalistic.

The n Ach level is obviously important for statesmen to watch and in many instances to try to do something about, particularly if a nation's economy is lagging. Take Britain, for example. A generation ago (around 1925) it ranked fifth among 25 countries where children's readers were scored for n Ach—and its economy was doing well. By 1950 the n Ach level had dropped to 27th out of 39 countries—well below the world average—and today, its leaders are feeling the severe economic effects of this loss in the spirit of enterprise.

ECONOMICS AND n ACH

If psychologists can detect n Ach levels in individuals or nations, particularly before their effects are widespread, can't the knowledge somehow be put to use to foster economic development? Obviously detection or diagnosis is not enough. What good is it to tell Britain (or India for that matter) that it needs more n Ach, a greater spirit of enterprise? In most such cases, informed observers of the local scene know very well that such a need exists, though they may be slower to discover it than the psychologist hovering over n Ach scores. What is needed is some method of developing n Ach in individuals or nations.

Since about 1960, psychologists in my research group at Harvard have been experimenting with techniques designed to accomplish this goal, chiefly among business executives whose work requires the action characteristics of people with high n Ach. Initially, we had real doubts as to whether we could succeed, partly because like most American psychologists we had

been strongly influenced by the psychoanalytic view that basic motives are laid down in childhood and cannot really be changed later, and partly because many studies of intensive psychotherapy and counseling have shown minor if any long-term personality effects. On the other hand we were encouraged by the nonprofessionals: those enthusiasts like Dale Carnegie, the Communist idealogue or the Church missionary, who felt they could change adults and in fact seemed to be doing so. At any rate we ran some brief (7 to 10 days) "total push" training courses for businessmen designed to increase their n Ach.

FOUR MAIN GOALS

In broad outline the courses had four main goals: (1) They were designed to teach the participants how to think, talk, and act like a person with high n Ach, based on our knowledge of such people gained through 17 years of research. For instance, men learned how to make up stories that would code high in n Ach (i.e., how to think in n Ach terms), how to set moderate goals for themselves in the ring toss game (and in life). (2) The courses stimulated the participants to set higher but carefully planned and realistic work goals for themselves over the next two years. Then we checked back with them every six months to see how well they were doing in terms of their own objectives. (3) The courses also utilized techniques for giving the participants knowledge about themselves. For instance, in playing the ring toss game, they could observe that they behaved differently from others—perhaps in refusing to adjust a goal downward after failure. This would then become a matter for group discussion and the man would have to explain what he had in mind in setting such unrealistic goals. Discussion could then lead on to what a man's ultimate goals in life were, how much he cared about actually improving performance v. making a good impression or having many friends. In this way the participants would be freer to realize their achievement goals without being blocked by old habits and attitudes. (4) The courses also usually created a group *esprit de corps* from learning about each other's hopes and fears, successes and failures, and from going through an emotional experience together, away from everyday life, in a retreat setting. This membership in a new group helps a man achieve his goals, partly because he knows he has their sympathy and support and partly because he knows they will be watching to see how well he does. The same effect has been noted in other therapy groups like Alcoholics Anonymous. We are not sure which of these course "inputs" is really absolutely essential—that remains a research question—but we were taking no chances at the outset in view of the general pessimism about such efforts, and we wanted to include any and all techniques that were thought to change people.

The courses have been given: to executives in a large American firm, and in several Mexican firms, to underachieving high school boys; and to businessmen in India from Bombay and from a small city—Kakinada in the state of Andhra Pradesh. In every instance save one (the Mexican case), it was possible to demonstrate statistically, some two years later, that the men who took the course had done better (made more money, got promoted faster, expanded their businesses faster) than comparable men who did not take the course or who took some other management course.

Consider the Kakinada results, for example. In the two years preceding the course 9 men, 18 percent of the 52 participants, had shown "unusual" enterprise in their businesses. In the 18 months following the course 25 of the men, in other words nearly 50 percent, were unusually active. And this was not due to a general upturn of business in India. Data from a control city, some forty-five miles away, show the same base rate of "unusually active" men as in Kakinada before the course—namely, about 20 percent. Something clearly happened in Kakinada: the owner of a small radio shop started a chemical plant; a banker was so successful in making commercial loans in an enterprising way that he was promoted to a much larger branch of his bank in Calcutta; the local political leader accomplished his goal (it was set in the course) to get the federal government to deepen the harbor and make it into an all-weather port; plans are far along for establishing a steel rolling mill, etc. All this took place without any substantial capital from the outside. In fact, the only costs were for our 10-day courses plus some brief follow-up visits every six months. The men are raising their own capital and using their own resources for getting business and industry moving in a city that had been considered stagnant and unenterprising.

The promise of such a method of developing achievement motivation seems very great. It has obvious applications in helping underdeveloped countries, or "pockets of poverty" in the United States, to move faster economically. It has great potential for businesses that need to "turn around" and take a more enterprising approach toward their growth and development. It may even be helpful in developing more *n* Ach among low-income groups. For instance, data show that lower-class Negro Americans have a very low level of *n* Ach. This is not surprising. Society has systematically discouraged and

McClelland

FIGURE 1

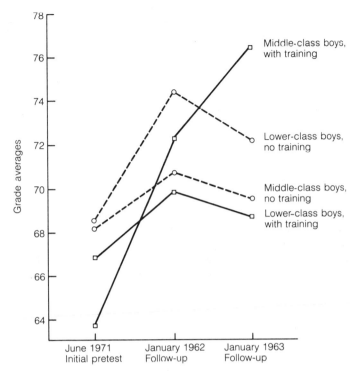

In a Harvard study, a group of underachieving 14-year-olds was given a six-week course designed to help them do better in school. Some of the boys were also given training in achievement motivation, or n Ach (solid lines). As graph reveals, the only boys who continued to improve after a two-year period were the middle-class boys with the special n Ach training. Psychologists suspect the lower-class boys dropped back, even with n Ach training, because they returned to an environment in which neither parents nor friends encouraged achievement.

blocked their achievement striving. But as the barriers to upward mobility are broken down, it will be necessary to help stimulate the motivation that will lead them to take advantage of new opportunities opening up.

EXTREME REACTIONS

But a word of caution: Whenever I speak of this research and its great potential, audience reaction tends to go to opposite extremes. Either people remain skeptical and argue that motives can't really be changed, that all we are doing is dressing Dale Carnegie up in fancy "psychologese," or they become converts and want instant course descriptions by a return mail to solve their local motivation problems. Either response is unjustified. What I have described here in a few pages has taken 20 years of patient research effort, and hundreds of thousands of dollars in basic research costs. What remains to be done will involve even larger sums and more time for development to turn a promising idea into something of wide practical utility.

ENCOURAGEMENT NEEDED

To take only one example, we have not yet learned how to develop n Ach really well among low-income groups. In our first effort—a summer course for bright underachieving 14-year-olds—we found that boys from the middle class improved steadily in grades in school over a two-year period, but boys from the lower class showed an improvement after the first year followed by a drop back to their beginning low grade average. (*See Figure 1.*) Why? We speculated that it was because they moved back into an environment in which neither parents nor friends encouraged achievement or upward mobility. In other words, it isn't enough to change a man's motivation if the environment in which he lives doesn't support at least to some degree his new efforts. Negroes striving to rise out of the ghetto frequently confront this problem: they are often faced by skepticism at home and suspicion on the job, so that even if their n Ach is raised, it can be lowered again by the heavy odds against their success. We must learn not only to raise n Ach but also to find methods of instructing people in how to manage it, to create a favorable environment in which it can flourish.

Many of these training techniques are now only in the pilot testing stage. It will take time and money to perfect them, but society should be willing to invest heavily in view of their tremendous potential for contributing to human betterment.

6

One More Time: How Do You Motivate Employees?

Not By Improving Work Conditions, Raising Salaries, or Shuffling Tasks

Frederick Herzberg

FOREWORD

KITA—the externally imposed attempt by management to "install a generator" in the employee—has been demonstrated to be a total failure, the author says. The absence of such "hygiene" factors as good supervisor-employee relations and liberal fringe benefits can make a worker unhappy, but their presence will not make him want to work harder. Essentially meaningless changes in the tasks that workers are assigned to do have not accomplished the desired objective either. The only way to motivate the employee is to give him challenging work in which he can assume responsibility.

Frederick Herzberg, who is Professor and Chairman of the Psychology Department at Case Western Reserve University, has devoted many years to the study of motivation in the United States and abroad. He is the author of *Work and the Nature of Man* (World Publishing Company, 1966).

How many articles, books, speeches, and workshops have pleaded plaintively, "How do I get an employee to do what I want him to do?"

The psychology of motivation is tremendously complex, and what has been unraveled with any degree of assurance is small indeed. But the dismal ratio of knowledge to speculation has not dampened the enthusiasm for new forms of snake oil that are constantly coming on the market, many of them with academic testimonials. Doubtless this article will have no depressing impact on the market for snake oil, but since the ideas expressed in it have been tested in many corporations and other organizations, it will help—I hope—to redress the imbalance in the aforementioned ratio.

'MOTIVATING' WITH KITA

In lectures to industry on the problem, I have found that the audiences are anxious for quick and practical answers, so I will begin with a straightforward, practical formula for moving people.

What is the simplest, surest, and

Author's note: I should like to acknowledge the contributions that Robert Ford of the American Telephone and Telegraph Company has made to the ideas expressed in this paper, and in particular to the successful application of these ideas in improving work performance and the job satisfaction of employees.

most direct way of getting someone to do something? Ask him? But if he responds that he does not want to do it, then that calls for a psychological consultation to determine the reason for his obstinacy. Tell him? His response shows that he does not understand you, and now an expert in communication methods has to be brought in to show you how to get through to him. Give him a monetary incentive? I do not need to remind the reader of the complexity and difficulty involved in setting up and administering an incentive system. Show him? This means a costly training program. We need a simple way.

Every audience contains the "direct action" manager who shouts, "Kick him!" And this type of manager is right. The surest and least circumlocuted way of getting someone to do something is to kick him in the pants—give him what might be called the KITA.

There are various forms of KITA, and here are some of them:

Negative physical KITA. This is a literal application of the term and was frequently used in the past. It has, however, three major drawbacks: (1) it is inelegant; (2) it contradicts the precious image of benevolence that most organizations cherish; and (3) since it is a physical attack, it directly stimulates the autonomic nervous system, and this often results in negative feedback—the employee may just kick you in return. These factors give rise to certain taboos against negative physical KITA.

The psychologist has come to the rescue of those who are no longer permitted to use negative physical KITA. He has uncovered infinite sources of psychological vulnerabilities and the appropriate methods to play tunes on them. "He took my rug away"; "I wonder what he meant by that"; "The boss is always going around me"—these symptomatic expressions of ego sores

that have been rubbed raw are the result of application of:

Negative Psychological KITA. This has several advantages over negative physical KITA. First, the cruelty is not visible; the bleeding is internal and comes much later. Second, since it affects the higher cortical centers of the brain with its inhibitory powers, it reduces the possibility of physical backlash. Third, since the number of psychological pains that a person can feel is almost infinite, the direction and site possibilities of the KITA are increased many times. Fourth, the person administering the kick can manage to be above it all and let the system accomplish the dirty work. Fifth, those who practice it receive some ego satisfaction (one upmanship), whereas they would find drawing blood abhorrent. Finally, if the employee does complain, he can always be accused of being paranoid, since there is no tangible evidence of an actual attack.

Now, what does negative KITA accomplish? If I kick you in the rear (physically or psychologically), who is motivated? *I* am motivated; you move! Negative KITA does not lead to motivation, but to movement. So:

Positive KITA. Let us consider motivation. If I say to you, "Do this for me or the company and in return I will give you a reward, an incentive, more status, a promotion, all the quid pro quos that exist in the industrial organization," am I motivating you? The overwhelming opinion I receive from management people is "Yes, this is motivation."

I have a year-old Schnauzer. When it was a small puppy and I wanted it to move, I kicked it in the rear and it moved. Now that I have finished its obedience training, I hold up a dog biscuit when I want the Schnauzer to move. In this instance, who is motivated—I or the dog? The dog wants the

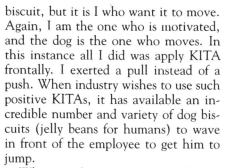
biscuit, but it is I who want it to move. Again, I am the one who is motivated, and the dog is the one who moves. In this instance all I did was apply KITA frontally. I exerted a pull instead of a push. When industry wishes to use such positive KITAs, it has available an incredible number and variety of dog biscuits (jelly beans for humans) to wave in front of the employee to get him to jump.

Why is it that managerial audiences are quick to see that negative KITA is not motivation while they are almost unanimous in their judgment that positive KITA is motivation? It is because negative KITA is rape, and positive KITA is seduction. But it is infinitely worse to be seduced than to be raped; the latter is an unfortunate occurrence, while the former signifies that you were a party to your own downfall. This is why positive KITA is so popular: it is a tradition; it is in the American way. The organization does not have to kick you; you kick yourself.

MYTHS ABOUT MOTIVATION

Why is KITA not motivation? If I kick my dog (from the front or the back), he will move. And when I want him to move again, what must I do? I must kick him again. Similarly, I can charge a man's battery, and then recharge it, and recharge it again. But it is only when he has his own generator that we can talk about motivation. He then needs no outside stimulation. He *wants* to do it.

With this in mind, we can review some positive KITA personnel practices that were developed as attempts to instill "motivation":

1. *Reducing time spent at work*—This represents a marvelous way of motivating people to work—getting them off the job! We have reduced (formally and informally) the time spent on the job over the last 50 or 60 years until we are finally on the way to the "63-day weekend." An interesting variant of this approach is the development of off-hour recreation programs. The philosophy here seems to be that those who play together, work together. The fact is that motivated people seek more hours of work, not fewer.

2. *Spiraling wages*—Have these motivated people? Yes, to seek the next wage increase. Some medievalists still can be heard to say that a good depression will get employees moving. They feel that if rising wages don't or won't do the job, perhaps reducing them will.

3. *Fringe benefits*—Industry has outdone the most welfare-minded of welfare states in dispensing cradle-to-the-grave succor. One company I know of had an informal "fringe benefit of the month club" going for a while. The cost of fringe benefits in this country has reached approximately 25% of the wage dollar, and we still cry for motivation.

People spend less time working for more money and more security than ever before, and the trend cannot be reversed. These benefits are no longer rewards; they are rights. A 6-day week is inhuman, a 10-hour day is exploitation, extended medical coverage is a basic decency, and stock options are the salvation of American initiative. Unless the ante is continuously raised, the psychological reaction of employees is that the company is turning back the clock.

When industry began to realize that both the economic nerve and the lazy nerve of their employees had insatiable appetites, it started to listen to the behavioral scientists who more out of a humanist tradition than from scientific study, criticized management for not knowing how to deal with people. The next KITA easily followed.

4. *Human relations training*—Over 30 years of teaching and, in many instances, of practicing psychological approaches to handling people have resulted in costly human relations programs and, in the end, the same question: How do you motivate workers? Here, too, escalations have taken place. Thirty years ago it was necessary to request, "Please don't spit on the floor." Today the same admonition requires three "please"s before the employee feels that his superior has demonstrated the psychologically proper attitudes toward him.

The failure of human relations training to produce motivation led to the conclusion that the supervisor or manager himself was not psychologically true to himself in his practice of interpersonal decency. So an advanced form of human relations KITA, sensitivity training, was unfolded.

5. *Sensitivity training*—Do you really, really understand yourself? Do you really, really, really trust the other man? Do you really, really, really, really cooperate? The failure of sensitivity training is now being explained, by those who have become opportunistic exploiters of the technique, as a failure to really (five times) conduct proper sensitivity training courses.

With the realization that there are only temporary gains from comfort and economic and interpersonal KITA, personnel managers concluded that the fault lay not in what they were doing, but in the employee's failure to appreciate what they were doing. This opened up the field of communications, a whole new area of "scientifically" sanctioned KITA.

6. *Communications*—The professor of communications was invited to join the faculty of management training programs and help in making employees understand what management was doing for them. House organs, briefing sessions, supervisory instruction on the importance of communication, and all sorts of propaganda have proliferated until today there is even an International Council of Industrial Editors. But no motivation resulted, and the obvious thought occurred that perhaps management was not hearing what the employees were saying. That led to the next KITA.

7. *Two-way communication*—Management ordered morale surveys, suggestion plans, and group participation programs. Then both employees and management were communicating and listening to each other more than ever, but without much improvement in motivation.

The behavioral scientists began to take another look at their conceptions and their data, and they took human relations one step further. A glimmer of truth was beginning to show through in the writings of the so-called higher-order-need psychologists. People, so they said, want to actualize themselves. Unfortunately, the "actualizing" psychologists got mixed up with the human relations psychologists, and a new KITA emerged.

8. *Job participation*—Though it may not have been the theoretical intention, job participation often became a "give them the big picture" approach. For example, if a man is tightening 10,000 nuts a day on an assembly line with a torque wrench, tell him he is building a Chevrolet. Another approach had the goal of giving the employee a *feeling* that he is determining, in some measure, what he does on his job. The goal was to provide a *sense* of achievement rather than a substantive achievement in his task. Real achieve-

ment, of course, requires a task that makes it possible.

But still there was no motivation. This led to the inevitable conclusion that the employees must be sick, and therefore to the next KITA.

9. *Employee counseling*—The initial use of this form of KITA in a systematic fashion can be credited to the Hawthorne experiment of the Western Electric Company during the early 1930s. At that time, it was found that the employees harbored irrational feelings that were interfering with the rational operation of the factory. Counseling in this instance was a means of letting the employees unburden themselves by talking to someone about their problems. Although the counseling techniques were primitive, the program was large indeed.

The counseling approach suffered as a result of experiences during World War II, when the programs themselves were found to be interfering with the operation of the organizations; the counselors had forgotten their role of benevolent listeners and were attempting to do something about the problems that they heard about. Psychological counseling, however, has managed to survive the negative impact of World War II experiences and today is beginning to flourish with renewed sophistication. But, alas, many of these programs, like all the others, do not seem to have lessened the pressure of demands to find out how to motivate workers.

Since KITA results only in short-term movement, it is safe to predict that the cost of these programs will increase steadily and new varieties will be developed as old positive KITA reach their satiation points.

HYGIENE vs. MOTIVATORS

Let me rephrase the perennial question this way: How do you install a generator in an employee? A brief review of my motivation hygiene theory of job attitudes is required before theoretical and practical suggestions can be offered. The theory was first drawn from an examination of events in the lives of engineers and accountants. At least 16 other investigations, using a wide variety of populations including some in the Communist countries have since been completed, making the original research one of the most replicated studies in the field of job attitudes.

The findings of these studies, along with corroboration from many other investigations using different procedures, suggest that the factors involved in producing job satisfaction and motivation are separate and distinct from the factors that lead to job dissatisfaction. Since separate factors need to be considered, depending on whether job satisfaction or job dissatisfaction is being examined, it follows that these two feelings are not opposites of each other. The opposite of job satisfaction is not job dissatisfaction but, rather, *no* job satisfaction; and similarly, the opposite of job dissatisfaction is not job satisfaction, but *no* job dissatisfaction.

Stating the concept presents a problem in semantics, for we normally think of satisfaction and dissatisfaction as opposites—i.e., is not satisfying must be dissatisfying, and vice versa. But when it comes to understanding the behavior of people in their jobs, more than play on words is involved.

Two different needs of man are involved here. One set of needs can be thought of as stemming from his animal nature—the built-in drive to avoid pain from the environment, plus all the learned drives which become conditioned to the basic biological needs. For example, hunger, a basic biological drive, makes it necessary to earn money, and then money becomes a specific drive. The other set of needs relates to that antique human characteristic, the ability to achieve and, through achievement, to experience psychological growth. The stimuli for the growth needs are tasks that induce growth; in the industrial setting, they are the *job content*. Contrariwise, the stimuli inducing pain-avoidance behavior are found in the *job environment*.

The growth or *motivator* factors that are intrinsic to the job are: achievement, recognition for achievement, the work itself, responsibility, and growth or advancement. The dissatisfaction-avoidance or *hygiene* (KITA) factors that are extrinsic to the job include: company policy and administration, supervision, interpersonal relationships, working conditions, salary, status, and security.

A composite of the factors that are involved in causing job satisfaction and job dissatisfaction, drawn from samples of 1,685 employees, is shown in *Exhibit 1*. The results indicate that motivators were the primary cause of satisfaction, and hygiene factors the primary cause of unhappiness on the job. The employees, studied in 12 different investigations, included lower-level supervisors, professional women, agricultural administrators, men about to retire from management positions, hospital maintenance personnel, manufacturing supervisors, nurses, food handlers, military officers, engineers, scientists, housekeepers, teachers, technicians, female assemblers, accountants, Finnish foremen, and Hungarian engineers.

They were asked what job events had occurred in their work that had led to extreme satisfaction or extreme dissat-

isfaction on their part. Their responses are broken down in the exhibit into percentages of total "positive" job events and of total "negative" job events. (The figures total more than 100% on both the "hygiene" and "motivators" sides because often at least two factors can be attributed to a single event; advancement, for instance, often accompanies assumption of responsibility.)

To illustrate, a typical response involving achievement that had a negative effect for the employee was, "I was unhappy because I didn't do the job successfully." A typical response in the small number of positive job events in the Company Policy and Administration grouping was, "I was happy because the company reorganized the section so that I didn't report any longer to the guy I didn't get along with."

As the lower right-hand part of the exhibit shows, of all the factors contributing to job satisfaction, 81% were motivators. And of all the factors contributing to the employees' dissatisfaction over their work, 69% involved hygiene elements.

ETERNAL TRIANGLE

There are three general philosophies of personnel management. The first is based on organizational theory, the second on industrial engineering, and the third on behavioral science.

The organizational theorist believes that human needs are either so irrational or so varied and adjustable to specific situations that the major function of personnel management is to be as pragmatic as the occasion demands. If jobs are organized in a proper manner, he reasons, the result will be the most efficient job structure, and the most favorable job attitudes will follow as a matter of course.

The industrial engineer holds that

Herzberg

EXHIBIT I ● FACTORS AFFECTING JOB ATTITUDES, AS REPORTED IN 12 INVESTIGATIONS

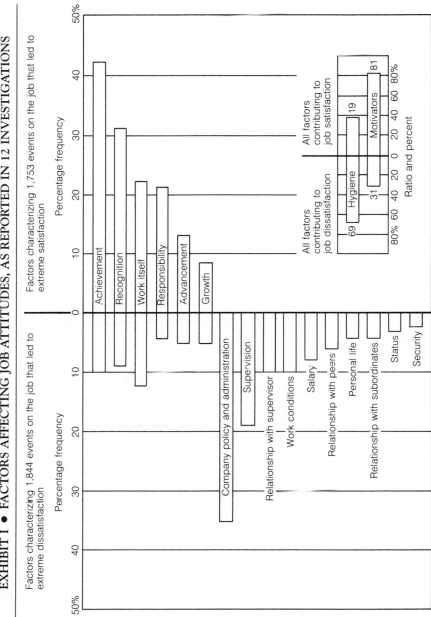

Factors characterizing 1,844 events on the job that led to extreme dissatisfaction

Factors characterizing 1,753 events on the job that led to extreme satisfaction

Percentage frequency

Percentage frequency

Achievement
Recognition
Work itself
Responsibility
Advancement
Growth

Company policy and administration
Supervision
Relationship with supervisor
Work conditions
Salary
Relationship with peers
Personal life
Relationship with subordinates
Status
Security

All factors contributing to job dissatisfaction

All factors contributing to job satisfaction

Hygiene 69 31
Motivators 19 81

Ratio and percent

man is mechanistically oriented and economically motivated and his needs are best met by attuning the individual to the most efficient work process. The goal of personnel management therefore should be to concoct the most appropriate incentive system and to design the specific working conditions in a way that facilitates the most efficient use of the human machine. By structuring jobs in a manner that leads to the most efficient operation, the engineer believes that he can obtain the optimal organization of work and the proper work attitudes.

The behavioral scientist focuses on group sentiments, attitudes of individual employees, and the organization's social and psychological climate. According to his persuasion, he emphasizes one or more of the various hygiene and motivator needs. His approach to personnel management generally emphasizes some form of human relations education, in the hope of instilling healthy employee attitudes and an organizational climate which he considers to be felicitous to human values. He believes that proper attitudes will lead to efficient job and organizational structure.

There is always a lively debate as to the overall effectiveness of the approaches of the organizational theorist and the industrial engineer. Manifestly they have achieved much. But the nagging question for the behavioral scientist has been: What is the cost in human problems that eventually cause more expense to the organization—for instance, turnover, absenteeism, errors, violation of safety rules, strikes, restriction of output, higher wages, and greater fringe benefits? On the other hand, the behavioral scientist is hard put to document much manifest improvement in personnel management, using his approach.

The three philosophies can be depicted as a triangle, as is done in *Exhibit II*, with each persuasion claiming the apex angle. The motivation-hygiene theory claims the same angle as industrial engineering, but for opposite goals. Rather than rationalizing the work to increase efficiency, the theory suggests that work be enriched to bring about effective utilization of personnel. Such a systematic attempt to motivate employees by manipulating the motivator factors is just beginning.

The term *job enrichment* describes this

EXHIBIT II • 'TRIANGLE' OF PHILOSOPHIES OF PERSONNEL MANAGEMENT

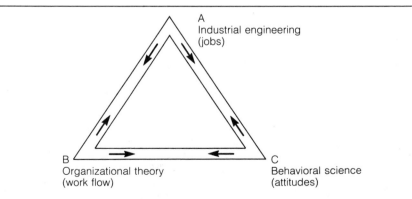

A
Industrial engineering
(jobs)

B
Organizational theory
(work flow)

C
Behavioral science
(attitudes)

embryonic movement. An older term, job enlargement should be avoided because it is associated with past failures stemming from a misunderstanding of the problem. Job enrichment provides the opportunity for the employee's psychological growth, while job enlargement merely makes a job structurally bigger. Since scientific job enrichment is very new, this article only suggests the principles and practical steps that have recently emerged from several successful experiments in industry.

JOB LOADING

In attempting to enrich an employee's job, management often succeeds in reducing the man's personal contribution, rather than giving him an opportunity for growth in his accustomed job. Such an endeavor, which I shall call horizontal job loading (as opposed to vertical loading, or providing motivator factors), has been the problem of earlier job enlargement programs. This activity merely enlarges the meaningless of the job. Some examples of this approach, and their effect, are:

- Challenging the employee by increasing the amount of production expected of him. If he tightens 10,000 bolts a day, see if he can tighten 20,000 bolts a day. The arithmetic involved shows that multiplying zero by zero still equals zero.
- Adding another meaningless task to the existing one, usually some routine clerical activity. The arithmetic here is adding zero to zero.
- Rotating the assignments of a number of jobs that need to be enriched. This means washing dishes for a while, then washing silverware. The arithmetic is substituting one zero for another zero.
- Improving the most difficult parts of the assignment in order to free the worker to accomplish more of the less challenging assignment. This tradi-

tional industrial engineering approach amounts to subtraction in the hope of accomplishing addition.

These are common forms of horizontal loading that frequently come up in preliminary brain-storming sessions on job enrichment. The principles of vertical loading have not all been worked out as yet, and they remain rather general, but I have furnished seven useful starting points for consideration in *Exhibit III.*

A SUCCESSFUL APPLICATION

An example from a highly successful job enrichment experiment can illustrate the distinction between horizontal and vertical loading of a job. The subjects of this study were the stockholder correspondents employed by a very large corporation. Seemingly, the task required of these carefully selected and highly trained correspondents was quite complex and challenging. But almost all indexes of performance and job attitudes were low, and exit interviewing confirmed that the challenge of the job existed merely as words.

A job enrichment project was initiated in the form of an experiment with one group, designated as an achieving unit, having its job enriched by the principles described in *Exhibit III.* A control group continued to do its job in the traditional way. (There were also two "uncommitted" groups of correspondents formed to measure the so-called Hawthorne Effect—that is, to gauge whether productivity and attitudes toward the job changed artificially merely because employees sensed that the company was paying more attention to them in doing something different or novel. The results for these groups were substantially the same as for the control group, and for the sake of simplicity I do not deal with them in this summary.)

EXHIBIT III • PRINCIPLES OF VERTICAL JOB LOADING

Principle	Motivators Involved
A. Removing some controls while retaining accountability	Responsibility and personal achievement
B. Increasing the accountability of individuals for own work	Responsibility and recognition
C. Giving a person a complete natural unit of work (module, division, area, and so on)	Responsibility, achievement, and recognition
D. Granting additional authority to an employee in his activity; job freedom	Responsibility, achievement, and recognition
E. Making periodic reports directly available to the worker himself rather than to the supervisor	Internal recognition
F. Introducing new and more difficult tasks not previously handled	Growth and learning
G. Assigning individuals specific or specialized tasks, enabling them to become experts	Responsibility, growth, and advancement

No changes in hygiene were introduced for either group other than those that would have been made anyway, such as normal pay increases.

The changes for the achieving unit were introduced in the first two months, averaging one per week of the seven motivators listed in *Exhibit III*. At the end of six months the members of the achieving unit were found to be outperforming their counterparts in the control group, and in addition indicated a marked increase in their liking for their jobs. Other results showed that the achieving group had lower absenteeism and, subsequently, a much higher rate of promotion.

Exhibit IV illustrates the changes in performance, measured in February and March, before the study period began, and at the end of each month of the study period. The shareholder service index represents quality of letters, including accuracy of information, and speed of response to stockholders' letters of inquiry. The index of a current month was averaged into the average of the two prior months, which means that improvement was harder to obtain if the indexes of the previous months were low. The "achievers" were performing less well before the six-month period started, and their performance service index continued to decline after the introduction of the motivators, evidently because of uncertainty over their newly granted responsibilities. In the third month, however, performance improved, and soon the members of this group had reached a high level of accomplishment.

Exhibit V shows the two groups' attitudes toward their job, measured at the end of March, just before the first motivator was introduced and again at the end of September. The correspondents were asked 16 questions, all involving motivation. A typical one was, "As you see it, how many opportunities do you feel that you have in your job for mak-

Herzberg (handwritten)

EXHIBIT IV • SHAREHOLDER SERVICE INDEX IN COMPANY EXPERIMENT
[Three-month cumulative average]

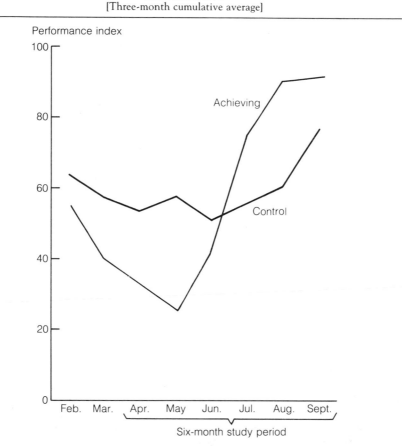

Performance index

Six-month study period

ing worthwhile contributions?" The answers were scaled from 1 to 80 with 80 as the maximum possible score. The achievers became much more positive about their job, while the attitude of the control unit remained about the same (the drop is not statistically significant).

How was the job of these correspondents restructured? *Exhibit VI* lists the suggestions made that were deemed to be horizontal loading, and the actual vertical loading changes that were incorporated in the job of the achieving unit. The capital letters under "Princi-

ple" after "Vertical loading" refer to the corresponding letters in *Exhibit III.* The reader will note that the rejected forms of horizontal loading correspond closely to the list of common manifestations of the phenomenon on page 59, left column.

STEPS TO JOB ENRICHMENT

Now that the motivator idea has been described in practice, here are the steps that managers should take in instituting the principle with their employees:

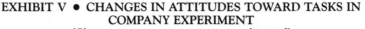

**EXHIBIT V • CHANGES IN ATTITUDES TOWARD TASKS IN
COMPANY EXPERIMENT**
[Changes in mean scores over six-month period]

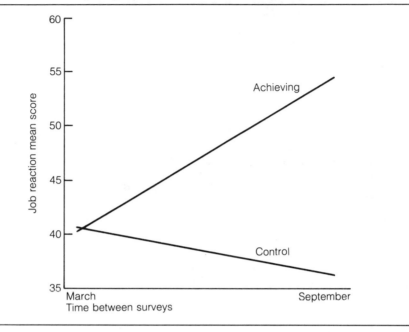

1. Select those jobs in which (a) the investment in industrial engineering does not make changes too costly, (b) attitudes are poor, (c) hygiene is becoming very costly, and (d) motivation will make no difference in performance.

2. Approach these jobs with the conviction that they can be changed. Years of tradition have led managers to believe that the content of the jobs is sacrosanct and the only scope of action that they have is in ways of stimulating people.

3. Brainstorm a list of changes that may enrich the jobs, without concern for their practicality.

4. Screen the list to eliminate suggestions that involve hygiene, rather than actual motivation.

5. Screen the list for generalities, such as "give them more responsibility," that are rarely followed in practice. This might seem obvious, but the motivator words have never left industry; the substance has just been rationalized and organized out. Words like "responsibility," "growth," "achievement," and "challenge," for example, have been elevated to the lyrics of the patriotic anthem for all organizations. It is the old problem typified by the pledge of allegiance to the flag being more important than contributions to the country—of following the form, rather than the substance.

6. Screen the list to eliminate any *horizontal* loading suggestions.

7. Avoid direct participation by the employees whose jobs are to be enriched. Ideas they have expressed previously certainly constitute a valuable

EXHIBIT VI ● ENLARGEMENT VS. ENRICHMENT OF CORRESPONDENTS' TASKS IN COMPANY EXPERIMENT

Horizontal Loading Suggestions (Rejected)	Vertical Loading Suggestions (Adopted)	Principle
Firm quotas could be set for letters to be answered each day, using a rate which would be hard to reach.	Subject matter experts were appointed within each unit for other members of the unit to consult with before seeking supervisory help. (The supervisor had been answering all specialized and difficult questions.)	G
The women could type the letters themselves as well as compose them, or take on any other clerical functions.	Correspondents signed their own names on letters. (The supervisor had been signing all letters.)	B
All difficult or complex inquiries could be channeled to a few women so that the remainder could achieve high rates of output. These jobs could be exchanged from time to time.	The work of the more experienced correspondents was proofread less frequently by supervisors and was done at the correspondents' desks, dropping verification from 100% to 10%. (Previously, all correspondents' letters had been checked by the supervisor.)	A
The women could be rotated through units handling different customers, and then sent back to their own units.	Production was discussed, but only in terms such as "a full day's work is expected." As time went on, this was no longer mentioned. (Before, the group had been constantly reminded of the number of letters that needed to be answered.)	D
	Outgoing mail went directly to the mailroom without going over supervisors' desks. (The letters had always been routed through the supervisors.)	A
	Correspondents were encouraged to answer letters in a more personalized way. (Reliance on the form-letter approach had been standard practice.)	C
	Each correspondent was held personally responsible for the quality and accuracy of letters. (This responsibility had been the province of the supervisor and the verifier.)	B, E

source for recommended changes, but their direct involvement contaminates the process with human relations *hygiene* and, more specifically, gives them only a *sense* of making a contribution. The job is to be changed, and it is the content that will produce the motivation, not attitudes about being involved or the challenge inherent in setting up a job. That process will be over shortly, and it is what the employees will be doing from then on that will determine their motivation. A sense of participation will result only in short-term movement.

8. In the initial attempts at job enrichment, set up a controlled experiment. At least two equivalent groups should be chosen, one an experimental unit in which the motivators are systematically introduced over a period of time, and the other one a control group in which no changes are made. For both groups, hygiene should be allowed to follow its natural course for the duration of the experiment. Pre- and post-installation tests of performance and job attitudes are necessary to evaluate the effectiveness of the job enrichment program. The attitude test must be limited to motivator items in order to divorce the employee's view of the job he is given from all the surrounding hygiene feelings that he might have.

9. Be prepared for a drop in performance in the experimental group the first few weeks. The changeover to a new job may lead to a temporary reduction in efficiency.

10. Expect your first-line supervisors to experience some anxiety and hostility over the changes you are making. The anxiety comes from their fear that the changes will result in poorer performance for their unit. Hostility will arise when the employees start assuming what the supervisors regard as their own responsibility for performance. The supervisor without checking duties to perform may then be left with little to do.

After a successful experiment, however, the supervisor usually discovers the supervisory and managerial functions he has neglected, or which were never his because all his time was given over to checking the work of his subordinates. For example, in the R&D division of one large chemical company I know of, the supervisors of the laboratory assistants were theoretically responsible for their training and evaluation. These functions, however, had come to be performed in a routine, unsubstantial fashion. After the job enrichment program, during which the supervisors were not merely passive observers of the assistants' performance, the supervisors actually were devoting their time to reviewing performance and administering thorough training.

What has been called an employee-centered style of supervision will come about not through education of supervisors, but by changing the jobs that they do.

CONCLUDING NOTE

Job enrichment will not be a one-time proposition, but a continuous management function. The initial changes, however, should last for a very long period of time. There are a number of reasons for this:

- The changes should bring the job up to the level of challenge commensurate with the skill that was hired.
- Those who have still more ability eventually will be able to demonstrate it better and win promotion to higher-level jobs.

Herzberg

- The very nature of motivators, as opposed to hygiene factors, is that they have a much longer term effect on employees' attitudes. Perhaps the job will have to be enriched again, but this will not occur as frequently as the need for hygiene.

Not all jobs can be enriched, nor do all jobs need to be enriched. If only a small percentage of the time and money that is now devoted to hygiene, however, were given to job enrichment efforts, the return in human satisfaction and economic gain would be one of the largest dividends that industry and society have ever reaped through their efforts at better personnel management.

The argument for job enrichment can be summed up quite simply: If you have someone on a job, use him. If you can't use him on the job, get rid of him, either via automation or by selecting someone with lesser ability. If you can't use him and you can't get rid of him, you will have a motivation problem.

7
Expectancy Theory

John P. Campbell, Marvin D. Dunnette,
Edward E. Lawler III & Karl E. Weick, Jr.

EXPECTANCY THEORY

Early cognitive theories. Concomitant with the development of <u>drive x</u> <u>habit theory</u>, <u>Lewin (1938)</u> and Tolman (1932) developed and investigated cognitive, or expectancy, theories of motivation. Even though Lewin was concerned with human subjects and Tolman worked largely with animals, much of their respective theorizing contained common elements. Basic to the cognitive view of motivation is the notion that individuals have cognitive *expectancies* concerning the outcomes that are likely to occur as the result of what they do and that individuals have preferences among outcomes. That is, an individual has an "idea" about possible consequences of his acts, and he makes conscious choices among consequences according to their probability of occurrence and their value to him.

Thus for the cognitive theorist it is the anticipation of reward that energizes behavior and the perceived value of various outcomes that gives behavior its direction. Tolman spoke of a *belief-value* matrix that specifies for each individual the value he places on particular outcomes and his belief that they can be attained.

Atkinson (1964) has compared drive theory and expectancy theory. Although he points out some differences, he emphasizes that both theories are actually quite similar and contain many of the same concepts. Both include the notion of a reward or favorable outcome that is desired, and both postulate a learned connection contained within the organism. For expectancy theory this learned connection is a behavior-outcome expectancy, and for drive theory it is an *S-R* habit strength.

However, the theories differ in two ways which are important for research on motivation in an organizational setting. For example, they differ in what they state is activated by the anticipation of reward. Expectancy theory sees the anticipation of a reward as functioning selectively on actions expected to lead to it. Drive theory views the magnitude of the anticipated goals as a source of general excitement—a nonselective influence on performance.

Expectancy theory is also much looser in specifying how expectancy-outcome connections are built up. Drive theory postulates that *S-R* habit strengths are built up through repeated associations of stimulus and response; that is, the reward or outcome must actually have followed the response to a particular stimulus in order for the *S-R*

Source: From "Expectancy Theory" by John P. Campbell, Marvin D. Dunnette, Edward E. Lawler III, and Karl E. Weick, Jr. in *Managerial Behavior, Performance, and Effectiveness*, pp. 343–48.

connection to operate in future choice behavior. Such a process is sufficient but not necessary for forming expectancy-outcome relationships. An individual may form expectancies vicariously (someone may tell him that complimenting the boss's wife leads to a promotion, for example) or by other symbolic means. This last point is crucial since the symbolic (cognitive) manipulation of various *S-R* situations seems quite descriptive of a great deal of human behavior.

These two differences make the cognitive or expectancy point of view much more useful for studying human motivation in an organizational setting. In fact, it is the one which has been given the most attention by theorists concerned with behavior in organizations.

Instrumentality-valence theory. Building on expectancy theory and its later amplifications by Atkinson (1958), W. Edwards (1954), Peak (1955), and Rotter (1955), Vroom (1964) has presented a process theory of work motivation that he calls *instrumentality theory*. His basic classes of variables are expectancies, valences, choices, outcomes, and instrumentalities.

Expectancy is defined as a belief concerning the likelihood that a particular act will be followed by a particular outcome. Presumably, the degree of belief can vary between 0 (complete lack of belief that it will follow) and 1 (complete certainty that it will). Note that it is the perception of the individual that is important, not the objective reality. This same concept has been referred to as *subjective probability* by others (e.g., W. Edwards, 1954).

Valence refers to the strength of an individual's preference for a particular outcome. An individual may have either a positive or a negative preference for an outcome; presumably, outcomes gain their valence as a function of the degree to which they are seen to be related to the needs of the individual. However, this last point is not dealt with concretely in Vroom's formulation. As an example of these two concepts, one might consider an increase in pay to be a possible outcome of a particular act. The theory would then deal with the valence of a wage increase for an individual and his expectancy that particular behaviors will be followed by a wage increase outcome. Again, valence refers to the perceived or expected value of an outcome, not its real or eventual value.

According to Vroom, outcomes take on a valence value because of their *instrumentality* for achieving other outcomes. Thus he is really postulating two classes of outcomes. In the organizational setting, the first class of outcomes might include such things as money, promotion, recognition, etc. Supposedly, these outcomes are directly linked to behavior. However, as Vroom implicitly suggests, wage increases or promotion may have no value by themselves. They are valuable in terms of their instrumental role in securing second level outcomes such as food, clothing, shelter, entertainment, and status, which are not obtained as the direct result of a particular action.

According to Vroom, instrumentality, like correlation, varies between $+1.0$ and -1.0. Thus a first level outcome may be seen as always leading to some desired second level outcome ($+1.0$) or as never leading to the second level outcome (-1.0). In Vroom's theory the formal definition of valence for a first level outcome is the sum of the products between its instrumentalities for all possible second level outcomes and their respective valences.

To sum up, Vroom's formulation postulates that the motivational force, or effort, an individual exerts is a function of (1) his expectancy that certain outcomes will result from his behavior (e.g., a raise in pay for increased effort) and (2) the valence, for him, of those outcomes. The valence of an outcome is in turn a function of its instrumentality for obtaining other outcomes and the valence of these other outcomes.

A hybrid expectancy model. Since his formulation first appeared, a number of investigators have attempted to extend Vroom's model to make it more explicit and more inclusive in terms of relevant variables (Graen, 1967; L.W. Porter & Lawler, 1968). Although we shall not discuss the contributions of these writers in detail, we would like to incorporate a number of their ideas in our own composite picture of an expanded expectancy model. However, any imperfections in what follows should be ascribed to us and not to them.

One major addition to Vroom's model is the necessity for a more concrete specification of the task or performance goals toward which work behavior is directed. Graen (1967) refers to this class of variables as *work roles*, but we prefer to retain the notion of *task goals*. Task goals may be specified externally by the organization or the work group, or internally by the individual's own value system. Examples of task goals include such things as production quotas, time limits for projects, quality standards, showing a certain amount of loyalty to the organization, exhibiting the right set of attitudes, etc.

We would also like to make more explicit a distinction between first and second level outcomes. First level outcomes are outcomes contingent on achieving the task goal or set of task goals. A potential first level outcome is synonymous with the term *incentive*,

and an outcome which is actually realized is synonymous with the term *reward*. The distinction is temporal. Like task goals, first level outcomes may be external or internal. Some examples of external first level outcomes granted by the organization are job security, pay, promotions, recognition, and increased autonomy. An individual may also set up his own internal incentives or reward himself with internally mediated outcomes such as ego satisfaction.

As pointed out in the discussion of Vroom's model first level outcomes may or may not be associated with a plethora of second level outcomes; that is, the externally or internally mediated rewards are instrumental in varying degrees for obtaining second level outcomes such as food, housing, material goods, community status, and freedom from anxiety.

The concepts of valence for first and second level outcomes and the instrumentality of first for second level outcomes are defined as before, but the notion of expectancy decomposes into two different variables. First, individuals may have expectancies concerning whether or not they will actually accomplish the task goal if they expend effort (expectancy I); that is, an individual makes a subjective probability estimate concerning his chances for reaching a particular goal, given a particular situation. For example, a manufacturing manager may think the odds of his getting a new product into production by the first of the year are about 3 to 1 (*i.e.*, expectancy I $= 0.75$). Perhaps the primary determiner of expectancy I is how the individual perceives his own job skills in the context of what is specified as his task goals and the various difficulties and external constraints standing in the way of accomplishing them. Certainly, then, an employee's perceptions of his own talents determine to a large degree the direction and intensity of his job behavior. This first kind of expectancy should be more salient for more complex and higher level tasks such as those involved in managing.

Second, individuals possess expectancies concerning whether or not achievement of specified task goals will actually be followed by the first level outcome (expectancy II). In other words, they form subjective probability estimates of the degree to which rewards are *contingent* on achieving task goals. The individual must ask himself what the probability is that his achievement of the goal will be rewarded by the organization. For example, the manufacturing manager may be virtually certain (expectancy II = 1.0) that if he does get the new product into production by the first of the year, he will receive a promotion and a substantial salary increase. Or, and this may be the more usual case, he may see no relationship at all between meeting the objective and getting a promotion and salary increase.

None of the authors cited so far have explicitly labeled these two kinds of expectancies. Indeed, in a laboratory or other experimental setting the distinction may not be necessary since the task may be so easy that accomplishing the goal is always a certainty (*i.e.*, expectancy I is 1.0 for everybody) or the contingency of reward on behavior may be certain and easily verified by the subject (*i.e.*, expectancy II is 1.0 for everybody). Vroom (1964) defines expectancy as an action-outcome relationship which is represented by an individual's subjective probability estimate that a particular set of behaviors will be followed by a particular outcome. Since Vroom presents no concrete definitions for the terms "action" and "outcome," his notion of expectancy could include

both expectancy I and expectancy II as defined above. Thus effort expenditure could be regarded as an action, and goal performance as an outcome; or performance could be considered behavior, and money an outcome. Vroom uses both kinds of examples to illustrate the expectancy variable and makes no conceptual distinction between them. However, in the organizational setting, the distinction seems quite necessary. Rewards may or may not be contingent on goal accomplishment, and the individual may or may not believe he has the wherewithal to reach the goal. A schematic representation of this hybrid model is shown in Figure 7.1.

We have purposely been rather vague concerning the exact form of the relationships between these different classes of variables. This schematic model is in no way meant to be a formal theory. To propose explicit multiplicative combinations or other configural or higher order functions is going a bit too far beyond our present measurement capability. Rather, we shall sum up the relationships contained in our expanded model as follows:

1. The valence of a first level outcome (incentive or reward) is a function of the instrumentality of that outcome for obtaining second level outcomes (need satisfactions) and the valences of the relevant second level outcomes.

2. The decision by an individual to work on a particular task and expend a certain amount of effort in that direction is a function of (*a*) his personal probability estimate that he can accomplish the task (expectancy I), (*b*) his personal probability estimate that his accomplishment of the task goal will be followed by certain first level outcomes or rewards (ex-

FIGURE 7.1 • A SCHEMATIC REPRESENTATION OF A HYBRID EXPECTANCY MODEL OF WORK MOTIVATION OUTLINING THE DETERMINANTS OF THE DIRECTION, AMPLITUDE, AND PERSISTENCE OF INDIVIDUAL EFFORT.

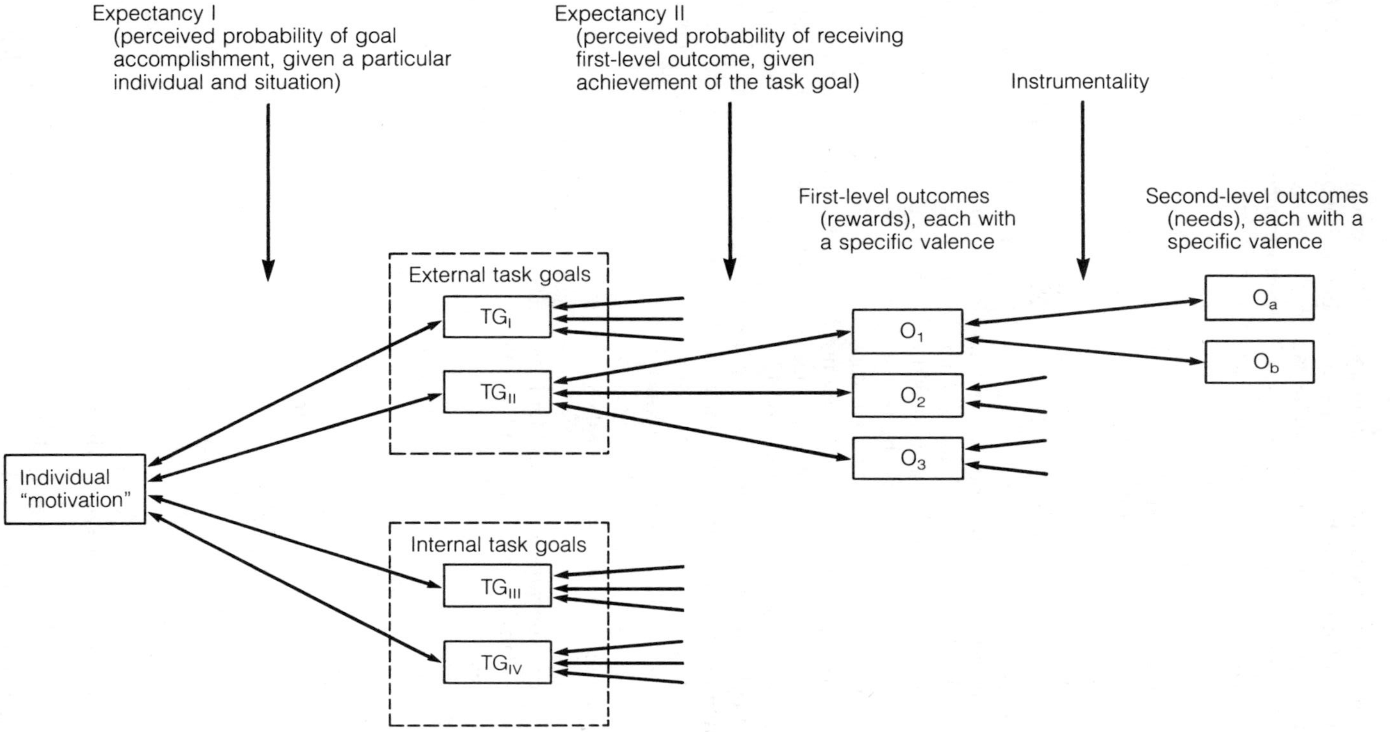

pectancy II), and (c) the valence of the first level outcomes.

3. The distinction between external and internal goals and rewards leads to a number of potential conflict situations for the individual. For example, an individual might estimate his chances for accomplishing a particular task as virtually certain (i.e., expectancy I = 1.0). However, the internal rewards which are virtually certain to follow (i.e., expectancy II = 1.0) may have a very low or even negative valence (e.g., feelings of extreme boredom or distaste). If external rewards, such as a lot of money, have a very high valence, a serious stress situation could result from outcomes which have conflicting valences. It would be to an organization's advantage to ensure positive valences for both internal and external rewards. Other conflict situations could be produced by high positive valences for outcomes and low estimates of type I expectancies (i.e., the individual does not think he can actually do the job).

Even though this kind of hybrid expectancy model seems to be a useful way of looking at organizational behavior and even though we have devoted more space to it, the reader should keep in mind that it is not the only process theory that one could use. Equity theory is its major competitor.

NOTES

1. K. Lewin, The Conceptual Representation and the Measurement of Psychological Forces (Durham, N.C.: Duke University Press, 1938).

2. E. C. Tolman, Purposive Behavior in Animals and Men (New York: Century. By permission of the University of California Press, 1932).

3. J. W. Atkinson, An Introduction to Motivation (Princeton, N.J.: Van Nostrand, 1964).

4. J. W. Atkinson (ed.), Motives in Fantasy, Action and Society (Princeton, N.J.: Van Nostrand, 1958).

5. W. Edwards, "The Theory of Decision Making," Psychological Bulletin, Vol. 51 (1954), pp. 380–417.

6. H. Peak, "Attitude and Motivation," in M. R. Jones (ed.), Nebraska Symposium on Motivation (Lincoln, Nebr.: University of Nebraska Press, 1955), pp. 149–188.

7. J. B. Rotter, "The Role of the Psychological Situation in Determining the Direction of Human Behavior," in M. R. Jones (ed.), Nebraska Symposium on Motivation (Lincoln, Nebr.: University of Nebraska Press, 1955).

8. V. H. Vroom, Work and Motivation (New York: Wiley, 1964).

9. G. B. Graen, Work Motivation: The Behavioral Effects of Job Content and Job Context Factors in an Employment Situation. Unpublished doctoral dissertation (University of Minnesota, 1967).

10. L. W. Porter and E. E. Lawler, Managerial Attitudes and Performance (Homewood, Ill.: Dorsey-Irwin, 1968).

11. Graen, op cit.

12. Vroom, op cit.

8

On the Folly of Rewarding A, While Hoping for B

Steven Kerr

Whether dealing with monkeys, rats, or human beings, it is hardly controversial to state that most organisms seek information concerning what activities are rewarded, and then seek to do (or at least pretend to do) those things, often to the virtual exclusion of activities not rewarded. The extent to which this occurs of course will depend on the perceived attractiveness of the rewards offered, but neither operant nor expectancy theorists would quarrel with the essence of this notion.

Nevertheless, numerous examples exist of reward systems that are fouled up in that behaviors which are rewarded are those which the rewarder is trying to *discourage*, while the behavior he desires is not being rewarded at all.

In an effort to understand and explain this phenomenon, this paper presents examples from society, from organizations in general, and from profit-making firms in particular. Data from a manufacturing company and information from an insurance firm are examined to demonstrate the consequences of such reward systems for the organizations involved, and possible reasons why such reward systems continue to exist are considered.

SOCIETAL EXAMPLES

Politics

Official goals are "purposely vague and general and do not indicate . . . the host of decisions that must be made among alternative ways of achieving official goals and the priority of multiple goals . . ." (8, p. 66). They usually may be relied on to offend absolutely no one, and in this sense can be considered high acceptance, low quality goals. An example might be "build better schools." Operative goals are higher in quality but lower in acceptance, since they specify where the money will come from, what alternative goals will be ignored, etc.

The American citizenry supposedly wants its candidates for public office to set forth operative goals, making their proposed programs "perfectly clear," specifying sources and uses of funds, etc. However, since operative goals are lower in acceptance, and since aspirants to public office need acceptance (from at least 50.1 percent of the people), most politicians prefer to speak only of official goals, at least until after the election. They of course would agree to speak at the operative level if "punished" for not doing so. The elec-

Source: From "On the Folly of Rewarding A, While Hoping for B." by Steven Kerr, in *Academy of Management Journal* 18, No. 4 (December 1975) pp. 769–82. Reprinted by permission.

Steven Kerr (Ph.D.—City University of New York) is Associate Professor of Organizational Behavior, College of Administrative Science, Ohio State University, Columbus, Ohio.

torate could do this by refusing to support candidates who do not speak at the operative level.

Instead, however, the American voter typically punishes (withholds support from) candidates who frankly discuss where the money will come from, rewards politicians who speak only of official goals, but hopes that candidates (despite the reward system) will discuss the issues operatively. It is academic whether it was moral for Nixon, for example, to refuse to discuss his 1968 "secret plan" to end the Vietnam war, his 1972 operative goals concerning the lifting of price controls, the reshuffling of his cabinet, etc. The point is that the reward system made such refusal rational.

It seems worth mentioning that no manuscript can adequately define what is "moral" and what is not. However, examination of costs and benefits, combined with knowledge of what motivates a particular individual, often will suffice to determine what for him is "rational."[1] If the reward system is so designed that it is irrational to be moral, this does not necessarily mean that immorality will result. But is this not asking for trouble?

War

If some oversimplification may be permitted, let it be assumed that the primary goal of the organization (Pentagon, Luftwaffe, or whatever) is to win. Let it be assumed further that the primary goal of most individuals on the front lines is to get home alive. Then

there appears to be an important conflict in goals—personally rational behavior by those at the bottom will endanger goal attainment by those at the top.

But not necessarily! It depends on how the reward system is set up. The Vietnam war was indeed a study of disobedience and rebellion, with terms such as "fragging" (killing one's own commanding officer) and "search and evade" becoming part of the military vocabulary. The difference in subordinates' acceptance of authority between World War II and Vietnam is reported to be considerable, and veterans of the Second World War often have been quoted as being outraged at the mutinous actions of many American soldiers in Vietnam.

Consider, however, some critical differences in the reward system in use during the two conflicts. What did the GI in World War II want? To go home. And when did he get to go home? When the war was won! If he disobeyed the orders to clean out the trenches and take the hills, the war would not be won and he would not go home. Furthermore, what were his chances of attaining his goal (getting home alive) if he obeyed the orders compared to his chances if he did not? What is being suggested is that the rational soldier in World War II, *whether patriotic or not*, probably found it expedient to obey.

Consider the reward system in use in Vietnam. What did the man at the bottom want? To go home. And when did he get to go home? When his tour of duty was over! This was the case *whether or not* the war was won. Furthermore, concerning the relative chance of getting home alive by obeying orders compared to the chance if they were disobeyed, it is worth noting that a mutineer in Vietnam was far more likely to

[1]In Simon's (10, pp. 76–77) terms, a decision is "subjectively rational" if it maximizes an individual's valued outcomes so far as his knowledge permits. A decision is "personally rational" if it is oriented toward the individual's goals.

be assigned rest and rehabilitation (on the assumption that fatigue was the cause) than he was to suffer any negative consequence.

In his description of the "zone of indifference," Barnard stated that "a person can and will accept a communication as authoritative only when . . . at the time of his decision, he believes it to be compatible with his personal interests as a whole" (1, p. 165). In light of the reward system used in Vietnam, would it not have been personally irrational for some orders to have been obeyed? Was not the military implementing a system which *rewarded* disobedience, while *hoping* that soldiers (despite the reward system) would obey orders?

Medicine

Theoretically, a physician can make either of two types of error, and intuitively one seems as bad as the other. A doctor can pronounce a patient sick when he is actually well, thus causing him needless anxiety and expense, curtailment of enjoyable foods and activities, and even physical danger by subjecting him to needless medication and surgery. Alternatively, a doctor can label a sick person as well, and thus avoid treating what may be a serious, even fatal ailment. It might be natural to conclude that physicians seek to minimize both types of error.

Such a conclusion would be wrong.[2] It is estimated that numerous Americans are presently afflicted with iatrogenic (physician *caused*) illnesses (9). This occurs when the doctor is approached by someone complaining of a

few stray symptoms. The doctor classifies and organizes these symptoms, gives them a name, and obligingly tells the patient what further symptoms may be expected. This information often acts as a self-fulfilling prophecy, with the result that from that day on the patient for all practical purposes is sick.

Why does this happen? Why are physicians so reluctant to sustain a type 2 error (pronouncing a sick person well) that they will tolerate many type 1 errors? Again, a look at the reward system is needed. The punishments for a type 2 error are real: guilt, embarrassment, and the threat of lawsuit and scandal. On the other hand, a type 1 error (labeling a well person sick) "is sometimes seen as sound clinical practice, indicating a healthy conservative approach to medicine" (9, p. 69). Type 1 errors also are likely to generate increased income and a stream of steady customers who, being well in a limited physiological sense, will not embarrass the doctor by dying abruptly.

Fellow physicians and the general public therefore are really *rewarding* type 1 errors and at the same time *hoping* fervently that doctors will try not to make them.

GENERAL ORGANIZATIONAL EXAMPLES

Rehabilitation Centers and Orphanages

In terms of the prime beneficiary classification (2, p. 42) organizations such as these are supposed to exist for the "public-in-contact," that is, clients. The orphanage therefore theoretically is interested in placing as many children as possible in good homes. However, often orphanages surround themselves with so many rules concerning adoption that it is nearly impossible to pry a child

---

[2]In one study (4) of 14,867 films for signs of tuberculosis, 1,216 positive readings turned out to be clinically negative; only 24 negative readings proved clinically active, a ratio of 50 to 1.

out of the place. Orphanages may deny adoption unless the applicants are a married couple, both of the same religion as the child, without history of emotional or vocational instability, with a specified minimum income and a private room for the child, etc.

If the primary goal is to place children in good homes, then the rules ought to constitute means toward that goal. Goal displacement results when these "means become ends-in-themselves that displace the original goals" (2, p. 229).

To some extent these rules are required by law. But the influence of the reward system on the orphanage's management should not be ignored. Consider, for example, that the:

1. Number of children enrolled often is the most important determinant of the size of the allocated budget.
2. Number of children under the director's care also will affect the size of his staff.
3. Total organizational size will determine largely the director's prestige at the annual conventions, in the community, etc.

Therefore, to the extent that staff size, total budget, and personal prestige are valued by the orphanage's executive personnel, it becomes rational for them to make it difficult for children to be adopted. After all, who wants to be the director of the smallest orphanage in the state?

If the reward system errs in the opposite direction, paying off only for placements, extensive goal displacement again is likely to result. A common example of vocational rehabilitation in many states, for example, consists of placing someone in a job for which he has little interest and few

qualifications, for two months or so, and then "rehabilitating" him again in another position. Such behavior is quite consistent with the prevailing reward system, which pays off for the number of individuals placed in any position for 60 days or more. Rehabilitation counselors also confess to competing with one another to place relatively skilled clients, sometimes ignoring persons with few skills who would be harder to place. Extensively disabled clients find that counselors often prefer to work with those whose disabilities are less severe.[3]

Universities

Society *hopes* that teachers will not neglect their teaching responsibilities but *rewards* them almost entirely for research and publications. This is most true at the large and prestigious universities. Cliches such as "good research and good teaching go together" notwithstanding, professors often find that they must choose between teaching and research oriented activities when allocating their time. Rewards for good teaching usually are limited to outstanding teacher awards, which are given to only a small percentage of good teachers and which usually bestow little money and fleeting prestige. Punishments for poor teaching also are rare.

Rewards for research and publications, on the other hand, and punishments for failure to accomplish these, are commonly administered by universities at which teachers are employed. Furthermore, publication oriented resumés usually will be well received at other universities, whereas teaching credentials, harder to document and quantify, are much less transferable.

[3]Personal interviews conducted during 1972–1973.

Consequently it is rational for university teachers to concentrate on research, even if to the detriment of teaching and at the expense of their students.

By the same token, it is rational for students to act based upon the goal displacement which has occurred within universities concerning what they are rewarded for. If it is assumed that a primary goal of a university is to transfer knowledge from teacher to student, then grades become identifiable as a means toward that goal, serving as motivational, control, and feedback devices to expedite the knowledge transfer. Instead, however, the grades themselves have become much more important for entrance to graduate school, successful employment, tuition refunds, parental respect, etc., than the knowledge or lack of knowledge they are supposed to signify.

It therefore should come as no surprise that information has surfaced in recent years concerning fraternity files for examinations, term paper writing services, organized cheating at the service academies, and the like. Such activities constitute a personally rational response to a reward system which pays off for grades rather than knowledge.

BUSINESS RELATED EXAMPLES

Ecology

Assume that the president of XYZ Corporation is confronted with the following alternatives:

1. Spend $11 million for antipollution equipment to keep from poisoning fish in the river adjacent to the plant; or
2. Do nothing, in violation of the law, and assume a one in ten

chance of being caught, with a resultant $1 million fine plus the necessity of buying the equipment.

Under this not unrealistic set of choices it requires no linear program to determine that XYZ Corporation can maximize its probabilities by flouting the law. Add the fact that XYZ's president is probably being rewarded by creditors, stockholders, and other salient parts of his task environment according to criteria totally unrelated to the number of fish poisoned, and his probable course of action becomes clear.

Evaluation of Training

It is axiomatic that those who care about a firm's well-being should insist that the organization get fair value for its expenditures. Yet it is commonly known that firms seldom bother to evaluate a new GRID, MBO, job enrichment program, or whatever, to see if the company is getting its money's worth. Why? Certainly it is not because people have not pointed out that this situation exists; numerous practitioner oriented articles are written each year to just this point.

The individuals (whether in personnel, manpower planning, or whatever) who normally would be responsible for conducting such evaluations are the same ones often charged with introducing the change effort in the work place. Having convinced top management to spend the money, they usually are quite animated afterwards in collecting vigorous vignettes and anecdotes about how successful the program was. The last thing many desire is a formal, systematic, and revealing evaluation. Although members of top management may actually *hope* for such systematic evaluation, their reward systems continue to *reward* ignorance in this area.

And if the personnel department abdicates its responsibility, who is to step into the breach? The change agent himself? Hardly! He is likely to be too busy collecting anecdotal "evidence" of his own, for use with his next client.

Miscellaneous

Many additional examples could be cited of systems which in fact are rewarding behaviors other than those supposedly desired by the rewarder. A few of these are described briefly below.

Most coaches disdain to discuss individual accomplishments, preferring to speak of teamwork, proper attitude, and a one-for-all spirit. Usually, however, rewards are distributed according to individual performance. The college basketball player who feeds his teammates instead of shooting will not compile impressive scoring statistics and is less likely to be drafted by the pros. The ballplayer who hits to right field to advance the runners will win neither the batting nor home run titles, and will be offered smaller raises. It therefore is rational for players to think of themselves first, and the team second.

In business organizations where rewards are dispensed for unit performance or for individual goals achieved, without regard for overall effectiveness, similar attitudes often are observed. Under most Management by Objectives (MBO) systems, goals in areas where quantification is difficult often go unspecified. The organization therefore often is in a position where it *hopes* for employee effort in the areas of team building, interpersonal relations, creativity, etc., but it formally *rewards* none of these. In cases where promotions and raises are formally tied to MBO, the system itself contains a paradox in that it "asks employees to set challenging, risky goals, only to face smaller paychecks and possibly damaged careers if these goals are not accomplished" (5, p. 40).

It is *hoped* that administrators will pay attention to long run costs and opportunities and will institute programs which will bear fruit later on. However, many organizational reward systems pay off for short run sales and earnings only. Under such circumstances it is personally rational for officials to sacrifice long term growth and profit (by selling off equipment and property, or by stifling research and development) for short term advantages. This probably is most pertinent in the public sector, with the result that many public officials are unwilling to implement programs which will not show benefits by election time.

As a final, clear-cut example of a fouled-up reward system, consider the cost-plus contract or its next of kin, the allocation of next year's budget as a direct function of this year's expenditures. It probably is conceivable that those who award such budgets and contracts really hope for economy and prudence in spending. It is obvious, however, that adopting the proverb "to him who spends shall more be given," rewards not economy, but spending itself.

TWO COMPANIES' EXPERIENCES

A Manufacturing Organization

A midwest manufacturer of industrial goods had been troubled for some time by aspects of its organizational climate it believed dysfunctional. For research purposes, interviews were conducted with many employees and a questionnaire was administered on a company-wide basis, including plants and offices in several American and Canadian locations. The company strongly encouraged employee participation in the survey, and made available time and space during the workday for completion of the instrument. All employees in attendance during the day of the survey completed the questionnaire. All instruments were collected directly by the researcher, who personally administered each session. Since no one employed by the firm handled the questionnaires, and since respondent names were not asked for it seems likely that the pledge of anonymity given was believed.

A modified version of the Expect Approval scale (7) was included as part of the questionnaire. The instrument asked respondents to indicate the degree of approval or disapproval they could expect if they performed each of the described actions. A seven point Likert scale was used, with one indicating that the action would probably bring strong disapproval and seven signifying likely strong approval.

Although normative data for this scale from studies of other organizations are unavailable, it is possible to examine fruitfully the data obtained from this survey in several ways. First, it may be worth noting that the questionnaire data corresponded closely to information gathered through interviews. Furthermore, as can be seen from the results summarized in Table 1, sizable

TABLE 1 • SUMMARY OF TWO DIVISIONS' DATA RELEVANT TO CONFORMING AND RISK-AVOIDANCE BEHAVIORS (EXTENT TO WHICH SUBJECTS EXPECT APPROVAL)

Dimension	Item	Division and Sample	Total Responses	Percentage of Workers Responding		
				1, 2, or 3 Disapproval	4	5, 6, or 7 Approval
Risk Avoidance	Making a risky decision based on the best information available at the time, but which turns out wrong.	A, levels 1–4 (lowest)	127	61	25	14
		A, levels 5–8	172	46	31	23
		A, levels 9 and above	17	41	30	30
		B, levels 1–4 (lowest)	31	58	26	16
		B, levels 5–8	19	42	42	16
		B, levels 9 and above	10	50	20	30
	Setting extremely high and challenging standards and goals, and then narrowly failing to make them.	A, levels 1–4	122	47	28	25
		A, levels 5–8	168	33	26	41
		A, levels 9+	17	24	6	70
		B, levels 1–4	31	48	23	29
		B, levels 5–8	18	17	33	50
		B, levels 9+	10	30	0	70

TABLE 1 (Continued)

Dimension	Item	Division and Sample	Total Responses	Percentage of Workers Responding		
				1, 2, or 3 Disapproval	4	5, 6, or 7 Approval
Risk Avoidance (continued)	Setting goals which are extremely easy to make and then making them.	A, levels 1–4	124	35	30	35
		A, levels 5–8	171	47	27	26
		A, levels 9 +	17	70	24	6
		B, levels 1–4	31	58	26	16
		B, levels 5–8	19	63	16	21
		B, levels 9 +	10	80	0	20
Conformity	Being a "yes man" and always agreeing with the boss.	A, levels 1–4	126	46	17	37
		A, levels 5–8	180	54	14	31
		A, levels 9 +	17	88	12	0
		B, levels 1–4	32	53	28	19
		B, levels 5–8	19	68	21	11
		B, levels 9 +	10	80	10	10
	Always going along with the majority.	A, levels 1–4	125	40	25	35
		A, levels 5–8	173	47	21	32
		A, levels 9 +	17	70	12	18
		B, levels 1–4	31	61	23	16
		B, levels 5–8	19	68	11	21
		B, levels 9 +	10	80	10	10
	Being careful to stay on the good side of everyone, so that everyone agrees that you are a great guy.	A, levels 1–4	124	45	18	37
		A, levels 5–8	173	45	22	33
		A, levels 9 +	17	64	6	30
		B, levels 1–4	31	54	23	23
		B, levels 5–8	19	73	11	16
		B, levels 9 +	10	80	10	10

differences between various work units, and between employees at different job levels within the same work unit, were obtained. This suggests that response bias effects (social desirability in particular loomed as a potential concern) are not likely to be severe.

Most importantly, comparisons between scores obtained on the Expect Approval scale and a statement of problems which were the reason for the survey revealed that the same behaviors which managers in each division thought dysfunctional were those which lower level employees claimed were rewarded. As compared to job levels 1 to 8 in Division B (see Table 1), those in Division A claimed a much higher acceptance by management of "conforming" activities. Between 31 and 37 percent of Division A employees at levels 1–8 stated that going along with the majority, agreeing with the boss, and staying on everyone's good side brought approval; only once (level 5–8 responses to one of the three items) did a majority suggest that such actions would generate disapproval.

Furthermore, responses from Division A workers at levels 1–4 indicate that behaviors geared toward risk avoidance were as likely to be rewarded as to be punished. Only at job levels 9 and above was it apparent that the reward system was positively reinforcing behaviors desired by top management. Overall, the same "tendencies toward conservatism and apple-polishing at the lower levels" which divisional management had complained about during the interviews were those claimed by subordinates to be the most rational course of action in light of the existing reward system. Management apparently was not getting the behaviors it was *hoping* for, but it certainly was getting the behaviors it was perceived by subordinates to be *rewarding*.

An Insurance Firm

The Group Health Claims Division of a large eastern insurance company provides another rich illustration of a reward system which reinforces behaviors not desired by top management.

Attempting to measure and reward accuracy in paying surgical claims, the firm systematically keeps track of the number of returned checks and letters of complaint received from policyholders. However, underpayments are likely to provoke cries of outrage from the insured, while overpayments often are accepted in courteous silence. Since it often is impossible to tell from the physician's statement which of two surgical procedures, with different allowable benefits, was performed, and since writing for clarifications will interfere with other standards used by the firm concerning "percentage of claims paid within two days of receipt," the new hire in more than one claims section is soon acquainted with the informal norm: "When in doubt, pay it out!"

The situation would be even worse were it not for the fact that other features of the firm's reward system tend to neutralize those described. For example, annual "merit" increases are given to all employees, in one of the following three amounts:

1. If the worker is "outstanding" (a select category, into which no more than two employees per section may be placed): 5 percent.

2. If the worker is "above average" (normally all workers not "outstanding" are so rated): 4 percent.

3. If the worker commits gross acts of negligence and irresponsibility for which he might be discharged in many other companies: 3 percent.

Now, since (a) the difference between the 5 percent theoretically attainable through hard work and the 4 percent attainable merely by living until the review date is small and (b) since insurance firms seldom dispense much of a salary increase in cash (rather, the worker's insurance benefits increase, causing him to be further overinsured), many employees are rather indifferent to the possibility of obtaining the extra one percent reward and therefore tend to ignore the norm concerning indiscriminant payments.

However, most employees are not indifferent to the rule which states that, should absences or latenesses total three or more in any six-month period, the entire 4 or 5 percent due at the next "merit" review must be forfeited. In this sense the firm may be described as *hoping* for performance, while *rewarding* attendance. What it gets, of course, is attendance. (If the absence-lateness rule appears to the reader to be stringent, it really is not. The company counts "times" rather than "days" absent, and a ten-day absence therefore counts the same as one lasting two days. A worker in danger of accumulating a third absence within six months merely has to remain ill (away from work) during his second absence until his first absence is more than six months old. The limiting factor is that at some point his salary ceases, and his sickness benefits take over. This usually is sufficient to get the younger workers to return, but for those with 20 or more years' service, the company provides sickness benefits of 90 percent of normal salary, tax-free! Therefore. . . .)

CAUSES

Extremely diverse instances of systems which reward behavior A although the rewarder apparently hopes for behavior B have been given. These are useful to illustrate the breadth and magnitude of the phenomenon, but the diversity increases the difficulty of determining commonalities and establishing causes. However, four general factors may be pertinent to an explanation of why fouled up reward systems seem to be so prevalent.

Fascination with an "Objective" Criterion

It has been mentioned elsewhere that:

> Most "objective" measures of productivity are objective only in that their subjective elements are a) determined in advance, rather than coming into play at the time of the formal evaluation, and b) well concealed on the rating instrument itself. Thus industrial firms seeking to devise objective rating systems first decide, in an arbitrary manner, what dimensions are to be rated, . . . usually including some items having little to do with organizational effectiveness while excluding others that do. Only then does Personnel Division churn out official-looking documents on which all dimensions chosen to be rated are assigned point values, categories, or whatever (6, p. 92).

Nonetheless, many individuals seek to establish simple, quantifiable standards against which to measure and reward performance. Such efforts may be successful in highly predictable areas within an organization, but are likely to cause goal displacement when applied anywhere else. Overconcern with attendance and lateness in the insurance firm and with number of people placed in the vocational rehabilitation division may have been largely responsible for the problems described in those organizations.

Overemphasis on Highly Visible Behaviors

Difficulties often stem from the fact that some parts of the task are highly visible while other parts are not. For example, publications are easier to demonstrate than teaching, and scoring baskets and hitting home runs are more readily observable than feeding teammates and advancing base runners. Similarly, the adverse consequences of pronouncing a sick person well are more visible than those sustained by labeling a well person sick. Team-building and creativity are other examples of behaviors which may not be rewarded simply because they are hard to observe.

Hypocrisy

In some of the instances described the rewarder may have been getting the desired behavior, notwithstanding claims that the behavior was not desired. This may be true, for example, of management's attitude toward apple-polishing in the manufacturing firm (a behavior which subordinates felt was rewarded, despite management's avowed dislike of the practice). This also may explain politicians' unwillingness to revise the penalties for disobedience of ecology laws, and the failure of top management to devise reward systems which would cause systematic evaluation of training and development programs.

Emphasis on Morality or Equity Rather than Efficiency

Sometimes consideration of other factors prevents the establishment of a system which rewards behaviors desired by the rewarder. The felt obligation of many Americans to vote for one candidate or another, for example, may impair their ability to withhold support from politicians who refuse to discuss the issues. Similarly, the concern for spreading the risks and costs of wartime military service may outweigh the advantage to be obtained by committing personnel to combat until the war is over.

It should be noted that only with respect to the first two causes are reward systems really paying off for other than desired behaviors. In the case of the third and fourth causes the system *is* rewarding behaviors desired by the rewarder, and the systems are fouled up only from the standpoints of those who believe the rewarder's public statements (cause 3), or those who seek to maximize efficiency rather than other outcomes (cause 4).

CONCLUSIONS

Modern organization theory requires a recognition that the members of organizations and society possess divergent goals and motives. It therefore is unlikely that managers and their subordinates will seek the same outcomes. Three possible remedies for this potential problem are suggested.

Selection

It is theoretically possible for organizations to employ only those individuals whose goals and motives are wholly consonant with those of management. In such cases the same behaviors judged by subordinates to be rational would be perceived by management as desirable. State-of-the-art reviews of selection techniques, however, provide scant grounds for hope that such an approach would be successful (for example, see 12).

Training

Another theoretical alternative is for the organization to admit those employees whose goals are not consonant with those of management and then, through training, socialization, or whatever, alter employee goals to make them consonant. However, research on the effectiveness of such training programs, though limited, provides further grounds for pessimism (for example, see 3).

Altering the Reward System

What would have been the result if:

1. Nixon had been assured by his advisors that he could not win re-election except by discussing the issues in detail?

2. Physicians' conduct was subjected to regular examination by review boards for type 1 errors (calling healthy people ill) and to penalties (fines, censure, etc.) for errors of either type?

3. The President of XYZ Corporation had to choose between (a) spending $11 million dollars for antipollution equipment, and (b) incurring a fifty-fifty chance of going to jail for five years?

Managers who complain that their workers are not motivated might do well to consider the possibility that they have installed reward systems which are paying off for behaviors other than those they are seeking. This, in part, is what happened in Vietnam, and this is what regularly frustrates societal efforts to bring about honest politicians, civic-minded managers, etc. This certainly is what happened in both the manufacturing and the insurance companies.

A first step for such managers might be to find out what behaviors currently are being rewarded. Perhaps an instrument similar to that used in the manufacturing firm could be useful for this purpose. Chances are excellent that these managers will be surprised by what they find—that their firms are not rewarding what they assume they are. In

fact, such undesirable behavior by organizational members as they have observed may be explained largely by the reward systems in use.

This is not to say that all organizational behavior is determined by formal rewards and punishments. Certainly it is true that in the absence of formal reinforcement some soldiers will be patriotic, some presidents will be ecology minded, and some orphanage directors will care about children. The point, however, is that in such cases the rewarder is not *causing* the behaviors desired but is only a fortunate bystander. For an organization to *act* upon its members, the formal reward system should positively reinforce desired behaviors, not constitute an obstacle to be overcome.

It might be wise to underscore the obvious fact that there is nothing really new in what has been said. In both theory and practice these matters have been mentioned before. Thus in many states Good Samaritan laws have been installed to protect doctors who stop to assist a stricken motorist. In states without such laws it is commonplace for doctors to refuse to stop for fear of involvement in a subsequent lawsuit. In college basketball additional penalties have been instituted against players who foul their opponents deliberately. It has long been argued by Milton Friedman and others that penalties should be altered so as to make it irrational to disobey the ecology laws, and so on.

By altering the reward system the organization escapes the necessity of selecting only desirable people or of trying to alter undesirable ones. In Skinnerian terms (as described in 11, p. 704), "As for responsibility and goodness—as commonly defined—no one . . . would want or need them. They refer to a man's behaving well despite the absence of positive reinforcement that is obviously sufficient to explain it. Where such reinforcement exists, 'no one needs goodness.'"

REFERENCES

1. Barnard, Chester, I. *The Functions of the Executive* (Cambridge, Mass.: Harvard University Press, 1964).

2. Blau, Peter M., and W. Richard Scott. *Formal Organizations* (San Francisco: Chandler, 1962).

3. Fiedler, Fred E. "Predicting the Effects of Leadership Training and Experience from the Contingency Model," *Journal of Applied Psychology*, Vol. 56 (1972), 114–119.

4. Garland, L. H. "Studies of the Accuracy of Diagnostic Procedures," *American Journal Roentgenological, Radium Therapy Nuclear Medicine*, Vol. 82 (1959), 25–38.

5. Kerr, Steven. "Some Modifications in MBO as an OD Strategy," *Academy of Management Proceedings*, 1973, pp. 39–42.

6. Kerr, Steven. "What Price Objectivity?" *American Sociologist*, Vol. 8 (1973), 92–93.

7. Litwin, G. H., and R. A. Stringer, Jr. *Motivation and Organizational Climate* (Boston: Harvard University Press, 1968).

8. Perrow, Charles. "The Analysis of Goals in Complex Organizations," in A. Etzioni (Ed.), *Readings on Modern Organizations* (Englewood Cliffs, N. J.: Prentice-Hall, 1969).

9. Scheff, Thomas J. "Decision Rules, Types of Error, and Their Consequences in Medical Diagnosis," in F. Massarik and P. Ratoosh (Eds.), *Mathematical Explorations in Behavioral Science* (Homewood, Ill.: Irwin, 1965).

10. Simon, Herbert A. *Administrative Behavior* (New York: Free Press, 1957).

11. Swanson, G. E. "Review Symposium: Beyond Freedom and Dignity," *American Journal of Sociology*, Vol. 78 (1972), 702–705.

12. Webster, E. *Decision Making in the Employment Interview* (Montreal: Industrial Relations Center, McGill University, 1964).

9
Motivation in Organizations: Toward Synthesis and Redirection
Barry M. Staw

It can be said that there is nothing so central to an organization's functioning as the motivation of its members. It can also be said that there has been more research on individual motivation than on any other topic within organizational behavior. Yet, somehow, most of the research in this area has either added little to what we already know from early experimental psychology (see, e.g., Thorndike, 1911; Tolman, 1932; Lewin, 1938), or has provided us with few insights which go beyond prevailing common sense. Recent work on the interaction of intrinsic and extrinsic motivation has helped to broaden the perspective of traditional motivation theory and that is why we have considered it in such depth. However, we must actively seek out other promising research questions if our understanding of motivation is to increase.

In the past decade, a great deal of research has, for example, gone into the question of whether a multiplicative model (*expectancy x valence*) is appropriate to specify motivational force (see Heneman and Schwab, 1972; Behling and Starke, 1973; House, Shapiro, and Wahba, 1974; and Mitchell, 1974, for reviews). This issue has been fraught with methodological and empirical difficulties (Schmidt, 1973; Connolly, in press) and shows little prospect of being

resolved. One might contend, therefore, that research on expectancy theory would be more fruitful if some of its basis questions were rephrased. Instead of testing the statistical significance of an expectancy model or comparing multiplicative versus additive models of motivation, one should ask under what conditions would individual motivation be expected to approximate a subjective expected utility (SEU) model, and when would it be less rational?

It may be true, for example, that many individuals and subgroups do not engage in detailed cognitive arithmetic to decide which organization to join and at what level to perform. Unlike the processes outlined in figures 2 and 3, many individuals may merely model the behavior of salient others or follow the path that appears appropriate for a person from a particular family background or socioeconomic group. Individuals may join an organization or perform at a certain level because it "seems the right thing to do," rather than its being the product of subjective expected utility. As Salancik has shown in a series of original studies (Salancik, 1974; Salancik and Conway, 1975), individuals may analyze their behavior in rationalistic terms only when faced with such a task presented to them by an outside researcher.

Although many studies testing expectancy models are subject to the bias that rationality has been retrospectively recalled (cf. Staw, 1975) rather than concurrently tapped by the researcher, these studies are still unimpressive in their support for the theory. The magnitude of unexplained variance should lead us to look for moderating variables. One such variable might be the fit between occupational status of the job and socioeconomic background of the role occupant. When the individual is upwardly mobile in status, his behavior may be better predicted by an expectancy-value model than when he is satisfied with his social station. Alternatively, if the individual's job occupies a small aspect of his "central life interest" (Dubin, Champoux, and Porter, 1975), the individual should be expected to do little cognitive work in deciding to join a particular organization or perform within it. Expectancy-value formulations may be appropriate only for the most important decisions an individual must make. For those un-involved in work, day-to-day performance questions or the choice of one of many perceived-to-be similar organizations (e.g., an auto worker's choice of Ford, GM, or Chrysler) may closely resemble impulse purchase decisions of consumers. Many workers may reserve their cognitive prowess for decisions about the allocation of leisure time and durable goods.

Finally, as discussed earlier, we should not expect individuals to engage *continually* in a cognitive motivational process. As noted in figure 3, individuals are most attentive to behavior-outcome contingencies in learning a new task or when confronted with a large discrepancy between present reward levels and a salient alternative (e.g., when a new pay plan is introduced). In other situations, the individual's behavior has probably become rou-

tinized and this patterning could be represented either in terms of an operant conditioning model (Skinner, 1953, 1974) or as a decision subroutine (March and Simon, 1958).

A DIVERGENT APPROACH

Mapping the cognitive antecedents of behavior is important and research should no doubt continue on it. But at the same time we should begin to examine alternative formulations of individual behavior. One strategy which is helpful in developing new theoretical propositions is to alter the point of view or perspective from which current theorizing addresses behavior.

Many existing theories of individual behavior can be viewed as formulations of individual adaptation to the environment. Certainly Skinner's theory of reinforcement and operant conditioning represents the view that man is extensively shaped by the reward/punishment contingencies around him. However, other motivational models can also be viewed, as White (1959) pointed out, as manifestations of an individual's motivation to be "competent" or positively adapted to his particular social and physical surroundings. For example, Festinger's (1957) theory of cognitive dissonance as well as the attribution models of Kelly (1969), Bem (1967, 1972), and Jones and Davis (1965) are theories about how individuals make sense of their physical and social worlds. Even the maximizing notions of expectancy theory and Simon's (1957) alternative of satisficing can be viewed in this way.

At the organizational level of analysis there has been a concomitant degree of theory development on how organizations can best be adapted to their environments. Work on centralization-decentralization (e.g., Blau and Schoenherr, 1971; Hage and Aiken, 1969; Mackenzie, 1975), integration and differentiation (e.g., Lawrence and Lorsch, 1967; Child, 1974, 1975; Khandwalla, 1974), and matrix organizational designs (Shull, 1965; Galbraith, 1973), are examples of this perspective. The central research question in this line of research has been how the particular structure of an organization interacts with characteristics of the organization's environment (such as uncertainty and technological change) to produce a given level of effectiveness.

Figure 5 represents the above two theoretical perspectives as the directed lines A and B. In figure 5, the organization is fitted within its environment, while top levels of the organization are shown to constitute the environment of lower participants. From a top-management perspective, societal institutions (including other organizations and the market economy) comprise the external

FIGURE 5 • FLOW OF INFLUENCE IN INTRA- AND EXTRAORGANIZATIONAL ENVIRONMENTS

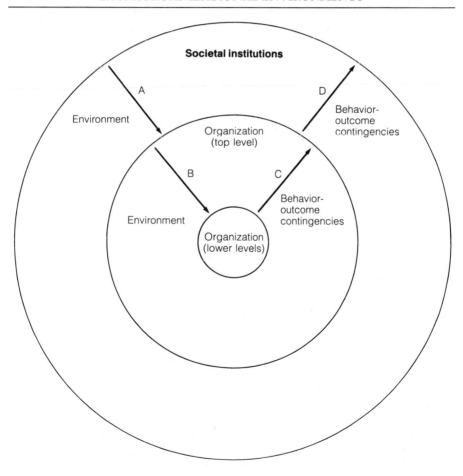

context in which behavior must be enacted. This environment determines many of the behavior-outcome contingencies which will shape and alter the organization's behavior. From the perspective of lower levels within the organization, the environment primarily consists of the actions and policies set by higher-level management. These policies frequently describe the behavior-outcome contingencies the lower-level participant faces on his job.

As illustrated in figure 5, each level in the organizational system tends to determine the behavior-outcome contingencies under which the lower level must operate. This is obviously an oversimplification, but it tends to fit a large body of theory and empirical research in organizational behavior. At the micro level, for example, organizational research is often concerned with the individual's response to incentive schemes, leadership practices, and control mechanisms exerted from higher levels in the organization. Individual behavior is studied largely to show why individuals respond positively to some actions and policies of management but negatively to others. In essence, much of the micro-level research has implicitly taken the perspective of higher management who attempt to control behavior-outcome contingencies and endeavor to increase worker response to them. From this perspective, the individual is viewed as an adaptive organism who responds to the reward contingencies facing him. Thus, if there is little positive response from the individual to a new program (e.g., job enlargement), the problem is conceptualized as due to the fact that the proper valences were not tapped (e.g., individuals may have low growth needs) or the contingencies between behavior and accomplishment or between accomplishment and reward were not clearly specified (e.g., task goals were not clearly set).

I would advocate that we enlarge our perspective of individuals in organizations, and that we attempt to creatively reverse our point of view. As shown in figure 5, there is an influence process that flows upward in the organization (cf. Mechanic, 1962) and also from the organization to its environment (cf. Thompson, 1967). By reversing our perspective, we not only recognize this upward influence but can build specific hypotheses which are not evident without it. This practice has already occurred to a large extent in the macro literature on organizations. Following Thompson's (1967) seminal work, the organization is viewed as an entity which attempts to shape its environment, reduce potential sources of uncertainty, and enlarge its bases of resources. The organization does not merely adapt to behavior-outcome contingencies facing it from the environment, but it alters these contingencies by *acting on* the environment. A number of empirical studies have tested this basic hypothesis (see, e.g., Selznick, 1949; Zald, 1967; Pfeffer, 1972, 1973).

Micro-level theory could profit by testing the same kinds of hypotheses that are now centered in the sociological literature. The individual should not be viewed as a passive acceptor of behavior-outcome contingencies or merely as an adapter to them, but also as an entity which strives to alter its environment. The individual, like the organization, strives to reduce sources of uncertainty in his day-to-day relations with superiors. One particular source of uncertainty the individual strives to reduce is uncertainty over the allocation of resources. From the individual's perspective, improvement may come in the form of increased control over reinforcement contingencies so that the individual is assured of a given level of reward for a specific behavior. In this regard it should be noted that unionization of the workplace brings increased power to workers and that this power is usually manifested in control over behavior-outcome contingencies. Union demands for weekly wages, rather than piece-rate incentives, and for the implementation of strict work rules can be interpreted as evidence for a demand for control over reinforcement contingencies.

A second method by which the individual may actively improve his situation in the organization is by ingratiation (Wortman and Linsenmeier, 1976). If the individual can manipulate his supervisor's attitudes and opinions of him, he can improve his share of resources allocated by the supervisor. Through ingratiation, the individual may receive more than he deserves for a given level of work or at least assure himself of a positive evaluation of his task output. (See chap. 4 for a complete discussion of the antecedents and consequences of ingratiating behavior.)

In developing a theory of individual action within the organizational environment, one caveat should be kept in mind: Individuals may indeed strive to reduce sources of uncertainty but they do not strive for high probabilities of receiving low rewards. This oversight in the macro-organizational literature has led to an overemphasis on environmental conditions leading to uncertainty and a virtual neglect of the scarcity-munificence of environments. As noted by Staw and Szwajkowski (1975), organizations strive to improve their quantities of resources in addition to reducing uncertainty in resource procurement. Thus, at the individual level of analysis, we must develop hypotheses which include both the magnitude of reinforcement received and the contin-gency between behavior and outcomes. A sample set of general hypotheses from which specific testable propositions can be derived is stated below:

Hypothesis 1: Individuals strive to increase the probability of receiving positive outcomes and to reduce the probability of receiving negative outcomes within the organization.

Hypothesis 2: Individuals attempt to control the reinforcement contingencies leading to both desirable and undesirable outcomes.

Hypothesis 3: If direct control of the reinforcement contingencies is impossible, individuals attempt to personally influence the allocator of resources so as to improve personal outcomes.

Hypothesis 4: If direct control of the reinforcement contingencies or indirect control through personal influence is impossible, individuals attempt to make the contingencies more predictable.

Hypothesis 5: Individuals strive to reduce the possibility of negative outcomes before attempting to control or make predictable positive outcomes from the organization.

From these hypotheses and others similar to them, it is possible to build a testable theory of upward influence in the organization. The individual, like the organization, may attempt to carve a niche for himself which is both highly munificent and low in uncertainty. The individual can attempt to do this in a one-to-one role relationship with his supervisor, and relations with subordinates and peers. Graen (1976), for example, has suggested that roles are negotiated between the superior and subordinate, and that the role-making process is determined by both interpersonal attraction and bargaining. We would contend that individuals generally follow a strategy of improving interpersonal attraction or ingratiation in one-to-one relationships with supervisors. Outright bargaining with supervisors runs the risk of future sanctions or negative outcomes, except when the individual's expertise is especially high or the individual is nearly irreplaceable. High-skill personnel, and especially those with ready opportunities in alternative organizations are, however, more likely to utilize either overt or implied bargaining in shaping their organizational roles. Low-skill personnel and those with fewer outside opportunities are more likely to use bargaining agents such as unions to help control behavior-outcome contingencies on the job.

A relevant question which follows from the above analysis is, "What are the consequences of behavior-outcome contingencies which are unpredictable or uncontrollable by the individual?" As implied by the above hypotheses, lack of individual control or predictive ability may be aversive to organizational participants. Several separate areas of research provide data which bear on this question.

Prediction of Behavior-Outcome Contingencies

The most familiar body of research data which is relevant to this issue is that of role conflict and ambiguity (Kahn et al., 1964). When the individual's task is inadequately defined or there is substantial disparity in demands placed upon the individual from his supervisor, peers, or subordinates, the individual may find the situation to be aversive. Under these conditions, the individual has been found to possess low job satisfaction, low trust in supervisors, and poor mental health (Kahn et al., 1964).

In a theoretical sense, both role conflict and ambiguity can be interpreted as factors which reduce the individual's ability to predict behavior-outcome contingencies. When an individual does not know what is expected of him due to the absence of information (i.e., role ambiguity) or conflicting information (i.e., role conflict), his predictive power is reduced. House and his associates' recent work on leadership (House, 1971; House and Dessler, 1974; Szilagyi and Sims, 1974) suggests that increased clarification and supervision (i.e., initiating structure) will improve individual attitudes and behavior on ambiguous tasks. However, when a task is already highly structured and routine, initiating structure has been found to be negatively related to task satisfaction. Presumably, once behavior-outcome contingencies are relatively clear, increased supervision and work directives add little of positive value and may be viewed by many workers as threatening.

If individuals do indeed strive to make the behavior-outcome contingencies they face more predictable, how can this fact be reconciled with the research and theory on achievement motivation that shows high achievers tend to seek out risk-taking situations (Atkinson and Raynor, 1974)? Fortunately, this paradox is more apparent than real. Individuals high in achievement motivation should not be viewed as deriving pleasure from uncertainty itself but from the *process of reducing it*. Behavior-outcome sequences which are either hopelessly impossible or trivially easy do not appeal to high achievers. They view 50-50 situations (termed "calculated risks" by McClelland) as most motivating because of the negative relationship between valence and expectancy (i.e., the most difficult tasks being the most rewarding) and the positive relationship between expectancy and goal attainment. Therefore, the primary contribution of achievement theory is to revise our expectancy-valence models so that the two factors of valence and expectancy are not independent. Achievement theory does not refute the notion that individuals strive to reduce uncertainty.

Control of Behavior-Outcome Contingencies

In recent years there have been a number of experimental studies designed to compare individuals' reactions to controllable and uncontrollable aversive outcomes (see Averill, 1973 and Glass and Singer, 1972, for reviews). Subjects in these studies are typically subjected to aversive stimuli and then either provided or not provided with information on how to terminate the stimulation (e.g., Corah and Boffa, 1970; Glass et al., 1971; Sherrod and Downs, 1974). In most of the studies in this area, subjects who can control aversive outcomes experience less stress than subjects without such control (see Wortman and Brehm, 1976).

Desire to control aversive outcomes makes sense intuitively and can be explained by any number of psychological theories. What is more compelling, in terms of testing an individual need or desire for control per se, is to examine the consequences of receiving positive outcomes under high and low choice. Tests of Brehm's (1966, 1972) theory of psychological reactance provide the most relevant data on individuals' striving for control.

Reactance

Brehm posited that when behavioral freedom is threatened, the individual will become motivationally aroused or experience reactance. The predicted

consequences of psychological reactance are efforts to restore freedom and an increased desire for any lost options. Among empirical studies designed to test reactance theory, it has been shown, for example, that subjects will devalue positive outcomes if they are "forced" to receive them. If the individual expects to choose his outcomes, he will react negatively if they are selected for him—even if they are the very outcomes he had previously preferred (see Hammock and Brehm, 1966). The implications of psychological reactance for applications of reinforcement theory in organizations are quite profound. Will the individual react negatively to the allocation of positive and negative outcomes by supervisors or will he react more positively if he can reduce his dependence on higher authorities?

An answer to this question is likely to be found by examining the parameters posited by Brehm as underlying psychological reactance. According to Brehm (1966, 1972), reactance should only result when there is an initial expectation of freedom, when this freedom is of importance to the individual, and when there is a significant threat of elimination of the freedom. In the experiment described above (Hammock and Brehm, 1966), for example, simply giving the preferred alternative to subjects with no expectation of control led to an increase in its evaluation. Thus, it would seem reasonable to conclude that in organizations with a tradition of hierarchical relations there should be no reactance aroused in employees who have come to expect a top-down approach. Reactance would be more of a problem in organizations with a history of participative management that attempt to institute hierarchical controls. Participation and freedom, following Brehm, are thus easier to expand than to contract.

Learned Helplessness

Recently, a large number of studies have been conducted on a related phenomenon labeled, "learned helplessness" (see Wortman and Brehm, 1976, for a review). In a series of studies using laboratory animals, Seligman (1975) and his associates have found that exposure to uncontrollable, inescapable electric shock leads to a reduction in subsequent avoidance learning. The learning that one's behavior and outcomes are independent apparently leads to a reduction in the ability to respond adaptively to future learning situations. This general finding has also been replicated in a number of task settings using human subjects (Hiroto and Seligman, 1975).

The practical implications of "learned helplessness" seem to conflict directly with those of reactance theory. One model posits that individuals react negatively to reductions in freedom and actively attempt to restore control, while the other posits that exposure to uncontrollable outcomes results in passive ac-

ceptance of any negative consequences. However, as noted by Wortman and Brehm (1976), it is possible to integrate learned helplessness and reactance into a single theoretical statement. Their model is presented in figure 6. If a person expects to be able to control or influence outcomes that are of importance to him (i.e., at point *a* in the figure), exposure to uncontrollable events should arouse psychological reactance and the individual should be motivated to re-exert control. But, if the individual comes to learn through extended helplessness training that he cannot control his environment, he will stop trying. When a person has no expectation of control (i.e., at point *b* in the figure) then reactance will *not* precede helplessness and the individual is predicted to quickly become a passive receiver of future outcomes. Wortman and Brehm report some tentative support for this model from animal research (e.g., Seligman and Maier, 1967; Sidman, Heinstein, and Conrad, 1957) and research using human sub-

FIGURE 6 ● THE INTEGRATIVE MODEL

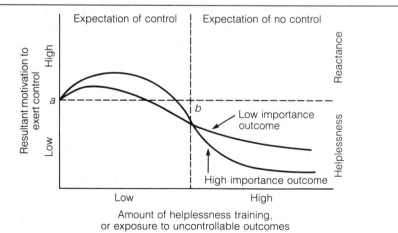

Amount of helplessness training,
or exposure to uncontrollable outcomes

From Wortman and Brehm, 1976

jects (e.g., Shaban and Welling, 1972; Glass and Singer, 1972; Krantz, Glass, and Snyder, 1974; Roth and Kuban, in press; Roth and Bootzin, 1974).

The Wortman and Brehm model of individuals' reaction to uncontrollable outcomes has some direct implications for everyday behavior, but these implications appear to turn on the critical variable of "expectation of control." Unfortunately, it is this same variable which is the most difficult to extrapolate across situations and individuals. Thus, following from the model, we must have some knowledge of both the history of upward and downward influence in the organization and the individual's personal reinforcement history in order to make accurate predictions. This is not a shortcoming of Wortman and Brehm's theory, but an empirical reality with which we must deal in applied research.

One factor which *is* a shortcoming of the Wortman and Brehm model is its lack of specificity of the notion of control. Much of the empirical work on reactance theory has dealt with the reduction of control over the distribution of outcomes, while the work on learned helplessness has been concerned with exposure to outcomes (primarily aversive) which are not contingent on the individual's actions. Thus, we can see that the crucial dimension of "exposure to uncontrollable outcomes" in figure 6 can be interpreted as either inability to influence the allocation of resources or merely as inability to predict the linkage between one's behavior and subsequent allocations by others. The reason that this vagary is so important is that the Wortman and Brehm model, as it stands, can be used to support either increased *or* decreased control by lower-order participants in an organizational setting. If one uses the argument that

predictive ability is the most important factor (citing the learned helplessness research as evidence), it is possible to conclude that the organization needs tighter top-down controls and increased power of supervisors to reward and punish contingently.[3] If, however, one uses the argument that control over resource allocation is the crucial factor (as per reactance theory), then one would be hesitant to institute any top-down controls which inhibit freedom and tend to avoid behavior modification schemes (Luthans and Krietner, 1975). Recall that reactance theory predicts that even positive outcomes may be devalued if they are not freely chosen by the individual.

It is my opinion that individuals do strive for control over their social environments and that one important source of control is that over behavior-outcome sequences. If no control is possible, then the ability to predict will be preferred by individuals over random or noncontingent outcomes. Thus, it is possible that individuals *will* prefer top-down controls and contingent reinforcement schemes over situations in which there is no apparent link between behavior and reward. However, this is not to deny that *control over the allocation of outcomes* is probably more preferred than a highly predictable supervisor who controls the rewards.

An alternative model to that of Wortman and Brehm is presented in figure 7. It shows that individuals follow a decision-making sequence in which they seek first to control and then, if control is not possible, to at least predict behavior-outcome sequences. If neither control nor prediction is perceived to be possible, the individual will either leave the field or become a passive acceptor of externally-imposed outcomes. In figure 7, expectations of con-

FIGURE 7 • FLOW DIAGRAM OF UPWARD CONTROL

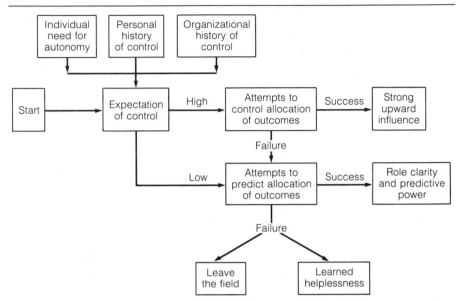

trol are shown as a moderating variable which determines where individuals begin this decision-making process. With no prior expectations of control, individuals are shown to strive primarily for prediction or clarity in behavior-outcome sequences. Clarity would be sought both in the specification of tasks to be completed and also in the rewards which would result from various levels of task performance. Individual differences in need for autonomy are also shown to affect the entry point in this decision process. With a low need for autonomy the individual may not be as interested in actual control over the allocation of resources as in predicting their distribution by supervisors. In addition, individual differences are relevant for one's personal history of control. Some individuals have had very little exposure to situations in which they were able to influence the allocation of external rewards, while others

(e.g., children raised on a communal farm) may have had little experience with highly authoritarian relationships. Finally, as touched upon earlier, the organization's own history of participative versus autocratic style of management will influence initial expectations of control.

As shown in the revised model of figure 7, if attempts at both control and prediction fail, the individual becomes resigned to his fate or decides to leave the field. This latter option is added to make the model applicable to real-world settings in which turnover is a definite option to the individual faced with uncontrollable outcomes. In laboratory research on learned helplessness, the subject either has no option to leave the field (especially in the studies using animal subjects) or this option is extremely restricted. In organizations, factors such as external labor market conditions, the educational or skill level of the individual, and his visibility to other organizations may determine ease of turnover.

SUMMARY AND CONCLUSIONS

The synthesis of motivation presented here is one in which the individual is an active constructor of his social reality. The individual is viewed not merely as an information processor confronting a number of possible behavioral paths—each with their attendant rewards and costs—but as an actor who can attempt to change the parameters or "givens" of traditional motivation models. The individual can bargain, cajole, and ingratiate in order to change the contingencies between behavior and outcomes. In addition, the individual may be able to change the valences attached to the particular outcomes he faces. (For example, an individual may consciously give up security and achievement to concentrate on social gratification.[4]) What we are facing therefore in describing a theory of individual motivation in organizations is a highly complex system in which individuals have constructed a social and physical niche for themselves within the larger environment. This niche is built upon relationships developed over time with supervisors, subordinates, and peers in the organization and rests, in part, upon a role negotiation process (Graen, 1976). This niche is also built upon the individual's idiosyncratic construction of his social reality (Berger and Luckman, 1967; Weick, 1969). The processes of self-perception, dissonance arousal and reduction, and psychological reactance are but a few of the ways by which individuals come to grips with their social world. We need to know more about how individuals psychologically cope with the demands placed upon them by an organization and how these demands are in turn changed, redefined, or met by subordinates.

To date, the investigation of individual motivation in organizations has been extremely narrow in both direction and scope. Nearly all efforts have been expended upon explaining the determinants of job choice, productivity, absenteeism, and turnover. While these are important criterion variables, they are not the only behaviors of interest in organizational systems and not the only behaviors related to organizational effectiveness. Similarly, nearly all efforts to explain motivation in organizations have focused upon either expectancy or reinforcement models of behavior. While these theories are certainly relevant, other psychological processes have been unduly neglected. Thus, there has been an unfortunate restriction in theory building at both the independent and dependent variable ends of our models. It is hoped that this chapter will serve as an impetus toward a broadening of our conceptualization of motivation and a reconsideration of established theory in the area.

NOTES

1. An experiment by Graen (1969) tested an expectancy model very similar to the one presented here. The present formulation also does not depart too greatly from the "within individuals" formulation of expectancy theory originally posited by Vroom (1946), and later advocated by Mitchell (1974) and Campbell and Pritchard (1976).

2. This point was also raised by Jerry Ross in a graduate seminar in organizational behavior at Northwestern University, 1976.

3. William E. Scott, for example, has previously used the learned helplessness literature as evidence for greater use of contingent reward systems.

4. This point was also raised by William Simons in a graduate organization behavior seminar at Northwestern University, 1976.

REFERENCES

Allport, F. H. A structuronomic conception of behavior: Individual and collective. *Journal of Abnormal and Social Psychology,* 1962, *64,* 3–30.

Allport, G. W. *Personality: A Psychological Interpretation.* New York: Holt, 1937.

Atkinson, J. W., and Raynor, J. O. *Motivation and Achievement.* New York: Wiley, 1974.

Averill, J. Personal control over aversive stimuli and its relationship to stress. *Psychological Bulletin,* 1973, *80,* 286–303.

Barnard, C. I. *The Functions of the Executive.* Cambridge, Mass.: Harvard University Press, 1938.

Behling, O., and Starke, F. The postulates of expectancy theory. *Academy of Management Journal,* 1973, *16,* 373–88.

Bern, D. J. Self-perception: The dependent variable of human performance. *Organizational Behavior and Human Performance,* 1967, *2,* 105–21.

———. Self-perception theory. In L. Berkowitz (ed.), *Advances in Experimental Social Psychology* (vol. 6), Academic Press, 1972.

Berger, P. L., and Luckman, T. *The Social Construction of Reality.* New York: Anchor, 1967.

Blau, P. M., and Schoenherr, R. A. *The Structure of Organizations.* New York: Basic Books, 1971.

Brehm, J. W. *A Theory of Psychological Reactance.* New York: Academic Press, 1966.

———. *Responses to Loss of Freedom: A Theory of Psychological Reactance.* Morristown, N.J.: General Learning Press, 1972.

Brehm, J. W., and Cohen, A. R. *Explorations in Cognitive Dissonance.* New York: Wiley, 1962.

Calder, B. J., Ross, M. and Insko, C. A. Attitude change and attitude attribution: Effects of incentive, choice, and consequences. *Journal of Personality and Social Psychology,* 1973, *25,* 84–100.

Calder, B. J., and Staw, B. M. The interaction of intrinsic and extrinsic motivation: Some methodological notes. *Journal of Personality and Social Psychology,* 1975, *31,* 76–80.

———. The self-perception of intrinsic and extrinsic motivation. *Journal of Personality and Social Psychology,* 1975, *31,* 599–605.

Campbell, D. T. Conformity in psychology's theories of acquired behavioral dispositions. In I. A. Berg and B. M. Bass (eds.) *Conformity and Deviation,* Harper and Brothers, 1961.

Campbell, J. P., Dunnette, M. D., Lawler, E. E., and Weick, K. E. *Managerial Behavior, Performance, and Effectiveness.* New York: McGraw-Hill, 1970.

Carlsmith, J. M., Collins, B. E., and Helmreich, R. L. Studies in forced compliance: The effect of pressure for compliance on attitude change produced by face-to-face role playing and anonymous essay writing. *Journal of Personality and Social Psychology,* 1966, *4,* 1–13.

Child, J. Managerial and organizational factors associated with company performance, Part I: A contingency analysis. *The Journal of Management Studies,* 1974, *11,* 175–89.

———. Managerial and organizational factors associated with company performance, Part II: A contingency analysis. *The Journal of Management Studies,* 1975, *12,* 12–27.

Collins, B. E., and Hoyt, M. F. Personal responsibility-for-consequences: An integration and extension of the forced compliance literature. *Journal of Experimental Social Psychology,* 1972, *8,* 558–94.

Connolly, T. Some conceptual and methodological issues in expectancy-type models of work motivation. *Academic Management Review,* in press.

Corah, N. L., and Boffa, J. Perceived control, self-observation, and response to aversive stimulation. *Journal of Personality and Social Psychology,* 1970.

Deci, E. L. The effects of externally mediated rewards on intrinsic motivation. *Journal of Personality and Social Psychology,* 1971, *18,* 105–15.

———. The effects of contingent and noncontingent rewards and controls on intrinsic motivation. *Organizational Behavior and Human Performance,* 1972, *8,* 217–29.

Dubin, R., Champoux, J. E., and Porter, L. W. Central life interests and organizational commitment of blue-collar and clerical workers. *Administrative Science Quarterly,* 1975, *20,* 411–21.

Edwards, W. The prediction of decision among bets. *Journal of Experimental Psychology,* 1955, *50,* 201–14.

Etzioni, A. *Complex Organizations.* New York: The Free Press, 1961.

Ferster, C. B., and Skinner, B. F. *Schedules of Reinforcement.* Appleton-Century-Crofts, 1957.

Festinger, L. *A Theory of Cognitive Dissonance.* Stanford University Press, 1957.

Festinger, L., and Carlsmith, J. M. Cognitive consequences of forced compliance. *Journal of Abnormal and Social Psychology,* 1959, *58,* 203–10.

Freedman, J. L. Attitudinal effects of inadequate justification. *Journal of Personality,* 1963, *31,* 371–85.

Galbraith, J. R. *Designing Complex Organizations.* Reading, Mass.: Addison-Wesley, 1973.

Galbraith, J. R., and Cummings, L. L. An empirical investigation of the motivational determinants of task performance: Interactive effects between instrumentality-valence and motivation-ability. *Organizational Behavior and Human Performance,* 1967, *2,* 237–57.

Glass, D. C., Reim, B., and Singer, J. E. Behavioral consequences of adaptation to controllable and uncontrollable noise. *Journal of Experimental Social Psychology,* 1971, *7,* 244–57.

Glass, D. C., and Singer, J. E. *Urban Stress.* New York: Academic Press, 1972.

Graen, G. Instrumentality theory of work motivation: Some experimental results and suggested modifications. *Journal of Applied Psychology Monograph,* 1969, *53,* 1–25.

———. Role making processes within complex organizations. In M. Dunnett (ed.) *Handbook of Industrial and Organizational Psychology.* Chicago: Rand McNally, 1976.

Hackman, J. R., and Lawler, E. E. Employee reactions to job characteristics. *Journal of Applied Psychology Monograph,* 1971, *55,* 259–86.

Hackman, J. R., and Oldham, G. R. Motivation through the design of work. *Organizational Behavior and Human Performance,* 1976, *16,* 250–79.

Hage, J., and Aiken, M. Routine technology, social structure and organization goals. *Administrative Science Quarterly,* 1969, *14,* 366–76.

Hammock, T., and Brehm, J. W. The attractiveness of choice alternatives when free-

dom is eliminated by a social agent. *Journal of Personality,* 1966, *34,* 546–54.

Hamner, W. C. Reinforcement theory and contingency management in organizational settings. In H. L. Tosi and W. C. Hamner (eds.) *Organizational Behavior and Management: A Contingency Approach.* Chicago: St. Clair Press, 1974.

Hamner, W. C., and Foster, L. W. Are intrinsic and extrinsic rewards additive? A test of Deci's cognitive evaluation theory of task motivation. *Organizational Behavior and Human Performance,* 1975, *14,* 398–415.

Hamner, W. C., and Hamner, E. P. Using positive reinforcement principles to increase worker productivity. *Organizational Dynamics,* April, 1976.

Heneman, H. G., and Schwab, D. P. Evaluation of research on expectancy theory predictions of employee performance. *Psychological Bulletin,* 1972, *78,* 1–9.

Hiroto, D. S., and Seligmen, M. E. P. Generally of learned helplessness in man. *Journal of Personality and Social Psychology,* 1975, *31,* 311–27.

House, R. J. A path-goal theory of leader effectiveness. *Administrative Science Quarterly,* 1971, *16,* 321–35.

House, R. J., and Dessler, G. The path-goal theory of leadership: Some post hoc and a priori tests. In J. G. Hunt (ed.), *Contingency Approaches to Leadership.* Carbondale, Illinois: Southern Illinois University Press, 1974.

House, R. J., Shapiro, H. J., and Wahba, M. A. Expectancy theory as a predictor of work behavior and attitude: A reevaluation of empirical evidence. *Decision Sciences.* 1974, *5,* 481–506.

Jones, E. E., and Davis, K. E. From acts to dispositions: The attribution process in person perception. In L. Berkowitz (ed.) *Advances in Experimental Social Psychology,* New York: Academic Press, 1965.

Kahn, R. L., Wolfe, D. M., Quinn, R. R., Snoek, J. D., and Rosenthal, R. N. *Organizational Stress: Studies in Role Conflict and Ambiguity.* New York: Wiley, 1964.

Katz, D., and Kahn, R. L. *The Social Psychology of Organizations.* New York: John Wiley, 1966.

Keller, F. S. *Learning: Reinforcement Theory* (2nd ed.). New York: Random House, 1969.

Kelley, H. H. Attribution theory in social psychology. In D. Levine (ed.) *Nebraska Symposium on Motivation* (vol. 15). Lincoln, Neb.: University of Nebraska Press, 1967.

————. The process of causal attribution. *American Psychologist*, 1974, *28*, 107–28.

Khandwalla, P. N. Mass output orientation of operations technology and organization structure. *Administrative Science Quarterly*, 1974, *19*, 74–97.

Kiesler, C. A., and Kiesler, S. B. *Conformity*. Reading, Massachusetts: Addison-Wesley, 1966.

Korman, A. K. *The Psychology of Motivation*. Englewood Cliffs, N. J.: Prentice-Hall, 1974.

Krantz, D. S., Glass, D. C., and Snyder, M. L. Helplessness, stress level, and the coronary-prone behavior pattern. *Journal of Experimental Social Psychology*, 1974, *10*, 284–300.

Kruglanski, A. W., Friedman, I., and Zeevi, G. The effects of extrinsic incentive on some qualitative aspects of task performance. *Journal of Personality*, 1971, *39*, 606–17.

Kruglanski, A. W., Alon, S., and Lewis, T. Retroactive misattribution and task enjoyment. *Journal of Experimental Social Psychology*, 1972, *8*, 493–501.

Latham, G. P., and Yukb, G. A. A review of research on the application of goal setting in organizations. *Academy of Management Journal*, 1975, *18*, 824–45.

Lawler, E. E. *Pay and Organizational Effectiveness: A Psychological View*. New York: McGraw-Hill, 1971.

————. *Motivation in Work Organizations*. Monterey, Calif.: Brooks/Cole, 1973.

Lawler, E. E., and Hackman, J. R. Impact of employee participation in the development of pay incentive plans: A field experiment. *Journal of Applied Psychology*, 1969, *53*, 467–71.

Lawler, E. E., Kuleck, W. J., and Rhode, J. G. Job choice and post decision dissonance. *Organizational Behavior and Human Performance*. 1975, *13*, 133–45.

Lawrence, P. R., and Lorsch, J. W. *Organization and Environment*. Boston: Harvard University, Graduate School of Business Administration, Division of Research.

Lepper, M. R., and Greene, D. Turning play into work: Effects of adult surveillance and extrinsic rewards on children's intrinsic motivation. *Journal of Personality and Social Psychology*, in press.

Lepper, M. R., Greene, D., and Nisbett, R. E. Undermining children's intrinsic interest with extrinsic rewards: A test of the "overjustification" hypothesis. *Journal of Personality and Social Psychology*, 1973, *28*, 129–37.

Lewin, K. *The Conceptual Representation and the Measurement of Psychological Forces*. Durham: Duke University Press, 1938.

Linder, D. E., Cooper, J., and Jones, E. E. Decision freedom as a determinant of the role of incentive magnitude in attitude change. *Journal of Personality and Social Psychology*, 1967, *6*, 245–54.

Locke, E. A. Personnel attitudes and motivation. *Annual Review of Psychology* (vol. 26), 1975.

Locke, E. A., Cartledge, N., and Koeppel, J. Motivational effects of knowledge of results: A goal-setting phenomenon? *Psychological Bulletin*, 1968, *70*, 474–85.

Luthans, F., and Kreitner, R. *Organizational Behavior Modification*. Glenview, Ill.: Scott, Foresman and Co., 1975.

Mackenzie, K. D. *A Theory of Group Structures*. Monograph, Lawrence, Kansas: University of Kansas, 1975.

March, J. G., and Simon, H. A. *Organizations*. New York: John Wiley, 1958.

McClelland, D. *The Achieving Society*. Princeton, N.J.: Van Nostrand, 1961.

————. The role of educational technology in developing achievement motivation. In D. C. McClelland and R. W. Steele (eds.) *Human Motivation: A Book of Readings*. Morristown, N.J.: General Learning Press, 1973a.

————. What is the effect of achievement motivation training in the schools? In D. C. McClelland and R. S. Steele (eds.) *Human Motivation: A Book of Readings*. Morristown, N.J.: General Learning Press, 1973b.

McClelland, D. C., and Winter, D. G. *Motivating Economic Achievement*. New York: Free Press, 1969.

Mechanic, D. Sources of power of lower participants in complex organizations. *Administrative Science Quarterly*, 1962, *7*, 249–364.

Miller, G. A. The magical number seven, plus or minus two: Some limits on our capacity for processing information. *Psychological Review*, 1956, *63*, 81–97.

Mitchell, T. R. Expectancy models of job satisfaction, occupational preference and effort: A theoretical, methodological, and empirical appraisal. *Psychological Bulletin*, 1974, *81*, 1053–77.

Mitchell, T. R., and Knudsen, B. W. Instrumentality theory predictions of students' attitudes towards business and their choice of business as an occupation. *Academy of Management Journal*, 1973, *16*, 41–52.

Nash, A. N., and Carroll, S. J. *The Management of Compensation.* Monterey, Calif.: Brooks/Cole, 1975.

Peak, H. Attitude and motivation. In M. R. Jones (ed.) *Nebraska Symposium on Motivation.* Lincoln: University of Nebraska Press, 1955, 149–88.

Pfeffer, J. Merger as a response to organizational interdependence. *Administrative Science Quarterly*, 1972, *17*, 382–94.

————. Size, composition, and function of hospital boards of directors: A study of organization-environment linkage. *Administrative Science Quarterly*, 1973, *18*, 349–64.

Porter, L. W., and Lawler, E. E. *Managerial Attitudes and Performance.* Homewood, Ill.: Irwin, 1968.

Rosenberg, M. J. Cognitive structure and attitudinal affect. *Journal of Abnormal and Social Psychology*, 1956, *53*, 367–72.

Ross, M. Salience of reward and intrinsic motivation. *Journal of Personality and Social Psychology*, 1975, *32*, 245–54.

Roth, S., and Bootzin, R. The effects of experimentally induced expectancies of external control: An investigation of learned helplessness. *Journal of Personality of Social Psychology*, 1974, *29*, 253–64.

Roth, S., and Kubal, L. The effects of noncontingent reinforcement of tasks of differing importance: Facilitation and learned helplessness. *Journal of Personality and Social Psychology*, in press.

Salancik, G. R. Inference of one's attitude from behavior recalled under linguistically manipulated cognitive sets. *Journal of Experimental Social Psychology*, 1974, *10*, 415–27.

Salancik, G. R., and Conway, M. Attitude inferences from salient and relevant cognitive content about behavior. *Journal of Personality and Social Psychology*, 1975, *32*, 829–40.

Schmidt, F. L. Implications of a measurement problem for expectancy theory research. *Organizational Behavior and Human Performance*, 1973, *10*, 243–51.

Scott, W. E. Activation theory and task design. *Organizational Behavior and Human Performance*, 1966, *1*, 3–30.

Seligman, M. E. P. *Helplessness.* San Francisco: W. H. Freeman, 1975.

Seligman, M. E. P., and Maier, S. F. Failure to escape traumatic shock. *Journal of Experimental Psychology*, 1967, *74*, 1–9.

Selznick, P. *TVA and the Grass Roots.* Berkeley: University of California Press, 1949.

Shaban, J., and Welling, G. The effects of two kinds of bureaucratic harassment. In D. C. Glass and J. Singer (eds.) *Urban Stress.* New York: Academic Press, 1972.

Sheard, J. L. Intrasubject prediction of preferences for organizational types. *Journal of Applied Psychology*, 1970, *54*, 248–52.

Sheridan, J. E., Richards, M. D., and Slocum, J. W. Comparative analysis of expectancy and heuristic models of decision behavior. *Journal of Applied Psychology*, 1975, *60*, 361–68.

Sherrod, D. R., and Downs, R. Environmental determinants of altruism: The effects of stimulus overload and perceived control on helping. *Journal of Experimental Social Psychology*, 1974, *10*, 468–79.

Shull, F. A. Matrix structure and project authority for optimizing organizational capacity. *Business Monograph* no. 1, Business Research Bureau, Southern Illinois University, 1965.

Sidman, M., Herrnstein, R. J., and Conrad, D. G. Maintenance of avoidance behavior by unavoidable shocks. *Journal of Comparative and Physiological Psychology*, 1957, *50*, 553–57.

Simon, H. A. *Administrative Behavior.* New York: Macmillan, 1957.

Skinner, B. F. *Science and Human Behavior.* New York: Macmillan, 1953.

————. *About Behaviorism,* New York: Alfred A. Knopf, 1974.

Slovic, P. From Shakespeare to Simon: Speculations—and some evidence about man's ability to process information. *Oregon Research Institute Monograph*, 1972, *12*, no. 2.

Spielberger, C. D., and DeNike, L. D. Descriptive behaviorism versus cognitive theory in verbal operant conditioning. *Psychological Review,* 1966, *73,* 306–25.

Staw, B. M. Attitudinal and behavioral consequences of changing a major organizational reward: A natural field experiment. *Journal of Personality and Social Psychology,* 1974, *6,* 742–51.

———. Attribution of the causes of performance: A new alternative interpretation of cross-sectional research on organizations. *Organizational Behavior and Human Performance,* 1975, *13,* 414–32.

———. *Intrinsic and Extrinsic Motivation.* Morristown, N. J.: General Learning Press, 1976.

Staw, B. M., Calder, B. J., and Hess, R. Situational norms and the effect of extrinsic rewards on intrinsic motivation. Working Paper, Northwestern University, 1976.

Staw, B. M., and Szwajkowski, E. The scarcity-munificence component of organizational environments and the commission of illegal acts. *Administrative Science Quarterly,* 1975, *20,* 345–54.

Szilagyi, S., and Sims, H. An exploration of the path-goal theory of leadership in a health care environment. *Academy of Management Journal,* 1974, *17,* 622–34.

Thompson, J. D. *Organizations in Action.* New York: McGraw-Hill, 1967.

Thorndike, E. L. *Animal Intelligence,* New York: Macmillan, 1911.

Tolman, E. C. *Purposive Behavior in Animals and Men.* New York: Appleton-Century Crofts, 1932.

———. Principles of performance. *Psychological Review,* 1955, *62,* 315–26.

Tosi, H. L., and Hamner, W. C. *Organizational Behavior and Management: A Contingency Approach.* Chicago: St. Clair Press, 1974.

Uhl, C. N., and Young, A. G. Resistance to extinction as a function of incentive, percentage of reinforcement, and number of nonreinforced trials. *Journal of Experimental Psychology,* 1967, *73,* 556–64.

Vroom, V. H. *Work and Motivation.* New York: John Wiley, 1964.

———. Organizational choice: A study of pre- and post-decision processes. *Organizational*

Behaviors and Human Performance, 1966, *1,* 212–25.

Vroom, V. H., and Deci, E. L. The stability of post-decision dissonance: A follow-up study of the job attitudes of business school graduates. *Organizational Behavior and Human Performance,* 1971, *6,* 36–49.

Wanous, J. P. Occupational preferences: Preferences of valence and instrumentality and objective data. *Journal of Applied Psychology,* 1972, *56,* 152–55.

Weick, K. E. Reduction of cognitive dissonance through task enhancement and effort expenditure. *Journal of Abnormal and Social Psychology,* 1964, *68,* 533–39.

———. *The Social Psychology of Organizing.* Reading, Mass.: Addison-Wesley, 1969.

———. Reward concepts: Dice or marbles, unpublished paper, Cornell University, 1974.

Weick, K. E., and Penner, D. D. Justification and productivity, unpublished manuscript, University of Minnesota, 1965.

Weiner, B. *Theories of Motivation: From Mechanism to Cognition.* Chicago: Rand McNally, 1972.

White, R. W. Motivation reconsidered: The concept of competence. *Psychological Review,* 1959, *66,* 297–333.

Willems, E. P. Go ye into all the world and modify behavior: An ecologist's view. *Representative Research in Social Psychology,* 1973, *4,* 93–105.

Woodworth, R. S. *Dynamic Psychology.* New York: Columbia University Press, 1918.

Wortman, C. B., and Brehm, J. W. Responses to uncontrollable outcomes: An integration of reactance theory and the learned helplessness model. In L. Berkowitz (ed.) *Advances in Experimental Social Psychology,* New York: Academic Press, 1976.

Wortman, C. B., and Linsenmeier, J. A. W. Interpersonal attraction and techniques of ingratiation in organizational settings. In B. Staw and G. Salancik (eds.) *New Directions in Organizational Behavior.* Chicago: St. Clair Press, 1977.

Zald, M. N. Urban differentiation, characteristics of boards of directors and organizational affectiveness. *American Journal of Sociology,* 1967, *73,* 261–72.

CHAPTER II

Group and Intergroup Behavior

People are social beings at work as well as at play. We form and associate in groups, and groups create their own norms, values, sentiments, membership criteria, roles, and aspirations. Most work groups also develop shared beliefs and attitudes about such things as the nature of the relationship between members and their employing organization, expectations about levels of work output and pay, what it takes to get ahead, and positive and negative consequences of trusting the organization or exhibiting loyalty to it.

Deciding whether to become a member of a group usually poses an *approach-avoidance conflict* for people. Joining has plus and minus connotations. Groups are a primary way people satisfy their desire for affiliation, their need for belonging. People working with and near each other form bonds—relationships—of friendship, camaraderie, and conversation. Yet, group membership always requires relinquishing some individuality—of personal identity and freedom of behavior—at least temporarily. Although groups vary, most norms demand some degree of conforming behavior, of acquiescence to "claims" made by other members or by the group, as one "price" of membership and thus for satisfying affiliation wants. As the result, decisions to join groups at work often are made with tentativeness and feelings of ambiguity.

The formation of groups in the workplace is more than just a way for people to satisfy their desires for affiliation. Ever since the days of the Industrial Revolution, workplace organizations have been constructed on the foundation principles of *specialization* and *division of labor* (Smith, 1776). In our complex organizations of today, few jobs can be done from start to finish by one person. Specialization allows an organization to use people's skills and efforts more systematically and to focus their knowledge and energy on a limited number of tasks. Employee learning curves are minimized.

With division of labor, people who perform a set of specialized functions are organizationally clustered in work groups, work groups in units or branches, branches in divisions or departments, divisions in companies or agencies, and so forth. Work groups attract people with like backgrounds; for example, professional training, socialization, and experience as accountants, teachers, production managers, or human resources managers; or, perhaps, people from similar sociodemographic backgrounds, for example, from "old line" New England families, or particular ethnic groups. All such shared backgrounds involve the socialization of people into common value/belief/behavior systems. We learn how to think and act like doctors, teachers, accountants, or credit managers; and, like Texans, Mainers, or Southern Californians.

Virtually all groups, and particularly purposeful, specialized, organizational groups, develop their own sets of norms (behavioral rules), values, stories, heroes, sagas, legends, myths, beliefs about their realities, and assumptions about things like the nature of their organizational environment and appropriate relations with other groups. When a group becomes institutionalized in an organization, such as a production unit or a branch office, these shared beliefs, values, and assumptions become the essence of an organizational subculture (Martin & Siehl, 1983). Most group subcultures have a resemblance to the overall organizational culture but also contain unique elements that form through the impacts of events, circumstances, and personalities, including (Ott, 1989, Ch. 4):

- The nature or type of business in which the organization is engaged,
- The *psychological script* or basic personality of the founder or other dominant early leaders, and
- The general culture of the society where the organization is located.

A specific group subculture develops from the learning members accumulate through their shared successes and failures experienced in solving problems that threatened the survival of the group and its identity or independence (Schein, 1985).

Putting aside the question of why work groups have at least partially unique subcultures, the fact remains that they usually are distinctive. Then, considering the normal loyalties that groups demand and the affiliational needs they meet, it becomes easy to understand why *ingroups* and *outgroups* and feelings of *we* and *they* and *we* versus *they* are so characteristic of life in organizations.

Group dynamics is the subfield of organization behavior "dedicated to achieving knowledge about the nature of groups, the laws of their development, and their interrelations with individuals, other groups, and larger institutions" (Cartwright & Zander, 1968). Kurt Lewin (See Chapter VI), perhaps the most influential social psychologist of this century (Marrow, 1969), is widely credited with creating and naming this field in which he has been a most influential contributor.

Lewin's group dynamics perspective was subsumed under the general heading *field theory*, which holds that a person's behavior is a function of the individual and her or his immediate environment—the group and the organizational context. (Excerpts from Lewin's chapter, "Group Decision and Social Change" are in Chapter VI.) For much of the decade of the 1940s, Lewin and his associates at the Massachusetts Institute of Technology's Research Center for Group Dynamics introduced concepts like *fields*, *force fields*, and *field forces* into the study of human behavior, focusing on things such as resistance to change and the effects of leadership on group performance. Perhaps Lewin's greatest single contribution, however, was to move the focus of behavioral theory and research from individuals to groups.

But the field of group dynamics has been more than Kurt Lewin. It has represented the first comprehensive pulling together of theories, research methods, and empirical findings from myriad social sciences. It is the acquisition of "knowledge about the. . . psychological and social forces associated with groups. . . . It refers to a field of inquiry dedicated to achieving knowledge about the nature of groups, the laws of their development, and their interrelations with individuals, other groups, and larger institutions" (Cartwright & Zander, 1968). Group dynamics is the accumulated contributions of many notable social scientists including R. F. Bales (1950), Alex Bavelas (1942), Dorwin Cartwright and Alvin Zander (1968), George Homans (1950), Jake Moreno (1934), T. M. Newcomb (1943), M. Sherif (1936), and William F. Whyte (1943, 1948).

Although definitions of a *group* vary, there is less disagreement here than there is about definitions of most other concepts of organizational behavior, such as *leader* and *motivation*. Usually, the term *group* refers to what is more technically known as a *primary group*—a group small enough to permit face-to-face interaction among its members and which remains in existence long enough for some personal relations, sentiments, and feelings of identification or belongingness to develop. Schein (1970) uses the term *psychological group* to mean much the same thing: "Any number of people who [1] interact with one another, [2] are psychologically aware of one another, and [3] perceive themselves to be a group." Over the years, many labels have been used to describe different types of groups, but for understanding organizational behavior, the most important types of groups probably are (Cohen, Fink, Gadon, & Willits, 1988, p. 69):

- *Formal, permanent groups:* Groups that are formally sanctioned, permanent fixtures in ongoing organizations. Groups of this type are the *building blocks* of organization structure, for example, a production work group, the staff of a small branch office, a product marketing group, or a military flight crew.
- *Formal, temporary groups:* Formally sanctioned, task-oriented groups with short lives. They are formed to accomplish a task, such as solving a problem or capitalizing on a specific opportunity, and then are disbanded. Some examples include task forces, committees, and project work teams in matrix organizations (Davis & Lawrence, 1977).
- *Informal groups:* People who associate voluntarily, primarily to satisfy social needs. Although informal groups at work may have goals and tasks (for example, bowling teams and luncheon bridge groups), their primary reasons for existence are friendship and affiliation. Although informal groups seldom are formally sanctioned by organizations, they are extremely important to the working of organizations. Their norms, values, beliefs, and expectations have significant impacts on work-related behavior and attitudes.

Groups in organizations of all types are of high importance and interest to students and practitioners of organizational behavior, both for what happens *in* them (and why) and what happens *between* them. Thus, this chapter contains seven important readings about some diverse aspects of group and intergroup dynamics.

Most of the readings in this book are presented chronologically in order to show the historical development. This chapter contains two subtopics, (1) intragroup dynamics (relations between individuals and groups) and (2) intergroup dynamics. By moving the placement of Irving Janis's "Groupthink," both subheadings fall into chronological sequence.

Groups cannot be discussed without considering important variables that are the subjects of other chapters, most importantly leadership, motivation, and the organizational context. However, to avoid repetition, subjects that are the topics of other chapters are introduced only tangentially.

Dynamics in Groups

The first reading describes research in the problematic area of group effects on individuals' decisions. In "Effects of Group Pressure Upon the Modification and Distortion of Judgments," Solomon Asch (1951) describes his famous investigations into ways individuals cope when a group's majority opinion is directly contrary to the facts of a situation. Asch put lone experimental subjects (college students) in rooms with people who had been instructed to give blatantly wrong answers to factual questions. Only the experimental subjects did not know what was going on. Although a slim majority of experimental subjects retained their independence and reported the facts accurately, a sizable minority of subjects *altered their judgment to match that of the majority.* When faced with a group opinion that was obviously wrong, they were not willing to report their observations as they saw them. They changed their judgments. Asch attributes peoples' decisions to retain independence of judgment or to yield to the majority, to several factors. The two most important factors are:

- The size of the majority and the extent of unanimity among members of the majority; and
- Identifiable, enduring differences among individuals, particularly character differences involving social relations.

Asch's experiments provide dramatic evidence of group impacts on people in organizations. From a managerial perspective, they show why it is extremely important to focus attention on the group's beliefs, values, composition, and activities. Nevertheless, for the most part, *informal groups* are outside of the formal organization's direct sphere of influence.

Twenty years after Asch's experiments, Irving Janis published the equally well-known study, "Groupthink," which is reprinted in this chapter. Like Asch, Janis explores pressures for conformance—the reasons why social conformity is encountered frequently in groups. But unlike Asch's experimental use of college students, Janis looked at high-level decision makers in times of real major fiascoes: the 1962 Bay of Pigs, the 1950 decision to send General MacArthur to the Yalu River, and the 1941 failure to prepare for the attack on Pearl Harbor. *Groupthink* is "the mode of thinking that persons engage in when *concurrence seeking* becomes so dominant in a cohesive in-group that it tends to override realistic appraisal of alternative courses of action. . . the desperate drive for consensus at any cost that suppresses dissent among the mighty in the corridors of power" (p. 44). Janis identifies eight symptoms of groupthink that are relatively easy to observe:

- An illusion of invulnerability;
- Collective construction of rationalizations which permit group members to ignore warnings or other forms of negative feedback;
- Unquestioning belief in the morality of the in-group;
- Strong, negative, stereotyped views about the leaders of enemy groups;
- Rapid application of pressure against group members who express even momentary doubts about virtually any illusions the group shares;
- Careful, conscious, personal avoidance of deviation from what appears to be a group consensus;
- Shared illusions of unanimity of opinion;
- Establishment of *mindguards*—people who "protect the leader and fellow members from adverse information that might break the complacency they shared about the effectiveness and morality of past decisions" (p. 74).

Janis concludes with an assessment of the negative influence of groupthink on executive decision making (including overestimation of the group's capability and self-imposed isolation from new or opposing information and points of view), and some preventive and remedial steps for groupthink.

Donald F. Roy examines a very different aspect of individual-group relationships in "'Banana Time': Job Satisfaction and Informal Interaction," which is reprinted here. He describes his subject of interest simply as workers' *psychological survival* in monotonous jobs (p. 158), but Roy's true interest is the workplace relationship among group cohesiveness, group goals, and job satisfaction. In "Banana Time," Roy focuses on interaction and job satisfaction. (In 1961, he followed this article with, "Efficiency and 'the Fix': Informal Intergroup Relations in a Piecework Machine Shop.") Roy took a job—by his description, a monotonous, repetitive, simple job—as a machine operator in order to collect information for the two studies. He concludes that workers in monotonous jobs survive psychologically through informal interaction. He watched machine operators keep from "going nuts" by talking and fooling around in a nonstop, highly stylized, and ritualistic manner. Roy found no evidence to support the then-prevailing belief that informal interaction on the job boosts productivity. In fact, quite the contrary. Roy predicts that productivity would increase if the "fooling around" were to cease. "As far as achievement of managerial goals is concerned, the most that could be suggested is that leavening the deadly boredom of individualized work routines with a concurrent flow of group festivities had a negative effect on turnover" (p. 166). Roy's article provides an important reminder that common sense expectations about people in groups aren't always valid. What would appear to be obviously correlated factors—informal interaction with co-workers, job satisfaction, and productivity—are not.

Dorwin Cartwright and Alvin Zander's contribution to this chapter is the introductory chapter "Origins of Group Dynamics" from their landmark volume, *Group Dynamics*. (Substantial portions of the original chapter have been deleted.) Cartwright and Zander define group dynamics as "a field of inquiry dedicated to advancing knowledge about the nature of groups, the laws of their development, and their interrelations with individuals, other groups, and larger institutions" (p. 7). The distinguishing characteristics of group dynamics—what separates group dynamics from numerous other groups of behavioral sciences that have investigated groups over the years—are:

1. Emphasis on theoretically significant empirical research; conceptual theories and personal observations are not adequate.

2. Interest in the dynamics and interdependence of phenomena. The dynamics are more important than static elements, single-variable theories, and structural schemes.

3. Broad interdisciplinary relevance, the importance of incorporating methods and knowledge from all of the social sciences, including sociology, psychology, and cultural anthropology.

4. "Potential applicability of its findings in efforts to improve the functioning of groups and their consequences on individuals and society" (p. 7). The results must be useful in social practice.

"Origins of Group Dynamics" provides a thorough analysis of the historical development of the field including the positive impetus provided by advancements in other professions, most notably group psychotherapy, education, and social group work, and social research techniques such as controlled observation and sociometry. Cartwright and Zander are *the* premiere chroniclers of group dynamics, and "Origins of Group Dynamics" is *the* outstanding overview of this field.

Intergroup Dynamics

Richard E. Walton and John M. Dutton's (1969) article, "The Management of Interdepartmental Conflict: A Model and Review," explores horizontal conflicts—conflicts across organization lines—rather than, for example, vertical conflicts between supervisors and subordinates. This model "includes five sets of related variables: antecedents to conflict, attributes of the lateral relationship, management of the interface, consequences of the relationship, and responses of higher executives" (p. 73). Together these comprise the antecedents, dynamics, and consequences of conflict. It is interesting to note that Walton and Dutton's first antecedent to (precursor of) interunit conflict is *mutual task dependence*—a first order consequence of specialization and division of labor. The Walton and Dutton model provides managers with a diagnostic tool for determining what needs to be changed to prevent or stop interdepartmental conflict, and strategies for achieving change.

In "Intergroup Problems in Organizations," which is reprinted in this chapter, Edgar H. Schein attacks "the overall problem [which], then, is how to establish high-productive, *collaborative* intergroup relations" (p. 80). The overall problem consists of two subproblems: (1) how groups can be effective at simultaneously meeting needs of members and organizational goals, and (2) how to design and "establish conditions *between groups* which will enhance the productivity of each without destroying intergroup relations and coordination" (p. 80). Schein identifies consequences of intergroup competition within and between the competing groups, citing experiments by Sherif and his associates (1961), and assesses the consequences of winning and losing. After a win-lose competition, losers often do not feel that they truly lost, tension between groups often rises, the heightened tension contributes to further breakdowns in communication and, in turn, stimulates perceptual distortions and mutual negative stereotyping.

Schein discusses the advantages of using laboratory training methods to reduce intergroup competition and the inherent problems that division of labor poses for the prevention of intergroup conflicts. "Interestingly enough, observations of cases would suggest that task-relevant conflict which improves overall effectiveness is greater under collaborative conditions because groups and members trust each other enough to be frank and open in sharing information and opinions" (p. 87).

The chapter's final selection is Jeffrey Pfeffer's "Coalitions," from his 1981 book, *Power in Organizations.* Whereas Walton and Dutton, and Schein are interested in what can be done to minimize negative impacts of intergroup competition, Pfeffer writes about the inevitability of conflict among organizational groups. Intergroup conflicts reflect inherent differences between perspectives (for example, between subculture beliefs and values) and ongoing competition for scarce organizational resources. *Coalitions* (usually formal temporary groups or informal groups) are means through which people gather power and support for political contests within organizations. (Also see the readings in Chapter V.) Like many other authors, Pfeffer argues that interdependence among people and groups results directly from the division of labor and specialization. It is a fundamental reason for the unceasing intergroup power struggles and for the formation and utilization of coalitions in and around organizations.

Pfeffer's "Coalitions" also weighs the advantages and disadvantages of building and using external as opposed to internal coalitions. For example, establishment of external coalitions for political action often is easier because the probability of being in competition with outsiders for scarce resources is lower. Nevertheless, internal and external coalition building strategies are "tricky" trade-off strategies involving high risks. As an alternative, he urges "judicious use of promotion opportunities" (p. 163) as a safer way to build a base of loyal supporters.

Power and influence are the subjects of Chapter V, but Pfeffer's article is included here because it presents an interesting and important counter-perspective to the more optimistic views of people and groups in organizations that characterize the other readings in this chapter. Although Pfeffer was schooled in the organizational behavior tradition, he has grown to be one of the most articulate spokespersons for the power perspective of organization (Shafritz & Ott, 1987, Chapter V).

REFERENCES

Asch, S. E. (1951). Effects of group pressure upon the modification and distortion of judgments. In, H. S. Guetzkow (Ed.), *Groups, leadership, and men* (pp. 177–190). Pittsburgh, PA: Carnegie Press.

Bales, R. F. (1950). *Interaction process analysis: A method for the study of small groups.* Reading, MA: Addison-Wesley.

Bavelas, A. (1942). Morale and training of leaders. In, G. Watson (Ed.), *Civilian morale.* Boston: Houghton Mifflin.

Cartwright, D., & Zander, A. (Eds.). (1968). *Group dynamics: Research and theory* (3d ed.). New York: Harper & Row.

Cohen, A. R., Fink, S. L., Gadon, H., & Willits, R. D. (1988). *Effective behavior in organizations* (4th ed.). Homewood, IL: Richard D. Irwin.

Davis, S. M., & Lawrence, P. R. (1977). *Matrix.* Reading, MA: Addison-Wesley.

Gouldner, A. (1960). The norm of reciprocity. *American Sociological Review, 25,* 161–178.

Homans, G. C. (1950). *The human group.* New York: Harcourt, Brace.

Janis, I. L. (November 1971). Groupthink. *Psychology Today,* 44–76.

Lewin, K. (1943). Forces behind food habits and methods of change. Washington, D.C.: *Bulletin of the National Research Council, 108,* 35–65.

Lewin, K. (June 1947). Frontiers in group dynamics: Concept, method and reality in social science; Social equilibria and social change. *Human Relations, 1* (1).

Lewin, K. (1951). *Field theory in social science.* New York: Harper & Row.

Lewin, K. (1952). Group decision and social change. In, G. E. Swanson, T. N. Newcomb, & E. L. Hartley (Eds.), *Reading in social psychology* (rev. ed.) (pp. 207–211). New York: Holt, Rinehart & Winston.

Lindzey, G. W. (Ed.). (1954). *The handbook of social psychology.* Cambridge, MA: Addison-Wesley.

Marrow, A. J. (1969). *The practical theorist: The life and work of Kurt Lewin.* New York: Basic Books.

Martin, J., & Siehl, C. (Autumn, 1983). Organizational culture and counterculture: An uneasy symbiosis. *Organizational Dynamics,* 52–64.

Moreno, J. L. (1934). *Who shall survive?: A new approach to human interrelations.* Washington, D.C.: Nervous and Mental Disease Publishing Co.

Newcomb, T. M. (1943). *Personality and social change.* New York: Dryden.

Ott, J. S. (1989). *The organizational culture perspective.* Chicago: The Dorsey Press.

Pfeffer, J. (1981). *Power in organizations.* Boston: Pitman Publishing Company.

Pondy, L. R. (1967). Organizational conflict: Concepts and models. *Administrative Science Quarterly, 12,* 296–320.

Roy, D. F. (1960). "Banana time": Job satisfaction and informal interaction. *Human Organization, 18,* 158–168.

Roy, D. F. (1961). Efficiency and "the fix": Informal intergroup relations in a piecework machine shop. In, S. M. Lipset & N. J. Smelser (Eds.), *The progress of a decade.* Englewood Cliffs, NJ: Prentice-Hall.

Schein, E. H. (1970). *Organizational psychology* (2d ed.). Englewood Cliffs, NJ: Prentice-Hall.

Schein, E. H. (1985). *Organizational culture and leadership.* San Francisco: Jossey-Bass.

Seashore, S. E. (1954). *Group cohesiveness in the industrial work group.* Ann Arbor: University of Michigan Press.

Shafritz, J. M., & Ott, J. S. (1987). *Classics of organization theory* (2d ed. rev. and expanded). Chicago: The Dorsey Press.

Sherif, M. (1936). *The psychology of social norms.* New York: Harper.

Sherif, M., Harvey, O. J., White, B. J., & Sherif, C. (1961). *Intergroup conflict and cooperation: The robbers' cave experiment.* Norman, OK: University Book Exchange.

Smith, A. (1776). *The wealth of nations* (Chapter 1, Of the division of labor).

Strauss, G. (1962). Tactics of lateral relationship: The purchasing agent. *Administrative Science Quarterly, 7,* 161–186.

Thibaut, J., & Kelly, H. (1959). *The social psychology of groups.* New York: John Wiley & Sons.

Thorndike, E. L. (1935). *The psychology of wants, interests, and attitudes.* New York: Appleton-Century.

Walton, R. E., & Dutton, J. M. (March, 1969). The management of interdepartmental conflict: A model and review. *Administrative Science Quarterly, 14* (1).

Walton, R. E., Dutton, J. M., & Fitch, H. G. (1966). A study of conflict in the process, structure, and attitudes of lateral relationships. In, A. H. Rubenstein & C. J. Haberstroh (Eds.), *Some theories of organization* (rev. ed.) (pp. 444–465). Homewood, IL: Richard D. Irwin.

Whyte, W. F., Jr. (1943). *Street corner society.* Chicago: University of Chicago Press.

Whyte, W. F., Jr. (1948). *Human relations in the restaurant industry.* New York: McGraw-Hill.

Zander, A. (1971). *Motives and goals in groups.* New York: Academic Press.

Zander, A. (1982). *Making groups effective.* San Francisco: Jossey-Bass.

10
Effects of Group Pressure Upon the Modification and Distortion of Judgments

Solomon E. Asch

We shall here describe in summary form the conception and first findings of a program of investigation into the conditions of independence and submission to group pressure. This program is based on a series of earlier studies conducted by the writer while a Fellow of the John Simon Guggenheim Memorial Foundation. The earlier experiments and the theoretical issues which prompted them are discussed in a forthcoming work by the writer on social psychology.

Our immediate object was to study the social and personal conditions that induce individuals to resist or to yield to group pressures when the latter are perceived to be *contrary to fact*. The issues which this problem raises are of obvious consequence for society; it can be of decisive importance whether or not a group will, under certain conditions, submit to existing pressures. Equally direct are the consequences for individuals and our understanding of them, since it is a decisive fact about a person whether he possesses the freedom to act independently, or whether he characteristically submits to group pressures.

The problem under investigation requires the direct observation of certain basic processes in the interaction between individuals, and between individuals and groups. To clarify these seems necessary if we are to make fundamental advances in the understand-ing of the formation and reorganization of attitudes, of the functioning of public opinion, and of the operation of propaganda. Today we do not possess an adequate theory of these central psychosocial processes. Empirical investigation has been predominantly controlled by general propositions concerning group influence which have as a rule been assumed but not tested. With few exceptions investigation has relied upon descriptive formulations concerning the operation of suggestion and prestige, the inadequacy of which is becoming increasingly obvious, and upon schematic applications of stimulus-response theory.

The bibliography lists articles representative of the current theoretical and empirical situation. Basic to the current approach has been the axiom that group pressures characteristically induce psychological changes *arbitrarily*, in far-reaching disregard of the material properties of the given conditions. This mode of thinking has almost exclusively stressed the slavish submission of individuals to group forces, has neglected to inquire into their possibilities for independence and for productive relations with the human environment, and has virtually denied the capacity of men under certain conditions to rise above group passion and prejudice. It was our aim to contribute to a clarification of

Source: From "Effects of Group Pressure Upon the Modification and Distortion of Judgments" by Solomon E. Asch, in *Groups, Leadership, and Men,* edited by Harold S. Guetzkow (Pittsburgh: Carnegie Press, 1951, pp. 177–190). Reprinted by permission from Carnegie Mellon University.

these questions, important both for theory and for their human implications, by means of direct observation of the effects of groups upon the decisions and evaluations of individuals.

THE EXPERIMENT AND FIRST RESULTS

To this end we developed an experimental technique which has served as the basis for the present series of studies. We employed the procedure of placing an individual in a relation of radical conflict with all the other members of a group, of measuring its effect upon him in quantitative terms, and of describing its psychological consequences. A group of eight individuals was instructed to judge a series of simple, clearly structured perceptual relations—to match the length of a given line with one of three unequal lines. Each member of the group announced his judgments publicly. In the midst of this monotonous "test" one individual found himself suddenly contradicted by the entire group, and this contradiction was repeated again and again in the course of the experiment. The group in question had, with the exception of one member, previously met with the experimenter and received instructions to respond at certain points with wrong—and unanimous—judgments. The errors of the majority were large (ranging between ½" and 1¾") and of an order not encountered under control conditions. The outstanding person—the critical subject—whom we had placed in the position of a *minority of one* in the midst of a *unanimous majority*—was the object of investigation. He faced, possibly for the first time in his life, a situation in which a group unanimously contradicted the evidence of his senses.

This procedure was the starting point of the investigation and the point of departure for the study of further problems. Its main features were the following: (1) The critical subject was submitted to two contradictory and irreconcilable forces—the evidence of his own experience of an utterly clear perceptual fact and the unanimous evidence of a group of equals. (2) Both forces were part of the immediate situation; the majority was concretely present, surrounding the subject physically. (3) The critical subject, who was requested together with all others to state his judgments publicly, was obliged to declare himself and to take a definite stand vis-à-vis the group. (4) The situation possessed a self-contained character. The critical subject could not avoid or evade the dilemma by reference to conditions external to the experimental situation. (It may be mentioned at this point that the forces generated by the given conditions acted so quickly upon the critical subjects that instances of suspicion were rare.)

The technique employed permitted a simple quantitative measure of the "majority effect" in terms of the frequency of errors in the direction of the distorted estimates of the majority. At the same time we were concerned from the start to obtain evidence of the ways in which the subjects perceived the group, to establish whether they became doubtful, whether they were tempted to join the majority. Most important, it was our object to establish the grounds of the subject's independence or yielding—whether, for example, the yielding subject was aware of the effect of the majority upon him, whether he abandoned his judgment deliberately or compulsively. To this end we constructed a comprehensive set of questions which served as the basis of an individual interview immediately following the experimental period. Toward the conclusion of the interview each subject was informed fully of the purpose of the experiment, of his role and of that of the majority. The reactions to the disclosure of the purpose of the experiment became in fact an integral part of the procedure. We may state here that the information derived from the interview became an indispensable source of evidence and insight into the psychological structure of the experimental situation, and in particular, of the nature of the individual differences. Also, it is not justified or advisable to allow the subject to leave without giving him a full explanation of the experimental conditions. The experimenter has a responsibility to the subject to clarify his doubts and to state the reasons for placing him in the experimental situation. When this is done most subjects react with interest and many express gratification at having lived through a striking

TABLE 1 • LENGTHS OF STANDARD AND COMPARISON LINES

Trials	Length of Standard Line (in inches)	Comparison Lines (in inches)			Correct Response	Group Response	Majority Error (in inches)
		1	2	3			
1	10	8¾	10	8	2	2	—
2	2	2	1	1½	1	1	—
3	3	3¾	4¼	3	3	1*	+ ¾
4	5	5	4	6½	1	2*	− 1.0
5	4	3	5	4	3	3	—
6	3	3¾	4¼	3	3	2*	+ 1¼
7	8	6¼	8	6¾	2	3*	− 1¼
8	5	5	4	6½	1	3*	+ 1½
9	8	6¼	8	6¾	2	1*	− 1¾
10	10	8¾	10	8	2	2	—
11	2	2	1	1½	1	1	—
12	3	3¾	4¼	3	3	1*	+ ¾
13	5	5	4	6½	1	2*	− 1.0
14	4	3	5	4	3	3	—
15	3	3¾	4¼	3	3	2*	+ 1¼
16	8	6¼	8	6¾	2	3*	− 1¼
17	5	5	4	6½	1	3*	+ 1½
18	8	6¼	8	6¾	2	1*	− 1¾

*Starred figures designate the erroneous estimates by the majority.

situation which has some bearing on wider human issues.

Both the members of the majority and the critical subjects were male college students. We shall report the results for a total of fifty critical subjects in this experiment. In Table 1 we summarize the successive comparison trials and the majority estimates. The quantitative results are clear and unambiguous.

1. There was a marked movement toward the majority. One-third of all the estimates in the critical group were errors identical with

or in the direction of the distorted estimates of the majority. The significance of this finding becomes clear in the light of the virtual absence of errors in control groups the members of which recorded their estimates in writing. The relevant data of the critical and control groups are summarized in Table 2.

2. At the same time the effect of the majority was far from complete. The preponderance of estimates in the critical group (68 per cent)

TABLE 2 ● DISTRIBUTION OF ERRORS IN EXPERIMENTAL AND CONTROL GROUPS

Number of Critical Errors	Critical Group* (N = 50)	Control Group (N = 37)
	F	F
0	13	35
1	4	1
2	5	1
3	6	
4	3	
5	4	
6	1	
7	2	
8	5	
9	3	
10	3	
11	1	
12	0	
Total	50	37
Mean	3.84	0.08

*All errors in the critical group were in the direction of the majority estimates.

was correct despite the pressure of the majority.

3. We found evidence of extreme individual differences. There were in the critical group subjects who remained independent without exception, and there were those who went nearly all the time with the majority. (The maximum possible number of errors was 12, while the actual range of errors was 0–11.) One-fourth of the critical subjects was completely independent; at the other extreme, one-third of the group displaced the estimates toward the majority in one-half or more of the trials.

The differences between the critical subjects in their reactions to the given conditions were equally striking. There were subjects who remained completely confident throughout. At the other extreme were those who became disoriented, doubt-ridden, and experienced a powerful impulse not to appear different from the majority.

For the purposes of illustration we include a brief description of one independent and one yielding subject.

Independent. After a few trials he appeared puzzled, hesitant. He announced all disagreeing answers in the form of "Three, sir; two, sir"; not so with the unanimous answers. At trial 4 he answered immediately after the first member of the group, shook his head, blinked, and whispered to his neighbor: "Can't help it, that's one." His later answers came in a whispered voice, accompanied by a deprecating smile. At one point he grinned embarrassedly, and whispered explosively to his neighbor: "I always disagree—darn it!" During the questioning, this subject's con-

stant refrain was: "I called them as I saw them, sir." He insisted that his estimates were right without, however, committing himself as to whether the others were wrong, remarking that "that's the way I see them and that's the way they see them." If he had to make a practical decision under similar circumstances, he declared, "I would follow my own view, though part of my reason would tell me that I might be wrong." Immediately following the experiment the majority engaged this subject in a brief discussion. When they pressed him to say whether the entire group was wrong and he alone right, he turned upon them defiantly, exclaiming: "You're *probably* right, but you may be wrong!" To the disclosure of the experiment this subject reacted with the statement that he felt "exultant and relieved," adding, "I do not deny that at times I had the feeling: 'to heck with it, I'll go along with the rest.'"

Yielding. This subject went with the majority in 11 out of 12 trials. He appeared nervous and somewhat confused, but he did not attempt to evade discussion; on the contrary, he was helpful and tried to answer to the best of his ability. He opened the discussion with the statement: "If I'd been the first I probably would have responded differently"; this was his way of stating that he had adopted the majority estimates. The primary factor in his case was loss of confidence. He perceived the majority as a decided group, acting without hesitation: "If they had been doubtful I probably would have changed, but they answered with such confidence." Certain of his errors, he explained, were due to the doubtful nature of the comparisons; in such instances he went with the majority. When the object of the experiment was explained, the subject volunteered: "I suspected about the middle—but tried to push it out of my mind." It is of interest that his suspicion was not able to restore his confidence and diminish the power of the majority. Equally striking is his report that he assumed the experiment to involve an "illusion" to which the others, but not he, were subject. This assumption too did not help to free him; on the contrary, he acted as if his divergence from the majority was a sign of defect. The principal impression this subject produced was of one so caught up by immediate difficulties that he lost clear reasons for his actions, and could make no reasonable decisions.

A FIRST ANALYSIS OF INDIVIDUAL DIFFERENCES

On the basis of the interview data described earlier, we undertook to differentiate and describe the major forms of reaction to the experimental situation, which we shall now briefly summarize.

Among the *independent* subjects we distinguished the following main categories:

1. Independence based on *confidence* in one's perception and experience. The most striking characteristic of these subjects is the vigor with which they withstand the group opposition. Though they are sensitive to the group, and experience the conflict, they show a resilience in coping with it, which is expressed in their continuing reliance on their perception and the effectiveness with which they shake off the oppressive group opposition.

2. Quite different are those subjects who are independent and *withdrawn*. These do not react in a spontaneously emotional way, but rather on the basis of explicit principles concerning the necessity of being an individual.

3. A third group of independent subjects manifest considerable tension

and *doubt*, but adhere to their judgments on the basis of a felt necessity to deal adequately with the task.

The following were the main categories of reaction among the *yielding* subjects, or those who went with the majority during one-half or more of the trials.

1. *Distortion of perception* under the stress of group pressure. In this category belong a very few subjects who yield completely, but are not aware that their estimates have been displaced or distorted by the majority. These subjects report that they came to perceive the majority estimates as correct.

2. *Distortion of judgment.* Most submitting subjects belong to this category. The factor of greatest importance in this group is a decision the subjects reach that their perceptions are inaccurate, and that those of the majority are correct. These subjects suffer from primary doubt and lack of confidence; on this basis they feel a strong tendency to join the majority.

3. *Distortion of action.* The subjects in this group do not suffer a modification of perception nor do they conclude that they are wrong. They yield because of an overmastering need not to appear different from or inferior to others, because of an inability to tolerate the appearance of defectiveness in the eyes of the group. These subjects suppress their observations and voice the majority position with awareness of what they are doing.

The results are sufficient to establish that independence and yielding are not psychologically homogeneous, that submission to group pressure (and freedom from pressure) can be the result of different psychological conditions. It should also be noted that the categories described above, being based exclusively on the subjects' reactions to the experimental conditions, are descriptive, not presuming to explain why a given individual responded in one way rather than another. The further exploration of the basis for the individual differences is a separate task upon which we are now at work.

EXPERIMENTAL VARIATIONS

The results described are clearly a joint function of two broadly different sets of conditions. They are determined first by the specific external conditions, by the particular character of the relation between social evidence and one's own experience. Second, the presence of pronounced individual differences points to the important role of personal factors, of factors connected with the individual's character structure. We reasoned that there are group conditions which would produce independence in all subjects, and that there probably are group conditions which would induce intensified yielding in many, though not in all. Accordingly we followed the procedure of *experimental variation,* systematically altering the quality of social evidence by means of systematic variation of group conditions. Secondly, we deemed it reasonable to assume that behavior under the experimental social pressure is significantly related to certain basic, relatively permanent characteristics of the individual. The investigation has moved in both of these directions. Because the study of the character-qualities which may be functionally connected with independence and yielding is still in progress, we shall limit the present account to a sketch of the representative experimental variations.

The Effect of Nonunanimous Majorities

Evidence obtained from the basic experiment suggested that the condition of being exposed *alone* to the opposition of a "compact majority" may have played a decisive role in determining the course and strength of the effects observed. Accordingly we undertook to investigate in a series of successive variations the effects of *nonunanimous* majorities. The technical problem of altering the uniformity of a majority is, in terms of our procedure, relatively simple. In most instances we merely directed one or more members of the instructed group to deviate from the majority in prescribed ways. It is obvious that we cannot hope to compare the performance of the same individual in two situations on the assumption that they remain independent of one another. At best we can investigate the effect of an earlier upon a later experimental condition. The comparison of different experimental situations therefore requires the use of different but comparable groups of critical subjects. This is the procedure we have followed. In the variations to be described we have maintained the conditions of the basic experiment (*e.g.,* the sex of the subjects, the size of the majority, the content of the task, and so on) save for the specific factor that was varied. The following were some of the variations we studied:

1. *The presence of a "true partner."* (a) In the midst of the majority were *two* naive, critical subjects. The subjects were separated, spatially, being seated in the fourth and eighth positions, respectively. Each therefore heard his judgment confirmed by one other person (provided the other person remained independent), one prior to, the

other subsequently to announcing his own judgment. In addition, each experienced a break in the unanimity of the majority. There were six pairs of critical subjects. (b) In a further variation the "partner" to the critical subject was a member of the group who had been instructed to respond correctly throughout. This procedure permits the exact control of the partner's responses. The partner was always seated in the fourth position; he therefore announced his estimates in each case before the critical subject.

The results clearly demonstrate that a disturbance of the unanimity of the majority markedly increased the independence of the critical subjects. The frequency of pro-majority errors dropped to 10.4 per cent of the total number of estimates in variation (a), and to 5.5 per cent in variation (b). These results are to be compared with the frequency of yielding to the unanimous majorities in the basic experiment, which was 32 per cent of the total number of estimates. It is clear that the presence in the field of *one other* individual who responded correctly was sufficient to deplete the power of the majority, and in some cases to destroy it. This finding is all the more striking in the light of other variations which demonstrate the effect of even small minorities provided they are unanimous. Indeed, we have been able to show that a unanimous majority of three is, under the given conditions, far more effective than a majority of eight containing one dissenter. That critical subjects will under these conditions free themselves of a majority of seven and join forces with one other person in the minority is, we believe, a result significant for theory. It points to a fundamental psychological difference between the condition of being alone and having a minimum of

human support. It further demonstrates that the effects obtained are not the result of a summation of influences proceeding from each member of the group; it is necessary to conceive the results as being relationally determined.

2. *Withdrawal of a "true partner."* What will be the effect of providing the critical subject with a partner who responds correctly and then withdrawing him? The critical subject started with a partner who responded correctly. The partner was a member of the majority who had been instructed to respond correctly and to "desert" to the majority in the middle of the experiment. This procedure permits the observation of the same subject in the course of transition from one condition to another. The withdrawal of the partner produced a powerful and unexpected result. We had assumed that the critical subject, having gone through the experience of opposing the majority with a minimum of support, would maintain his independence when alone. Contrary to this expectation, we found that the experience of having had and then lost a partner restored the majority effect to its full force, the proportion of errors rising to 28.5 per cent of all judgments, in contrast to the preceding level of 5.5 per cent. Further experimentation is needed to establish whether the critical subjects were responding to the sheer fact of being alone, or to the fact that the partner abandoned them.

3. *Late arrival of a "true partner."* The critical subject started as a minority of one in the midst of a unanimous majority. Toward the conclusion of the experiment one member of the majority "broke" away and began announcing correct estimates. This procedure, which reverses the order of conditions of the preceding experiment, permits

the observation of the transition from being alone to being a member of a pair against a majority. It is obvious that those critical subjects who were independent when alone would continue to be so when joined by another partner. The variation is therefore of significance primarily for those subjects who yielded during the first phase of the experiment. The appearance of the late partner exerts a freeing effect, reducing the level to 8.7 per cent. Those who had previously yielded also became markedly more independent, but not completely so, continuing to yield more than previously independent subjects. The reports of the subjects do not cast much light on the factors responsible for the result. It is our impression that having once committed himself to yielding, the individual finds it difficult and painful to change his direction. To do so is tantamount to a public admission that he has not acted rightly. He therefore follows the precarious course he has already chosen in order to maintain an outward semblance of consistency and conviction.

4. *The presence of a "compromise partner."* The majority was consistently extremist, always matching the standard with the most unequal line. One instructed subject (who, as in the other variations, preceded the critical subject) also responded incorrectly, but his estimates were always intermediate between the truth and the majority position. The critical subject therefore faced an extremist majority whose unanimity was broken by one more moderately erring person. Under these conditions the frequency of errors was reduced but not significantly. However, the lack of unanimity determined in a strikingly consistent way the *direction* of the errors. The preponderance of the errors, 75.7 per cent of the total, was moderate, whereas in a parallel experiment in which the majority was unanimously extremist (*i.e.,* with the "compromise" partner excluded), the incidence of moderate errors was reduced to 42 per cent of the total. As might be expected, in a unanimously moderate majority, the errors of the critical subjects were without exception moderate.

The Role of Majority Size

To gain further understanding of the majority effect, we varied the size of the majority in several different variations. The majorities, which were in each case unanimous, consisted of 16, 8, 4, 3, and 2 persons, respectively. In addition, we studied the limited case in which the critical subject was opposed by one instructed subject. Table 3 contains the means and the range of errors under each condition.

With the opposition reduced to one, the majority effect all but disappeared. When the opposition proceeded from a group of two, it produced a measurable though small distortion, the errors being 12.8 per cent of the total number of estimates. The effect appeared in full

TABLE 3 • ERRORS OF CRITICAL SUBJECTS WITH UNANIMOUS
MAJORITIES OF DIFFERENT SIZE

Size of majority	Control	1	2	3	4	8	16
N	37	10	15	10	10	50	12
Mean number of errors	0.08	0.33	1.53	4.0	4.20	3.84	3.75
Range of errors	0–2	0–1	0–5	1–12	0–11	0–11	0–10

force with a majority of three. Larger majorities of four, eight, and sixteen did not produce effects greater than a majority of three.

The effect of a majority is often silent, revealing little of its operation to the subject, and often hiding it from the experimenter. To examine the range of effects it is capable of inducing, decisive variations of conditions are necessary. An indication of one effect is furnished by the following variation in which the conditions of the basic experiment were simply reversed. Here the majority, consisting of a group of sixteen, was naive; in the midst of it we placed a single individual who responded wrongly according to instructions. Under these conditions the members of the naive majority reacted to the lone dissenter with amusement and disdain. Contagious laughter spread through the group at the droll minority of one. Of significance is the fact that the members lack awareness that they draw their strength from the majority, and that their reactions would change radically if they faced the dissenter individually. In fact, the attitude of derision in the majority turns to seriousness and increased respect as soon as the minority is increased to three. These observations demonstrate the role of social support as a source of power and stability, in contrast to the preceding investigations which stressed the effects of withdrawal of social support, or to be more exact, the effects of social opposition. Both aspects must be explicitly considered in a unified formulation of the effects of group conditions on the formation and change of judgments.

The Role of the Stimulus-Situation

It is obviously not possible to divorce the quality and course of the group forces which act upon the individual from the specific stimulus-conditions.

Of necessity the structure of the situation molds the group forces and determines their direction as well as their strength. Indeed, this was the reason that we took pains in the investigations described above to center the issue between the individual and the group around an elementary and fundamental matter of fact. And there can be no doubt that the resulting reactions were directly a function of the contradiction between the objectively grasped relations and the majority position.

These general considerations are sufficient to establish the need of varying the stimulus-conditions and of observing their effect on the resulting group forces. We are at present conducting a series of investigations in which certain aspects of the stimulus-situation are systematically altered.

One of the dimensions we are examining is the magnitude of discrepancies above the threshold. Our technique permits an easy variation of this factor, since we can increase or decrease at will the deviation of the majority from the given objective conditions. Hitherto we have studied the effect of a relatively moderate range of discrepancies. Within the limits of our procedure we find that different magnitudes of discrepancy produce approximately the same amount of yielding. However, the quality of yielding alters: As the majority becomes more extreme, there occurs a significant increase in the frequency of "compromise" errors. Further experiments are planned in which the discrepancies in question will be extremely large and small.

We have also varied systematically the structural clarity of the task, including in separate variations judgments based on mental standards. In agreement with other investigators, we find that the majority effect grows stronger as the situation diminishes in clarity. Concurrently, however, the disturbance of the subjects and the conflict-quality of the situation decrease markedly. We consider it of significance that the majority achieves its most pronounced effect when it acts most painlessly.

was proposed that these are functionally dependent on relatively enduring character differences, in particular those pertaining to the person's social relations.

SUMMARY

We have investigated the effects upon individuals of majority opinions when the latter were seen to be in a direction contrary to fact. By means of a simple technique we produced a radical divergence between a majority and a minority, and observed the ways in which individuals coped with the resulting difficulty. Despite the stress of the given conditions, a substantial proportion of individuals retained their independence throughout. At the same time a substantial minority yielded, modifying their judgments in accordance with the majority. Independence and yielding are a joint function of the following major factors: (1) The character of the stimulus situation. Variations in structural clarity have a decisive effect: With diminishing clarity of the stimulus-conditions the majority effect increases. (2) The character of the group forces. Individuals are highly sensitive to the structural qualities of group opposition. In particular, we demonstrated the great importance of the factor of unanimity. Also, the majority effect is a function of the size of group opposition. (3) The character of the individual. There were wide, and indeed, striking differences among individuals within the same experimental situation. The hypothesis

BIBLIOGRAPHY

1. Asch, S. E. Studies in the principles of judgments and attitudes: II. Determination of judgments by group and by ego-standards. *J. soc. Psychol.*, 1940, *12*, 433–465.

2. ———. The doctrine of suggestion, prestige and imitation in social psychology. *Psychol. Rev.*, 1948, *55*, 250–276.

3. Asch, S. E., Block, H., and Hertzman, M. Studies in the principles of judgments and attitudes. I. Two basic principles of judgment. *J. Psychol.* 1938, *5*, 219–251.

4. Coffin, E. E. Some conditions of suggestion and suggestibility: A study of certain attitudinal and situational factors influencing the process of suggestion. *Psychol. Monogr.*, 1941, *53*, No. 4.

5. Lewis, H. B. Studies in the principles of judgments and attitudes: IV. The operation of prestige suggestion. *J. soc. Psychol.*, 1941, *14*, 229–256.

6. Lorge, I. Prestige, suggestion, and attitudes. *J. soc. Psychol.*, 1936, *7*, 386–402.

7. Miller, N. E. and Dollard, J. *Social Learning and Imitation.* New Haven: Yale University Press, 1941.

8. Moore, H. T. The comparative influence of majority and expert opinion. *Amer. J. Psychol.*, 1921, *32*, 16–20.

9. Sherif, M. A study of some social factors in perception. *Arch. Psychol.*, N.Y. 1935, No. 187.

10. Thorndike, E. L. *The Psychology of Wants, Interests, and Attitudes.* New York: D. Appleton-Century Company, Inc., 1935.

11

"Banana Time": Job Satisfaction and Informal Interaction

Donald F. Roy*

This paper undertakes description and exploratory analysis of the social interaction which took place within a small work group of factory machine operatives during a two-month period of participant observation. The factual and ideational materials which it presents lie at an intersection of two lines of research interest and should, in their dual bearings, contribute to both. Since the operatives were engaged in work which involved the repetition of very simple operations over an extra-long workday, six days a week, they were faced with the problem of dealing with a formidable "beast of monotony." Revelation of how the group utilized its resources to combat that "beast" should merit the attention of those who are seeking solution to the practical problem of job satisfaction, or employee morale. It should also provide insights for those who are trying to penetrate the mysteries of the small group.

Convergence of these two lines of interest is, of course, no new thing. Among the host of writers and researchers who have suggested connections between "group" and "joy in work" are Walker and Guest, observers of social interaction on the automobile assembly line.[1] They quote assembly-line workers as saying, "We have a lot of fun and talk all the time,"[2] and, "If it weren't for the talking and fooling, you'd go nuts."[3]

My account of how one group of machine operators kept from "going nuts" in a situation of monotonous work activity attempts to lay bare the tissues of interaction which made up the content of their adjustment. The talking, fun, and fooling which provided solution to the elemental problem of "psychological survival" will be described according to their embodiment in intra-group relations. In addition, an unusual opportunity for close observation of behavior involved in the maintenance of group equilibrium was afforded by the fortuitous introduction of a "natural experiment." My unwitting injection of explosive materials into the stream of interaction resulted in sudden, but temporary, loss of group interaction.

My fellow operatives and I spent our long days of simple, repetitive work in relative isolation from other employees of the factory. Our line of machines was sealed off from other work areas of the

*Dr. Roy is in the Department of Sociology, Duke University, Durham, North Carolina.

[1] Charles R. Walker and Robert H. Guest, *The Man on the Assembly Line*, Harvard University Press, Cambridge, 1952.

[2] *Ibid.*, p. 77.

[3] *Ibid.*, p. 68.

Source: From "'Banana Time': Job Satisfaction and Informal Interaction" by Donald F. Roy in *Human Organization*, 18 (1960). Reproduced by permission of the Society for Applied Anthropology.

plant by the four walls of the clicking room. The one door of this room was usually closed. Even when it was kept open, during periods of hot weather, the consequences were not social; it opened on an uninhabited storage room of the shipping department. Not even the sounds of work activity going on elsewhere in the factory carried to this isolated work place. There were occasional contacts with "outside" employees, usually on matters connected with the work; but, with the exception of the daily calls of one fellow who came to pick up finished materials for the next step in processing, such visits were sporadic and infrequent.

Moreover, face-to-face contact with members of the managerial hierarchy were few and far between. No one bearing the title of foreman ever came around. The only company official who showed himself more than once during the two-month observation period was the plant superintendent. Evidently overloaded with supervisory duties and production problems which kept him busy elsewhere, he managed to pay his respects every week or two. His visits were in the nature of short, businesslike, but friendly exchanges. Otherwise he confined his observable communications with the group to occasional utilization of a public address system. During the two-month period, the company president and the chief chemist paid one friendly call apiece. One man, who may or may not have been of managerial status, was seen on various occasions lurking about in a manner which excited suspicion. Although no observable consequences accrued from the peculiar visitations of this silent fellow, it was assumed that he was some sort of efficiency expert, and he was referred to as "The Snooper."

As far as our work group was concerned, this was truly a situation of laissez-faire management. There was no interference from staff experts, no hounding by time-study engineers or personnel men hot on the scent of efficiency or good human relations. Nor were there any signs of industrial democracy in the form of safety, recreational, or production committees. There was an international union, and there was a highly publicized union-management cooperation program; but actual interactional processes of cooperation were carried on somewhere beyond my range of observation and without participation of members of my work group. Furthermore, these union-management get-togethers had no determinable connection with the problem of "toughing out" a twelve-hour day at monotonous work.

Our work group was thus not only abandoned to its own resources for creating job satisfaction, but left without that basic reservoir of ill-will toward management which can sometimes be counted on to stimulate the development of interesting activities to occupy hand and brain. Lacking was the challenge of intergroup conflict, that perennial source of creative experience to fill the otherwise empty hours of meaningless work routine.[4]

The clicking machines were housed in a room approximately thirty by twenty-four feet. They were four in number, set in a row, and so arranged along one wall that the busy operator could, merely by raising his head from his work, freshen his reveries with a glance through one of three large barred windows. To the rear of one of the end machines sat a long cutting table; here the operators cut up rolls of plastic ma-

[4] Donald F. Roy, "Work Satisfaction and Social Reward in Quota Achievement: An Analysis of Piecework Incentive," *American Sociological Review*, XVIII (October, 1953), 507–514.

terials into small sheets manageable for further processing at the clickers. Behind the machine at the opposite end of the line sat another table which was intermittently the work station of a female employee who performed sundry scissors operations of a more intricate nature on raincoat parts. Boxed in on all sides by shelves and stocks of materials, this latter locus of work appeared a cell within a cell.

The clickers were of the genus punching machines; of mechanical construction similar to that of the better-known punch presses, their leading features were hammer and block. The hammer, or punching head, was approximately eight inches by twelve inches at its flat striking surface. The descent upon the block was initially forced by the operator, who exerted pressure on a handle attached to the side of the hammer head. A few inches of travel downward established electrical connection for a sharp, power-driven blow. The hammer also traveled, by manual guidance, in a horizontal plane to and from, and in an arc around, the central column of the machine. Thus the operator, up to the point of establishing electrical connections for the sudden and irrevocable downward thrust, had flexibility in maneuvering his instrument over the larger surface of the block. The latter, approximately twenty-four inches wide, eighteen inches deep, and ten inches thick, was made, like a butcher's block, of inlaid hardwood; it was set in the machine at a convenient waist height. On it the operator placed his materials, one sheet at a time if leather, stacks of sheets if plastic, to be cut with steel dies of assorted sizes and shapes. The particular die in use would be moved, by hand, from spot to spot over the materials each time a cut was made; less frequently, materials would be shifted on

the block as the operator saw need for such adjustment.

Introduction to the new job, with its relatively simple machine skills and work routines, was accomplished with what proved to be, in my experience, an all-time minimum at job training. The clicking machine assigned to me was situated at one end of the row. Here the superintendent and one of the operators gave a few brief demonstrations, accompanied by bits of advice which included a warning to keep hands clear of the descending hammer. After a short practice period, at the end of which the superintendent expressed satisfaction with progress and potentialities, I was left to develop my learning curve with no other supervision than that afforded by members of the work group. Further advice and assistance did come, from time to time, from my fellow operatives, some times upon request, sometimes unsolicited.

THE WORK GROUP

Absorbed at first in three related goals of improving my clicking skill, increasing my rate of output, and keeping my left hand unclicked, I paid little attention to my fellow operatives save to observe that they were friendly, middle aged, foreign-born, full of advice, and very talkative. Their names, according to the way they addressed each other, were George, Ike, and Sammy.[5] George, a stocky fellow in his late fifties, operated the machine at the opposite end of the line; he, I later discovered, had emigrated in early youth from a country in Southeastern Europe. Ike, stationed at George's left, was tall, slender, in his early fifties, and Jewish; he had come from Eastern Europe in his youth. Sammy, number three man in the line,

[5] All names used are fictitious.

and my neighbor, was heavy set, in his late fifties, and Jewish; he had escaped from a country in Eastern Europe just before Hitler's legions had moved in. All three men had been downwardly mobile as to occupation in recent years. George and Sammy had been proprietors of small businesses; the former had been "wiped out" when his uninsured establishment burned down; the latter had been entrepreneuring on a small scale before he left all behind him to flee the Germans. According to his account, Ike had left a highly skilled trade which he had practiced for years in Chicago.

I discovered also that the clicker line represented a ranking system in descending order from George to myself. George not only had top seniority for the group, but functioned as a sort of leadman. His superior status was marked in the fact that he received five cents more per hour than the other clickermen, put in the longest workday, made daily contact, outside the workroom, with the superintendent on work matters which concerned the entire line, and communicated to the rest of us the directives which he received. The narrow margin of superordination was seen in the fact that directives were always relayed in the superintendent's name; they were on the order of, "You'd better let that go now, and get on the green. Joe says they're running low on the fifth floor," or, "Joe says he wants two boxes of the 3-die today." The narrow margin was also seen in the fact that the superintendent would communicate directly with his operatives over the public address system; and, on occasion, Ike or Sammy would leave the workroom to confer with him for decisions or advice in regard to work orders.

Ike was next to George in seniority, then Sammy. I was, of course, low man on the totem pole. Other indices to status differentiation lay in informal interaction, to be described later.

With one exception, job status tended to be matched by length of workday. George worked a thirteen-hour day, from 7 A.M. to 8:30 P.M. Ike worked eleven hours, from 7 A.M. to 6:30 P.M.; occasionally he worked until 7 or 7:30 for an eleven and a half- or a twelve-hour day. Sammy put in a nine hour day, from 8 A.M. to 5:30 P.M. My twelve hours spanned from 8 A.M. to 8:30 P.M. We had a half hour for lunch, from 12 to 12:30.

The female who worked at the secluded table behind George's machine put in a regular plant-wide eight-hour shift from 8 to 4:30. Two women held this job during the period of my employment; Mable was succeeded by Baby. Both were Negroes; and in their late twenties.

A fifth clicker operator, an Arabian *emigré* called Boo, worked a night shift by himself. He usually arrived about 7 P.M. to take over Ike's machine.

THE WORK

It was evident to me, before my first workday drew to a weary close, that my clicking career was going to be a grim process of fighting the clock, the particular timepiece in this situation being an old-fashioned alarm clock which ticked away on a shelf near George's machine. I had struggled through many dreary rounds with the minutes and hours during the various phases of my industrial experience, but never had I been confronted with such a dismal combination of working conditions as the extra-long workday, the infinitesimal cerebral excitation, and the extreme limitation of physical movement. The contrast with a recent stint in the California oil fields was striking. This was no eight-hour day of racing hither and yon over desert and foothills with a rollicking crew of "roustabouts" on a variety of repair missions at oil wells, pipe lines, and storage tanks. Here there were no afternoon dallyings to search the sands for horned toads, tarantulas, and rattlesnakes, or to climb old wooden derricks for raven's nests, with an eye out, of course, for the tell-tale streak of dust in the distance which gave ample warning of the approach of the boss. This was standing all day in one spot beside three old codgers in a dingy room looking out through barred windows at the bare walls of a brick warehouse, leg movements largely restricted to the shifting of body weight from one foot to the other, hand and arm movements confined, for the most part, to a simple repetitive sequence of place the die,———punch the clicker,———place the die,——— punch the clicker, and intellectual activity reduced to computing the hours to quitting time. It is true that from time to time a fresh stack of sheets would have to be substituted for the clicked-out old one; but the stack would have been prepared by someone else, and the exchange would be only a minute or two in the making. Now and then a box of finished work would have to be moved back out of the way, and an empty box brought up; but the moving back and the bringing up involved only a step or two. And there was the half hour for lunch, and occasional trips to the lavatory or the drinking fountain to break up the day into digestible parts. But after each momentary respite, hammer and die were moving again: click,———move die,——— click,———move die.

Before the end of the first day, Monotony was joined by his twin brother, Fatigue. I got tired. My legs ached, and my feet hurt. Early in the afternoon I discovered a tall stool and moved it up to my machine to "take the load off my feet." But the superintendent dropped in to see how I was "doing" and promptly informed me that "we don't sit down on this job." My reverie toyed with the idea of quitting the job and looking for other work.

The next day was the same: the monotony of the work, the tired legs and sore feet and thoughts of quitting.

THE GAME OF WORK

In discussing the factory operative's struggle to "cling to the remnants of joy in work," Henri de Man makes the general observations that "it is psychologically impossible to deprive any kind of work of all its positive emotional elements," that the worker will find *some* meaning in any activity assigned to him, a "certain scope for initiative which can satisfy after a fashion the instinct for play and the creative impulse," that "even in the Taylor system there is found luxury of self-determination."[6] De Man cites the case of one worker who wrapped 13,000 incandescent bulbs a day; she found her outlet for creative impulse, her self-determination, her meaning in work by varying her wrapping movements a little from time to time.[7]

So did I search for *some* meaning in my continuous mincing of plastic sheets into small ovals, fingers, and trapezoids. The richness of possibility for creative expression previously discovered in my experience with the "Taylor system"[8] did not reveal itself here. There was no piecework, so no piecework game. There was no conflict with manage-

[6] Henri de Man, *The Psychology of Socialism*, Henry Holt and Company, New York, 1927, pp. 80–81.

[7] de Man. *The Psychology of Socialism*.

[8] Roy, "Work Satisfaction and Social Reward . . ."

ment, so no war game. But, like the light bulb wrapper, I did find a "certain scope for initiative," and out of this slight freedom to vary activity, I developed a game of work.

The game developed was quite simple, so elementary, in fact, that its playing was reminiscent of rainy-day preoccupations in childhood, when attention could be centered by the hour on colored bits of things of assorted sizes and shapes. But this adult activity was not mere pottering and piddling; what it lacked in the earlier imaginative content, it made up for in clean-cut structure. Fundamentally involved were: a) variation in color of the materials cut, b) variation in shapes of the dies used, and c) a process called "scraping the block." The basic procedure which ordered the particular combination of components employed could be stated in the form: "As soon as I do so many of these, I'll get to do those." If, for example, production scheduled for the day featured small, rectangular strips in three colors, the game might go: "As soon as I finish a thousand of the green ones, I'll click some brown ones." And, with success in attaining the objective of working with brown materials, a new goal of "I'll get to do the white ones" might be set. Or the new goal might involve switching dies.

Scraping the block made the game more interesting by adding to the number of possible variations in its playing; and, what was perhaps more important, provided the only substantial reward, save for going to the lavatory or getting a drink of water, on days when work with one die and one color of material was scheduled. As a physical operation, scraping the block was fairly simple; it involved application of a coarse file to the upper surface of the block to remove roughness and unevenness resulting from the wear and tear of die pene-

tration. But, as part of the intellectual and emotional content of the game of work, it could be in itself a source of variation in activity. The upper left-hand corner of the block could be chewed up in the clicking of 1,000 white trapezoid pieces, then scraped. Next, the upper right-hand corner, and so on until the entire block had been worked over. Then, on the next round of scraping by quadrants, there was the possibility of a change of color or die to green trapezoid or white oval pieces.

Thus the game of work might be described as a continuous sequence of short-range production goals with achievement rewards in the form of activity change. The superiority of this relatively complex and self-determined system over the technically simple and outside-controlled job satisfaction injections experienced by Milner at the beginner's table in a shop of the feather industry should be immediately apparent:

> Twice a day our work was completely changed to break the monotony. First Jennie would give us feathers of a brilliant green, then bright orange or a light blue or black. The "ohs" and "ahs" that came from the girls at each change was proof enough that this was an effective way of breaking the monotony of the tedious work.[9]

But a hasty conclusion that I was having lots of fun playing my clicking game should be avoided. These games were not as interesting in the experiencing as they might seem to be from the telling. Emotional tone of the activity was low, and intellectual currents weak. Such rewards as scraping the block or "getting to do the blue ones" were not very exciting, and the stretches of repetitive movement involved in achiev-

[9] Lucille Milner, *Education of An American Liberal*, Horizon Press, New York, 1954, p. 97.

ing them were long enough to permit lapses into obsessive reverie. Henri de Man speaks of "clinging to the remnants of joy in work," and this situation represented just that. How tenacious the clinging was, how long I could have "stuck it out" with my remnants, was never determined. Before the first week was out this adjustment to the work situation was complicated by other developments. The game of work continued, but in a different context. Its influence became decidedly subordinated to, if not completely overshadowed by, another source of job satisfaction.

INFORMAL SOCIAL ACTIVITY OF THE WORK GROUP: TIMES AND THEMES

The change came about when I began to take serious note of the social activity going on around me; my attentiveness to this activity came with growing involvement in it. What I heard at first, before I started to listen, was a stream of disconnected bits of communication which did not make much sense. Foreign accents were strong and referents were not joined to coherent contexts of meaning. It was just "jabbering." What I saw at first, before I began to observe, was occasional flurries of horseplay so simple and unvarying in pattern and so childish in quality that they made no strong bid for attention. For example, Ike would regularly switch off the power at Sammy's machine whenever Sammy made a trip to the lavatory or the drinking fountain. Correlatively, Sammy invariably fell victim to the plot by making no attempt to operate his clicking hammer after returning to the shop. And, as the simple pattern went, this blind stumbling into the trap was always followed by indignation and reproach from Sammy, smirking satisfaction from Ike, and mild paternal scolding from

George. My interest in this procedure was at first confined to wondering when Ike would weary of his tedious joke or when Sammy would learn to check his power switch before trying the hammer.

But, as I began to pay closer attention, as I began to develop familiarity with the communication system, the disconnected became connected, the nonsense made sense, the obscure became clear, and the silly actually funny. And, as the content of the interaction took on more and more meaning, the interaction began to reveal structure. There were "times" and "themes," and roles to serve their enaction. The interaction had subtleties, and I began to savor and appreciate them. I started to record what hitherto had seemed unimportant.

Times

This emerging awareness of structure and meaning included recognition that the long day's grind was broken by interruptions of a kind other than the formally instituted or idiosyncratically developed disjunctions in work routine previously described. These additional interruptions appeared in daily repetition in an ordered series of informal interactions. They were, in part, but only in part and in very rough comparison, similar to those common fractures of the production process known as the coffee break, the coke break, and the cigarette break. Their distinction lay in frequency of occurrence and in brevity. As phases of the daily series, they occurred almost hourly, and so short were they in duration that they disrupted work activity only slightly. Their significance lay not so much in their function as rest pauses, although it cannot be denied that physical refreshment was involved. Nor did their chief importance lie in the accentuation of progress points in the passage of time, although they could perform that function far more strikingly than the hour hand on the dull face of George's alarm clock. If the daily series of interruptions be likened to a clock, then the comparison might best be made with a special kind of cuckoo clock, one with a cuckoo which can provide variation in its announcements and can create such an interest in them that the intervening minutes become filled with intellectual content. The major significance of the interactional interruptions lay in such a carryover of interest. The physical interplay which momentarily halted work activity would initiate verbal exchanges and thought processes to occupy group members until the next interruption. The group interactions thus not only marked off the time; they gave it content and hurried it along.

Most of the breaks in the daily series were designated as "times" in the parlance of the clicker operators, and they featured the consumption of food or drink of one sort or another. There was coffee time, peach time, banana time, fish time, coke time, and, of course, lunch time. Other interruptions, which formed part of the series but were not verbally recognized as times, were window time, pickup time, and the staggered quitting times of Sammy and Ike. These latter unnamed times did not involve the partaking of refreshments.

My attention was first drawn to this times business during my first week of employment when I was encouraged to join in the sharing of two peaches. It was Sammy who provided the peaches; he drew them from his lunch box after making the announcement, "Peach time!" On this first occasion I refused the proffered fruit, but thereafter regularly consumed my half peach. Sammy continued to provide the peaches and to make the "Peach time!" announcement, although there were days when

Ike would remind him that it was peach time, urging him to hurry up with the mid-morning snack. Ike invariably complained about the quality of the fruit, and his complaints fed the fires of continued banter between peach donor and critical recipient. I did find the fruit a bit on the scrubby side but felt, before I achieved insight into the function of peach time, that Ike was showing poor manners by looking a gift horse in the mouth. I wondered why Sammy continued to share his peaches with such an ingrate.

Banana time followed peach time by approximately an hour. Sammy again provided the refreshments, namely, one banana. There was, however, no four-way sharing of Sammy's banana. Ike would gulp it down by himself after surreptitiously extracting it from Sammy's lunch box, kept on a shelf behind Sammy's work station. Each morning, after making the snatch, Ike would call out, "Banana time!" and proceed to down his prize while Sammy made futile protests and denunciations. George would join in with mild remonstrances, sometimes scolding Sammy for making so much fuss. The banana was one which Sammy brought for his own consumption at lunch time; he never did get to eat his banana, but kept bringing one for his lunch. At first this daily theft startled and amazed me. Then I grew to look forward to the daily seizure and the verbal interaction which followed.

Window time came next. It followed banana time as a regular consequence of Ike's castigation by the indignant Sammy. After "taking" repeated references to himself as a person badly lacking in morality and character, Ike would "finally" retaliate by opening the window which faced Sammy's machine, to let the "cold air" blow in on Sammy. The slandering which would, in its echolalic repetition, wear down Ike's patience and forbearance usually took the form of the invidious comparison: "George is a good daddy! Ike is a bad man! A very bad man!" Opening the window would take a little time to accomplish and would involve a great deal of verbal interplay between Ike and Sammy, both before and after the event. Ike would threaten, make feints toward the window, then finally open it. Sammy would protest, argue, and make claims that the air blowing in on him would give him a cold; he would eventually have to leave his machine to close the window. Sometimes the weather was slightly chilly, and the draft from the window unpleasant; but cool or hot, windy or still, window time arrived each day. (I assume that it was originally a cold season development.) George's part in this interplay, in spite of the "good daddy" laudations, was to encourage Ike in his window work. He would stress the tonic values of fresh air and chide Sammy for his unappreciativeness.

Following window time came lunch time, a formally designated half-hour for the midday repast and rest break. At this time, informal interaction would feature exchanges between Ike and George. The former would start eating his lunch a few minutes before noon, and the latter, in his role as straw boss, would censure him for malobservance of the rules. Ike's off-beat luncheon usually involved a previous tampering with George's alarm clock. Ike would set the clock ahead a few minutes in order to maintain his eating schedule without detection, and George would discover these small daylight saving changes.

The first "time" interruption of the day I did not share. It occurred soon after I arrived on the job, at eight o'clock. George and Ike would share a small pot of coffee brewed on George's hot plate.

Pickup time, fish time, and coke time came in the afternoon. I name it pickup time to represent the official visit of the man who made daily calls to cart away boxes of clicked materials. The arrival of the pickup man, a Negro, was always a noisy one, like the arrival of a daily passenger train in an isolated small town. Interaction attained a quick peak of intensity to crowd into a few minutes all communications, necessary and otherwise. Exchanges invariably included loud depreciations by the pickup man of the amount of work accomplished in the clicking department during the preceding twenty-four hours. Such scoffing would be on the order of "Is that all you've got done? What do you boys do all day?" These devaluations would be countered with allusions to the "soft job" enjoyed by the pickup man. During the course of the exchanges news items would be dropped, some of serious import, such as reports of accomplished or impending layoffs in the various plants of the company, or of gains or losses in orders for company products. Most of the news items, however, involved bits of information on plant employees told in a light vein. Information relayed by the clicker operators was usually told about each other, mainly in the form of summaries of the most recent kidding sequences. Some of this material was repetitive, carried over from day to day. Sammy would be the butt of most of this newscasting, although he would make occasional counter-reports on Ike and George. An invariable part of the interactional content of pickup time was Ike's introduction of the pickup man to George. "Meet Mr. Papeatis!" Ike would say in mock solemnity and dignity. Each day the pickup man "met" Mr. Papeatis, to the obvious irritation of the latter. Another pickup time invariably would bring Baby (or Mable) into the interaction. George would always issue the loud warning to the pickup man: "Now I want you to stay away from Baby! She's Henry's girl!" Henry was a burly Negro with a booming bass voice who made infrequent trips to the clicking room with lift-truck loads of materials. He was reputedly quite a ladies' man among the colored population of the factory. George's warning to "Stay away from Baby!" was issued to every Negro who entered the shop. Baby's only part in this was to laugh at the horseplay.

About mid-afternoon came fish time. George and Ike would stop work for a few minutes to consume some sort of pickled fish which Ike provided. Neither Sammy nor I partook of this nourishment, nor were we invited. For this omission I was grateful; the fish, brought in a newspaper and with head and tail intact, produced a reverse effect on my appetite. George and Ike seemed to share a great liking for fish. Each Friday night, as a regular ritual, they would enjoy a fish dinner together at a nearby restaurant. On these nights Ike would work until 8:30 and leave the plant with George.

Coke time came late in the afternoon, and was an occasion for total participation. The four of us took turns in buying the drinks and in making the trip for them to a fourth floor vending machine. Through George's manipulation of the situation, it eventually became my daily chore to go after the cokes; the straw boss had noted that I made a much faster trip to the fourth floor and back than Sammy or Ike.

Sammy left the plant at 5:30, and Ike ordinarily retired from the scene an hour and a half later. These quitting times were not marked by any distinctive interaction save the one regular exchange between Sammy and George over the former's "early washup." Sammy's tendency was to crowd his washing up toward five o'clock, and it was

George's concern to keep it from further creeping advance. After Ike's departure came Boo's arrival. Boo's was a striking personality productive of a change in topics of conversation to fill in the last hour of the long workday.

Themes

To put flesh, so to speak, on this interactional frame of "times," my work group had developed various "themes" of verbal interplay which had become standardized in their repetition. These topics of conversation ranged in quality from an extreme of nonsensical chatter to another extreme of serious discourse. Unlike the times, these themes flowed one into the other in no particular sequence of predictability. Serious conversation could suddenly melt into horseplay, and vice versa. In the middle of a serious discussion on the high cost of living, Ike might drop a weight behind the easily startled Sammy, or hit him over the head with a dusty paper sack. Interaction would immediately drop to a low comedy exchange of slaps, threats, guffaws, and disapprobations which would invariably include a ten-minute echolalia of "Ike is a bad man, a very bad man! George is a good daddy, a very fine man!" Or, on the other hand, a stream of such invidious comparisons as followed a surreptitious switching-off of Sammy's machine by the playful Ike might merge suddenly into a discussion of the pros and cons of saving for one's funeral.

"Kidding themes" were usually started by George or Ike, and Sammy was usually the butt of the joke. Sometimes Ike would have to "take it," seldom George. One favorite kidding theme involved Sammy's alleged receipt of $100 a month from his son. The points stressed were that Sammy did not have to work long hours, or did not have to work at all, because he had a son to support him. George would always point out that he sent money to his daughter; she did not send money to him. Sammy received occasional calls from his wife, and his claim that these calls were requests to shop for groceries on the way home were greeted with feigned disbelief. Sammy was ribbed for being closely watched, bossed, and henpecked by his wife, and the expression "Are you man or mouse?" became an echolalic utterance, used both in and out of the original context.

Ike, who shared his machine and the work scheduled for it with Boo, the night operator, came in for constant invidious comparison on the subject of output. The socially isolated Boo, who chose work rather than sleep on his lonely night shift, kept up a high level of performance, and George never tired of pointing this out to Ike. It so happened that Boo, an Arabian Moslem from Palestine, had no use for Jews in general; and Ike, who was Jewish, had no use for Boo in particular. Whenever George would extol Boo's previous night's production, Ike would try to turn the conversation into a general discussion on the need for educating the Arabs. George, never permitting the development of serious discussion on this topic, would repeat a smirking warning, "You watch out for Boo! He's got a long knife!"

The "poom poom" theme was one that caused no sting. It would come up several times a day to be enjoyed as unbarbed fun by the three older clicker operators. Ike was usually the one to raise the question, "How many times you go poom poom last night?" The person questioned usually replied with claims of being "too old for poom poom." If this theme did develop a goat, it was I. When it was pointed out that I was a younger man, this provided further grist for the poom poom mill. I soon grew

weary of this poom poom business, so dear to the hearts of the three old satyrs, and, knowing where the conversation would inevitably lead, winced whenever Ike brought up the subject.

I grew almost as sick of a kidding theme which developed from some personal information contributed during a serious conversation on property ownership and high taxes. I dropped a few remarks about two acres of land which I owned in one of the western states, and from then on I had to listen to questions, advice, and general nonsensical comment in regard to "Danelly's farm."[10] This "farm" soon became stocked with horses, cows, pigs, chickens, ducks, and the various and sundry domesticated beasts so tunefully listed in "Old McDonald Had a Farm." George was a persistent offender with this theme. Where the others seemed to be mainly interested in statistics on livestock, crops, etc., George's teasing centered on a generous offering to help with the household chores while I worked in the fields. He would drone on, *ad nauseam*, "When I come to visit you, you will never have to worry about the housework, Danelly. I'll stay around the house when you go out to dig the potatoes and milk the cows; I'll stay in and peel potatoes and help your wife do the dishes." Danelly always found it difficult to change the subject on George, once the latter started to bear down on the farm theme.

Another kidding theme which developed out of serious discussion could be labelled "helping Danelly find a cheaper apartment." It became known to the group that Danelly had a pending housing problem, that he would need new

[10] This spelling is the closest I can come to the appellation given me in George's broken English and adopted by other members of the group.

quarters for his family when the permanent resident of his temporary summer dwelling returned from a vacation. This information engendered at first a great deal of sympathetic concern and, of course, advice on apartment hunting. Development into a kidding theme was immediately related to previous exchanges between Ike and George on the quality of their respective dwelling areas. Ike lived in "Lawndale," and George dwelt in the "Woodlawn" area. The new pattern featured the reading aloud of bogus "apartment for rent" ads in newspapers which were brought into the shop. Studying his paper at lunchtime, George would call out, "Here's an apartment for you, Danelly! Five rooms, stove heat, $20 a month, Lawndale Avenue!" Later, Ike would read from his paper, "Here's one! Six rooms, stove heat, dirt floor. $18.50 a month! At 55th and Woodlawn." Bantering would then go on in regard to the quality of housing or population in the two areas. The search for an apartment for Danelly was not successful.

Serious themes included the relating of major misfortunes suffered in the past by group members. George referred again and again to the loss, by fire, of his business establishment. Ike's chief complaints centered around a chronically ill wife who had undergone various operations and periods of hospital care. Ike spoke with discouragement of the expenses attendant upon hiring a housekeeper for himself and his children; he referred with disappointment and disgust to a teen-age son, an inept lad who "couldn't even fix his own lunch. He couldn't even make himself a sandwich!" Sammy's reminiscences centered on the loss of a flourishing business when he had to flee Europe ahead of Nazi invasion.

But all serious topics were not tales of woe. One favorite serious theme which

was optimistic in tone could be called either "Danelly's future" or "getting Danelly a better job." It was known that I had been attending "college," the magic door to opportunity although my specific course of study remained somewhat obscure. Suggestions poured forth on good lines of work to get into, and these suggestions were backed with accounts of friends, and friends of friends, who had made good via the academic route. My answer to the expected question, "Why are you working here?" always stressed the "lots of overtime" feature, and this explanation seemed to suffice for short-range goals.

There was one theme of especially solemn import, the "professor theme." This theme might also be termed "George's daughter's marriage theme"; for the recent marriage of George's only child was inextricably bound up with George's connection with higher learning. The daughter had married the son of a professor who instructed in one of the local colleges. This professor theme was not in the strictest sense a conversation piece; when the subject came up, George did all the talking. The two Jewish operatives remained silent as they listened with deep respect, if not actual awe, to George's accounts of the Big Wedding which, including the wedding pictures, entailed an expense of $1,000. It was monologue, but there was listening, there was communication, the sacred communication of a temple, when George told of going for Sunday afternoon walks on the Midway with the professor, or of joining the professor for a Sunday dinner. Whenever he spoke of the professor, his daughter, the wedding, or even of the new son-in-law, who remained for the most part in the background, a sort of incidental like the wedding cake, George was complete master of the interaction. His manner, in speaking to the rank-and-file of clicker operators, was indeed that of master deigning to notice his underlings. I came to the conclusion that it was the professor connection, not the straw-boss-ship or extra nickel an hour, which provided the fount of George's superior status in the group.

If the professor theme may be regarded as the cream of verbal interaction, the "chatter themes" should be classed as the dregs. The chatter themes were hardly themes at all; perhaps they should be labeled "verbal states," or "oral autisms." Some were of doubtful status as communication; they were like the howl or cry of an animal responding to its own physiological state. They were exclamations, ejaculations, snatches of song or doggerel, talkings-to-oneself, mutterings. Their classification as themes would rest on their repetitive character. They were echolalic utterances, repeated over and over. An already mentioned example would be Sammy's repetition of "George is a good daddy, a very fine man! Ike is a bad man, a very bad man!" Also, Sammy's repetition of "Don't bother me! Can't you see I'm busy? I'm a very busy man!" for ten minutes after Ike had dropped a weight behind him would fit the classification. Ike would shout "Mamariba!" at intervals between repetition of bits of verse, such as:

Mama on the bed,
Papa on the floor,
Baby in the crib
Says giver some more!

Sometimes the three operators would pick up one of these simple chatterings in a sort of chorus. "Are you man or mouse? I ask you, are you man or mouse?" was a favorite of this type.

So initial discouragement with the meagerness of social interaction I now recognized as due to lack of observation. The interaction was there, in constant flow. It captured attention and held interest to make the long day pass. The twelve hours of "click,————move die,————click,———— move die" became as easy to endure as eight hours of varied activity in the oil fields or eight hours of playing the piecework game in a machine shop. The "beast of boredom" was gentled to the harmlessness of a kitten.

BLACK FRIDAY: DISINTEGRATION OF THE GROUP

But all this was before "Black Friday." Events of that dark day shattered the edifice of interaction, its framework of times and mosaic of themes, and reduced the work situation to a state of social atomization and machine-tending drudgery. The explosive element was introduced deliberately, but without prevision of its consequences.

On Black Friday, Sammy was not present; he was on vacation. There was no peach time that morning, of course, and no banana time. But George and Ike held their coffee time, as usual; and a steady flow of themes was filling the morning quite adequately. It seemed like a normal day in the making, at least one which was going to meet the somewhat reduced expectations created by Sammy's absence.

Suddenly I was possessed of an inspiration for modification of the professor theme. When the idea struck, I was working at Sammy's machine, clicking out leather parts for billfolds. It was not difficult to get the attention of close neighbor Ike to suggest *sotto voce*, "Why don't you tell him you saw the professor teaching in a barber college on Madison Street? . . . Make it near Halsted Street."

Ike thought this one over for a few minutes, and caught the vision of its possibilities. After an interval of steady application to his clicking, he informed the unsuspecting George of his near West Side discovery; he had seen the professor busy at his instructing in a barber college in the lower reaches of Hobohemia.

George reacted to this announcement with stony silence. The burden of questioning Ike for further details on his discovery fell upon me. Ike had not elaborated his story very much before we realized that the show was not going over. George kept getting redder in the face, and more tight-lipped; he slammed into his clicking with increased vigor. I made one last weak attempt to keep the play on the road by remarking that barber colleges paid pretty well. George turned to hiss at me, "You'll have to go to Kankakee with Ike!" I dropped the subject. Ike whispered to me, "George is sore!"

George was indeed sore. He didn't say another word the rest of the morning. There was no conversation at lunchtime, nor was there any after lunch. A pall of silence had fallen over the clicker room. Fish time fell a casualty. George did not touch the coke I brought for him. A very long, very dreary afternoon dragged on. Finally, after Ike left for home, George broke the silence to reveal his feelings to me:

> Ike acts like a five-year-old, not a man! He doesn't even have the respect of the niggers. But he's got to act like a man around here! He's always fooling around! I'm going to stop that! I'm going to show him his place!
>
> . . . Jews will ruin you, if you let them. I don't care if he sings, but the first time he mentions my name, I'm going to shut him up! It's always "Meet Mr. Papeatis! George is a good daddy!" And all that. He's paid to work! If he doesn't work, I'm going to tell Joe! [The superintendent.]

Then came a succession of dismal workdays devoid of times and barren of themes. Ike did not sing, nor did he recite bawdy verse. The shop songbird was caught in the grip of icy winter. What meager communication there was took a sequence of patterns which proved interesting only in retrospect.

For three days, George would not speak to Ike. Ike made several weak attempts to break the wall of silence which George had put between them, but George did not respond; it was as if he did not hear. George would speak to me, on infrequent occasions, and so would Ike. They did not speak to each other.

On the third day George advised me of his new communication policy, designed for dealing with Ike, and for Sammy, too, when the latter returned to work. Interaction was now on a "strictly business" basis, with emphasis to be placed on raising the level of shop output. The effect of this new policy on production remained indeterminate. Before the fourth day had ended, George got carried away by his narrowed interests to the point of making sarcastic remarks about the poor work performances of the absent Sammy. Although addressed to me, these caustic depreciations were obviously for the benefit of Ike. Later in the day Ike spoke to me, for George's benefit, of Sammy's outstanding ability to turn out billfold parts. For the next four days, the prevailing silence of the shop was occasionally broken by either harsh criticism or fulsome praise of Sammy's outstanding workmanship. I did not risk replying to either impeachment or panegyric for fear of involvement in further situational deteriorations.

Twelve-hour days were creeping again at snail's pace. The strictly business communications were of no help, and the sporadic bursts of distaste or enthusiasm for Sammy's clicking ability helped very little. With the return of boredom, came a return of fatigue. My legs tired as the afternoons dragged on, and I became engaged in conscious efforts to rest one by shifting my weight to the other. I would pause in my work to stare through the barred windows at the grimy brick wall across the alley; and, turning my head, I would notice that Ike was staring at the wall too. George would do very little work after Ike left the shop at night. He would sit in a chair and complain of weariness and sore feet.

In desperation, I fell back on my game of work, my blues and greens and whites, my ovals and trapezoids, and my scraping the block. I came to surpass Boo, the energetic night worker, in volume of output. George referred to me as a "day Boo" (day-shift Boo) and suggested that I "keep" Sammy's machine. I managed to avoid this promotion, and consequent estrangement with Sammy, by pleading attachment to my own machine.

When Sammy returned to work, discovery of the cleavage between George and Ike left him stunned. "They were the best of friends!" he said to me in bewilderment.

George now offered Sammy direct, savage criticisms of his work. For several days the good-natured Sammy endured these verbal aggressions without losing his temper; but when George shouted at him, "You work like a preacher!" Sammy became very angry, indeed. I had a few anxious moments when I thought that the two old friends were going to come to blows.

Then, thirteen days after Black Friday, came an abrupt change in the pattern of interaction. George and Ike spoke to each other again, in friendly conversation:

I noticed Ike talking to George after lunch. The two had newspapers of fish at George's cabinet. Ike was excited; he said, "I'll pull up a chair!" The two ate for ten minutes. . . . It seems that they went up to the 22nd Street Exchange together during lunch period to cash pay checks.

That afternoon Ike and Sammy started to play again, and Ike burst once more into song. Old themes reappeared as suddenly as the desert flowers in spring. At first, George managed to maintain some show of the dignity of superordination. When Ike started to sing snatches of "You Are My Sunshine," George suggested that he get "more production." Then Ike backed up George in pressuring Sammy for more production. Sammy turned this exhortation into low comedy by calling Ike a "slave driver" and by shouting over and over again, "Don't bother me! I'm a busy man!" On one occasion, as if almost overcome with joy and excitement, Sammy cried out, "Don't bother me! I'll tell Rothman! [the company president] I'll tell the union! Don't mention my name! I hate you!"

I knew that George was definitely back into the spirit of the thing when he called to Sammy, "Are you man or mouse?" He kept up the "man or mouse" chatter for some time.

George was for a time reluctant to accept fruit when it was offered to him, and he did not make a final capitulation to coke time until five days after renewal of the fun and fooling. Strictly speaking, there never was a return to banana time, peach time, or window time. However, the sharing and snitching of fruit did go on once more, and the window in front of Sammy's machine played a more prominent part than ever in the renaissance of horseplay in the clicker room. In fact, the "rush to the window" became an integral part of increasingly complex themes and repeated sequences of intereaction. This window rushing became especially bound up with new developments which featured what may be termed the "anal gesture."[11] Introduced by Ike, and given backing by an enthusiastic, very playful George, the anal gesture became a key component of fun and fooling during the remaining weeks of my stay in the shop:

> Ike broke wind, and put his head in his hand on the block as Sammy grabbed a rod and made a mock rush to open the window. He beat Ike on the head, and George threw some water on him, playfully. In came the Negro head of the Leather Department; he remarked jokingly that we should take out the machines and make a playroom out of the shop.

Of course, George's demand for greater production was metamorphized into horseplay. His shout of "Production please!" became a chatter theme to accompany the varied antics of Ike and Sammy.

The professor theme was dropped completely. George never again mentioned his Sunday walks on the Midway with the professor.

CONCLUSIONS

Speculative assessment of the possible significance of my observations on information interaction in the clicking

room may be set forth in a series of general statements.

Practical Application

First, in regard to possible practical application to problems of industrial management, these observations seem to support the generally accepted notion that one key source of job satisfaction lies in the informal interaction shared by members of a work group. In the clicking room situation the spontaneous development of a patterned combination of horseplay, serious conversation, and frequent sharing of food and drink reduced the monotony of simple, repetitive operations to the point where a regular schedule of long work days became livable. This kind of group interplay may be termed "consumatory" in the sense indicated by Dewey, when he makes a basic distinction between "instrumental" and "consumatory" communication.[12] The enjoyment of communication "for its own sake" as "mere sociabilities," as "free, aimless social intercourse," brings job satisfaction, at least job endurance, to work situations largely bereft of creative experience.

In regard to another managerial concern, employee productivity, any appraisal of the influence of group interaction upon clicking-room output could be no more than roughly impressionistic. I obtained no evidence to warrant a claim that banana time, or any of its accompaniments in consumatory interaction, boosted production. To the contrary, my diary recordings express an occasional perplexity in the form of "How does this company manage to stay in business?" However, I did not obtain sufficient evidence to indicate that, under the prevailing conditions of laissez-faire management, the output of our

[11] I have been puzzled to note widespread appreciation of this gesture in the "consumatory" communication of the working men of this nation. For the present I leave it to clinical psychologists to account for the nature and pervasiveness of this social bond and confine myself to joining offended readers in the hope that someday our industrial workers will achieve such a level of refinement in thought and action that their behavior will be no more distressing to us than that of the college students who fill out our questionnaires.

[12] John Dewey, *Experience and Nature*, Open Court Publishing Co., Chicago, 1925, pp. 202–206.

group would have been more impressive if the playful cavorting of three middle-aged gentlemen about the barred windows had never been. As far as achievement of managerial goals is concerned, the most that could be suggested is that leavening the deadly boredom of individualized work routines with a concurrent flow of group festivities had a negative effect on turnover. I left the group, with sad reluctance, under the pressure of strong urgings to accept a research fellowship which would involve no factory toil. My fellow clickers stayed with their machines to carry on their labors in the spirit of banana time.

Theoretical Considerations

Secondly, possible contribution to ongoing sociological inquiry into the behavior of small groups in general, and factory work groups, in particular, may lie in one or more of the following ideational products of my clicking-room experience:

1. In their day-long confinement together in a small room spatially and socially isolated from other work areas of the factory the Clicking Department employees found themselves ecologically situated for development of a "natural" group. Such a development did take place; from worker intercommunications did emerge the full-blown sociocultural system of consummatory interactions which I came to share, observe, and record in the process of my socialization.

2. These interactions had a content which could be abstracted from the total existential flow of observable doings and sayings for labelling and objective consideration. That is, they represented a distinctive sub-culture, with its recurring patterns of reciprocal influencings which I have described as times and themes.

3. From these interactions may also be abstracted a social structure of statuses and roles. This structure may be discerned in the carrying out of the various informal activities which provide the content of the sub-culture of the group. The times and themes were performed with a system of roles which formed a sort of pecking hierarchy. Horseplay had its initiators and its victims, its amplifiers and its chorus; kidding had its attackers and attacked, its least attacked and its most attacked, its ready acceptors of attack and its strong resistors to attack. The fun went on with the participation of all, but within the controlling frame of status, a matter of who can say or do what to whom and get away with it.

4. In both the cultural content and the social structure of clicker group interaction could be seen the permeation of influences which flowed from the various multiple group memberships of the participants. Past and present "other-group" experiences or anticipated "outside" social connections provided significant materials for the building of themes and for the establishment and maintenance of status and role relationships. The impact of reference group affiliations on clicking-room interaction was notably revealed in the sacred, status-conferring expression of the professor theme. This impact was brought into very sharp focus in developments which followed my attempt to degrade the topic, and correlatively, to demote George.

5. Stability of the clicking-room social system was never threatened by immediate outside pressures. Ours was not an instrumental group, subject to disintegration in a losing struggle against environmental obstacles or oppositions. It was not striving for corporate goals; nor was it faced with the enmity of other groups. It was strictly

a consumatory group, devoted to the maintenance of patterns of self-entertainment. Under existing conditions, disruption of unity could come only from within.

Potentials for breakdown were endemic in the interpersonal interactions involved in conducting the group's activities. Patterns of fun and fooling had developed within a matrix of frustration. Tensions born of long hours of relatively meaningless work were released in the mock aggressions of horseplay. In the recurrent attack, defense, and counterattack there continually lurked the possibility that words or gestures harmless in conscious intent might cross the subtle boundary of accepted, playful aggression to be perceived as real assault. While such an occurrence might incur displeasure no more lasting than necessary for the quick clarification or creation of kidding norms, it might also spark a charge of hostility sufficient to disorganize the group.

A contributory potential for breakdown from within lay in the dissimilar "other group" experiences of the operators. These other-group affiliations and identifications could provide differences in tastes and sensitivities, including appreciation of humor, differences which could make maintenance of consensus in regard to kidding norms a hazardous process of trial and error adjustments.

6. The risk involved in this trial and error determination of consensus on fun and fooling in a touchy situation of frustration—mock aggression—was made evident when I attempted to introduce alterations in the professor theme. The group disintegrated, *instanter.* That is, there was an abrupt cessation of the interactions which constituted our groupness. Although both George and I were solidly linked in other-group affiliations with the higher learning, there was not enough agree-

ment in our attitudes toward university professors to prevent the interactional development which shattered our factory play group. George perceived my offered alterations as a real attack, and he responded with strong hostility directed against Ike, the perceived assailant, and Sammy, a fellow traveler.

My innovations, if accepted, would have lowered the tone of the sacred professor theme, if not to "Stay Away From Baby" ribaldry, then at least to the verbal slapstick level of "finding Danelly an apartment." Such a downgrading of George's reference group would, in turn, have downgraded George. His status in the shop group hinged largely upon his claimed relations with the professor.

7. Integration of our group was fully restored after a series of changes in the patterning and quality of clicking-room interaction. It might be said that reintegration took place *in* these changes, that the series was a progressive one of step-by-step improvement in relations, that re-equilibration was in process during the three weeks that passed between initial communication collapse and complete return to "normal" interaction.

The cycle of loss and recovery of equilibrium may be crudely charted according to the following sequence of phases: a) the stony silence of "not speaking"; b) the confining of communication to formal matters connected with work routines; c) the return of informal give-and-take in the form of harshly sarcastic kidding, mainly on the subject of work performance, addressed to a neutral go-between for the "benefit" of the object of aggression; d) highly emotional direct attack, and counterattack, in the form of criticism and defense of work performance; e) a sudden rapprochement expressed in serious, dignified, but friendly conversation; f) return to informal interaction in the form of mutually enjoyed mock aggression; g) return to informal inter-action in the form of regular patterns of sharing food and drink.

The group had disintegrated when George withdrew from participation; and, since the rest of us were at all times ready for rapprochement, reintegration was dependent upon his "return." Therefore, each change of phase in interaction on the road to recovery could be said to represent an increment of return on George's part. Or, conversely, each phase could represent an increment of reacceptance of punished deviants. Perhaps more generally applicable to description of a variety of reunion situations would be conceptualization of the phase changes as increments of reassociation without an atomistic differentiation of the "movements" of individuals.

8. To point out that George played a key role in this particular case of re-equilibration is not to suggest that the homeostatic controls of a social system may be located in a type of role or in a patterning of role relationships. Such controls could be but partially described in terms of human interaction; they would be functional to the total configuration of conditions within the field of influence. The automatic controls of a mechanical system operate as such only under certain achieved and controlled conditions. The human body recovers from disease when conditions for such homeostasis are "right." The clicking-room group regained equilibrium under certain undetermined conditions. One of a number of other possible outcomes could have developed had conditions not been favorable for recovery.

For purposes of illustration, and from reflection on the case, I would consider the following as possibly necessary conditions for reintegration of our group: a)

continued monotony of work operations; b) continued lack of a comparatively adequate substitute for the fun and fooling release from work tensions; c) inability of the operatives to escape from the work situation or from each other, within the work situation. George could not fire Ike or Sammy to remove them from his presence, and it would have been difficult for the three middle-aged men to find other jobs if they were to quit the shop. Shop space was small; and the machines close together. Like a submarine crew, they had to "live together"; d) Lack of conflicting definitions of the situation after Ike's perception of George's reaction to the "barber college" attack. George's anger and his punishment of the offenders was perceived as justified; e) Lack of introduction of new issues or causes which might have carried justification for new attacks and counter-attacks, thus leading interaction into a spiral of conflict and crystallization of conflict norms. For instance, had George reported his offenders to the superintendent for their poor work performance; had he, in his anger, committed some offense which would have led to reporting of a grievance to local union officials; had he made his anti-Semitic remarks in the presence of Ike or Sammy, or had I relayed these remarks to them; had I tried to "take over" Sammy's machine, as George had urged; then the interactional outcome might have been permanent disintegration of the group.

9. Whether or not the particular patterning of interactional change previously noted is somehow typical of a "re-equilibration process" is not a major question here. My purpose in discriminating the seven changes is primarily to suggest that re-equilibration, when it does occur, may be described in observable phases and that the emergence of each succeeding phase should be depen-

dent upon the configuration of conditions of the preceding one. Alternative eventual outcomes may change in their probabilities, as the phases succeed each other, just as prognosis for recovery in sickness may change as the disease situation changes.

10. Finally, discrimination of phase changes in social process may have practical as well as scientific value. Trained and skillful administrators might follow the practice in medicine of introducing aids to re-equilibration when diagnosis shows that they are needed.

12

Origins of Group Dynamics

Dorwin Cartwright & Alvin Zander

Whether one wishes to understand or to improve human behavior, it is necessary to know a great deal about the nature of groups. Neither a coherent view of man nor an advanced social technology is possible without dependable answers to a host of questions concerning the operation of groups, how individuals relate to groups, and how groups relate to larger society. When, and under what conditions, do groups form? What conditions are necessary for their growth and effective functioning? What factors foster the decline and disintegration of groups? How do groups affect the behavior, thinking, motivation, and adjustment of individuals? What makes some groups have powerful influence over members while other groups exert little or none? What characteristics of individuals are important determinants of the properties of groups? What determines the nature of relations between groups? When groups are part of a larger social system, what circumstances make them strengthen or weaken the more inclusive organization? How does the social environment of a group affect its properties? Questions like these *must* be answered before we will have a real understanding of human nature and human behavior. They must be answered, too, before we can hope to design an optimal society and bring it into being.

The student of group dynamics is interested in acquiring knowledge about the nature of groups and especially about the psychological and social forces associated with groups.

What, then, is group dynamics? The phrase has gained popular familiarity since World War II but, unfortunately, with its increasing circulation its meaning has become imprecise. According to one rather frequent usage, group dynamics refers to a sort of political ideology concerning the ways in which groups should be organized and managed. This ideology emphasizes the importance of democratic leadership, the participation of members in decisions, and the gains both to society and to individuals to be obtained through cooperative activities in groups. The critics of this view have sometimes caricatured it as making "togetherness" the supreme virtue, advocating that everything be done jointly in groups that have and need no leader because everyone participates fully and equally. A second popular usage of the term group dynamics has it refer to a set of techniques, such as role playing, buzz-sessions, observation and feedback of group process, and group decision, which have been employed widely during the past decade or two in training programs designed to improve skill in human relations and in the management of conferences and committees. These techniques have been identified most closely with the National Training Laboratories whose annual training programs at Bethel, Maine, have become widely known.

Source: From *Group Dynamics*, 3rd ed., by Dorwin Cartwright and Alvin Zander, pp. 4–21. Copyright © 1968 by Dorwin Cartwright and Alvin Zander. Reprinted by permission of Harper & Row Publishers, Inc.

183

According to the third usage of the term group dynamics, it refers to a field of inquiry dedicated to achieving knowledge about the nature of groups, the laws of their development, and their interrelations with individuals, other groups, and larger institutions.

It is not possible, of course, to legislate how terms are to be used in a language. Nevertheless, it is important for clarity of thinking and communication to distinguish among these three quite distinct things which have been given the same label in popular discussions. Everyone has an ideology, even though he may not be able to state it very explicitly, concerning the ways in which group life should be organized. Those responsible for the management of groups and the training of people for participation in groups can fulfill their responsibilities only by the use of techniques of one sort or another. But there is no rigidly fixed correspondence between a particular ideology about the "ideal" nature of groups and the use of particular techniques of management and training. And it should be obvious that the search for a better understanding of the nature of group life need not be linked to a particular ideology or adherence to certain techniques of management. In this book we shall limit our usage of the term group dynamics to refer to the field of inquiry dedicated to advancing knowledge about the nature of group life.

Group dynamics, in this sense, is a branch of knowledge or an intellectual specialization. Being concerned with human behavior and social relationships, it can be located within the social sciences. And yet it cannot be identified readily as a subpart of any of the traditional academic disciplines. In order to gain a better understanding of how group dynamics differs from other familiar fields, let us consider briefly some of its distinguishing characteristics.

1. Emphasis on theoretically significant empirical research. We noted above that an interest in groups can be found throughout history and that such an interest cannot, therefore, distinguish group dynamics from its predecessors. The difference lies, rather, in the way this interest is exploited. Until the beginning of the present century those who were curious about the nature of groups relied primarily upon personal experience and historical records to provide answers to their questions. Not being burdened by the necessity of accounting for an accumulation of carefully gathered empirical data, writers in this speculative era devoted their energies to the creation of comprehensive theoretical treatments of groups. These theoretical systems, especially the ones produced during the nineteenth century, were elaborate and widely inclusive, having been created by men of outstanding intellectual ability. The list of names from this era contains such impressive thinkers as Cooley, Durkheim, Freud, Giddings, LeBon, McDougall, Ross, Tarde, Tönnies, and Wundt. Their ideas can still be seen in contemporary discussions of group life.

By the second decade of this century an empiricist rebellion had begun in social science, principally in the United States and especially in psychology and sociology. Instead of being content with speculation about the nature of groups, a few people began to seek out facts and to attempt to distinguish between objective data and subjective impression. Although rather simple empirical questions initially guided this research, a fundamentally new criterion for evaluating knowledge about groups was established. Instead of asking merely whether some proposition about the nature of groups is plausible and logically consistent, those interested in groups began to demand that the proposition be supported by reliable data that can be reproduced by an independent investigator. Major effort went into the devising and improving of techniques of empirical research that would provide reliability of measurement, standardization of observation, effective experimental design, and the statistical analysis of data. When, in the late 1930's, group dynamics began to emerge as an identifiable field the empiricist rebellion was well along in social psychology and sociology, and from the outset group dynamics could employ the research methods characteristic of an empirical science. In fact, group dynamics is to be distinguished from its intellectual predecessors primarily by its basic reliance on careful observation, quantification, measurement, and experimentation.

But one should not identify group dynamics too closely with extreme empiricism. Even in its earliest days, work in group dynamics displayed an interest in the construction of theory and the derivation of testable hypotheses from theory, and it has come progressively to maintain a close interplay between data collection and the advancement of theory.

2. Interest in dynamics and interdependence of phenomena. Although the phrase group dynamics specifies groups as the object of study, it also focuses attention more sharply on questions about the dynamics of group life. The student of group dynamics is not satisfied with just a description of the properties of groups or of events associated with groups. Nor is he content with a classification of types of groups or of forms of group behavior. He wants to know how the phenomena he ob-

serves depend on one another and what new phenomena might result from the creation of conditions never before observed. In short, he seeks to discover general principles concerning what conditions produce what effects.

This search requires the asking of many detailed questions about the interdependence among specific phenomena. If a change of membership occurs in a group, which other features of the group will change and which will remain stable? Under what conditions does a group tend to undergo a change of leadership? What are the pressures in a group which bring about the uniformity of thinking among its members? What conditions inhibit creativity among group members? What changes in a group will heighten productivity, lower it, or not affect it at all? If the cohesiveness of a group is raised, which other of its features will change? Answers to questions like these reveal how certain properties and processes depend on others.

Theories of group dynamics attempt to formulate lawful relations among phenomena such as these. As these theories have been elaborated, they have guided work in group dynamics toward the intensive investigation of such things as change, resistance to change, social pressures, influence, coercion, power, cohesion, attraction, rejection, interdependence, equilibrium, and instability. Terms like these, by suggesting the operation of psychological and social forces, refer to the dynamic aspects of groups and play an important role in theories of group dynamics.

3. Interdisciplinary relevance. It is important to recognize that research on the dynamics of groups has not been associated exclusively with any one of the social science disciplines. Sociologists have, of course, devoted great energy to

the study of groups, as illustrated by investigations of the family, gangs, work groups, military units, and voluntary associations. Psychologists have directed their attention to many of the same kinds of groups, concentrating for the most part on the ways groups influence the behavior, attitudes, and personalities of individuals and the effects of characteristics of individuals on group functioning. Cultural anthropologists, while investigating many of the same topics as sociologists and psychologists, have contributed data on groups living under conditions quite different from those of modern industrial society. Political scientists have extended their traditional interest in large institutions to include studies of the functioning of legislative groups, pressure groups, and the effects of group membership on voting. And economists have come increasingly to collect data on the way decisions to spend or save money are made in the family, how family needs and relationships affect the size of the labor force, how goals of unions affect policies in business, and how decisions having economic consequences are reached in businesses of various kinds. Since an interest in groups is shared by the various social science disciplines, it is clear that any general knowledge about the dynamics of groups has significance widely throughout the social sciences.

4. Potential applicability of findings to social practice. Everyone who feels a responsibility for improving the functioning of groups and the quality of their consequences for individuals and society must base his actions upon some more or less explicit view of the effects that will be produced by different conditions and procedures. Anyone who is concerned with improving the quality of work in a research team, the effectiveness of a Sunday school class, the

morale of a military unit, with decreasing the destructive consequences of intergroup conflict, or with attaining any socially desirable objective through groups, can make his efforts more effective by basing them on a firm knowledge of the laws governing group life.

The various professions that specialize in dealing with particular needs of individuals and of society have much to gain from advances in the scientific study of groups. One outstanding development in the more advanced societies during the past century has been the increasing differentiation undergone by the traditional professions of medicine, law, education, and theology. Today there are people who receive extensive training and devote their lives to such professional specialities as labor-management mediation, public health education, marriage counseling, human relations training, intergroup relations, social group work, pastoral counseling, hospital administration, adult education, public administration, psychiatry, and clinical psychology—just to mention a few. The professionalization of practice in these many areas has brought about a self-conscious desire to improve standards and the establishment of requirements for proper training. The major universities now have professional schools in many of these fields to provide such training. As this training has been extended and rationalized, members of these professions have become increasingly aware of the need for knowledge of the basic findings and principles produced in the social sciences. All of these professions must work with people, not simply as individuals but in groups and through social institutions. It should not be surprising, therefore, to find that courses in group dynamics are becoming more and more common in the professional schools, that people trained in group dynamics are being employed by agencies concerned with professional practice, and that group dynamics research is often carried out in connection with the work of such agencies.

In summary, then, we have proposed that group dynamics should be defined as a field of inquiry dedicated to advancing knowledge about the nature of groups, the laws of their development, and their interrelations with individuals, other groups, and larger institutions. It may be identified by four distinguishing characteristics: *(a)* an emphasis on theoretically significant empirical research, *(b)* an interest in dynamics and the interdependence among phenomena, *(c)* a broad relevance to all the social sciences, and *(d)* the potential applicability of its findings in efforts to improve the functioning of groups and their consequences on individuals and society. Thus conceived, group dynamics need not be associated with any particular ideology concerning the ways in which groups should be organized and managed nor with the use of any particular techniques of group management. In fact, it is a basic objective of group dynamics to provide a better scientific basis for ideology and practice.

CONDITIONS FOSTERING THE RISE OF GROUP DYNAMICS

Group dynamics began, as an identifiable field of inquiry, in the United States toward the end of the 1930's. Its origination as a distinct specialty is associated primarily with Kurt Lewin (1890–1947) who popularized the term group dynamics, made significant contributions to both research and theory in group dynamics, and in 1945 established the first organization devoted explicitly to research on group dynamics. Lewin's contribution was of great importance, but, as we shall see in detail,

group dynamics was not the creation of just one person. It was, in fact, the result of many developments that occurred over a period of several years and in several different disciplines and professions. Viewed in historical perspective, group dynamics can be seen as the convergence of certain trends within the social sciences and, more broadly, as the product of the particular society in which it arose.

The time and place of the rise of group dynamics were, of course, not accidental. American society in the 1930's provided the kind of conditions required for the emergence of such an intellectual movement. And, over the years since that time, only certain countries have afforded a favorable environment for its growth. To date, group dynamics has taken root primarily in the United States and the countries of northwestern Europe, although there have also been important developments in Israel, Japan, and India. Three major conditions seem to have been required for its rise and subsequent growth.

A SUPPORTIVE SOCIETY

If any field of inquiry is to prosper, it must exist in a surrounding society which is sufficiently supportive to provide the institutional resources required. By the end of the 1930's cultural and economic conditions in the United States were favorable for the emergence and growth of group dynamics. Great value was placed on science, technology, rational problem-solving, and progress. There was a fundamental conviction that in a democracy human nature and society can be deliberately improved by education, religion, legislation, and hard work. American industry had grown so rapidly, it was believed, not only because of abundant natural resources but especially because it had acquired technological and administrative "know how." The heroes of American progress were inventors, like Bell, Edison, Franklin, Fulton, and Whitney, and industrialists who fashioned new social organizations for efficient mass production. Although there had grown up a myth about the inventor as a lone wolf working in his own tool shed, research was already becoming a large-scale operation—just how big may be seen in the fact that private and public expenditures for research in the United States in 1930 amounted to more than $160,000,000 and increased, even during the depression years, to nearly $350,000,000 by 1940.

Most of this research was, of course, in the natural and biological sciences and in engineering and medicine. The idea that research could be directed profitably to the solution of social problems gained acceptance much more slowly. But even in the 1930's significant resources were being allotted to the social sciences. The dramatic use of intelligence testing during World War I had stimulated research on human abilities and the application of testing procedures in school systems, industry, and government. "Scientific management," though slow to recognize the importance of social factors, was laying the groundwork for a scientific approach to the management of organizations. The belief that the solution of "social problems" could be facilitated by systematic fact-finding was gaining acceptance. Thomas and Znaniecki (45) had, by 1920, demonstrated that the difficulties accompanying the absorption of immigrants into American society could be investigated systematically; several research centers had been created to advance knowledge and to improve practice with respect to the welfare of children; by the early 1930's practices in social work and juvenile courts were being modified on the basis of findings

from an impressive series of studies on juvenile gangs in Chicago that had been conducted by Thrasher (46) and Shaw (40); and, enough research had been completed on intergroup relations by 1939 so that Myrdal (31) could write a comprehensive treatment of the "Negro problem" in America. Symptomatic of the belief in the feasibility of empirical research on social problems was the establishment in 1936 of the Society for the Psychological Study of Social Issues with 333 charter members. Thus, when the rapid expansion of group dynamics began after World War II, there were important segments of American society prepared to provide financial support for such research. Support came not only from academic institutions and foundations but also from business, the Federal Government, and various organizations concerned with improving human relations.

DEVELOPED PROFESSIONS

The attempt to formulate a coherent view of the nature of group life may be motivated by intellectual curiosity or by the desire to improve social practice. A study of the conditions bringing the field of group dynamics into existence reveals that both of these motivations played an important role. Interest in groups and a recognition of their importance in society were apparent early among social scientists, who according to a common stereotype are motivated by idle curiosity. But it should be also noted that some of the most influential early systematic writing about the nature of groups came from the pens of people working in the professions, people whose motivation has often been said to be purely practical. Before considering the social scientific background of group dynamics, we will describe briefly some of the developments within the professions that facilitated its rise.

Cartwright
+ Zander

By the 1930's a large number of distinct professions had come into existence in the United States, probably more than in any other country. Many of these worked directly with groups of people, and as they became concerned with improving the quality of their practice they undertook to codify procedures and to discover general principles for dealing with groups. It gradually became evident, more quickly in some professions than in others, that generalizations from experience can go only so far and that systematic research is required to produce a deeper understanding of group life. Thus, when group dynamics began to emerge as a distinct field, the leaders of some of the professions were well prepared to foster the idea that systematic research on group life could make a significant contribution to their professions. As a result, several professions helped to create a favorable atmosphere for the financing of group dynamics research, provided from their accumulated experience a broad systematic conception of group functioning from which hypotheses for research could be drawn, afforded facilities in which research could be conducted, and furnished the beginnings of a technology for creating and manipulating variables in experimentation on groups. Four professions played an especially important part in the origin and growth of group dynamics.

1. Social Group Work.
2. Group Psychotherapy.
3. Education.
4. Administration.

DEVELOPED SOCIAL SCIENCE

In considering the conditions that stimulated the present approach to group dynamics within the social sciences, it is essential to recognize that this approach could originate only because certain advances had been accomplished in the social sciences at large. Thus, the rise of group dynamics required not only a supportive society and developed professions but also developed social sciences.

A basic premise of group dynamics is that the methods of science can be employed in the study of groups. This assumption could be entertained seriously only after the more general belief had gained acceptance that man, his behavior, and his social relations can be properly subjected to scientific investigation. And, any question about the utilization of scientific methods for learning about human behavior and social relations could not rise, of course, before the methods of science were well developed. It was only in the nineteenth century that serious discussions of this possibility occurred. Comte's extensive treatment of positivism in 1830 provided a major advance in the self-conscious examination of basic assumptions about the possibility of subjecting human and social phenomena to scientific investigation; and the controversies over evolutionary theories of man in the last half of the century resulted in a drastically new view of the possibility of extending the scientific enterprise to human behavior. Not until the last decades of the nineteenth century were there many people actually observing, measuring, or conducting experiments on human behavior. The first psychological laboratory was established only in 1879.

The Reality of Groups. An important part of the early progress in social science consisted in clarifying certain basic assumptions about the reality of social phenomena. The first extensions of the scientific method of human behavior occurred in close proximity to biology. Techniques of experimentation and measurement were first applied to investigations of the responses of organisms to stimulation of the sense organs and to modification of responses due to repeated stimulation. There was never much doubt about the "existence" of individual organisms, but when attention turned to groups of people and to social institutions, a great confusion arose. Discussion of these matters invoked terms like "group mind," "collective representations," "collective unconscious," and "culture." And people argued heatedly as to whether such terms refer to any real phenomena or whether they are mere "abstractions" or "analogies." On the whole, the disciplines concerned with institutions (anthropology, economics, political science, and sociology) have freely attributed concrete reality to supra-individual entities, whereas psychology, with its interest in the physiological bases of behavior, has been reluctant to admit existence to anything other than the behavior of organisms. But in all these disciplines there have been conflicts between "institutionalists" and "behavioral scientists."

It may appear strange that social scientists should get involved in philosophical considerations about the nature of reality. As a matter of fact, however, the social scientist's view of reality makes a great deal of difference to his scientific behavior. In the first place, it determines what things he is prepared to subject to empirical investigation. Lewin pointed out this fact succinctly in the following statement (**22**, 190):

> Labeling something as "nonexistent" is equivalent to declaring it "out of bounds" for the scientist. Attributing "existence" to an item automatically makes it a duty of the scientist to consider this item as an object of research; it includes the necessity of considering its properties as "facts" which cannot be neglected in the total

system of theories; finally, it implies that the terms with which one refers to the item are acceptable as scientific "concepts" (rather than as "mere words").

Secondly, the history of science shows a close interaction between the techniques of research which at any time are available and the prevailing assumptions about reality. Insistence on the existence of phenomena that cannot at that time be objectively observed, measured, or experimentally manipulated accomplishes little of scientific value if it does not lead to the invention of appropriate techniques of empirical research. As a practical matter, the scientist is justified in excluding from consideration allegedly real entities whose empirical investigation appears impossible. And yet, as soon as a new technique makes it possible to treat empirically some new entity, this entity immediately acquires "reality" for the scientist. As Lewin noted (**22**, 193), "The taboo against believing in the existence of a social entity is probably most effectively broken by handling this entity experimentally."

The history of the "group mind" controversy well illustrates these points. The early insistence on the reality of the "group mind," before techniques for investigating such phenomena were developed, contributed little to their scientific study. Allport's denial of the reality of the group actually had a strongly liberating influence on social psychologists, for he was saying, in effect, "Let us not be immobilized by insisting on the reality of things which we cannot now deal with by means of existing techniques of research." He, and likeminded psychologists, were then able to embark upon a remarkably fruitful program of research on the attitudes of individuals toward institutions and on the behavior of individuals in social settings. Although this view of

Cartwright & Zander

reality was too limited to encourage the empirical study of properties of groups, it did stimulate the development of research techniques that subsequently made a broader view of reality scientifically feasible. Until these techniques were in existence those who persisted in attributing reality to groups and institutions were forced to rely on purely descriptive studies or armchair speculation from personal experience, and such work was legitimately criticized as being "subjective" since the objective techniques of science were rarely applied to such phenomena.

Development of Techniques of Research. Of extreme importance for the origin of group dynamics, then, was the shaping of research techniques that could be extended to research on groups. This process, of course, took time. It began in the last half of the nineteenth century with the rise of experimental psychology. Over the subsequent years more and more aspects of human experience and behavior were subjected to techniques of measurement and experimentation. Thus, for example, during the first third of this century impressive gains were made in the measurement of attitudes. Noteworthy among these were the scale of "social distance" developed by Bogardus (8), the comprehensive treatment of problems of scaling by Thurstone (47) and Thurstone and Chave (48), and the much simpler scaling technique of Likert (24). Parallel to these developments, and interacting with them, were major advances in statistics. By the late 1930s, powerful statistical methods had been fashioned, which made possible efficient experimental designs and the evaluation of the significance of quantitative findings. These advances were important, of course, not only for the rise of group dynamics but for progress in all the behavioral sciences.

Within this general development we may note three methodological gains contributing specifically to the rise of group dynamics.

1. Experiments on individual behavior in groups. As noted above, research in group dynamics is deeply indebted to experimental psychology for the invention of techniques for conducting experiments on the conditions affecting human behavior. But experimental psychology did not concern itself, at first, with social variables; it was only toward the beginning of the present century that a few investigators embarked upon experimental research designed to investigate the effects of social variables upon the behavior of individuals.

2. Controlled observation of social interaction. One might think that the most obvious device for learning about the nature of group functioning would be simply to watch groups in action. Indeed, this procedure has been employed by chroniclers and reporters throughout history and has continued to be a source of data, perhaps most impressively as employed by social anthropologists in their reports of the behavior, culture, and social structure of primitive societies. The major drawback of the procedure as a scientific technique is that the reports given by observers (the scientific data) depend to such a high degree upon the skill, sensitivity, and interpretive predilections of the observer. The first serious attempts to refine methods of observation, so that objective and quantitative data might be obtained, occurred around 1930 in the field of child psychology. A great amount of effort went into the construction of categories of observation that would permit an observer simply to indicate the presence or absence of a particular kind of behavior or social interaction during

the period of observation. Typically, reliability was heightened by restricting observation to rather overt interactions whose "meaning" could be revealed in a short span of time and whose classification required little interpretation by the observer. Methods were also developed for sampling the interactions of a large group of people over a long time so that efficient estimates of the total interaction could be made on the basis of more limited observations. By use of such procedures and by careful training of observers quantitative data of high reliability were obtained. The principal researchers responsible for these important advances were Goodenough (15), Jack (19), Olson (34), Parten (35), and Thomas (44).

3. Sociometry. A somewhat different approach to the study of groups is to ask questions of the members. Data obtained in this manner can, of course, reflect only those things the individual is able, and willing, to report. Nevertheless, such subjective reports from the members of a group might be expected to add valuable information to the more objective observations of behavior. Of the many devices for obtaining information from group members one of the earliest and most commonly used is the sociometric test, which was invented by Moreno (30). Although based essentially on subjective reports of individuals, the sociometric test provides quantifiable data about patterns of attractions and repulsions existing in a group. The publication by Moreno (30) in 1934 of a major book based on experience with the test and the establishment in 1937 of a journal, *Sociometry,* ushered in a prodigious amount of research employing the sociometric test and numerous variations of it.

The significance of sociometry for group dynamics lay both in the provision of a useful technique for research on groups and in the attention it directed to such features of groups as social position, patterns of friendship, subgroup formation, and, more generally, informal structure.

BEGINNINGS OF GROUP DYNAMICS

By the mid-1930's conditions were ripe within the social sciences for a rapid advance in empirical research on groups. And, in fact, a great burst of such activity did take place in America just prior to the entry of the United States into World War II. This research, moreover, began to display quite clearly the characteristics that are now associated with work in group dynamics. Within a period of approximately five years several important research projects were undertaken, more or less independently of one another but all sharing these distinctive features. We now briefly consider four of the more influential of these.

EXPERIMENTAL CREATION OF SOCIAL NORMS

In 1936 Sherif (42) published a book containing a systematic theoretical analysis of the concept *social norm* and an ingenious experimental investigation of the origin of social norms among groups of people. Probably the most important feature of this book was its bringing together of ideas and observations from sociology and anthropology and techniques of laboratory experimentation from experimental psychology. Sherif began by accepting the existence of customs, traditions, standards, rules, values, fashions, and other criteria of conduct (which he subsumed under the general label, social norm). Further, he agreed with Durkheim that

Cartwright & Zander

such "collective representations" have, from the point of view of the individual, the properties of exteriority and constraint. At the same time, however, he agreed with F. H. Allport that social norms have been too often treated as something mystical and that scientific progress can be achieved only by subjecting phenomena to acceptable techniques of empirical research. He proposed that social norms should be viewed simultaneously in two ways: (a) as the product of social interaction and (b) as social stimuli which impinge upon any given individual who is a member of a group having these norms. Conceived in this way, it would be possible to study experimentally the origin of social norms and their influence on individuals.

In formulating his research problem, Sherif drew heavily upon the findings of Gestalt psychology in the field of perception. He noted that this work had established that there need not necessarily be a fixed point-to-point correlation between the physical stimulus and the experience and behavior it arouses. The frame of reference a person brings to a situation influences in no small way how he sees that situation. Sherif proposed that psychologically a social norm functions as such a frame of reference. Thus, if two people with different norms face the same situation (for example, a Mohammedan and a Christian confront a meal of pork chops), they will see it and react to it in widely different ways. For each, however, the norm serves to give meaning and to provide a stable way of reacting to the environment.

Having thus related social norms to the psychology of perception, Sherif proceeded to ask how norms arise. It occurred to him that he might gain insight into this problem by placing people in a situation that had no clear structure and

in which they would not be able to bring to bear any previously acquired frame of reference or social norm. Sherif stated the general objective of his research as follows (**42**, 90–91):

. . . What will an individual do when he is placed in an objectively unstable situation in which all basis of comparison, as far as the external field of stimulation is concerned, is absent? In other words, what will he do when the external frame of reference is eliminated, in so far as the aspect in which we are interested is concerned? Will he give a hodgepodge of erratic judgments? Or will he establish a point of reference of his own? *Consistent* results in this situation may be taken as the index of a subjectively evolved frame of reference. . . .

Coming to the social level we can push our problem further. What will a group of people do in the same unstable situation? Will the different individuals in the group give a hodgepodge of judgments? Or will there be established a common norm peculiar to the particular group situation and depending upon the presence of these individuals together and their influence upon one another? If they in time come to perceive the uncertain and unstable situation which they face in common in such a way as to give it some sort of order, perceiving it as ordered by a frame of reference developed among them in the course of the experiment, and if this frame of reference is peculiar to the group, then we may say that we have at least the prototype of the psychological process involved in the formation of a norm in a group.

In order to subject these questions to experimental investigation. Sherif made use of what is known in psychology as the autokinetic effect. It had previously been shown in perceptual research that if a subject looks at a stationary point of light in an otherwise dark room he will soon see it as moving. Furthermore, there are considerable individual differences in the extent of perceived motion. Sherif's experiment consisted of placing subjects individually in the darkened room and getting judgments of the extent of apparent motion. He found that upon repeated test the subject establishes a range within which his judgments fall and that this range is peculiar to each individual. Sherif then repeated the experiment, but this time having groups of subjects observe the light and report aloud their judgments. Now he found that the individual ranges of judgment converged to a group range that was peculiar to the group. In additional variations Sherif was able to show that (**42,** 104):

> When the individual, in whom a range and a norm within that range are first developed in the individual situation, is put into a group situation, together with other individuals who also come into the situation with their own ranges and norms established in their own individual sessions, the ranges and norms tend to converge.

Moreover, "when a member of a group faces the same situation subsequently *alone,* after once the range and norm of his group have been established, he perceives the situation in terms of the range and norm that he brings from the group situation" (**42,** 105).

Sherif's study did much to establish the feasibility of subjecting group phenomena to experimental investigation. It should be noted that he did not choose to study social norms existing in any natural group. Instead, he formed new groups in the laboratory and observed the development of an entirely new social norm. Although Sherif's experimental situation might seem artificial, and even trivial, to the anthropologist or sociologist, this very artificiality gave the findings a generality not ordinarily achieved by naturalistic research. By subjecting a group-level concept,

like social norm, to psychological analysis, Sherif helped obliterate what he considered to be the unfortunate categorical separation of individual and group. And his research helped establish among psychologists the view that certain properties of groups have reality, for, as he concluded, "the fact that the norm thus established is peculiar to the group suggests that there is a factual psychological basis in the contentions of social psychologists and sociologists who maintain that new and supra-individual qualities arise in the group situations" (**42,** 105).

SOCIAL ANCHORAGE OF ATTITUDES

During the years 1935–39, Newcomb (**32**) was conducting an intensive investigation of the same general kind of problem that interested Sherif but with quite different methods. Newcomb selected a "natural" rather than a "laboratory" setting in which to study the operation of social norms and social influence processes, and he relied primarily upon techniques of attitude measurement, sociometry, and interviewing to obtain his data. Bennington College was the site of his study, the entire student body were his subjects, and attitudes toward political affairs provided the content of the social norms.

It was first established that the prevailing political atmosphere of the campus was "liberal" and that entering students, who came predominantly from "conservative" homes, brought with them attitudes that deviated from the college culture. The power of the college community to change attitudes of students was demonstrated by the fact that each year senior students were more liberal than freshmen. The most significant feature of this study, how-

Cartwright + Zander

ever, was its careful documentation of the ways in which these influences operated. Newcomb showed, for example, how the community "rewarded" students for adopting the approved attitudes. Thus, a sociometric-like test, in which students chose those "most worthy to represent the College at an intercollegiate gathering," revealed that the students thus chosen in each class were distinctly less conservative than those not so chosen. And, those students enjoying a reputation for having a close identification with the college, for being "good citizens," were also relatively more liberal in their political attitudes. By means of several ingenious devices Newcomb was able to discover the student's "subjective role," or self-view of his own relationship to the student community. Analysis of these data revealed several different ways in which students accommodated to the social pressures of the community. Of particular interest in this analysis was the evidence of conflicting group loyalties between membership in the college community and membership in the family group and some of the conditions determining the relative influence of each.

Newcomb's study showed that the attitudes of individuals are strongly rooted in the groups to which people belong, that the influence of a group upon an individual's attitudes depends upon the nature of the relationship between the individual and the group, and that groups evaluate members, partially at least, on the basis of their conformity to group norms. Although most of these points had been made in one form or another by writers in the speculative era of social science, this study was especially significant because it provided detailed, objective, and quantitative evidence. It thereby demonstrated, as

Sherif's study did in a different way, the feasibility of conducting scientific research on important features of group life.

GROUPS IN STREET CORNER SOCIETY

The sociological and anthropological background of group dynamics is most apparent in the third important study of this era. In 1937 W. F. Whyte moved into one of the slums of Boston to begin a three and one-half year study of social clubs, political organizations, and racketeering. His method was that of "the participant observer," which had been most highly developed in anthropological research. More specifically, he drew upon the experience of Warner and Arensberg which was derived from the "Yankee City" studies. In various ways he gained admittance to the social and political life of the community and faithfully kept notes of the various happenings that he observed or heard about. In the resulting book, Whyte (51) reported in vivid detail on the structure, culture, and functioning of the Norton Street gang and the Italian Community Club. The importance of these social groups in the life of their members and in the political structure of the larger society was extensively documented.

In the interpretation and systematization of his findings, Whyte was greatly influenced by the "interactionist" point of view that was then being developed by Arensberg and Chapple, and that was subsequently presented by such writers as Chapple (10), Bales (4), and Homans (18). The orientation derived by Mayo and his colleagues from the Western Electric studies is also evident in Whyte's analysis of his data. Although he made no effort to quantify the interactions he observed, Whyte's great care for detail lent a strong flavor of objectivity to his account of the interactions among the people he observed. His "higher order" concepts, like social structure, cohesion, leadership, and status, were clearly related to the more directly observable interactions among people, thus giving them a close tie with empirical reality.

The major importance of this study for subsequent work in group dynamics was three-fold: (a) It dramatized, and described in painstaking detail, the great significance of groups in the lives of individuals and in the functioning of larger social systems. (b) It gave impetus to the interpretation of group properties and processes in terms of interactions among individuals. (c) It generated a number of hypotheses concerning the relations among such variables as initiation of interaction, leadership, status, mutual obligations, and group cohesion. These hypotheses have served to guide much of Whyte's later work on groups as well as the research of many others.

EXPERIMENTAL MANIPULATION OF GROUP ATMOSPHERE

By far the most influential work in the emerging study of group dynamics was that of Lewin, Lippitt, and White (23, 25, Chap. 25). Conducted at the Iowa Child Welfare Research Station between 1937 and 1940, these investigations of group atmosphere and styles of leadership accomplished a creative synthesis of the various trends and developments considered above. In describing the background of this research, Lippitt noted that the issue of what constitutes "good" leadership had come to the fore in the professions of social

group work, education, and administration, and he observed that, with the exception of the Western Electric studies, remarkably little research had been conducted to help guide practice in these professions. In setting up his theoretical problem, he drew explicitly on the previous work in social, clinical, and child psychology, sociology, cultural anthropology, and political science. And in designing his research, he made use, with important modifications, of the available techniques of experimental psychology, controlled observation, and sociometry. This work, then, relied heavily upon previous advances in social science and the professions, but it had an originality and significance which immediately produced a marked impact on all these fields.

The basic objective of this research was to study the influences upon the group as a whole and upon individual members of certain experimentally induced "group atmospheres," or "styles of leadership." Groups of ten- and eleven-year-old children were formed to meet regularly over a period of several weeks under the leadership of an adult, who induced the different group atmospheres. In creating these groups care was taken to assure their intial comparability; by utilizing the sociometric test, playground observations, and teacher interviews, the structural properties of the various groups were made as similar as possible; on the basis of school records and interviews with the children, the backgrounds and individual characteristics of the members were equated for all the groups; and the same group activities and physical setting were employed in every group.

The experimental manipulation consisted of having the adult leaders behave in a prescribed fashion in each experimental treatment, and in order to rule out the differential effects of the personalities of the leaders, each one led a group under each of the experimental conditions. Three types of leadership, or group atmosphere, were investigated: democratic, autocratic, and laissez-faire.

In the light of present-day knowledge it is clear that a considerable number of separable variables were combined within each style of leadership. Perhaps for this very reason, however, the effects produced in the behavior of the group members were large and dramatic. For example, rather severe forms of scapegoating occurred in the autocratic groups, and at the end of the experiment the children in some of the autocratic groups proceeded to destroy the things they had constructed. Each group, moreover, developed a characteristic level of aggressiveness, and it was demonstrated that when individual members were transferred from one group to another their aggressiveness changed to approach the new group level. An interesting insight into the dynamics of aggression was provided by the rather violent emotional "explosion" which took place when some of the groups that had reacted submissively to autocratic leadership were given a new, more permissive leader.

As might be expected from the fact that this research was both original and concerned with emotionally loaded matters of political ideology, it was immediately subjected to criticism, both justified and unjustified. But the major effect on the social sciences and relevant professions was to open up new vistas and to raise the level of aspiration. The creation of "miniature political systems" in the laboratory and the demonstration of their power to influence the behavior and social relations of people made it clear that practical problems of group management could be subjected to the experimental method and that social scientists could employ the methods of science to solve problems of vital significance to society.

Of major importance for subsequent research in group dynamics was the way in which Lewin formulated the essential purpose of these experiments. The problem of leadership was chosen for investigation, in part, because of its practical importance in education, social group work, administration, and political affairs. Nevertheless, in creating the different types of leadership in the laboratory the intention was not to mirror or to simulate any "pure types" that might exist in society. The purpose was rather to lay bare some of the more important ways in which leader behavior may vary and to discover how various styles of leadership influence the properties of groups and the behavior of members. As Lewin put it (**21**, 74), the purpose "was not to duplicate any given autocracy or democracy or to study an 'ideal' autocracy or democracy, but to create set-ups which would give insight into the underlying group dynamics." This statement, published in 1939, appears to be the earliest use by Lewin of the phrase group dynamics.

It is important to note rather carefully how Lewin generalized the research problem. He might have viewed this research primarily as a contribution to the technology of group management in social work or education. Or he might have placed it in the context of research on leadership. Actually, however, he stated the problem in a most abstract way as one of learning about the underlying dynamics of group life. He believed that it was possible to construct a coherent body of empirical knowledge about the nature of group life that would be meaningful when specified for any particular kind of group. Thus, he envisioned a general theory of groups that could be brought to bear on such apparently diverse matters as family life, work groups, classrooms, committees, military units, and the community. Furthermore, he saw such specific problems as leadership, status, communication, social norms, group atmosphere, and intergroup relations as part of the general problem of understanding the nature of group dynamics. Almost immediately, Lewin and those associated with him began various research projects designed to contribute information relevant to a general theory of group dynamics. Thus, French conducted a laboratory experiment designed to compare the effects of fear and frustration on organized versus unorganized groups. Bavelas (6) undertook an experiment to determine whether the actual behavior of leaders of youth groups could be significantly modified through training. Later, Bavelas suggested to Lewin the cluster of ideas that became known as "group decision." With America's entry into the war, he and French, in association with Marrow (26), explored group decision and related techniques as a means of improving industrial production; and Margaret Mead interested Lewin in studying problems related to wartime food shortages, with the result that Radke together with others (20, 36) conducted experiments on group decision as a means of changing food habits.

SUMMARY

Group dynamics is a field of inquiry dedicated to advancing knowledge about the nature of groups, the laws of their development, and their interrelations with individuals, other groups, and larger institutions. It may be identified by its reliance upon empirical research for obtaining data of theoretical significance, its emphasis in research and theory upon the dynamic aspects of group life, its broad relevance to all the social sciences, and the potential applicability of its findings to the improvement of social practice.

It became an identifiable field toward the end of the 1930's in the United States and has experienced a rapid growth since that time. Its rise was fostered by certain conditions that were particularly favorable in the United States just prior to World War II. These same conditions have facilitated its growth here and in certain other countries since that time. Of particular importance among these has been the acceptance by significant segments of society of the belief that research on groups is feasible and ultimately useful. This belief was initially encouraged by a strong interest in groups among such professions as social group work, group psychotherapy, education, and administration. It was made feasible because the social sciences had attained sufficient progress, by clarifying basic assumptions about the reality of groups and by designing research techniques for the study of groups, to permit empirical research on the functioning of groups.

By the end of the 1930's several trends converged with the result that a new field of group dynamics began to take shape. The practical and theoretical importance of groups was by then documented empirically. The feasibility of conducting objective and quantitative research on the dynamics of group life was no longer debatable. And the reality of groups had been removed from the realm of mysticism and placed squarely within the domain of empirical social science. Group norms could be objectively measured, even created experimentally in the laboratory, and

Cartwright + Zander

some of the processes by which they influence the behavior and attitudes of individuals had been determined. The dependence of certain emotional states of individuals upon the prevailing group atmosphere had been established. And different styles of leadership had been created experimentally and shown to produce marked consequences on the functioning of groups. After the interruption imposed by World War II, rapid advances were made in constructing a systematic, and empirically based, body of knowledge concerning the dynamics of group life.

REFERENCES

1. Allport, F. H. *Social psychology.* Boston: Houghton Mifflin, 1924.
2. Allport, G. W. The historical background of modern social psychology. In G. Lindzey (Ed.), *Handbook of social psychology.* Cambridge, Mass.: Addison-Wesley, 1954. Pp. 3–56.
3. Bach, G. R. *Intensive group psychotherapy.* New York: Ronald Press, 1954.
4. Bales, R. F. *Interaction process analysis.* Cambridge, Mass.: Addison-Wesley, 1950.
5. Barnard, C. I. *The functions of the executive.* Cambridge, Mass.: Harvard Univ. Press, 1938.
6. Bavelas, A. Morale and training of leaders. In G. Watson (Ed.), *Civilian morale.* Boston: Houghton Mifflin, 1942.
7. Bion, W. R. Experiences in groups. I–VI. *Human Relations,* 1948–1950, **1,** 314–320, 487–496; **2,** 13–22, 295–303; **3,** 3–14, 395–402.
8. Bogardus, E. S. Measuring social distance. *Journal of Applied Sociology,* 1925, 9, 299–308.
9. Busch, H. M. *Leadership in group work.* New York: Association Press, 1934.
10. Chapple, E. D. Measuring human relations: An introduction to the study of interaction of individuals, *Genetic Psychology Monographs,* 1940, **22,** 3–147.
11. Coyle, G. L. *Social process in organized groups.* New York: Rinehart, 1930.

12. Dashiell, J. F. Experimental studies of the influence of social situations on the behavior of individual human adults. In C. C. Murchison (Ed.), *Handbook of social psychology,* Worcester, Mass.: Clark Univ. Press, 1935. Pp. 1097–1158.
13. Follett, M. P. *The new state, group organization, the solution of popular government.* New York: Longmans, Green, 1918.
14. Follett, M. P. *Creative experience.* New York: Longmans, Green, 1924.
15. Goodenough, F. L. Measuring behavior traits by means of repeated short samples. *Journal of Juvenile Research,* 1928, **12,** 230–235.
16. Gordon, K. Group judgments in the field of lifted weights. *Journal of Experimental Psychology,* 1924, **7,** 398–400.
17. Haire, M. Group dynamics in the industrial situation. In A. Kornhauser, R. Dubin, & A. M. Ross (Eds.), *Industrial conflict.* New York: McGraw-Hill, 1954. Pp. 373–385.
18. Homans, G. C. *The human group.* New York: McGraw-Hill, 1954. Pp. 373–385.
19. Jack, L. M. An experimental study of ascendent behavior in preschool children. *Univ. of Iowa Studies in Child Welfare,* 1934, **9,** (3).
20. Lewin, K. Forces behind food habits and methods of change. *Bulletin of the National Research Council,* 1943, **108,** 35–65.
21. Lewin, K. *Resolving social conflicts.* New York: Harper, 1948.
22. Lewin, K. *Field theory in social science.* New York: Harper, 1951.
23. Lewin, K., Lippitt, R., & White, R. Patterns of aggressive behavior in experimentally created "social climates." *Journal of Social Psychology,* 1939, **10,** 271–299.
24. Likert, R. A technique for the measurement of attitudes. *Archives of Psychology,* 1932, No. 140.
25. Lippitt, R. An experimental study of authoritarian and democratic group atmospheres. *Univ. of Iowa Studies in Child Welfare,* 1940, **16** (3), 43–195.
26. Marrow, A. J. *Making management human.* New York: McGraw-Hill, 1957.
27. Mayo, E. *The human problems of an industrial civilization.* New York: Macmillan, 1933.

28. Moede, W. *Experimentelle massenpsychologie*. Leipzig: S. Hirzel, 1920.

29. Moore, H. T. The comparative influence of majority and expert opinion. *American Journal of Psychology*, 1921, **32**, 16–20.

30. Moreno, J. L. *Who shall survive?* Washington, D. C.: Nervous and Mental Diseases Publishing Co., 1934.

31. Myrdal, G. *An American dilemma*. New York: Harper, 1944.

32. Newcomb, T. M. *Personality and social change*. New York: Dryden, 1943.

33. Newstetter, W., Feldstein, M., & Newcomb, T. M. *Group adjustment, a study in experimental sociology*. Cleveland: Western Reserve Univ., School of Applied Social Sciences, 1938.

34. Olson, W. C., & Cunningham, E. M. Time-sampling techniques. *Child Development*, 1934, **5**, 41–58.

35. Parten, M. B. Social participation among preschool children. *Journal of Abnormal and Social Psychology*, 1932, **27**, 243–269.

36. Radke, M., & Klisurich, D. Experiments in changing food habits. *Journal of American Dietetics Association*, 1947, **23**, 403–409.

37. Redl, F., & Wineman, D. *Children who hate*. Glencoe, Ill.: Free Press, 1951.

38. Roethlisberger, F. J., & Dickson, W. J. *Management and the worker*. Cambridge, Mass.: Harvard Univ. Press, 1939.

39. Scheidlinger, S. *Psychoanalysis and group behavior*. New York: Norton, 1952.

40. Shaw, C. R. *The jack roller*. Chicago: Univ. of Chicago Press, 1939.

41. Shaw, M. E. A comparison of individuals and small groups in the rational solution of complex problems. *American Journal of Psychology*. 1932, **44**, 491–504.

42. Sherif, M. *The psychology of social norms*. New York: Harper, 1936.

43. Slavson, S. R. *Analytic group psychotherapy*. New York: Columbia Univ. Press. 1950.

44. Thomas, D. S. An attempt to develop precise measurement in the social behavior field. *Sociologus*, 1933, **9**, 1–21.

45. Thomas, W. I., & Znaniecki, F. *The Polish peasant in Europe and America*. Boston: Badger, 1918.

46. Thrasher, F. *The gang*. Chicago: Univ. of Chicago Press, 1927.

47. Thurstone, L. L. Attitudes can be measured. *American Journal of Sociology*, 1928, **33**, 529–554.

48. Thurstone, L. L., & Chave, E. J. *The measurement of attitude*. Chicago: Univ. of Chicago Press, 1929.

49. Triplett, N. The dynamogenic factors in pacemaking and competition. *American Journal of Psychology*, 1897, **9**, 507–533.

50. Watson, G. B. Do groups think more effectively than individuals? *Journal of Abnormal and Social Psychology*, 1928, **23**, 328–336.

51. Whyte, W. F., Jr. *Street corner society*. Chicago: Univ. of Chicago Press, 1943.

52. Whyte, W. H., Jr. *The organization man*. New York: Simon and Schuster, 1956.

53. Wilson, A. T. M. Some aspects of social process. *Journal of Social Issues*, 1951 (Suppl. Series 5).

54. Wilson, G., & Ryland, G. *Social group work practice*. Boston: Houghton Mifflin, 1949.

13

The Management of Interdepartmental Conflict: A Model and Review

Richard E. Walton & John M. Dutton

Horizontal interactions are seldom shown on the organizational chart, but transactions along this dimension are often at least as important as vertical interactions (Simpson, 1959; Landsberger, 1961; Burns and Stalker, 1961). This paper presents a general model of interdepartmental conflict and its management, together with a review of the relevant literature.[1] The model includes five sets of related variables: antecedents to conflict, attributes of the lateral relationship, management of the interface, consequences of the relationship, and responses of higher executives. Figure 1 shows the general relationship among these sets of variables.

The general model is postulated as applicable to all lateral relations between any two organizational units (departments, divisions, sections, and so on) that engage in any type of transaction, including joint decision making, exchanging information, providing expertise or advice, and auditing or inspecting.

ANTECEDENTS TO INTERUNIT CONFLICT AND COLLABORATION

Manifest conflict results largely from factors which originate outside the particular lateral relationship under consideration or which antedate the relationship. Hypotheses and models that use external factors to predict lateral relations have been advanced by March and Simon (1958), Thompson (1961), Caplow (1964), Lawrence and Lorsch (1967a, b) and Pondy (1967). The present model describes nine major types of antecedents: mutual dependence, asymmetries, rewards, organizational differentiation, role dissatisfaction, ambiguities, common resources, communication obstacles, and personal skills and traits.

Mutual Task Dependence

Mutual task dependence is the key variable in the relevance of the interunit conflict model in general and the impact of the postulated conflict antecedents in particular. Task dependence is the extent to which two units depend upon each other for assistance, information, compliance, or other coordinative acts in the performance of their respective tasks. It is assumed here that dependence is mutual and can range from low to high. Asymmetry in the interdependence is treated later.

According to Miller (1959), the

[1]This research was supported by a grant from the McKinsey Foundation for Management Research, Inc.

Source: From "The Management of Interdepartmental Conflict: A Model and Review" by Richard E. Walton and John M. Dutton in *Administrative Science Quarterly,* 14, no 1 (March 1969), pp. 73–84. Copyright © 1969 Administrative Science Quarterly. Reprinted with permission.

FIGURE 1 ● GENERAL MODEL OF INTERUNIT CONFLICT.

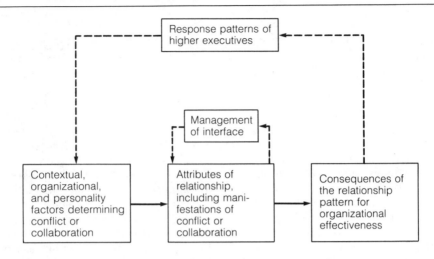

more performance of one unit depends on the performance of all other units, the more likely is the system to perform without external control. Other studies, however, Dutton and Walton (1966), for example, indicate that task interdependence not only provides an incentive for collaboration, but also presents an occasion for conflict and the means for bargaining over interdepartmental issues. A related factor, task overload, has similarly mixed potential for conflict and collaboration. Overload conditions may intensify the problem of scarce resources and lead to bargaining; may increase tension, frustration, and aggression; and may decrease the time available for the social interactions that would enable the units to contain their conflict. On the other hand, overload may place a premium on mutual assistance. The net directional effects of high task interdependence and overload are therefore uncertain.

Other implications of the extent of mutual task dependence are more predictable. High task interdependence and overload tend to heighten the intensity of either interunit antagonisms

or friendliness, increase the magnitude of the consequences of unit conflict for organizational performance, and contribute to the difficulty of changing an ongoing pattern.

Task-related Asymmetries

Symmetrical interdependence and symmetrical patterns of initiation between units promote collaboration; asymmetrical interdependence leads to conflict. For example, in a study by Dalton (1959), a staff group resented the asymmetries in their relationship with line groups. The staff group had to understand the problems of the line groups, had to get along with them, promote their ideas, and justify their existence; but none of these relations were reciprocal requirements imposed on the line groups. Strauss (1962) reported that asymmetrical high dependence of purchasing agents on another group led them to make more attempts to influence the terms of requisitions they received and thereby force interaction to flow both ways.

The adverse effects of asymmetrical conditions are sometimes related to the

Walton & Dutton

fact that one unit has little incentive to coordinate. The more dependent unit may try to increase the incentive of the more independent unit to cooperate by interfering with their task performance. The assumption is that once the independent unit is made aware of their need for the cooperation of the dependent unit (i.e., to desist from interfering acts), they will behave more cooperatively (supply the assistance necessary). This tactic may indeed achieve its purpose, and the conflict-interfering acts may cease; but frequently interference elicits a retaliatory response.

Conflict is also produced by differences in the way units are ranked along various dimensions of organizational status, namely direction of initiation of action, prestige, power, and knowledge. Seiler (1963) studied in an organization in which it was generally agreed that research had more prestige than engineering and engineering had more prestige than production. When the sequential pattern of initiation and influence followed this status ordering, it was accepted. However, where a lower-status industrial engineering group needed to direct the higher-status research group to carry out routine tests, the result was a breakdown in relationships between the departments.

Inconsistency between the distribution of knowledge among departments and the lateral influence patterns are also a source of conflict. Lawrence and Lorsch (1967a) advanced the idea that the more the influence of each unit is consistent with key competitive factors, the more effectively will interunit issues be resolved. They noted that in container firms, customer delivery and product quality were crucial for competitive success; therefore, sales and production were required to have the most influence in the resolution of interunit conflict. By contrast, in the food indus-

try, where market expertise and food science were essential, sales and research were required to be the more influential. Landsberger (1961) also found that the locus of power among three plants in the same industry was affected by their different market positions.

Zald (1962) in a study of correctional institutions offered a power-balance proposition about the effect of relative power: assuming task interdependence and divergent values among three units (teachers, cottage parents, and social service workers), conflict is most likely to occur between units that are unable to control the situation and those perceived as being in control. He found that the patterns of conflict among these three units were generally consistent with predictions based on this power-balance hypothesis.

Performance Criteria and Rewards

Interunit conflict results when each of the interdependent departments has responsibility for only one side of a dilemma embedded in organizational tasks. Dutton and Walton (1966) noted that the preference of production units for long, economical runs conflicted with the preference of sales units for quick delivery to good customers. Dalton (1959) observed that staff units valued change, because that was one way they proved their worth; whereas line units valued stability, because change reflected unfavorably upon them or inconvenienced them. Also, staff units were strongly committed to preserving the integrity of control and rule systems, whereas line personnel believed they could be more effective by flexible reinterpretation of control and incentive schemes, and by ignoring many discipline and safety violations. A study by Strauss (1962) showed that engineers preferred to order brand items, whereas purchasing agents sought specifications suitable for several vendors. Similar instances abound. Landsberger (1961) postulated several basic dilemmas which probably underlie many interdepartmental differences: flexibility versus stability; criteria for short-run versus long-run performance; emphasis on measurable results versus attention to intangible results; maximizing organizational goals versus responding to other societal needs.

Although the dilemmas may be inherent in the total task, the reward system designed by management can serve either to sharpen or to blunt their divisive effective: the more the evaluations and rewards of higher management emphasize the separate performance of each department rather than their combined performance, the more conflict.

Close, one-to-one supervisory styles have generally been assumed to promote more conflict among peers than general supervision in which the superior also deals with subordinates as a group (Likert 1961). One might speculate that group supervisory patterns are taken to indicate emphasis on group rather than individual performance criteria; and that group patterns allow the supervisor to observe the process and to reward cooperative acts.

Organizational Differentiation

Litwak (1961) postulated that uniform tasks require a bureaucratic type of organization, characterized by impersonality of relations, prior specification of job authority, emphasis on hierarchical authority, separation of policy and administration, and emphasis on general rules and specialization; whereas nonuniform tasks require a human-relations organization with the contrasting characteristics. In contemporary society, most large-scale organizations have to deal with both uniform and nonuniform tasks, and must combine these contradictory forms of social relations into a professional model. Litwak regards the inclusions of these contradictory forms as a source of organizational conflict.

Lawrence and Lorsch (1967a) emphasized the effects of differentiation. Where each unit (such as research, sales, or production) performs a different type of task and copes with a different segment of the environment, the units will develop significant internal differences. Such units may differ from each other (*a*) in the degree of structure, that is, tightness of rules, narrowness of span of supervisory control, frequency and specificity of performance review; and in the orientation of its members; (*b*) toward the environment, such as, new scientific knowledge versus customer problems and market opportunities versus costs of raw materials and processing; (*c*) toward time, such as planning time perspective; and (*d*) toward other people, such as, openness and permissiveness of interpersonal relationships. Lawrence and Lorsch measured these differences in six plastics organizations with the results shown in Table 1.

Lawrence and Lorsch believe this fourfold differentiation is largely a response to the degree of uncertainty in the environments of the different departments. They use a notion of optimum degree of differentiation, which depends upon the task environments. Thus, either overdifferentiation or underdifferentiation has implications for the coordinative process. Although greater differentiation apparently results in more *potential* for conflict, these authors do not assume that more manifest conflict will automatically result. In their study of six plastics organizations, the degree of integration did not, in fact, vary strictly with the degree of differentiation.

Walten & Dutton

TABLE 1 ● DIFFERENCES RELATED TO ENVIRONMENT
OF DEPARTMENTS.*

Departments	Orientation Toward Environment	Orientation Toward Time	Degree of Formality in Departmental Structure	Permissiveness versus Directiveness in Orientation Toward Others
Applied research	Techno-economic	Long	Medium	Medium
Sales	Market	Short	High	Low
Production	Techno-economic	Short	High	High

*After Lawrence and Lorsch (1967).

Role Dissatisfaction

Role dissatisfaction, stemming from a variety of sources, can be a source of conflict. Blocking status aspirations in purchasing agents (Strauss, 1962) and in staff members (Dalton, 1959) led to conflict with other units. In these cases, professionals felt they lacked recognition and opportunities for advancement. Similarly, White (1961) stated that members might feel that the growth of their units and its external status did not meet their needs, and therefore might enter another unit or withdraw from contacts which were painful reminders of the lack of status. Where one unit informally reports on the activities of another unit, resentment can occur, as with staff units reporting to management on production irregularities (Dalton, 1959). Argyris (1964) and Dalton (1959) both argued that role dissatisfaction and conflict followed where one unit with the same or less status set standards for another.

Where there is role dissatisfaction, ambiguities in the definition of work responsibilities further increase the likelihood of interunit conflict. Landsberger (1961) pointed out that ambiguities tempted the dissatisfied unit to engage in offensive maneuvers so as to improve its lot, and thus induced other units to engage in defensive maneuvers.

Role dissatisfaction and ambiguity are related to more basic organizational variables, including growth rate, organizational level, and hierarchical differences. Organizational growth appears to have offsetting consequences. Slower rates of organizational growth and of opportunities for promotion increase role dissatisfaction, but are also accompanied by fewer ambiguities. Interfaces higher in the organization are more likely to be marked by conflict to redefine departmental responsibilities. At the higher levels, jurisdictional boundaries are less clear (Pondy, 1967), and the participants perceive more opportunity to achieve some restructuring. Steep and heavily emphasized hierarchical differences in status, power, and rewards were seen by Thompson (1961) as responsible for some lateral conflict, because these factors tended to activate and to legitimate individual aspiration for increased status and power and tended to lead to increased upward orientation toward the desires of one's superiors, rather than to problem orientation and increased horizontal coordination.

Ambiguities

In addition to its interaction with role dissatisfaction, ambiguity contributes to interunit conflict in several other ways. Difficulty in assigning credit or blame between two departments increases the likelihood of conflict between units. Dalton (1959) attributed part of the staff-line conflict he observed to the fact that although improvements required collaboration between line and staff units, it was later difficult to assess the contribution of each unit. Similarly, disputes resulted between production and sales units, when it could not be determined which department made a mistake (Dutton and Walton, 1966).

Low routinization and uncertainty of means to goals increase the potential for interunit conflict. This proposition is supported by Zald (1962) in his study of interunit conflict in five correctional institutions. Similarly, ambiguity in the criteria used to evaluate the performance of a unit may also create tension, frustration, and conflict (Kahn, Wolfe, et al., 1964). Organization planning, which includes clarity of rule definition, correlated positively with measures of lateral coordination and problem solving in a study of ten hospitals by Georgopoulos and Mann (1962).

Dependence on Common Resources

Conflict potential exists when two units depend upon a common pool of scarce organizational resources, such as, physical space, equipment, manpower, operating funds, capital funds, central staff resources, and centralized services (e.g., typing and drafting). If the two units have interdependent tasks, the competition for scarce resources will tend to decrease interunit problem solving and coordination. Also, if competition for scarce resources is not mediated by some third unit and they must agree on their allocation, they will come into direct conflict.

Communication Obstacles

Semantic difficulties can impede communications essential for cooperation. Strauss (1964) observed that differences in training of purchasing agents and engineers contributed to their conflicts. March and Simon (1958) stated that organizational channeling of information introduced bias.

Common experience reduces communication barriers and provides common referents. Miller (1959) proposed that the less units know about each other's job, the less collaboration and that lack of knowledge can lead to unreasonable interunit demands through ignorance. Cozer (1956) argued that accommodation is especially dependent on knowledge of the power of the other unit.

Personal Skills and Traits

Walton and McKersie (1965), reviewing experimental studies, found that certain personality attributes, such as high authoritarianism, high dogmatism, and low self-esteem, increased conflict behavior. Kahn et al. (1964: 256) found that in objective role conflict persons who scored lower on neurotic anxiety scales tended to depart more from "cordial, congenial, trusting, respecting, and understanding relations," and introverts tended to lose their confidence, trust, and respect for work associates more than extroverts.

Most interunit relationships are mixed-motive situations, which require high behavioral flexibility to manage optimally. A person with a narrower range of behavioral skills is less likely to exploit the integrative potential fully in an interunit relationship. He may either engage in bargaining to the exclusion of collaborative problem solving, or withdraw or become passive (Walton and McKersie, 1966). Dalton (1959) and Thompson (1960) found that personal dissimilarities, such as, background, values, education, age, social patterns lowered the probability of interpersonal rapport between unit representatives, and in turn decreased the amount of collaboration between their respective units. Personal status incongruities between departmental representatives, that is, the degree to which they differed in rank orderings in various status dimensions (such as length of service, age, education, ethnicity, esteem in eyes of superiors, pay and so on) increase the tendency for conflict (Dutton and Walton, 1966).

Personal satisfaction with the internal climate of one's unit decreases the likelihood that a member will initiate interunit conflict. Seiler (1963) observed that in one firm, constructive handling of interdepartmental differences occurred in part because the members of each department derived social satisfaction from their work associates, had high job interest and good opportunities for promotions, and were not in conflict with each other.

Attributes

INTERDEPARTMENTAL RELATIONSHIP

Tactics of Conflict and Indicators of Collaboration

The literature on interdepartmental relations has been most vivid in its description of manifest conflict and collaboration processes. Dalton (1959) observed that staff units were encouraged by top management to monitor and report on the activities of line units, and the line units retaliated by resisting the ideas of the staff units and discouraging their promotions. He also observed power struggles between line units and documented the conflict tactics of coalitions, distortion of information, and misappropriation of resources.

Strauss (1962) observed the tactics of purchasing agents who wished to increase their authority and influence over decisions shared with engineering and production. The purchasing agents made restrictive rules for the other units, evaded their rules, relied on personal contacts and persuasion to subvert the other units, and altered organization structure.

Focusing on positive relations, Georgopoulos and Mann (1962) used coordination as their broadest concept, which included "the extent to which the various interdependent parts of an organization function each according to the needs and requirements of the other parts of the total system." In a study of ten hospitals, they found that over-all coordination correlated positively with (a) shared expectations, (b) absence of intraorganizational tension, (c) awareness of problems and solving of problems, and (d) ease of communication.

System Characteristics of an Interunit Relationship

Attempting to incorporate aspects of the approaches just described, Walton (1966) developed a theory which also explains the system dynamics of conflict and collaboration in the interunit relationship. Three components of the relationship are considered: (a) exchange of information in the joint decision process, (b) structure of interunit interactions and decision making, and (c) attitudes toward the other unit. Two opposite types of relationships, "integrative" and "distributive," are postulated as frequently encountered systems of interunit behavior (see Table 2). This particular model now appears to be most applicable to lateral relations where the dominant transaction at the interface is joint decision making; where there is relative symmetry in interdependency; and where the transactions required are relatively frequent and important.

In the most general sense, the chain of assumptions underlying Walton's systems theory of lateral relationships (and explaining the distributive syndrome, in particular) is as follows: First, an ante-

TABLE 2 • COMPONENTS AND CHARACTERISTICS OF
CONTRASTING TYPES OF LATERAL RELATIONSHIPS.*

Component	Type of Lateral Relationship	
	Integrative	Distributive
Form of joint decision process	Problem-solving: free exchange of information, conscientious accuracy in transmitting information	Bargaining: careful rationing, and deliberate distortion of information
Structure of interaction and framework of decision	Flexible, informal, open	Rigid, formal, circumscribed
Attitudes toward other unit	Positive attitudes: trust, friendliness, inclusion of other unit	Negative attitudes: suspicion, hostility, dissociation from other unit

*After Walton (1966).

cedent, say goal competition between participants engaged in joint decision making, induces the units to engage in concealment and distortion tactics in their exchange of information, such that joint decision making takes on the character of bargaining. Second, in order to ration and distort information effectively and systematically, a unit will attempt to place limitations on the interactions and other behavior of their counterpart in order to make them more predictable and keep them within certain boundaries. Third, the way information is handled (concealment, distortion, etc.) and the way interactions are patterned (circumscribed, rigid, etc.) results in suspicion and hostility. Furthermore, these negative attitudes have a feedback effect which tend to reinforce the same interaction structure and information-handling pattern.

Regardless of the antecedents, the theory hypothesizes that the conflict relationship will become fixed as a result of: the tendency to generalize a conflictful orientation to the many areas of in-

terunit decision making, the self-reinforcing nature of the various elements of a relationship pattern, the reciprocal nature of a conflictful orientation between units, and the tendency toward socialization and institutionalization of these orientations within a unit.

The individual propositions contained in the model are generally supported by a review of the relevant literature in experimental social psychology (Walton, 1966). The hypothesized variation of attributes of a relationship are also generally supported by a comparative field study of production-sales relationships in six plants (Walton, Dutton, and Fitch, 1966). The hypothesized dominant cause-effect relationships among process, structure, and attitude are anecdotally supported in a comparison of two plants (Dutton and Walton, 1966).

The theory suggests that the total lateral relationship is influenced or determined by contextual factors operating first upon the way the parties exchange information, with the effects on interaction structure and interunit trust as subsequent reactions. However, although the process of exchanging information may be the most frequent determinant, it is not exclusively the point of entry in the lateral relationship. For instance, personality and status may first influence attitudes such as trust and friendliness in which case the pattern of information exchange and interaction structure are a secondary reaction.

MANAGEMENT OF THE INTERFACE

The relationship between units is largely a function of the conflict potential inherent in the factors already discussed; but it is also subject to control by the participants, their effectiveness depending upon how much conscious effort they invest in management of the interface and the appropriateness of the techniques they use.

Interface conflict will be managed best where the attention devoted to interface management corresponds to the degree of differentiation between departments. Lawrence and Lorsch (1967a) compared integrative devices used by three high-performing organizations selected from industries with high, medium, and low differentiation. The most differentiated firm had the most elaborate array of interface management techniques, including a separate integrative department with the primary purpose of coordinating the basic functional units, permanent teams consisting of representatives of members from functional units together with the integrative department, direct contact across hierarchies at all levels, procedures for appeal to a common superior, and a coordination system involving written communications. As expected, when all three organizations were compared, the same rank order obtained for

the differentiation scores as for the degree of elaboration of integrative devices. Explicit conflict-resolution mechanisms can be overelaborate, however. For example, a formal coordinative unit was used between slightly differentiated units in a *low*-performing unit. Lawrence and Lorsch concluded that the units were not sufficiently differentiated to justify the coordinative unit, and the result was that the superfluous unit added noise to the system, actually decreasing coordination.

In their comparison of six plastics firms, Lawrence and Lorsch found that three factors promoted effective resolution of interdepartmental conflict and thus high organizational performance. First, where there is a separate coordinating person or unit, the coordinating unit will be most effective if its degree of structure and the goal, time, and interpersonal orientations of its personnel are intermediate between those of the units linked. Second, where there is a separate coordinating unit, conflict resolution will be more effective if its personnel have relatively high influence based on perceived expertise, and if they are evaluated and rewarded on overall performance measures embracing the activities of the several departments. Third, interunit cooperation will be more effectively achieved and over-all organizational performance will be higher to the extent that managers openly confront differences rather than smooth them over or force decisions. The more subtle aspects of confrontation are discussed by Schmidt and Tannenbaum (1960) and Walton (1968), who analyze the advantages and risks of confronting differences, the timing and skill required, as well as the conditions under which confrontation is most appropriate.

Seiler (1963) also observed techniques for management of interunit conflict. A department may keep its own records, so as to reduce requests for information and thus avoid distasteful contact; a junior member may be assigned as the liaison person, where his presence will not arouse status conflict; and inventories may be introduced to reduce scheduling interdependence.

CONSEQUENCES OF INTERUNIT CONFLICT

The manifest characteristics of interunit conflict include: a competitive orientation, bargaining and restrictions on information, circumscribed interaction patterns, and antagonistic feelings. To determine whether the conflict has an adverse effect on organizational performance, one must assess the consequences of these characteristics. Whether a competitive orientation is in fact energizing or debilitating for members of the unit will depend in part on the personalities of the participants. For some, competition is motivating and arouses energies not otherwise available for organizational tasks; for others conflict is a major threat. Whether competitive energy will contribute to over-all performance depends upon whether a unit can improve its performance without interfering with the performance of another unit.

Another factor governing the motivational effect of conflict is the degree of symmetry in tactics between units. Crozier (1961) reported that managers who were not able to retaliate when conflict was initiated responded by withdrawing commitment from their job. Seiler (1963) postulated that internal social stability, value sharing between units, and a legitimate authority hierarchy between units were important in influencing whether interunit competition would result in destructive conflict.

According to Strauss (1964), the competitive orientation that accompanies conflict behavior may also contribute to a system of checks and balances, increase the availability of new ideas to compete with established ones, and decrease the type of collusion among middle managers, deprives higher-level top management of information.

It seems reasonable to assume that the more important the interdependence, the more a restriction on interunit information becomes damaging. When a lateral relationship involves joint decision making, each unit can bias the decisions in its own favor by controlling information relevant to these decisions. Even minor concealment or distortion can be of great importance, if the decisions are key ones.

The structural attributes of a conflictful relationship are not necessarily variable in the lateral relationship, as for example, the number of liaison contacts between departments, which may be specified by higher authorities. Whether a structural attribute has a positive or an adverse effect on over-all performance depends on factors other than structure. For example, in a conflictful pattern more problems are referred to the superiors. On the one hand, referral may overload a superior; on the other, a superior may find himself more informed about operations and subordinates. Similarly, referral of problems requiring new policy may also be organizationally useful. Also, the inability of a decision-making pair to change decision rules or apply them flexibly may result in decisions that are not innovative. However, given the larger network of task relationships in which the pair is embedded, the inflexibility may produce a degree of predictability, which is valuable for some other reason.

Channeling all interunit interactions through a few liaison persons in a con-

Walton & Dutton

flict syndrome often reduces over-all performance; for where other persons are either affected by an interunit decision or have potentially relevant information or opinions, ignoring their contribution decreases the quality of the decisions and lowers the commitment to decisions.

Apart from their influence on the quality of decisions, the attributes of an interunit relationship may impinge upon coordinative activities. For example, a tendency to avoid contact can result in implementation that lacks coordination. The seriousness of the effect of conflict in decreasing the rate of interaction between the units therefore depends in part upon how much coordination is required to implement joint decisions.

Conflict relationships involve sterotyping and include *attitudes* of low friendliness, low trust, and low respect. Such attitudes indirectly affect performance. For example, low trust limits the flow of relevant task information and decreases coordinative interactions. Furthermore, some persons experience psychological strain when other persons dislike or distrust them. Dalton (1959: 95) reported that staff men were shocked by the need to engage in conflict that required them to use their interpersonal skills as much as their academic skills. The stress of this interpersonal or intergroup climate may result in higher turnover or withdrawal from interdepartmental relations.

A positive by-product of interunit rivalry is more unit cohesion, which contributes to cooperation within the unit. Each unit may become more receptive to directives from their own hierarchy; but sometimes the centralization of control within the unit causes frustration in subordinates (Seiler, 1963). Competition may serve as a useful training device. Managers' insight into how the respective goals of interdependent units contribute to over-all goals may be sharpened. Negotiating and policymaking skills of prospective top managers may be increased, and tolerance of unavoidable conflict may be developed.

Some of the postulated relationships between attributes of a conflictful syndrome and consequences for over-all performance are shown in Table 3. Each of the relationships is subject to limiting conditions, some of which were noted earlier. The point being made is that conclusions about the effect of a generally competitive or conflictful relationship can only be made on the basis of an analysis of the specific components of the pattern together with an analysis of the task. Comparative field data are needed to evaluate the validity of the concept of an optimum degree of competitiveness and rivalry. The optimum might be expected to vary, depending upon the type of interunit interdependence, the type of work of each unit, and the personalities of unit representatives.

RESPONSES OF HIGHER EXECUTIVES

Response Tendencies of Executives

The response of executives refers to how superiors react to information about subordinate organizational units; that is, to low performance and attributes of the interunit relationship itself. Here "low performance" means inadequate productivity, low adaptability, or inability of the units to conserve their human and other resources.

A manager's response is a combination of his habitual patterns, emotional reactions, and deliberate responses. This idiosyncratic element in the system of interunit conflict shown in Fig-

TABLE 3 • CONSEQUENCES OF INTERUNIT CONFLICT.

Attributes of Conflictful Lateral Relationships	Illustrative Consequences
Competition in general	Motivates or debilitates Provides checks and balances
Concealment and distortion	Lowers quality of decisions
Channeled interunit contacts	Enhances stability in the system
Rigidity, formality in decision procedures	Enhances stability in the system Lowers adaptability to change
Appeals to superiors for decisions	Provides more contact for superiors May increase or decrease quality of decisions
Decreased rate of interunit interaction	Hinders coordination and implementation of tasks
Low trust, suspicion, hostility	Psychological strain and turnover of personnel or decrease in individual performance

ure 1 is a major problem in developing a general explanatory or predictive model of the total system. For the same reason, however, it is an opportunity for improving the interunit relationship. Several automatic responses to low performance can be noted for illustration. If the joint performance of two units is considered inadequate, higher executives may place particular emphasis on observable, short-run measures of performance for each subunit. Thus, poor performance, whatever its source, may lead to the very rewards, controls, and styles of supervision here shown to be antecedents to conflict. If the relationships hypothesized are valid, reinforcing feedback will lead to more interunit conflict and still lower performance. White (1961) reported that higher executives who were dissatisfied with the performance of subordinate units frequently responded by reorganizing the units. The feelings of status depreciation or power deprivation and the ambiguity which frequently follow a reorganization may increase the potential for conflict.

Executive Responses in Relation to Model

The model has implications both for determining what needs changing and for developing a strategy for achieving the change. Executive responses can either reinforce and intensify a conflict pattern, or create pressures to change it. Much depends upon how sophisticated a diagnostic model the manager uses. Ideally he would take into account all the valid implications of a model of the antecedents, dynamics, and consequences of conflict.

The model as a diagnostic tool. Cause-and-effect relationships can be traced back through the model as follows:

1. Are there manifestations of conflict or low collaboration in the lateral relationship? If not, this interunit conflict model is not relevant. If so, determine the particular aspects of the relationship processes that are impinging upon performance; for instance, distortion of information, infrequent interaction, and lack of mutual assistance.

2. Are these dysfunctional elements of the conflict process inherent in a competitive interunit relationship? If not, determine how the management activities at the interface are inadequate, and whether these can be modified by suggesting or requiring changes in them. If they are, determine what particular contextual variables are responsible for the competitive orientation; for example, scarce resources, competitive reward system, asymmetrical task interdependence, or personalities of key liaison personnel.

3. Which of the contextual factors that create the interunit conflict are not inherent in the technology or are not essential parts of the administrative apparatus? Determine which of these might be modified to have a significant influence on the relationship.

An exhaustive treatment of the factors which are instrumental in altering a conflictful interunit relationship and which executives can modify would review the entire model. Instead, only a few relevant executive responses that have been treated in the literature are considered.

Thompson (1960) identified three areas of executive response: First, "Within limits, administrative allocations (of rewards, status symbols, resources, etc.) determine the relative deprivation experienced by organizational members, and thereby control potential conflict inherent in modern technologies" (392). Second, "To the extent that recruitment and selection procedures limit or maintain it within manageable pattern, the organization can manage the potential conflict in latent role diversity" (394). By latent role diversity, Thompson means differences in socioeconomic status, ethnic background, and so on. Third, "By varying the distinctiveness of the organization, the proportion of members exposed, and the frequency and regularity of their exposure, the organization gains a measure of control over conflict stemming from potential reactions to competing pressures" (396). Here he is referring to organizational conflict induced by ideas or pressures from the organization's environment.

Landsberger (1961) states that horizontal differences in authority can be more strongly supported by organizational logic, and need be less dependent on arbitrary fiat than vertical authority. On the other hand, differences in lateral authority are less obvious and are less likely to be stated explicitly, and therefore tend toward conflict. Consequently, one executive response is to make explicit rules allocating final authority for decisions on interunit activities, so as to depersonalize the order. A related response is for higher executives to develop rules to cover an increasing proportion of interunit transactions, and thereby confine decisions to exceptional situations, a practice noted by both Brown (1960) and Landsberger (1961).

Pondy (1967) refers to other devices which are not only available to those who manage the interface, but which can also be included in the executive response repertory: reducing dependence on common resources, transfer pricing between units, loosening schedules, or introducing buffer inventories. Litwak (1961) suggests many "mechanisms or segregation," used to reduce the conflict generated by contradictory social forms which modern organizations must incorporate, including stricter role separation between those for whom affect and those for whom strict objectivity is important; physical separation, such as moving the research facility away from the production facility; and transferral occupations, such as engineers who maintain involvement with a product from research to production stages.

Implications of the model for change of strategy. Ideally, higher executives would develop a strategy for modifying the level of interunit conflict and collaboration which not only acts on the problem diagnosed, but also takes into account the self-perpetuating characteristics of conflict relationships. The analysis of the dynamics of lateral relationship not only underscored the self-reinforcing tendencies of conflictful processes of information exchange, interaction patterns, and attitudes between units; it is also stressed the reciprocal and regenerative tendencies of conflictful approaches to the interface.

These self-reinforcing, regenerative and reciprocal tendencies lead to persistence of a conflict process; therefore, higher management needs to engage in activities designed to replace existing patterns. Blake, Shepard and Mouton (1964), and Walton (1968) have outlined theories and techniques of third-party consulting interventions. The underlying assumption is that the units must find a new culture in which to view and understand each other. Various techniques of re-education can be used to change intergroup perceptions based on stereotypes, misunderstanding the intention of others, and past history of hostile relations. Thus, whether higher executives conclude that basic contextual factors or techniques for interface management need to be modified, change effort will be effective only if it includes some interventions which help change the existing pattern.

CONCLUSIONS

Several features of the model of interunit conflict deserve emphasis: First, no a priori assumption is made that interunit conflict should be reduced. Second, the model recognizes a large number of potential determinants of conflict and conflict-reinforcement syndromes. Third, the model incorporates contextual and structural factors emphasized by sociologists and economists, as well as interpersonal interaction phenomena studied by social psychologists. These approaches are integrated in the explanatory model and in the action implications of the model. Fourth, the model of the internal dynamics of the relationship particularly throws light on the problems of unfreezing the existing patterns. Fifth, the ability to manage interunit conflict is shown to require sophistication in executive response.

REFERENCES

Argyris, Chris. 1964. *Integrating the individual and the organization.* New York: Wiley.

Blake, R. R., and H. A. Shephard, and J. S. Mouton. 1964. *Intergroup conflict in organizations.* Ann Arbor: Foundation for Research on Human Behavior.

Brown, Wilfred. 1960. *Explorations in management.* London: Tavistock.

Burns, T., and G. M. Stalker. 1961. *The management of innovation.* London: Tavistock.

Caplow, T. 1964. *Principles of organization.* New York: Harcourt, Brace and World.

Cozer, L. A. 1956. *The functions of social conflict.* Glencoe, Illinois: Free Press.

Crozier, Michel. 1961. "Human relations at the management level in a bureaucratic system of organization." *Human Organization,* 20: 51–64.

Dalton, M. 1959. *Men who manage.* New York: Wiley.

Dutton, J. M., and R. E. Walton. 1966. "Interdepartmental conflict and cooperation: two contrasting studies." *Human Organization,* 25: 207–220.

Georgopoulos, B., and F. Mann. 1962. *The community general hospital.* New York: Macmillan.

Kahn, R. L., D. M. Wolfe, R. P. Quinn, J. D. Snoek, and R. A. Rosenthal. 1964. *Organizational stress: Studies in role conflict and ambiguity.* New York: Wiley.

Landsberger, H. A. 1961. "The horizontal dimension in a bureaucracy." *Administrative Science Quarterly*, 6: 298–333.

Lawrence, P. R., and J. W. Lorsch. 1967a. *Organization and environment.* Boston: Division of Research, Graduate School of Business Administration, Harvard University. 1967b. "Differentiation and integration in complex organizations." *Administrative Science Quarterly*, 12: 1–47.

Likert, R. 1961. *New patterns of management.* New York: McGraw-Hill.

Litwak, E. 1961. "Models of bureaucracy which permit conflict." *American Journal of Sociology*, 67: 177–184.

March, J. G., and H. A. Simon. 1958. *Organizations.* New York: Wiley.

Miller, E. J. 1959. "Technology, territory and time." *Human Relations*, 12: 243–272.

Pondy, L. R. 1967. "Organizational conflict: concepts and models." *Administrative Science Quarterly*, 12: 296–320.

Schmidt, W., and R. Tannenbaum. 1960. "The management of differences." *Harvard Business Review*, 38 (November-December): 107–115.

Seiler, J. A. 1963. "Diagnosing interdepartmental conflict." *Harvard Business Review*, 41 (September-October): 121–132.

Simpson, R. L. 1959. "Vertical and horizontal communication in formal organization." *Administrative Science Quarterly*, 4: 188–196.

Strauss, G. 1962. "Tactics of lateral relationship: The purchasing agent." *Administrative Science Quarterly*, 7: 161–186. 1964. "Work-flow frictions, interfunctional, rivalry, and professionalism: A case study of purchasing agents." *Human Organization*, 23: 137–149.

Thompson, J. D. 1960. "Organizational management of conflict." *Administrative Science Quarterly*, 4: 389–409.

Thompson, V. A. 1961. *Modern organization.* New York: Alfred A. Knopf.

Walton, R. E. 1966. "Theory of conflict in lateral organizational relationships." In J. R. Lawrence (ed.). *Operational research and the social sciences*, 409–428. London: Tavistock. 1968. "Interpersonal confrontation and basic third-party roles." *Journal of Applied Behavioral Sciences.*

Walton, R. E., J. M. Dutton, and H. G. Fitch. 1966. "A study of conflict in the process, structure, and attitudes of lateral relationships." In Haberstroh and Rubenstein (eds.), *Some theories of organization.* Revised edition: 444–465. Homewood, Illinois: Irwin.

Walton, R. E., and R. B. McKersie. 1965. *A behavioral theory of labor negotiations.* New York: McGraw-Hill. 1966. "Behavioral dilemmas in mixed-motive decision making." *Behavioral Science*, 11: 370–384.

White, J. 1961. "Management conflict and social structure." *American Journal of Sociology*, 67: 185–191.

Zald, M. N. 1962. "Power balance and staff conflict in correctional institutions." *Administrative Science Quarterly*, 7: 22–49.

14
Group and Intergroup Relationships
Edgar H. Schein

INTERGROUP PROBLEMS IN ORGANIZATIONS

The first major problem of groups in organizations is how to make them effective in fulfilling both organizational goals and the needs of their members. The second major problem is how to establish conditions *between groups* which will enhance the productivity of each without destroying intergroup relations and coordination. This problem exists because as groups become more committed to their own goals and norms, they are likely to become competitive with one another and seek to undermine their rivals' activities, thereby becoming a liability to the organization as a whole. The over-all problem, then, is how to establish high-productive, *collaborative* intergroup relations.

Some Consequences of Intergroup Competition

The consequences of intergroup competition were first studied systematically by Sherif in an ingeniously designed setting. He organized a boys' camp in such a way that two groups would form and would become competitive. Sherif then studied the effects of the competition and tried various devices for re-establishing collaborative relationships between the groups.[14] Since his original

experiments, there have been many replications with adult groups; the phenomena are so constant that it has been possible to make a demonstration exercise out of the experiment.[15] The effects can be described in terms of the following categories:

A. What happens *within* each competing group?

1. Each group becomes more closely knit and elicits greater loyalty from its members; members close ranks and bury some of their internal differences.

2. Group climate changes from informal, casual, playful to work- and task-oriented; concern for members' psychological needs declines while concern for task accomplishment increases.

3. Leadership patterns tend to change from more democratic toward more autocratic; the group becomes more willing to tolerate autocratic leadership.

4. Each group becomes more highly structured and organized.

5. Each group demands more loyalty and conformity from its

[14]M. Sherif, O. J. Harvey, B. J. White, W. R. Hood, and Carolyn Sherif. *Intergroup conflict and cooperation; the robbers cave experiment.* Norman, Okla.: Univ. Book Exchange, 1961.

[15]R. R. Blake and Jane S. Mouton. Reactions to intergroup competition under win-lose conditions. *Management Science*, 1961, 7, 420–435.

Source: From Edgar H. Schein, *Organizational Psychology*, 2nd edition, pp. 80–89, Copyright © 1970. Reprinted by permission of Prentice-Hall, Inc., Englewood Cliffs, New Jersey.

Schein

members in order to be able to present a "solid front."

B. What happens *between* the competing groups?

1. Each group begins to see the other groups as the enemy, rather than merely a neutral object.

2. Each group begins to experience distortions of perceptions—it tends to perceive only the best parts of itself, denying its weaknesses, and tends to perceive only the worst parts of the other group, denying its strengths; each group is likely to develop a negative stereotype of the other ("they don't play fair like we do").

3. Hostility toward the other group increases while interaction and communication with the other group decrease; thus it becomes easier to maintain negative stereotypes and more difficult to correct perceptual distortions.

4. If the groups are forced into interaction—for example, if they are forced to listen to representatives plead their own and the others' cause in reference to some task—each group is likely to listen more closely to their own representative and not to listen to the representative of the other group, except to find fault with his presentation; in other words, group members tend to listen only for that which supports their own position and stereotype.

Thus far, I have listed some consequences of the competition itself, with-

out reference to the consequences if one group actually wins out over the other. Before listing those effects, I would like to draw attention to the generality of the above reactions. Whether one is talking about sports teams, or interfraternity competition, or labor-management disputes, or interdepartmental competition as between sales and production in an industrial organization, or about international relations and the competition between the Soviet Union and the United States, the same phenomena tend to occur. If you will give just a little thought to competing groups of which you have been a member, you will begin to recognize most of the psychological responses described. I want to stress that these responses can be very useful to the group in making it more effective and highly motivated in task accomplishment. However, the same factors which improve *intra*group effectiveness may have negative consequences for *inter*group effectiveness. For example, as we have seen in labor-management or international disputes, if the groups perceive themselves as competitors, they find it more difficult to resolve their differences.

Let us next look at the consequences of winning and losing, as in a situation where several groups are bidding to have their proposal accepted for a contract or as a solution to some problem, or in a labor-management negotiation being decided by an arbitrator, or in the typical athletic contest. Many intraorganizational situations become win-or-lose affairs, hence it is of particular importance to examine their consequences.

C. What happens to the *winner*?

1. Winner retains its cohesion and may become even more cohesive.

2. Winner tends to release tension, lose its fighting spirit,

become complacent, casual, and playful (the "fat and happy" state).

3. Winner tends toward high intragroup cooperation and concern for members' needs, and low concern for work and task accomplishment.

4. Winner tends to be complacent and to feel that winning has confirmed the positive stereotype of itself and the negative stereotype of the "enemy" group; there is little basis for reevaluating perceptions, or reexamining group operations in order to learn how to improve them.

D. What happens to the *loser?*

1. If the situation permits because of some ambiguity in the decision (say, if judges have rendered it or if the game was close), there is a strong tendency for the loser to deny or distort the reality of losing; instead, the loser will find psychological escapes like "the judges were biased," "the judges didn't really understand our solution," "the rules of the game were not clearly explained to us," "if luck had not been against us at the one key point, we would have won," and so on.

2. If loss is accepted, the losing group tends to splinter, unresolved conflicts come to the surface, fights break out, all in the effort to find a cause for the loss.

3. Loser is more tense, ready to work harder, and desperate to find someone or something to blame—the leader, itself, the judges who decided against

them, the rules of the game (the "lean and hungry" state).

4. Loser tends toward low intragroup cooperation, low concern for members' needs, and high concern for recouping by working harder.

5. Loser tends to learn a lot about itself as a group because positive stereotype of itself and negative stereotype of the other group are upset by the loss, forcing a reevaluation of perceptions; as a consequence, loser is likely to reorganize and become more cohesive and effective, once the loss has been accepted realistically.

The net effect of the win-lose situation is often that the loser is not convinced that he lost, and that intergroup tension is higher than before the competition began.

Reducing the Negative Consequences of Intergroup Competition

The gains of intergroup competition may under some conditions outweigh the negative consequences. It may be desirable to have work groups pitted against one another or to have departments become cohesive loyal units, even if interdepartmental coordination suffers. Other times, however, the negative consequences outweigh the gains, and management seeks ways of reducing intergroup tension. Many of the ideas to be mentioned about how this might be accomplished also come from the basic researches of Sherif and Blake; they have been tested and found to be successful. As we will see, the problems derive not so much from being unable to think of ways for reducing intergroup conflict as from being *unable to implement some of the most effective ways.*

Scheur

The fundamental problem of intergroup competition is the conflict of goals and the breakdown of interaction and communication between the groups; this breakdown in turn permits and stimulates perceptual distortion and mutual negative stereotyping. The basic strategy of reducing conflict, therefore, is to find goals upon which groups can agree and to reestablish valid communication between the groups. The tactics to employ in implementing this strategy can be any combination of the following:

Locating a common enemy. For example, the competing teams of each league can compose an all-star team to play the other league, or conflicts between sales and production can be reduced if both can harness their efforts to helping their company successfully compete against another company. The conflict here is merely shifted to a higher level.

Inventing a negotiation strategy which brings subgroups of the competing groups into interaction with each other. The isolated group representative cannot abandon his group position but a subgroup which is given some power can not only permit itself to be influenced by its counterpart negotiation team, but will have the strength to influence the remainder of the group.

Locating a superordinate goal. Such a goal can be a brand-new task which requires the cooperative effort of the previously competing groups or can be a task like analyzing and reducing the intergroup conflict itself. For example, the previously competing sales and production departments can be given the task of developing a new product line which will be both cheap to produce and in great customer demand; or, with the help of an outside consultant, the competing groups can be invited to examine their own behavior and re-evaluate the gains and losses from competition.

Reducing Intergroup Competition through Laboratory Training Methods. The last procedure mentioned above has been tried by a number of psychologists, notably Blake, with considerable success.[16] Assuming the organization recognizes that it has a problem, and assuming it is ready to expose this problem to an outside consultant, the laboratory approach to reducing conflict might proceed as follows: (1) The competing groups are both brought into a training setting and the goals are stated to be an exploration of mutual perceptions and mutual relations. (2) Each group is then invited to discuss its perceptions of and attitudes toward itself and the other group. (3) In the presence of both groups, representatives publicly share the perceptions of self and other which the groups have generated, while the groups are obligated to remain silent (the objective is simply to report to the other group as accurately as possible the images that each group has developed in private). (4) Before any exchange has taken place, the groups return to private sessions to digest and analyze what they have heard; there is a great likelihood that the representative reports have revealed great discrepancies to each group between its self-image and the image that the other group holds of it; the private session is partly devoted to an analysis of the reasons for the discrepancies, which forces each group to review its actual behavior toward the other group and the possible consequences of that behavior, regardless of its intentions. (5) In public session, again work-

[16]R. R. Blake, and Jane S. Mouton. Headquarters—field team training for organizational improvement. *J. of the Amer. Soc. of Training Directors*, 1962, 16.

ing through representatives, each group shares with the other what discrepancies they have uncovered and their analysis of the possible reasons for them, with the focus on the actual behavior exhibited. (6) Following this mutual exposure, a more open exploration is then permitted between the two groups on the *now-shared goal* of identifying further reasons for perceptual distortions.

Interspersed with these steps will be short lectures and reading assignments on the psychology of intergroup conflict, the bases for perceptual distortion, psychological defense-mechanisms, and so on. The goal is to bring the psychological dynamics of the situation into conscious awareness and to refocus the groups on the common goal of exploring jointly the problem they share. In order to do this, they must have valid data about each other, which is provided through the artifice of the representative reports.

The Blake model described above deals with the entire group. Various other approaches have been tried which start with members. For example, groups A and B can be divided into pairs composed of an A and B member. Each pair can be given the assignment of developing a joint product which uses the best ideas from the A product and the B product. Or, in each pair, members may be asked to argue for the product of the opposing group. It has been shown in a number of experiments that one way of changing attitudes is to ask a person to play the role of an advocate of the new attitude to be learned.[17] The very act of arguing for another product, even if it is purely an exercise, exposes the person to some of its virtues which he had previously denied. A practical application

of these points might be to have some members of the sales department spend some time in the production department and be asked to represent the production point of view to some third party, or to have some production people join sales teams to learn the sales point of view.

Most of the approaches cited depend on a recognition of some problem by the organization and a willingness on the part of the competing groups to participate in some training effort to reduce negative consequences. The reality, however, is that most organizations neither recognize the problem nor are willing to invest time and energy in resolving it. Some of the unwillingness also arises from each competing group's recognition that in becoming more cooperative it may lose some of its own identity and integrity as a group. Rather than risk this, the group may prefer to continue the competition. This may well be the reason why, in international relations, nations refuse to engage in what seem like perfectly simple ways of resolving their differences. They resist partly in order to protect their integrity. Consequently, the *implementation* of strategies and tactics for reducing the negative consequences of intergroup competition is often a greater problem than the development of such strategies and tactics.

Preventing Intergroup Conflict

Because of the great difficulties of reducing intergroup conflict once it has developed, it may be desirable to prevent its occurrence in the first place. How can this be done? Paradoxically, a strategy of prevention must bring into question the fundamental premise upon which organization through division of labor rests. Once it has been decided by a superordinate authority to divide up functions among different departments

[17] I. L. Janis and B. T. King. The influence of role playing on opinion change. *J. abnorm. soc. Psychol.*, 1954, 69, 211–218.

Schein

or groups, a bias has already been introduced toward intergroup competition; for in doing its own job well, each group must to some degree compete for scarce resources and rewards from the superordinate authority. The very concept of division of labor implies a reduction of communication and interaction between groups, thus making it possible for perceptual distortions to occur.

The organization planner who wishes to avoid intergroup competition need not abandon the concept of division of labor, but he should follow some of the steps listed below in creating and handling his different functional groups.

1. Relatively greater emphasis given to *total organizational effectiveness* and the role of departments in contributing to it; departments measured and rewarded on the basis of their *contribution* to the total effort rather than their individual effectiveness.

2. *High interaction* and *frequent communication* stimulated between groups to work on problems of intergroup coordination and help; organizational *rewards given partly on the basis of help* which groups give to each other.

3. Frequent *rotation of members* among groups or departments to stimulate high degree of mutual understanding and empathy for one anothers' problems.

4. *Avoidance of any win-lose situation;* groups never put into the position of competing for some organizational reward; emphasis always placed on pooling resources to maximize organizational effectiveness; rewards shared equally with all the groups or departments.

Most managers find the last of the above points particularly difficult to accept because of the strong belief that performance can be improved by pitting people or groups against one another in a competitive situation. This may indeed be true in the short run, and in some cases may work in the long run, but the negative consequences we have described are undeniably a product of a competitive win-lose situation. Consequently, if a manager wishes to prevent such consequences, he must face the possibility that he may have to abandon competitive relationships altogether and seek to substitute intergroup collaboration toward organizational goals. Implementing such a preventive strategy is often more difficult, partly because most people are inexperienced in stimulating and managing collaborative relationships. Yet it is clear from observing organizations such as those using the Scanlon Plan not only that it is possible to establish collaborative relationships, even between labor and management, but also that where this has been done, organizational and group effectiveness have been as high as or higher than under competitive conditions.

THE PROBLEM OF INTEGRATION IN PERSPECTIVE

I have discussed two basic issues in this chapter, both dealing with psychological groups: (1) the development of groups within organizations which can fulfill both the needs of the organization and the psychological needs of its members; and (2) the problems of intergroup competition and conflict. To achieve maximum integration, the organization should be able to create conditions which will facilitate a balance between organizational goals and member needs and which will minimize disintegrative competition between the subunits of the total organization.

Groups are highly complex sets of relationships. There are no easy generalizations about the conditions under which they will be effective, but with suitable training, many kinds of groups can become more effective than they have been. Consequently, group-dynamics training by laboratory methods may be a more promising approach to effectiveness than attempting *a priori* to determine the right membership, type of leadership, and organization. All the factors must be taken into account, with training perhaps weighted more heavily than it has been, though the training itself can be carefully undertaken.

The creation of psychologically meaningful and effective groups does not solve all of the organization's problems if such groups compete and conflict with each other. We examined some of the consequences of competition under win-lose conditions and outlined two basic approaches for dealing with the problem: (1) reducing conflict by increasing communication and locating superordinate goals, and (2) preventing conflict by establishing from the outset organizational conditions which stimulate collaboration rather than competition.

It is important to recognize that the preventive strategy does not imply absence of disagreement and artificial "sweetness and light" within or between groups. Conflict and disagreement at the level of the group or organizational *task* is not only desirable but essential for the achievement of the best solutions to problems. What is harmful is *interpersonal* or *intergroup* conflict in which the task is not as important as gaining advantage over the other person or group. The negative consequences we described, such as mutual negative stereotyping, fall into this latter category and undermine rather than aid over-all task performance. And it is these kinds of conflicts which can be reduced by establishing collaborative relationships. Interestingly, enough, observations of cases would suggest that task-relevant conflict which improves over-all effectiveness is greater under collaborative conditions because groups and members trust each other enough to be frank and open in sharing information and opinions. In the competitive situation, each group is committed to hiding its special resources from the other groups, thus preventing effective integration of all resources in the organization.

15

Groupthink: The Desperate Drive for Consensus at Any Cost

Irving L. Janis

"How could we have been so stupid?" President John F. Kennedy asked after he and a close group of advisers had blundered into the Bay of Pigs invasion. For the last two years I have been studying that question, as it applies not only to the Bay of Pigs decision-makers but also to those who led the United States into such other major fiascos as the failure to be prepared for the attack on Pearl Harbor, the Korean War stalemate and the escalation of the Vietnam War.

Stupidity certainly is not the explanation. The men who participated in making the Bay of Pigs decision, for instance, comprised one of the greatest arrays of intellectual talent in the history of American Government—Dean Rusk, Robert McNamara, Douglas Dillon, Robert Kennedy, McGeorge Bundy, Arthur Schlesinger Jr., Allen Dulles and others.

It also seemed to me that explanations were incomplete if they concentrated only on disturbances in the behavior of each individual within a decision-making body: temporary emotional states of elation, fear, or anger that reduce a man's mental efficiency, for example, or chronic blind spots arising from a man's social prejudices or idiosyncratic biases.

I preferred to broaden the picture by looking at the fiascos from the standpoint of group dynamics as it has been explored over the past three decades, first by the great social psychologist Kurt Lewin and later in many experimental situations by myself and other behavioral scientists. My conclusion after poring over hundreds of relevant documents—historical reports about formal group meetings and informal conversations among the members—is that the groups that committed the fiascos were victims of what I call "groupthink."

"Groupy." In each case study, I was surprised to discover the extent to which each group displayed the typical phenomena of social conformity that are regularly encountered in studies of group dynamics among ordinary citizens. For example, some of the phenomena appear to be completely in line with findings from social-psychological experiments showing that powerful social pressures are brought to bear by the members of a cohesive group whenever a dissident begins to voice his objections to a group consensus. Other phenomena are reminiscent of the shared illusions observed in encounter groups and friendship cliques when the members simultaneously reach a peak of "groupy" feelings.

Above all, there are numerous indications pointing to the development of group norms that bolster morale at the expense of critical thinking. One of the most common norms appears to be that

Source: From "Groupthink" by Irving L. Janis in *Psychology Today Magazine.* Copyright © 1971 American Psychological Association. Reprinted with permission from *Psychology Today Magazine.*

of remaining loyal to the group by sticking with the policies to which the group has already committed itself, even when those policies are obviously working out badly and have unintended consequences that disturb the conscience of each member. This is one of the key characteristics of groupthink.

1984. I use the term groupthink as a quick and easy way to refer to the mode of thinking that persons engage in when *concurrence-seeking* becomes so dominant in a cohesive ingroup that it tends to override realistic appraisal of alternative courses of action. Groupthink is a term of the same order as the words in the newspeak vocabulary George Orwell used in his dismaying world of *1984.* In that context, groupthink takes on an invidious connotation. Exactly such a connotation is intended, since the term refers to a deterioration in mental efficiency, reality testing and moral judgments as a result of group pressures.

The symptoms of groupthink arise when the members of decision-making groups become motivated to avoid being too harsh in their judgments of their leaders' or their colleagues' ideas. They adopt a soft line of criticism, even in their own thinking. At their meetings, all the members are amiable and seek complete concurrence on every important issue, with no bickering or conflict to spoil the cozy, "we-feeling" atmosphere.

Kill. Paradoxically, soft-headed groups are often hard-hearted when it comes to dealing with outgroups or enemies. They find it relatively easy to resort to dehumanizing solutions—they will readily authorize bombing attacks that kill large numbers of civilians in the name of the noble cause of persuading an unfriendly government to negotiate at the peace table. They are unlikely to pursue the more difficult and

controversial issues that arise when alternatives to a harsh military solution come up for discussion. Nor are they inclined to raise ethical issues that carry the implication that *this fine group of ours, with its humanitarianism and its high-minded principles, might be capable of adopting a course of action that is inhumane and immoral.*

Norms. There is evidence from a number of social-psychological studies that as the members of a group feel more accepted by the others, which is a central feature of increased group cohesiveness, they display less overt conformity to group norms. Thus we would expect that the more cohesive a group becomes, the less the members will feel constrained to censor what they say out of fear of being socially punished for antagonizing the leader or any of their fellow members.

In contrast, the groupthink type of conformity tends to increase as group cohesiveness increases. Groupthink involves nondeliberate suppression of critical thoughts as a result of internalization of the group's norms, which is quite different from deliberate suppression on the basis of external threats of social punishment. The more cohesive the group, the greater the inner compulsion on the part of each member to avoid creating disunity, which inclines him to believe in the soundness of whatever proposals are promoted by the leader or by a majority of the group's members.

In a cohesive group, the danger is not so much that each individual will fail to reveal his objections to what the others propose but that he will think the proposal is a good one, without attempting to carry out a careful, critical scrutiny of the pros and cons of the alternatives. When groupthink becomes dominant, there also is considerable suppression of deviant thoughts, but it takes the form of each person's deciding that his misgivings are not relevant and should be set aside, that the benefit of the doubt regarding any lingering uncertainties should be given to the group consensus.

Stress. I do not mean to imply that all cohesive groups necessarily suffer from groupthink. All ingroups may have a mild tendency toward groupthink, displaying one or another of the symptoms from time to time, but it need not be so dominant as to influence the quality of the group's final decision. Neither do I mean to imply that there is anything necessarily inefficient or harmful about group decisions in general. On the contrary, a group whose members have properly defined roles, with traditions concerning the procedures to follow in pursuing a critical inquiry, probably is capable of making better decisions than any individual group member working alone.

The problem is that the advantages of having decisions made by groups are often lost because of powerful psychological pressures that arise when the members work closely together, share the same set of values and, above all, face a crisis situation that puts everyone under intense stress.

The main principle of groupthink, which I offer in the spirit of Parkinson's Law, is this: *The more amiability and esprit de corps there is among the members of a policy-making ingroup, the greater the danger that independent critical thinking will be replaced by groupthink, which is likely to result in irrational and dehumanizing actions directed against outgroups.*

Symptoms. In my studies of high-level governmental decision-makers, both civilian and military, I have found eight main symptoms of groupthink.

1. INVULNERABILITY. Most or all of the members of the ingroup share an illusion of invulnerability that provides for them some degree of reassurance about obvious dangers and leads them to become over-optimistic and willing to take extraordinary risks. It also causes them to fail to respond to clear warnings of danger.

The Kennedy ingroup, which uncritically accepted the Central Intelligence Agency's disastrous Bay of Pigs plan, operated on the false assumption that they could keep secret the fact that the United States was responsible for the invasion of Cuba. Even after news of the plan began to leak out, their belief remained unshaken. They failed even to consider the danger that awaited them: a worldwide revulsion against the U.S.

A similar attitude appeared among the members of President Lyndon B. Johnson's ingroup, the "Tuesday Cabinet," which kept escalating the Vietnam War despite repeated setbacks and failures. "There was a belief," Bill Moyers commented after he resigned, "that if we indicated a willingness to use our power, they [the North Vietnamese] would get the message and back away from an all-out confrontation. . . . There was a confidence—it was never bragged about, it was just there—that when the chips were really down, the other people would fold."

A most poignant example of an illusion of invulnerability involves the ingroup around Admiral H. E. Kimmel, which failed to prepare for the possibility of a Japanese attack on Pearl Harbor despite repeated warnings. Informed by his intelligence chief that radio contact with Japanese aircraft carriers had been lost, Kimmel joked about it: "What, you don't know where the carriers are? Do you mean to say that they could be rounding Diamond Head (at Honolulu) and you wouldn't know it?" The carriers were in fact moving full-steam toward Kimmel's command post at the time. Laughing together about a danger signal, which labels it as a purely laughing matter, is a characteristic manifestation of groupthink.

2. RATIONALE. As we see, victims of groupthink ignore warnings; they also collectively construct rationalizations in order to discount warnings and other forms of negative feedback that, taken seriously, might lead the group members to reconsider their assumptions each time they recommit themselves to past decisions. Why did the Johnson ingroup avoid reconsidering its escalation policy when time and again the expectations on which they based their decisions turned out to be wrong? James C. Thompson, Jr., a Harvard historian who spent five years as an observing participant in both the State Department and the White House, tells us that the policymakers avoided critical discussion of their prior decisions and continually invented new rationalizations so that they could sincerely recommit themselves to defeating the North Vietnamese.

In the fall of 1964, before the bombing of North Vietnam began, some of the policymakers predicted that six weeks of air strikes would induce the North Vietnamese to seek peace talks. When someone asked, "What if they don't?" the answer was that another four weeks certainly would do the trick.

Later, after each setback, the ingroup agreed that by investing just a bit more effort (by stepping up the bomb tonnage a bit, for instance), their course of action would prove to be right. *The Pentagon Papers* bear out those observations.

In *The Limits of Intervention*, Townsend Hoopes, who was acting Secretary of the Air Force under Johnson, says that Walt W. Rostow in particular showed a remarkable capacity for what has been called "instant rationalization." According to Hoopes, Rostow buttressed the group's optimisim about being on the road to victory by culling

selected scraps of evidence from news reports or, if necessary, by inventing "plausible" forecasts that had no basis in evidence at all.

Admiral Kimmel's group rationalized away their warnings, too. Right up to December 7, 1941, they convinced themselves that the Japanese would never dare attempt a full-scale surprise assault against Hawaii because Japan's leaders would realize that it would precipitate an all-out war which the United States would surely win. They made no attempt to look at the situation through the eyes of the Japanese leaders—another manifestation of groupthink.

3. MORALITY. Victims of groupthink believe unquestioningly in the inherent morality of their ingroup; this belief inclines the members to ignore the ethical or moral consequences of their decisions.

Evidence that this symptom is at work usually is of a negative kind—the things that are left unsaid in group meetings. At least two influential persons had doubts about the morality of the Bay of Pigs adventure. One of them, Arthur Schlesinger Jr., presented his strong objections in a memorandum to President Kennedy and Secretary of State Rusk but suppressed them when he attended meetings of the Kennedy team. The other, Senator J. William Fulbright, was not a member of the group, but the President invited him to express his misgivings in a speech to the policymakers. However, when Fulbright finished speaking the President moved on to other agenda items without asking for reactions of the group.

David Kraslow and Stuart H. Loory, in *The Secret Search for Peace in Vietnam*, report that during 1966 President Johnson's ingroup was concerned primarily with selecting bomb targets in North Vietnam. They based their selections on four factors—the military advantage, the risk to American aircraft and pilots, the danger of forcing other countries into the fighting, and the danger of heavy civilian casualties. At their regular Tuesday luncheons, they weighed these factors the way school teachers grade examination papers, averaging them out. Though evidence on this point is scant, I suspect that the group's ritualistic adherence to a standardized procedure induced the members to feel morally justified in their destructive way of dealing with the Vietnamese people—after all, the danger of heavy civilian casualties from U.S. air strikes was taken into account on their checklists.

4. STEREOTYPES. Victims of groupthink hold stereotyped views of the leaders of enemy groups: they are so evil that genuine attempts at negotiating differences with them are unwarranted, or they are too weak or too stupid to deal effectively with whatever attempts the ingroup makes to defeat their purposes, no matter how risky the attempts are.

Kennedy's groupthinkers believed that Premier Fidel Castro's air force was so ineffectual that obsolete B-26s could knock it out completely in a surprise attack before the invasion began. They also believed that Castro's army was so weak that a small Cuban-exile brigade could establish a well-protected beachhead at the Bay of Pigs. In addition, they believed that Castro was not smart enough to put down any possible internal uprisings in support of the exiles. They were wrong on all three assumptions. Though much of the blame was attributable to faulty intelligence, the point is that none of Kennedy's advisers even questioned the CIA planners about these assumptions.

The Johnson advisers' sloganistic thinking about "the Communist apparatus" that was "working all around the world" (as Dean Rusk put it) led them to overlook the powerful nationalistic strivings of the North Vietnamese government and its efforts to ward off Chinese domination. The crudest of all stereotypes used by Johnson's inner circle to justify their policies was the domino theory ("If we don't stop the Reds in South Vietnam, tomorrow they will be in Hawaii and next week they will be in San Francisco," Johnson once said). The group so firmly accepted this stereotype that it became almost impossible for any adviser to introduce a more sophisticated viewpoint.

In the documents on Pearl Harbor, it is clear to see that the Navy commanders stationed in Hawaii had a naive image of Japan as a midget that would not dare to strike a blow against a powerful giant.

5. PRESSURE. Victims of groupthink apply direct pressure to any individual who momentarily expresses doubts about any of the group's shared illusions or who questions the validity of the arguments supporting a policy alternative favored by the majority. This gambit reinforces the concurrence-seeking norm that loyal members are expected to maintain.

President Kennedy probably was more active than anyone else in raising skeptical questions during the Bay of Pigs meetings, and yet he seems to have encouraged the group's docile, uncritical acceptance of defective arguments in favor of the CIA's plan. At every meeting, he allowed the CIA representatives to dominate the discussion. He permitted them to give their immediate refutations in response to each tentative doubt that one of the others expressed, instead of asking whether anyone shared the doubt or wanted to pursue the implications of the new worrisome issue that had just been raised.

And at the most crucial meeting, when he was calling on each member to give his vote for or against the plan, he did not call on Arthur Schlesinger, the one man there who was known by the President to have serious misgivings.

Historian Thomson informs us that whenever a member of Johnson's in-group began to express doubts, the group used subtle social pressures to "domesticate" him. To start with, the dissenter was made to feel at home provided that he lived up to two restrictions: 1) that he did not voice his doubts to outsiders, which would play into the hands of the opposition; and 2) that he kept his criticisms within the bounds of acceptable deviation, which meant not challenging any of the fundamental assumptions that went into the group's prior commitments. One such "domesticated dissenter" was Bill Moyers. When Moyers arrived at a meeting, Thomson tells us, the President greeted him with, "Well, here comes Mr. Stop-the-Bombing."

6. SELF-CENSORSHIP. Victims of groupthink avoid deviating from what appears to be group consensus; they keep silent about their misgivings and even minimize to themselves the importance of their doubts.

As we have seen, Schlesinger was not at all hesitant about presenting his strong objections to the Bay of Pigs plan in a memorandum to the President and the Secretary of State. But he became keenly aware of his tendency to suppress objections at the White House meetings. "In the months after the Bay of Pigs, I bitterly reproached myself for having kept so silent during those crucial discussions in the cabinet room," Schlesinger writes in A *Thousand Days,* "I can only explain my failure to do more than raise a few timid questions by reporting that one's impulse to blow the whistle on this nonsense was simply undone by the circumstances of the discussion."

7. UNANIMITY. Victims of groupthink share an illusion of unanimity within the group concerning almost all judgments expressed by members who speak in favor of the majority view. This symptom results partly from the preceding one, whose effects are augmented by the false assumption that any individual who remains silent during any part of the discussion is in full accord with what the others are saying.

When a group of persons who respect each other's opinions arrives at a unanimous view, each member is likely to feel that the belief must be true. This reliance on consensual validation within the group tends to replace individual critical thinking and reality testing, unless there are clear-cut disagreements among the members. In contemplating a course of action such as the invasion of Cuba, it is painful for the members to confront disagreements within their group, particularly if it becomes apparent that there are widely divergent views about whether the preferred course of action is too risky to undertake at all. Such disagreements are likely to arouse anxieties about making a serious error. Once the sense of unanimity is shattered, the members no longer can feel complacently confident about the decision they are inclined to make. Each man must then face the annoying realization that there are troublesome uncertainties and he must diligently seek out the best information he can get in order to decide for himself exactly how serious the risks might be. This is one of the unpleasant consequences of being in a group of hard-headed, critical thinkers.

To avoid such an unpleasant state, the members often become inclined, without quite realizing it, to prevent latent disagreements from surfacing when they are about to initiate a risky, course of action. The group leader and the members support each other in playing up the areas of convergence in their thinking, at the expense of fully exploring divergencies that might reveal unsettled issues.

"Our meetings took place in a curious atmosphere of assumed consensus," Schlesinger writes. His additional comments clearly show that, curiously, the consensus was an illusion—an illusion that could be maintained only because the major participants did not reveal their own reasoning or discuss their idiosyncratic assumptions and vague reservations. Evidence from several sources makes it clear that even the three principals—President Kennedy, Rusk and McNamara—had widely differing assumptions about the invasion plan.

8. MINDGUARDS. Victims of groupthink sometimes appoint themselves as mindguards to protect the leader and fellow members from adverse information that might break the complacency they shared about the effectiveness and morality of past decisions. At a large birthday party for his wife, Attorney General Robert F. Kennedy, who had been constantly informed about the Cuban invasion plan, took Schlesinger aside and asked him why he was opposed. Kennedy listened coldly and said, "You may be right or you may be wrong, but the President has made his mind up. Don't push it any further. Now is the time for everyone to help him all they can."

Rusk also functioned as a highly effective mindguard by failing to transmit to the group the strong objections of three "outsiders" who had learned of the invasion plan—Undersecretary of State Chester Bowles, USIA Director Edward R. Murrow, and Rusk's intelligence chief, Roger Hilsman. Had Rusk done so, their warnings might have reinforced Schlesinger's memorandum and jolted some of Kennedy's ingroup, if not the President himself, into reconsidering the decision.

Products. When a group of executives frequently displays most or all of these interrelated symptoms, a detailed study of their deliberations is likely to reveal a number of immediate consequences. These consequences are, in effect, products of poor decision-making practices because they lead to inadequate solutions to the problems under discussion.

First, the group limits its discussions to a few alternative courses of action (often only two) without an initial survey of all the alternatives that might be worthy of consideration.

Second, the group fails to reexamine the course of action initially preferred by the majority after they learn of risks and drawbacks they had not considered originally.

Third, the members spend little or no time discussing whether there are nonobvious gains they may have overlooked or ways of reducing the seemingly prohibitive costs that made rejected alternatives appear undesirable to them.

Fourth, members make little or no attempt to obtain information from experts within their own organizations who might be able to supply more precise estimates of potential losses and gains.

Fifth, members show positive interest in facts and opinions that support their preferred policy, they tend to ignore facts and opinions that do not.

Sixth, members spend little time deliberating about how the chosen policy might be hindered by bureaucratic inertia, sabotaged by political opponents, or temporarily derailed by common accidents. Consequently, they fail to work out contingency plans to cope with foreseeable setbacks that could endanger the overall success of their chosen course.

Support. The search for an explanation of why groupthink occurs has led me through a quagmire of complicated theoretical issues in the murky area of human motivation. My belief, based on recent social psychological research, is that we can best understand the various symptoms of groupthink as a mutual effort among the group members to maintain self-esteem and emotional equanimity by providing social support to each other, especially at times when they share responsibility for making vital decisions.

Even when no important decision is pending, the typical administrator will begin to doubt the wisdom and morality of his past decisions each time he receives information about setbacks, particularly if the information is accompanied by negative feedback from prominent men who originally had been his supporters. It should not be surprising, therefore, to find that individual members strive to develop unanimity and esprit de corps that will help bolster each other's morale, to create an optimistic outlook about the success of pending decisions, and to reaffirm the positive value of past policies to which all of them are committed.

Pride. Shared illusions of invulnerability, for example, can reduce anxiety about taking risks. Rationalizations help members believe that the risks are really not so bad after all. The assumption of inherent morality helps the members to avoid feelings of shame or guilt. Negative stereotypes function as stress-reduc-

ing devices to enhance a sense of moral righteousness as well as pride in a lofty mission.

The mutual enhancement of self-esteem and morale may have functional value in enabling the members to maintain their capacity to take action, but it has maladaptive consequences insofar as concurrence-seeking tendencies interfere with critical, rational capacities and lead to serious errors of judgment.

While I have limited my study to decision-making bodies in government, groupthink symptoms appear in business, industry and any other field where small, cohesive groups make the decisions. It is vital, then, for all sorts of people—and especially group leaders—to know what steps they can take to prevent groupthink.

Remedies. To counterpoint my case studies of the major fiascos, I have also investigated two highly successful group enterprises, the formulation of the Marshall Plan in the Truman Administration and the handling of the Cuban missile crisis by President Kennedy and his advisers. I have found it instructive to examine the steps Kennedy took to change his group's decision-making processes. These changes ensured that the mistakes made by his Bay of Pigs ingroup were not repeated by the missile-crisis ingroup, even though the membership of both groups was essentially the same.

The following recommendations for preventing groupthink incorporate many of the good practices I discovered to be characteristic of the Marshall Plan and missile crisis groups:

1. The leader of a policy-forming group should assign the role of critical evaluator to each member, encouraging the group to give high priority to open airing of objections and doubts. This

practice needs to be reinforced by the leader's acceptance of criticism of his own judgments in order to discourage members from soft-pedaling their disagreements and from allowing their striving for concurrence to inhibit critical thinking.

2. When the key members of a hierarchy assign a policy-planning mission to any group within their organization, they should adopt an impartial stance instead of stating preferences and expectations at the beginning. This will encourage open inquiry and impartial probing of a wide range of policy alternatives.

3. The organization routinely should set up several outside policy-planning and evaluation groups to work on the same policy question, each deliberating under a different leader. This can prevent the insulation of an in-group.

4. At intervals before the group reaches a final consensus, the leader should require each member to discuss the group's deliberations with associates in his own unit of the organization—assuming that those associates can be trusted to adhere to the same security regulations that govern the policy-makers—and then to report back their reactions to the group.

5. The group should invite one or more outside experts to each meeting on a staggered basis and encourage the experts to challenge the views of the core members.

6. At every general meeting of the group, whenever the agenda calls for an evaluation of policy alternatives, at least one member should play devil's advocate, functioning as a good lawyer in challenging the testimony of those who advocate the majority position.

7. Whenever the policy issue involves relations with a rival nation or organization, the group should devote a sizable block of time, perhaps an entire session, to a survey of all warning signals from the rivals and should write alternative scenarios on the rivals' intentions.

8. When the group is surveying policy alternatives for feasibility and effectiveness, it should from time to time divide into two or more subgroups to meet separately, under different chairmen, and then come back together to hammer out differences.

9. After reaching a preliminary consensus about what seems to be the best policy, the group should hold a "second-chance" meeting at which every member expresses as vividly as he can all his residual doubts, and rethinks the entire issue before making a definitive choice.

How. These recommendations have their disadvantages. To encourage the open airing of objections, for instance, might lead to prolonged and costly debates when a rapidly growing crisis requires immediate solution. It also could cause rejection, depression and anger. A leader's failure to set a norm might create cleavage between leader and members that could develop into a disruptive power struggle if the leader looks on the emerging consensus as anathema. Setting up outside evaluation groups might increase the risk of security leakage. Still, inventive executives who know their way around the organizational maze probably can figure out how to apply one or another of the prescriptions successfully, without harmful side effects.

They also could benefit from the advice of outside experts in the administrative and behavioral sciences. Though these experts have much to offer, they have had few chances to work on policy-making machinery within large organizations. As matters now stand, executives innovate only when they need new procedures to avoid repeating serious errors that have deflated their self-images.

In this era of atomic warheads, urban disorganization and ecocatastrophes, it seems to me that policymakers should collaborate with behavioral scientists and give top priority to preventing groupthink and its attendant fiascos.

16

Coalitions

Jeffrey Pfeffer

Having considered some of the processes through which power is used in an unobtrusive fashion and in such a way as to legitimate and rationalize the decision results, our attention will focus next on some processes through which additional power and support is mustered for political contests within organizations. Organizations are, above all else, systems of interdependent activity. Because of the division of labor and specialization of tasks which occur within formal organizations, interdependence is created among subunits and positions. By interdependence we mean that in order for one subunit to accomplish something, it requires the efforts and cooperation of other subunits. In order for the sales department to sell the product, it may have to rely on production for satisfactory delivery times and product reliability. In order for production to keep its costs down, it may have to rely on the purchasing department to provide high quality input supplies on an assured basis. This interdependence within organizations means that there is often a great deal of contact across subunit boundaries. And, this interdependence means that the potential for both conflict and cooperation exists. The interdependence creates conflict because the goals and values within each of the various interacting organizational units may not be consonant. The potential for cooperation and coalition formation exists because organizational partici-

pants are used to working with and through others in order to get things done.

Thus, organizational politics may involve the formation of coalitions with others either inside or outside of the formally designated organizational boundaries. In some sense, the use of the outside expert can be viewed as a coalition formation strategy with an external party. In that case, the inside subunit or groups form a coalition with an outside expert or set of experts to advocate their position on a set of decision issues. Since the expert is presumably value neutral and objective, the visibility and explicitness of the coalition formation process is lower than in the instances to be described later.

Although there is an extensive theory of coalition formation and coalition size developed in the literature on political science (cf. Riker, 1962; Leiserson, 1970), there are two difficulties in transferring that literature directly to the issue of analyzing coalition formation in formal organizations. The literature in political science has been virtually exclusively developed in one of two contexts: the study of voting blocs and coalitions in legislatures (e.g., Rosenthal, 1970) or the study of coalition formation in small, experimental groups (e.g., Gamson, 1964).

Neither context is representative of the situation confronted within formal organizations. In the legislature con-

Source: From *Power in Organizations* by Jeffrey Pfeffer. Copyright © 1981 by Jeffrey Pfeffer. Reprinted with permission from Ballinger Publishing Company.

text, it is individuals who are bargaining, log-rolling, and forming coalitions, whereas one of the distinctive features of formal organizations is the fact that much of the activity takes place on the level of the organizational subunit. Additionally, the degree of socialization, interdependence, and consequently, solidarity is somewhat different in the two contexts. Most organizations have much more elaborate control and socialization systems, which means that there exists an ideology of an overarching organizational goal and there is probably more trust and commonly shared values than in legislatures. The small, experimental groups have suffered until quite recently from the fact that they were constructed so as to have no history and to play a very short sequence of games. In contrast, in an ongoing organization, there is a history and a future to social interaction which constrains the strategies participants will use against each other and which provides some moderation and stability to the action.

The second problem, which is in some sense even more troublesome, is that most theories of coalition formation and operation proceed from assumptions of rationality and calculation which are not completely consistent with either observed events or theories of social behavior from psychology or sociology. We could pick on many such premises, but one of the most prominent will serve to illustrate this point. One of the theoretical ideas emerging from coalition research is that participants in the political struggle seek to form coalitions that are of the minimum winning size (Riker, 1962). This is because of the assumption that although actors want to win in order to share in the rewards acquired by the winning coalition, they want to share these rewards with as few others as possible; hence, a

coalition of the smallest size necessary to win is the most desirable. Importing these ideas into an organizational context, one would predict that a decision would be made whenever enough support was mustered behind one position or the other to ensure that a decision could be made.

But this is not what is observed in many instances. Many times, long after the preponderance of support in an organization has come down on one side of an issue, the discussion, debate, and decision process continues in an attempt to build a broader base of support for the decision. Indeed, the goal of building consensus behind some policy or decision is one that is empirically observable in many choice situations. The desire for widely shared consensus at times means that making the decision rapidly or as soon as it is politically possible to do so is sacrificed in the interests of getting as many organizational interests as possible behind the decision. One difference from the theory of the minimal winning coalition is that the situation addressed by the traditional, political science theories of coalitions is one in which the decision making ends the action, and a policy is decided and the rewards are divided. In ongoing organizations, implementation of and commitment to the decision may be as important, if not more so, than the decision itself. Making a decision in a context in which there is enough opposition so that implementation in an interdependent set of actors is problematic, is probably an almost useless activity. Many excellent decisions have been doomed by implementation problems. Thus, in formal organizations instead of the observation of the principle of the minimum winning coalition size, what is observed more often is the maximum possible coalition size principle. In this case, the making of a decision is delayed until all the interests that can possibly be lined up in support of the decision have been approached and courted. It is only when it becomes clear that almost no additional concessions or political action can produce additional support for the decision, that the decision will be finally made. Although this principle presumes some lack of immediate time pressure, this practice of consensus building is frequently followed even when there is some pressure for fairly rapid action. As Bucher (1970:45) has noted, "most of the opposition to an idea is worked through . . . or else the proposal dies."

Yet another difference involves the zero versus increasing sum nature of the game being played. Studies of coalition behavior in experimental groups or legislatures take a situation or construct a situation in which the total rewards to be distributed among the participants are fixed at the outset. By contrast, competition and conflict among those interacting in the situation in organizations are on occasion somewhat more like a varying sum game in which one party's gain may not be the other's loss. Even when, as in the case of budget allocations or promotion decisions, there is a relatively fixed sum to be distributed, because of the values and norms stressing the goals and success of the total organization, the losers can be given symbolic assurances that the choice maximizes their long-term welfare and increases the overall well-being of the total organization. We will consider the symbolic use of political language in detail in the next chapter. For the moment we assert that the myth of organizational goals serves to transform the decision situation into somewhat less a zero-sum game than what typically is faced in the arena of legislative politics or experimental games.

What this means is that although the analysis of coalition formation and coalition behavior in organizations can start with ideas from political science, it will have to develop its own theory and empirical base because of the differences between organizational contexts and legislative and small-group contexts. We have already suggested one difference in the argument about the size of the coalition desired. One could refine that argument to further suggest that the attempt to maximize the size of the coalition will be observed more in situations in which commitment and motivation in the organization has a stronger normative (as contrasted with utilitarian) basis. Thus, the consensus building and coalition size maximization which is described is more likely to be observed in universities or social service agencies than in business firms; within business firms, is more likely to be observed in organizations which rely heavily on shared values, socialization, and inculturation as forms of control (Ouchi and Jaeger, 1978).

We have also implicitly suggested that coalition formation activity will be more prevalent to the extent that there is more task and resource interdependence within the organization. The creation of self-contained subunits or the provision of slack resources, both of which reduce interdependence among subunits (Galbraith, 1973), will tend to reduce the coalition formation activity. An extension of this argument would maintain that coalition formation activity would increase and revolve around those decisions within the organization that involve task or resource interdependence. So, the most political activity in terms of attempting to garner support and allies for one's position can be observed in situations in which there is a higher degree of resource interdependence within the organization. The amount of coalition formation activity will be reduced to the extent that units face environments of more resources or are less interdependent.

BUILDING EXTERNAL CONSTITUENCIES

There are two foci for coalition formation activity. The first focus is outward to groups in contact with the organization, and the second focus is within the organization to other social actors whose support may be obtained. Both types of supporters are sought, and each has its own advantages and disadvantages. Allies external to the organization are less likely to be in direct competition with the subunit in question for resources, power, or decision outcomes within the organization. It is, in some sense, more feasible to expect to find a symbiotic rather than competitive relationship with an external group or organization. By the same token, however, allies within the organization are closer to the actual decision process and therefore are somewhat more valuable in influencing decision outcomes. An external ally may have less conflict of interest with the internal subunit. However, because of its distance and lack of direct involvement in the decision process, the external group can apply pressure to the organization but can less easily intervene in the decision process to advocate and selectively use information. Allies more proximately connected to the decision sequence are potentially more helpful in affecting the decision outcome.

Another cost of building and using alliances with participants outside of the organization is that such an activity can be viewed as being disloyal to the organization and its goals. As argued previously, the ideology of most organizations suggests the existence of a common goal or set of goals sought by those within the organization. To build alliances with external groups suggests a rejection of the organization's interests for selfish interests of the subunit, a view which is likely to be seen as going against the norms of internal cooperation and goal sharing. For this reason, it might be hypothesized that the building of external alliances and constituencies will be done somewhat more circumspectly, particularly in contexts in which the concept or belief in shared goals and values within the organization is particularly strong.

At the same time, it is clear that in many organizational contexts subunits attempt to develop relationships with external groups as a way of enhancing their power within the organization and increasing the likelihood of getting their way in organizational decisions. This process can be illustrated with several examples.

At a small electronics firm in the Southwest, the purchase of components and raw materials had been centralized and delegated to a purchasing department. This department had instituted procedures to select vendors and evaluate their quality as well as to ensure that price and quality control standards were met. The manufacturing operation within the firm, then, dealt through the purchasing department to obtain necessary supplies. Over time conflict developed between the two units. Manufacturing was most concerned about having enough materials of high enough quality on a timely basis. The manufacturing unit was much less concerned with the cost of the materials, and whether or not the suppliers had favorable or unfavorable credit terms. The unit was particularly unconcerned with the bureaucratic niceties of the procurement process, the filling out of requisitions, obtaining bids, evaluating vendors, and placing of orders. Finally, manufacturing went to the president of the company and argued that it should be allowed to purchase directly. This would fulfill its requirements more satisfactorily and also permit the corporation to save money by eliminating the purchasing department.

Having gone through the process of establishing relationships with certain vendors for various supply requirements, purchasing had, of course, developed close and at times personal relationships with these vendors. The vendors could not be sure that if the acquisition process were changed, they would still be able to generate the same volume of business. In addition, they had grown accustomed to the procedures and people in purchasing. To change and develop a new set of relationships would be time consuming and uncertain. Thus, the external constituency, those currently selling to the firm, was there to be mobilized.

The purchasing personnel informed the current vendors about what was going on within the firm and, furthermore, implied that if manufacturing took over the ordering, it was not too likely that the same business relationships would be maintained. The various vendors then wrote to the president of the firm, noting that the procedures and practices followed by the purchasing department in this firm and by similar departments in other firms enabled the vendors to plan production rates, quality standards, and specifications for the product. If the firm were to use another acquisition process, it was possible that order delivery, product reliability and willingness to work with the firm might be harmed. The firm, as previously noted, was relatively small. Input quality and delivery were important factors in controlling manufacturing costs, in ensuring product quality and, therefore, in affecting the success of the firm. Rather than risk offending these necessary and powerful suppliers for the sole reason of satisfying a subunit within the

firm, the president maintained the present organizational arrangements. The future of purchasing thus was more secure than ever and the department had even more power than before.

As another example, consider the power of many accounting groups within business schools. In some instances, accounting has been able to institute its own separate master's degree program. In other instances accounting has been able to offer the largest number of doctoral courses. Typically, accounting faculty are paid somewhat more than other faculty within the school. Accounting students and faculty may receive more financial support from the school. This has tended to come about in those cases in which the accounting group has been able to build strong relationships with the professional accounting community, and this professional constituency has become active in donating money and other forms of support to the school. Once this relationship is established, every time a suggestion is made to cut down accounting enrollments, equalize resources across groups, or in some other way shift power within the schools, the accounting faculty quickly call up their external supporters who place pressure on the school to continue to favor accounting. The implied threat is that if accounting is not maintained in its favored position, the donated resources, which are of use to other groups as well, will dry up.

Finally, no setting is better for illustrating the development of external constituencies than governmental agencies. Agencies that deliver social services, money, or other benefits to various groups typically develop effective contact with those groups so that these external constituencies can be mobilized if funding is about to be reduced or the program cut back in some other way. Although this constituency building is done throughout government, it was quite evident in the various poverty, housing, and training programs that were the legacy of Lyndon Johnson's War on Poverty Program. One of the things mandated by these programs was the development of community-based organizations to help with the delivery of services and with the policy formulation and management of these various activities on the local level. Ironically, these community action boards, manpower planning agencies, and housing and development boards were then politically organized and potent supporters of the various programs that were the domain of their related government bureaucracies. Any attempt to reduce funding for a given program would trigger an immediate outcry of protest from the local groups that had been established by the program itself. In this case the agency did not have to try very hard to establish an external constituency which would support it in internal struggles for resources; such organizations were decreed by the very content of the legislation which established the programs in the first place.

Building external constituencies requires contact with some organizations or groups outside the organization that are interdependent with the organization and that can be mobilized to support related internal subunits. Thus, although this strategy is certainly used, it is one that is not as readily open to every participant within the organization. However, all organizational actors can engage in building coalitions and alliances with others within the organization.

INTERNAL ALLIANCES

Just as in the case of building external constituencies, internal alliances are founded on common interests among the various participants. Internal alliances are likely to be particularly sought by the less powerful actors in the organization. Because of their limited power, the best way to ensure that these less powerful actors can achieve their interests in the organization is by finding common interests with others, particularly those with more power. Pfeffer and Salancik (1977a), for example, noted that knowledge of the internal power distribution was more highly related to resource allocations, controlling other factors, for those departments that were themselves less powerful. They argued that it was particularly necessary for the less powerful university departments to know the distribution of power because it was these departments that would find it most necessary to form alliances and find powerful sponsorship for their interests. Thus, one can predict that organizational coalitions are more likely to be sought more vigorously by the less powerful social actors within an organization.

Coalitions with other groups on issues where common positions can be identified make it possible for each group to obtain its desired outcomes. Two examples will serve to illustrate this point. We have already described the grocery store corporation in which personnel did not have much power and in which issues of employee relations and management development had for a long period been ignored because they were excluded from the agenda of high level meetings. That same corporation and example also illustrates the importance of allies within the organization.

As noted before, none of the staff groups had much power, for the power in the firm was held by retailing, the store management function. The most powerful of the groups, however, was the legal department. Lawyers held a certain expertise and a mystique regarding that expertise that brought power. In addition, some of the members of the board of directors were themselves lawyers. With the increasing amount of litigation, not only concerning employee relations, but also dealing with advertising, product quality, and product liability, legal constraints and contingencies were slowly being recognized as being more important to the firm.

The personnel staff individual had come into contact with the legal department on some fair employment litigation. The personnel staff member had performed statistical analyses and had participated in a very helpful and competent manner in designing hiring and evaluation procedures to solve the current problems and help prevent new ones. As a consequence of that contact, the personnel and the legal departments formed an alliance. This alliance was based on their common interest of increasing the corporation's concern with compliance issues and a respect for the type of technical expertise represented in both departments that was helpful in dealing with these issues. It was, if you will, these two departments allied against the retailing department. In the various meetings that occurred concerning the litigation, the personnel staff member would point out how well the legal department had handled the negotiations and managed the case and how the department should be consulted earlier and more frequently on these issues before they came to litigation. The head of the legal department came out quite strongly in favor of the kinds of training and survey and analysis activities that the personnel unit wanted to undertake. In fact, when the key personnel staff member threatened to quit, the legal department went to the president of the corporation and argued that to replace his expertise by using outsiders would be substantially more expensive and the department offered him an alternative of various consulting relationships and affiliations. It

is clear that the two departments' reinforcement of each other was mutually beneficial. However, personnel, the lower power function, particularly benefited from the support for its objectives provided by the chief corporate counsel. Later, when personnel's attempts to introduce new procedures, training, and evaluation were resisted by the tradition-bound retailing section, there was recourse to the legal necessity and legal support for these activities. With this outside expertise in support, personnel activity was greatly expanded in both power and scope at the corporation.

The second example has to do with the introduction of a workload measurement system at a professional school. The school was comprised of various disciplines because, as is the case for many professional schools, the school was interdisciplinary. One or two of the groups in the school were heavily burdened by the task of supervising graduate projects. These were specialties that were quite popular with the students, and many chose to do their required projects under the tutelage of persons from those disciplines. One or two of the other groups were heavily burdened by the necessity of teaching a large number of hours. Even though the formal teaching load was the same for all, some courses met only three hours a week while others met four and one-half hours, or 50% more. Because of the distribution of elective and required courses, two of the groups had much more than their share of longer courses.

A proposal was floated to provide explicit teaching credit and thus, course relief for the supervision of these graduate projects. Such a proposal, however, was favored only by the two groups that did most of this work. At the same time, the two groups that did most of the four and one-half hour course teaching were interested in adjusting the workload measurement and allocation system to recognize the fact that an n-course load teaching all classes that met three hours was not the same as an n-course load teaching classes that met for four and one-half hours. There was not a lot of support for that idea as again only a small portion of the entire school was affected. What finally happened was that the two sets of groups formed a coalition. The group burdened with project supervision supported the measurement and assignment of workload on the basis of classroom hours rather than courses, while the other group supported, in turn, the measurement and provision of teaching credit for the supervision of graduate projects. In the end, both had their workloads reduced. With the passage of the combined proposal, each group was able to benefit by its joint action with the other.

This last example illustrates an important point about coalitions, that they are unstable and shift depending on the particular issues involved. Bucher (1970: 34) has noted:

> Most coalitions are shifting alliances, depending upon the issues. As issues come up, faculty within the department who are concerned shop around seeking out those who might be allies in relation to the particular issue.

Politics indeed makes strange bedfellows. As long as there is enough commonality on a set of issues so a deal can be made, the other characteristics of the coalition participants may not be relevant. The type of analysis used in Chapter 2 in the discussion of interests at New York University is an example of one kind of methodology for identifying potential coalitions that can be formed around particular concerns.

COALITION BUILDING THROUGH PROMOTIONS

The preceding discussion of coalition development has been couched in terms of issue trade-offs. Subunit A supports B on one issue of concern to B, and B in turn supports A on some other issue that is of concern to A. Such log-rolling requires the identification of a set of issues of mutual concern and working out the terms of the exchange. Both parts of the transaction may be tricky, particularly for those not well-schooled in political activity.

An alternative way of building support within the organization is through the judicious use of promotion opportunities. In John De Lorean's account of his time as a General Motors executive, he provides evidence for the use of this strategy by Fred Donner in his efforts to consolidate the power of the finance group at GM:

> From him (Donner) developed what I call "promotion of the unobvious choice." This means promoting someone who was not regarded as a contender for the post. Doing so not only puts "your man" in position, but it earns for you his undying loyalty because he owes his corporate life to you. . . . A study of the past ten years of General Motors top executives and an examination of their business biographies makes it obvious that some men with undistinguished business careers moved to the top and in many cases occupy positions of power within the corporation today. An understanding of their benefactors makes their ascension more explicable (Wright, 1979: 41).

In a similar vein, Perrow (1972) has argued that nepotism practiced within the organization may not produce high quality employees but will probably produce loyal supporters. Coalitions are formed, then, by placing allies or supporters in key positions in other departments. This ensures the support of those other units when it is needed. When such placements are unjustified on meritocratic grounds, there is even more insecurity and loyalty engendered in those promoted, making them particularly reliable allies.

Although this strategy is most often discussed in terms of building personal power, it clearly also impacts the power of organizational subunits. In the large retailing organization previously described, the fact that persons were appointed from retailing to head departments of personnel, public relations, industrial relations, and so forth, who had absolutely no background in those areas, ensured that the power and reach of the retailing point of view would be maintained without opposition in the higher management ranks. People got the jobs because they were from the retailing department and loyal to it, and they and everyone else knew it. Professional competence or even experience in the area being managed was not only not a requirement, it was frequently seen as a detriment.

EVERYBODY'S A WINNER

One of the nice aspects of coalition formation in organizations is that the rewards are frequently not zero-sum, in the sense that one's gain comes at another's expense. One of the strategies that may be used to build consensus and a large coalition within the organization is to attempt to make all participants winners, to give all the major groups or interests something from the decision.

This strategy in use can be seen in the Bethlehem Steel example introduced in the last chapter. Recall that the corporation had to choose a new chief executive officer from among three leading candidates: Trautlein, a financial man, Schubert, the public relations and lobbying person, and Walter Williams, the steel operations man. The choice, because it reflected the company's concern for what were to be the strategic issues in the immediate future, took on enormous symbolic significance. Steel manufacturing types were worried that control was about to pass

to either an accountant or a governmental relations type. Finance forces within the firm were concerned that control would remain with steel manufacturing and the company would be unable to raise capital and manage diversification. What the company did, of course, was to promote everyone while giving the chief executive title to Trautlein:

> Donald H. Trautlein, a 53-year-old former Price, Waterhouse & Co. accountant, was named chairman and chief executive officer of Bethlehem Steel Corporation. . . . The move clearly reflects concern . . . about maintaining and improving Bethlehem's financial health. . . . Two other highly touted candidates—Richard F. Schubert . . . and Walter F. Williams . . . also were promoted. Mr. Schubert will become one of Bethlehem's four vice chairmen and Mr. Williams will take over the president's office with the additional new title of chief operating officer (Sease, 1980b: 6).

Note that a new title was created, that of chief operating officer, to provide a sense of balance between the financial side of the firm, represented by Trautlein, and the operations side, represented by Williams. Williams also got Schubert's old title of president, but Schubert was promoted to vice chairman which apparently satisfied him:

> Mr. Schubert . . . said he had never viewed himself as the leading candidate. Mr. Schubert added that the "clear intent" of Mr. Foy's choices for promotion "is to develop the strongest possible team concept" (Sease, 1980b: 6).

This is scarcely the only instance in which positions and titles have been created in order to bring into a coalition various interests within the organization. The win-lose aspects of organizational politics can be downplayed and more support and commitment generated for the adopted policies either by proliferating positions or by rotating subunits through them in a predetermined fashion.

There is a clearly tremendous need for the systematic investigation of coalition behavior within organizations. It seems evident that coalitions and alliances are important in the exercise of power and in the making of decisions within organizations. For the analyst of organizational power and politics, it would be useful to know more specifically under what circumstances these alliances form and when and how potential coalitions become activated. The formation of coalitions requires the information that one participant's interests are coincident in some important respect with another's. Indeed, it is probably the lack of knowledge about the preferences and beliefs of others within the organization that constitutes a major barrier to the formation of coalitions. One of the functions of informal social communication networks within organizations is the exchange of this type of information so that when decisions arise, the process of searching for allies is facilitated. If this is the case, then another component of political skill is a knowledge of subunit perceptions and positions on decision issues within the organization. It is not only important to know the distribution of power; it is also critical to know how the various participants stand so that alliances can be formed.

REFERENCES

Bucher, Rue. 1970. Social process and power in a medical school. In *Power in organizations*, ed. Mayer N. Zald, pp. 3–48. Nashville, TN: Vanderbilt University Press.

Galbraith, Jay R. 1973. *Designing complex organizations*. Reading, MA: Addison-Wesley.

Gamson, William A. 1964. Experimental studies of coalition formation. In *Advances in experimental social psychology*, Vol. 1, ed. Leonard Berkowitz, pp. 81–110. New York: Academic Press.

Leiserson, Michael. 1970. Coalition government in Japan. In *The study of coalition behavior*, ed. Sven Groennings, E. W. Kelley, and Michael Leiserson, pp. 80–102. New York: Holt, Rinehart and Winston.

Ouchi, William G. 1980. Markets, bureaucracies, and clans. *Administrative Science Quarterly* 25:129–141.

———; and Jaeger, Alfred M. 1978. Type Z organization: stability in the midst of mobility. *Academy of Management Review* 3:305–314.

Perrow, Charles, 1972. *Complex organizations: a critical essay*. Glenview, IL: Scott, Foresman.

Pfeffer, Jeffrey, and Salancik, Gerald R. 1974. Organizational decision making as a political process: the case of a university budget. *Administrative Science Quarterly* 19:135–151.

———, 1977a. Administrator effectiveness: the effects of advocacy and information on resource allocations. *Human Relations* 30:641–656.

Riker, William H. 1962. *The theory of political coalitions*. New Haven, CT: Yale University Press.

Rosenthal, Howard. 1970. Size of coalition and electoral outcomes in the Fourth French Republic. In *The study of coalition behavior*, ed. Sven Groennings, E. W. Kelley, and Michael Leiserson, pp. 43–59. New York: Holt, Rinehart and Winston.

Sease, Douglas R. 1980a. Steel's priorities may determine winner in race for Lewis Foy's job at Bethlehem. *Wall Street Journal*, January 16, 1980, p. 5.

———. 1980b. Bethlehem Steel picks Donald Trautlein, an accountant, to be its chief executive. *Wall Street Journal*, February 1, 1980, p. 6.

Wright, J. Patrick. 1979. *On a clear day you can see General Motors: John Z. DeLorean's look inside the automotive giant*. Grosse Point, MI: Wright Enterprises.

CHAPTER III

LEADERSHIP

WHAT IS LEADERSHIP?

Over the years, the importance attributed to the position of leaders has led innumerable practitioners and theorists to ask the seemingly unanswerable question: "What does it take to be an effective leader?", and almost as many behavioral scientists have tried to offer answers. This chapter discusses some of the more important approaches that have been proposed in answer to this most basic but elusive question of leadership.

Although we need to have an understanding of what leadership is in order to discuss it, it is important to realize that there are no clear-cut, universally accepted definitions of what it is. Lombardo and McCall (1978, p. 3) describe the situation well. "'Leadership' is one of the most magnetic words in the English language. Mention it, and a perceptible aura of excitement, almost mystical in nature appears . . . [Yet] if leadership is bright orange, leadership research is slate gray." Complicating this is the fact that we also need to distinguish between *leadership* (or *leader*) and *management* (or *manager*). Although the two functions and roles overlap substantially, *manager* implies that authority has been formally granted to an individual by an organization. *Management* involves power (usually formal authority) bestowed on the occupant of a position by a higher organizational authority. With the power of management comes responsibility and accountability for the use of organizational resources. In contrast, *leader* implies effective use of influence that is rather independent of the authority granted to one because of position. Leadership cannot be bestowed upon a person by a higher authority. Effective managers also must be leaders, and many leaders become managers, but the two sets of roles and functions differ.

Leadership has been defined in countless ways. A few examples include:

- "The influence people exercise over each other" (Lorch, 1978, p. 203).
- "Influence based on inspiration, admiration, or appeal to follower's aspirations" (Barton, 1985, p. 312).
- "The exercise of authority, whether formal or informal, in directing and coordinating the work of others" (Shafritz, 1988, p. 318).

*This chapter was written collaboratively with David Sullivan, formerly at the Department of Public Administration, University of Maine; currently Town Administrator of Windham, New Hampshire.

243

One group of authors recently began defining a successful leader as one who is able to transform an organization when situations call for such action (Bennis, 1984; Bennis & Nanus, 1985; Tichy, 1980; Tichy & Devanna, 1986). Probably the most widely accepted current definitions view leadership as an interpersonal process through which one individual influences the attitudes, beliefs, and especially the behavior of one or more other people (Richardson and Baldwin, 1976).

The subject of leadership raises many complex issues that have plagued behavioral scientists for generations: For example, what gives a manager or a leader legitimacy? Shafritz (1988, p. 324) describes *legitimacy* as "a characteristic of a social institution, such as a government or a family [or an organization], whereby it has both a legal and a perceived right to make binding decisions." Thus, managers presumably have legitimacy because of the legal and perceived rights that accompany their organizational positions. In contrast, the legitimacy of a leader—separate and distinct from the legitimacy of a manager—cannot be addressed without introducing the concept of *charisma*. Charisma is "leadership based on the compelling personality of the leader rather than on formal position" (Shafritz 1988, p. 89).

The concept was first articulated by the German sociologist, Max Weber, who distinguished charismatic authority from the traditional authority of a monarch and the legal authority one receives by virtue of law—such as the authority that legitimizes organizational executives.

Despite the differences and the unresolved questions, two important definitional givens are evident: First, leadership involves a relationship between people in which influence and power are unevenly distributed on a legitimate basis; and second, a leader cannot function in isolation. In order for there to be a leader, someone must follow (Fiedler and Chemers, 1974, p. 4). In his enduring chapter, "The Executive Functions" (1938), which is reprinted in this chapter, Chester Barnard defines three essential functions of leaders or executives: to provide a system of communication, to promote the securing of essential efforts, and to formulate and define the purposes and goals of an organization. He was decades ahead of his times in arguing that the most critical function of a chief executive is to establish and communicate a system of organizational values among organizational members. If the value system is clear and strong, the day-to-day concerns will take care of themselves.

TRAIT THEORIES

Over the years, studies of leadership have taken different approaches based on divergent perspectives. The trait approach to leadership dominated into the 1950s. The trait theories assume that leaders possess traits which are fundamentally different from followers. A *trait* is a "personality attribute or a way of interacting with others which is independent of the situation, that is, a characteristic of the person rather than of the situation" (Fiedler and Chemers, 1974, p. 22). Advocates of trait theory believe that some individuals have characteristics and qualities which enable them to "rise above the population," to assume responsibilities not everyone can execute, and therefore to become leaders (Hampton et al., 1982, p. 566). Under trait theory, the task of the behavioral sciences is to identify those traits and learn how to identify people who possess them.

It is no longer fashionable to contend that people will be effective leaders because they possess certain traits—without also considering other variables that influence leadership effectiveness. The arguments against trait theory are persuasive and come from a number of points of view. First, trait theory has largely fallen out of favor because reality never matched the theory. Instead, starting in the late 1950s, it started to become standard practice to view leadership as a relationship, an interaction between individuals. The interaction was called a *transaction*, so the term *transactional leadership* became the umbrella label encompassing many theories of leadership of the 1950s, 1960s, and 1970s. Second, the situation strongly influences leadership. As Stogdill (1948) stated, the situation has an active influence in determining the qualities, characteristics, and skills needed in a leader.

Probably the most damaging criticism of trait theory, however, has been its lack of ability to identify which traits make an effective leader. Even among the traits that have been most commonly cited—intelligence, energy, achievement, dependability, and socioeconomic status—there is a lack of consensus across studies. Leadership involves more than possessing certain traits. A leader may be effective in one setting and ineffective in another. It depends on the situation (Fiedler, 1969).

TRANSACTIONAL APPROACHES TO LEADERSHIP

The transactional approaches to leadership had early beginnings in the 1930s but did not emerge as the dominant view of leadership until the 1950s. Two primary forces were behind the ascendancy: (1) frustration and disappointment with the trait theories, and (2) dramatic post–World War II advances in the applied behavioral sciences.

Whereas the trait approaches view leadership as something(s) inherent in a leader, the transactional approaches see leadership as a set of functions and roles that develop from an interaction between two or more people. The interaction between a person who leads and those who follow is labeled a *transaction*—much the same as in *Transactional Analysis* (Berne, 1964; Harris, 1967; James & Jongeward, 1971). Although there are vast differences in emphasis among groupings of transactional leadership theories, all of them focus on the transaction—what happens and why, and what directly and indirectly influences or shapes it. Thus, for example, the transactional theorist Fiedler (1966) emphasizes the leader—but in the context of the match between leaders and followers. In contrast, Hersey and Blanchard (1969) focus on subordinates—but in a leader-follower context.

Leadership Style Theories

The early transactional leadership theories tended to assume that people have relatively fixed styles and thus were often labeled *leadership style theories*. Many of the more recent theories also involve leadership styles, but because the earlier assumption of style inflexibility has been abandoned, they usually are called *situational* or *contingency approaches.* But once again in both cases, leadership is seen as a transaction. Whereas the central question for the trait approach is, *who exerts leadership?*, the quest of the transactional approaches is to determine *how leadership is established and exerted.*

Leadership style-oriented transactional approaches all follow in the tradition of the famous Lewin, Lippitt, and White (1939) studies of the effectiveness of leadership styles on group productivity. Lewin, Lippitt, and White studied groups of 10-year-old children engaged in hobby activities. The leader in each group was classified as authoritarian, democratic, or laissez-faire oriented. Authoritarian leaders determined all policies, set all work assignments, and were personal in their criticisms. They were product (or task) oriented and practiced initiating structure. Democratic-oriented leaders shared decision-making powers with subordinates, decisions about assignments were left to the group, and they participated in group activities but tried not to monopolize. They used high levels of consideration. Laissez-faire-oriented leaders allowed freedom for individual and group decision making, provided information (or supplies) only when requested, and did not participate in the group except when called upon. They function more as facilitators.

Groups with democratic-oriented leaders were the most satisfied and productive. The authoritarian-led groups showed the most aggressive behavior and were the least satisfied, but they were highly productive (possibly because of fear of the leader.) The groups with laissez-faire-oriented leaders showed low satisfaction, low production, and were behaviorally aggressive toward group members and other groups.

The leadership style-oriented transactional approaches attempt to identify styles of leader behavior which result in effective group performance. Probably the best known groups of studies using this approach were conducted at the University of Michigan and at Ohio State University. They were widely known as *the Michigan studies* and *the Ohio State studies.*

Most of the Michigan studies analyzed two extreme leadership styles, *product-oriented* and *employee-oriented.* A product-oriented leadership style focuses on accomplishing the task of the organization producing the product. This style is exhibited in such activities as setting organizational or group goals, assigning work to subordinates, and constantly evaluating performance. The employee-oriented leadership style pays more attention to how well subordinates are doing and to their feelings and attitudes.

Typically, the Michigan studies had subordinates rate their supervisors on the degree to which "he treats people under him without considering their feelings," or "he does personal favors for the people under him" (Fleishman and Harris, 1962, p.10). Findings from the Michigan studies have shown that high productivity may be associated with either style of leadership, but product-oriented leaders tend to be confronted more often and their employees have more job dissatisfaction, high turnover rates, and higher absenteeism rates (Fleishman and Harris, 1962, p. 53). Finally, other studies have shown that work output is correlated with the freedom supervisors give to workers, and employees produce more under loose supervision than under close supervision.

One of the best known of the Michigan studies is reported in Robert Kahn and Daniel Katz's 1962 article, "Leadership Practices in Relation to Productivity and Morals," which is reprinted in this chapter. Kahn and Katz discuss some of their findings that successfully relate the influence of four groups of variables—the supervisor's role, the closeness of supervision, the quality of supportiveness, and the amount of group cohesiveness—on the productivity of organizational groups and the level of morale groups exhibits.

Like the University of Michigan studies, the Ohio State studies classified leader behavior as either product-oriented or employee-oriented, but they used different terminology: *initiation of structure* and *consideration*. The Ohio State studies treat the two behaviors as independent dimensions rather than as scalar opposites. In other words, a leader can rank high on consideration and either high or low on initiation of structure. Thus, leaders can be grouped into four quadrants.

Initiation of structure is "the leader's behavior in delineating the relationship between himself and members of the work group and in endeavoring to establish well-defined patterns of organization, channels of command, and methods of procedure" (Bozeman, 1979, p. 208). It is a variety of leader actions used "to get the work out." The leader plans, directs, sets standards, and controls the work of subordinates.

Consideration is "any action which the leader takes to perceive the human needs of his subordinates and to support the subordinates in their own attempts to satisfy their needs" (Hampton et al., 1982, p. 569). Or as stated by Stogdill, consideration is "any behavior indicative of friendship, mutual trust, respect, and warmth in the relationship between the leader and a member of his staff" (Bozeman, 1979, p. 208).

The Ohio State studies found the productivity of individuals and groups to be higher when the leader initiates structure than when they do not. Some studies have found consideration positively related to productivity, while others show a negative effect or no effect at all. As far as satisfaction, studies have shown the initiation of structure to be received differently by different people in different situations. For example, House's (1971) work illustrated that the larger the organization, the more employees need some stability, order, and direction. At the other extreme, considerate behavior has almost always been shown to increase employee satisfaction (Fleishman and Harris, p. 47).

The Ohio State studies contain interesting parallels to the Michigan studies. So although the Hersey and Blanchard (1969) article does not chronologically follow Kahn and Katz, it is reprinted here for comparison. Hersey and Blanchard reject the idea that there is one best leadership style for all situations. They use the maturity of the work groups as a variable influencing the effectiveness of the style used. In their 1969 article, "Life Cycle Theory of Leadership," Hersey and Blanchard emphasize that leadership should be appropriate for a given situation. Using *initiation of structure* and *consideration* for dimensions, they develop a matrix with four leadership styles: telling, selling, participating, and delegating. When a work group is not mature enough to assume a task, the leader needs to be high in initiation (task) and low in consideration (relationship) behavior, in order to help the group understand what is required of them. On the other hand, when a group is mature, the leader should be high in consideration (relationship) and low in initiation (task) behavior, because the group is able to complete its task without much guidance. Although the model is conceptually intriguing, a major weakness is its lack of a "systematic measurement device to measure maturity" (Schein, 1980).

Returning now to a chronological approach to the development of transactional leadership theories, we move to perhaps the best known organizational behaviorist of all times, Douglas M. McGregor. McGregor's chapter "An Analysis of Leadership" from *The Human Side of Enterprise* (1960), which is included in this chapter, points out that the trait approach was "not unimportant, but those (characteristics of the leader) which are essential differ considerably depending upon the circumstances" (p. 180). McGregor discusses leadership as a relationship between the leader and the situation. As McGregor asserts, "the research during the past has shown that we must look beyond the personal qualifications of the leader if we wish to understand what leadership is" (p. 182). McGregor argues that managers have to change their recruiting policies to better prepare all individuals for a possible leadership position, because it is no longer feasible to assume that certain preselected individuals will become future leaders. In essence it is possible for anyone to be a leader, depending on the situation.

Situational or Contingency Approaches

McGregor's observations provide an excellent lead-in to a direct consideration of the *situational* or *contingency* approaches to transactional leadership. Probably, the earliest situationist was the classical organizational philosopher, Mary Parker Follett. In her 1926 article, "The Giving of Orders," Follett discusses how orders should be given in any organization: They should be depersonalized "to unite all concerned in a study of the situation, to discover the law of the situation and obey that" (p. 33). Follett thus argues for a *participatory leadership style* where employees and employers cooperate to assess the situation and decide what should be done at that moment—in that situation. Once the *law of the situation* is discovered, "the employee can issue it to the employer as well as employer to employee" (p. 33). This manner of giving orders facilitates better attitudes within an organization because nobody is necessarily under another person; rather all take their cues from the situation.

The early style approach to transactional leadership assumed that leaders can be trained to act in the appropriate way as called for by their organization. This has proven to be a major weakness. When leaders return to their organization after leadership training sessions, they seldom exhibit behavior changes (Barton and Chappell, 1985, p. 316). Despite training, department heads will not necessarily act considerately toward subordinates if their own supervisors do not act supportively toward them. One obvious implication is that changes must be introduced into an organization as a whole—not just to certain employees.

In practice, leaders apply different styles in different situations (Barton and Chappell, 1985, p. 316). Thus, the "pure" leadership style emphasis has given way to the contingency approaches. Unlike the trait theory and leadership style approaches, the contingency approaches take into consideration many factors that may influence a leader's style. It recognizes that a successful leader in one type of organization may not be successful in another simply because it differs from the previous one. Its situation (or context) is different, and the choice of a style needs to be contingent upon the situation. As Stogdill (1974) notes, the contingency theories stress:

1. The type, structure, size, and purpose of the organization;
2. The external environment in which the organization functions;
3. The orientation, values, goals, and expectations of the leader, his superiors, and subordinates; and
4. The expert or professional knowledge required of the position.

The contingency approaches assert that different leadership styles will differ in their effects in different situations. The situation (not traits or styles themselves) determines whether a leadership style or a particular leader will be effective. Thus, contingency theorists maintain that there is no "one best way" of effective leadership.

Tannenbaum and Schmidt (1958, 1973) conducted one of the first studies that actually indicated a need for leaders to evaluate the situational factors prior to the implementation of a particular leadership style (Blunt, 1981). Tannenbaum and Schmidt grouped leader decision-making behavior into seven categories along a continuum from *boss-centered* to *subordinate-centered.* Each category is based on a single variable: the degree of participation in making decisions that is allowed to subordinates. For example:

- Category 1 assumes that the leader makes all decisions and announces them to subordinates.
- Category 7 assumes that the leader defines limits but allows the group to define the problem and to make the final decision.

Tannenbaum and Schmidt also specify three factors that influence where along their continuum a decision will be made. These factors are: forces in the leader, forces of the subordinates, and forces in the situation.

> The successful manager of men can be primarily characterized neither as a strong leader nor as a permissive one. Rather, he is one who maintains a high batting average in accurately assessing the forces that determine what his most appropriate behavior at any given time should be and in actually being able to behave accordingly (Tannenbaum and Schmidt, 1973, p. 180).

Whereas Tannenbaum and Schmidt have focused mostly on variables involving followers, Fred Fiedler has emphasized the leader (but still from a transactional perspective). In "The Contingency Model: A Theory of Leadership Effectiveness" (included in this chapter), Fiedler discusses a study done with the Belgian Naval

Forces. Some earlier leadership theorists had believed that leaders could be trained to adopt styles that are suitable for situations, but Fiedler found the opposite to be true. It is easier to change the work environment, the situation, to fit a leader's style. A person's underlying leadership style depends upon one's personality. According to Fiedler, a leader's personality is not likely to change because of a few lectures or a few weeks of intensive training. Therefore, an organization should not choose a leader who fits a situation, but should change the situation to mesh with the style of its leader. (See also, Cooper & Robertson, 1988, p. 84.)

Concerns About Leadership Theory

Warren Bennis seems to have always been one who astutely leads theory into transitional stages. Leadership is no exception. His work in the late 1950s and early 1960s was traditionally transactional; for example, his 1961 *Harvard Business Review* article, "Revisionist Theory of Leadership." But, like Bennis's writings about organizations in general during the late 1960s, he started to question generally accepted views on leadership. Were we really learning anything new or of use about leadership that had practical value? His chapter, "Mortal Stakes: Where Have All the Leaders Gone?" (reprinted here), is from a 1976 book whose title expresses the depth of Bennis's frustration: *The Unconscious Conspiracy: Why Leaders Can't Lead.*

In "Where Have All the Leaders Gone?", Bennis ponders why we no longer have leaders like those of old. He argues that today's leaders are confused: The gap between expectations and reality is widening. However, he remains optimistic that managers can learn to lead, to have a perspective of the future, and to practice the strategic functions of leadership. Bennis coined the phrase *social architects* to describe what he considers to be the most important roles and formations of organizational leaders: understanding the organizational culture, having a sense of vision, and encouraging individuals to be innovative.

CULTURAL AND TRANSFORMATIVE THEORIES

A growing number of leadership theorists recently have moved past the transactional approaches to write about leadership from an organizational culture perspective or, as it is sometimes called, a symbolic management perspective (Shafritz & Ott, 1987; Ott, 1989). Once again, Warren Bennis has been one of the frontrunners in the transition away from transactional approaches (Bennis, 1984; Bennis & Nanus, 1985), but he has lots of company. One of the most articulate statements of the organizational culture perspective on leadership is Thomas J. Sergiovanni's "Leadership as Cultural Expression" (1984), which is included as a reading in this chapter. Sergiovanni argues that leadership is an artifact—a product of organizational culture. The particular shape and style of leadership in an organization is not a function of individuals or of training programs: Rather, it has to do with the mixture of organizational culture and the *density* of leadership competence.

According to Sergiovanni, the real value of leadership "rests with the meanings which actions import to others than in the actions themselves" (pg. 106). Leadership communicates the culture. Thus, leadership needs to be symbolic and strategic. In this context, Sergiovanni proposes 10 principles of quality leadership which result in leadership being less a management technique and more a *cultural expression*. If leadership is effective, norms, beliefs, and principles will emerge in an organization to which members give allegiance. Sergiovanni's conceptualization of leadership has much in common with Chester Barnard's writing of 50 years ago. Barnard truly was a remarkable prophet.

Transformational leadership or *transformative leadership* is a second recent slant on leadership that is theoretically consistent with the organizational culture perspective. Whereas the transactional theories of leadership apply primarily to leadership roles, functions, and behavior *within* an existing organizational culture, transformative leadership is about leadership to *change* a culture. *Transactional leadership focuses on incremental change: Transformative leadership is about radical change.* Lee Iacocca (1984) is the most visible current embodiment of a transformative leader. It is interesting to note that transformational leadership theories have many similarities with the trait theories of leadership. Transformational leadership borders on "great man" theory: Leaders are born, not made. In many ways, leadership theory is once again involved in seeking to find the basis of leadership in traits—rather than in relational and cultural factors.

Noel Tichy and David Ulrich's 1984 *Sloan Management Review* article, "The Leadership Challenge—A Call for the Transformational Leader" (reprinted in this chapter) describes a transformational leader as "one who must develop and communicate a new vision and get others not only to see the vision but also to commit themselves to it" (p. 59). They describe transformational leaders as those rare individuals who can lead employees through their fears and uncertainties to the realization of the vision. This requires transformational leadership—leadership that successfully changes peoples' perceptions of the organization. Transformational change is more than a rational, technical, incremental approach to change. The leader's primary function is to lead and support through carefully conceived change stages, acting as a *cheerleader* and as a *belief model*—verbally and nonverbally communicating belief in the benefits to all that will accrue from the changes.

During the last fifty years, leadership theory has wound its way torturously over twisting and often seemingly fruitless paths. For every gain in understanding, there have been more new questions to answer. The search for a comprehensive theory of leadership is a seemingly neverending quest. Since the 1940s, the search has led us through trait theories, myriad transactional approaches, and now transformative/cultural theories. No one truly believes that the answers have been found to the most basic questions of leadership. Many of us, when confronted with the practical realities of leading, particularly in complex organizations, share Bennis's frustrations. We find ourselves asking: Why can't leaders lead? Where have all the leaders gone? Even the readings that follow do not hold all of the answers. However, they are among the very best attempts at providing insight.

REFERENCES

Allaire, Y., & Firsirotu, M. (Spring, 1985). How to implement radical strategies in large organizations. *Sloan Management Review, 26*(3), 19–34.

Argyris, C. (1957). *Personality and organization.* New York: Harper & Row.

Argyris, C. (1964). *Integrating the individual and the organization.* New York: John Wiley.

Barnard, C. I. (1968). *The functions of the executive.* Cambridge, MA: Harvard University Press. (Originally published in 1938.)

Barton, R., & Chappell, W. L., Jr. (1985). *Public administration: The work of government.* Glenview, IL: Scott, Foresman and Company.

Beckhard, R. (1988). The executive management of transformational change. In R. H. Kilmann & T. J. Covin (Eds.), *Corporate transformation* (pp. 89–101). San Francisco: Jossey-Bass.

Bennis, W. G. (1961). Revisionist theory of leadership. *Harvard Business Review, 39.*

Bennis, W. G. (1976). Mortal stakes: Where have all the leaders gone? In W. G. Bennis, *The unconscious conspiracy: Why leaders can't lead* (pp. 143–156). New York: AMACOM.

Bennis, W. G. (1984). Transformative power and leadership. In T. J. Sergiovanni & J. E. Corbally (Eds.), *Leadership and organizational culture* (pp. 64–71). Urbana, IL: University of Illinois Press.

Bennis, W. G., & Nanus, B. (1985). *Leaders: The strategies for taking charge.* New York: Harper & Row.

Berne, E. (1964). *Games people play.* New York: Grove Press.

Bird, C. (1940). *Social psychology.* New York: Appleton-Century.

Blake, R. T., & Mouton, J. S. (1969). *Building a dynamic corporation through grid organization development.* Reading, MA: Addison-Wesley Publishing Company.

Blunt, B. E. (1981). *Organizational leadership.* Ann Arbor, MI: University Microfilm International.

Bozeman, B. (1979). *Public management and policy analysis.* New York: St. Martin's Press.

Cattell, R. B. (1951). New concepts for measuring leadership in terms of group syntality. *Human Relations, 4,* 161–184.

Cooper, C. L., & Robertson, I. (Eds.). (1988). *International review of industrial and organizational psychology.* New York: John Wiley.

Deal, T. E. (1985). Cultural change: Opportunity, silent killer, or metamorphosis? In R. H. Kilmann, M. J. Saxton, & R. Serpa (Eds.), *Gaining control of the corporate culture* (pp. 292–331). San Francisco: Jossey-Bass.

Dublin, R. (1951). *Human relations in administration.* Englewood Cliffs, NJ: Prentice-Hall.

Dunnette, M. D. (1976). *Handbook of industrial and organizational psychology.* Chicago: Rand McNally.

Fiedler, F. E. (1967). *A theory of leadership effectiveness.* New York: McGraw-Hill.

Fiedler, F. E. (March, 1969). Style or circumstance: The leadership enigma. *Psychology Today 2*(10), 38–43.

Fiedler, F. E. (1966). The contingency model: A theory of leadership effectiveness. In C. W. Backman & P. F. Secord (Eds.), *Problems in social psychology* (pp. 278–289). New York: McGraw-Hill.

Fiedler, F. E., & Chemers, M. M. (1974). *Leadership style and effective management.* Glenview, IL: Scott, Foresman and Company.

Fiedler, F. E., Chemers, M. M., & Mahar, L. (1976). *Improving leadership effectiveness: The leader match concept.* New York: John Wiley & Sons.

Fleishman, E. A., & Harris, E. F. (1962). Patterns of leadership behavior related to employee grievances and turnover. *Personnel Psychology, 15,* 43–56.

Fleishman, E. A., & Hunt, J. G. (1973). *Current developments in the study of leadership.* Carbondale, IL: Southern Illinois University Press.

Follett, M. P. (1926). The giving of orders. In H. C. Metcalf (Ed.), *Scientific foundations of business administration.* Baltimore, MD: Williams & Wilkins Company.

Hampton, D. R., Summer, C. E., & Webber, R. A. (1982). *Organizational behavior and the practice of management.* Glenview, IL: Scott, Foresman and Company.

Harris, T. A. (1968). *I'm OK—You're OK.* New York: Harper & Row.

Hemphill, J. K. (1950). *Leader behavior description.* Columbus, OH: Ohio State University Press.

Hersey, P., & Blanchard, K. H. (May, 1969). Life cycle theory of leadership. *Training and Development Journal,* 26–34.

House, R. J. (1971). Path-goal theory of leadership effectiveness. *Administrative Sciences Quarterly, 16,* 321–338.

House, R. J., & Mitchell, T. M. (Autumn, 1974). Path-goal theory of leadership. *Journal of Contemporary Business, 3*(4), 81–97.

Iacocca, L. (1984). *Iacocca, an autobiography.* Toronto: Bantam Books.

James, M., & Jongeward, D. (1973). *Born to win.* Reading, MA: Addison-Wesley Publishing Company.

Jennings, E. E. (1962). *The executive, autocrat, bureaucrat, democrat.* New York: Harper & Row.

Jennings, E. E. (1967). *Executive success: Stresses, problems and adjustment.* New York: Appleton-Century-Crofts.

Kahn, R. L., & Katz, D. (1962). Leadership practices in relation to productivity and morale. In D. Cartwright & A. Zander (Eds.), *Group dynamics* (2d ed.) (pp. 554–570). New York: Harper & Row.

Leavitt, H. J. (June, 1962). Applied organizational change: A summary and evaluation of the power equalization approaches. Seminar in the Social Science of Organizations. Pittsburgh, PA.

Lewin, K., Lippitt, R., & White, R. K. Patterns of aggressive behavior in experimentally created social climates. *Journal of Social Psychology, 10,* 271–299.

Likert, R. (1961). *New patterns of management.* New York: McGraw-Hill.

Lombardo, M. M., & McCall, M. W., Jr., (1978). Leadership. In M. W. McCall, Jr., & M. M. Lombardo (Eds.), *Leadership: Where else can we go?* (pp. 3–34). Durham, NC: Duke University Press.

Mann, R. D. (1979). A review of the relationships between personality and performance in small groups. *Psychological Bulletin, 56,* 241–270.

McGregor, D. M. (1960). *The human side of enterprise.* New York: McGraw-Hill.

Nigro, F. A., & Nigro, L. G. (1980). *Modern public administration.* New York: Harper & Row.

Ott, J. S. (1989). *The organizational culture perspective.* Chicago: The Dorsey Press.

Schein, E. H. (1980). *Organizational psychology* (3d ed.). Englewood Cliffs, NJ: Prentice-Hall.

Schön, D. A. (1984). Leadership as reflection-in-action. In T. J. Sergiovanni & J. E. Corbally (Eds.), *Leadership and organizational culture* (pp. 36–63). Urbana, IL: University of Illinois Press.

Selznick, P. (1957). *Leadership in administration: A sociological interpretation.* New York: Harper & Row.

Sergiovanni, T. J. (1984). Leadership as cultural expression. In T. J. Sergiovanni & J. E. Corbally (Eds.), *Leadership and organizational culture* (pp. 105–114). Urbana, IL: University of Illinois Press.

Shafritz, J. M. (1988). *The Dorsey dictionary of politics and government.* Chicago: The Dorsey Press.

Shafritz, J. M., & Ott, J. S. (1987). *Classics of organization theory* (2d ed., rev. and expanded). Chicago: The Dorsey Press.

Stogdill, R. M. (1948). Personal factors associated with leadership: A survey of the literature. *Journal of Psychology, 25,* 35–71.

Stogdill, R. M. (1974). *Handbook of leadership: A study of theory and research.* New York: The Free Press.

Stogdill, R. M., & Coons, A. E. (Eds.). (1957). *Leader behavior: Its description and measurement.* Columbus, OH: Ohio State University Press.

Tannenbaum, R. J., & Schmidt, W. H. (March–April, 1958). How to choose a leadership pattern. *Harvard Business Review, 36*(2), 95–101.

Tannenbaum, R. J., & Schmidt, W. H. (May–June, 1973). How to choose a leadership pattern. *Harvard Business Review, 51*(3), 1–10.

Tannenbaum, R. J., Weschler, I. R., & Massarik, F. (1961). *Leadership and organization.* New York: McGraw-Hill.

Tichy, N. M. (1983). *Managing strategic change: Technical, political and cultural dynamics.* New York: John Wiley & Sons.

Tichy, N. M., & Devanna, M. A. (1986). *The transformational leader.* New York, John Wiley & Sons.

Tichy, N. M., & Ulrich, D. O. (1984). The leadership challenge—a call for the transformational leader. *Sloan Management Review, 26,* 59–68.

Vroom, V. H. (Winter, 1976). Can leaders learn to lead? *Organizational Dynamics.*

Vroom, Victor, H., & Yetton, P. W. (1973). *Leadership and decision making.* Pittsburgh, PA: University of Pittsburgh Press.

Zaleznik, A. (1967). *Human dilemmas of leadership.* New York: Harper & Row.

17
The Giving of Orders
Mary Parker Follett

To some men the matter of giving orders seems a very simple affair; they expect to issue their own orders and have them obeyed without question. Yet, on the other hand, the shrewd common sense of many a business executive has shown him that the issuing of orders is surrounded by many difficulties; that to demand an unquestioning obedience to orders not approved, not perhaps even understood, is bad business policy. Moreover, psychology, as well as our own observation, shows us not only that you cannot get people to do things most satisfactorily by ordering them or exhorting them; but also that even reasoning with them, even convincing them intellectually, may not be enough. Even the "consent of the governed" will not do all the work it is supposed to do, an important consideration for those who are advocating employee representation. For all our past life, our early training, our later experience, all our emotions, beliefs, prejudices, every desire that we have, have formed certain habits of mind that the psychologists call habit-patterns, action-patterns, motor-sets.

Therefore it will do little good merely to get intellectual agreement; unless you change the habit-patterns of people, you have not really changed your people. Business administration, industrial organization, should build up certain habit-patterns, that is, certain mental

attitudes. For instance, the farmer has a general disposition to "go it alone," and this is being changed by the activities of the co-operatives, that is, note, *by the farmer's own activities.* So the workman has often a general disposition of antagonism to his employers which cannot be changed by argument or exhortation, but only through certain activities which will create a different disposition. One of my trade union friends told me that he remembered when he was a quite small boy hearing his father, who worked in a shoe-shop, railing daily against his boss. So he grew up believing that it was inherent in the nature of things that the workman should be against his employer. I know many working men who have a prejudice against getting college men into factories. You could all give me examples of attitudes among your employees which you would like to change. We want, for instance, to create an attitude of respect for expert opinion.

If we analyse this matter a little further we shall see that we have to do three things. I am now going to use psychological language: (1) build up certain attitudes; (2) provide for the release of these attitudes; (3) augment the released response as it is being carried out. What does this mean in the language of business? A psychologist has given us the example of the salesman. The salesman first creates in you the at-

Source: From "The Giving of Orders" by Mary Parker Follett, in *Scientific Foundations of Business Administration* (Baltimore: Williams & Wilkins Co., 1926). Copyright © 1926 The Williams and Wilkins Company. Reproduced by permission.

titude that you want his article; then, at just the "psychological" moment, he produces his contract blank which you may sign and thus release that attitude; then if, as you are preparing to sign, some one comes in and tells you how pleased he has been with his purchase of this article, that augments the response which is being released.

If we apply this to the subject of orders and obedience, we see that people can obey an order only if previous habit-patterns are appealed to or new ones created. When the employer is considering an order, he should also be thinking of the way to form the habits which will ensure its being carried out. We should first lead the salesmen selling shoes or the bank clerk cashing cheques to see the desirability of a different method. Then the rules of the store or bank should be so changed as to make it possible for salesman or cashier to adopt the new method. In the third place they could be made more ready to follow the new method by convincing in advance some one individual who will set an example of the others. You can usually convince one or two or three ahead of the rank and file. This last step you all know from your experience to be good tactics; it is what the psychologists call intensifying the attitude to be released. But we find that the released attitude is not by one release fixed as a habit; it takes a good many responses to do that.

This is an important consideration for us, for from one point of view business success depends largely on this— namely, whether our business is so organized and administered that it tends to form certain habits, certain mental attitudes. It has been hard for many old-fashioned employers to understand that *orders will not take the place of training.* I want to italicize that. Many a time an employer has been angry because, as he

expressed it, a workman "wouldn't" do so and so, when the truth of the matter was that the workman couldn't, actually couldn't, do as ordered because he could not go contrary to life-long habits. This whole subject might be taken up under the heading of education, for there we could give many instances of the attempt to make arbitrary authority take the place of training. In history, the aftermath of all revolutions shows us the results of the lack of training.

In this matter of prepared-in-advance behaviour patterns—that is, in preparing the way for the reception of orders, psychology makes a contribution when it points out that the same words often rouse in us a quite different response when heard in certain places and on certain occasions. A boy may respond differently to the same suggestion when made by his teacher and when made by his schoolmate. Moreover, he may respond differently to the same suggestion made by the teacher in the schoolroom and made by the teacher when they are taking a walk together. Applying this to the giving of orders, we see that the place in which orders are given, the circumstances under which they are given, may make all the difference in the world as to the response which we get. Hand them down a long way from President or Works Manager and the effect is weakened. One might say that the strength of favourable response to an order is in inverse ratio to the distance the order travels. Production efficiency is always in danger of being affected whenever the long-distance order is substituted for the face-to-face suggestion. There is, however, another reason for that which I shall consider in a moment.

All that we said in the foregoing paper of integration and circular behaviour applies directly to the anticipation of response in giving orders. We spoke then of what the psychologists call linear and circular behaviour. Linear behaviour would be, to quote from Dr. Cabot's review of my book, *Creative Experience,* when an order is accepted as passively as the woodshed accepts the wood. In circular behaviour you get a "come-back." But we all know that we get the come-back every day of our life, and we must certainly allow for it, or for what is more elegantly called circular behaviour, in the giving of orders. Following out the thought of the previous paper, I should say that the giving of orders and the receiving of orders ought to be a matter of integration through circular behaviour, and that we should seek methods to bring this about.

Psychology has another important contribution to make on this subject of issuing orders or giving directions: before the integration can be made between order-giver and order-receiver, there is often an integration to be made within one or both of the individuals concerned. There are often two dissociated paths in the individual; if you are clever enough to recognize these, you can sometimes forestall a Freudian conflict, make the integration appear before there is an acute stage.

To explain what I mean, let me run over briefly a social worker's case. The girl's parents had been divorced and the girl placed with a jolly, easy-going, slack and untidy family, consisting of the father and mother and eleven children, sons and daughters. Gracie was very happy here, but when the social worker in charge of the case found that the living conditions involved a good deal of promiscuity, she thought the girl should be placed elsewhere. She therefore took her to call on an aunt who had a home with some refinement of living, where they had "high tastes," as one of the family said. This aunt wished to have Gracie live with her, and Gracie de-

cided that she would like to do so. The social worker, however, in order to test her, said, "But I thought you were so happy where you are." "Can't I be happy and high, too?" the girl replied. There were two wishes here, you see. The social worker by removing the girl to the aunt may have forestalled a Freudian conflict, the dissociated paths may have been united. I do not know the outcome of this story, but it indicates a method of dealing with our co-directors—make them "happy and high, too."

Business administration has often to consider how to deal with the dissociated paths in individuals or groups, but the methods of doing this successfully have been developed much further in some departments than in others. We have as yet hardly recognized this as part of the technique of dealing with employees, yet the clever salesman knows that it is the chief part of his job. The prospective buyer wants the article and does not want it. The able salesman does not suppress the arguments in the mind of the purchaser against buying, for then the purchaser might be sorry afterwards for his purchase, and that would not be good salesmanship. Unless he can unite, integrate, in the purchaser's mind, the reasons for buying and the reasons for not buying, his future sales will be imperilled, he will not be the highest grade salesman.

Please note that this goes beyond what the psychologist whom I quoted at the beginning of this section told us. He said, "the salesman must create in you the attitude that you want his article." Yes, but only if he creates this attitude by integration, not by suppression.

Apply all this to orders. An order often leaves the individual to whom it is given with two dissociated paths; an order should seek to unite, to integrate, dissociated paths. Court decisions often settle arbitrarily which of two ways is to be followed without showing a possible integration of the two, that is, the individual is often left with an internal conflict on his hands. This is what both courts and business administration should try to prevent, the internal conflicts of individuals or groups.

In discussing the preparation for giving orders, I have not spoken at all of the appeal to certain instincts made so important by many writers. Some writers, for instance, emphasize the instinct of self-assertion; this would be violated by too rigid orders or too clumsily-exercised authority. Other writers, of equal standing, tell us that there is an instinct of submission to authority. I cannot discuss this for we should first have to define instincts, too long an undertaking for us now. Moreover, the exaggerated interest in instincts of recent years, an interest which in many cases has received rather crude expression, is now subsiding. Or, rather, it is being replaced by the more fruitful interest in habits.

There is much more that we could learn from psychology about the forming of habits and the preparation for giving orders than I can even hint at now. But there is one point, already spoken of by implication, that I wish to consider more explicitly—namely, the manner of giving orders. Probably more industrial trouble has been caused by the manner in which orders are given than in any other way. In the *Report on Strikes and Lockouts,* a British government publication, the cause of a number of strikes is given as "alleged harassing conduct of the foreman," "alleged tyrannical conduct of an under-foreman," "alleged overbearing conduct of officials." The explicit statement, however, of the tyranny of superior officers as the direct cause of strikes is I should say, unusual, yet resentment smoulders and breaks out in other issues. And the demand for better treatment is often explicit enough. We find it made by the metal and woodworking trades in an aircraft factory, who declared that any treatment of men without regard to their feelings of self-respect would be answered by a stoppage of work. We find it put in certain agreements with employers that "the men must be treated with proper respect, and threats and abusive language must not be used."

What happens to man, *in* a man, when an order is given in a disagreeable manner by foreman, head of department, his immediate superior in store, bank or factory? The man addressed feels that his self-respect is attacked, that one of his most inner sanctuaries is invaded. He loses his temper or becomes sullen or is on the defensive; he begins thinking of his "rights"—a fatal attitude for any of us. In the language we have been using, the wrong behaviour pattern is aroused, the wrong motor-set; that is, he is now "set" to act in a way which is not going to benefit the enterprise in which he is engaged.

There is a more subtle psychological point here, too; the more you are "bossed" the more your activity of thought will take place within the bossing-pattern, and your part in that pattern seems usually to be opposition to the bossing.

This complaint of the abusive language and the tyrannical treatment of the one just above the worker is an old story to us all, but there is an opposite extreme which is far too little considered. The immediate superior officer is often so close to the worker that he does not exercise the proper duties of his position. Far from taking on himself an aggressive authority, he has often evaded one of the chief problems of his job: how to do what is implied in the fact that he has been put in a position over others. The head of the woman's cloak department in a store will call out, "Say, Sadie, you're 36, aren't you? There's a woman down in the Back Bay kicking about something she says you promised yesterday." "Well, I like that," says Sadie, "Some of those Back Bay women would kick in Heaven." And that perhaps is about all that happens. Of course, the Back Bay lady has to be appeased, but there is often no study of what has taken place for the benefit of the store. I do not mean that a lack of connection between such incidents and the improvement of store technique is universal, but it certainly exists far too often and is one of the problems of those officials who are just above the heads of departments. Naturally, a woman does not want to get on bad terms with her fellow employees with whom she talks and works all day long. Consider the chief operator of the telephone exchanges, remembering that the chief operator is a member of the union, and that the manager is not.

Now what is our problem here? How can we avoid the two extremes: too great bossism in giving orders, and practically no orders given? I am going to ask how *you* are avoiding these extremes. My solution is to depersonalize the giving of orders, to unite all concerned in a study of the situation, to discover the law of the situation and obey that. Until we do this I do not think we shall have the most successful business administration. This is what does take place, what has to take place, when there is a question between two men in positions of equal authority. The head of the sales departments does not give orders to the head of the production department, or vice versa. Each studies the market and the final decision is made as the market demands. This is, ideally, what should take place between foremen and rank and file, between any

head and his subordinates. One *person* should not give orders to another *person*, but both should agree to take their orders from the situation. If orders are simply part of the situation, the question of someone giving and someone receiving does not come up. Both accept the orders given by the situation. Employers accept the orders given by the situation; employees accept the orders given by the situation. This gives, does it not, a slightly different aspect to the whole of business administration through the entire plant?

We have here, I think, one of the largest contributions of scientific management: it tends to depersonalize orders. From one point of view, one might call the essence of scientific management the attempt to find the law of the situation. With scientific management the managers are as much under orders as the workers, for both obey the law of the situation. Our job is not how to get people to obey orders, but how to devise methods by which we can best *discover* the order integral to a particular situation. When that is found, the employee can issue it to the employer, as well as employer to employee. This often happens easily and naturally. My cook or my stenographer points out the law of the situation, and I, if I recognize it as such, accept it, even although it may reverse some "order" I have given.

If those in supervisory positions should depersonalize orders, then there would be no overbearing authority on the one hand, nor on the other that dangerous *laissez-aller* which comes from the fear of exercising authority. Of course we should exercise authority, but always the authority of the situation. I do not say that we have found the way to a frictionless existence, far from it, but we now understand the place which we mean to give to friction. We intend to set it to work for us as the engineer does when he puts the belt over the pulley. There will be just as much, probably more, room for disagreement in the method I am advocating. The situation will often be seen differently, often be interpreted differently. But we shall know what to do with it, we shall have found a method of dealing with it.

I call it depersonalizing because there is not time to go any further into the matter. I think it really is a matter of *repersonalizing*. We, persons, have relations with each other, but we should find them in and through the whole situation. We cannot have any sound relations with each other as long as we take them out of that setting which gives them their meaning and value. This divorcing of persons and the situation does a great deal of harm. I have just said that scientific management depersonalizes; the deeper philosophy of scientific management shows us personal relations within the whole setting of that thing of which they are a part.

There is much psychology, modern psychology particularly, which tends to divorce person and situation. What I am referring to is the present zest for "personality studies." When some difficulty arises, we often hear the psychologist whose specialty is personality studies say, "Study the psychology of that man." And this is very good advice, but only if at the same time we study the entire situation. To leave out the whole situation, however, is so common a blunder in the studies of these psychologists that it constitutes a serious weakness in their work. And as those of you who are personnel directors have more to do, I suppose, with those psychologists who have taken personality for their specialty than with any others, I wish you would watch and see how often you find that this limitation detracts from the value of their conclusions.

I said above that we should substitute for the long-distance order the face-to-face suggestion. I think we can now see a more cogent reason for this than the one then given. It is not the face-to-face suggestion that we want so much as the joint study of the problem, and such joint study can be made best by the employee and his immediate superior or employee and special expert on that question.

I began this talk by emphasizing the advisability of preparing in advance the attitude necessary for the carrying out of orders, as in the previous paper we considered preparing the attitude for integration; but we have now, in our consideration of the joint study of situations, in our emphasis on obeying the law of the situation, perhaps got a little beyond that, or rather we have now to consider in what sense we wish to take the psychologist's doctrine of prepared-in-advance attitudes. By itself this would not take us far, for everyone is studying psychology nowadays, and our employees are going to be just as active in preparing us as we in preparing them! Indeed, a girl working in a factory said to me, "We had a course in psychology last winter, and I see now that you have to be pretty careful how you put things to the managers if you want them to consider favourably what you're asking for." If this prepared-in-advance idea were all that the psychologists think it, it would have to be printed privately as secret doctrine. But the truth is that the best preparation for integration in the matter of orders or in anything else, is a joint study of the situation. We should not try to create the attitude we *want*, although that is the usual phrase, but the attitude required for cooperative study and decision. This holds good even for the salesman. We said above that when the salesman is told that he should create in the prospective buyer the attitude that he wants the article, he ought also to be told that he should do this by integration rather than by suppression. We have now a hint of *how* he is to attain this integration.

I have spoken of the importance of changing some of the language of business personnel relations. We considered whether the words "grievances," "complaints," or Ford's "trouble specialists" did not arouse the wrong behaviour-patterns. I think "order" certainly does. If that word is not to mean any longer external authority, arbitrary authority, but the law of the situation, then we need a new word for it. It is often the order that people resent as much as the thing ordered. People do not like to be ordered even to take a holiday. I have often seen instances of this. The wish to govern one's own life is, of course, one of the most fundamental feelings in every human being. To call this "the instinct of self-assertion," "the instinct of initiative," does not express it wholly. I think it is told in the life of some famous American that when he was a boy and his mother said, "Go get a pail of water," he always replied, "I won't," before taking up the pail and fetching the water. This is significant; he resented the command, the command of a person; but he went and got the water, not, I believe, because he had to, but because he recognized the demand of the situation. *That,* he knew he had to obey; *that,* he was willing to obey. And this kind of obedience is not opposed to the wish to govern one's self, but each is involved in the other; both are part of the same fundamental urge at the root of one's being. We have here something far more profound than "the egoistic impulse" or "the instinct of self-assertion." We have the very essence of the human being.

This subject of orders has led us into the heart of the whole question of authority and consent. When we conceive of authority and consent as parts of an inclusive situation, does that not throw a flood of light on this question? The point of view here presented gets rid of several dilemmas which have seemed to puzzle people in dealing with consent. The feeling of being "under" someone, of "subordination," of "servility," of being "at the will of another," comes out again and again in the shop stewards movement and in the testimony before the Coal Commission. One man said before the Coal Commission, "It is all right to work *with* anyone; what is disagreeable is to feel too distinctly that you are working *under* anyone." *With* is a pretty good preposition, not because it connotes democracy, but because it connotes functional unity, a much more profound conception than that of democracy as usually held. The study of the situation involves the *with* preposition. Then Sadie is not left alone by the head of the cloak department, nor does she have to obey her. The head of the department says, "Let's see how such cases had better be handled, then we'll abide by that." Sadie is not under the head of the department, but both are *under* the situation.

Twice I have had a servant applying for a place ask me if she would be treated as a menial. When the first woman asked me that, I had no idea what she meant, I thought perhaps she did not want to do the roughest work, but later I came to the conclusion that to be treated as a menial meant to be obliged to be under someone, to follow orders without using one's own judgment. If we believe that what heightens self-respect increases efficiency, we shall be on our guard here.

Very closely connected with this is the matter of pride in one's work. If an order goes against what the craftsman or the clerk thinks is the way of doing his work which will bring the best results, he is justified in not wishing to obey that order. Could not that difficulty be met by a joint study of the situation? It is said that it is characteristic of the British workman to feel, "I know my job and won't be told how." The peculiarities of the British workman might be met by a joint study of the situation, it being understood that he probably has more to contribute to that study than anyone else. . . .

There is another dilemma which has to be met by everyone who is in what is called a position of authority: how can you expect people merely to obey orders and at the same time to take that degree of responsibility which they should take? Indeed, in my experience, the people who enjoy following orders blindly, without any thought on their own part, are those who like thus to get rid of responsibility. But the taking of responsibility, each according to his capacity, each according to his function in the whole . . . , this taking of responsibility is usually the most vital matter in the life of every human being, just as the allotting of responsibility is the most important part of business administration.

A young trade unionist said to me, "How much dignity can I have as a mere employee?" He can have all the dignity in the world if he is allowed to make his fullest contribution to the plant *and to assume definitely the responsibility therefor.*

I think one of the gravest problems before us is how to make the reconciliation between receiving orders and taking responsibility. And I think the reconciliation can be made through our conception of the law of the situation. . . .

We have considered the subject of symbols. It is often very apparent that an order is a symbol. The referee in the game stands watch in hand, and says, "Go." It is an order, but order only as symbol. I may say to an employee, "Do so and so," but I should say it only because we have both agreed, openly or tacitly, that that which I am ordering done is the best thing to be done. The order is then a symbol. And if it is a philosophical and psychological truth that we owe obedience only to a functional unity to which we are contributing, we should remember that a more accurate way of stating that would be to say that our obligation is to a unifying, to a process.

This brings us now to one of our most serious problems in this matter of orders. It is important, but we can touch on it only briefly; it is what we spoke of . . . as the evolving situation. I am trying to show here that the order must be integral to the situation and must be recognized as such. But we saw that the situation was always developing. If the situation is never stationary, then the order should never be stationary, so to speak; how to prevent it from being so is our problem. The situation is changing while orders are being carried out, because, by and through orders being carried out. How is the order to keep up with the situation? External orders never can, only those drawn fresh from the situation.

Moreover, if taking a *responsible* attitude toward experience involves recognizing the evolving situation, a *conscious* attitude toward experience means that we note the change which the developing situation makes in ourselves; the situation does not change without changing us.

To summarize, . . . integration being the basic law of life, orders should be the composite conclusion of those who give and those who receive them; more than this, that they should be the integration of the people concerned and the situation; even more than this, that they should be the integration involved in the evolving situation. If you accept my three fundamental statements on this subject: (1) that the order should be the law of the situation; (2) that the situation is always evolving; (3) that orders should involve circular not linear behaviour—then we see that our old conception of orders has somewhat changed, and that there should therefore follow definite changes in business practice.

There is a problem so closely connected with the giving of orders that I want to put it before you for future discussion. After we have decided on our orders, we have to consider how much and what kind of supervision is necessary or advisable in order that they shall be carried out. We all know that many workers object to being watched. What does that mean, how far is it justifiable? How can the objectionable element be avoided and at the same time necessary supervision given? I do not think that this matter has been studied sufficiently. When I asked a very intelligent girl what she thought would be the result of profit sharing and employee representation in the factory where she worked, she replied joyfully, "We shan't need foremen any more." While her entire ignoring of the fact that the foreman has other duties than keeping workers on their jobs was amusing, one wants to go beyond one's amusement and find out what this objection to being watched really means.

In a case in Scotland arising under the Minimum Wage Act, the overman was called in to testify whether or not a certain workman did his work properly. The examination was as follows:

Magistrate: "But isn't it your duty under the Mines Act to visit each working place twice a day?"

Overman: "Yes."

Magistrate: "Don't you do it?"

Overman: "Yes."

Magistrate: "Then why didn't you ever see him work?"

Overman: "They always stop work when they see an overman coming and sit down and wait till he's gone— even take out their pipes, if it's a mine free from gas. They won't let anyone watch them."

An equally extreme standard was enforced for a part of the war period at a Clyde engineering works. The chairman of shop stewards was told one morning that there was a grievance at the smithy. He found one of the blacksmiths in a rage because the managing director in his ordinary morning's walk through the works had stopped for five minutes or so and watched this man's fire. After a shop meeting the chairman took up a deputation to the director and secured the promise that this should not happen again. At the next works meeting the chairman reported the incident to the body of workers, with the result that a similar demand was made throughout the works and practically acceded to, so that the director hardly dared to stop at all in his morning's walk.

I have seen similar instances cited. Many workmen feel that being watched is unbearable. What can we do about it? How can we get proper supervision without this watching which a worker resents? Supervision is necessary; supervision is resented—how are we going to make the integration there? Some say, "Let the workers elect the supervisors." I do not believe in that.

There are three other points closely connected with the subject of this paper which I should like merely to point out. First, when and how do you point out mistakes, misconduct? One principle can surely guide us here: don't blame for the sake of blaming, make what you have to say accomplish something; say it in that form, at that time, under those circumstances, which will make it a real education to your subordinate. Secondly, since it is recognized that the one who gives the orders is not as a rule a very popular person, the management sometimes tries to offset this by allowing the person who has this onus upon him to give any pleasant news to the workers, to have the credit of any innovation which the workers very much desire. One manager told me that he always tried to do this. I suppose that this is good behaviouristic psychology, and yet I am not sure that it is a method I wholly like. It is quite different, however, in the case of a mistaken order having been given; then I think the one who made the mistake should certainly be the one to rectify it, not as a matter of strategy, but because it is better for him too. It is better for all of us not only to acknowledge our mistakes, but to do something about them. If a foreman discharges someone and it is decided to reinstate the man, it is obviously not only good tactics but a square deal to the foreman to allow him to do the reinstating.

There is, of course, a great deal more to this matter of giving orders than we have been able to touch on; far from exhausting the subject, I feel that I have only given hints. I have been told that the artillery men suffered more mentally in the war than others, and the reason assigned for this was that their work was directed from a distance. The combination of numbers by which they focused their fire was telephoned to them. The result was also at a distance. Their activity was not closely enough connected with the actual situation at either end.

18
The Executive Functions
Chester I. Barnard

The coördination of efforts essential to a system of coöperation requires, as we have seen, an organization system of communication. Such a system of communication implies centers or points of interconnection and can only operate as these centers are occupied by persons who are called executives. It might be said, then, that the function of executives is to serve as channels of communication so far as communications must pass through central positions. But since the object of the communication system is coördination of all aspects of organization, it follows that the functions of executives relate to all the work essential to the vitality and endurance of an organization, so far, at least, as it must be accomplished through formal coördination.

It is important to observe, however, that not all work done by persons who occupy executive positions is in connection with the executive functions, the coördination of activities of others. Some of the work of such persons, though *organization* work, is not executive. For example, if the president of a corporation goes out personally to sell products of his company or engages in some of the production work, these are not executive services. If the president of a university gives lectures to a class of students, this is not executive work. If the head of a government department spends time on complaints or disputes about services rendered by the depart-

ment, this is not necessarily executive work. Executive work is not that *of* the organization, but the specialized work of *maintaining* the organization in operation.

Probably all executives do a considerable amount of nonexecutive work. Sometimes this work is more valuable than the executive work they do. This intermixture of functions is a matter of convenience and often of economy, because of the scarcity of abilities; or there may be other reasons for it. As a result of the combination of executive with non-executive functions, however, it is difficult in practice merely by comparison of titles or of nominal functions to determine the comparative methods of executive work in different organizations. If we mean by executive functions the specialized work of maintaining systems of coöperative effort, we may best proceed for general purposes to find out what work has to be done, and then, when desirable, to trace out who are doing that work in a particular organization.

This is especially true because executive work is itself often complexly organized. In an organization of moderate size there may be a hundred persons who are engaged part of the time in executive work; and some of them, for example clerks or stenographers, are not executives in any ordinary sense. Nevertheless, the activities of these persons constitute the executive organiza-

Source: Reprinted by permission of the publishers from *The Functions of the Executive* by Chester I. Barnard, Cambridge, Massachusetts: Harvard University Press, Copyright © 1938, 1968 by the President and Fellows of Harvard College; © 1966 by Grace F. N. Barnard.

tion. It is to the functions of this organization as a special unit that our attention should be given primarily, the distribution of work between persons or positions being for general purposes quite of secondary importance. This chapter will be devoted to the functions of the executive organization as a whole which exists exclusively for the coördination of the efforts of the entire organization.

The executive functions serve to maintain a system of cooperative effort. They are impersonal. The functions are not, as so frequently stated, to manage a group of persons. I do not think a correct understanding of executive work can be had if this narrower, convenient, but strictly speaking erroneous, conception obtains. It is not even quite correct to say that the executive functions are to manage the system of coöperative efforts. As a whole it is managed by itself, not by the executive organization, which is a part of it. The functions with which we are concerned are like those of the nervous system, including the brain, in relation to the rest of the body. It exists to maintain the bodily system by directing those actions which are necessary more effectively to adjust to the environment, but it can hardly be said to manage the body, a large part of whose functions are independent of it and upon which it in turn depends.

The essential executive functions, as I shall present them, correspond to the elements of organization as already stated in Chapter VII and presented in some detail in Part III. They are, first, to provide the system of communication; second, to promote the securing of essential efforts; and, third, to formulate and define purpose. Since the elements of organization are interrelated and interdependent, the executive functions are so likewise; nevertheless they are subject to considerable specialization and as functions are to a substantial degree separable in practice. We shall deal with them only as found in complex, though not necessarily large, organizations.

I. THE MAINTENANCE OF ORGANIZATION COMMUNICATION

We have noticed in previous chapters that, when a complex of more than one unit is in question, centers of communication and corresponding executives are necessary. The need of a definite system of communication creates the first task of the organizer and is the immediate origin of executive organization. If the purpose of an organization is conceived initially in the mind of one person, he is likely very early to find necessary the selection of lieutenants; and if the organization is spontaneous its very first task is likely to be the selection of a leader. Since communication will be accomplished only through the agency of persons, the selection of persons for executive functions is the concrete method of establishing the *means* of communication, though it must be immediately followed by the creation of positions, that is, a *system* of communication; and, especially in established organizations, the positions will exist to be filled in the event of vacancies.

In other words, communication position and the "locating" of the services of a person are complementary phases of the same thing. The center of communication is the organization service of a person at a place. Persons without positions cannot function as executives, they mean nothing but potentiality. Conversely, positions vacant are as defunct as dead nerve centers. This is why executives, when functioning strictly as executives, are unable to appraise men in the abstract, in an organization vacuum, as it were. Men are neither good nor bad, but only good or bad in this or that position. This is why they not infrequently "change the organization," the arrangement of positions, if men suitable to fill them are not available. In fact, "executive organization" in practice cannot be divorced from "executive personnel"; and "executive personnel" is without important meaning except in conjunction with a specific arrangement of positions.

Therefore, the problem of the establishment and maintenance of the system of communication, that is, the primary task of the executive organization, is perpetually that of obtaining the coalescence of the two phases, executive personnel and executive positions. Each phase in turn is the strategic factor of the executive problem—first one, then the other phase, must be adjusted. This is the central problem of the executive functions. Its solution is not in itself sufficient to accomplish the work of all these functions; but no others can be accomplished without it, and none well unless it is well done.

Although this communication function has two phases, it is usually necessary in practice to deal with one phase at a time, and the problems of each phase are of quite different kinds. The problems of positions are those of location and the geographical, temporal, social, and functional specializations of unit and group organizations. The personnel problems are a special case of general personnel problems— the recruiting of contributors who have appropriate qualifications, and the development of the inducements, incentives, persuasion, and objective authority that can make those qualifications effective executive services in the organization.

I. The Scheme of Organization

Let us call the first phase of the function—the definition of organization positions—the "scheme of organization." This is the aspect of organization which receives relatively excessive formal attention because it can apparently be reduced to organization charts, specifications of duties, and descriptions of divisions of labor, etc. It rests upon or represents a coördination chiefly of the work to be done by the organization, that is, its purposes broken up into subsidiary purposes, specializations, tasks, etc., which will be discussed in Section III of this chapter; the kind and quantity of *services* of personnel that can be obtained; the kind and quantity of *persons* that must be included in the coöperative system for this purpose; the inducements that are required; and the places at which and the times when these factors can be combined, which will not be specifically discussed here.[1]

It is evident that these are mutually dependent factors, and that they all involve other executive functions which we shall discuss later. So far as the *scheme* of organization is separately attacked, it is always on the assumption that it is then the strategic factor, the other factors of organization remaining fixed for the time being; but since the underlying purpose of any change in a scheme of organization is to affect these other factors as a whole favorably, any scheme of organization at any given time represents necessarily a result of previous successive approximations through a period of time. It has always necessarily to be attacked on the basis of the present situation.

---

[1]See Chapter X, "The Basis and Kinds of Specializations," and Section III of the present chapter.

II. Personnel

The scheme of organization is dependent not only upon the general factors of the organization as a whole, but likewise, as we have indicated, on the availability of various kinds of services for the executive positions. This becomes in its turn the strategic factor. In general, the principles of the economy of incentives apply here as well as to other more general personnel problems. The balance of factors and the technical problems of this special class, however, are not only different from those generally to be found in other spheres of organization economy but are highly special in different types of organizations.

The most important single contribution required of the executive, certainly the most universal qualification, is loyalty, domination by the organization personality. This is the first necessity because the lines of communication cannot function at all unless the personal contributions of executives will be present at the required positions, at the times necessary, without default for ordinary personal reasons. This, as a personal qualification, is known in secular organizations as the quality of "responsibility"; in political organizations as "regularity"; in governmental organizations as fealty or loyalty; in religious organizations as "complete submission" to the faith and to the hierarchy of objective religious authority.

The contribution of personal loyalty and submission is least susceptible to tangible inducements. It cannot be bought either by material inducements or by other positive incentives, except all other things be equal. This is as true of industrial organizations, I believe, as of any others. It is rather generally understood that although money or other material inducements must usually be paid to responsible persons, responsibility itself does not arise from such inducements.

However, love of prestige is, in general, a much more important inducement in the case of executives than with the rest of the personnel. Interest in work and pride in organization are other incentives that usually must be present. These facts are much obscured as respects commercial organizations, where material inducements appear to be the effective factors partly because such inducements are more readily offered in such organizations and partly because, since the other incentives are often equal as between such organizations, material inducements are the only available differential factor. It also becomes an important secondary factor to individuals in many cases, because prestige and official responsibilities impose heavy material burdens on them. Hence neither churches nor socialistic states have been able to escape the necessity of direct or indirect material inducements for high dignitaries or officials. But this is probably incidental and superficial in all organizations. It appears to be true that in all of them adequate incentives to executive services are difficult to offer. Those most available in the present age are tangible, materialistic; but on the whole they are both insufficient and often abortive.[2]

---

[2]After much experience, I am convinced that the most ineffective services in a continuing effort are in one sense those of volunteers, or of semi-volunteers; for example, half-pay workers. What appears to be inexpensive is in fact very expensive, because non-material incentives—such as prestige, toleration of too great personal interest in the work with its accompanying fads and "pet" projects, the yielding to exaggerated conceptions of individual importance—are causes of internal friction and many other undesirable consequences. Yet in many emergency situations, and in a large part of political, charitable, civic, educational, and religious organization work, often indispensable services cannot be obtained by material incentives.

Following loyalty, responsibility, and capacity to be dominated by organization personality, come the more specific personal abilities. They are roughly divided into two classes: relatively general abilities, involving general alertness, comprehensiveness of interest, flexibility, faculty of adjustment, poise, courage, etc.; and specialized abilities based on particular aptitudes and acquired techniques. The first kind is relatively difficult to appraise because it depends upon innate characteristics developed through general experience. It is not greatly susceptible of immediate inculcation. The second kind may be less rare because the division of labor, that is, organization itself, fosters it automatically, and because it is susceptible to development (at a cost) by training and education. We deliberately and more and more turn out specialists; but we do not develop general executives well by specific efforts, and we know very little about how to do it.

The higher the positions in the line of authority, the more general the abilities required. The scarcity of such abilities, together with the necessity for keeping the lines of authority as short as feasible, controls the organization of executive work. It leads to the reduction of the number of formally executive positions to the minimum, a measure made possible by creating about the executives in many cases staffs of specialists who supplement them in time, energy, and technical capacities. This is made feasible by elaborate and often delicate arrangements to correct error resulting from the faults of over-specialization and the paucity of line executives.

The operation of such systems of complex executive organization requires the highest development of the executive arts. Its various forms and techniques are most definitely exemplified in the armies and navies of the major powers, the Postal Administrations of several European countries, the Bell Telephone System, some of the great railway systems, and the Catholic Church; and perhaps in the political organization of the British Empire.[3] One of the first limitations of world-wide or even a much more restricted international organization is the necessity for the development of these forms and techniques far beyond their present status.

Thus, jointly with the development of the scheme of organization, the selection, promotion, demotion, and dismissal of men becomes the essence of maintaining the system of communication without which no organization can exist. The selection in part, but especially the promotion, demotion, and dismissal of men, depend upon the exercise of supervision or what is often called "control."

Control relates directly, and in conscious application chiefly, to the work of the organization as a whole rather than to the work of executives as such. But so heavily dependent is the success of coöperation upon the functioning of the executive organization that practically the control is over executives for the most part. If the work of an organization is not successful, if it is inefficient, if it cannot maintain the services of its personnel, the conclusion is that its "management" is wrong; that is, that the scheme of communication or the associated personnel or both, that is, the

[3]From a structural point of view the organization of the United States of America is especially noteworthy, but from the viewpoint of the executive functions it is intended to be defective; that is, the system of States Rights or dual sovereignty and the separation of legislative, judicial, and executive departments precludes a common center of authoritative communication in American government as a formal organization. It is intended or expected that the requirements will be met by informal organization.

executive department directly related, are at fault. This is, sometimes at least, not true, but often it is. Moreover, for the correction of such faults the first reliance is upon executive organization. The methods by which control is exercised are, of course, numerous and largely technical to each organization, and need not be further discussed here.

III. Informal Executive Organizations

So far we have considered the first executive function only as it relates to the formal communication system. It has been emphasized several times in this treatise that informal organization is essential to formal organizations, particularly with reference to communication. This is true not only of the organization as a whole, or of its ultimate subordinate units, but also of that special part which we call the executive organization. The communication function of executives includes the maintenance of informal executive organization as an essential means of communication.

Although I have never heard it stated that this is an executive function or that such a thing as an informal executive organization exists, in all the good organizations I have observed the most careful attention is paid to it. In all of them informal organizations operate. This is usually not apparent except to those directly concerned.

The general method of maintaining an informal executive organization is so to operate and to select and promote executives that a general condition of compatibility of personnel is maintained. Perhaps often and certainly occasionally men cannot be promoted or selected, or even must be relieved, because they cannot function, because they "do not fit," where there is no question of formal competence. This

question of "fitness" involves such matters as education, experience, age, sex, personal distinctions, prestige, race, nationality, faith, politics, sectional antecedents; and such very specific personal traits as manners, speech, personal appearance, etc. It goes by few if any rules, except those based at least nominally on other, formal, considerations. It represents in its best sense the political aspects of personal relationship in formal organization. I suspect it to be most highly developed in political, labor, church, and university organizations, for the very reason that the intangible types of personal services are relatively more important in them than in most other, especially industrial, organizations. But it is certainly of major importance in all organizations.

This compatibility is promoted by educational requirements (armies, navies, churches, schools); by requirement of certain background (European armies, navies, labor unions, Soviet and Fascist governments, political parties); by conferences and conventions; by specifically social activities; by class distinctions connected with privileges and "authority" (in armies, navies, churches, universities). A certain conformity is required by unwritten understanding that can sometimes be formally enforced, expressed for its negative aspect by the phrase "conduct unbecoming a gentleman and an officer." There are, however, innumerable other processes, many of which are not consciously employed for this purpose.

It must not be understood that the desired degree of compatibility is always the same or is the maximum possible. On the contrary it seems to me to be often the case that excessive compatibility or harmony is deleterious, resulting in "single track minds" and excessively crystallized attitudes and in the destruction of personal responsibility;

but I know from experience in operating with new emergency organizations, in which there was no time and little immediate basis for the growth of an informal organization properly coördinated with formal organization that it is almost impossible to secure effective and efficient coöperation without it.

The functions of informal executive organizations are the communication of intangible facts, opinions, suggestions, suspicions, that cannot pass through formal channels without raising issues calling for decisions, without dissipating dignity and objective authority, and without overloading executive positions; also to minimize excessive cliques of political types arising from too great divergence of interests and views; to promote self-discipline of the group; and to make possible the development of important personal influences in the organization. There are probably other functions.

I shall comment on only two functions of informal executive organization. The necessity for avoiding formal issues, that is, for avoiding the issuance of numerous formal orders except on routine matters and except in emergencies, is important.[4] I know of major executives who issue an order or judgment settling an important issue rather seldom, although they are functioning all the time. The obvious desire of politicians to avoid important issues (and to

impose them on their opponents) is based upon a thorough sense of organization. Neither authority nor coöperative disposition (largely the same things) will stand much overt division on formal issues in the present stage of human development. Hence most laws, executive orders, decisions, etc., are in effect formal notice that all is well— there is agreement, authority is not questioned.

The question of personal influence is very subtle. Probably most good organizations have somewhere a Colonel House; and many men not only exercise beneficent influence far beyond that implied by their formal status, but most of them, at the time, would lose their influence if they had corresponding formal status. The reason may be that many men have personal qualifications of high order that will not operate under the stress of commensurate official responsibility. By analogy I may mention the golfers of first class skill who cannot "stand up" in public tournaments.

To summarize: the first executive function is to develop and maintain a system of communication. This involves jointly a scheme of organization and an executive personnel. The processes by which the latter is accomplished include chiefly the selection of men and the offering of incentives; techniques of control permitting effectiveness in promoting, demoting, and dismissing men; and finally the securing of an informal organization in which the essential property is compatibility of personnel. The chief functions of this informal organization are expansion of the means of communication with reduction in the necessity for formal decisions, the minimizing of undesirable influences, and the promotion of desirable influences concordant with the scheme of formal responsibilities.

[4]When writing these lines I tried to recall an important general decision made by me on my initiative as a telephone executive within two years. I could recall none, although on reviewing the record I found several. On the other hand, I can still recall without any record many major decisions made by me "out of hand" when I was a Relief Administrator. I probably averaged at least five a day for eighteen months. In the latter case I worked with a very noble group but a very poor informal organization under emergency conditions.

II. THE SECURING OF ESSENTIAL SERVICES FROM INDIVIDUALS

The second function of the executive organization is to promote the securing of the personal services that constitute the material of organizations.

The work divides into two main divisions: (I) the bringing of persons into coöperative relationship with the organization; (II) the eliciting of the services after such persons have been brought into that relationship.

I

The characteristic fact of the first division is that the organization is acting upon persons who are in every sense outside it. Such action is necessary not merely to secure the personnel of new organizations, or to supply the material for the growth of existing organizations, but also to replace the losses that continually take place by reason of death, resignation, "backsliding," emigration, discharge, excommunication, ostracism. These factors of growth or replacement of contributors require bringing persons by organization effort within range of the consideration of the incentives available in order to induce some of these persons to attach themselves to the organization. Accordingly the task involves two parts: (*a*) bringing persons within reach of specific effort to secure services, and (*b*) the application of that effort when they have been brought near enough. Often both parts of the task occupy the efforts of the same persons or parts of an organization; but they are clearly distinct elements and considerable specialization is found with respect to them.

(*a*) Bringing persons within reach of recruiting or proselyting influence is a task which differs in practical emphasis

among organizations in respect both to scope and to method. Some religious organizations—especially the Catholic Church, several Protestant Churches, the Mormon Church, for example— have as ideal goals the attachment of all persons to their organizations, and the wide world is the field of proselyting propaganda. During many decades the United States of America invited all who could reach its shores to become American citizens. Other organizations, having limits on the volume of their activities, restrict the field of propaganda. Thus many nations in effect now restrict substantial growth to those who acquire a national status by birth; the American Legion restricts its membership to those who have acquired a status by certain type of previous service, etc. Others restrict their fields practically on the basis of proportions. Thus universities "in principle" are open to all or to all with educational and character qualifications but may restrict their appeals to geographical, racial, and class proportions so as to preserve the cosmopolitan character of their bodies, or to preserve predominance of nationals, etc. Industrial and commercial organizations are theoretically limited usually by considerations of social compatibility and additionally by the costs of propaganda. They usually attempt no appeal when the geographic remoteness makes it ineffective.

Although the scope of the field of propaganda is for most organizations not clearly conceived or stated and as a problem only requires active consideration at intervals usually long, the question is nevertheless fundamental. This is best indicated by the methods practically employed in connection with it. In churches the organization of mission work and its territorial scope are the best indications of its importance. In most governments, at present, the accretion of members takes the form of stimulating reproduction by active promotional efforts, as in France and Italy, for example, or by the ease of acquiring citizenship and free land, as until recently in the United States. In many industrial organizations foreign recruiting was once an important aspect of their work, and directly or indirectly the appeal for contributors of capital or credit has been fundamentally international in scope until recent exchange restrictions. In fact, the most universal aspect of industrial organization appeal has been in respect to this type of contributor—for many practical purposes he is not usually regarded as the material of organization, though in the present study he is.

(*b*) The effort to induce specific persons who by the general appeal are brought into contact with an organization actually to become identified with it constitutes the more regular and routine work of securing contributors. This involves in its general aspects the method of persuasion which has already been described, the establishment of inducements and incentives, and direct negotiation. The methods required are indefinitely large in number and of very wide variety.[5] It would not be useful here to add to what has already been said in Chapter XI on the economy of incentives. It is only necessary to emphasize again that fundamentally most persons potentially available are not susceptible at any given time of being induced to give service to any particular organization, large or small.

II

Although the work of recruiting is important in most organizations, and especially so in those which are new or rapidly expanding or which have high "turnover," nevertheless in established and enduring organizations the eliciting of the quantity and quality of efforts from their adherents is usually more important and occupies the greater part of personnel effort. Because of the more tangible character of "membership," being an "employee," etc., recruiting is apt to receive more attention as a field of personnel work than the business of promoting the actual output of efforts and influences, which are the real material of organization.[6] Membership, nominal adherence, is merely the starting point; and the minimum contributions which can be conceived as enabling retention of such connection would generally be insufficient for the survival of active or productive organization. Hence every church, every government, every other important organization, has to intensify or multiply the contributions which its members will make above the level of volume which would occur if no such effort were made. Thus churches must strengthen the faith, secure compliance by public and private acknowledgments of faith or devotion, and secure material contributions from their members. Governments are concerned with increasing the quality of the citizenry—promoting national solidarity, loyalty, patriotism, discipline, and competence. Other organizations are similarly occupied in securing loyalty, reliability, responsibility, enthusiasm, quality of efforts, output.

[5]I must repeat that although the emphasis is on the employee group of contributors, so far as industrial organizations are concerned, nevertheless "customers" are equally included. The principles broadly discussed here relate to salesmanship as well as employing persons.

[6]As an instance, note the great attention in civil service regulations, and also in political appointments, to obtaining and retaining employment, and the relatively small attention to services.

In short, every organization to survive must deliberately attend to the maintenance and growth of its authority to do the things necessary for coördination, effectiveness, and efficiency. This, as we have seen, depends upon its appeal to persons who are already related to the organization.

The methods, the inducements and incentives, by which this is done have already been in general indicated in our discussion of incentives and authority. As executive functions they may be distinguished as the maintenance of morale, the maintenance of the scheme of inducements, the maintenance of schemes of deterrents, supervision and control, inspection, education and training.

III. THE FORMULATION OF PURPOSE AND OBJECTIVES

The third executive function is to formulate and define the purposes, objectives, ends, of the organization. It has already been made clear that, strictly speaking, purpose is defined more nearly by the aggregate of action taken than by any formulation in words; but that the aggregate of action is a residuum of the decisions relative to purpose and the environment, resulting in closer and closer approximations to the concrete acts. It has also been emphasized that purpose is something that must be accepted by all the contributors to the system of efforts. Again, it has been stated that purpose must be broken into fragments, specific objectives, not only ordered in time so that detailed purpose and detailed action follow in the series of progressive coöperation, but also ordered contemporaneously into the specializations—geographical, social, and functional—that each unit organization implies. It is more apparent here than with other ex-

ecutive functions that it is an entire executive organization that formulates, redefines, breaks into details, and decides on the innumerable simultaneous and progressive actions that are the stream of syntheses constituting purpose or action. No single executive can under any conditions accomplish this function alone, but only that part of it which relates to his position in the executive organization.

Hence the critical aspect of this function is the assignment of responsibility—the delegation of objective authority. Thus in one sense this function is that of the scheme of positions, the system of communication, already discussed. That is its potential aspect. Its other aspect is the actual decisions and conduct which make the scheme a working system. Accordingly, the general executive states that "this is the purpose, this the objective, this the direction, in general terms, in which we wish to move, before next year." His department heads, or the heads of his main territorial divisions, say to their departments or suborganizations: "This means for us these things now, then others next month, then others later, to be better defined after experience." Their subdepartment or division heads say: "This means for us such and such operations now at these places, such others at those places, something today here, others tomorrow there." Then district or bureau chiefs in turn become more and more specific, their sub-chiefs still more so as to place, group, time, until finally purpose is merely jobs, specific groups, definite men, definite times, accomplished results. But meanwhile, back and forth, up and down, the communications pass, reporting obstacles, difficulties, impossibilities, accomplishments; redefining, modifying purposes level after level.

Thus the organization for the definition of purpose is the organization for the specification of work to do; and the specifications are made in their final stage when and where the work is being done. I suspect that at least nine-tenths of all organization activity is on the responsibility, the authority, and the specifications of those who make the last contributions, who apply personal energies to the final concrete objectives. There is no meaning to personal specialization, personal experience, personal training, personal location, personal ability, eyes and ears, arms and legs, brains and emotions, if this is not so. What must be added to the indispensable authority, responsibility, and capability of each contributor is the indispensable coördination. This requires a pyramiding of the formulation of purpose that becomes more and more general as the number of units of basic organization becomes larger, and more and more remote in future time. Responsibility for abstract, generalizing, prospective, long-run decision is delegated *up* the line, responsibility for definition, action, remains always at the base where the authority for effort resides.

The formulation and definition of purpose is then a widely distributed function only the more general part of which is executive. In this fact lies the most important inherent difficulty in the operation of coöperative systems—the necessity for indoctrinating those at the lower levels with general purposes, the major decisions, so that they remain cohesive and able to make the ultimate detailed decisions coherent; and the necessity, for those at the higher levels, of constantly understanding the concrete conditions and the specific decisions of

the "ultimate" contributors from which and from whom executives are often insulated. Without that up-and-down-the-line coördination of purposeful decisions, general decisions and general purposes are mere intellectual processes in an organization vacuum, insulated from realities by layers of misunderstanding. The function of formulating grand purposes and providing for their redefinition is one which needs sensitive systems of communication, experience in interpretation, imagination, and delegation of responsibility.

Perhaps there are none who could consider even so extremely condensed and general a description of the excutive functions as has here been presented without perceiving that these functions are merely elements in an organic whole. It is their combination in a working system that makes an organization.

This combination involves two opposite incitements to action. First, the concrete interaction and mutual adjustment of the executive functions are partly to be determined by the factors of the environment of the organization—the specific coöperative system as a whole and its environment. This involves fundamentally the logical processes of analysis and the discrimination of the strategic factors. We shall consider this aspect in the following chapter. Second, the combination equally depends upon the maintenance of the vitality of action—the will to effort. This is the moral aspect, the element of morale, the ultimate reason for coöperation, to which Chapter XVII will be given.

19
An Analysis of Leadership
Douglas M. McGregor

Are successful managers born or "made"? Does success as a manager rest on the possession of a certain core of abilities and traits, or are there many combinations of characteristics which can result in successful industrial leadership? Is managerial leadership—or its potential—a property of the individual, or is it a term for describing a relationship between people? Will the managerial job twenty years from now require the same basic abilities and personality traits as it does today?

The previous chapters of this volume suggest tentative answers to these questions. Knowledge gained from research in the social sciences sheds additional light on these and other questions relevant to leadership in industry. It does not provide final, definitive answers. There is much yet to be learned. But the accumulated evidence points with high probability toward certain ones among a number of possible assumptions.

Prior to the 1930s it was widely believed that leadership was a property of the individual, that a limited number of people were uniquely endowed with abilities and traits which made it possible for them to become leaders. Moreover, these abilities and traits were believed to be inherited rather than acquired.

As a consequence of these beliefs, re-search studies in this field were directed toward the identification of the universal characteristics of leadership so that potential leaders might be more readily identified. A large number of studies were published—many based on arm-chair theorizing, but some utilizing biographical or other empirical data.

Examinations of this literature reveals an imposing number of supposedly essential characteristics of the successful leader—over a hundred, in fact, even after elimination of obvious duplication and overlap of terms. The search still continues in some quarters. Every few months a new list appears based on the latest analysis. And each new list differs in some respects from the earlier ones.

However, social science research in this field since the 1930s has taken new directions. Some social scientists have become interested in studying the behavior as well as the personal characteristics of leaders. As a result, some quite different ideas about the nature of leadership have emerged.

The research in this field in the last twenty years has been prolific. A recent summary cites 111 references, of which six were published prior to 1930. As a result of such work, a number of generalizations about leadership may be stated with reasonable certainty. Among these, the following are particularly significant for management.

Source: From "An Analysis of Leadership" by Douglas McGregor, in *The Human Side of Enterprise*, pp. 179–189. Copyright © 1960 McGraw-Hill Book Company. Reprinted by permission.

GENERALIZATIONS FROM RECENT RESEARCH

It is quite unlikely that there is a single basic pattern of abilities and personality traits characteristic of all leaders. The personality characteristics of the leader are not unimportant, but those which are essential differ considerably depending upon the circumstances. The requirements for successful political leadership are different from those for industrial management or military or educational leadership. Failure is as frequent as success in transfers of leaders from one type of social institution to another. The reasons are perhaps evident in the light of the discussion in earlier chapters of this volume.

Even within a single institution such as industry, different circumstances require different leadership characteristics. Comparisons of successful industrial leaders in different historical periods, in different cultures, in different industries, or even in different companies have made this fairly obvious. The leadership requirements of a young, struggling company, for example, are quite different from those of a large, well-established firm.

Within the individual company different functions (sales, finance, production) demand rather different abilities and skills of leadership. Managers who are successful in one function are sometimes, but by no means always, successful in another. The same is true of leadership at different organizational levels. Every successful foreman would not make a successful president (or vice versa!). Yet each may be an effective leader.

On the other hand, leaders who differ notably in abilities and traits are sometimes equally successful when they succeed each other in a given situation.

Within rather wide limits, weaknesses in certain characteristics can be compensated by strength in others. This is particularly evident in partnerships and executive teams in which leadership functions are, in fact, *shared.* The very idea of the team implies different and supplementary patterns of abilities among the members.

Many characteristics which have been alleged to be essential to the leader turn out not to differentiate the successful leader from unsuccessful ones. In fact, some of these—integrity, ambition, judgment, for example—are to be found not merely in the leader, but in any successful member of an organization.

Finally, among the characteristics essential for leadership are skills and attitudes which can be acquired or modified extensively through learning. These include competence in planning and initiating action, in problem solving, in keeping communication channels open and functioning effectively, in accepting responsibility, and in the skills of social interaction. Such skills are not inherited, nor is their acquisition dependent on the possession of any unique pattern of inborn characteristics.

It is, of course, true that the few outstanding leaders in any field have been unusually gifted people, but these preeminent leaders differ widely among themselves in their strengths and weaknesses. They do not possess a pattern of leadership characteristics in common. The evidence to date does not prove conclusively that there is no basic universal core of personal qualifications for leadership. However, few of the social scientists who have worked extensively during recent years in this field would regard this as a promising possibility for further work. On the contrary, the research during the past two decades has shown that we must look beyond the personal qualifications of the leader if we wish to understand what leadership is.

LEADERSHIP IS A RELATIONSHIP

There are at least four major variables now known to be involved in leadership: (1) the characteristics of the leader; (2) the attitudes, needs, and other personal characteristics of the followers; (3) characteristics of the organization, such as its purpose, its structure, the nature of the tasks to be performed; and (4) the social, economic, and political milieu. The personal characteristics required for effective performance as a leader vary, depending on the other factors.

This is an important research finding. *It means that leadership is not a property of the individual, but a complex relationship among these variables.* The old argument over whether the leader makes history or history makes the leader is resolved by this conception. Both assertions are true within limits.

The relationship between the leader and the situation is essentially circular. Organization structure and policy, for example, are established by top management. Once established, they set limits on the leadership patterns which will be acceptable within the company. However, influences from above (a change in top management with an accompanying change in philosophy), from below (following recognition of a union and adjustment to collective bargaining, for example), or from outside (social legislation, changes in the market, etc.) bring about changes in these organizational characteristics. Some of these may lead to a redefinition of acceptable leadership patterns. The changes which occurred in the leader-

ship of the Ford Motor Company after Henry Ford I retired provide a dramatic illustration.

The same thing is true of the influence of the broader milieu. The social values, the economic and political conditions, the general standard of living, the level of education of the population, and other factors characteristic of the late 1800s had much to do with the kinds of people who were successful as industrial leaders during that era. Those men in turn helped to shape the nature of the industrial environment. Their influence affected the character of our society profoundly.

Today, industry requires a very different type of industrial leader than it did in 1900. Similarly, today's leaders are helping to shape industrial organizations which tomorrow will require people quite different from themselves in key positions.

An important point with respect to these situational influences on leadership is that they operate selectively—in subtle and unnoticed as well as in obvious ways—to reward conformity with acceptable patterns of behavior and to punish deviance from these. The differing situations from company to company, and from unit to unit within a company, each have their selective consequences. The observable managerial "types" in certain companies are illustrative of this phenomenon. One consequence of this selectivity is the tendency to "weed out" deviant individuals, some of whom might nevertheless become effective, perhaps outstanding, leaders.

Even if there is no single universal pattern of characteristics of the leader, it is conceivable at least that there might be certain universal characteristics *of the relationship* between the leader and the other situational factors which are essential for optimum organized human effort in all situations. This is doubtful. Consider, for example, the relationship of an industrial manager with a group of native employees in an underdeveloped country on the one hand, and with a group of United States workmen who are members of a well-established international union on the other. Moreover, even if research finally indicates that there are such universal requirements of the relationship, there will still be more than one way of achieving them. For example, if "mutual confidence" between the leader and the led is a universal requirement, it is obvious that there are many ways of developing and maintaining this confidence.

We have already considered some of the significant conditions for the success of certain relationships involving interdependence in industrial organizations today. To achieve these conditions, the supervisor requires skills and attitudes, *but these can be acquired by people who differ widely in their inborn traits and abilities.* In fact, one of the important lessons from research and experience in this field is that the attempt to train supervisors to adopt a single leadership "style" yields poorer results than encouraging them to create the essential conditions *in their individual ways* and with due regard for their own particular situations. Note also in this connection how organization structure and management philosophy may either encourage or inhibit the supervisor in establishing these conditions.

It does not follow from these considerations that *any* individual can become a successful leader in a given situation. It *does* follow that successful leadership is not dependent on the possession of a single universal pattern of inborn traits and abilities. It seems likely that leadership potential (considering the tremendous variety of situations for which leadership is required) is broadly rather than narrowly distributed in the population.

Research findings to date suggest, then, that it is more fruitful to consider leadership as a relationship between the leader and the situation than as a universal pattern of characteristics possessed by certain people. The differences in requirements for successful leadership in different situations are more striking than the similarities. Moreover, research studies emphasize the importance of leadership skills and attitudes which can be acquired and are, therefore, not inborn characteristics of the individual.

It has often happened in the physical sciences that what was once believed to be an inherent property of objects—gravity, for example, or electrical "magnetism," or mass—has turned out to be a complex relationship between internal and external factors. The same thing happens in the social sciences, and leadership is but one example.

IMPLICATIONS FOR MANAGEMENT

What is the practical relevance for management of these findings of social science research in the field of leadership? First, if we accept the point of view that leadership consists of a relationship between the leader, his followers, the organization, and the social milieu, and if we recognize that these situational factors are subject to substantial changes with time, we must recognize that we cannot predict the personal characteristics of the managerial resources that an organization will require a decade or two hence. Even if we can list the positions to be filled, we cannot define very adequately the essential characteristics of the people who will be needed in those situations at that time. *One of management's major tasks, therefore, is to provide a heterogeneous supply of human resources from which individuals can be selected to fill a variety of specific but unpredictable needs.*

This is a blow to those who have hoped that the outcome of research would be to provide them with methods by which they could select today the top management of tomorrow. It is a boon to those who have feared the consequences of the "crown prince" approach to management development. It carries other practical implications of some importance.

With the modern emphasis on career employment and promotion from within, management must pay more than casual attention to its recruitment practices. It would seem logical that this process should tap a variety of sources: liberal arts as well as technical graduates, small colleges as well as big universities, institutions in different geographic regions, etc. It may be necessary, moreover, to look carefully at the criteria for selection of college recruits if heterogeneity is a goal. The college senior who graduates in the top 10 per cent of his class may come from a narrow segment of the range of potential leaders for industry. What of the student who has, perhaps for reasons unrelated to intellectual capacity, graduated in the middle of his class because he got A's in some subjects and C's and D's in others? What of the student whose academic achievement was only average because the education system never really challenged him?

As a matter of fact there is not much evidence that high academic achievement represents a necessary characteristic for industrial leadership. There may be a positive correlation, but it is not large enough to provide a basis for a recruitment policy. In fact, the current

President of the United States would have been passed over at graduation by any management recruiter who relied on this correlation! It may be, on the contrary, that the *intellectual* capacity required for effective leadership in many industrial management positions is no greater than that required for graduation from a good college. Of course, there are positions requiring high intellectual capacity, but it does not follow that there is a one-to-one correlation between this characteristic and success as an industrial leader. (This question of intellectual capacity is, of course, only one reason why industry seeks the bulk of its potential managerial resources among college graduates today. There are other factors involved: confidence and social poise, skill acquired through participation in extracurricular activities, personal ambition and drive, etc. These, however, are relatively independent of class standing.)

It may be argued that intellectual *achievement*, as measured by consistently high grades in all subjects, is evidence of motivation and willingness to work. Perhaps it is—in the academic setting—but it is also evidence of willingness to conform to the quite arbitrary demands of the educational system. There is little reason for assuming that high motivation and hard work *in school* are the best predictors of motivation and effort in later life. There are a good many examples to the contrary.

A second implication from research findings about leadership is that a management development program should involve many people within the organization rather than a select few. The fact that some companies have been reasonably successful in developing a selected small group of managerial trainees may well be an artifact—an example of the operation of the "self-fulfilling prophecy." If these companies had been equally concerned to develop managerial talent within a much broader sample, they might have accomplished this purpose with no greater percentage of failures. And, if the generalizations above are sound, they would have had a richer, more valuable pool of leadership resources to draw on as a result.

Third, management should have as a goal the development of the unique capacities and potentialities of each individual rather than common objectives for all participants. This is a purpose which is honored on paper much more than in practice. It is difficult to achieve, particularly in the big company, but if we want heterogeneous leadership resources to meet the unpredictable needs of the future we certainly won't get them by subjecting all our managerial trainees to the same treatment.

Moreover, this process of developing heterogeneous resources must be continuous; it is never completed. Few human beings ever realize all of their potentialities for growth, even though some may reach a practical limit with respect to certain capacities. Each individual is unique, and it is this uniqueness we will constantly encourage and nourish if we are truly concerned to develop leaders for the industry of tomorrow.

Fourth, the promotion policies of the company should be so administered that these heterogeneous resources are actually considered when openings occur. There is little value in developing a wide range of talent if only a small and possibly limited segment of it constitutes the field of candidates when a particular position is being filled.

In view of the selective operation of situational variables referred to above, there may be legitimate questions concerning the value of an *exclusive* policy of "promotion from within." It is conceivable that in a large and reasonably decentralized company sufficient heterogeneity can be maintained by transfers of managerial talent between divisions, but it is probable that fairly strenuous efforts will be required to offset the normal tendency to create and maintain a "type," a homogeneous pattern of leadership within a given organization. Without such efforts competent individuals who don't "fit the pattern" are likely to be passed over or to leave because their talents are not rewarded. Many industrial organizations, for example, would not easily tolerate the strong individualism of a young Charles Kettering today.

Finally, if leadership is a function—a complex relation between leader and situation—we ought to be clear that every promising recruit is *not* a potential member of top management. Some people in some companies will become outstanding leaders as foremen, or as plant superintendents, or as professional specialists. Many of these would not be effective leaders in top management positions, at least under the circumstances prevailing in the company.

If we take seriously the implications of the research findings in this field, we will place high value on such people. We will seek to enable them to develop to the fullest their potentialities in the role they can fill best. And we will find ways to reward them which will persuade them that we consider outstanding leadership *at any level* to be a precious thing.

REFERENCES

Bennis, Warren G., "Leadership theory and administrative behavior," *Administrative Science Quarterly*, vol. 4, no. 3, 1959.

Fortune Editors, *The executive life.* New York: Doubleday & Company, Inc., 1956.

Gibb, Cecil A., "Leadership," in Gardner Lindzey (ed.), *Handbook of social psychology.* Reading, Mass.: Addison-Wesley Publishing Company, 1954, vol. II.

Ginzberg, Eli, *What makes an executive.* New York: Columbia University Press, 1955.

Knickerbocker, Irving, "Leadership: A conception and some implications," *Journal of Social Issues,* vol. 4, no. 3, 1948.

Selznick, Philip, *Leadership in administration.* Evanston, Ill.: Row, Peterson & Company, 1957.

4 Factors
1. Differentiation of role
2. closeness of supervision
3. orientation
4. group rel.

20
Leadership Practices in Relation to Productivity and Morale
Robert L. Kahn & Daniel Katz

In applying the principles discovered in laboratory studies to life situations, there is always the problem of the generality and meaningfulness of the findings. Can the more complex social situation be interpreted adequately in terms of the results of laboratory experiments? Will the use of the generalization from the group experiment be effective in the life situation, where the game is being played for higher stakes, and where people are playing for keeps? The direct study of natural groups and organizations may not necessarily challenge the validity of laboratory research, but it can demonstrate its importance or its triviality.

In a program of research on human relations in group organization, the Survey Research Center of the University of Michigan has attempted a direct attack upon the conditions and causes of worker productivity and worker morale through field studies, surveys and field experiments. In this program, the initial research was not planned around tight mathematical models of the hypothetico-deductive variety but was more empirically oriented, seeking to discover and explore those variables which assumed significant proportions in the industrial situations studied. Nevertheless, the contributions of the Lewinian school, the self-realization notions of Dewey and Rogers, and the realistic analyses of institutional structure by Allport and Mayo and Roethlisberger had a good deal to do with the directions of the research.

Field studies of this sort have the great advantage over laboratory situations of dealing directly with social realities and thus meeting the problem of applicability and generalization to social phenomena, provided they can deal with variables at some level of generality. They suffer, however, in comparison to laboratory experiments with respect to control in the identification and manipulation of variables. In the Human Relations Program, therefore, methodological emphasis was placed upon checks and controls in the field studies undertaken. Unquantified anthropological observation was replaced by standardized interviews with care-

This chapter was prepared especially for this volume. The findings and many of the interpretations are taken from several of the major studies in the program of human relations research conducted by the Survey Research Center of the University of Michigan. This program is supported by grants from the Office of Naval Research and the Rockefeller Foundation, and by contracts with the organizations in which the studies were conducted. The studies cited were directed by Gerald Gurin, Eugene Jacobson, Robert L. Kahn, Nathan Maccoby, Floyd C. Mann, Nancy C. Morse, and Donald C. Pelz. The results of these studies are presented more fully in the publications listed following this chapter.

fully defined samples of respondents. Impressionistic accounts of attitude and morale, as in the Hawthorne studies, were replaced with measures of workers' psychological responses. Effects of supervisory practices were not judged on the basis of what management assumed the results to be. Independently derived measures were employed in testing relationships between factors. For example, supervisory behavior was measured independently of its effects upon productivity and morale of workers. Interestingly enough, this is the first time such measurements have ever been taken in an effort to get at the functional relationships in an ongoing organization. Moreover, where productivity was taken as the dependent variable, supervisory practice as the independent variable, and morale as the intervening variable, the groups which were compared were equated on all the technological factors which could affect productivity.

Studies in this program of research have now been conducted in a variety of industrial situations, and in civilian and military agencies. These include the home office of an insurance company, maintenance-of-way section gangs on a railroad, an electric utility, an automotive manufacturer, a tractor company, an appliance manufacturer, and two agencies of the federal government. Some of the major research findings emerging from these projects are summarized in the following pages.

DIFFERENTIATION OF SUPERVISORY ROLE

The supervisor with the better productive record plays a more differentiated role than the supervisor with the poor productive record; that is, he does not perform the same functions as the rank and file worker, but assumes more of the functions traditionally associated with leadership. Foremen of railroad section gangs, for example, were found to differ with respect to the amount of time they spent in planning the work and performing special skilled tasks (Table 1). In general, the foremen with the better production records devoted more time

TABLE 1 • RELATION OF WHAT FOREMAN REPORTS DOING ON
THE JOB TO SECTION PRODUCTIVITY
(Section Gangs on a Railroad)

	Supervisory Duties		Non-Supervisory Duties			
	Planning; Skilled Tasks	Providing Materials to Men; Watching Men	Same Things Men Do	Keeping up Track	Number of Duties Mentioned*	N
Foremen of high-producing sections	42	41	8	7	98	36
		83		15		
Foremen of low-producing sections	25	42	15	14	96	36
		67		29		

*The responses total more than 72 because many foremen gave more than one answer.

TABLE 2 • RELATION OF MEN'S PERCEPTION OF FOREMAN'S PLANNING ABILITY TO SECTION PRODUCTIVITY
(Section Gangs on a Railroad)

Question: "How good is the foreman at figuring work out ahead of time?"

	Very Good	Pretty Good	So-so and Not Very Good	Not Ascertained	Total	N
Men in high-producing sections	38%	48%	2%	12%	100%	156
Men in low-producing sections	27%	54%	10%	9%	100%	142

to these aspects of their work, according to their own report. They were also perceived by their men as possessing superior planning ability (Table 2). Similarly, in a company manufacturing heavy agricultural and road-building equipment, both the foremen and the men of high producing sections evaluated the quality of planning as superior to that of most other groups.

Another indication of the ability of the high-producing supervisor to differentiate his own function from that of the men is the amount of time which he gives to the work of actual supervision, as contrasted to the time allocated to activities which are not uniquely those of the supervisor. In the studies of clerical workers, railroad workers, and workers in heavy industry, the supervisors with the better production records gave a larger proportion of their time to supervisory functions, especially to the interpersonal aspects of their job. The supervisors of the lower-producing sections were more likely to spend their time in tasks which the men themselves were performing, or in the paper-work aspects of their jobs (Table 3).

The reverse side of this picture was also revealed in the railroad study, in which statements made by the section hands in low-producing sections indicated a tendency for an informal leader to arise in these sections. For example, in the low sections there was more frequently some one member of the group who "spoke up for the men when they wanted something." Apparently the informal organization in the low group compensated in some respects for the abdication or misdirected leadership of the foremen, but not without some losses in total effectiveness (Table 4).

The recognition by the supervisor of the importance of giving more time to his leadership role was also reflected in the morale findings. In the tractor company, for example, the men supervised by foremen who reported spending more than half their time in actual supervision not only had higher production records, but were more satisfied with the company than the men whose supervisors gave their time primarily to other aspects of the job.

Moreover, in the same company the men with the highest morale as measured in terms of satisfaction with job, supervisor, and company were those who perceived their supervisors as performing a number of broad, supportive functions. Almost all employees, of high or low morale, reported that their

TABLE 3 • RELATION OF TIME SPENT IN SUPERVISION TO
SECTION PRODUCTIVITY (Sections in an Insurance Company; Section
Gangs on a Railroad; Work Groups
in a Tractor Factory)

Questions:
  Insurance company—"What proportion of your time is given to supervisory matters?
    What proportion to other duties?"
  Railroad—"How much of your time do you usually spend in supervising, and how much
    in straight production work?"
  Tractor factory—"How much of your time do you usually spend in supervising the men,
    and how much in other things like planning the work, making out reports, and
    dealing with people outside your section?"

Section Productivity	50% or More of Time Spent in Supervising	Less than 50% of Time Spent in Supervising	Not Ascertained, or Can't Separate Functions	Total	N
Insurance company					
High	75%	17%	8%	100%	12
Low	33	59	8	100	12
Railroad					
High	55	31	14	100	36
Low	25	61	14	100	36
Tractor factory					
97–101%	69	31	0	100	52
91–96%	59	41	0	100	71
86–90%	48	52	0	100	89
80–85%	41	59	0	100	69
50–79%	54	46	0	100	35

supervisors enforced the rules and kept production up, but the high morale employees also reported that their supervisors performed such other functions as on-the-job training, recommending people for promotion and transfer, and communicating relevant information about the work and the company.

The differentiated role of the supervisor apparently affects the productivity of the group in two ways. The attention given to planning has a direct effect upon output in the coordination and organization of the tasks of the group. This is a type of skill of an engineering or institutional sort, in that the technical know-how of the supervisor is brought to bear upon the ordering of the work of the group on a long range basis. The second way in which the supervisor affects productivity is more indirect. He can increase or decrease the motivation of his employees to produce. These two abilities are not necessarily correlated in the same supervisors. But our evidence indicates that either the engineering skill or the human relations skill can increase the performance of the group. The relative importance of these two factors is determined in good part by the degree of freedom in the situation for the given skill to be effectively manifested. If the company is so tightly organized and so centrally controlled that

TABLE 4 ● RELATION OF MEN'S PERCEPTION OF A GROUP SPOKESMAN TO SECTION PRODUCTIVITY
(Section Gangs on a Railroad)

Question: "Is there some one man in the section who speaks up for the men when they want something?"

	Yes	No	Not Ascertained*	Total	N
Men in high-producing sections	9%	47%	44%	100%	156
Men in low-producing sections	17%	37%	46%	100%	142

*Consists primarily of employees of whom this question was not asked.

TABLE 5 ● RELATION OF CLOSENESS OF SUPERVISION OF EMPLOYEES TO SECTION PRODUCTIVITY
(Sections in an Insurance Company)

	Close Supervision	General Supervision	Not Ascertained	N
Heads of high-producing sections	6	5	1	12
Heads of low-producing sections	11	1	0	12

Note. —The findings are based upon an over-all code which defines closeness of supervision as the degree to which the supervisor checks up on his employees frequently, gives them detailed and frequent instructions and, in general, limits the employees' freedom to do the work in their own way. This over-all code is derived from the supervisors' discussions of their jobs.

the tasks of even the smallest work groups are prescribed, then the first-level supervisor with extremely high planning ability will not affect the productive process.

CLOSENESS OF SUPERVISION

A second major dimension which appears to discriminate between high- and low-producing supervisors is the closeness with which they supervise, or the degree to which they delegate authority. Although the high supervisors spend more time performing the supervisory functions, they do not supervise as closely as their low-producing colleagues. This general characteristic is reflected in a number of specific research findings. In the insurance study, low-producing supervisors were found to check up on their employees more frequently, to give them more detailed and more frequent work instructions, and in general to limit their freedom to do the work in their own way (Table 5). In the company manufacturing earth-moving equipment, the high-producing workers reported more often that they set their own pace on the job (Table 6).

Closeness of supervision is an interesting example of the necessity for distinguishing between the engineering (or institutional) skill of the supervisor and

TABLE 6 ● RELATION OF MEN'S PERCEPTIONS OF PACE-SETTING
FACTORS TO INDIVIDUAL PRODUCTIVITY
(Employees in an Insurance Company)

Question: "What is the most important in setting the pace for your work?"

Employees with Pro-ductivity of:	Set Own Pace	Speed of Line Sets Pace	Speed of Machines, Condition of Tools, Set My Pace	Pressure for Pro-duction Sets Pace	Other, Unspecified and Not Ascertained	T	N
100–119%	46%	14%	17%	9%	14%	100%	327
90–99%	38	12	27	12	11	100	762
80–89%	39	11	27	10	13	100	452
70–79%	38	11	27	9	15	100	269
40–69%	37	5	31	7	20	100	275

his human relations skill in motivating people. Close supervision often is employed as an institutional device for insuring that workers follow their job assignments correctly and assiduously. But this very practice also has negative morale and motivation implications, and some supervisors may give more freedom to their employees as a way of increasing their motivation. The greater freedom may produce positive results through the satisfaction that the individual has in participation and in self-determination. There is considerable evidence to support this interpretation in the research findings. In the tractor company studied, workers who perceived their foremen as supervising them less closely were better satisfied with their jobs and with the company.

In the same study, each worker was asked how much he had to say about the way his own job was done, and whether he would like to have more or less to say on this subject. Workers who reported having a lot to say about their own work wanted no less, and were relatively high on the three dimensions of morale—sat-

isfaction with job, supervisor, and company. Workers who reported having little say about how their jobs should be done wanted more autonomy in this area, and were relatively dissatisfied with their jobs, their supervisors, and the company. Apparently, close supervision can interfere with the gratification of some strongly felt needs.

There is a great deal of evidence that this factor of closeness of supervision, which is very important, is by no means determined at the first level of supervision. Rather, the first-level supervisor tends to offer to his men the style of supervision which he experiences with his own supervisor. Or to put it another way, the style of supervision which is characteristic of first-level supervisors reflects in considerable degree the organizational climate which exists at higher levels in the management hierarchy. Among the many findings which bear out this interpretation are the following: In the insurance study the low-producing supervisors reported that they were under closer supervision from above than did the high-producing su-

TABLE 7 • RELATION OF CLOSENESS OF SUPERVISION OF SECTION HEAD BY HIS SUPERIOR TO SECTION PRODUCTIVITY
(Section Heads in an Insurance Company)

	Close or Fairly Close Supervision	Fairly General or Quite General Supervision	Not Ascertained	N
On high section heads	2	9	1	12
On low section heads	8	4	0	12

Note—Closeness of supervision is based on an over-all code, and was defined for coding purposes as the degree to which the section head was given freedom to handle his own problems by his superiors, as compared with the degree to which the superior was directly involved in running the section.

TABLE 8 • RELATION OF FOREMEN'S PERCEPTION OF OPPORTUNITY FOR PLANNING TO SECTION PRODUCTIVITY
(Foremen in a Tractor Factory)

Foreman Question: "Are you able to plan your work ahead as much as you would like?"

Foremen of Sections with Productivity of:	Can Plan Ahead as Much as Needed	Sometimes Have Trouble Planning Far Enough Ahead	Usually Can't or Hardly Ever Can Plan Ahead	Total	N
97–101%	37%	42%	21%	100%	52
91–96%	51	32	17	100	71
86–90%	29	41	30	100	89
80–85%	29	46	25	100	69
50–79%	14	40	46	100	35

pervisors (Table 7). In the agricultural equipment factory, foremen of high-producing sections indicated relatively more freedom or scope of authority. They stated that they were able to plan their own work as much and as far ahead as they wanted to (Table 8). In the railroad study there was a tendency for the foremen of high-producing gangs to report relatively less pressure from above and to be more satisfied with the amount of authority which they had on

their job, although these findings were not statistically significant.

There is an additional analysis which bears on the notion that supervisory behavior at the first level is conditioned in great degree by practices of higher management. The general hypothesis was that the relationships between the behavior of first-level supervisors and the attitudes of their employees are importantly conditioned by the organizational milieu in which the first-level supervisors are functioning, and particularly by the amount of their power or influence in the department—"their potential degree of control over the social environment in which their employees are functioning." In other words, the foreman who is given so little freedom or authority by his supervisors that he is unable to exert a meaningful influence on the environment in which he and his employees function will be ineffective in dealing with employees, regardless of his human relations skills. His intended supportive actions may even have a negative effect on employee attitudes, insofar as they encourage expectations which cannot be met by him. The data from this analysis of supervisors in a public utility in general support the hypothesis. Under high-influence supervisors, 19 of 28 correlations between supervisory practices and employee attitudes are positive, though small. Under low-influence supervisors, 20 out of 28 are zero or negative.

EMPLOYEE-ORIENTATION

A third dimension of supervision which has been demonstrated to be consistently related to productivity is a syndrome of characteristics which can be called "employee-orientation." The employee-oriented supervisor, in contrast to the production-oriented or institution-oriented supervisor, gives major attention to creating employee motivation. The specific ways in which he does this may vary from situation to situation, but they contribute to a supportive personal relationship between himself and his work group members. Thus in the railroad study, the workers in high-producing groups more frequently characterized their foremen as taking a personal interest in them and their off-the-job problems. This finding was re-

peated in a study in heavy industry, in which the high-producing employees reported that their foremen took a personal interest in them. High-producing foremen also were more likely to say that the men wanted them to take a personal interest in them, whereas the low-producing foremen were more likely to have the perception that the men resented such a demonstration of interest. It is quite possible that this difference in perception is in part cause and in part effect. The low-producing foreman has a less satisfactory relationship with his employees and he may well be right in thinking that they want no more of the kind of relationship which he offers. At the same time, his conviction that they wish to minimize the relationship undoubtedly contributes to the psychological distance between him and the work group.

Even more consistent relationships were found in those behavior areas which not only reflect smooth interpersonal dealings, but also offer tangible evidence of the supportive intentions of the supervisor. Thus, in the railroad study the high-producing foremen were said by their men to be more understanding and less punitive when mistakes were made (Table 9). They were also more likely to groom employees for promotion by teaching them new things (Table 10).

In the insurance study, the high-producing supervisors were more employee-oriented and less production-oriented than their low-producing colleagues. The low supervisors emphasized production and technical aspects of the job, and tended to think of their employees as "people to get the work done," in contrast to emphasizing training people, taking an interest in employees, and considering them primarily as individual human beings. In the same study, the supervisors were asked the question,

Kahn+katz

TABLE 9 • RELATION OF MEN'S PERCEPTION OF FOREMAN'S REACTION TO BAD JOBS TO SECTION PRODUCTIVITY
(Section Gangs on a Railroad)

Question: "What does the foreman do when you do a bad job?"

	Foreman Punitive	Foreman Nonpunitive	Not Ascertained	Total	N
Men in high-producing sections	35%	54%	11%	100%	156
Men in low-producing sections	50%	36%	14%	100%	142

TABLE 10 • RELATION OF WAYS FOREMAN TRAINS MEN FOR BETTER JOBS TO SECTION PRODUCTIVITY
(Section Gangs on a Railroad)

Question: "In what way [does the foreman train men for better jobs]?"

	Teaches Men New Techniques and Duties	Teaches Men Better or Easier Ways of Doing Usual Jobs	Doesn't Train Men	Not Ascertained	Total	N
Men in high-producing sections	29%	21%	33%	17%	100%	156
Men in low-producing sections	17%	24%	44%	15%	100%	142

"Some people feel the job of supervisor is tough because they stand between the workers and management. Do you feel that this is a problem?" The high-producing supervisors were predominantly employee-identified, according to their own report. The low-producing supervisors were, for the most part, management-identified. This general statement was borne out by the supervisors' reactions to two aspects of company policy which at the time of the study constituted problems in morale or employee motivation. In both of these areas, the placement policy and the dining room setup, the high-producing supervisors were more critical and more aware of the situations as sources of employee disaffection than were the low-producing supervisors.

In the study of industrial workers, there was a whole cluster of findings which seems to fit this framework. The employees with highest production records were more likely to report a good over-all relationship with their foreman, in terms of the quality of his supervision, the way they got along with him, and the interest he took in them. In addition, they reported good communications with him; they said that the foreman let them know how they were doing, that he was easy to talk to, that it usually helped to talk over a problem with him, and that he took care of things right away (Table 11). This indicates both a supportive relationship and an effective role in the larger structure. It is perhaps a reflection of the importance of the supervisor's ability to understand and identify himself with the employees that, in this study, the foremen who had previously belonged to a labor organization had better production records than those who had not.

In this study, also, the employee-identification of the higher-producing supervisors was associated with a greater criticism of certain company policies, although at the same time high-producing supervisors were better satisfied with many aspects of their own jobs, and felt that their own superiors were well pleased with their work. But it was the high-producing foremen who in greater numbers felt that their own supervisors were doing less than a very good job, and were no more than fairly good at handling people.

A number of the supervisory characteristics which we have included in the concept of employee-orientation have important effects upon employee satisfaction as well as productivity. This is particularly true for the foreman's giving reasons for forthcoming changes on the job, demonstrating to employees that he holds other aspects of the work situation to be as important as high productivity, and that his concept of reasonable performance is not excessive. In the tractor company, these characteristics were related to job satisfaction, satisfaction with supervision, and satisfaction with the company as a whole.

A related finding appeared when each employee was asked who in the work situation took the greatest interest in him. The workers who felt that the foreman took the greatest interest in them also were getting the greatest psychological return from their employment in terms of satisfaction with job, supervisor, and company.

There is evidence that the quality of employee-orientation, like closeness of supervision, is in part determined by organizational characteristics and is not merely the reflection of personality traits.[1] For example, the tractor foremen who were reported by their men to make a practice of explaining in advance any changes in the job situation said that they were similarly treated by their own supervisors. The replication of supervisory behavior at successive echelons of large organizations is a phenomenon which deserves further study, particularly to reveal the motivational basis for such behavior and the environmental cues on which it depends.

GROUP RELATIONSHIPS

The fourth factor which seems to be emerging as a major determinant of productivity in industrial situations involves relationships in the work group. Such a variable was tentatively identified in the insurance study. Employees in the higher-producing groups tended to express a more favorable evaluation of their section (work group) and of their division. This was based on overall coded ratings of the interview content, and also on specific responses to

[1]Research findings in this area are reported by Ralph M. Stogdill in "Studies in Naval Leadership, Part II," in Guetzkow, H. (Ed.), *Groups, leadership, and men.* Pittsburgh: Carnegie Press, 1951.

**TABLE 11 ● RELATION OF EMPLOYEE PERCEPTIONS OF
SUPERVISORY BEHAVIOR TO PRODUCTIVITY**
(Workers in a Tractor Factory)

	Employees with Productivity of				
	100–119%	90–99%	80–89%	70–79%	40–69%
*Over-all relationship with foreman**					
Better than most	24%	21%	17%	16%	14%
About the same as most	71	73	77	76	78
Not as good as most	4	5	5	7	7
Not ascertained	1	1	1	1	1
Total	100%	100%	100%	100%	100%
Foreman interest in employee†					
Great deal or quite a lot	47%	45%	46%	40%	38%
Little or none	50	54	52	59	61
Not ascertained	3	1	2	1	1
Total	100%	100%	100%	100%	100%
Foreman communication to employee‡					
Always or usually know	59%	60%	54%	49%	55%
A lot of times I don't know or hardly ever know	39	39	45	50	45
Not ascertained	2	1	1	1	0
Total	100%	100%	100%	100%	100%
Foreman accessibility for discussion§					
Easy to talk to about most things	78%	76%	78%	67%	70%
Hard to talk to about many things	22	22	22	33	29
Not ascertained	0	2	0	0	1
Total	100%	100%	100%	100%	100%
Foreman action following discussion ‖					
Usually or always does some good	54%	47%	47%	38%	44%
Sometimes does some good	30	34	35	40	33
Usually does no good or hardly ever does any good	16	18	16	22	22
Not ascertained	0	1	2	0	1
Total	100%	100%	100%	100%	100%

(*continued*)

TABLE 11 (Continued)

	Employees with Productivity of				
	100–119%	90–99%	80–89%	70–79%	40–69%
Foreman promptness in taking action¶					
Takes care of things right away	55%	52%	51%	43%	52%
Sometimes takes care of things right away, sometimes doesn't	28	30	28	32	27
Foreman promptness in taking action¶					
Lets things go	16	17	20	25	20
Not ascertained	1	1	1	0	1
Total	100%	100%	100%	100%	100%
Number	327	762	452	269	275

*"On the whole, how would you say you get along with your foreman?"

†"How much interest does your foreman take in you on the job?" (Significant between .05 and .10 level.)

‡"Does your foreman let you know how you're doing? Do you know where you stand with him?"

§"If you have a problem you would like to talk over with your foreman how easy is it to talk to him?"

‖ "If you talk over a problem with your foreman, does it do any good?"

¶"If there is something that needs to be taken care of, will your foreman do it right away or will he let it go?" (Significant between .05 and .10 level.)

the question, "How do you think your section compares with other sections in the company in getting a job done?" Several interpretations of this finding are possible. On the one hand it is conceivable that the employees in high-producing groups were simply reporting what they knew to be the objective fact—that their groups had superior work records. However, it is also possible that high involvement in the work group was the cause, and high productivity the effect. Finally, and perhaps most probably, there is the possibility that pride or involvement in the work group and productivity are interacting variables, and that an increase in either one tends to bring about an increase in the other (Table 12).

In the railroad study, both the men and the foremen in high-producing groups evaluated their group performances as better than most, even though they had no formal channels of communication through which to learn of the productivity of other groups.

In the factory manufacturing earth-moving equipment, this area was further explored. It was found that high-producing employees more often said that their groups were better than most others at putting out work. They also

Kahn+Katz

TABLE 12 • RELATION OF EMPLOYEE EVALUATION OF WORK GROUP TO SECTION PRODUCTIVITY
(Employees in an Insurance Company)

	High Pride	Medium Pride	Low Pride	Total	N*
Employees in high-producing sections	33%	37%	30%	100%	143
Employees in low-producing sections	10%	41%	49%	100%	142

Note. —Evaluation of work group is an index score obtained by summing coders' ratings of responses to the following items:

1. "How well do you think your section compares with other sections in the company in getting a job done?"

2. "How well do you think your division compares with other divisions in the company in getting a job done?"

3. An over-all coder rating of the respondent's degree of identification with his section; and

4. An over-all coder rating of the respondent's degree of identification with his division.

*There were 66 employees in high sections and 68 in low sections who could not be coded on one or more items of this index.

TABLE 13 • RELATION OF EMPLOYEE EVALUATION OF WORK GROUP TO PRODUCTIVITY (Workers in a Tractor Factory)

Employee question: "When it comes to putting out work, how does your work group compare to others?"

Employees with Productivity of:	Better Than Most	The Same as Most	Not as Good as Most	Not Ascertained	Total	N
100–119%	33%	63%	2%	2%	100%	327
90–99%	32	65	2	1	100	762
80–89%	28	67	3	2	100	452
70–79%	26	67	7	0	100	269
40–69%	21	67	11	1	100	275

reported that they felt they were "really a part of their group," in contrast to the lower producers who were more likely to say that they were "included in some ways but not in others," or that they did not really feel that they were members of the group. Moreover, foremen of the higher-producing groups cited their sections as better than most in the way in which their men helped one another out on the job. Foremen of low-producing groups said their sections were not as good as most in this respect. Nor were these responses merely reflecting some

TABLE 14 • RELATION OF GROUP BELONGINGNESS TO
PRODUCTIVITY (Workers in a Tractor Factory)

Employee question: "Do you feel you are really a part of your work group?" (Significant
between .05 and .10 level.)

Employees with Productivity of:	Really a Part	Included in Most Ways	Included in Some Ways	Not Ascertained	Total	N
100–119%	58%	24%	10%	8%	100%	327
90–99%	56	29	10	5	100	762
80–89%	51	31	13	5	100	452
70–79%	52	28	10	10	100	269
40–69%	46	31	15	8	100	275

general effect for the group (Table 13). There was no difference between high and low producers in the characteristics they ascribed to their groups in the areas of skill, know-how, education, and the like. All this tends to support the notion of team spirit or cohesiveness in the work group as a factor in productivity.

The relationships in the primary group are also important among the determinants of morale, especially satisfaction with the job and with the larger organization. Workers in the tractor company who reported that they really felt a part of their work group, and that they would prefer their present jobs to identical jobs in other groups, tended to be high in satisfaction with job and company (Table 14).

Thus in the area of group relationships, as in others, we find that the twin criteria of productivity and morale have many determinants in common. This suggests again that the effect of supervisory behavior on motivation may be basic to understanding productivity differences. Yet the coexistence of high morale and low productivity, or more frequently, low morale and high produc-

tivity, is sufficiently common so that no consistent relationship between productivity and morale has appeared in any of these research studies. One explanation of this discrepancy has already been suggested, namely, that the supervisor can increase productivity in two fairly independent ways: either through his engineering skill or through his ability to motivate his men. Another major explanation is that productivity can be increased in some instances by company practices involving negative sanctions which affect morale adversely.

It is possible also that the lack of a consistently high correlation between morale and productivity in these studies reflects the fact that we are dealing with only one measure of the over-all costs of production, namely, the amount at one point in time. If we were to include the costs of turnover, absence, and scrap loss, the correlation with morale might be higher. For example, in the case of a company with high production at a given point in time because of negative sanctions, the impression of over-all efficiency might change if we also had measures of turnover and quality of product.

Kahn + Katz

CONCLUSION

We have considered some research findings which suggest four classes of variables to be consistently related to the productivity of an organizational group and to the psychological returns which the group offers its members. These classes of variables—the supervisor's ability to play a differentiated role, the degree of delegation of authority or closeness of supervision, the quality of supportiveness or employee-orientation, and the amount of group cohesiveness—have been developed from a program of studies conducted in complex, ongoing organizations, the majority of them in business or industry.

In reviewing these research findings, one finds confirmation for much of the recent product of small group experimentation by Lewinian psychologists and others. Lewin's work on the decision-making process, the research of Lippitt and White on leadership climate and style, Bavelas' experiments with on-the-job autonomy in pace-setting, the Harwood project of Coch and French, the communications studies of Festinger and his colleagues—all offer results which are in substantial agreement with the findings reported here. Such agreement is especially significant in the light of the differences between most of the small group studies and the work of the Human Relations Program, in method, theory, and research site.

There is much in the experience of the program, however, which reinforces the ideas with which this chapter was begun—that it is necessary to study complex social situations and organizations directly, as well as to attempt laboratory abstractions of their most significant problems and characteristics. This is true not only because such studies facilitate generalization of research results (if they are not phenotypical relationships), but also because a direct grappling with the live organization tends to orient the researcher toward the most real and significant dimensions of organizational structure and function. The study of living organizations, particularly under conditions of change, suggests serious limitations in attempting to understand organizational change in terms of the primary group alone, and even more drastic difficulties in attempting to induce change by dealing only with the primary group. This wholistic emphasis upon the interrelationships in the total structure is of course consistent with the Lewinian point of view.

Primary work groups exist only in a larger organizational context, and many an unsuccessful industrial training program testifies to the almost insurmountable difficulties of producing change by means which fail to take adequate account of that context. To put it another way, the psychological field is an intervening construct and as such is not directly susceptible to manipulation; the field changes when the social psychological environment changes, and such alterations usually involve broad segments of the organization in addition to the group in which change is proposed. The awareness of industrial employees of these organizational characteristics is great. These results suggest that the full motivation of workers in a complex organizational system can be tapped only when some system of functional representation assures them of an element of control in the larger organization as well as the primary group.

REFERENCES

1. Jacobson, E., Kahn, R., Mann, F., & Morse, Nancy C. (Eds.). Human relations research in large organizations. *Journal of Social Issues*, 1951, 7, No. 3.

2. Katz, D., & Kahn, R. L. Human organization and worker motivation. In L. R. Tripp (Ed.), *Industrial productivity*. Madison, Wisconsin: Industrial Relations Research Association, 1951.

3. Katz, D., Kahn, R. L., Jacobson, E., Morse, Nancy C., & Campbell, A. The Survey Research Center's ONR program. In H. Guetzkow (Ed.), *Groups, leadership and men*. Pittsburgh: Carnegie Press, 1951.

4. Katz, D., & Kahn, R. L. Some recent findings in human relations research in industry. In G. E. Swanson, T. M. Newcomb, & E. L. Hartley (Eds.), *Readings in social psychology*. (Revised) New York: Holt, 1952.

5. Katz, D., Maccoby, N., Gurin, G., & Floor, Lucretia. *Productivity, supervision, and morale among railroad workers*. Ann Arbor, Mich.: Survey Research Center, 1951.

6. Katz, D., Maccoby, N., & Morse, Nancy C. *Productivity, supervision and morale in an office situation. Part I*. Ann Arbor, Mich.: Survey Research Center, 1951.

7. Pelz, D. C. *Power and leadership in the first-line supervisor*. Ann Arbor, Mich.: Survey Research Center, 1951.

21

The Contingency Model: A Theory of Leadership Effectiveness[1]

Fred E. Fiedler

Leadership, as a problem in social psychology, has dealt primarily with two questions, namely, how one becomes a leader, and how one can become a *good* leader, that is, how one develops effective group performance. Since a number of excellent reviews (e.g., Stogdill, 1948; Gibb, 1954; Mann, 1959; Bass, 1960), have already dealt with the first question we shall not be concerned with it in the present paper.

The second question, whether a given leader will be more or less effective than others in similar situations, has been a more difficult problem of research and has received correspondingly less attention in the psychological literature. The theoretical status of the problem is well reflected by Browne and Cohn's (1958) statement that ". . . leadership literature is a mass of content without coagulating substances to bring it together or to produce coordination . . ." McGrath (1962), in

making a similar point, ascribed this situation to the tendency of investigators to select different variables and to work with idiosyncratic measures and definitions of leadership. He also pointed out, however, that most researchers in this area have gravitated toward two presumably crucial clusters of leadership attitudes and behaviors. These are the critical, directive, autocratic, task-oriented versus the democratic, permissive, considerate, person-oriented type of leadership. While this categorization is admittedly oversimplified, the major controversy in this area has been between the more orthodox viewpoint, reflected in traditional supervisory training and military doctrine that the leader should be decisive and forceful, that he should do the planning and thinking for the groups, and that he should coordinate, direct and evaluate his men's actions. The other viewpoint, reflected in the newer human relations oriented training and in the philosophy behind non-directive and brain-storming technique stresses the need for democratic, permissive, group-oriented leadership techniques. Both schools of thought have strong adherents and there is evidence supporting both points of view (Gibb, 1954; Hare, 1962).

While one can always rationalize that contradictory findings by other investigators are due to poor research de-

[1]The present paper is mainly based on research conducted under Office of Naval Research Contracts 170–106, N6–ori–07135 (Fred E. Fiedler, Principal Investigator) and RN 177–472, Noor 1834(36). (Fred E. Fiedler, C. E. Osgood, L. M. Stolurow, and H. C. Triandis, Principal Investigators.) The writer is especially indebted to his colleagues, A. R. Bass, L. J. Cronbach, M. Fishbein, J. E. McGrath, W. A. T. Meuwese, C. E. Osgood, H. C. Triandis, and L. R. Tucker, who offered invaluable suggestions and criticisms at various stages of the work.

Source: From "The Contingency Model: A Theory of Leadership Effectiveness" by Fred E. Fiedler, in *Problems in Social Psychology,* edited by Carl W. Backman and Paul F. Secord, pp. 279–289. New York: McGraw-Hill Book Company, 1970. Reprinted by permission of the author.

sign, or different tests and criteria, such problems present difficulties if they appear in one's own research. We have, during the past thirteen years, conducted a large number of studies on leadership and group performance, using the same operational definitions and essentially similar leader attitude measures. The inconsistencies which we obtained in our own research program demanded an integrative theoretical formulation which would adequately account for the seemingly confusing results.

The studies which we conducted used as the major predictor of group performance an interpersonal perception or attitude score which is derived from the leader's description of his most and of his least preferred co-workers. He is asked to think of all others with whom he has ever worked, and then to describe first the person with whom he worked best (his most preferred coworker) and then the person with whom he could work least well (his least preferred co-worker, or LPC). These descriptions are obtained, wherever possible, before the leader is assigned to his team. However, even when we deal with already existing groups, these descriptions tend to be of individuals whom the subject has known in the past rather than of persons with whom he works at the time of testing.

The descriptions are typically made on 20 eight-point bi-polar adjective scales, similar to Osgood's Semantic Differential (Osgood, et al., 1957), e.g.,

Pleasant _:_:_:_:_:_:_:_ Unpleasant

Friendly _:_:_:_:_:_:_:_ Unfriendly

These items are scaled on an evaluative dimension, giving a score of 8 to the most favorable pole (i.e., Friendly, Pleasant) and a score of 1 to the least favorable pole. Two main scores have been derived from these descriptions. The first one, which was used in our earlier studies, is based on the profile similarity measure D (Cronbach and Gleser, 1953) between the descriptions of the most and of the least preferred co-worker. This core, called the Assumed Similarity between Opposites, or ASo, indicates the degree to which the individual perceives the two opposites on his co-worker continuum as similar or different. The second score is simply based on the individual's description of his least preferred co-worker, LPC, and indicates the degree to which the subject evaluates his LPC in a relatively favorable or unfavorable manner. The two measures are highly correlated (.80 to .95) and will here be treated as interchangeable.

We have had considerable difficulty in interpreting these scores since they appear to be uncorrelated with the usual personality and attitude measures. They are, however, related to the Ohio State University studies' "Initiation of structure" and "Consideration" dimensions (Stogdill and Coons, 1957). Extensive content analysis (Meuwese and Oonk, 1960; Julian and McGrath, 1963; Morris and Fiedler, 1964) and a series of studies by Hawkins (1962) as well as research by Bass, Fiedler, and Krueger (1964) have given consistent results. These indicate that the person with high LPC or ASo, who perceives his least preferred co-worker in a relatively favorable, accepting manner, tends to be more accepting, permissive, considerate, and person-oriented in his relations with group members. The person who perceives his most and least preferred co-workers as quite different, and who sees his least preferred coworker in a very unfavorable, rejecting manner tends to be directive, task-oriented and controlling on task relevant group behaviors in his interactions.

ASo and LPC scores correlated highly with group performance in a wide variety of studies, although, as mentioned above, not consistently in the same direction. For example, in two samples of high school basketball teams the sociometrically chosen leader's ASo score correlated −.69 and −.58 with the percent of games won by teams and −.51 with the accuracy of surveying of civil engineer teams (Fiedler, 1954), and the melter foreman's ASo score correlated −.52 with tonnage output of open-hearth shops (Cleven and Fiedler, 1956). These negative correlations indicate that *low* ASo or LPC scores were associated with good group performance, i.e., that these groups performed better under managing, directive leaders than under more permissive, accepting leaders. However, while the ASo score of the sociometrically accepted company manager correlated also negatively (−.70) with the net income of consumer cooperatives, the board chairman's ASo score under the same circumstances correlated +.62 (Godfrey, Fiedler, and Hall, 1959). Thus, groups with different tasks seemed to require different leader attitudes. In a more recent study of group creativity in Holland, the leader's LPC score correlated with performance +.75 in religiously homogeneous groups with formally appointed leaders, but −.72 in religiously heterogeneous groups; and while the correlation was +.75 in homogeneous groups with appointed leaders it was −.64 in homogeneous groups having emergent (sociometrically nominated leaders). (Fiedler, Meuwese and Oonk, 1961).

The results of these investigations clearly showed that the direction and magnitude of the correlations were contingent upon the nature of the group-task situation with which the leader had to deal. Our problem resolved itself then into (a) developing a meaningful system for categorizing group-task situations; (b) inducing the underlying theoretical model which would integrate the seemingly inconsistent results obtained in our studies, and (c) testing the validity of the model by adequate research.

DEVELOPMENT OF THE MODEL

Key definitions. We shall here be concerned solely with "interacting" rather than "co-acting" task groups. By an interacting task group we mean a face-to-face team situation (such as a basketball team) in which the members work *interdependently* on a common goal. In groups of this type, the individual's contributions cannot readily be separated from total group performance. In a co-acting group, however, such as a bowling or a rifle team, the group performance is generally determined by summing the members' individual performance scores.

We shall define the leader as the group member who is officially appointed or elected to direct and coordinate group action. In groups in which no one has been so designated, we have identified the informal leader by means of sociometric preference questions such as asking group members to name the person who was most influential in the group, or whom they would most prefer to have as a leader in a similar task.

The leader's effectiveness is here defined in terms of the group's performance on the assigned primary task. Thus, although a company manager may have, as one of his tasks, the job of maintaining good relations with his customers, his main job, and the one on which he is in the final analysis evaluated, consists of the long range profitability of the company. Good relations with customers, or high morale and low labor turnover may well contribute to success, but they would not be the basic criteria by this definition.

The categorization of group-task situations. Leadership is essentially a problem of wielding influence and power. When we say that different types of groups require different types of leadership we imply that they require a different relationship by which the leader wields power and influence. Since it is easier to wield power in some groups than in others, an attempt to categorize groups might well begin by asking what conditions in the group-task situation will facilitate or inhibit the leader's exercise of power. On the basis of our previous work we postulated three important aspects in the total situation which influence the leader's role.

1. *Leader-member relations.* The leader who is personally attractive to his group members, and who is respected by his group, enjoys considerable power (French, 1956). In fact, if he has the confidence and loyalty of his men he has less need of official rank. This dimension can generally be measured by means of sociometric indices or by group atmosphere scales (Cf. Fiedler, 1962) which indicate the degree to which the leader experiences the groups as pleasant and well disposed toward him.

2. *Task structure.* The task generally implies an order "from above" which incorporates the authority of the superior organization. The group member who refuses to comply must be prepared to face disciplinary action by the higher authority. For example, a squad member who fails to perform a lawful command of his sergeant may have to answer to his regimental commander. However, compliance with a task order can be enforced only if the task is relatively well structured, i.e., if it is capable of being programmed, or spelled out step by step. One cannot effectively force a group to perform well on an unstructured task such as developing a new product or writing a good play.

Thus, the leader who has a structured task can depend on the backing of his superior organizations, but if he has an unstructured task the leader must rely on his own resources to inspire and motivate his men. The unstructured task thus provides the leader with much less effective power than does the highly structured task.

We operationalized this dimension by utilizing four of the aspects which Shaw (1962) recently proposed for the classification of group task. These are, (*a*) decision *verifiability*, the degree to which the correctness of the solution can be demonstrated objectively; (*b*) *good clarity*, the degree to which the task requirements are clearly stated or known to the group; (*c*) *goal path multiplicity*, the degree to which there are many or few procedures available for performing the task (reverse scoring); and (*d*) *solution specificity*, the degree to which there is one rather than an infinite number of correct solutions (e.g., writing a story vs. solving an equation). Ratings based on these four dimensions have yielded interrater reliabilities of .80 to .90.

3. *Position power.* The third dimension is defined by the power inherent in the position of leadership irrespective of the occupant's personal relations with his members. This includes the rewards and punishments which are officially or traditionally at the leader's disposal, his authority as defined by the group's rules and by-laws, and the organizational support given to him in dealing with his men. This dimension can be operationally defined by means of a check list (Fiedler, 1964) containing items such as "Leader can effect promotion or demotion," "Leader enjoys special rank and status in real life which sets him apart

FIGURE 1 • A MODEL FOR THE CLASSIFICATION OF GROUP-TASK SITUATIONS.

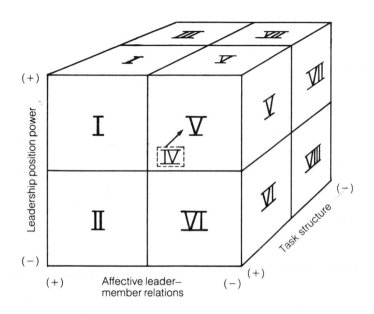

from, and above his group members." The medium interrater agreement of four independent judges rating 35 group situations was .95.

A three dimensional group classification. Group-task situations can now be rated on the basis of the three dimensions of leader-member relations, task structure, and position power. This locates each group in a three dimensional space. A rough categorization can be accomplished by halving each of the dimensions so that we obtain an eight celled cube (Fig. 1). We can now determine whether the correlations between leader attitudes and group performance within each of these eight cells, or octants, are relatively similar in magnitude and direction. If they are, we can infer that the group classification has been successfully accomplished since it shows

that groups falling within the same octant require similar leader attitudes.

An earlier paper has summarized 52 group-task situations which are based on our previous studies (Fiedler, 1964). These 52 group-task situations have been ordered into the eight octants. As can be seen from Table 1, groups falling within the same octant show correlations between the leader's ASo or LPC score and the group performance criterion which are relatively similar in magnitude and direction. We can thus infer that the group classification has been accomplished with at least reasonable success.

Consideration of Figure 1 suggests a further classification of the cells in term of the effective power which the group-task situation places at the leader's disposal, or more precisely, the favorable-

TABLE 1 • MEDIAN CORRELATION BETWEEN LEADER LPC AND GROUP PERFORMANCE IN VARIOUS OCTANTS

	Leader-Member Relations	Task Structure	Position Power	Median Correlation	Number of Relations Included in Median
Octant I	Good	Structured	Strong	$-.52$	2
Octant II	Good	Structured	Weak	$-.58$	3
Octant III	Good	Unstructured	Strong	$-.41$	4
Octant IV	Good	Unstructured	Weak	$.47$	10
Octant V	Mod. poor	Structured	Strong	$.42$	6
Octant VI	Mod. poor	Structured	Weak		0
Octant VII	Mod. poor	Unstructured	Strong	$.05$	10
Octant VIII	Mod. poor	Unstructured	Weak	$-.43$	12

ness of the situation for the leader's exercise of his power and influence.

Such an ordering can be accomplished without difficulty at the extreme poles of the continuum. A liked and trusted leader with high rank and a structured task is in a more favorable position than is a disliked and powerless leader with an ambiguous task. The intermediate steps pose certain theoretical and methodological problems. To collapse a three-dimensional system into a unidimensional one implies in Coombs' terms a partial order or a lexicographic system for which there is no unique solution. Such an ordering must, therefore, be done either intuitively or in accordance with some reasonable assumptions. In the present instance we have postulated that the most important dimension in the system is the leader-member relationship since the highly liked and respected leader is less in need of position power or the power of the higher authority incorporated in the task structure. The second-most important dimension in most group-task situations is the task structure since a leader with a highly structured task does not require a powerful leader position.

(For example, privates or non-commissioned officers in the army are at times called upon to lead or instruct officers in certain highly structured tasks such as demonstrating a new weapon, or, for example, teaching medical officers close order drill—though not in unstructured tasks such as planning new policies on strategy.) This leads us here to order the group-task situations first on leader-member relations, then on task structure, and finally on position power. While admittedly not a unique solution, the resulting ordering constitutes a reasonable continuum which indicates the degree of the leader's effective power in the group.[2]

As was already apparent from Table 1, the relationship between leader attitudes and group performance is contingent upon the accurate classification of the group-task situation. A more mean-

[2]Another cell should be added which contains real-life groups which reject their leader. Exercise of power would be very difficult in this situation and such a cell should be placed at the extreme negative end of the continuum. Such cases are treated in the section on validation.

FIGURE 2 ● CORRELATIONS OF LEADER LPC AND GROUP PERFORMANCE PLOTTED AGAINST OCTANTS

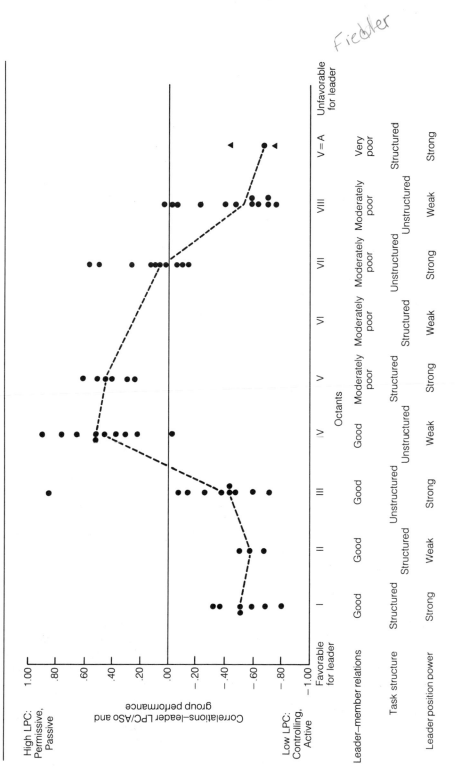

ingful model of this contingency relationship emerges when we now plot the correlation between *LPC* or *ASo* and group performance on the one hand, against the octants ordered on the effective power, or favorableness-for-the-leader dimension on the other. This is shown on Figure 2. Note that each point in the plot is a *correlation* predicting leadership performance or group effectiveness. The plot therefore represents 53 *sets of groups* totalling over 800 separate groups.

As Figure 2 shows, managing, controlling, directive (low *LPC*) leaders perform most effectively either under very favorable or under very unfavorable situations. Hence we obtain negative correlations between *LPC* and group performance scores. Considerate, permissive, accepting leaders obtain optimal group performance under situations intermediate in favorableness. These are situations in which (*a*) the task is structured, but the leader is disliked and must, therefore, be diplomatic; (*b*) the liked leader has an ambiguous, unstructured task and must, therefore, draw upon the creativity and cooperation of his members. Here we obtain positive correlations between *LPC* and group performance scores. Where the task is highly structured and the leader is well-liked, non-directive behavior or permissive attitudes (such as asking how the group ought to proceed with a missile count-down) is neither appropriate nor beneficial. Where the situation is quite unfavorable, e.g., where the disliked chairman of a volunteer group faces an ambiguous task, the leader might as well be autocratic and directive since a positive, non-directive leadership style under these conditions might result in complete inactivity on the part of the group. This model, thus, tends to shed some light on the apparent inconsistencies in our

own data as well as in data obtained by other investigators.

EMPIRICAL TESTS EXTENSION OF THE MODEL

The basic hypothesis of the model suggests that the directive, controlling, task oriented (low *LPC*) leader will be most successful in group-task situations which are either very favorable or else very unfavorable for the leader. The permissive, considerate, human relations oriented (high *LPC*) leader will perform best under conditions which are intermediate in favorableness. This hypothesis was tested by re-analyzing data from previous studies as well as by a major experiment specifically designed to test the model. Both are briefly described below.

Re-analyses of Previous Studies

As we indicated before, there is reason to believe that the relationship between the leader and his members is the most important of the three dimensions for classifying group-task situations. The problem of exercising leadership will be a relatively easy one in group-task situations in which the leader is not only liked by his crew and gets along well with his group, but in which the task is structured and the leader has a relatively powerful position. The situation will be somewhat more difficult if the leader under these circumstances has an only moderately good relationship with his group members, and it will be quite difficult if the leader-member relations are very poor, if the group members reject or actively dislike the leader. Ordinarily this does not occur in laboratory studies. It does happen, however, that real-life groups strongly reject leaders—sometimes to the point of sabotaging the task. Since such a situation would present a very difficult problem in

TABLE 2 • CORRELATIONS BETWEEN AIRCRAFT COMMANDER'S (AC's) ASo SCORE AND RADAR BOMB SCORES UNDER DIFFERENT PATTERNS OF SOCIOMETRIC CHOICES IN B-29 BOMBER CREWS*

	RHO	N
AC is most preferred crew member and chooses keymen (K)	$-.81$	10
AC is most preferred crew member and is neutral to K	$-.14$	6
AC is most preferred crew member and does not choose K	$.43$	6
AC is not most preferred crew member but chooses K	$-.03$	18
AC is not most preferred crew member and is neutral to K	$-.80$	5
AC is not most preferred crew member and does not choose K	$-.67$	7

*Table adapted from Fiedler (1955).

leadership, we would expect better performance from the task-oriented, controlling leader, and hence a negative correlation between the leader's ASo or LPC score and his group's performance. This result appeared in one study of bomber crews for which we already had the appropriate data, and it was tested by new analyses in two other studies.

Bomber Crew Study. A study was conducted on B-29 bomber crews (Fiedler, 1955) where the criterion of performance consisted of radar bomb scores. This is the average circular error, or accuracy of hitting the target by means of radar procedures. The crews were classified on the basis of their relationship between the aircraft commander and his crew. The crews were ordered on whether or not (a) the aircraft commander was the most chosen member of the crew, and (b) the aircraft commander sociometrically endorsed his keymen on his radar bombing team (the radar observer and navigator).

The results of this analysis are presented in Table 2. As can be seen, the correlations between ASo and crew performance are highly negative in crews having very good and very poor leader-group relations, but they tend to be positive in the intermediate range.

Anti-aircraft Artillery Crews. A second set of data came from a study of anti-aircraft artillery crews (Hutchins and Fiedler, 1960). Here the criterion of crew performance consisted of scores indicating the "location and acquisition" of unidentified aircraft. These crews were subdivided on the basis of leader-crew relations by separately correlating the leader's LPC score with group performance (a) for the ten crews which most highly chose their crew commander, (b) the ten which were in the intermediate range, and (c) the ten crews which gave the least favorable sociometric choices to their leader. These data are presented in Table 3.

Consumer Cooperative Companies. Finally we reanalyzed data from a study of 31 consumer cooperatives (Godfrey, Fiedler and Hall, 1959) in which the criterion of performance consisted of the per cent of company net income over a three-year period. The companies were subdivided into those in which the general manager was sociometrically chosen (a) by his board of directors as well as by his staff of assistant managers, (b) those in which the general manager was chosen by his board but not his staff, or (c) by his staff but not his board, and (d) the companies in

TABLE 3 • CORRELATIONS BETWEEN LEADER LPC SCORES AND ANTI-AIRCRAFT ARTILLERY CREW PERFORMANCE

	RHO	N
Most highly chosen crew commanders	−.34	10
Middle range in sociometric choices	.49	10
Lowest chosen crew commanders	−.42	10

TABLE 4 • CORRELATIONS BETWEEN GENERAL MANAGER'S ASo SCORE AND COMPANY NET INCOME

	RHO	N
Gen. mgr. is mostly chosen by board and staff (ASo perf.)	−.67	10
Gen. mgr. is chosen by board, but rejected by staff	.20	6
Gen. mgr. is rejected by board, but chosen by staff	.26	6
Gen. mgr. is rejected by board and staff	−.75	7

which the general manager was rejected, or not chosen, by both board of directors and staff. (Table 4.)

As these tables, and Figure 3 show, the task-oriented, managing, low *LPC* leaders performed best under very favorable and under very unfavorable situations, while the permissive, considerate leaders performed best under conditions intermediate in favorableness. These data, therefore, clearly support the hypothesis derived from the model.

Experimental Test of the Contingency Model

In cooperation with the Belgian Naval Forces we recently conducted a major study which served in part as a specific test of the model. Only aspects immediately relevant to the test are here described. The investigation was conducted in Belgium where the French and Dutch speaking (or Flemish) sectors of the country have been involved in a long standing and frequently acrimonious dispute. This conflict centers about the use of language, but it also involves a host of other cultural factors which differentiate the 60 per cent Flemish and 40 per cent French speaking population groups in Wallonie and Brussels. This "linguistic problem" which is rooted in the beginning of Belgium's national history, has in recent years been the cause of continuous public controversy, frequent protest meetings, and occasional riots.

The linguistic problem is of particular interest here since a group, consisting of members whose mother tongue, culture, and attitudes differ, will clearly present a more difficult problem in leadership than a group whose members share the same language and culture. We were thus able to test the major hypothesis of the model as well as to extend the research by investigating the type of leadership which linguistically and culturally heterogeneous groups require.

Design. The experiment was conducted at the naval training center at

FIGURE 3 ● CORRELATIONS BETWEEN LEADER LPC OR ASo SCORES AND GROUP PERFORMANCE UNDER THREE CONDITIONS OF LEADER ACCEPTANCE BY THE GROUP IN STUDIES OF BOMBER CREWS, ANTI-AIRCRAFT ARTILLERY CREWS AND CONSUMER COOPERATIVES.

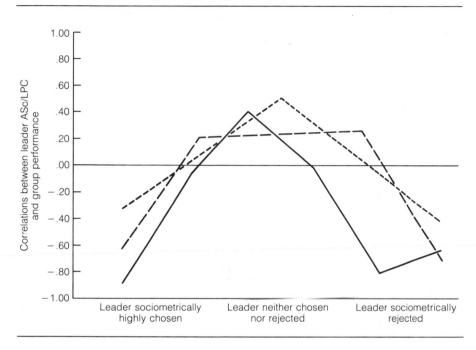

Ste. Croix-Bruges.[3] It utilized 48 career petty officers and 240 recruits who had been selected from a pool of 546 men on the basis of a pre-test in which we obtained *LPC*, intelligence, attitude, and language comprehension scores.

The experiment was specifically designed to incorporate the three major group classification dimensions shown on Figure 1, namely, leader-member relations, position power, and task structure. It also added the additional

[3]This investigation was conducted in collaboration with Dr. J. M. Nuttin (Jr.) and his students while the author was Ford Faculty Research Fellow at the University of Louvain, 1963–1964. The experiment, undertaken with permission of Commodore L. Petitjean, then Chief of Staff of the Belgian Naval Forces, was carried out at the Centre de Formation Navale, Ste. Croix-Bruges. The writer wishes to express his especial gratitude and appreciation to the commandant of the center, Captain V. Van Laethem, who not only made

the personnel and the facilities of the center available to us, but whose active participation in the planning and the execution of the project made this study possible. We are also most grateful to Dr. U. Bouvier, Director of the Center for Social Studies, Ministry of Defense, to Capt. W. Cafferata, USN, the senior U.S. Naval representative of the Military Assistance and Advisory Group, Brussels, and to Cmdr. J. Robison, U.S. Naval Attache in Brussels, who provided liaison and guidance.

dimension of group homogeneity vs. heterogeneity. Specifically, 48 groups had leaders with high position power (petty officers) while 48 had leaders with low position power (recruits); 48 groups began with the unstructured task, while the other 48 groups began with two structured tasks; 48 groups were homogeneous, consisting of three French or three Dutch speaking men, while the other 48 groups were heterogeneous, consisting of a French speaking leader and two Flemish members, or a Dutch speaking, Flemish leader and two French speaking members. The quality of the leader-member relations was measured as in our previous studies by means of a group atmosphere scale which the leader completed after each task session.

Group Performance Criteria. Two essentially identical structured tasks were administrated. Each lasted 25 minutes and required the groups to find the shortest route for a ship which, given certain fuel capacity and required ports of call, had to make a round trip calling at respectively ten or twelve ports. The tasks were objectively scored on the basis of sea miles required for the trip. Appropriate corrections and penalties were assigned for errors.

The unstructured task required the groups to compose a letter to young men of 16 and 17 years, urging them to choose the Belgian Navy as a career. The letter was to be approximately 200 words in length and had to be completed in 35 minutes. Each of the letters, depending upon the language in which it was written, was then rated by Dutch or by French speaking judges on style and use of language, as well as interest value, originality, and persuasiveness. Estimated reliability was .92 and .86 for Dutch and French speaking judges, respectively.

It should be noted in this connection that the task of writing a letter is not as unstructured as might have been desirable for this experiment. The form of any letter of this type is fairly standardized, and its content was, of course, suggested by the instructions. The navy officers with whom we consulted throughout the study considered it unwise, however, to give a highly unstructured task, such as writing a fable or proposing a new policy, since tasks of this nature were likely to threaten the men and to cause resentment and poor cooperation. High and low task-structure is, therefore, less well differentiated in this study than it has been in previous investigations.

Results. The contingency model specifies that the controlling, managing, low *LPC* leaders will be most effective either in very favorable or else in relatively unfavorable group-task situations, while the permissive, considerate, high *LPC* leaders will be more effective in situations intermediate in difficulty.

The basic test of the hypothesis requires, therefore, that we order the group-task situations, represented in this experiment, in terms of the difficulty which they are likely to present for the leader. Since there are 16 cells in the design, the size of the sample within each cell (namely 6 groups) is, of course, extremely small. However, where the conditions are reasonably replicated by other cells, the relationship can be estimated from the median rank-order correlations.

The hypothesis can be tested most readily with correlations of leader *LPC* and group performance in homogeneous groups on the more reliably scorable second structured task. These conditions approximate most closely those represented on Figure 3, on bomber and antiaircraft crews and consumer cooperatives. We have here made the fairly obvious assumption that the powerful leader or the leader who feels liked and accepted faces an easier group-task situation than low ranking leaders and those who see the groups as unpleasant and tense. Each situation is represented by two cells of six groups, each. Since there were two orders of presentation—half the groups worked first on the structured task, the other half on the unstructured task, arranging the group-task situations in order of favorableness for the leader then gives us the following results:

	Order 1	Order 2
High group atmosphere and high position power	− .77	− .77
High group atmosphere and low position power	+ .60	+ .50
Low group atmosphere and high position power	+ .16	+ .01
Low group atmosphere and low position power	− .16	− .43

These are, of course, the trends in size and magnitude of correlations which the model predicts. Low *LPC* leaders are again most effective in favorable and unfavorable group-task situations: the more permissive, considerate high *LPC* leaders were more effective in the intermediate situations.

Extending the model to include heterogeneous groups requires that we make a number of additional assumptions for weighting each of the group-task dimensions so that all 48 cells (i.e., 16 cells × 3 tasks) can be reasonably ordered on the same scale. We have here assigned equal weights of 3 to the favorable poles of the major dimensions, i.e., to homogeneity, high group

atmosphere, and high position power. A weight of one was assigned to the first structured task, and a weight of two to the second structured task on the assumption that the structured task makes the group-task situation somewhat more favorable than the unstructured task, and that the practice and learning effect inherent in performing a second, practically identical task, will make the group-task situation still more favorable for the leader. Finally, a weight of one was given to the "second presentation," that is, the group task which occurred toward the end of the session, on the assumption that the leader by that time had gotten to know his group members and had learned to work with them more effectively, thus again increasing the favorableness of his group-task situation to a certain extent.

The resulting weighting system leads to a scale from 12 to 0 points, with 12 as the most favorable pole. If we now plot the median correlation coefficients of the 48 group-task situations against the scale indicating the favorableness of the situation for the leader, we obtain the curve presented on Figure 4.

As can be seen, we again obtain a curvilinear relationship which resembles that shown on Figure 2. Heterogeneous groups with low position power and/or poor leader-member relations fall below point 6 on the scale, and thus tend to perform better with controlling, directive, low *LPC* leaders. Only under otherwise very favorable conditions do heterogeneous groups perform better with permissive, considerate high *LPC* leaders, that is, in group-task situations characterized by high group atmosphere as well as high position power, four of the six correlations (66%) are positive, while only five of eighteen (28%) are positive in the less favorable group-task situations.

It is interesting to note that the curve

FIGURE 4 • MEDIAN CORRELATIONS BETWEEN LEADER *LCP* AND GROUP PERFORMANCE SCORES PLOTTED AGAINST FAVORABLENESS-FOR-LEADER SCALE IN THE BELGIAN NAVY STUDY.

Code for two-digit numbers figure indicating the type of group involved

Composition	Position Power	High Group Atmos.	Low Group Atmos.	Task	1st Pres.	2nd Pres.
Homogeneous	High	1	5	Structured I	1	2
Homogeneous	Low	2	6	Structured II	3	4
Heterogeneous	High	3	7	Unstructured	5	6
Heterogeneous	Low	4	8			

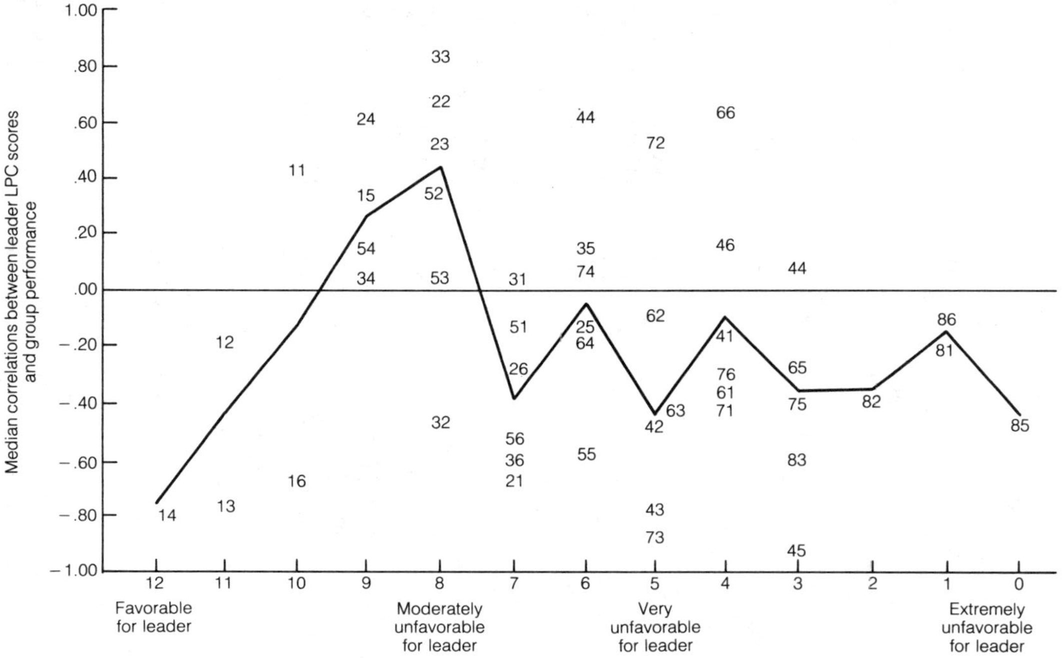

is rather flat and characterized by relatively low negative correlations as we go toward the very unfavorable end of the scale. This result supports Meuwese's (1964) recent study which showed that correlations between leader *LPC* as well as between leader intelligence and group performance tend to become attenuated under conditions of relative stress. These findings suggest that the leader's ability to influence and control the group decreases beyond a certain point of stress and difficulty in the group-task situation.

DISCUSSION

The contingency model seeks to reconcile results which up to now had to be considered inconsistent and difficult to understand. We have here attempted to develop a theoretical framework which can provide guidance for further research. While the model will undoubtedly undergo modifications and elaboration as data become available, it provides an additional step toward a better understanding of leadership processes required in different situations. We have here tried to specify exactly the type of leadership which different group task-situations require.

The model has a number of important implications for selection and training, as well as for the placement of leaders and organizational strategy. Our research suggests, first of all, that we can utilize a very broad spectrum of individuals for positions of leadership. The problem becomes one of placement and training rather than of selection since both the permissive, democratic, human-relations oriented, and the managing, autocratic, task-oriented leader can be effectively utilized. Leaders can be trained to recognize their own style of leadership as well as the conditions which are most compatible with their style.

The model also points to a variety of administrative and supervisory strategies which the organization can adopt to fit the group-task situation to the needs of the leader. Tasks can, after all, be structured to a greater or lesser extent by giving very specific and detailed, or vague and general instructions; the position power of the group leader can be increased or decreased and even the congeniality of a group, and its acceptance of the leader can be affected by appropriate administration action, such as for instance increasing or decreasing the group's homogeneity.

The model also throws new light on phenomena which were rather difficult to fit into our usual ideas about measurement in social psychology. Why, for example, should groups differ so markedly in their performance on nearly parallel tasks? The model—and our data—show that the situation becomes easier for the leader as the group moves from the novel to the already known group-task situations. The leaders who excel under relatively novel and therefore more difficult conditions are not necessarily those who excel under those which are more routine, or better known and therefore more favorable. Likewise, we find that different types of task structure require different types of leader behavior. Thus, in a research project's early phases the project director tends to be democratic and permissive; everyone is urged to contribute to the plan and to criticize all aspects of the design. This situation changes radically in the more structured phase when the research design is frozen and the experiment is underway. Here the research director tends to become managing, controlling, and highly autocratic and woe betide the assistant who attempts to be creative in giving instructions to subjects, or in his timing of tests. A similar situation is often found in business organizations where the routine operation tends to be well structured and calls for a managing, directive leadership. The situation becomes suddenly unstructured when a crisis occurs. Under these conditions the number of discussions, meetings, and conferences increases sharply so as to give everyone an opportunity to express his views.

At best, this model is of course only a partial theory of leadership. The leader's intellectual and task-relevant abilities, and the members' skills and motivation, all play a role in affecting the group's performance. It is to be hoped that these other important aspects of group interaction can be incorporated into the model in the not too distant future.

REFERENCES

Bass, A. R., Fiedler, F. E., and Krueger, S. Personality correlates of assumed similarity (ASo) and related scores. Urbana, Ill.: Group Effectiveness Research Laboratory, University of Illinois, 1964.

Bass, B. M. *Leadership psychology and organizational behavior.* New York: Harper Brothers, 1960.

Browne, C. G., and Cohn, T. S. (Eds.) *The study of leadership.* Danville, Illinois. The Interstate Printers and Publishers, 1958.

Cleven, W. A., and Fiedler, F. E. Interpersonal perceptions of open hearth foremen and steel production. *J. appl. Psychol.* 1956. 40, 312–314.

Cronbach, J. J., and Gleser, Goldene C. Assessing similarity between profiles. *Psychol. Bull.*, 1953, 50, 456–473.

Fiedler, F. E. Assumed similarity measures as predictors of team effectiveness. *J. abnorm. soc. Psychol.*, 1954, 49, 381–388.

Fiedler, F. E. Leader attitudes, group climate, and group creativity. *J. abnorm. soc. Psychol.*, 1962, 64. 308–318.

Fiedler, F. E. A contingency model of leadership effectiveness. In L. Berkowitz (Ed.) *Advances in experimental social psychology.* New York: Academic Press, 1964. Vol. I.

Fiedler, F. E., and Meuwese, W. A. T. The leader's contribution to performance in cohesive and uncohesive groups. *J. abnorm. soc. Psychol.*, 1963, 67, 83–87.

Fiedler, F. E., Meuwese, W. A. T., and Oonk, Sophie. Performance of laboratory tasks requiring group creativity. *Acta Psychologica,* 1961, 18, 100–119.

French, J. R. P., Jr. A formal theory of social power. *Psychol. Rev.*, 1956, 63, 181–194.

Gibb, C. A. "Leadership" in G. Lindzey (Ed.) *Handbook of social psychology,* Vol. II, Cambridge, Mass.: Addison-Wesley, 1954.

Godfrey, Eleanor P., Fiedler, F. E., and Hall, D. M. *Boards, management, and company success.* Danville, Illinois: Interstate Printers and Publishers, 1959.

Hare, A. P. *Handbook of small group research.* New York: Free Press, 1962.

Hawkins, C. A study of factors mediating a relationship between leader rating behavior and group productivity. Unpublished Ph.D. dissertion, University of Minnesota, 1962.

Hutchins, E. B., and Fiedler, F. E. Task-oriented and quasi-therapeutic role functions of the leader in small military groups. *Sociometry,* 1960, 23, 293–406.

Julian, J. W., and McGrath, J. E. The influence of leader and member behavior on the adjustment and task effectiveness of negotiation groups. Urbana, Ill.: Group Effectiveness Research Laboratory, University of Illinois, 1963.

McGrath, J. E. A summary of small group research studies. Arlington, Va.: Human Sciences Research Inc., 1962 (Litho.).

Mann, R. D. A review of the relationship between personality and performance in small groups. *Psychol. Bull.*, 1959, 56, 241–270.

Meuwese, W. A. T. The effect of the leader's ability and interpersonal attitudes on group creativity under varying conditions of stress. Unpublished doctoral dissertation, University of Amsterdam, 1964.

Morris, C. G., and Fiedler, F. E. Application of a new system of interaction analysis to be relationships between leader attitudes and behavior in problem solving groups. Urbana, Ill.: Group Effectiveness Research Laboratory, University of Illinois, 1964.

Osgood, C. A., Suci, G. A., and Tannenbaum, P. H. *The measurement of meaning.* Urbana, Ill.: University of Illinois Press, 1957.

Shaw, M. E. Annual Technical Report, 1962. Gainesville, Florida: University of Florida, 1962 (Mimeo.).

Stogdill, R. Personal factors associated with leadership: a survey of the literature. *J. of Psychol.*, 1948, 25, 35–71.

Stogdill, R. M., and Coons, A. E. Leader behavior: its description and measurement. Columbus, Ohio: Ohio State University, *Research Monograph*, No. 88, 1957.

22

Life Cycle Theory of Leadership

Paul Hersey &
Kenneth H. Blanchard

The recognition of task and relationships as two important dimensions of leader behavior has pervaded the works of management theorists[1] over the years. These two dimensions have been variously labeled as "autocratic" and "democratic"; "authoritarian" and "equalitarian"; "employee-oriented" and "production-oriented"; "goal achievement" and "group maintenance"; "task-ability" and "likeability"; "instrumental" and "expressive"; "efficiency" and "effectiveness." The difference between these concepts and task and relationships seems to be more semantic than real.

For some time, it was believed that task and relationships were either/or styles of leader behavior and, therefore, should be depicted as a single dimension along a continuum, moving from very authoritarian (task) leader behavior at one end to very democratic (relationships) leader behavior at the other.[2]

OHIO STATE LEADERSHIP STUDIES

In more recent years, the feeling that task and relationships were either/or leadership styles has been dispelled. In particular, the leadership studies initiated in 1945 by the Bureau of Business Research at Ohio State University[3] questioned whether leader behavior could be depicted on a single continuum.

In attempting to describe *how* a leader carries out his activities, the Ohio State staff identified "Initiating Structure" (task) and "Consideration" (relationships) as the two most important dimensions of leadership. "Initiating Structure" refers to "the leader's behavior in delineating the relationship between himself and members of the work-group and in endeavoring to establish well-defined patterns of organization, channels of communication, and methods of procedure." On the other hand, "Consideration" refers to "behavior indicative of friendship, mutual trust, respect, and warmth in the relationship between the leader and the members of his staff."[4]

In the leadership studies that followed the Ohio State staff found that leadership styles vary considerably from leader to leader. The behavior of some leaders is characterized by rigidly structuring activities of followers in terms of *task* accomplishments, while others concentrate on building and maintaining good personal *relationships* between themselves and their followers. Other leaders have styles characterized by both task and relationships behavior. There are even some individuals in leadership

Source: From "Life Cycle Theory of Leadership" by Paul Hersey and Kenneth H. Blanchard, in *Training and Development Journal.* Copyright © 1969 *Training and Development Journal,* American Society for Training and Development. Reprinted with permission. All rights reserved.

FIGURE 1 • THE OHIO STATE LEADERSHIP QUADRANTS

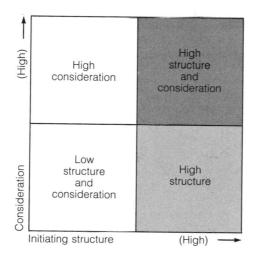

positions whose behavior tends to provide little structure or development of interpersonal relationships. No dominant style appears. Instead, various combinations are evident. Thus, task and relationships are not either/or leadership styles as an authoritarian-democratic continuum suggests. Instead, these patterns of leader behavior are separate and distinct dimensions which can be plotted on two separate axes, rather than a single continuum. Thus, the Ohio State studies resulted in the development of four quadrants to illustrate leadership styles in terms of Initiating Structure (task) and Consideration (relationships) as shown in Figure 1.

THE MANAGERIAL GRID

Robert R. Blake and Jane S. Mouton[5] in their Managerial Grid have popularized the task and relationships dimen-

sions of leadership and have used them extensively in organization and management development programs.

In the Managerial Grid, five different types of leadership based on concern for production (task) and concern for people (relationships) are located in the four quadrants identified by the Ohio State studies.

Concern for *production* is illustrated on the horizontal axis. Production becomes more important to the leader as his rating advances on the horizontal scale. A leader with a rating of 9 has a maximum concern for production.

Concern for people is illustrated on the vertical axis. People become more important to the leader as his rating progresses up the vertical axis. A leader with a rating of 9 on the vertical axis has a maximum concern for people.

The Managerial Grid, in essence, has given popular terminology to five points within the four quadrants identified by the Ohio State studies.

FIGURE 2 • THE MANAGERIAL GRID LEADERSHIP STYLES

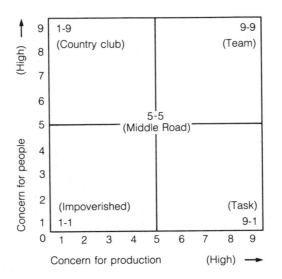

SUGGESTING A "BEST" STYLE OF LEADERSHIP

After identifying task and relationships as two central dimensions of any leadership situation, some management writers have suggested a "best" style of leadership. Most of these writers have supported either an integrated leader behavior style (high task and high relationships) or a permissive, democratic, human relations approach (high relationships).

Andrew W. Halpin,[6] of the original Ohio State staff, in a study of school superintendents, pointed out that according to his findings "effective or desirable leadership behavior is characterized by high ratings on both Initiating Structure and Consideration. Conversely, ineffective or undesirable leadership behavior is marked by low ratings on both dimensions." Thus, Halpin seemed to conclude that the high Con-

sideration and high Initiating Structure style is theoretically the ideal or "best" leader behavior, while the style low on both dimensions is theoretically the "worst."

Blake and Mouton in their Managerial Grid also imply that the most desirable leadership style is "team management" (maximum concern for production and people) and the least desirable is "impoverished management" (minimum concern for production and people). In fact, they have developed training programs designed to change the behavior of managers toward this "team" style.[7]

LEADERSHIP STYLE SHOULD VARY WITH THE SITUATION

While the Ohio State and the Managerial Grid people seem to suggest this is a "best" style of leadership,[8] recent evidence from empirical studies clearly shows that there is no single all purpose leadership style which is universally successful.

Some of the most convincing evidence which dispels the idea of a single "best" style of leader behavior was gathered and published by A. K. Korman[9] in 1966. Korman attempted to review all the studies which examined the relationship between the Ohio State behavior dimensions of Initiating Structure (task) and Consideration (relationships) and various measures of effectiveness, including group productivity, salary, performance under stress, administrative reputation, work group grievances, absenteeism, and turnover. Korman reviewed over twenty-five studies and concluded that:

Despite the fact that "consideration" and "Initiating Structure" have become almost bywords in American industrial psychology, it seems apparent that very little is now known as to how these variables may predict work group performance and the conditions which affect such predictions. At the current time, we cannot even say whether they have any predictive significance at all.

Thus, Korman found the use of Consideration and Initiating Structure had no significant predictive value in terms of effectiveness as situations changed. *This suggests that since situations differ, so must leader style.*

Fred E. Fiedler,[10] in testing his contingency model of leadership in over fifty studies covering a span of fifteen years (1951–1967), concluded that both directive, task-oriented leaders and non-directive, human relations-oriented leaders are successful under some conditions. Fiedler argues:

While one can never say that something is impossible, and while someone may well discover the all-purpose leadership style or behavior at some future time, our own data and those which have come out of sound research by other investigators do not promise such miraculous cures.

A number of other investigators[11] besides Korman and Fiedler have also shown that different leadership situations require different leader styles.

In summary, empirical studies tend to show that there is no normative (best) style of leadership; that successful leaders are those who can adapt their leader behavior to meet the needs of their followers and the particular situation. Effectiveness is dependent upon the leader, the followers, and other situational elements. In managing for effectiveness a leader must be able to diagnose his own leader behavior in light of his environment. Some of the variables other than his followers which he should examine include the organization, superiors, associates, and job demands. This list is not all inclusive, but contains interacting components which used to be important to a leader in many different organizational settings.

ADDING AN EFFECTIVENESS DIMENSION

To measure more accurately how well a leader operates within a given situation, an "effectiveness dimension" should be added to the two-dimension Ohio State model. This is illustrated in Figure 3.

By adding an effectiveness dimension to the Ohio State model, a three-dimensional model is created.[12] This Leader Effectiveness Model attempts to integrate the concepts of leader style with situational demands of a specific environment. When the leader's style is appropriate in a given environment measured by results, it is termed *effective*; when his style is inappropriate to a

FIGURE 3 • ADDING AN EFFECTIVENESS DIMENSION

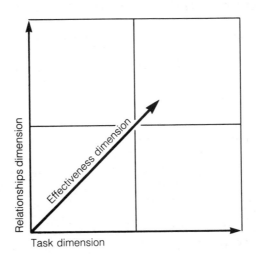

given environment, it is termed *ineffective*.

If a leader's effectiveness is determined by the interaction of his style and environment (followers and other situational variables), it follows that any of the four styles depicted in the Ohio State model may be effective or ineffective depending on the environment.

Thus, there is *no* single ideal leader behavior style which is appropriate in all situations. For example, the high task and high relationships style is appropriate only in certain situations, but is inappropriate in others. In basically crisis-oriented organizations like the military or the police, there is considerable evidence that the most appropriate style would be high task, since under combat or riot conditions success often depends upon immediate response to orders. Time demands do not permit talking things over or explaining decisions. For success, behavior must be automatic.

While a high task style might be effective for a combat officer, it might not

be effective in other situations even within the military. This was pointed out when the officers trained at West Point were sent to command outposts in the Dew Line, which was part of an advanced warning system. The scientific personnel involved, living in close quarters in an Arctic region, did not respond favorably to the task-oriented behavior of these combat trained officers. The level of education and maturity of these people was such that they did not need a great deal of structure in their work. In fact, they tended to resent it.

Other studies of scientific and research-oriented personnel show also that many of these people desire, or need, only a limited amount of socio-emotional support. Therefore, there are situations in which the low task and relationships style, which has been assumed by some authors to be theoretically a poor leadership style, may be an appropriate style.

In summary, an effective leader must be able to *diagnose* the demands of the environment and then either *adapt* his leader style to fit these demands, or develop the means to *change* some or all of the other variables.

ATTITUDINAL VS. BEHAVIORAL MODELS

In examining the dimensions of the Managerial Grid (*concern* for production and *concern* for people), one can see that these are attitudinal dimensions. That is, concern is a feeling or emotion toward something. On the other hand, the dimensions of the Ohio State Model (Initiating Structure and Consideration) and the Leader Effectiveness Model (task and relationships) are dimensions of *observed* behavior. Thus, the Ohio State and Leader Effectiveness Models measure *how* people behave, while the Managerial Grid measures *predisposition* toward production and people. As discussed earlier, the Leader Effectiveness Model is an outgrowth of the Ohio State Model but is distinct from it in that it adds an effectiveness dimension to the two dimensions of behavior.

Although the Managerial Grid and the Leader Effectiveness Model measure different aspects of leadership, they are not incompatible. A conflict develops, however, because behavioral assumptions have often been drawn from analysis of the attitudinal dimensions of the Managerial Grid.[13] While high *concern* for both production and people is desirable in many organizations, managers having a high concern for both people and production do not always find it appropriate in all situations to initiate a high degree of structure and provide a high degree of socio-emotional support.

For example, if a manager's subordinates are emotionally mature and can take responsibility for themselves, his appropriate style of leadership may be low task and low relationships. In this case, the manager permits these subordinates to participate in the planning, organizing, and controlling of their own operation. He plays a background role, providing socio-emotional support only when necessary. Consequently, it is assumptions about behavior drawn from the Managerial Grid and not the Grid itself that are inconsistent with the Leader Effectiveness Model.

Korman,[14] in his extensive review of studies examining the Ohio State concepts of Initiating Structure and Consideration, concluded that:

> What is needed . . . in future concurrent (and predictive) studies is not just recognition of this factor of "situational determinants" but, rather, a systematic conceptualization of situational variance as it might relate to leadership behavior (Initiating Structure and Consideration).

In discussing this conclusion, Korman suggests the possibility of a curvilinear relationship rather than a simple linear relationship between Structure and Consideration and other variables. The Life Cycle Theory of Leadership which we have developed is based on a curvilinear relationship between task and relationships and "maturity." This theory will attempt to provide a leader with some understanding of the relationship between an effective style of leadership and the level of maturity of one's followers. The emphasis in the Life Cycle Theory of Leadership will be on the followers. As Fillmore H. Sanford has indicated, there is some justification for regarding the followers "as the most crucial factor in any leadership event."[15] Followers in any situation are vital, not only because individually they accept or reject the leader, but as a group they actually determine whatever personal power he may have.

According to Life Cycle Theory, as the level of maturity of one's follow-

FIGURE 4 • LIFE CYCLE THEORY OF LEADERSHIP

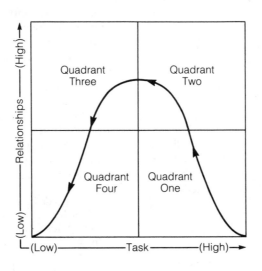

ers continues to increase, appropriate leader behavior not only requires less and less structure (task) but also less and less socio-emotional support (relationships). This cycle can be illustrated in the four quadrants of the basic styles portion of the Leader Effectiveness Model as shown in Figure 4.

Maturity is defined in Life Cycle Theory by the relative independence,[16] ability to take responsibility, and achievement-motivation[17] of an individual or group. These components of maturity are often influenced by level of education and amount of experience. While age is a factor, it is not directly related to maturity as used in the Life Cycle. Our concern is for psychological age, not chronological age. Beginning with structured task behavior which is appropriate for working and immature people, Life Cycle Theory suggests that leader behavior should move from: (1) high task-low relationships behavior to (2) high task-high relationships and (3) high relationships-low task behavior to

(4) low task-low relationships behavior, if one's followers progress from immaturity to maturity.

PARENT-CHILD EXAMPLE

An illustration of this Life Cycle Theory familiar to everyone is the parent-child relationship. As a child begins to mature, it is appropriate for the parent to provide more socio-emotional support and less structure. Experience shows us that if the parent provides too much relationships before a child is somewhat mature, this behavior is often misinterpreted by the child as permissiveness. Thus it is appropriate to increase one's relationships behavior as the child is able to increase his maturity or capacity to take responsibility.

A child when first born is unable to control much of his own environment. Consequently, his parents must initiate almost all structure, *i.e.*, that is, dress the child, feed the child, bathe the child, turn the child over, etc. While it is appropriate for a parent to show love and affection toward a child, this is different than the mutual trust and respect which characterizes relationships behavior. Consequently, the most appropriate style for a parent to use with his children during the early preschool years may be high task-low relationships (quadrant 1).

Even when the child begins to attend school, the parent must provide a great deal of structure. The child is still not mature enough to accept much responsibility on his own. It may become appropriate at this state, as the child matures, for the parent to increase his relationships behavior by showing more trust and respect for his child. At this point, the parent's behavior could be characterized as high task-high relationships (quadrant 2).

Gradually as the child moves into high school and/or college, he begins to seek and accept more and more responsibility for his own behavior. It is during this time that a parent should begin to engage in less structured behavior and provide more socio-emotional support (quadrant 3). This does not mean that the child's life will have less structure, but it will now be internally imposed by the "young man" rather than externally by the parent. When this happens the cycle as depicted on the Leader Effectiveness Model begins to become a backward bending curve. The child is not only able to structure many of the activities in which he engages, but is also able to provide self-control over his interpersonal and emotional needs.

As the child begins to make his own living, start his own family, and take full responsibility for his actions, a decrease in structure and socio-emotional support by the parents becomes appropriate. In reality, the umbilical cord has been severed and the child is now "on his own." At this stage of the parent-child relationship, a low task-low relationships style seems to be most appropriate (quadrant 4).

Although the Life Cycle suggests a basic style for different levels of maturity in meeting specific contingencies, it may be necessary to vary one's style anywhere within the four quadrants to deal appropriately with this event. For example, even when a young man is away at college and his parents are using a high relationships style with him, it might be appropriate for them to initiate some structure with their son if they discover that he is not behaving in as mature a way as expected (he has become a discipline problem). A change in parental behavior might even be necessary later in life after a son (or daughter) has had a family of his own for a number of years. If this son, for example, suddenly begins to experience marital difficulties and his family begins to disintegrate, it might be appropriate for his parents temporarily to increase their socio-emotional support.

OTHER ASPECTS OF THE LIFE CYCLE

The parent-child relationship is only one example of the Life Cycle. This cycle is also discernible in other organizations in the interaction between superiors and subordinates. An interesting example is found in Research and Development work. In working with highly trained and educated Research and Development personnel, the most effective leader behavior style might be low task-low relationships. However, during the early stages of a particular project, the director must impose a certain amount of structure as the requirements and limitations of the project are established. Once these limitations are understood, the R & D director moves rapidly through the *"project cycle"* back to the mature low task-low relationships style.

In a college setting, the Life Cycle Theory has been validated in studying the teacher-student relationship. Effective teaching of lower division students (freshmen and sophomores) has been characterized by structured behavior on the part of the teacher as he reinforces appropriate patterns in attendance and study habits, while more relationships behavior seems to be appropriate for working with upper division undergraduates and Master's students. And finally the cycle seems to be completed as a teacher begins to work with mature Ph.D. candidates, who need very little guidance or socio-emotional support.

We realize that most groups in our society do not reach the backward bending aspect of the cycle. But there is some evidence that as the level of education and experience of a group increases, appropriate movement in this direction will take place. However, the demands of the job may often be a limiting factor on the development of maturity in workers. For example, an assembly line operation in an automobile plant is so highly structured that it offers little opportunity for the maturing process to occur. With such monotonous tasks, workers are given minimal control over their environment and are often encouraged to be passive, dependent, and subordinate.

LIFE CYCLE AND SPAN OF CONTROL

For years it has been argued by many management writers that one man can *supervise* only a relatively few people; therefore, all managers should have a limited span of control. For example, Harold Koontz and Cyril O'Donnell[18] state that:

In every organization it must be decided how many subordinates a superior can manage. Students of management have found that this number is usually four to eight subordinates at the upper levels of organization and eight to fifteen or more at the lower levels.

While the suggested number of subordinates which one can supervise varies anywhere from three to thirty, the principle usually states that the number should decrease as one moves higher in the organization. Top management should have fewer subordinates to supervise than lower level managers. Yet the Life Cycle Theory of Leadership suggests that span of control may not depend on the level of the management hierarchy but should be a function of the maturity of the individuals being supervised. The more independent, able to take responsibility, and achievement-motivated one's subordinates are, the more people a manager can supervise. It is theoretically possible to supervise an infinite number of subordinates if everyone is completely mature and able to be responsible for his own job. This does not mean there is less control, but these subordinates are self-controlled rather than externally controlled by their superior. Since people occupying higher level jobs in an organization tend to be more "mature" and therefore need less close supervision than people occupying lower level jobs, it seems reasonable to assume that top managers should be able to supervise more subordinates than their counterparts at lower levels.[19]

CONCLUSIONS

Rensis Likert[20] found in his research that supervisors with the best records of performance were employee-centered (high relationships), while job-centered (high task) supervisors were found more often to have low-producing sections. While this relationship seemed to exist, Likert raised the question of which variable was the causal factor. Is the style of the supervisor causing the level of production or is the level of production encouraging the style of the managers? As Likert suggests, it may very well be that high-producing sections allow for general supervision rather than close supervision and relationship behavior rather than task behavior. The supervisor soon learns that his subordinates are mature enough to structure their own environment, thus leaving him time for other kinds of activities. At the same time a low-producing section may leave the supervisor with no choice but to be job-centered. If he attempted to use a relationships style this may be misunderstood and interpreted as reinforcement for their low level of performance. The point is, the supervisor must change appropriately.

CHANGING STYLE

The problem with the conclusions of Likert and other behavioral scientists comes in implementation. Practitioners read that employee-centered supervisors tend to have higher-producing sections than job-centered supervisors. Wanting to implement these findings overnight, they encourage all supervisors to become more employee-oriented. Consequently, a foreman who has been operating as a task-oriented authoritarian leader for many years may be encouraged to change his style—"get in step with the times." Upon returning from a "human relations" training program, the foreman will probably try to utilize some of the new relationships techniques he has recently been taught. The problem is that his personality is not compatible with the new concepts, but he tries to use them anyway. As long as things are

running smoothly, there is no difficulty. However, the minute an important issue or crisis develops he tends to revert to his old basic style and becomes inconsistent, vacillating between the new relationships style he has been taught, and his old task style which has the force of habit behind it.

This idea was supported in a study conducted by the General Electric Company at one of its turbine and generator plants. In this study, the leadership styles of about 90 foremen were analyzed and rated as "democratic," "authoritarian" or "mixed." In discussing the findings, Saul W. Gellerman[21] reported that:

> The lowest morale in the plant was found among those men whose foremen were rated *between* the democratic and authoritarian extremes. The GE research team felt that these foremen might have varied inconsistently in their tactics, permissive at one moment and hard-fisted the next, in a way that left their men frustrated and unable to anticipate how they would be treated. The naturally autocratic supervisor who is exposed to human relations training may behave in exactly such a manner . . . a pattern which will probably make him even harder to work for than he was before being "enlightened."

Thus, changing the style of managers is a difficult process, and one that takes considerable time to accomplish. Expecting miracles overnight will only lead to frustration and uneasiness for both managers and their subordinates. Yet industry invests many millions of dollars annually for training and development programs which concentrate on effecting change in the style of managers. As Fiedler[22] suggests:

> A person's leadership style . . . reflects the individual's basic motivational and need structure. At best it takes one, two, or three years of intensive psychotherapy to effect changes in personality structure.

It is difficult to see how we can change in more than a few cases an equally important set of core values in a few hours of lectures and role playing or even in the course of a more intensive training program of one or two weeks.

Fiedler's point is well-taken. It is indeed difficult to effect changes in the styles of managers overnight. However, it is not completely hopeless. But, at best, it is a slow and expensive process which requires creative planning and patience. In fact, Likert[23] found that it takes from three to seven years, depending on the size and complexity of the organization, to effectively implement a new management theory.

> Haste is self-defeating because of the anxieties and stresses it creates. There is no substitute for ample time to enable the members of an organization to reach the level of skillful and easy, habitual use of the new leadership . . .

CHANGING PERFORMANCE

Not only is it difficult to effect changes in the styles of managers overnight, but the question that we raise is whether it is even appropriate. It is questionable whether a work group whose performance has been continually low would suddenly leap to high productivity with the introduction of an employee-centered supervisor. In fact, they might take advantage of him and view him as a "soft-touch." These workers lack maturity and are not ready for more responsibility. Thus the supervisor must bring them along slowly, becoming more employee-centered and less job-centered as they mature. When an individual's performance is low, one cannot expect drastic changes overnight, regardless of changes in expectations or other incentives. The key is often reinforcing positively *"successive approximations."* By successive approximations we mean be-

havior which comes closer and closer to the supervisor's expectations of good performance. Similar to the child learning some new behavior, a manager should not expect high levels of performance at the outset. As a parent or teacher, we would use positive reinforcement as the child's behavior approaches the desired level of performance. Therefore, the manager must be aware of any progress of his subordinates so that he is in a position to reinforce appropriately improved performance.

Change through the cycle from quadrant 1 to quadrant 2, 3, and then 4 must be gradual. This process by its very nature cannot be revolutionary but must be evolutionary—gradual developmental changes, a result of planned growth and the creation of mutual trust and respect.

REFERENCES

1. As examples see the following: Robert F. Bales, "Task Roles and Social Roles in Problem-Solving Groups," in *Readings in Social Psychology*, E. E. Maccoby, T. M. Newcomb and E. L. Hartley (eds.), Holt, Rinehart and Winston, 1958; Chester I. Barnard, *The Functions of the Executive*, Harvard University Press, 1938; Dorwin Cartwright and Alvin Zander (eds.), *Group Dynamics: Research and Theory*, second edition, Row, Peterson and Co., 1960; D. Katz, N. Maccoby, and Nancy C. Morse, *Productivity Supervision, and Morale in an Office Situation*, The Darel Press, Inc., 1950; Talcott Parsons, *The Social System*, The Free Press, 1951.

2. Robert Tannenbaum and Warren H. Schmidt, "How to Choose a Leadership Pattern," *Harvard Business Review*, Mar.–Apr. 1957, pp. 95–101.

3. Roger M. Stogdill and Alvin E. Coons (eds.), *Leader Behavior: Its Description and Measurement*, Research Monograph No. 88, Bureau of Business Research, The Ohio State Univ., 1957.

4. Stogdill and Coons, *Leader Behavior . . .* See also Andrew W. Halpin. *The Leadership Behavior of School Superintendents*,

Midwest Administration Center, The University of Chicago, 1959.

5. Robert R. Blake and Jane S. Mouton, *The Managerial Grid,* Gulf Publishing, 1964.

6. Halpin, *The Leadership Behavior of School Superintendents.*

7. Robert R. Blake, *et al.,* "Breakthrough in Organization Development," *Harvard Business Review,* Nov.–Dec. 1964.

8. See also, Rensis Likert, *New Patterns of Management,* McGraw-Hill, 1961.

9. A. K. Korman, "'Consideration,' 'Initiating Structure,' and Organizational Criteria—A Review," *Personnel Psychology: A Journal of Applied Research,* Vol. 19, No. 4, (Winter, 1966), pp. 349–361.

10. Fred E. Fiedler, *A Theory of Leadership Effectiveness.* McGraw-Hill, 1967.

11. See C. A. Gibb, "Leadership"; A. P. Hare, *Handbook of Small Group Research,* Wiley, 1965; and D. C. Pelz, "Leadership Within a Hierarchial Organization," *Journal of Social Issues,* 1961, 7, pp. 49–55.

12. Paul Hersey and Kenneth H. Blanchard, *Leader Behavior,* Management Education & Development, Inc., 1967; see also Hersey and Blanchard, *Management of Organizational Behavior: Utilizing Human Resources,* Prentice-Hall, Inc., (in Press); and William J. Reddin, "The 3-D Management Style Theory," *Training and Development Journal,* Apr. 1967.

13. Fred E. Fiedler in his Contingency Model of Leadership Effectiveness (Fiedler, *A Theory of Leadership Effectiveness*) tends to make behavioral assumptions from data gathered from an attitudinal measure of leadership style. A leader is asked to evaluate his least preferred co-worker (LPC) on a series of Semantic Differential type scales. Leaders are classified as high or low LPC depending on the favorableness with which they rate their LPC.

14. Korman, "'Consideration,' 'Initiating Structure' and Organizational Criteria—A Review."

15. Fillmore H. Sanford, *Authoritarianism and Leadership,* Institute for Research in Human Relations, 1950.

16. Chris Argyris, *Personality and Organization,* Harper & Row, Publishers, Inc., 1957; *Interpersonal Competence and Organizational Effectiveness,* Dorsey Press, 1962; and *Integrating the Individual and the Organization,* Wiley, 1964.

17. David C. McClelland, J. W. Atkinson, R. A. Clark, and E. L. Lowell, *The Achievement Motive,* Appleton-Century-Crafts, Inc., 1953, and *The Achieving Society,* D. Van Nostrand Co., 1961.

18. Harold Koontz and Cyril O'Donnell, *Principles of Management,* fourth edition, McGraw-Hill, 1968.

19. Support for this discussion is provided by Peter F. Drucker, *The Practice of Management,* Harper & Bros., 1954, pp. 139–40.

20. Rensis Likert, *New Patterns of Management,* McGraw-Hill, 1961.

21. Saul Gellerman, *Motivation and Productivity,* American Management Assn., 1963.

22. Fiedler, *A Theory of Leadership Effectiveness.*

23. Likert, *New Patterns of Management.*

23
Mortal Stakes: Where Have All the Leaders Gone?
Warren G. Bennis

"Where have all the leaders gone?" They are, as a paraphrase of that haunting song could remind us, "long time passing."

All the leaders whom the young respect are dead. F.D.R., who could challenge a nation to rise above fear, is gone. Churchill, who could demand and get blood, sweat, and tears, is gone. Schweitzer, who from the jungles of Lambarene could inspire mankind with a reverence for life, is gone. Einstein, who could give us that sense of unity in infinity, of cosmic harmony, is gone. Gandhi, the Kennedys, Martin Luther King—all lie slain, as if to prove the mortal risk in telling us that we can be greater, better than we are.

The stage is littered with fallen leaders. A president reelected with the greatest plurality in history resigns in disgrace. The vice-president he twice chose as qualified to succeed him is driven from office as a common crook. Since 1973, the governments of all nine Common Market countries have changed hands. In nine recent months, nine more major governments have fallen. Shaky coalitions exist in Finland, Belgium, and Israel. Minority governments rule precariously in Britain, Denmark, and Sweden. Portugal overturned its fascist dictatorship and, as of this writing, has still not settled on a right-wing or left-wing dominated government. In Ethiopia, the King of Kings died a captive in his palace.

Where have all the leaders gone?

Those who remain—the successors, the survivors—are the Fords and Rockefellers who come to power without election, the struggling corporate chieftains, the university presidents, the city managers, the state governors. True leaders today are an endangered species. And why? Because of the whirl of events and circumstances beyond rational control.

There is a high turnover, an appalling mortality—whether occupational or actuarial—among leaders. In recent years the typical college president has lasted about four years. Men capable of leading institutions often refuse to accept such pressures, such risks. President Ford has had great difficulty getting the top men he wanted to accept Cabinet jobs. We see what James Reston of *The New York Times* calls "burntout cases," the debris of leaders. We see Peter Principle leaders rising to their final levels of incompetence. It has been said if a Martian were to demand, "Take me to your leader," Earthlings would not know where to take him. Administrative sclerosis around the world, in political office, in all administrative offices, breeds suspicion and distrust. A bumper sticker glimpsed in Massachusetts sums it up: "IMPEACH SOMEONE!"

Source: Reprinted, by permission of the publisher, from *The Unconscious Conspiracy: Why Leaders Can't Lead* by Warren G. Bennis, pp. 143–156, copyright © 1976 AMACOM, a division of American Management Association, New York. All rights reserved.

We see people dropping out—not just college students but leaders of large institutions and businesses—to seek some Walden utopia without responsibility. We see more and more managers turning into Swiss gnomes who do not *lead* but attempt to barely manage.

A scientist at the University of Michigan has recently discussed what he considers to be the ten basic dangers to our society. First on his list of ten, and most significant, is the possibility of some kind of nuclear war or accident which would destroy the entire human race. The second basic challenge facing us is the prospect of a worldwide epidemic, disease, famine, or depression. The scientist's No. 3 in terms of the key problems which can bring about the destruction of society is *the quality of the management and leadership of our institutions.*

I think he's right. And, in effect, here we are: virtually without leaders. In the past year or so, we've seen four senior Congressional leaders, committee chairmen, deposed. In the new Congress, the new junior members have the power. Whether they can exercise it intelligently and responsibly is increasingly a question. The Congress used to get much more work done when there were some towering giants in those chambers: the "whales," as Lyndon Johnson called them—Rayburn, George, Vandenberg, Johnson himself. They were arrogant and sometimes oppressive, but nevertheless they managed to produce an aura that seemed to say things were getting done. Now there is scant attention to the basic issues of our times. The landscape of American politics is peculiarly flat and characterless.

In business, also, the landscape is flat. The giants that come to mind—Ford, Edison, Rockefeller, Morgan, Schwab, Sloan, Kettering—are no more. Nixon's business intimates were really outside the business establishment, entrepreneurs without widespread acceptance as leaders or spokesmen. And President Gerald Ford seems to get on best with the Washington *vice-presidents* of major corporations (a vice-president syndrome, as it were). Max Ways, in *Fortune* magazine, talks about the absence of business leaders in New York University's Hall of Fame. Of the 99 people selected, only 10 are business leaders. Education is more highly represented—Mark Hopkins, Nicholas Murray Butler, Mary Lyon, Horace Mann, Alice Freeman Palmer, Robert Hutchins, Booker T. Washington are among those honored.

But these giants in the field of education belong to yesterday's world. Today we see what appears to be a growing invisibility and blandness among educational leaders. Haverford College President Jack Coleman writes nostalgically about a vanished age: "Gone are the days when academic administrators offered leadership on a broad scale, whether it was on educational affairs or pressing public matters of the day." Is there now a college president who might, like Wilson, aspire to be President of the United States?

What about our cities, their management and leadership? My own city of Cincinnati hired one of the outstanding city managers in the nation—Bob Turner, a former president of the International City Managers Association. On March 1, 1975, after just three years on the job, he left—unable to realize the goals that he brought with him. (He is becoming a corporate executive, hoping for greater scope.) And in Detroit the first black mayor, Coleman Young, said to a jubilant crowd at his inauguration, "As of this moment, we're going to turn this city around." Less than a year later, Mayor Young in his "State of the City" address confessed that he had not been able to realize any of his goals, including the reduction of crime and the revitalization of industry in Detroit. It is as if the problems that people in leadership face are out of control.

There was a different time, when Carlisle could write about institutions as being the lengthened shadow of one man. And there was Pope Urban IV, whose retinue would greet him with a chant. *"Deus es. Deus es,"* they would intone—to which he could reply, "It is somewhat strong, but really very pleasant." Leaders do not hear that kind of chant today. They have very few moments for hearing something adulatory or even merely pleasant.

A student at my university wrote me a letter after a talk he had heard me give. "Where," he asked, "is education to go in a society that becomes more and more dreamless each day?"

What shall I reply? What has dulled the image, not only of society, but of its leaders? We hunger for greatness, but what we find is, at best, efficient managers or, at worst, amoral gnomes lost in narrow orbits.

Why have we become a dreamless society? In the case of educational leaders, Haverford's Jack Coleman suggests that we have fallen into a "popularity trap." "We have asked too soon and too often whether our immediate constituents would like our programs and policies. Like other leaders of the day, we read polls."

It wasn't always that way. Not long ago a relative of M. Cary Thomas was describing that venerable woman's presidential years at Bryn Mawr College. An eager undergraduate asked, "Was she liked?" The answer was short: "I'm sure the question never crossed her mind."

Harry McPherson, a former counsel to President Lyndon Johnson, has some trenchant observations on leaders: "First, the media have overexposed public men, showing their feet and in some cases their whole bodies of clay. Television burns up new personalities quickly.

"Two, political, economic, and social changes which various leaders offered as remedies for the nation's ills are perceived as having failed or only partially succeeded."

Are leaders an endangered species?

The Problems and the Pressures

I have spent most of my life studying the best, the most rational, the most productive forms of organization and of leadership, whether of corporate, governmental, educational, or other institutions. Now, as I begin my fifth year of governing the nation's second largest urban multiversity—whose problems reflect in microcosm those of any complex organization—I can look back upon both accomplishments and failures.

I can compare what a specialist, a theorist, blithely believed *should* be done with what, in an imperfect world, *can* be done. I can compare what is desirable with what is possible. I know, as any leader of any organization—public, corporate, institutional—knows from experience, that the challenge is not for an omnipotent, omniscient "man on a white horse" but for a fallible, bewildered, often impotent individual to get one foot in the stirrup.

That is so because he confronts problems which may have no solutions or, at best, only proximate solutions. He confronts innumerable, diverse, and warring constituencies, whose separate goals and drives may be irreconcilable. The test, then, for any leader today is first to discover just *what* he does confront and then devise the best, the optimum, ways of making that reality potentially manageable.

Let me first try to set forth the conflicting demands—the turbulent, explosive environment—which make that task so difficult.

Foremost is *the loss of autonomy.* Time was when the leader could decide—period. A Henry Ford or a Carnegie could issue a ukase—and everyone would automatically obey. Their successors' hands are now tied in innumerable ways: by governmental requirements, by union rules, by the moral—and sometimes legal—pressures of organized consumers and environmentalists. As a supposed leader, I watch with envy the superior autonomy of the man mowing the university lawn. He is in complete control of the machine he rides, the total arbiter of which swath to cut where and when. I cannot match him.

The greatest problem facing today's institution is *the concatenation of external forces that impinge and impose upon it events outside the skin boundary of the organization.* Fifty years ago this external environment was fairly placid, like an ocean on a calm day, predictable, regular, not terribly eventful. Now that ocean is turbulent and highly interdependent and pivotal. In my own institution right now, the key people for me to reckon with are not only the students, the faculty, and my own management group, but people external to the university—the city manager, the city council members, the state legislature, the federal government, alumni, and parents. There is an incessant, dissonant clamor out there. And because the university is a brilliant example of an institution that has blunted and diffused its main purposes—through a proliferation of dependence on external patronage structures—its autonomy has declined to the point where our boundary system is like Swiss cheese. Because of

these pressures, every leader must create, in effect, a department of "external affairs"—a secretary of state, as it were, to deal with external constituencies.

At the same time Henry Kissinger, a *real* secretary of state, finds foreign affairs thwarted by *internal constitutencies* which undo his long, laborious, and precarious negotiations.

With this comes *a new movement of populism*—not the barn burners of the Grange days, not Bryan and his advocates of free silver against gold's "crown of thorns," but the fragmentation, the caucusization, of constituencies. On our campus, as I have mentioned in these pages, we have innumerable organized pressure groups—and the same phenomenon exists, more or less, in all large institutions. There is a loss of consensus, of community. We have a new form of politics in which people do not march on cities but march on particular bureaus or departments within our institutions.

We have become *a litigious society,* where individuals and groups more and more resort to the courts to determine issues which previously might have been settled privately. A hockey pro, injured in his sport, bypasses the institutional procedures to bring formal suit. My own university faces a suit from a woman, a black, for her loss of the administrative position I had thought she could fill. Even a law review has been sued—for rejecting an article.

In New Jersey, a federal judge has ordered 28 state senators to stand trial for violating the constitutional rights of the 29th member, a woman, by excluding her from their party caucus (they did so because she was "leaking" their deliberations to the press). In a Columbus, Ohio, test case, the Supreme Court ruled that secondary-school students may not be suspended, disciplinarily, without formal charges and a hearing—

that the loss of a single day's education is a deprivation of property. A federal court in Washington has just awarded $10,000 to each of the thousands of May 1970 antiwar demonstrators who it found had been illegally arrested and confined. Without questioning the merits of any particular case, the overriding fact is clear that the hands of all administrators are increasingly tied by real or potential legal issues. I find I must consult our lawyers even over small, trivial decisions.

With the neopopulism comes the phenomenon which I have described as *arribismo*. The U.S. brand of *arribismo* distinguishes all those diverse Americans who are trying to find themselves along race lines, sex lines, ethnic lines, even age lines—all at different stages of their social identity and their economic and political power.

And the neopopulism and the *arribismo* are accompanied by a related development that we might call the *psychology of entitlement*. It asserts one's right to things that one might not deserve through merit or achievement, simply because one's whole group has been deprived—by racism or whatever—from normal enjoyment of them. It demands x number of jobs regardless of individual qualifications.

These pressure groups are not united but fragmented. They go their *separate and often conflicting ways*. It is they who are telling us that the old dream of the melting pot, of assimilation, does not work. They have never been *beyond* the melting pot; rather, they have been *behind* it. They say, "Forget about your mainstream. We just want to be *us*"— blacks, homosexuals, Chicanos, women's libbers, or Menominee Indians seizing an empty Catholic monastery.

Meanwhile, the country is trying to cope with the *Roosevelt legacy*, the post-Depression development in the public

sector of those areas of welfare, social service, and education that the private sector was unwilling or unable to handle. As Lord Keynes wrote: "Progress lies in the growth and the recognition of semi-autonomous bodies within the states. Large business corporations, when they have reached a certain age and size, approximate the status of public corporations rather than that of the individualistic private enterprise." The Keynesian prophecy is upon us. When David Rockefeller goes to London, he is greeted as if he were a chief of state (and some of his empires are bigger than many states). But, in addition to the semiautonomous, often global corporations, rivaling governments, which Lord Keynes envisioned, we also have public-sector institutions which he could scarcely have imagined. The largest employment sector of our society, which is growing at the fastest rate, is local and state government. *Higher education, which less than 20 years ago was 50 percent private and 50 percent public, is now about 85 percent public and is expected to be 90 percent public by 1980.*

And, *where a century ago 90 percent of all Americans were self-employed, today 90 percent now work in what can be called bureaucracies.* They are members of some kind of corporate family. They might be called "juristic" persons; that is, they work within the sovereignty of a legal entity called a corporation or bureaucracy. Juristic persons do not control their own actions; hence they cannot place the same faith in each other that they might if they were self-employed.

And along with the growth of public-sector institutions, we have seen its handmaiden—a *cat's cradle of regulations which tend to restrict or reduce the institution's autonomy in decision making.* What we now have is a situation where many of the decisions being made by any major organization, public or private, have to do with factors that are partly outside the control, and definitely outside the governing perimeter, of the organization itself.

To take just one example, the university, the Buckley Amendment makes all records available to students and parents. It obviously changes every aspect of information sharing and the way recommendations are written about students.

Leaders are becoming an endangered species, also, because *the external forces and the internal constituents, themselves with diverse expectations and demands and desires, isolate the man at the top* as the sole "boundary" person trying somehow to negotiate between them. Growing tension, conflict, goal divergence develop between the internal and external demands. In my own city a Kroger's or a P&G must consider both external as well as internal problems, whether nitrates or price labeling. Or take the effects of "affirmative action" on what used to be autonomous decisions made by the organization. The overload of these demands from within and without the institution is enormous.

Within the community, we have not only a loss of consensus over basic values, we have as well a polarization. We have not a consensus but a dissensus.

Finally, consider the change of values among the young, as reflected in the surveys done recently by Yankelovich. We've gone from concern for *quantity*— that is, *more*—toward considerations of *quality*—that is, *better*. The old culture focused on the concept of *independence*, whereas the new culture moves toward the concept of *interdependence* of nations, institutions, individuals, all natural species. What youth is saying is that we need a new "declaration of interdependence." That we must move from conquest of nature toward living in harmony with it, from competition toward cooperation, from doing and planning toward being, from the primacy of technology toward considerations of social justice and equity, from the dictates of organizational convenience toward the aspirations of self-realization and learning, from authoritarianism and dogmatism toward more participation, from uniformity and centralization toward diversity and pluralism, from the concept of work as hard and unavoidable, from life as nasty, brutish, and short toward work as purpose and self-fulfilment, a recognition of leisure as a valid activity in itself.

The people who are joining our organizations and institutions today are those who seek, who represent, the latter part of each of those dichotomies. They are the New Culture.

Why "Leaders" Don't "Lead"

These, then, are the problems of leadership today. We have the new and important emergence of a Roosevelt-Keynes revolution, new politics, new dependencies, new constituencies, new values. The consequence of these pressures is a loss of the institution's autonomy to determine its own destiny.

So why are "leaders" not "leading"?

One reason, I fear, is that many of us don't have the faintest concept of what leadership is all about. Leading does not mean managing; the difference between the two is crucial. There are many institutions I know that are very well *managed* and very poorly *led*. They may excel in the ability to handle all the routine inputs each day, yet they may never ask whether the routine should be preserved at all.

As I noted earlier, frequently my most enthusiastic deputies unwittingly do their best to keep me from working any fundamental change in the institution. I think all of us find that acting on routine problems, just because they are the easiest, often blocks us from getting involved in the bigger ones.

In recent years I have talked to many new presidents of widely ranging enterprises. Almost every one of them feels that the biggest mistake he made at the start was to *take on too much,* as if proving oneself depended on providing instant solutions and success was dependent on immediate achievement. The instant solutions often led to *pseudo-solutions* for problems not fully analyzed. People follow the old army game. They do not want to take responsibility for, or bear the consequences of, decisions that they should properly make. Everybody tries to dump those "wet babies" on the boss's desk—defenseless and unequipped as he is.

Today's leader is often baffled or frustrated by a new kind of politics, which arises from significant interaction with various governmental agencies, relevant laws and regulations, the courts, the media, the consumers, and so on. It is the politics of maintaining institutional "inner-directedness" and mastery in times of rapid change. Many institution leaders do not want to face up to the need for politicking. Not long ago, when the director of the New York Health Corporation resigned, he declared, "I already see indications of the corporation and its cause being made a political football in the current campaign. I'm not a politician. I do not wish to become involved in the political issues here." And yet, in a previous article, he had said that he found himself "at the center of a series of ferocious struggles for money, power, and jobs among the combatants, political leaders, labor leaders, minority groups, medical militants, medical-school deans, doctors and nurses, and many of his own administrative subordinates." The corporation he headed has an $800 million budget and is responsible for capital construction of more than $1 billion; it employs 40,000 people, including 7,500 doctors and almost 15,000 nurses and nurse's aides. It embraces 19 hospitals with 15,000 beds and numerous outpatient clinics and emergency rooms that treat 2,000,000 New Yorkers a year. And he's *surprised* that he's into politics—and doesn't like it!

When our own university could admit only 187 medical-school applicants out of 8,000, we immediately angered some 23,000 would-be constituents—24,000 parents and applicants minus the successful applicants and their parents, who were pleased. Those who were unhappy immediately brought pressure on councilmen and legislators. What resulted was proposals to legislate restrictions on our autonomy—for example, to bar out-of-state students. We could resent and oppose that, and we did. But we should not have been surprised by it. We should have known that such decisions automatically *become* political.

The high turnover and the appalling mortality among leaders remain. The landscape continues flat. The problems seem insoluble—to the degree that we are becoming a dreamless society. Now we hear that butterflies are to be listed as a threatened species. Can we allow leaders to go the same route?

24
Leadership as Cultural Expression
Thomas J. Sergiovanni

How often it seems in leadership that battles are won but wars are lost; that progress is made event by event with no qualitative organizational effect; that administrative energies are expended and routine competence is maintained with no commensurate hint of excellence or greatness. Thanks to sound management, research centers increase the number of research contracts won but decline in reputation; courses are revised according to logical principles of curriculum development, but programs do not excell; new resources are obtained by rational administrative efforts but excellence escapes; and technically superb plans are developed to redistribute existing resources with declines in morale and overall productivity. These apparent contradictions in part can be explained by differentiating between tactical and strategic leadership. Tactical leadership involves analyses which lead to administrative action and means of minor magnitude, which are of small scale, and which serve larger purposes. Strategic leadership, by contrast, is the art and science of enlisting support for broader policies and purposes and for devising longer-range plans.

It seems trite to note that quality leadership requires balanced attention to both tactical and strategic requirements. Despite this common knowledge, leadership research and practice reflect a bias in favor of the tactical. At best, attention to the tactical at the expense of the strategic maintains day-by-day organizational competence, but excellence remains out of reach. In part, the emphasis on tactical requirements of leadership reflects the broader management culture of Western society. Such values as efficiency, specificity, rationality, measurability, and objectivity combined with the belief that good management is tough-minded are part of this culture. Results-oriented management is the slogan; the bottom line is worshiped; and the direct, in-control manager is admired. Leadership is broadly defined as achieving objectives effectively and efficiently. Leadership theory puts the emphasis on the leader's behavior and on results. The metaphors of the battlefield are often used to remind us that one must be hard-nosed, and that the going is tough. Evaluation is quick and to the point and success is determined on the basis of short-term accomplishments. Key to this management culture is the assumption that ambiguity is an organizational ill to be rooted out by rational management techniques. Good administrators manage with certainty, are decisive, and can back up action with rational and logical arguments. Given these cultural demands no wonder that the tactical requirements of leadership are em-

Source: From "Leadership as Cultural Expression" by Thomas J. Sergiovanni, in *Leadership and Organizational Culture: New Perspectives on Administrative Theory and Practice,* edited by Thomas J. Sergiovanni and John E. Corbally. Copyright © 1984 by the Board of Trustees of the University of Illinois. Reprinted by permission of University of Illinois Press.

phasized. Missing from these tactical issues are holistic values of purpose, goodness, and importance. Missing is an emphasis on long-term quality.

In recent years conventional views of management and leadership have been called to question. Theorists, for example, are coming to realize that uncertainty and ambiguity are not only natural but desirable (March 1980; Pascale 1978). Further, cultural aspects of organization are being offered as better able to account for the artificial, purposive, and practical aspects of organizational life.

There is more to leadership than meets the tactical eye. The real value of leadership rests with the meanings which actions import to others than in the actions themselves. A complete rendering of leadership requires that we move beyond the obvious to the subtle, beyond the immediate to the long range, beyond actions to meanings, beyond viewing organizations and groups within social systems to cultural entities. These are the strategic issues which will be discussed in this chapter.

Let's take as an example the important tactical skill of mastering a contingency approach to leadership, characterized by careful reading of situations and by applying the right doses of the correct mix of leadership styles. Combine this tactical skill with a leader who has certain purposes, beliefs, and commitment to what the school or university is and can be and who can communicate these in a fashion which rallies others to the cause, and we are achieving proper balance. One would not want to choose between the tactical and strategic in this case, but if I had to make such a choice, my vote would be with the latter. What a leader stands for is more important than what he or she does. The meanings a leader communicates to others is more important than

his or her specific leadership style. Critical to understanding this relationship is a view that humans, beyond rudimentary animalistic tendencies, do not behave but act. Actions differ from behavior in that they are born of preconceptions, assumptions, and motives, and these are imbedded with meanings. Leadership acts are expressions of culture. Leadership as cultural expression seeks to build unity and order within an organization by giving attention to purposes, historical and philosophical tradition, and ideals and norms which define the way of life within the organization and which provide the bases for socializing members and obtaining their compliance.

Developing and nurturing organizational value patterns and norms represent a response to felt needs of individuals and groups for order, stability, and meaning. The concept of "center" is used by Shils (1961) to describe this need. Organizational centers represent the focus of values, sentiments, and beliefs which provide the cultural cement needed to hold people together in groups and groups into an organizational federation. Lacking an official center, "wild" centers emerge within the organization as a natural response to felt needs. Wild centers are only accidentally compatible with the official, thus the "domestication" of wild centers is important to leadership as cultural expression.

Recognizing that organizations often resemble multicultural societies and that subgroups must of necessity maintain individual and cherished identities, the domestication process seeks *minimally* to build a cultural federation of compatibility which provides enough common identity, enough common meanings, and enough of a basis for committed action for the organization to function in spirited concert.

TABLE 1 • THE 10–P MODEL OF LEADERSHIP

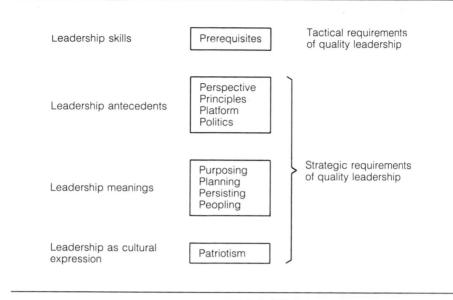

Leadership skills	Prerequisites	Tactical requirements of quality leadership
Leadership antecedents	Perspective Principles Platform Politics	
Leadership meanings	Purposing Planning Persisting Peopling	Strategic requirements of quality leadership
Leadership as cultural expression	Patriotism	

Leadership as cultural expression results from the complex interplay of several dimensions, prime among which are leadership skills, antecedents, and meanings. Leadership skills have been traditionally emphasized in the management literature, are considered important in the complex interplay of dimensions, and represent tactical requirements. Less considered have been antecedents and meanings—dimensions which comprise strategic requirements. From leadership skills, meanings, antecedents, and culture can be extracted ten principles of quality leadership. These principles are depicted in Table 1. There is always a risk in reducing the subtle and complex to a handful of abbreviated and specific principles. I accept this risk in order to provide busy professionals with a useful and easily remembered framework. The risk will be reduced if we agree that the ten principles are not meant to be recited as one would a litany, but are offered to bring to one's consciousness a cognitive map of the requirements for quality in leadership. A careful reading of other chapters in this section will reveal that most of the principles have already been considered, either directly or indirectly. This rendering, therefore, should be viewed in part as a summary and in part as an extension and synthesis which seeks an integrated image of quality dimensions in leadership (Sergiovanni 1981, 1982).

The first principle to be considered is that of *prerequisites*. Prerequisites refer to the various leadership skills needed to develop and maintain basic leadership competence. Such skills as mastering and using various contingency leadership theories, conflict management tactics, team management principles, shared decision-making models, and group process techniques are examples of basic leadership requirements. Leadership skills are tactical in the sense that they are situationally specific, of short duration, and focused on specific objectives or outcomes. Successful leadership is not likely to be within the reach of those who are not competent in the basic leadership skills, but competence and excellence are different. To move beyond routine competence one must shift attention from the tactical to the strategic. The remaining principles are strategic in nature. They give meaning and direction to the leadership skills.

The next group of four principles are leadership antecedents in the sense that they represent conditions, feelings, assumptions, cognitive maps, and attitudes of the leader which determine his or her reality and which guide his or her decisions, actions, and behavior. As antecedents vary among leaders, so does leadership quality and meaning.

Perspective refers to the ability of the leader to be able to differentiate between the tactical and strategic and to understand how they are related. One with perspective brings a broader, patient, more long-range view to his or her leadership responsibilities which enables the sorting of trivial from important events and outcomes and the determining of worth. What the leader stands for and believes about schooling, the place of education in society, how schools should be organized and operated, and how people should be treated comprise the guiding *principles* which bring integrity and meaning to leadership. Leaders stand for certain ideals and principles which become cornerstones of their very being. In a recent *Wall Street Journal*-Gallup poll, for example, integrity was the factor considered most important for advancement by chief executives of 282 of the nation's largest firms in describing characteristics of subordinates. The number one failing of weak managers, by contrast, was limited point of view. Integrity suggests that the leader values

something important and is able to communicate this value to others.

Platform refers to the articulation of one's principles into an operational framework. Platforms are governing in the sense that they represent a set of criteria and an implicit standard from which decisions are made. One's teaching platform governs the decisions he or she makes about teaching and provides a set of ideals which make teaching decisions sensible to a person. Educational and management platforms, so essential to quality in leadership, operate in much the same fashion.

Politics is the final leadership antecedent to be considered. At its simplest level, leadership can be defined as the ability of an individual to influence another individual or group in a fashion which helps to achieve certain desired goals. In schools and universities political behavior is a key ingredient in successful leadership. Schools and universities, like other arenas of public administration, are political organizations characterized by multiple interest groups, unclear and competing goals, diffuse sources of power, and ambiguous lines of authority. Unlike the simple business firm or owner-operated store, the educational administrator typically cannot exercise direct authority to obtain compliance or cooperation from others. Often, groups to be influenced are outside the organization itself, or are outside of the administrator's authority. Typically, the administrator must obtain voluntary cooperation, support, and good will from others to get things done. Sensitivity to *politics* and knowledge that the leader is typically dependent upon the good wishes and voluntary compliance of others if he or she is to be effective in the long haul is thus a necessary leadership antecedent.

The next group of leadership principles reflects the *meanings* theme. Key to quality in leadership and quality in educational organizations is that academics and others find their work to be interesting, satisfying, and meaningful. Meaning suggests as well that people believe in what they are doing and appreciate its importance to the organization, to society, and to themselves. Leadership meanings can be summed in the four principles: purposing, planning, persisting, and peopling.

Purposing breathes life and meaning into the day-to-day activities of people at work. It helps people to interpret their contributions, their successes and failures, their efforts and energies in light of the organization's purposes. Through this process, seemingly ordinary events become meaningful with subsequent motivational benefits to the organization. In addition, purposing is the means by which leaders articulate the antecedents of principle and platform. It represents as well the rallying point for bringing together all human resources into a common cause.

Planning is the articulation of purpose into concrete but long-term operational programs. Planning sketches out the major structures and design to be implemented, the major steps to be taken, and the major milestones to be achieved. The time frame is long-range and planning as a strategic requirement of leadership should not be confused with such tactical requirements as management by objectives, the specification of short-term outcomes or results, or the various scheduling devices such as Gantt or PERT (Program Evaluation Review Technique). Despite the usefulness of such tactics in the short range, they can mislead if they are not part of a more long-range plan.

Tactical planning responses by universities to shifting marketplace demands on educational programs is a case in point. Such responses typically include reallocating existing resources from low to high demand areas. The tactical logic of such reallocation rests in changes in the ratios of FTEs (Full Time Equivalents) to instructional units. Thus, such areas as fine arts, social science, education, and the humanities are today's losers to such high-demand areas as science, engineering, and business administration. The domination of tactical logic and short-term planning responses to marketplace demands gives attention to the "body" of the university at the expense of its "soul." A strategic view of planning would seek to balance marketplace demands against images of what constitutes the concept university and would seek to protect the integrity of these images. Further, as demands once again shift in favor of today's losers, as they most surely will, undue commitments to short-range planning will result in the university being in a strategically poor position to face newer pressures and to maintain long-term quality.

Persisting refers to the attention leaders give to important principles, issues, goals, and outcomes. Symbolically how an administrator uses time is a form of administrative attention which communicates meanings to others in the school. It is assumed by most that an administrator gives attention to the events and activities he or she values. As others learn the value of this activity to the leader, they are also likely to give it attention. Administrative attention, then, can be considered as a form of modeling for others who work in the school. Through administrative attention, the leader contributes to setting the tone or climate of the school and communicates to others the goals and activities which should enjoy high priority.

The social-psychological effects of administrative attention tend to occur whether or not they are intended. An elementary school principal might, for example, espouse an educational platform which suggests a deep commitment to building a strong educational program sensitive to individual needs of students, taught by a happy committed faculty, and supported by his or her school community. But this platform is likely to be ignored in favor of the one which students, teachers, and parents infer on the basis of administrative attention. Protestations to the contrary, if most of the principal's time is spent on the many trivial activities associated with routine administrative maintenance, observers will learn that "running a smooth ship" is the goal of real value to the principal and the school.

Peopling recognizes that little can be accomplished by the leader without the good wishes of others. More than mere compliance from others is necessary if excellence is sought. Instead, the leader seeks to fine tune and match more closely the goals, objectives, and desires of people with those of the organization. Growth and development of the human organization enjoys equal status, as a tactical objective, with increased organizational outputs. Indeed, lower levels of organizational achievement might well be appropriate in the short term if human values would otherwise be endangered. When considered in the long term, an undisputed link exists between the satisfaction and development of the human organization and increased organizational performance, both in quantity and quality. Peopling is a key strategic requirement of quality leadership. Accepting short-term gains which compromise the quality of life which people enjoy in schools and universities simply does not make strategic sense.

When leadership skills, antecedents, and meanings are successfully articulated into practice, we come to see leadership as less a behavioral style or management technique and as more a cultural expression. Here, a set of norms, beliefs, and principles emerge to which organizational members give allegiance. These represent a strong bond which brings people together to work on behalf of the organization. Indeed a culture emerges which details what is important and provides guidelines that govern behavior. The principle of *patriotism* is key to viewing leadership as cultural expression. In highly effective organizations workers share a set of common beliefs, and reach a set of common agreements which govern what will be done and how it will be done. Members express loyalty or patriotism to this way of life. Organizational patriots are committed to purposes, they work hard, believe in what they are doing, feel a sense of excitement for the organization and its work, and find their own contributions to the organization meaningful if not inspirational.

In sum, organizational patriotism can be defined as commitment and loyalty to the characteristics which give an organization or organizational subunits unique meaning. This meaning is part of the unit's culture and is implicit in its governing platforms. Goals, sense of mission, philosophy, expected ways of operating, and images of excellence are examples. The more explicit these are and the more patriotic are members, the more likely that excellence can be attained.

Symbolic Aspects of Leadership

Studies of leadership give too much attention to the instrumental and behavioral aspects and not enough to symbolic and cultural. The principles presented here, by contrast, give attention to the more informal, subtle, and symbolic aspects of leadership. Symbols evoke and bring to the forefront one's history. Meanings are raised to one's consciousness and through these meanings one is able to link on to some aspect of his or her world. But evoked meanings from any given object are never quite the same for everyone and thus need to be tied together into persistent cultural strands which define the organization's mission and activities. Answers to such questions as what is this organization about, what is of value here, what do we believe in, why do we function the way we do, and how are we unique come from such a definition. Persistent cultural strands introduce an orderliness to one's organizational life, provide one with a sense of purpose, and enrich existing meanings.

But symbols are more than superficial images tossed around for public effect. As Ricoeur (1974, 299) suggests, "I am convinced that we must think not *behind* the symbols, but starting from symbols, according to symbols, that their substance is indestructible, that they constitute the *revealing* substrata of speech which lives among men. In short, the symbol gives *rise* to the thought." He cautions against glib responses or even reading between the lines in attempting to figure out the meaning of symbols, preferring that the symbols themselves do the work. Symbols should be allowed to raise one's consciousness and unravel one's history.

Some have argued that most aspects of the school's culture are unrealistic and unattainable. Indeed, the word symbol suggests that aspirations and beliefs may be more shadow than real. Should this matter? Probably not. What is important is that the group's cultural imperatives represent a common rallying cry and provide a standard to which the group strives. Some point out that the domestication of organizational cultures is either autocratic (for example,

merely a rephrasing of the center-periphery struggle described by Schön, 1971) or unrealistic given the strength of wild centers which exist in multicultural societies. Though an enriched, domesticated center would be ideal from an administrative perspective, the likely domesticated center is a federated one whereby enough common values are articulated to give people common purpose and common meanings but where cherished local values are protected. Over time, compatibility increases as center and periphery values each take on characteristics of each other.

Our Tacit Understanding of Excellence

Many of the leadership principles articulated here are given credibility by other authors who wrote chapters for this section. The current popular interest of management theorists implicit in Japanese management practices reveals as well insights and prescriptions which resemble the ten principles (Ouchi 1981; Pascale and Athos 1981). These principles have been historically espoused in the writings of the human resources theorists (Argyris, Bennis, Likert, Maslow, and McGregor, for example) though perhaps not in an integrated and systematic leadership model. But perhaps the most convincing evidence comes from our own tacit understanding of excellence in organizations.

In his presentations on high-performing systems, Peter Vaill often asks listeners to engage in an exercise designed to raise to consciousness tacit understanding of high-performing systems. Adopting his strategy here, take a moment to recall in your life experiences that one group, team, unit, or organization which, when compared with all others from your personal experience, was the most high-performing.

You might go back to your teen years and recall a childhood or high school group, or perhaps to your experiences as a family member, or as a member of some social group or fraternity, or perhaps your military years, or to your experiences on a sports or sandlot team. Perhaps your attention will focus more on the world of work and you might recall some job you had, either recent or past, which included membership in a particularly high-performing group. Whatever the case, recall how the system operated. How did you feel about membership in the group? What made you work so hard? What accounted for your enthusiasm? Why did you enjoy being associated with the group? What was the system trying to accomplish? How loyal were you and why? How meaningful was your membership and why? Chances are that your analysis of this system highlights many of the quality leadership "P's" proposed here. Repeat this exercise, limiting yourself to schools or universities and work groups within these institutions with which you are familiar even though you may not have been a member. Recall the one most effective, most excellent, most high-performing from among all your experiences with these groups. Describe the system, what it valued, and how it worked. Take the time to sketch out some ideas on a sheet of paper. Again, compare your analysis with the quality leadership "P's." You should find a remarkable resemblance between the two.

Debates over such issues as skills versus meanings or tactics versus strategy can be misleading. This chapter, for example, is not a plea to substitute the heroic for the technocratic; to abandon sound management principles for the symbolic; to replace administrators with poets and artists. The issues of concern should be ones of balance and integration. It is clear that presently, in educational administration, the leadership emphasis is not balanced but tilts too much in the direction of leadership skills and the prerequisite management techniques they suggest.

The function of such skills is not to stand alone or even to be "added in" but to be integrated into a larger focus. This integration is suggested in the following quality leadership equation:

$$QL = LS (LA + LM + LCE)$$

Quality leadership (QL) results from the compounding effects of leadership skills (LS) *interacting with* leadership antecedents (LA), meanings (LM), and cultural expression (LCE). In sum, the 10–P model of leadership is offered as an interdependent and interlocking network. Though conveniently sorted into four categories of skills, antecedents, meanings, and cultural expression, the art of leadership is celebrated in their integration in practice.

REFERENCES

March, James G. (1980). "How We Talk and How We Act: Administrative Theory and Administrative Life." David D. Henry Lecture, University of Illinois, Urbana-Champaign.

Ouchi, William (1981). *Theory Z: How American Business Can Meet the Japanese Challenge.* Reading, Mass.: Addison-Wesley.

Pascale, Richard T. (1978). "Zen and the Art of Management." *Harvard Business Review* 56(2), 1953–62.

Pascale, Richard T., and Anthony G. Athos (1981). *The Art of Japanese Management.* New York: Simon and Schuster.

Ricoeur, Paul (1974). "The Hermeneutics of Symbols and Philosophical Reflections." Translated by Charles Freilich. In Don Ihde, ed. *The Conflict of Interpretations: Essays in Hermeneutics.* Evanston, Ill.: Northwestern University Press.

Schön, Donald A. (1971). *Beyond the Stable State.* New York: Random House.

Sergiovanni, Thomas J. (1981). "Symbolism in Leadership (What Great Leaders Know That Ordinary Ones Do Not)." Occasional paper, Institute of Educational Administration, Melbourne.

——— (1982). "Quality Leadership: Requirements and Principles." *Educational Leadership* 39(5), 330–36.

Shils, Edward (1961). "Centre and Periphery." In *The Logic of Personal Knowledge: Essays Presented to Michael Polanyi.* London: Routledge & Kegan Paul, pp. 117–31.

25

The Leadership Challenge—A Call for the Transformational Leader

Noel M. Tichy & David O. Ulrich

Some optimists are heralding in the age of higher productivity, a transition to a service economy, and a brighter competitive picture for U.S. corporations in world markets. We certainly would like to believe that the future will be brighter, but our temperament is more cautious. We feel that the years it took for most U.S. companies to get "fat and flabby" are not going to be reversed by a crash diet for one or two years. Whether we continue to gradually decline as a world competitive economy will largely be determined by the quality of leadership in the top echelons of our business and government organizations. Thus, it is our belief that now is the time for organizations to *change* their corporate lifestyles.

To revitalize organizations such as General Motors, American Telephone and Telegraph, General Electric, Honeywell, Ford, Burroughs, Chase Manhattan Bank, Citibank, U.S. Steel, Union Carbide, Texas Instruments, and Control Data—just to mention a few companies currently undergoing major transformations—a new brand of leadership is necessary. Instead of managers who continue to move organizations along historical tracks, the new leaders must *transform* the organizations and head them down new tracks. What is required of this kind of leader is an ability to help the organization develop a vision of what it can be, to mobilize the organization to accept and work toward achieving the new vision, and to institutionalize the changes that must last over time. Unless the creation of this breed of leaders becomes a national agenda, we are not very optimistic about the revitalization of the U.S. economy.

We call these new leaders transformational leaders, for they must create something new out of something old: out of an old vision, they must develop and communicate a new vision and get others not only to see the vision but also to commit themselves to it. Where transactional managers make only minor adjustments in the organization's mission, structure, and human resource management, transformational leaders not only make major changes in these three areas but they also evoke fundamental changes in the basic political and cultural systems of the organization. The revamping of the political and cultural systems is what most distinguishes the transformational leader from the transactional one.

Source: Reprinted from "The Leadership Challenge—A Call for the Transformational Leader" by N. M. Tichy and D. O. Ulrich in *Sloan Management Review* (Fall 1984), pp. 59–68, by permission of the publisher. Copyright © 1984 by the Sloan Management Review Association. All rights reserved.

LEE IACOCCA: A TRANSFORMATIONAL LEADER

One of the most dramatic examples of transformational leadership and organizational revitalization in the early 1980s has been the leadership of Lee Iacocca, the chairman of Chrysler Corporation. He provided the leadership to transform a company from the brink of bankruptcy to profitability. He created a vision of success and mobilized large factions of key employees toward enacting that vision while simultaneously downsizing the workforce by 60,000 employees. As a result of Iacocca's leadership, by 1984 Chrysler had earned record profits, had attained high levels of employee morale, and had helped employees generate a sense of meaning in their work.

Until Lee Iacocca took over at Chrysler, the basic internal political structure had been unchanged for decades. It was clear who reaped what benefits from the organization, how the pie was to be divided, and who could exercise what power. Nonetheless, Mr. Iacocca knew that he needed to alter these political traditions, starting with a new definition of Chrysler's link to external stakeholders. Therefore, the government was given a great deal of control over Chrysler in return for the guaranteed loan that staved off bankruptcy. Modification of the political system required other adjustments, including the "trimming of fat" in the management ranks, limiting financial rewards for all employees, and receiving major concessions for the UAW. An indicator of a significant political shift was the inclusion of Douglas Frazer on the Chrysler Board of Directors as part of UAW concessions.

Equally dramatic was the change in the organization's cultural system. First, the company had to recognize its unique status as a recipient of a federal bailout. This bailout came with a stigma, thus Mr. Iacocca's job was to change the company's cultural values from a loser's to a winner's feeling. Still, he realized that employees were not going to be winners unless they could, in cultural norms, be more efficient and innovative than their competitors. The molding and shaping of the new culture was clearly and visibly led by Mr. Iacocca, who not only used internal communication as a vehicle to signal change but also used his own personal appearance in Chrysler ads to reinforce these changes. Quickly, the internal culture was transformed to that of a lean and hungry team looking for victory. Whether Chrysler will be able to sustain this organizational phenomenon over time remains to be seen. If it does, it will provide a solid corporate example of what Burns referred to as a transforming leader.[1]

Lee Iacocca's high visibility and notoriety may be the *important* missing elements in management today: there seems to be a paucity of transformational leader role models at all levels of the organization.

ORGANIZATIONAL DYNAMICS OF CHANGE

Assumption One: Trigger Events Indicate Change Is Needed

Organizations do not change unless there is a trigger which indicates change is needed. This trigger can be as extreme as the Chrysler impending bankruptcy or as moderate as an abstract future-oriented fear that an organization may lose its competitiveness. For example, General Electric's trigger for change is a view that by 1990 the company will not be world competitive unless major changes occur in productivity, innovation, and marketing. Thus, Chairman Jack Welch sees his role as that of transforming GE even though it does not face imminent doom. Nonetheless, the trick for him is to *activate* the trigger; otherwise, complacency may prevail. Similarly, for AT&T, technological, competitive, and political forces have led it to undertake its massive transformation. For General Motors, economic factors of world competition, shifting consumer preferences, and technological change have driven it to change.

In a decade of increased information, international competition, and technological advances, triggers for change

have become commonplace and very pressing. However, not all potential trigger events lead to organizational responses, and not all triggers lead to change. Nonetheless, the trigger must create a *felt need* in organizational leaders. Without this felt need, the "boiled frog phenomenon" is likely to occur.

The Boiled Frog. This phenomenon is based on a classic experiment in biology. A frog which is placed in a pan of cold water but which still has the freedom to jump out can be boiled if the temperature change is gradual, for it is not aware of the barely detectable changing heat threshold. In contrast, a frog dropped in a pot of boiling water

TABLE 1 • A LIST OF TECHNICAL, POLITICAL, AND CULTURAL SYSTEM RESISTANCES

Technical System Resistances Include:

Habit and inertia. Habit and inertia cause task-related resistance to change. Individuals who have always done things one way may not be politically or culturally resistant to change, but may have trouble, for technical reasons, changing behavior patterns. Example: some office workers may have difficulty shifting from electric typewriters to word processors.

Fear of the unknown or loss of organizational predictability. Not knowing or having difficulty predicting the future creates anxiety and hence resistance in many individuals. Example: the introduction of automated office equipment has often been accompanied by such resistances.

Sunk costs. Organizations, even when realizing that there are potential payoffs from a change, are often unable to enact a change because of the sunk costs of the organizations' resources in the old way of doing things.

Political System Resistances Include:

Powerful coalitions. A common threat is found in the conflict between the old guard and the new guard. One interpretation of the exit of Archie McGill, former president of the newly formed AT&T American Bell, is that the backlash of the old-guard coalition exacted its price on the leader of the new-guard coalition.

Resource limitations. In the days when the economic pie was steadily expanding and resources were much less limited, change was easier to enact as every part could gain— such was the nature of labor management agreements in the auto industry for decades. Now that the pie is shrinking decisions need to be made as to who shares a smaller set of resources. These zero-sum decisions are much more politically difficult. As more and more U.S. companies deal with productivity, downsizing, and divestiture, political resistance will be triggered.

will immediately jump out: it has a felt need to survive. In a similar vein, many organizations that are insensitive to gradually changing organizational thresholds are likely to become "boiled frogs"; they act in ignorant bliss of environmental triggers and eventually are doomed to failure. This failure, in part, is a result of the organization having no felt need to change.

Assumption Two: A Change Unleashes Mixed Feelings

A felt need for change unleashes a mix of forces, both a positive impetus for change as well as a strong negative individual and organizational resistance. These forces of resistance are generated in each of three interrelated systems—technical, political, cultural—

which must be managed in the process of organizational transitions (see Table 1).[2] Individual and organizational resistance to change in these three systems must be overcome if an organization is to be revitalized.[3]

Managing technical systems refers to managing the coordination of technology, capital information, and people in order to produce products or services desired and used in the external marketplace. Managing political systems refers to managing the allocation of organizational rewards such as money, status, power, and career opportunities and to exercising power so employees and departments perceive equity and justice. Managing cultural systems refers to managing the set of shared values and norms which guides the behavior of members of the organization.

TABLE 1 (Continued)

Indictment quality of change: Perhaps the most significant resistance to change comes from leaders having to indict their own past decisions and behaviors to bring about a change. Example: Roger Smith, chairman and CEO of GM, must implicitly indict his own past behavior as a member of senior management when he suggests changes in GM's operations. Psychologically, it is very difficult for people to change when they were party to creating the problems they are trying to change. It is much easier for a leader from the outside, such as Lee Iacocca, who does not have to indict himself every time he says something is wrong with the organization.

Cultural System Resistances Include:

Selective perception (cultural filters). An organization's culture may highlight certain elements of the organization, making it difficult for members to conceive of other ways of doing things. An organization's culture channels that which people perceive as possible; thus, innovation may come from outsiders or deviants who are not as channeled in their perceptions.

Security based on the past. Transition requires people to give up the old ways of doing things. There is security in the past, and one of the problems is getting people to overcome the tendency to want to return to the "good old days." Example: today, there are still significant members of the white-collar workforce at GM who are waiting for the "good old days" to return.

Lack of climate for change. Organizations often vary in their conduciveness to change. Cultures that require a great deal of conformity often lack much receptivity to change. Example: GM with its years of internally developed managers must overcome a limited climate for change.

When a needed change is perceived by the organizational leaders, the dominant group in the organization must experience a dissatisfaction with the status quo. For example, in the late 1970s John DeButts, chairman and chief executive officer of AT&T, was not satisfied with the long-term viability of AT&T as a regulated telephone monopoly in the age of computers and satellite communication systems. Likewise, when Roger Smith became CEO at General Motors in the early 1980s, he could hardly be satisfied with presiding over GM's first financial loss since the depression. In these two cases, the felt need provided the impetus for transition; yet, such impetus is not uniformly positive.

The technical, political, and cultural resistances are most evident during early stages of an organizational transformation. At GM the early 1980s were marked by tremendous uncertainty concerning many technical issues such as marketing strategy, production strategy, organization design, factory automation, and development of international management. Politically, many powerful coalitions were threatened. The UAW was forced to make wage concessions and accept staffing reductions. The white-collar workers saw their benefits being cut and witnessed major layoffs within the managerial ranks. Culturally, the once dominant managerial style no longer fit the environmental pressures for change: the "GM way" was no longer the right way.

One must be wary of these resistances to change as they can lead to organizational stagnation rather than revitalization. In fact, some managers at GM in late 1983 were waiting for "the good old days" to return. Such resistance exemplifies a dysfunctional reaction to the felt need. As indicated in Figure 1, a key to whether resistant forces will lead to little or inadequate change and hence organizational decline or revitalization lies in an organization's leadership. Defensive, transactional leadership will not rechannel the resistant forces. A case in point is International Harvester which appears to have had a defensive transactional leadership. Thus, in the early 1980s, International Harvester lacked a new vision which would inspire employees to engage in new behaviors. In contrast, Lee Iacocca has been a transformational leader at Chrysler by creating a vision, mobilizing employees, and working toward the institutionalization of Chrysler's transition.

Assumption Three: Quick-Fix Leadership Leads to Decline

Overcoming resistance to change requires transformational leadership, not defensive, transactional managers who are in search of the one minute quick fix. The transformational leader needs to avoid the trap of simple, quick-fix solutions to major organizational problems. Today, many versions of this quick-fix mentality abound: the book, *One Minute Manager,* has become a best seller in companies in need of basic transformation.[4] Likewise, *In Search of Excellence* has become a cookbook for change.[5] In fact, a number of CEOs have taken the eight characteristics of the "excellent" companies and are trying to blindly impose them on their organizations without first examining their appropriateness. For example, many faltering organizations try to copy such company practices as Hewlett-Packard's (HP) statement of company values. Because they read that HP has a clearly articulated statement of company values—the HP equivalent of the ten commandments—they want to create their list of ten commandments. The scenario which has been carried

FIGURE 1 • TRANSFORMATIONAL LEADERSHIP

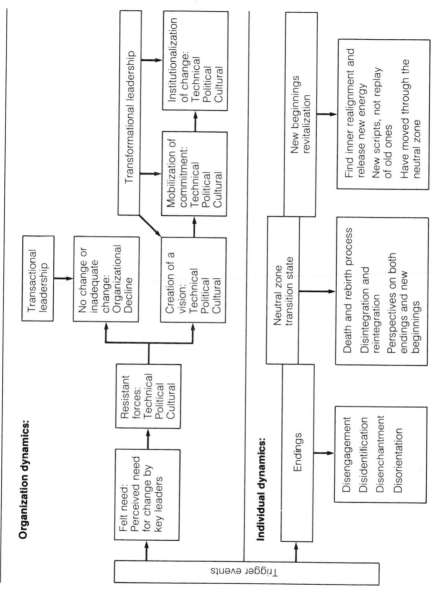

349

out in many major U.S. firms in the past year goes something like this: the CEO wants to develop the company value statement, so he organizes an off-site meeting in order to spend a couple of days developing the company XYZ corporate value statement. The session is usually quite enlightening—managers become quite thoughtful, and soul-searching takes place. At the end of the session, the group is able to list the XYZ company's "ten commandments." The CEO is delighted that they are now well on the way to a major cultural change. He brings the ten commandments back to the corporation and calls in the staff to begin the communication program so that all company employees can learn the new cultural values. This about ends the transformational process.

The problem with the ten-commandments quick fix is that the CEOs tend to overlook the lesson Moses learned several thousand years ago—namely, getting the ten commandments written down and communicated is the easy part; getting them implemented is the challenge. How many thousands of years has it been since Moses received the ten commandments, and yet today there still seems to be an implementation challenge. Transformational leadership is different from defensive, transactional leadership. Lee Iacocca did not have to read about what others did to find a recipe for his company's success.

Assumption Four: Revitalization Requires Transformational Leadership

There are three identifiable programs of activity associated with transformational leadership.

1. *Creation of a Vision.* The transformational leader must provide the organization with a vision of a desired future state. While this task may be shared with other key members of the organization, the vision remains the core responsibility of the transformational leader. The leader needs to integrate analytic, creative, intuitive, and deductive thinking. Each leader must create a vision which gives direction to the organization while being congruent with the leader's and the organization's philosophy and style.

For example, in the early 1980s at GM, after several years of committee work and staff analysis, a vision of the future was drafted which included a mission statement and eight objectives for the company. This statement was the first articulation of a strategic vision for General Motors since Alfred Sloan's leadership. This new vision was developed consistently with the leadership philosophy and style of Roger Smith. Many people were involved in carefully assessing opportunities and constraints for General Motors. Meticulous staff work culminated in committee discussions to evoke agreement and commitment to the mission statement. Through this process a vision was created which paved the way for the next phases of the transformation at GM.

At Chrysler, Lee Iacocca developed a vision without committee work or heavy staff involvement. Instead, he relied more on his intuitive and directive leadership, philosophy, and style. Both GM and Chrysler ended up with a new vision because of transformational leaders proactively shaping a new organization mission and vision. The long-term challenge to organizational revitalization is not "how" the visions are created but the extent to which the visions correctly respond to environmental pressures and transitions within the organization.

2. *Mobilization of Commitment.* Here, the organization, or at least a critical mass of it, accepts the new mission and

vision and makes it happen. At General Motors, Roger Smith took his top 900 executives on a five-day retreat to share and discuss the vision. The event lasted five days not because it takes that long to share a one-paragraph mission statement and eight objectives, but because the process of evolving commitment and mobilizing support requires a great deal of dialogue and exchange. It should be noted that mobilization of commitment must go well beyond five-day retreats; nevertheless, it is in the phase that transformational leaders get deeper understanding of their *followers*. Maccoby acknowledges that leaders who guide organizations through revitalization are distinct from previous leaders and gamesmen who spearheaded managers to be winners in the growth days of the 1960s and early 1970s. Today, Maccoby argues:

> The positive traits of the gamesman, enthusiasm, risk taking, meritocratic fairness, fit America in a period of unlimited economic growth, hunger for novelty, and an unquestioned career ethic. The negative traits for manipulation, seduction, and the perpetual adolescent need for adventure were always problems, causing distrust and unnecessary crises. The gamesman's daring, the willingness to innovate and take risks are still needed. Companies that rely on conservative company men in finance to run technically based organizations (for example, auto and steel) lose the competitive edge. But unless their negative traits are transformed or controlled, even gifted gamesmen become liabilities as leaders in a new economic reality. A period of limited resources and cutbacks, when the team can no longer be controlled by the promise of more, and one person's gains may be another's loss, leadership with values of caring and integrity and a vision of self-development must create the trust that no one will be penalized for cooperation and that sacrifice as well as rewards are equitable.[6]

After transformational leaders create a vision and mobilize commitment, they must determine how to institutionalize the new mission and vision.

3. *Institutionalization of Change*. Organizations will not be revitalized unless new patterns of behavior within the organization are adopted. Transformational leaders need to transmit their vision into reality, their mission into action, their philosophy into practice. New realities, action, and practices must be shared throughout the organization. Alterations in communication, decision making, and problem-solving systems are tools through which transitions are shared so that visions become a reality. At a deeper level, institutionalization of change requires shaping and reinforcement of a new culture that fits with the revitalized organization. The human resource systems of selection, development, appraisal, and reward are major levers for institutionalizing change.

INDIVIDUAL DYNAMICS OF CHANGE

The previous section outlined requisite processes for organizational revitalization. Although organizational steps are necessary, they are not sufficient in creating and implementing change. In managing transitions, a more problematic set of forces which focuses on individual psychodynamics of change must be understood and managed. Major transitions unleash powerful conflicting forces in people. The change invokes simultaneous positive and negative personal feelings of fear and hope, anxiety and relief, pressure and stimulation, leaving the old and accepting a new direction, loss of meaning and new meaning, threat to self-esteem and new sense of value. The challenge for transformational leaders is to recognize these mixed emotions, act to help people move from negative to positive emotions, and mobilize and focus energy that is necessary for individual renewal and organizational revitalization.

Figure 1 provides a set of concepts for understanding the individual dynamics of transitions. The concepts, drawn from the work by Bridges, propose a three-phase process of individual change: first come endings, followed by neutral zones, and then new beginnings.[7] During each of these phases, an identifiable set of psychological tasks can be identified which individuals need to successfully complete in order to accept change.

The Three-Phase Process

Endings. All individual transitions start with endings. Endings must be accepted and understood before transitions can begin. Employees who refuse to accept the fact that traditional behaviors have ended will be unable to adopt new behaviors. The first task is to disengage, which often accompanies a physical transaction. For example, when transferring from one job to another, individuals must learn to accept the new physical setting and disengage from the old position: when transferred employees continually return to visit former colleagues, this is a sign that they have inadequately disengaged. The second task is to disidentify. Individual self-identity is often tied to a job position in such a way that when a plant manager is transferred to corporate staff to work in the marketing department, he or she must disidentify with the plant and its people and with the self-esteem felt as a plant manager. At a deeper personal level, individual transactions require disenchantment. Disenchantment entails recognizing that the enchantment or positive feelings associated with past situations will not be possible to replicate

in the future. Chrysler, GM, AT&T, or U.S. Steel employees who remember the "good old days" need to become disenchanted with those feelings: the present reality is different and self-worth cannot be recaptured by longing for or thinking about the past. A new enchantment centered on new circumstances needs to be built. Finally, individuals need to experience and work through disorientation which reflects the loss of familiar trappings. As mature organizations become revitalized, individuals must disengage, disidentify, disenchant, and disorient with past practices and discover in new organizations a new sense of worth or value.

To help individuals cope with endings, transformational leaders need to replace past glories with future opportunities. However, leaders must also acknowledge individual resistances and senses of loss in a transitional period while encouraging employees to face and accept failures as learning opportunities. Holding on to past accomplishments and memories without coming to grips with failure and the need to change may be why companies such as W.T. Grant, International Harvester, and Braniff were unsuccessful at revitalization. There is a sense of dying in all endings, and it does not help to treat transactions as if the past can be buried without effort. Yet, one should see the past as providing new directions.

Neutral Zone. The key to individuals being able to fully change may be in the second phase which Bridges terms the neutral zone.[8] This phase can be interpreted as a seemingly unproductive "time out" when individuals feel disconnected from people and things of the past and emotionally unconnected with the present. In reality, this phase is a time of reorientation where individuals complete endings and begin new patterns of behavior. Often Western culture, especially in the U.S., avoids this experience and treats the neutral zone like a busy street, to be crossed as fast as possible and certainly not a place to contemplate and experience. However, running across the neutral zone too hurriedly does not allow the ending to occur nor the new beginning to properly start. A death and rebirth process is necessary so that organizational members can work through the disintegration and reintegration. To pass through the neutral zone requires taking the time and thought to gain perspective on both the endings—what went wrong, why it needs to be changed, and what must be overcome in both attitude and behavioral change—and the new beginning—what the new priorities are, why they are needed, and what new attitudes and behaviors will be required. It is in this phase that the most skillful transformational leadership is called upon.

A timid, bureaucratic leader who often reels in the good old days will not provide the needed support to help individuals cross through the neutral zone. On the other hand, the militaristic dictatorial leader who tries to force a "new beginning" and does not allow people to work through their own feelings and emotions may also fail to bring about change. The purported backlash toward the "brash" Archie McGill at American Bell in June 1983 may have been an example of trying to force people through the neutral zone in order to get to a new beginning. Archie McGill was known to rant and rave about the stodgy, old fashioned, and noninnovative "bell-shaped men" at AT&T. While he was trying to help and lead individuals to become innovative and marketing orientated, he may not have allowed them to accept the endings inherent in the transition. Although his enthusiasm may have been well placed,

he may have lacked the sensitivity to individual endings and neutral phases of transactions.

Failure to lead individuals through the neutral zone may result in aborted new beginnings. In 1983, International Harvester appeared to be stuck in the neutral zone. In order for International Harvester to make a new beginning, it must enable people to find a new identification with the future organization while accepting the end of the old organization. Such a transformation has successfully occurred at Chrysler Corporation where morale and esprit de corps grew with the new vision implanted by Lee Iacocca. In the end, organizational revitalization can only occur if individuals accept past failures and engage in new behaviors and attitudes.

New Beginnings. After individuals accept endings by working through neutral zones, they are able to work with new enthusiasm and commitment. New beginnings are characterized by employees learning from the past rather than reveling in it, looking for new scripts rather than acting out old ones, and being positive and excited about current and future work opportunities rather than dwelling on past successes or failures. When Mr. Iacocca implemented his vision at Chrysler, many long-term employees discovered new beginnings. They saw the new Chrysler as an opportunity to succeed, and they worked with a renewed vigor.

WHAT QUALITIES DO TRANSFORMATIONAL LEADERS POSSESS?

So what does it take to transform an organization's technical, political, and cultural systems? The transformational leader must possess a deep understanding, whether it be intuitive or learned, of organizations and their place both in society at large and in the lives of individuals. The ability to build a new institution requires the kind of political dialogue our founding fathers had when Jefferson, Hamilton, Adams, and others debated issues of justice, equity, separation of powers, checks and balances, and freedom. This language may sound foreign to corporate settings but when major organization revitalization is being undertaken, all of these concepts merit some level of examination. At Chrysler, issues of equity, justice, power, and freedom underlay many of Mr. Iacocca's decisions. Thus, as a start, transformational leaders need to understand concepts of equity, power, freedom, and the dynamics of decision making. In addition to modifying systems, transformational leaders must understand and realign cultural systems.

In addition to managing political and cultural systems, transformational leaders must make difficult decisions quickly. Leaders need to know when to push and when to back off. Finally, transformational leaders are often seen as creators of their own luck. These leaders seize opportunities and know when to act so that casual observers may perceive luck as a plausible explanation for their success; whereas, in reality it is a transformational leader who knows when to jump and when not to jump. Again, Mr. Iacocca can be viewed either as a very lucky person or as the possessor of a great ability to judge when to act and when not to act.

THE SIGNIFICANCE OF CORPORATE CULTURES

Much has been written about organizational cultures in recent years.[9] We suggest that every organization has a culture, or a patterned set of activities that reflects the organization's underlying values. Cultures don't occur randomly. They occur because leaders spend time on and reward some behaviors and practices more than others. These practices become the foundation of the organization's culture. At HP, for example, Bill Hewlett and Dave Packard spent time wandering around, informally meeting with and talking to employees. Such leadership behavior set the HP cultural tone of caring about and listening to people. Similarly, Tom Watson, Sr., at IBM spent a great deal of time with customers. His practice led to a company culture of commitment to customers. Indeed, corporate cultures exist. Leaders can shape cultures by carefully monitoring where and how they spend their time and by encouraging and rewarding employees to behave in certain ways.

Culture plays two central roles in organizations. First, it provides organizational members with a way of understanding and making sense of events and symbols. Thus, when employees are confronted with certain complex problems, they "know" how to approach them the "right" way. Like the Eskimos who have a vocabulary that differentiates the five types of snow, organizations create vocabularies to describe how things are done in the organization. At IBM, it is very clear to all insiders how to form a task force and to solve problems since task forces and problem solving are a way of life in IBM's culture.

Second, culture provides meaning. It embodies a set of values which helps justify why certain behaviors are encouraged at the exclusion of other behaviors. Companies with strong cultures have been able to commit people to the organization and have them identify very personally and closely with the organization's success. Superficially, this is seen in the "hoopla" activities associated with an IBM sales meeting, a

Tupperware party, or an Amway distributor meeting. Outsiders often ridicule such activities, yet they are part of the process by which some successful companies manage cultural meaning. On one level, corporate culture is analogous to rituals carried out in religious groups. The key point in assessing culture is to realize that in order to transform an organization the culture that provides meaning must be assessed and revamped. The transformational leader needs to articulate new values and norms and then to use multiple change levers ranging from role modeling, symbolic acts, creation of rituals, and revamping of human resource systems and management processes to support new cultural messages.

CONCLUSION

Based on the premise that the pressure for basic organizational change will intensify and not diminish, we strongly believe that transformational leadership, not transactional management, is required for revitalizing our organizations. Ultimately, it is up to our leaders to choose the right kind of leadership and corporate lifestyle.

REFERENCES

1. See J. M. Burns, *Leadership* (New York: Harper & Row, 1978).

2. See N. M. Tichy, *Managing Strategic Change: Technical, Political and Cultural Dynamics* (New York: John Wiley & Sons, 1983).

3. Ibid.

4. See K. H. Blanchard and S. Johnson, *The One Minute Manager* (New York: Berkeley Books, 1982).

5. See T. J. Peters and R. J. Waterman, Jr., *In Search of Excellence* (New York: Harper & Row, 1982).

6. See M. Maccoby, *The Leader* (New York: Ballantine Books, 1981).

7. See W. Bridges, *Making Sense of Life's Transitions* (New York: Addison-Wesley, 1980).

8. Ibid.

9. See: T. E. Deal and A. A. Kennedy, *Corporate Cultures* (Reading, MA: Addison-Wesley, 1982); "Corporate Culture: The Hard-to-Change Values That Spell Success or Failure," *Business Week*, 27 October 1980, pp. 148–160; W. Ulrich, "HRM and Culture: History, Rituals, and Myths," *Human Resource Management* (23/2) Summer 1984.

CHAPTER IV

People in Organizations: The Context

In 1959, Warren Bennis observed that such classical organization theorists as Frederick Winslow Taylor, Henry Gantt, and Henri Fayol (see Shafritz & Ott, 1987, Chapter I) were fixated on structural variables (such as the chain of command, centralization and decentralization, and span of control) to the extent that they almost seem to think about "organizations without people." In contrast, the human relations-oriented organizational behaviorists of the late 1950s and 1960s were so enamored with people and groups (with personal growth, group development, sensitivity training groups, and human relations training) that they seemed to think only about "people without organizations." Bennis's observation was equally applicable to the early industrial/organizational psychologists—to the pre-Hawthorne and pre-Theory X and Theory Y value system-based social scientists who worked with organizational behavior, but not from an organizational behavior perspective (see the *Introduction*). However, between the 1930s and the 1950s and 1960s, *organizational behavior* reversed its field and in the process almost forgot (or at least ignored) the substantial influences that organization systems and structures have on the people and groups in and around them.

Many things in the organizational context influence and are influenced by organizational behavior. To list only a few:

- *The type of business in which an organization is engaged.* The business of banking places different demands on and yields different rewards to employees than does making and marketing new television game shows.
- *The legal relationship between an organization and people who work for it.* Typically, there are different impacts on organizational behavior in, for example, a family-owned business, a publicly held investor-owned company, a nonprofit organization, and a government agency.
- *The nature of the perceived relationships between an organization and its environment at large.* The prevailing perception in some organizations seems to be that they exist in a hostile world, where the media, general public, other types of organizations (such as government agencies, legislatures, or private corporations), and sometimes even clientele or customers (as well as direct competitors) all are immediate or potential enemies or threats. In contrast,

356

the prevailing view in other organizations is more one of the organization existing in harmony with its environment.
* *The structure of the organization*—the subject of this chapter.

This chapter primarily addresses structure, specifically how organization structure affects organizational behavior. The decision to so limit the discussion and articles requires the chapter to exclude the external environment (Dill, 1958; Churchman, 1968; Galbraith, 1973), and take a *closed system* rather than an *open system* view of organization (Shafritz & Ott, 1987, Chapter IV). This allows us to concentrate on a single viewpoint of organizational structure.

When someone refers to organization structure, usually he or she is talking about the relatively stable relationships among the positions or groups of positions (such as the units, divisions, and departments) that comprise an organization, along with the organized procedures and methods that define how things are designed for work to flow through it. Structure is the design of an organization, its units, and its production processes. It is the set of specific patterns of differentiation and integration of tasks and activities in an organization (Thompson, 1967; Miles, 1980). *Differentiation* is the (conceptual) dividing up of a total system into its component parts (units, groups, and people) which perform specialized tasks. (In essence, *differentiation* is a more sophisticated way of saying *division of labor*). *Integration* is how the divided-up parts and specialized tasks are linked together to form a coordinated whole.

To be more concrete, a widely read article by Lyman Porter and Edward Lawler (1965) identifies the properties of organization structure that, according to an extensive search of the then published literature, most affect individual and group attitudes and on-the-job behavior. Their list of structural properties includes:

* *Organization levels* (the number of levels and in which one—or how high—one is situated),
* *Line or staff* roles of organization units,
* *Span of control,*
* *Size of units,*
* *Size of the total organization,*
* *Organization shape* (flat or tall), and
* *Centralized or decentralized* authority and responsibility.

The structure—an organization's shape, size, procedures, production technology, position descriptions, reporting arrangements, and coordinating relationships—affects the feelings and emotions, and therefore the behavior of the people and groups inside them. There are incongruencies between the needs of a mature personality and of formal organization—between the growth trends of healthy people and the requirements of organizations (Argyris, 1957b). The impacts of structure on behavior partially result from the unique functions structure performs. In each organization, structure defines the unique ways labor is divided, how specialized roles and functions are to be coordinated (related to each other and to other organizational levels and functions), how information is to flow among people and groups, and how the system of controls (how tasks are measured, evaluated, and altered) is to work (Organ & Bateman, 1986). Structure establishes how *roles, expectations,* and *resource allocations* are defined for people and groups in any given organization. Structure is a primary reason why *organizational behavior* differs from mere *behavior,* and thus why organizational behavior developed as a separate field of study within the applied behavioral sciences.

The first article in this chapter is Robert Merton's (1940, 1957) analysis of how one form of organization structure—*bureaucracy*—impinges on the personalities of people who work inside them. Merton uses *bureaucracy* to mean the pervasive form of organization that Max Weber (1922) described in *Wirtschat und Gesellschaft.* In this use, *bureaucracy* is neither an epithet per se, nor is it limited in applicability to government agencies. According to Merton, bureaucracy exerts constant pressures on people to be methodical and disciplined, to conform to patterns of obligations. These pressures eventually cause people to adhere to rules as an end rather than a means—as a matter of blind conformance. Bureaucratic structure also stresses depersonalized relations, and power and authority gained by virtue of organizational position rather than by thought or action. Without question, Merton sees bureaucratic structure as more than *affecting* organizational behavior and thinking: it also *determines and controls.* As a form of organization, bureaucracy has its advantages: order, predictability, stability, professionalism, and consistency (Shafritz & Ott, 1987, Chapter I). Nevertheless, the behavioral consequences of bureaucratic structure are mostly negative, including reduced organizational flexibility and efficiency and, adapting a phrase coined by Merton, eventually *bureaupathological personalities* of members.

Sociotechnical systems is commonly used to mean the interactive relationships or the *fit* between work technology, organization structure, and social interactions of the workplace. Most sociotechnical system studies involve investigations of how work processes (technology) and work teams (social systems) can be structured (organization) to maximize productivity and at the same time satisfy employees' desires for affiliation and, in some work settings, needs for safety that only close groups can provide. The Tavistock Institute of London has been closely identified with *sociotechnical systems* research and consulting since the 1950s. The best known of the Tavistock sociotechnical systems studies have been set in British coal mines (Trist and Bamforth, 1951; Trist, Higgin, Murray & Pollock, 1965) and weaving mills of India (Rice, 1953). These studies became the forerunners of many widely publicized sociotechnical systems-style work reorganization efforts, such as in the Scandinavian automobile industry (Thorsrud, 1968); "Procter & Gamble's plant in Lima, Ohio; Alcan's cold rolling mill in Quebec; Shell's refinery in Teesport, England; and Norsk Hydro's fertilizer plant in Porsgrunn, Norway" (Walton, 1975, p. 117).

Whereas Robert Merton was interested in the effects of bureaucratic structure on personality, Eric Trist, Kenneth Bamforth, and their associates at the Tavistock Institute studied the links between work technology, organization structure, and social structure. In their famous 1951 article, "Some Social and Psychological Consequences of the Longwall Method of Coal-Getting" (reprinted in this chapter), Trist and Bamforth found that management's attempts to increase coal mining productivity by moving to the *longwall method* (a technology analogous to mass production) had very negative repercussions. At the time of its introduction in the late 1940s, the longwall method of coal-getting represented a major technological improvement. Prior to that time, coal had been mined by self-selecting, highly mutually supportive, self-regulating small groups (often pairs) who performed the entire cycle of extraction operations. The pairs faced grave dangers together working far under the earth, watched out for each other, and jointly decided when to change working places and procedures in the face of dangers. The pair system also provided each man with someone to talk with about fears and anxieties.

The longwall method changed everything. Miners no longer worked in long-established small groups. They worked in long lines, using new machinery that required them to face the wall, with a substantial distance between each man. When work pressure increased, there was no close associate to talk with about stress and anxiety or even people close enough for bantering. Introduction of the new structural and technological systems destroyed important social systems; hence, productivity and morale became major problems. "It is difficult to see how these problems can be solved effectively without restoring responsible autonomy to primary groups throughout the system and ensuring that each of these groups has a satisfying subwhole as its work task, and some scope for flexibility in workpace" (Trist & Bamforth, 1951, p. 38). The longwall coal study, along with several other socio-technical system studies that appeared at about the same time (for example, Jaques, 1950; Rice, 1953; Rice, Hill & Trist, 1950), represented a major turning point in the *practice* of organizational behavior. The coal companies *listened* to the workers (through the reporting of the behavioral scientists) and modified the technical system to mesh with the workers' social system needs.

In an earlier article, Robert Merton questions the long-term impacts of organizations' conformity requirements on the personalities—*the beingness*—of organization members. The concluding chapter of *The Organization Man* (1956), by William H. Whyte, Jr., which is reprinted here, returns us to Merton's question. In 1954, this nation had been shaken, perhaps as never before, by the apparent ease with which the Chinese had succeeded in "brainwashing" U.S. prisoners of war in Korea. For the first time in this nation's history, some of our soldiers, who were only required to provide captors with their "name, rank, and serial number" (under international agreement), aided their Chinese captors by identifying informal leaders among their fellow prisoners, revealing prisoner escape plans, confessing to illegal and immoral actions supposedly taken against the Chinese, and publicly denouncing the United States. Two years later Whyte's book, which culminated several years of research into the willingness of several hundred young U.S. managers to conform to organizational and role expectations, exploded onto the national scene. Where was America's rugged individualism? Had we become a nation of sheep?

Whyte quotes from Alexis de Tocqueville's *Democracy in America* (1847): If America ever destroyed its genius, "it would be . . . by making the individual come to regard himself as a hostage to prevailing opinion, by creating, in sum, a tyranny of the majority" (Whyte, 1956, p. 396). Whyte asserts this is occurring with the *Corporate American, the organization man of today:* "He is not only other-directed, to borrow David Riesman's concept, he is articulating a philosophy which tells him it is right to be that way" (p. 396). When Whyte wrote *The Organization Man,* he was not pessimistic about peoples' abilities to withstand pressures to conform. Quite the contrary—despite the evidence of his research. His solution lies in:

- Increased consciousness of the worth of individualism;
- Reexamination of the worth of designing work to allow individuals to be involved in a total effort, not just to increase efficiency or effectiveness, but also to allow individuals to build self-respect;
- Reduced amounts of time people at work spend in meetings. Require people to think creatively at least some of the time; and
- Reduced emphasis on professionals being "company men"—on organizational commitment. Instead, increase peoples' allegiances to their career. (Also see the article in this chapter by Alvin Gouldner.)

Despite Whyte's professed lack of pessimism, he concludes on a less than optimistic note. "[The organization man] must *fight* the organization . . . for the demands for his surrender are constant and powerful, and the more he has come to like the life of organization the more difficult does he find it to resist these demands, or even to recognize them. . . . The peace of mind offered by organization remains a surrender, and no less so for being offered in benevolence. That is the problem" (p. 404). Thirty years later, in the 1980s, many of Whyte's themes and warnings are reappearing in the literature of the *organizational culture perspective* of organization theory (Ott, 1989).

Alvin Gouldner's (1957) legendary analysis, "Cosmopolitans and Locals: Toward an Analysis of Latent Social Roles—I, "also provides important insights about coping with organizational pressures to conform, even though this was not Gouldner's primary purpose in writing the article. "Cosmopolitans and Locals," which is included in this chapter, identifies two types of latent organizational roles or identities, *cosmopolitans* and *locals.* The important reference groups and orientations for *locals* are *inside* the organization, whereas for *cosmopolitans* they are *outside* (usually in their profession). Gouldner's study found differences between cosmopolitans and locals in terms of their degree of influenceability, level of participation in the organization, willingness to accept organizational rules, and informal relations at work. If our primary orientations and reference groups are outside of our employing organization, we are more inclined to retain our individuality, and less willing to commit ourselves to the organization—to allow it to attempt to influence how we think and act.

The final selection of the chapter, "'Democracy' as Hierarchy and Alienation," by Frederick Thayer (1981), poses a potent but simple hypothesis: People in organizations are alienated by hierarchy. "The fundamental source of alienation is *hierarchy* . . ." (p. 46). By definition, hierarchical relations are impersonal. "Interactions within any hierarchical structure are those of *ruling* and *being ruled, issuing commands* and *obeying them, repressing* and *being repressed*" (p. 52). Employee alienation can be ended by eradicating hierarchy, and alienation cannot be eradicated so long as hierarchy remains. "Where hierarchy is concerned, then, there is no choice between Ellul, Marx, and others. All of them accept hierarchy, and their proposed cures for alienation involve only more of the same" (p. 52).

This chapter demonstrates how the structural impacts of organizational contexts affect the thinking and behavior of individuals and groups. Robert Merton and William Whyte examine organizational control over human lives and question whether we can withstand organizational pressures to conform. Frederick Thayer contends that hierarchy and alienation are inseparable. Trist and Bamforth report on how changing the technology of coal mining caused changes in organizational structure and, in turn, broke down functionally important social systems. Alvin Gouldner reports on how the one's basic career orientation and reference group choice allows or restricts one's psychological freedom inside an organization. Five very different, fascinating—and in some cases, controversial—articles about effects of structural organizational context on behavior in organizations.

REFERENCES

Argyris, C. (1957a). *Personality and organization.* New York: Harper.

Argyris, C. (1957b). The individual and organization: Some problems of mutual adjustment. *Administrative Science Quarterly, 2,* 1–24.

Bennis, W. G. (1959). Leadership theory and administrative behavior: The problem of authority. *Administrative Science Quarterly, 4,* 259–301.

Churchman, C. W. (1968). *The systems approach.* New York: Dell Books.

Dalton, M. (June, 1950). Conflicts between staff and line managerial officers. *American Sociological Review, 15,* 342–351.

Dalton, M. (1959). *Men who manage.* New York: John Wiley.

Dill, W. R. (1958). Environment as an influence on managerial autonomy. *Administrative Science Quarterly, 2,* 409–443.

Entwisle, D., & Walton, J. (1961). Observations on the span of control. *Administrative Science Quarterly, 5,* 522–533.

Galbraith, J. R. (1973). *Designing complex organizations.* Reading, MA: Addison-Wesley Publishing.

Gouldner, A. W. (December, 1957). Cosmopolitans and locals: Toward an analysis of latent social roles—I. *Administrative Science Quarterly, 2*(3).

Hall, R. H. (1972). *Organizations: Structure and process.* Englewood Cliffs, NJ: Prentice-Hall.

Herzberg, F., Mausner, B., & Snyderman, B. (1959). *The motivation to work* (2d ed.). New York: John Wiley.

Jaques, E. (1950). Collaborative group methods in a wage negotiation situation (The Glacier Project—I). *Human Relations, 3*(3).

Katz, D., & Kahn, R. L. (1966). *The social psychology of organizations.* New York: John Wiley & Sons.

Lawrence, P. R. (1958). *The changing of organizational behavior patterns: A case study of de-*

centralization. Cambridge, MA: Harvard University, Graduate School of Business Administration.

Merton, R. K. (1957). Bureaucratic structure and personality. In, R. K. Merton, *Social theory and social structure* (rev. & enl. ed.). New York: The Free Press. A revised version of an article of the same title that appeared in *Social Forces, 18* (1940).

Miles, R. H. (1980). *Macro organizational behavior.* Santa Monica, CA: Goodyear Publishing.

Mills, T. (October, 1976). Altering the social structure in coal mining: A case study. *Monthly Labor Review,* 3–10.

Organ, D. W., & Bateman, T. (1986). *Organizational behavior: An applied psychological approach* (3rd ed.). Plano, TX: Business Publications, Inc.

Ott, J. S. (1989). *The organizational culture perspective.* Chicago: The Dorsey Press.

Porter, L. W. (1962). Job attitudes in management: I. Perceived deficiencies in need fulfillment as a function of job level. *Journal of Applied Psychology, 46,* 375–384.

Porter, L. W., & Lawler, E. E., III. (1964). The effects of tall vs. flat organization structures on managerial job satisfaction. *Personnel Psychology, 17,* 135–148.

Porter, L. W., & Lawler, E. E., III. (1965). Properties of organization structure in relation to job attitudes and job behavior. *Psychological Bulletin, 64*(1), 23–51.

Rice, A. K. (1953). Productivity and social organization in an Indian weaving shed: An examination of some aspects of the sociotechnical system of an experimental automatic loom shed. *Human Relations, 6,* 297–329.

Rice, A. K., Hill, J. M. M., & Trist, E. L. (1950). The representation of labour turnover as a social process (The Glacier Project—II). *Human Relations, 3*(4).

Shafritz, J. M., & Ott, J. S. (1987). *Classics of organization theory* (2d ed.). Chicago: The Dorsey Press.

Thayer, F. C. (1981). *An end to hierarchy and competition: Administration in the post–affluent world* (2d ed.). New York: New Viewpoints.

Thompson, J. D. (1967). *Organizations in action.* New York: McGraw-Hill.

Thorsrud, D. E. (1968). Sociotechnical approach to job design and organization development. *Management International Review, 8,* 120–131.

Tocqueville, A. de (1847). *Democracy in America* (7th ed.). New York: Walker.

Trist, E. L. (1960). *Socio-technical systems.* London: Tavistock Institute of Human Relations.

Trist, E. L., & Bamforth, K. (1951). Some social and psychological consequences of the longwall method of coal-getting. *Human Relations, 4,* 3–38.

Trist, E. L., Higgin, G. W., Murray, H., & Pollock, A. B. (1965). *Organizational choice.* London: Tavistock Institute of Human Relations.

Walton, R. E. (1975). From Hawthorne to Topeka and Kalmar. In, E. L. Cass & F. G. Zimmer (Eds.), *Man and work in society* (pp. 116–129). New York: Western Electric Co.

Weber, M. (1922). Bureaucracy. In, H. Gerth & C. W. Mills (Eds.), *Max Weber: Essays in sociology.* Oxford, U.K.: Oxford University Press.

Whyte, W. F. (1961). *Men at work.* Homewood, IL: The Dorsey Press.

Whyte, W. H., Jr. (1956). *The organization man.* New York: Simon and Schuster.

Worthy, J. C. (1950). Organizational structure and employee morale. *American Sociological Review, 15,* 169–179.

26
Bureaucratic Structure and Personality
Robert K. Merton

A formal, rationally organized social structure involves clearly defined patterns of activity in which, ideally, every series of actions is functionally related to the purposes of the organization.[1] In such an organization there is integrated a series of offices, of hierarchized statuses, in which inhere a number of obligations and privileges closely defined by limited and specific rules. Each of these offices contains an area of imputed competence and responsibility. Authority, the power of control which derives from an acknowledged status, inheres in the office and not in the particular person who performs the official role. Official action ordinarily occurs within the framework of preexisting rules of the organization. The system of prescribed relations between the various offices involves a considerable degree of formality and clearly defined social distance between the occupants of these positions. Formality is manifested by means of a more or less complicated social ritual which symbolizes and supports the pecking order of the various offices. Such formality, which is integrated with the distribution of authority within the system, serves to minimize friction by largely restricting (official) contact to modes which are previously defined by the rules of the organization. Ready calculability of others' behavior and a stable set of mutual expectations is thus built up. Moreover, formality facilitates the interaction of the occu-

pants of offices despite their (possibly hostile) private attitudes toward one another. In this way, the subordinate is protected from the arbitrary action of his superior, since the actions of both are constrained by a mutually recognized set of rules. Specific procedural devices foster objectivity and restrain the "quick passage of impulse into action."[2]

THE STRUCTURE OF BUREAUCRACY

The ideal type of such formal organization is bureaucracy and, in many respects, the classical analysis of bureaucracy is that by Max Weber.[3] As Weber indicates, bureaucracy involves a clear-cut division of integrated activities which are regarded as duties inherent in the office. A system of differentiated controls and sanctions is stated in the regulations. The assignment of roles occurs on the basis of technical qualifications which are ascertained through formalized, impersonal procedures (*e.g.*, examinations). Within the structure of hierarchically arranged authority, the activities of "trained and salaried experts" are governed by general, abstract, and clearly defined rules which preclude the necessity for the issuance of specific instructions for each specific case. The generality of the rules requires the constant use of *categorization*, whereby individual problems and cases are

Source: Reprinted with permission of The Free Press, a Division of MacMillan, Inc., from *Social Theory and Social Structure*, revised and enlarged edition, by Robert K. Merton. Copyright © 1957 by The Free Press, renewed 1985 by Robert K. Merton.

classified on the basis of designated criteria and are treated accordingly. The pure type of bureaucratic official is appointed, either by a superior or through the exercise of impersonal competition; he is not elected. A measure of flexibility in the bureaucracy is attained by electing higher functionaries who presumably express the will of the electorate (*e.g.*, a body of citizens or a board of directors). The election of higher officials is designed to affect the purposes of the organization, but the technical procedures for attaining these ends are carried out by continuing bureaucratic personnel.[4]

Most bureaucratic offices involve the expectation of life-long tenure, in the absence of disturbing factors which may decrease the size of the organization. Bureaucracy maximizes vocational security.[5] The function of security of tenure, pensions, incremental salaries and regularized procedures for promotion is to ensure the devoted performance of official duties, without regard for extraneous pressures.[6] The chief merit of bureaucracy is its technical efficiency, with a premium placed on precision, speed, expert control, continuity, discretion, and optimal returns on input. The structure is one which approaches the complete elimination of personalized relationships and nonrational considerations (hostility, anxiety, affectual involvements, etc.).

With increasing bureaucratization, it becomes plain to all who would see that man is to a very important degree controlled by his social relations to the instruments of production. This can no longer seem only a tenet of Marxism, but a stubborn fact to be acknowledged by all, quite apart from their ideological persuasion. Bureaucratization makes readily visible what was previously dim and obscure. More and more people discover that to work, they must

be employed. For to work, one must have tools and equipment. And the tools and equipment are increasingly available only in bureaucracies, private or public. Consequently, one must be employed by the bureaucracies in order to have access to tools in order to work in order to live. It is in this sense that bureaucratization entails separation of individuals from the instruments of production, as in modern capitalistic enterprise or in state communistic enterprise (of the midcentury variety), just as in the postfeudal army, bureaucratization entailed complete separation from the instruments of destruction. Typically, the worker no longer owns his tools nor the soldier, his weapons. And in this special sense, more and more people become workers, either blue collar or white collar or stiff shirt. So develops, for example, the new type of scientific worker, as the scientist is "separated" from his technical equipment—after all, the physicist does not ordinarily own his cyclotron. To work at his research, he must be employed by a bureaucracy with laboratory resources.

Bureaucracy is administration which almost completely avoids public discussion of its techniques, although there may occur public discussion of its policies.[7] This secrecy is confined neither to public nor to private bureaucracies. It is held to be necessary to keep valuable information from private economic competitors or from foreign and potentially hostile political groups. And though it is not often so called, espionage among competitors is perhaps as common, if not as intricately organized, in systems of private economic enterprise as in systems of national states. Cost figures, lists of clients, new technical processes, plans for production—all these are typically regarded as essential secrets of private economic bureaucracies which might be revealed if the bases of all decisions and policies had to be publicly defended.

THE DYSFUNCTIONS OF BUREAUCRACY

In these bold outlines, the positive attainments and functions of bureaucratic organization are emphasized and the internal stresses and strains of such structures are almost wholly neglected. The community at large, however, evidently emphasizes the imperfections of bureaucracy, as is suggested by the fact that the "horrid hybrid," bureaucrat, has become an epithet, a *Schimpfwort*.

The transition to a study of the negative aspects of bureaucracy is afforded by the application of Veblen's concept of "trained incapacity," Dewey's notion of "occupational psychosis" or Warnotte's view of "professional deformation." Trained incapacity refers to that state of affairs in which one's abilities function as inadequacies or blind spots. Actions based upon training and skills which have been successfully applied in the past may result in inappropriate responses *under changed conditions*. An inadequate flexibility in the application of skills, will, in a changing milieu, result in more or less serious maladjustments.[8] Thus, to adopt a barnyard illustration used in this connection by Burke, chickens may be readily conditioned to interpret the sound of a bell as a signal for food. The same bell may now be used to summon the trained chickens to their doom as they are assembled to suffer decapitation. In general, one adopts measures in keeping with one's past training and, under new conditions which are not recognized as *significantly* different, the very soundness of this training may lead to the adoption of the wrong procedures. Again, in Burke's almost echolalic phrase, "people may be unfitted by being fit in an unfit

fitness"; their training may become an incapacity.

Dewey's concept of occupational psychosis rests upon much the same observations. As a result of their day to day routines, people develop special preferences, antipathies, discriminations and emphases.[9] (The term psychosis is used by Dewey to denote a "pronounced character of the mind.") These psychoses develop through demands put upon the individual by the particular organization of his occupational role.

The concepts of both Veblen and Dewey refer to a fundamental ambivalence. Any action can be considered in terms of what it attains or what it fails to attain. "A way of seeing is also a way of not seeing—a focus upon object A involves a neglect of object B."[10] In his discussion, Weber is almost exclusively concerned with what the bureaucratic structure attains: precision, reliability, efficiency. This same structure may be examined from another perspective provided by the ambivalence. What are the limitations of the organizations designed to attain these goals?

For reasons which we have already noted, the bureaucratic structure exerts a constant pressure upon the official to be "methodical, prudent, disciplined." If the bureaucracy is to operate successfully, it must attain a high degree of reliability of behavior, an unusual degree of conformity with prescribed patterns of action. Hence, the fundamental importance of discipline which may be as highly developed in a religious or economic bureaucracy as in the army. Discipline can be effective only if the ideal patterns are buttressed by strong sentiments which entail devotion to one's duties, a keen sense of the limitation of one's authority and competence, and methodical performance of routine activities. The efficacy of social structure depends ultimately upon infusing group participants with appropriate attitudes and sentiments. As we shall see, there are definite arrangements in the bureaucracy for inculcating and reinforcing these sentiments.

At the moment, it suffices to observe that in order to ensure discipline (the necessary reliability of response), these sentiments are often more intense than is technically necessary. There is a margin of safety, so to speak, in the pressure exerted by these sentiments upon the bureaucrat to conform to his patterned obligations, in much the same sense that added allowances (precautionary overestimations) are made by the engineer in designing the supports for a bridge. But this very emphasis leads to a transference of the sentiments from the *aims* of the organization onto the particular details of behavior required by the rules. Adherence to the rules, originally conceived as a means, becomes transformed into an end-in-itself; there occurs the familiar process of *displacement of goals* whereby "an instrumental value becomes a terminal value."[11] Discipline, readily interpreted as conformance with regulations, whatever the situation, is seen not as a measure designed for specific purposes but becomes an immediate value in the life-organization of the bureaucrat. This emphasis, resulting from the displacement of the original goals, develops into rigidities and an inability to adjust readily. Formalism, even ritualism, ensues with an unchallenged insistence upon punctilious adherence to formalized procedures.[12] This may be exaggerated to the point where primary concern with conformity to the rules interferes with the achievement of the purposes of the organization, in which case we have the familiar phenomenon of the technicism or red tape of the official. An extreme product of this process of displacement of goals is the bureaucratic virtuoso,

who never forgets a single rule binding his action and hence is unable to assist many of his clients.[13] A case in point, where strict recognition of the limits of authority and literal adherence to rules produced this result, is the pathetic plight of Bernt Balchen, Admiral Byrd's pilot in the flight over the South Pole.

> According to a ruling of the department of labor Bernt Balchen . . . cannot receive his citizenship papers. Balchen, a native of Norway, declared his intention in 1927. It is held that he has failed to meet the condition of five years' continuous residence in the United States. The Byrd antarctic voyage took him out of the country, although he was on a ship carrying the American flag, was an invaluable member of the American expedition, and in a region to which there is an American claim because of the exploration and occupation of it by Americans, this region being Little America.
>
> The bureau of naturalization explains that it cannot proceed on the assumption that Little America is American soil. That would be *trespass on international questions* where it has no sanction. So far as the bureau is concerned, Balchen was out of the country and *technically* has not complied with the law of naturalization.[14]

STRUCTURAL SOURCES OF OVERCONFORMITY

Such inadequacies in orientation which involve trained incapacity clearly derive from structural sources. The process may be briefly recapitulated. (1) An effective bureaucracy demands reliability of response and strict devotion to regulations. (2) Such devotion to the rules leads to their transformation into absolutes; they are no longer conceived as relative to a set of purposes. (3) This interferes with ready adaptation under special conditions not clearly envisaged by those who drew up the general rules. (4) Thus, the very elements which conduce toward efficiency in general produce inefficiency in specific instances. Full realization of the inadequacy is seldom attained by members of the group who have not divorced themselves from the meanings which the rules have for them. These rules in time become symbolic in cast, rather than strictly utilitarian.

Thus far, we have treated the ingrained sentiments making for rigorous discipline simply as data, as given. However, definite features of the bureaucratic structure may be seen to conduce to these sentiments. The bureaucrat's official life is planned for him in terms of a graded career, through the organizational devices of promotion by seniority, pensions, incremental salaries, etc., all of which are designed to provide incentives for disciplined action and conformity to the official regulations.[15] The official is tacitly expected to and largely does adapt his thoughts, feelings and actions to the prospect of this career. But *these very devices* which increase the probability of conformance also lead to an over-concern with strict adherence to regulations which induces timidity, conservatism, and technicism. Displacement of sentiments from goals onto means is fostered by the tremendous symbolic significance of the means (rules).

Another feature of the bureaucratic structure tends to produce much the same result. Functionaries have the sense of a common destiny for all those who work together. They share the same interests, especially since there is relatively little competition in so far as promotion is in terms of seniority. Ingroup aggression is thus minimized and this arrangement is therefore conceived to be positively functional for the bureaucracy. However, the *esprit de corps* and informal social organization which typically develops in such situations often leads the personnel to defend their entrenched interests rather than to assist their clientele and elected higher officials. As President Lowell reports, if the bureaucrats believe that their status is not adequately recognized by an incoming elected official, detailed information will be withheld from him, leading him to errors for which he is held responsible. Or, if he seeks to dominate fully, and thus violates the sentiment of self-integrity of the bureaucrats, he may have documents brought to him in such numbers that he cannot manage to sign them all, let alone read them.[16] This illustrates the defensive informal organization which tends to arise whenever there is an apparent threat to the integrity of the group.[17]

It would be much too facile and partly erroneous to attribute such resistance by bureaucrats simply to vested interests. Vested interests oppose any new order which either eliminates or at least makes uncertain their differential advantage deriving from the current arrangements. This is undoubtedly involved in part in bureaucratic resistance to change but another process is perhaps more significant. As we have seen, bureaucratic officials affectively identify themselves with their way of life. They have a pride of craft which leads them to resist change in established routines; at least, those changes which are felt to be imposed by others. This nonlogical pride of craft is a familiar pattern found even, to judge from Sutherland's *Professional Thief,* among pickpockets who, despite the risk, delight in mastering the prestige-bearing feat of "beating a left breech" (picking the left front trousers pocket).

In a stimulating paper, Hughes has applied the concepts of "secular" and "sacred" to various types of division of labor; "the sacredness" of caste and *Stände* prerogatives contrasts sharply with the increasing secularism of occupational differentiation in our society.[18] However, as our discussion suggests, there may ensue, in particular vocations and in particular types of organization, the *process of sanctification* (viewed as the counterpart of the process of secularization). This is to say that through sentiment-formation, emotional dependence upon bureaucratic symbols and status, and affective involvement in spheres of competence and authority, there develop prerogatives involving attitudes of moral legitimacy which are established as values in their own right, and are no longer viewed as merely technical means for expediting administration. One may note a tendency for certain bureaucratic norms, originally introduced for technical reasons, to become rigidified and sacred, although, as Durkheim would say, they are *laïque en apparence*.[19] Durkheim has touched on this general process in his description of the attitudes and values which persist in the organic solidarity of a highly differentiated society.

PRIMARY VERSUS SECONDARY RELATIONS

Another feature of the bureaucratic structure, the stress on depersonalization of relationships, also plays its part in the bureaucrat's trained incapacity. The personality pattern of the bureaucrat is nucleated about this norm of impersonality. Both this and the categorizing tendency, which develops from the dominant role of general, abstract rules, tend to produce conflict in the bureaucrat's contacts with the public or clientele. Since functionaries minimize personal relations and resort to categorization, the peculiarities of individual cases are often ignored. But the client who, quite understandably, is convinced of the special features of *his* own problem often objects to such categorical treatment. Stereotyped behavior is not adapted to the exigencies of individual problems. The impersonal treatment of affairs which are at times of great personal significance to the client gives rise to the charge of "arrogance" and "haughtiness" of the bureaucrat. Thus, at the Greenwich Employment Exchange, the unemployed worker who is securing his insurance payment resents what he deems to be "the impersonality and, at times, the apparent abruptness and even harshness of his treatment by the clerks. . . . Some men complain of the superior attitude which the clerks have."[20]

Still another source of conflict with the public derives from the bureaucratic structure. The bureaucrat, in part irrespective of his position with*in* the hierarchy, acts as a representative of the power and prestige of the entire structure. In his official role he is vested with definite authority. This often leads to an actually or apparently domineering attitude, which may only be exaggerated by a discrepancy between his position within the hierarchy and his position with reference to the public.[21] Protest and recourse to other officials on the part of the client are often ineffective or largely precluded by the previously mentioned *esprit de corps* which joins the officials into a more or less solidary in-group. This source of conflict *may* be minimized in private enterprise since the client can register an effective protest by transferring his trade to another organization within the competitive system. But with the monopolistic nature of the public organization, no such alternative is possible. Moreover, in this case, tension is increased because of a discrepancy between ideology and fact: the governmental personnel are held to be "servants of the people," but in fact they are often superordinate, and release of tension can seldom be afforded by turning to other agencies for the necessary service.[22] This tension is in part attributable to the confusion of the status of bureaucrat and client; the client may consider himself socially superior to the official who is at the moment dominant.[23]

Thus, with respect to the relations between officials and clientele, one structural source of conflict is the pressure for formal and impersonal treatment when individual, personalized consideration is desired by the client. The conflict may be viewed, then, as deriving from the introduction of inappropriate attitudes and relationships. Conflict *within* the bureaucratic structure arises from the converse situation, namely, when personalized relationships are substituted for the structurally required impersonal relationships. This type of conflict may be characterized as follows.

The bureaucracy, as we have seen, is organized as a secondary, formal group. The normal responses involved in this organized network of social expectations are supported by affective attitudes of members of the group. Since the group is oriented toward secondary norms of impersonality, any failure to conform to these norms will arouse antagonism from those who have identified themselves with the legitimacy of these rules. Hence, the substitution of personal for impersonal treatment within the structure is met with widespread disapproval and is characterized by such epithets as graft, favoritism, nepotism, apple-polishing, etc. These epithets are clearly manifestations of injured sentiments.[24] The function of such virtually automatic resentment can be clearly seen in terms of the requirements of bureaucratic structure.

Bureaucracy is a secondary group structure designed to carry on certain activities which cannot be satisfactorily performed on the basis of primary group criteria.[25] Hence behavior which runs counter to these formalized norms becomes the object of emotionalized disapproval. This constitutes a functionally significant defence set up against tendencies which jeopardize the performance of socially necessary activities. To be sure, these reactions are not rationally determined practices explicitly designed for the fulfillment of this function. Rather, viewed in terms of the individual's interpretation of the situation, such resentment is simply an immediate response opposing the "dishonesty" of those who violate the rules of the game. However, this subjective frame of reference notwithstanding, these reactions serve the latent function of maintaining the essential structural elements of bureaucracy by reaffirming the necessity for formalized, secondary relations and by helping to prevent the disintegration of the bureaucratic structure which would occur should these be supplanted by personalized relations. This type of conflict may be generically described as the intrusion of primary group attitudes when secondary group attitudes are institutionally demanded, just as the bureaucrat-client conflict often derives from interaction on impersonal terms when personal treatment is individually demanded.[26]

PROBLEMS FOR RESEARCH

The trend towards increasing bureaucratization in Western Society, which Weber had long since foreseen, is not the sole reason for sociologists to turn their attention to this field. Empirical studies of the interaction of bureaucracy and personality should especially increase our understanding of social structure. A large number of specific questions invite our attention. To what extent are particular personality types selected and modified by the various bureaucracies (private enterprise, public service, the quasi-legal political machine, religious orders)? Inasmuch as ascendancy and submission are held to be traits of personality, despite their variability in different stimulus-situations, do bureaucracies select personalities of particularly submissive or ascendant tendencies? And since various studies have shown that these traits can be modified, does participation in bureaucratic office tend to increase ascendant tendencies? Do various systems of recruitment (*e.g.*, patronage, open competition involving specialized knowledge or general mental capacity, practical experience) select different personality types?[27] Does promotion through seniority lessen competitive anxieties and enhance administrative efficiency? A detailed examination of mechanisms for imbuing the bureaucratic codes with affect would be instructive both sociologically and psychologically. Does the general anonymity of civil service decisions tend to restrict the area of prestige-symbols to a narrowly defined inner circle? Is there a tendency for differential association to be especially marked among bureaucrats?

The range of theoretically significant and practically important questions would seem to be limited only by the accessibility of the concrete data. Studies of religious, educational, military, economic, and political bureaucracies dealing with the interdependence of social organization and personality formation should constitute an avenue for fruitful research. On that avenue, the functional analysis of concrete structures may yet build a Solomon's House for sociologists.

NOTES

1. For a development of the concept of "rational organization," see Karl Mannheim, *Mensch und Gesellschaft im Zeitalter des Umbaus* (Leiden: A. W. Sijthoff, 1935), esp. 28 ff.

2. H. D. Lasswell, *Politics* (New York: McGraw-Hill, 1936), 120–21.

3. Max Weber, *Wirtschaft und Gesellschaft* (Tübingen: J. C. B. Mohr, 1922), Pt. III, chap. 6; 650–678. For a brief summary of Weber's discussion, see Talcott Parsons, *The Structure of Social Action*, esp. 506 ff. For a description, which is not a caricature, of the bureaucrat as a personality type, see C. Rabany, "Les types sociaux: le fonctionnaire," *Revue générale d'administration* 88 (1907), 5–28.

4. Karl Mannheim, *Ideology and Utopia* (New York: Harcourt Brace Jovanovich, 1936), 18n., 105 ff. See also Ramsay Muir, *Peers and Bureaucrats* (London: Constable, 1910), 12–13.

5. E. G. Cahen-Salvador suggests that the personnel of bureaucracies is largely constituted by those who value security above all else. See his "La situation matérielle et morale des fonctionnaires," *Revue politique et parlementaire* (1926), 319.

6. H. J. Laski, "Bureaucracy," *Encyclopedia of the Social Sciences*. This article is written primarily from the standpoint of the political scientist rather than that of the sociologist.

7. Weber, *op. cit.*, 671.

8. For a stimulating discussion and application of these concepts, see Kenneth Burke, *Permanence and Change* (New York: New Republic, 1935), pp. 50 ff.; Daniel Warnotte, "Bureaucratie et Fonctionnarisme," *Revue de l'Institut de Sociologie* 17 (1937), 245.

9. *Ibid.*, 58–59.

10. *Ibid.*, 70.

11. This process has often been observed in various connections. Wundt's *heterogony of ends* is a case in point; Max Weber's *Paradoxie der Folgen* is another. See also MacIver's observations on the transformation of civilization into culture and Lasswell's remark that "the human animal distinguishes himself by his infinite capacity for making ends of his means." See Merton, "The unanticipated consequences of purposive social action," *American Sociological Review* 1 (1936), 894–904. In terms of the psychological mechanisms involved, this process has been analyzed most fully by Gordon W. Allport, in his discussion of what he calls "the functional autonomy of motives." Allport emends

the earlier formulations of Woodworth, Tolman, and William Stern, and arrives at a statement of the process from the standpoint of individual motivation. He does not consider those phases of the social structure which conduce toward the "transformation of motives." The formulation adopted in this paper is thus complementary to Allport's analysis; the one stressing the psychological mechanisms involved, the other considering the constraints of the social structure. The convergence of psychology and sociology toward this central concept suggests that it may well constitute one of the conceptual bridges between the two disciplines. See Gordon W. Allport, *Personality* (New York: Henry Holt & Co., 1937), chap. 7.

12. See E. C. Hughes, "Institutional office and the person," *American Journal of Sociology*, 43 (1937), 404–413; E. T. Hiller, "Social structure in relation to the person," *Social Forces* 16 (1937), 34–4.

13. Mannheim, *Ideology and Utopia*, 106.

14. Quoted from the *Chicago Tribune* (June 24, 1931, p. 10) by Thurman Arnold, *The Symbols of Government* (New Haven: Yale University Press, 1935), 201–2. (My italics.)

15. Mannheim, *Mensch und Gesellschaft*, 32–33. Mannheim stresses the importance of the "Lebensplan" and the "Amtskarriere." See the comments by Hughes, *op. cit.*, 413.

16. A. L. Lowell, *The Government of England* (New York, 1908). I, 189 ff.

17. For an instructive description of the development of such a defensive organization in a group of workers, see F. J. Roethlisberger and W. J. Dickson, *Management and the Worker* (Boston: Harvard School of Business Administration, 1934).

18. E. C. Hughes, "Personality types and the division of labor," *American Journal of Sociology* 33 (1928), 754–768. Much the same distinction is drawn by Leopold von Wiese and Howard Becker, *Systematic Sociology* (New York: John Wiley & Sons, 1932), 222–25 et passim.

19. Hughes recognizes one phase of this process of sanctification when he writes that professional training "carries with it as a by-product assimilation of the candidate to a set of professional attitudes and controls, *a professional conscience and solidar-*

ity. The profession claims and aims to become a moral unit." Hughes, *op. cit.*, 762, (italics inserted). In this same connection, Sumner's concept of *pathos*, as the halo of sentiment which protects a social value from criticism, is particularly relevant, inasmuch as it affords a clue to the mechanism involved in the process of sanctification. See his *Folkways*, 180–181.

20. "'They treat you like a lump of dirt they do. I see a navvy reach across the counter and shake one of them by the collar the other day. The rest of us felt like cheering. Of course he lost his benefit over it. . . . But the clerk deserved it for his sassy way.'" (E. W. Bakke, *The Unemployed Man*, 79–80). Note that the domineering attitude was *imputed* by the unemployed client who is in a state of tension due to his loss of status and self-esteem in a society where the ideology is still current that an "able man" can always find a job. That the imputation of arrogance stems largely from the client's state of mind is seen from Bakke's own observation that "the clerks were rushed, and had no time for pleasantries, but there was little sign of harshness or a superiority feeling in their treatment of the men." In so far as there is an objective basis for the imputation of arrogant behavior to bureaucrats, it may possibly be explained by the following juxtaposed statements. "Auch der moderne, sei es öffentliche, sei es private, Beamte erstrebt immer und geniesst meist den Beherrschten gegenüber eine spezifisch gehobene, 'ständische' soziale Schätzung." (Weber, *op. cit.*, 652.) "In persons in whom the craving for prestige is uppermost, hostility usually takes the form of a desire to humiliate others." K. Horney, *The Neurotic Personality of Our Time*, 178–79.

21. In this connection, note the relevance of Koffka's comments on certain features of the pecking-order of birds. "If one compares the behavior of the bird at the top of the pecking list, the despot, with that of one very far down, the second or third from the last, then one finds the latter much more cruel to the few others over whom he lords it than the former in this treatment of all members. As soon as one removes from the group all members above the penultimate, his behavior becomes milder and may even become very friendly. . . . It is not difficult to find analogies to this in human societies, and

therefore one side of such behavior must be primarily the effects of the social groupings, and not of individual characteristics." K. Koffka, *Principles of Gestalt Psychology* (New York: Harcourt Brace Jovanovich, 1935), 668–9.

22. At this point the political machine often becomes functionally significant. As Steffens and others have shown, highly personalized relations and the abrogation of formal rules (red tape) by the machine often satisfy the needs of individual "clients" more fully than the formalized mechanism of governmental bureaucracy. See the slight elaboration of this as set forth in Chapter I.

23. As one of the unemployed men remarked about the clerks at the Greenwich Employment Exchange: "'And the bloody blokes wouldn't have their jobs if it wasn't for us men out of a job either. That's what gets me about their holding their noses up.'" Bakke, *op. cit.,* 80. See also H. D. Lasswell and G. Almond, "Aggressive behavior by clients towards public relief administrators," *American Political Science Review* 28 (1934), 643–55.

24. The diagnostic significance of such linguistic indices as epithets has scarcely been explored by the sociologist. Sumner properly observes that epithets produce "summary criticisms" and definitions of social situations. Dollard also notes that "epithets frequently define the central issues in a society," and Sapir has rightly emphasized the importance of context of situations in appraising the significance of epithets. Of equal relevance is Linton's

observation that "in case histories the way in which the community felt about a particular episode is, if anything, more important to our study than the actual behavior. . . ." A sociological study of "vocabularies of encomium and opprobrium" should lead to valuable findings.

25. *Cf.* Ellsworth Faris, *The Nature of Human Nature* (New York: McGraw-Hill, 1937), 41 ff.

26. Community disapproval of many forms of behavior may be analyzed in terms of one or the other of these patterns of substitution of culturally inappropriate types of relationship. Thus, prostitution constitutes a type-case where coitus, a form of intimacy which is institutionally defined as symbolic of the most "sacred" primary group relationship, is placed within a contractual context, symbolized by the exchange of that most impersonal of all symbols, money. See Kingsley Davis, "The sociology of prostitution," *American Sociological Review* 2 (1937), 744–55.

27. Among recent studies of recruitment to bureaucracy are: Reinhard Bendix, *Higher Civil Servants in American Society* (Boulder: University of Colorado Press, 1949); Dwaine Marwick, *Career Perspectives in a Bureaucratic Setting* (Ann Arbor: University of Michigan Press, 1954); R. K. Kelsall, *Higher Civil Servants in Britain* (London: Routledge & Kegan Paul, 1955); W. L. Warner and J. C. Abegglen, *Occupational Mobility in American Business and Industry* (Minneapolis: University of Minnesota Press, 1955).

27

Some Social and Psychological Consequences of the Longwall Method of Coal-Getting[1]

An Examination of the Psychological Situation and Defences of a Work Group in Relation to the Social Structure and Technological Content of the Work System

E. L. Trist & K. W. Bamforth[2]

INTRODUCTION: A PERSPECTIVE FROM RECENT INNOVATIONS

A number of innovations in work organization at the coal-face have been making a sporadic and rather guarded appearance since the change-over of the industry to nationalization. During the past two years the authors have been following the course of these developments. Though differing from each other, they have had the common effect of increasing productivity, at least to some extent, and sometimes the in-

crease reported has reached a level definitely above the upper limit customarily achieved by good workmen using similar equipment under conventional conditions. They have been accompanied by impressive changes in the social quality of the work-life of face teams. Greater cohesiveness has appeared in groups, and greater personal satisfaction has been reported by individuals. Decreases have also been indicated in sickness and absenteeism.

In the account to follow, the longwall method will be regarded as a technological system expressive of the prevailing outlook of mass-production engineering and as a social structure consisting of the occupational roles that have been institutionalized in its use. These interactive technological and sociological patterns will be assumed to exist as forces having psychological effects in the life-space of the face-worker, who must either take a role and perform a task in the system they compose or abandon his attempt to work at

[1] The study reported here is one part of a larger project on which the Tavistock Institute of Human Relations has for some time been engaged, concerned with the conditions likely to increase the effectiveness of the "dissemination of information" about new social techniques developed in industry. This project was initiated by the Human Factors Panel of the Committee on Industrial Productivity set up by the Lord President of the Council under the Scientific Adviser to the Government. It has been administered by the Medical Research Council. No responsibility, however, attaches to either of these bodies for the contents of this paper, a shortened version of which has been discussed by the Medical Research Subcommittee of the National Coal Board.

[2] The field work necessary for this study has been lessened by the fact that Mr. K. W. Bamforth was himself formerly a miner and worked at the coal-face for 18 years.

Source: From "Some Social and Psychological Consequences of the Longwall Method of Coal-Getting" by E. L. Trist and K. W. Bamforth in *Human Relations, 4,* (1951). Reprinted by permission of Plenum Publishing Corporation.

the coal-face. His own contribution to the field of determinants arises from the nature and quality of the attitudes and relationships he develops in performing one of these tasks and in taking one of these roles. Together, the forces and their effects constitute the psycho-social whole which is the object of study.

THE CHARACTER OF THE PRE-MECHANIZED EQUILIBRIUM AND THE NATURE OF ITS DISTURBANCE

1. Hand-got Systems and the Responsible Autonomy of the Pair-Based Work Group

The outstanding feature of the social pattern with which the pre-mechanized equilibrium was associated is its emphasis on small group organization at the coal-face. The groups themselves were interdependent working pairs to whom one or two extra individuals might be attached. It was common practice for two colliers—a hewer and his mate—to make their own contract with the colliery management and to work their own small face with the assistance of a boy "trammer." This working unit could function equally well in a variety of engineering layouts both of the advance and retreat type, whether step-wise or direct. Sometimes it extended its numbers to seven or eight, when three or four colliers, and their attendant trammers, would work together.[3]

A primary work-organization of this type has the advantage of placing responsibility for the complete coal-getting task squarely on the shoulders of a single, small, face-to-face group which experiences the entire cycle of operations within the compass of its membership. For each participant the task has

[3]Hand-got methods contained a number of variants, but discussion of these is beyond present scope.

total significance and dynamic closure. Though the contract may have been in the name of the hewer, it was regarded as a joint undertaking. Leadership and "supervision" were internal to the group, which had a quality of *responsible autonomy*. The capacity of these groups for self-regulation was a function of the wholeness of their work task, this connection being represented in their contractual status. A whole has power as an independent detachment, but a part requires external control.

Within these pair-based units was contained the full range of coal-face skills; each collier being an all-round workman, usually able to substitute for his mate. Though his equipment was simple, his tasks were multiple. The "underground skill" on which their efficient and safe execution depended was almost entirely person-carried. He had craft pride and artisan independence. These qualities obviated status difficulties and contributed to responsible autonomy.

Choice of workmates posed a crucial question. These choices were made by the men themselves, sociometrically, under full pressure of the reality situation and with long-standing knowledge of each other. Stable relationships tended to result, which frequently endured over many years. In circumstances where a man was injured or killed, it was not uncommon for his mate to care for his family. These work relationships were often reinforced by kinship ties, the contract system and the small group autonomy allowing a close but spontaneous connection to be maintained between family and occupation, which avoided tying the one to the other. In segregated mining communities the link between kinship and occupation can be oppressive as well as supportive; against this danger, "exogamous" choice was a safeguard. But against too emotional a relationship, more likely to develop between non-kin associates, kinship barriers were in turn a safeguard.

The wholeness of the work task, the multiplicity of the skills of the individual, and the self-selection of the group were congruent attributes of a pattern of responsible autonomy that characterized the pair-based face teams of hand-got mining.

2. The Adaptability of the Small Group to the Underground Situation

Being able to work their own short faces continuously, these pair, or near pair, groups could stop at whatever point may have been reached by the end of a shift. The flexibility in work pace so allowed had special advantages in the underground situation; for when bad conditions were encountered, the extraction process in a series of stalls could proceed unevenly in correspondence with the uneven distribution of these bad conditions, which tend to occur now in one and now in another section along a seam. Even under good conditions, groups of this kind were free to set their own targets, so that aspirations levels with respect to production could be adjusted to the age and stamina of the individuals concerned.

In the underground situation external dangers must be faced in darkness. Darkness also awakens internal dangers. The need to share with others anxieties aroused by this double threat may be taken as self-evident. In view of the restricted range of effective communication, these others have to be immediately present. Their number therefore is limited. These conditions point to the strong need in the underground worker for a role in a small primary group.

A second characteristic of the underground situation is the wide dispersal of particular activities, in view of the large area over which operations generally are extended. The small groups of the hand-got systems tended to become isolated from each other even when working in the same series of stalls; the isolation of the group, as of the individual, being intensified by the darkness. Under these conditions there is no possibility of continuous supervision, in the factory sense, from any individual external to the primary work group.

The small group, capable of responsible autonomy, and able to vary its work pace in correspondence with changing conditions, would appear to be the type of social structure ideally adapted to the underground situation. It is instructive that the traditional work systems, evolved from the experience of successive generations, should have been founded on a group with these attributes.

But to earn a living under hand-got conditions often entailed physical effort of a formidable order, and possession of exceptional skill was required to extract a bare existence from a hard seam with a bad roof. To tram tubs was "horse-work." Trammers were commonly identified by scabs, called "buttons," on the bone joints of their backs, caused by catching the roof while pushing and holding tubs on and off "the gates." Hand-got conditions still obtain, for by no means all faces are serviced by conveyors and coal-cutters. In some circumstances this equipment is unsuitable. But hardness of work is a separate consideration from the quality of the group.

3. The Counter Balance of the Large Undifferentiated Collectivity

The psychological disadvantages of a work system, the small group organization of which is based on pair relationships, raises issues of a far-reaching kind only recently submitted to study in group dynamics (4). It would appear that the self-enclosed character of the relationship makes it difficult for groups of this kind to combine effectively in differentiated structures of a somewhat larger social magnitude, though this inability does not seem to hold in respect of much larger collectivities of a simpler mass character. But in premechanized mining there was no technological necessity for intermediate structures, equivalent to factory departments, to make their appearance between the small pair-based primary units and the larger collectivities called into action by situations of crisis and common danger. To meet situations requiring the mobilization of the large mass group, mining communities have developed traditions generally recognized as above the norm commonly attained by occupational groups in our society. This supranormative quality was present also in the traditions of the small pair-based organizations. But between these extremes there was little experience.

Sociologically, this situation is not atypical of industries which, though large-scale, have experienced delay in undergoing mechanization. The pair-based face teams corresponded to the technological simplicity of the hand-got methods, with their short faces, autonomously worked and loosely co-ordinated on a district basis. The mass collectivities reflected the large-scale size of the pit as an overall industrial unit. Absent were structures at the level of the factory department, whose process-linked, fractionated role-systems, dependent on external supervision, were antithetical alike to the pattern of small group autonomy and to the artisan outlook of the collier.

In the pre-mechanized pattern, the pair-based primaries and the large relatively undifferentiated collectivities composed a dynamically interrelated system that permitted an enduring social balance. The intense reciprocities of the former, with their personal and family significance, and the diffuse identifications of the latter, with their community and class connectedness, were mutually supportive. The face teams could bear the responsibility of their autonomy through the security of their dependence on the united collectivity of the pit.

Difficulties arose largely from rivalries and conflicts between the various pairs and small teams. A common form of "graft" was to bribe the deputy in order to secure a good "benk," i.e. a "length" with a "rack roof," under which the coal was notoriously soft and easy to work. Trammers were encouraged to resort to sharp practices to obtain adequate supplies of tubs. As supplies were often short, the amount of coal a working pair could send up depended not a little on the prowess of their trammer. Going early to work, he would turn two or three tubs on their sides in his "gate," maintaining he had taken only one. Ensuing disputes caused frequent fights both underground and in the community. In the common saying, it was he who could lie, cheat, or bully the most who made the best trammer. All this was accepted as part of the system.

Inter-team conflict provided a channel for aggression that preserved intact the loyalties on which the small group depended. In the large group aggression received structured expression in trade union resistance. If the struggle was harsh, it was at least direct and understandable. It was not the insidious kind that knocked the bottom out of life, leaving those concerned without a sense of a scheme in things—the "anomie" described by Halliday (2) after the transition to the longwall. The system as a whole contained its bad in a way that did not destroy its good. The balance persisted, albeit that work was of the hardest, rewards often meagre, and the social climate rough at times and even violent.

4. Mechanization and the Problem of Intermediate Organization

With the advent of coal-cutters and mechanical conveyors, the degree of technological complexity of the coal-getting task was raised to a different level. Mechanisation made possible the working of a single long face in place of a series of short faces. In thin seams short faces increase costs, since a large number of "gates" have to be "ripped" up several feet above the height of the seam to create haulage and travelling facilities. In British coal, seams less than 4 ft. in thickness are common, so that there was a tendency to make full use of the possibility of working optimally long rather than optimally short faces. For this reason, and for others also, discussion of which is beyond present scope, the longwall method came into being. Applicable to thick as well as to thin seams, it became the general method of coal-getting in the British industry, enabling the average type of pit, which may contain three or four seams of different thickness, to work its entire coal economically, and to develop its layout and organize its production in terms of a single, self-consistent plan. In America, where thick seams are the rule, mechanization has developed in terms of shorter faces and room-and-pillar techniques.

The associated characteristics of mechanized complexity, and of largeness as regards the scale of the primary production unit, created a situation in which it was impossible for the method to develop as a technological system without bringing into existence a work relationship structure radically different from that associated with hand-got procedures. The artisan type of pair, composed of the skilled man and his mate, assisted by one or more labourers, was out of keeping as a model for the type of work group required. Need arose for a unit more of the size and differentiated complexity of a small factory department. A structure of intermediate social magnitude began therefore to emerge. The basic pattern round which the work relationships of the longwall production unit were organized became the cycle group of 40–50 men, their shot-firer and shift "deputies," who were responsible to the pit management for the working as a whole. Only in relation to this total cycle group could various smaller subgroups secure function and acquire social form.

This centring of the new system on a differentiated structure of intermediate social magnitude disturbed the simple balance that had existed between the very small and very large traditional groups, and impaired the quality of responsible autonomy. The psychological and sociological problems posed by the technological needs of the longwall system were those with respect to which experience in the industry was least, and towards which its traditions were antithetical. The consequences of this conflict between the demands of the new situation and the resources available from past experience will be taken up in the light of the detailed account, which will now be presented, of the longwall system itself.

5. The Lack of Recognition of the Nature of the Difficulties

Anyone who has listened to the talk of older miners who have experienced in their own work-lives the change-over to the longwall cannot fail to be impressed by the confused mourning for the past that still goes on in them together with a dismay over the present coloured by despair and indignation. To the clinical worker the quality of these talks has at times a ring that is familiar. Those with rehabilitation experience will recognize it as similar to the quality of feeling expressed by rehabilitees when ventilating the aftermath in themselves of an impairment accepted as irreversible.

THE STRESS OF MASS PRODUCTION IN THE UNDERGROUND SITUATION

1. The Interaction of Bad Conditions and Bad Work

Differentiated, rigidly sequenced work systems, organized on mass-production lines to deal with large quantities of material on a multi-shift cycle, are a basic feature of the factory pattern. Even in the factory situation, their maintenance at a level which allows full and continuous realization of their technological potentialities creates a difficult problem of industrial management. In the underground situation these difficulties are of a higher order, it being virtually impossible to establish the kind of constant background to the task that is taken for granted in the factory. A very large variety of unfavourable and changing environmental conditions is encountered at the coal-face, many of which are impossible to predict. Others, though predictable, are impossible to alter.

2. The Strain of Cycle Control

The main burden of keeping down the number of cycle stoppages falls on the deputy, who is the only person in the face area with cycle, as distinct from task, responsibility. Discussion with groups of deputies readily yields

evidence of the strain involved. A common and reality-based complaint is that the authority of the deputy is incommensurate with responsibility of this order. The background to this complaint is the fact, noted in the discussion of the hand-got systems, that, in view of the darkness and the spread out character of the work, there is no possibility of close supervision. Responsibility for seeing to it that bad work is not done, however bad the conditions, rests with the face-workers themselves. But the responsible autonomy of some, especially, of the occupational sub-groups has been impaired in the longwall method. This problem will be taken up in succeeding sections.

As a result, management complain of lack of support from the men, who are accused of being concerned only with their own fractional tasks and unwilling to take broader cycle responsibility. The parallel complaint of the workers is of being driven and tricked by management, who are resented as outsiders— intermittent visitors and "stick" men, who interfere without sharing the hard, physical work and in-group life of the face. On occasions, for example, the deputy is reduced to bargaining with the men as to whether they will agree to carry out essential bye-work. The complaint of the men is that deputies' promises are rarely kept, and that they have gone unpaid too often to be again easily persuaded. The deputy's answer is that the under-manager or manager has refused to uphold his case. Whether he presented it, how he presented it, or what reasons may have dictated the managerial view are a type of issue on which effective communication back to the man breaks down. The deputy has equally little chance of increasing the insight of the workmen into their own tendency to drive sharp bargains.

The strain of cycle control tends to

produce a group "culture" of angry and suspicious bargaining over which both management and men are in collusion. There is displacement both upwards and downwards of the tensions generated. The "hell" that breaks loose in the under-manager's office when news comes in that the fillers are unlikely to fill off in one or more faces resounds through the pit.

3. The Norm of Low Productivity

In all work at the coal-face two distinct tasks are simultaneously present; those that belong to the production cycle being always to some extent carried out on the background of a second activity arising from the need to contend with interferences, actual or threatened, emanating from the underground situation. The activity of the "ground" has always to be dealt with, and ability to contend with this second or background task comprises the common fund of underground skill shared alike by all experienced face-workers. This common skill is of a higher order than that required simply to carry out, as such, any of the operations belonging to the production cycle. For these, initial training is short, and may be measured in months; it is longest for those, such as cutting, where the engineering component is largest. But the specifically mining skill of contending with underground conditions, and of maintaining a high level of performance when difficulties arise, is developed only as the result of several years of experience at the face. A work-system basically appropriate to the underground situation requires to have built into its organization the findings of this experience. Unless this has been done, it will not only fail to engage the face-worker to the limit of his capabilities, but will restrict him to a level of performance below his potentiality.

The evidence suggests that the longwall method acts in this way. The crises of cycle stoppages and the stress of the deputy's role are but symptoms of a wider situation characterized by the establishment of a norm of low productivity, as the only adaptive method of handling, in the contingencies of the underground situation, a complicated, rigid, and large-scale work system, borrowed with too little modification from an engineering culture appropriate to the radically different situation of the factory. At the time the longwall method developed, there were no precedents for the adaptive underground application of a machine technology. In the absence of relevant experience in the mining tradition itself it was almost inevitable that heavy culture-borrowing of this kind should have taken place. There was also no psychological or sociological knowledge in existence at that time which might have assisted in lessening the difficulties.

As regards the special difficulties which stem from the large-scale character of the longwall production unit, it may be noted that less acute problems appear to have arisen at equal or even higher levels of mechanization, with room-and-pillar techniques. Here the scale of operations is less, in view of the shorter expanse of the faces; while adaptability to the changing circumstances of underground conditions appears to have been correspondingly greater. It must not, however, be inferred from room-and-pillar experience that the development of a high level of functional efficiency is impossible in a large-scale mechanized unit; rather, that the problems presented are more difficult. The difficulties occur very largely in the field of social organization. In the succeeding sections consideration will be given to problems of group relationships in the various occupational sub-groups of the longwall system.

THE SPECIAL SITUATION OF THE FILLING SHIFT

1. Isolated Dependence

Relationships between members of the filling shift are characterized by an absence of functional interdependence, which arises from the absence of role differentiation in the twenty identical tasks performed by the shift aggregate. The filler is the modern version of the second collier of the older hand-got systems, whose hewer has departed to the cutting shift. While his former mate has acquired a new partner in the back man on the coal-cutter, and is serviced by a new group of labourers—gummers, as distinct from trammers—the filler is alone in his stint, the dimensions of which are those of the short face formerly worked in common. The advent of mechanization has changed but little the character of filling, except that the filler has, in his air pick, the assistance of one power-driven tool and, instead of a hand-pushed tub, a mechanically driven conveyor on to which to load his coal.

The effect of the introduction of mechanized methods of face preparation and conveying, along with the retention of manual filling, has been not only to isolate the filler from those with whom he formerly shared the coal-getting task as a whole, but to make him one of a large aggregate serviced by the same small group of preparation workers. In place of an actually present partner, who belonged to him solely as the second member of an interdependent pair, he has acquired an "absent group," whom he must share with nineteen others. The temporal distance separating

him from this absent group is increased by the interval of the ripping shift.

The preparation group itself is so loosely organized that its boundaries are difficult to determine. If thought of as centred on the two cutters, the extent of the filler's dependence on earlier activities is such that the cutting group must be expanded to include the two borers as well as the four gummers. Since in addition he is dependent on the belt-men, these latter, representing transformed but likewise absent versions of trammers formerly under his own eye, must also be included in his absent group. While, in the time perspective of the present, the filler has no relationships of functional interdependence with other fillers on his own shift, in the time perspective of the past he must contend with a complex set of dependent relationships with the entire series of preparation workers who have preceded him in the face. These relationships are dependent rather than interdependent since, within a given cycle period, they operate only in one direction.

Difficulties are increased still further by the fact that the concern of this succession of pairs is with the entire 180–200 yds. of the face. For them the face is a single continuous region, whereas for the fillers it is differentiated into a series of short adjacent sections. For the individual filler it is the 8–10 yds. of his own length. In the corner of this length he usually chalks up his name, but these chalk marks mean little more than just the name to traversing pairs, to whom individual fillers are personally little known. The structure of the preparation tasks as continuous activities covering the entire expanse of the face gives the succession of traversing pairs no functional relationship with the discrete tasks of individual fillers. The absent, internally disconnected

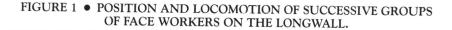

FIGURE 1 • POSITION AND LOCOMOTION OF SUCCESSIVE GROUPS OF FACE WORKERS ON THE LONGWALL.

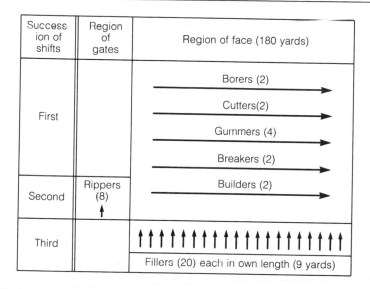

group on which he is dependent takes no functional cognizance of the existence of the filler as an individual. In view of the far-reaching community, as well as work, separation that exists between the preparation and the filling shifts (produced by the time-table arrangements), actual cognizance tends also to be minimal. The pattern of these relationships is shown in *Figure 1*, where the picture presented is one in which, within the period of a given cycle, the fillers are left "alone with each other" and at the mercy of the rest.

2. Unequal Men with Equal Stints under Unequal Conditions

The fillers, as has been shown, have no secure relationships in face of the differential incidence of the bad conditions they may encounter or of the bad work they may inherit from the preparation workers on whom they are dependent. The men who face these unequal conditions are themselves unequal; but the

lengths of face they clear are the same. The detailed implications of this situation are set out in *Table I*, where the differential incidence of some of the most common types of bad conditions and of bad work, in the different lengths of a typical face, is shown in relation to the variations in skill, conscientiousness, and stamina in a typical group of fillers, fractionated into informal sub-groups interspersed with isolates.

The local arrival of certain types of bad conditions, such as rolls that move across the face, can be anticipated, so that anxiety piles up. The passage across a face of a roll that continues for different periods of time in various lengths is shown in *Figure 2*. As regards bad work left by the other shifts, the filler is in the situation of never knowing what he may find, so that anxiety of a second kind arises that tends to produce chronic uncertainty and irritation. There is little doubt that these two circumstances contribute to the wide-

TABLE I • CUMULATIVE AND DIFFERENTIAL INCIDENCE OF BAD CONDITIONS AND BAD WORK IN THE FILLING SHIFT

(This table has been built up as a "model" of the situation from the experience of a group of face-workers who acted as informants. It relates the effect of bad conditions and bad work, traversing the face unevenly, to the unequal personal and group qualities of the fillers.)

X indicates local distribution of difficulty in typical examples of different kinds of bad conditions and bad work.

Types of Adverse Factor	Positions Across the Face of 20 Fillers																			
	1	2	3	4	5	6	7	8	9	10	11	12	13	14	15	16	17	18	19	20
Loose roof—roof broken up by weight or natural "slips" (cracks) making it difficult to support; extra time required for timbering reduces that for filling.				X	X	X				X				X	X	X				
Faults—sudden changes in slope of seam either up or down, producing bad conditions capable of anticipation, possibly lasting over a considerable period.	X	X																X		
Rolls—temporary unevenness in floor or roof reducing working height and producing severely cramped conditions in thin seams. As above for anticipation and duration.	X				X										X					
Roof weight—roof sagging down—especially in middle positions along the face where weight is greatest; not dissimilar to above in effect.						X	X								X	X				
Rising floor—from natural bad stone floor, or from the cut having been made into the coal so that the gas in the coal lifts up the floor, or from naturally inferior coal which is left down but which lifts (gas).				X		X								X	X					

	3	1	–	3	7	5	2	1	–	3	2	1	–	3	4	2	2	2	–	3
Bad boring—holes bored short so that coal at the back of the undercut is unaffected by shot (hard backs); heavy extraction task with air pick at end of shift, when tired; or holes too low, so that shot leaves coal clinging to roof (sticky tops). Both these conditions tend to occur through naturally hard coal and certain types of roof.															X		X			
Uneven cut—from the coal cutter having gone up into the coal. This reduces the filler's working height, cf. rolls, and the tonnage on which his wages depend. Also, as with rolls, faults, etc., it means that 3-ft. props have to be inserted in 2-ft. 6-in. height, which means sinking them in floor (dirting props) as an additional unremunerated task.	X				X	X				X	X				X	X				
Gummings left in—failure on the part of the gummers to clear coal from undercut so that coal cannot drop and shot is wasted. The result is a solid mass of hard coal, requiring constant use of air pick and backbreaking effort. The amount left in varies.				X	X	X				X	X			X	X		X			
Belt trouble—the belt may not have been set in a straight line, or bad joints may have been made, or it may not have been made tight enough. On top-delivery belts coal going back on the bottom belt very soon stops it. Belt stoppages may produce exceedingly awkward delays, especially if conditions are otherwise bad.					X	X	X													
*Total	3	1	–	3	7	5	2	1	–	3	2	1	–	3	4	2	2	2	–	3

383

(continued)

TABLE 1 (Continued)

Types of Adverse Factor	Positions Across the Face of 20 Fillers																			
	1	2	3	4	5	6	7	8	9	10	11	12	13	14	15	16	17	18	19	20
**Skill	+												−	+		−		−		+
**Stamina				+			−								−		+			
**Conscientiousness				−											+		−			
***Sub-group membership	a	a	a	l	b	b	l	c	c	d	d	l	e	e	e	l	f	f		

*These numbers simply indicate the fact that several different kinds of things often go wrong in the same length. Severity varies. At one extreme there may be a series of minor nuisances, at the other one major interference. When conditions seriously deteriorate the interaction of factors and effects is such that some degree of disturbance is apt to be felt from most quarters at one or other point along the face.

**Plus or minus ratings have been given for supra- or infra-norm group status on the three attributes of skill, stamina and conscientiousness on the job, which represent the type of judgments of each other that men need to make, and do in fact make.

***Members of the same informal sub-group are indicated by the same letter; l = Isolate.

FIGURE 2 ● THE COURSE OF A ROLL, OR FAULT ACROSS A LONGWALL FACE.

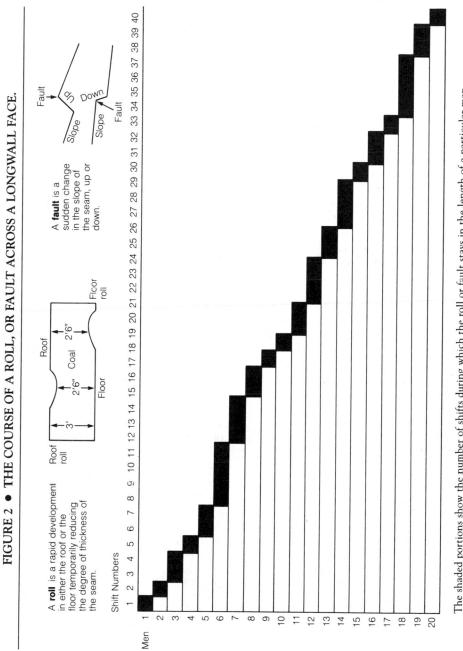

A **roll** is a rapid development in either the roof or the floor temporarily reducing the degree of thickness of the seam.

A **fault** is a sudden change in the slope of the seam, up or down.

The shaded portions show the number of shifts during which the roll or fault stays in the length of a particular man.

spread incidence of psycho-somatic and kindred neurotic disorders among those concerned.

The degree of stress arising when men experience the full weight of this situation could have been explored only in a therapeutic relationship. But many instances were given of neurotic episodes occurring on shift—of men sitting in their lengths in stony silence, attacking their coal in towering rage, or leaving the face in panic. In a situation of dependent isolation with the odds unequal both as regards his own resources and what is required of him, the individual inevitably erects protective defences, and these are elaborated and shared in the work group. An account of the main pattern of group defences will now be given. These defences are reactive rather than adaptive. Their effectiveness therefore is only partial. But without them life at the longwall would be intolerable for all but those whose level of personal adjustment is rather better than that attained by most individuals in the course of their development.

FOUR TYPES OF GROUP DEFENCE

1. Informal Organization

The functional isolation of the filler within his own group, which leaves him "officially" alone with his "coals," is met by an attempt to develop informal, small-group organization in which private arrangements to help each other out are made among neighbours, in twos, threes, or fours. But these solely interpersonal arrangements are undependable and open to manipulation for anti-social and competitive as well as for mutually protective ends. A number of isolates is left over. The total face group is incapable, except defensively,

of acting as a socially responsible whole, since not even private allegiances are owed outside the small informal groups. These in turn are without responsible autonomy; the absence of institutionalized mutual obligation means that there are no statutory group tasks, and each individual can be held ultimately responsible only for clearing his own length. Internal "rows" the more easily break up the informal "coalitions," whose morale tends to be of the clique type.

Examples were, however, given to the writers of stable groups who stuck to each other and worked well over long periods. One informant said of these: "Here things are more like the old times in the pit." Groups of this kind were envied and also criticized for being "too close." They appeared sometimes to be held together by a natural leader, and at others to be made up of individuals of generally good personality. Most informants were agreed that there was a tendency for the extremes to sort themselves out; there were "good" and "bad" faces as well as "good" and "bad" cliques within a particular face aggregate. But all this happened as it might. There was no support from the system.

Isolates, it appears, are either individualists—who "won't even share timber"—or men with bad reputations, with whom others refuse to work. Amongst these are the unconscientious—who "won't help out at the end of a shift" and who are frequently absent—and the helpless—who "cannot learn to look after themselves under bad conditions." Others, whose stamina is deficient (whether through age, illness, or neurosis) and whose lengths are often uncleared in consequence, are dropped from the informal groups.

Only to a very limited extent, therefore, does his informal group organization meet the filler's need for a secure role in a primary group within his own shift. In view of the extent of his dependence on the performance of those in the other two shifts, his need for this foundation is greater than that of any of the other occupational groups, while the resources available to him are fewer.

2. Reactive Individualism

His small group failing, the filler is thrown on to himself and against others. The second defence against isolation is the development of a reactive individualism, in which a reserve of personal secrecy is apt to be maintained. Among his own shift mates there is competitive intrigue for the better places—middle positions are avoided; from these "it is a long way to creep"—and for jobs in workings where conditions are good there is a scramble.

On some faces described to the writers, fear of victimization was rife, particularly in the form of being sent to work in a "bad place"; the deputy being more easily turned into a persecutor in view of the guilt arising from the intrigue and deception which the men practised both against him and against each other. Against the deputy, advantage is taken of the scope afforded in the underground situation for petty deception over such matters as time of leaving the pit, or the "measure that is sent up" (amount of coal filled on to the conveyor). With the deputy, however, men are also prepared to enter into alliance against each other, often for very good reasons—to stop mates from going absent and by so doing throwing more work on to the others.

As regards outside groups, practices of bribing members of the other shifts in the hope of getting a "good deal" in one's own length were mentioned by several informants. Tobacco is taken to the cutter; gummers are stood a pint on Sunday. These practices are to be regarded as symptoms of a state of affairs rather than as widespread in themselves.

The effect of this defensive individualism is to reduce the sense of secure identification in the larger pit collectivity, which was the second principle on which the older equilibrium was based.

Nowhere is the mistrust that shift mates have of each other more in evidence than in controversies over byework "slipping off the note." On what is referred to as the "big note" is entered all the contract and bye-work done during the week by the shift aggregate. This note is issued to one man called "the number man" since he is identified by his check-number. In no sense is this individual a representative appointed by his mates. Only rarely is he an informal leader. Customarily he is a "corner man," whose length adjoins the main gate, i.e., the man most conveniently within reach of the deputy. When asked about bye-work he does not always know what has been done at the far ends of the face and he is under no obligation to stop his own work to find out. But though a number of men will grouse about their pay being short, mentioning this or that item as having "slipped off the note," very few ever bother to check up. There are men who have worked on a face for three or four years and never once seen their own big note. Yet these are among the more ready to accuse the corner man or the deputy. The corner man is suspected at least of never forgetting to make the most of his own assignments. To the deputy is ascribed the intention of keeping the costs of his district down. Conspiracy between the two is often alleged. Only when a major rumpus occurs are such suspicions put to the test, but showdowns of this kind are avoided as apt to peter out in squabbles proving nothing.

The competition, intrigue, unwillingness to put allegations to the test and the reserve of personal secrecy, are parts of one pattern. Whatever their personal wishes, men feel under pressure to be out for themselves, since the social structure in which they work denies them membership in any group that can legitimize interdependence. In this respect reactive individualism makes a basic interpretation of the social structure of the filling shift and is the only form of authorized behaviour.

3. Mutual Scapegoating

Fillers almost never see those who work on the "back shifts," and this absence of contact gives full scope for mutual and irresponsible scapegoating. When there is a crisis, and the filling shift is unable to fill off, the "buck" is passed to the other shifts—or vice versa if disorganization has occurred elsewhere. It is frequently also passed to the deputy, who is blamed for not finding substitutes, and to repair men, brought in, but too old to stand the pace.

For these to pass the buck back to the fillers is fruitless. As they do not exist as a responsible whole, they, as a group, are not there to take the blame, and the individual filler can always exempt himself. Since bad conditions and bad work interact so closely, it is usually difficult to pin blame specifically. Mutual scapegoating is a self-perpetuating system, in which nothing is resolved and no one feels guilty. For all concerned to remain in collusion with such a system is a defence which allows each to make his "anonymous contribution" to the "group mentality," (4) which sabotages both the goal of cycle productivity and the needs of the individual for a membership in a satisfying work-group. So far as this pattern obtains, all strike at each other in a mock war in which no one is hurt yet all suffer.

This defence can also be seen as a "back-handed" attempt to recover the supportive unity lost through reactive individualism in a way that is consistent with it. For all to be "in the bad" together is at least a way of being together. If one's contribution to a group is to help carry the badness of others, the group's contribution to oneself is to allow one to leave some of one's own badness in the group by being granted, for example, the privilege of withdrawal so that one's absence is sanctioned on a fair share of occasions. This "formula" provides a workable scheme since the tacit agreement is only too plausibly maintained that the badness both of the group and of the individual are exclusively effects of the system which the group is compelled to operate without having power to change, i.e., these effects are regarded as "induced" rather than also as "own" forces. The group and the individual can therefore deny and get rid of their own badness by ascribing it to the system. The good of the group becomes its power to preserve the good of individual members by limiting the degree of their exposure to the bad system. The alternative would be constructive limitation of its real deficiencies so that it might be operated with more productive results and a higher degree of mutual satisfaction.

Not that the system is felt as entirely bad since it is the means by which a living is earned. Moreover, under present conditions this living is a good one, both in terms of wages and of community status. But the benefits which these "goods" bring are not realized in the work activities of the group. They lie outside the work system, which is tolerated as a means to external ends rather than accepted also as an end in itself, worthy of whole-hearted pursuit in virtue of the internal satisfactions it affords. When these different aspects of the matter are put together the expectation emerges of a balance being struck which would allow things to tick over, though with a degree of social illness costly alike to productivity and to personal well-being. This expectation accords with reality.

4. Self-Compensatory Absenteeism

Withdrawal is the fourth form of defence, complementing mutual scapegoating, and absenteeism is to be regarded as a recognized social technique within this pattern. For example, one filler, returning from his week's holiday with pay, complained that the first two shifts had "knocked it all out of him." The gummings had been left in. His coal was solid. He had had the air-pick on all day. "I've tried cursing 'em but it's no use, and pleading with 'em but it's no use. I'll take a day off for this."

When conditions on a face deteriorate, especially in ways that are predictable, absenteeism among fillers sometimes piles up to a point where the remainder have to stay down an extra two or three hours in order to clear the face. Should this situation repeat itself for more than a day or two, those coming on shift often meet at the pit-head baths before presenting themselves for work. If less than a certain number arrive, all go home.

Absenteeism of this self-compensatory type, though carried out as an act of aggrieved defiance against a system, felt in these circumstances as persecutory, is an attempt on the part of the individual to prolong his work life at the coal-face. For without the respite of occasional absences, he feels that he would soon become unable to carry on. In view of the accentuated differences both in wages and in status between face workers and repair, haulage, or surface personnel, the goal of remaining at the coal-face for as long as possible would appear to operate as a powerful motivational force in determining the behaviour of the ordinary face-worker.

The following is some of the material obtained in interviews and discussions. Fear of being "too old for the face at forty," or even thirty-five, was a frequently expressed anxiety, made more acute by personal experience of the painful tensions in miners' families, where a father relegated to the surface at £5 19s. 3d. a week must face a son, still in his early twenties, earning more than twice this wage. Instances were reported of quarrels between brothers, among whom long-standing but mild neurotic rivalries had existed that severely disturbed the larger family when the older, through sickness, often of a psycho-somatic kind, had been forced to leave the face. In the culture of the mining family a face-worker husband is the object of special care on the part of his wife. There were men who felt that the privilege of this care, the emotional need for which was now stronger, was no longer merited once their *élite* position had been forfeited and their potency as bread-winners reduced. The dilemma of this situation is that fear of the loss of this care and acceptance of its continuing offer are both unbearable.

Absenteeism of this self-compensatory type is a socially structured activity operated in accordance with a complex code that governs both the occasions and amounts regarded as permissible. It is a psycho-social defence motivated by the wish to remain at the coal-face, and is a species of "institutional" conduct with a functional role in the total social system in which the longwall method plays a central part.

This, and the other three defences discussed, play a dynamically interrelated part in forming the culture[4] of the work group, though naturally the intensity to which the pattern is present varies widely, and there are faces where the group atmosphere remains for long periods relatively immune from these influences. These are apt, however, to be "fair-weather" faces.

The danger is that habituation to working in a bad system has the compensation of enabling those concerned to leave too much both of their own and of their group's "badness" *in the system.* It then ties them to it through the fact that it does this, despite their hatred of it. As well as its faults, it is their own hatred that they hate in the system— and there is usually stubborn refusal to recognize such projections in work—no less than in therapy-groups. A characteristic of faces with a bad group atmosphere is the protesting yet excited collusion of all concerned with the state of affairs. This is in contrast to the more independently critical and realistic attitude of those in groups where the pattern is less complete and less intense.

---

[4]The concept of "culture" as a psycho-social technique developed by a group in a structurally determined situation has been outlined by Trist, "Culture as a Psycho-Social Process," contributed to a symposium on The Concept of Culture, British Association, Section (H), Anthropology and Archeology, Birmingham Meeting, 1950. This viewpoint develops that of Curle, and Curle and Trist, "Transitional Communities and Social Reconnection," *Human Relations,* Vol. I, No. 1, pp. 42–68, and No. 2, pp. 240–288; and is akin to that of Ruesch, "Experiments in Psychotherapy, II: Individual Social Techniques," *The Journal of Social Psychology,* 1949, 29, 3–28; and Ruesch and Bateson, "Structure and Process in Social Relations," *Psychiatry,* 1949, Vol. XII, 2, pp. 105–124.

CONCLUSIONS

The fact that the desperate economic incentives of the between-war period no longer operate means a greater intolerance of unsatisfying or difficult working conditions, or systems or organization, among miners, even though they may not always be clear as to the exact nature of the resentment or hostility which they often appear to feel. The persistence of socially ineffective structures at the coal-face is likely to be a major factor in preventing a rise of morale, in discouraging recruitment, and in increasing labour turnover.

The innovations in social organization of face-work groups, which have begun to appear, and the success of some of these developments, suggest that the organizational changes brought about by nationalization provide a not inappropriate opportunity for the experimental working through of problems of the types which have been indicated. It can certainly be said with some confidence that within the industry there exist the necessary resources and creativity to allow widespread constructive developments to take place.

As regards the longwall system, the first need is for systematic study and evaluation of the changes so far tried.[5] It seems to the present writers, however, that a qualitative change will have to be effected in the general character of the method, so that a social as well as a technological whole can come into existence. Only if this is achieved can the relationships of the cycle work-group be successfully integrated and a new social balance be created.

---

[5]One of the most interesting of these is "An Experiment in Continuous Longwall Mining at Bolsover Colliery," W. V. Sheppard, The Institution of Mining Engineers, Annual General Meeting, Jan. 1951.

The immediate problems are to develop formal small-group organization on the filling shift and to work out an acceptable solution to the authority questions in the cutting team. But it is difficult to see how these problems can be solved effectively without restoring responsible autonomy to primary groups throughout the system and ensuring that each of these groups has a satisfying sub-whole as its work task, and some scope for flexibility in work-pace. Only if this is done will the stress of the deputy's role be reduced and his task of maintaining the cycle receive spontaneous support from the primary work groups.

It is likely that any attempts in this direction would require to take advantage of the recent trend of training face-workers for more than one role, so that interchangeability of tasks would be possible within work teams. Moreover, the problem of shift segregation will not be overcome until the situation is altered in which one large group is permanently organised round the day shift and the others round the back shifts.

Some interchange between roles in preparation and filling tasks would seem worth consideration. Once preparation workers and fillers could experience each other's situations, mutual understanding and tolerance would be likely to increase.

It is to be borne in mind that developments in room-and-pillar methods appear to be stressing the value of the strongly-knit primary work-group and that the most recent advances in mechanization, such as power loaders or strippers, both require work teams of this kind.

REFERENCES

1. Dickson, D. E. "The Morbid Miner," *Edin. Med. J.*, 1936, p. 696.

2. Halliday, J. L. *Psychosocial Medicine: A Study of the Sick Society*, Heinemann, London, 1949.

3. Morris, J. N. "Coal Miners," *Lancet*, Vol. II, 1947, p. 341.

4. Bion, W. R. "Experiences in Groups, III," *Human Relations*, Vol. II, No. 1, January, 1949, pp. 13–22.

28

The Organization Man: Conclusion

William H. Whyte, Jr.

Here, finally, is the apotheosis of the Social Ethic. Some might summarize the suburban temper in different terms—pragmatism, perhaps, or utilitarianism—and their intonation would depend on their own outlook. But the dominant motif is unmistakable. Not just as something expedient, but as something right, the organization transients have put social usefulness at the core of their beliefs. Adaptation has become more than a necessity; in a life in which everything changes, it has become almost a constant.

Since I am using suburbia as a vehicle to bring together many strands, it can be asked if it is fair to generalize from such places to organization man in general. I am talking about values, and the suburbanites themselves provide evidence that their values are a great deal more than a function of the physical environment. That they respond to the pressure of the court or the tight-knit block is not so significant. They have to. What is significant is how they feel about these pressures—and how, ideally, they think a person should feel about them.

Their children, for example. In building the school system the suburbanites have had to face the question, and if the passing-phase explanation were correct, we could find the answer in the kind of well-roundedness they

ask for. In deciding what the children needed most to learn, or least, parents might reason that since the children were already so well instructed by the environment in social skills the schools should teach them not to overcompensate. For the sake of mental health, if nothing else, it would follow that the schools would emphasize the more neglected, inner aspect of the child to the end that personality development be truly balanced. In this light, the more asocial, intellectual disciplines could be utilized as highly pragmatic tools—not to mention any utility their content might have.

But this, we know, is not the way the great majority of parents feel. They do not wish the great cycle of which they are a part reversed, but intensified. It is an age of group action, they well agree, and skilled as they are in the ways of group living, it is a source of pride to them, rather than concern, that their children may be even more so. As some parents point out, they themselves have had to learn adjustment the hard way, without the benefit of an education anywhere near as contemporary, or socially-conscious, as that the schools are now offering. If they have made their adjustments as successfully as they have, they wonder, how much more successfully may their children when they come of age?

Source: From *The Organization Man* (pp. 392–404) by William H. Whyte, Jr., New York: Simon & Schuster, Inc. Copyright © 1956, 1984 by William H. Whyte, Jr. Reprinted by permission of Simon & Schuster, Inc.

Let us now broaden our view to organization man in general and ask what this climate of thought portends. If, as I believe, the people I have been examining in this book are representative of the main stream of organization life, one thing seems clear. If ever there was a generation of technicians, theirs is it. No generation has been so well equipped, psychologically as well as technically, to cope with the intricacies of vast organizations; none has been so well equipped to lead a meaningful community life; and none probably will be so adaptable to the constant shifts in environment that organization life is so increasingly demanding of them. In the better sense of the word, they are becoming the interchangeables of our society and they accept the role with understanding. They are all, as they say, in the same boat.

But where is the boat going? No one seems to have the faintest idea; nor, for that matter, do they see much point in even raising the question. Once people liked to think, at least, that they were in control of their destinies, but few of the younger organization people cherish such notions. Most see themselves as objects more acted upon than acting— and their future, therefore, determined as much by the system as by themselves.

In a word, they *accept,* and if we do not find this comforting at least we should recognize that it would be odd if they did not feel this confidence. For them society has in fact been good— very, very good—for there has been a succession of fairly beneficent environments: college, the paternalistic, if not always pleasant, military life, then, perhaps, graduate work through the G.I. Bill of Rights, a corporation apprenticeship during a period of industrial expansion and high prosperity, and, for some, the camaraderie of communities like Park Forest. The system, they instinctively conclude, is essentially benevolent.

No one should begrudge them the prosperity that has helped make them feel this way. If we have to have problems, after all, the adversities of good times are as worthy as any to have to worry about. Nor should we regard the emphasis on co-operation as a reversal of our national character. When the suburbanites speak of re-establishing the spirit of the frontier communities, there is a truth in their analogy. Our country was born as a series of highly communal enterprises, and though the individualist may have opened the frontier, it was the co-operative who settled it. So throughout our history. Our national genius has always lain in our adaptability, in our distrust of dogma and doctrine, in our regard for the opinion of others, and in this respect the organization people are true products of the American past. "The more equal social conditions become," De Tocqueville, no friend of conformity, presciently observed, "the more men display this reciprocal disposition to oblige each other."

And there is the crux. When De Tocqueville wrote this a century ago it was the double-edged nature of this disposition that haunted him. He understood its virtue; he was an aristocrat and he confessed that he missed the excellence of the few in the good of the many, but he saw clearly that our egalitarianism and our ease of social co-operation were the great fruits of democracy. We could not sustain these virtues without suffering their defects. But could we keep them in balance? De Tocqueville made a prophecy. If America ever destroyed its genius it would be by intensifying the social virtues at the expense of others, by making the individual come to regard himself as a hostage to prevailing opinion, by creating, in sum, a tyranny of the majority.

And this is what the organization man is doing. He is doing it for what he feels are good reasons, but this only makes the tyranny more powerful, not less. At the very time when the pressures of our highly organized society make so stringent a demand on the individual, he is himself compounding the impact. He is not only other-directed, to borrow David Riesman's concept, he is articulating a philosophy which tells him it is right to be that way.

My charge against the Social Ethic, then, is on precisely the grounds of contemporary usefulness it so venerates. It is not, I submit, suited to the needs of "modern man," but is instead reinforcing precisely that which least needs to be emphasized, and at the expense of that which does. Here is my bill of particulars.

It is redundant. In some societies individualism has been carried to such extremes as to endanger the society itself, and there exist today examples of individualism corrupted into a narrow egoism which prevents effective co-operation. This is a danger, there is no question of that. But is it today as pressing a danger as the obverse—a climate which inhibits individual initiative and imagination, and the courage to exercise it against group opinion? Society is itself an education in the extrovert values, and I think it can be rightfully argued that rarely has there been a society which has preached them so hard. No man is an island unto himself, but how John Donne would writhe to hear how often, and for what reasons, the thought is so tiresomely repeated.

It is premature. To preach technique before content, the skills of getting along isolated from why and to what end the getting along is for, does not produce maturity. It produces a sort of permanent prematurity, and this is true not only of the child being taught life adjustment but of the organization man being taught well-roundedness. This is a sterile concept, and those who believe that they have mastered human relations can blind themselves to the true bases of co-operation. People don't co-operate just to co-operate; they co-operate for substantive reasons, to achieve certain goals, and unless these are comprehended the little manipulations for morale, team spirit, and such are fruitless.

And they can be worse than fruitless. Held up as the end-all of organization leadership, the skills of human relations easily tempt the new administrator into the practice of a tyranny more subtle and more pervasive than that which he means to supplant. No one wants to see the old authoritarian return, but at least it could be said of him that what he wanted primarily from you was your sweat. The new man wants your soul.

It is delusory. It is easy to fight obvious tyranny; it is not easy to fight benevolence, and few things are more calculated to rob the individual of his defenses than the idea that his interests and those of society can be wholly compatible. The good society is the one in which they are most compatible, but they never can be completely so, and one who lets The Organization be the judge ultimately sacrifices himself. Like the good society, the good organization encourages individual expression, and many have done so. But there always remains some conflict between the individual and The Organization. Is The Organization to be the arbiter? The Organization will look to its own interests, but it will look to the individual's *only as The Organization interprets them.*

It is static. Organization of itself has no dynamic. The dynamic is in the individual and thus he must not only question how The Organization interprets his interests, he must question how it interprets its own. The bold new plan he feels is necessary, for example. He cannot trust that The Organization will recognize this. Most probably, it will not. It is the nature of a new idea to confound current consensus—even the mildly new idea. It might be patently in order, but, unfortunately, the group has a vested interest in its miseries as well as its pleasures, and irrational as this may be, many a member of organization life can recall instances where the group clung to known disadvantages rather than risk the anarchies of change.

It is self-destructive. The quest for normalcy, as we have seen in suburbia, is one of the great breeders of neuroses, and the Social Ethic only serves to exacerbate them. What is normalcy? We practice a great mutual deception. Everyone knows that they themselves are different—that they are shy in company, perhaps, or dislike many things most people seem to like—but they are not sure that other people are different too. Like the norms of personality testing, they see about them the sum of efforts of people like themselves to seem as normal as others and possibly a little more so. It is hard enough to learn to live with our inadequacies, and we need not make ourselves more miserable by a spurious ideal of middle-class adjustment. Adjustment to what? Nobody really knows—and the tragedy is that they don't realize that the so-confident-seeming other people don't know either.

Now let us ask if these defects are inevitable. Does The Organization *have* to require acquiescence? Many critics of American civilization, European critics in particular, see our spiritual conformities as an unavoidable consequence of an industrial society, and further growth and prosperity of our kind, they believe, will lead to the ultimate dehumanization of man. The external similarities of American life, in short, they hold as inextricably related to the inner similarities.

We should never allow ourselves to be complacent about the external similarities of American life, or use prosperity as an apologia for Babbittry. But it is a retrograde point of view that fails to recognize that these similarities are in great part a consequence of making the benefits of our civilization available to more people. The monotonous regularity of ranch-type houses that can so easily appall us is not the product of an inner desire for uniformity so much as the fact that modular construction is a condition of moderate-cost housing. This kind of housing is no more or less a pressure for inner conformity than the rows of identical brownstones of the 1890s or, for that matter, the identical brick fronts of the 1700s.

Science and technology do not have to be antithetical to individualism. To hold that they must be antithetical, as many European intellectuals do, is a sort of utopianism in reverse. For a century Europeans projected their dreams into America; now they are projecting their fears, and in so doing they are falling into the very trap they accuse us of. Attributing a power to the machine that we have never felt, they speak of it almost as if it were animistic and had a will of its own over and above the control of man. Thus they see our failures as inevitable, and those few who are consistent enough to pursue the logic of their charge imply that there is no hope to be found except through a retreat to the past. *

This is a hopelessly pessimistic view. The fault is not in the pressures of industrial society—an agrarian society has pressures as powerful—but in the stance we assume before these pressures. If we reverse our current emphases, we will not reverse progress, for individualism is more necessary, not less, than it ever was.

This does not mean a "return" to the Protestant Ethic as preached a century ago. It is futile to speak of individalism as if unrestrained self-interest will some-

---

* In *Tomorrow Is Already Here,* to cite one example, Robert Jungk touches on many of the things I have gone into in this book, but his underlying premise seems to be that it is morally wrong for man to try to control his environment the way Americans are doing. In this indictment he fails to distinguish between the kinds of control, and with little qualification he equates aberrations like "soul engineering" with such activities as trying to find better air medicine techniques, scientific agriculture, etc. This is very sloppy thinking. One kind of activity represents man's attempt to control his physical environment; the other is an attempt at social manipulation, and its relation to science lies only in its pretensions.

Where man uses science to control the physical, the result is to enlarge the area of his potential freedom. This point shouldn't need to be labored, but some of our own critics similarly fail to distinguish between control of the physical and control of the social, with the result that they see the I.B.M. machine, fluorescent lighting, and the like as symbols of spiritual decline. This false personalization of the inanimate seems to me a very sentimental viewpoint and one that militates against any comprehension of the real problems. The I.B.M. machine has no ethic of its own; what it does is enable one or two people to do the amount of computing work that formerly required many more people. If people often use it stupidly, it is their stupidity, not the machine's, and a return to the abacus would not exorcise the failing. People can be treated as drudges just as effectively without modern machines.

---

how produce the greater good. It is for this reason, perhaps, that the right wing has remained a comparatively negative force in American thought. Even more than those who preach the Social Ethic slough over the individual's rights against society, the right sloughs over the individual's obligations to society— and the lack of realism is sensed by the middle as well as the left.

The pendulum analogy that suggests itself would be misleading, for it implies a return to some ideal state of balance. What we need is not to return but to reinterpret, to apply to our problems the basic idea of individualism, not ancient particulars. The doctrines of the nineteenth-century businessman and our modern society are disparate, but that they are disparate is little cause for us to assume that individualism must be too. The central ideal—that the individual, rather than society, must be the paramount end—animated Western thought long before the Industrial Revolution, or Calvinism, or Puritanism, and it is as vital and as applicable today as ever.

But what is the *"solution"?* many ask. There is no solution. The conflict between individual and society has always involved dilemma; it always will, and it is intellectual arrogance to think a program would solve it. Certainly the current experience does suggest a few steps we can profitably take, and I would like to suggest several. Common to all, however, must be a fundamental shift of emphasis, and if this is evaded, any change will exist largely on the level of language. The organization man has a tremendous affinity for vogue words by which the status quo can be described as dynamic advance, and "individualism," alas, is such a word. Let us beware, then, the hard-sell, twelve-point program. Many have been touted as in the name of individual expression, but as those suppressed by them will sense, they are usually organization-serving loyalty devices that fool only those who administrate them.

This caveat made, let me suggest several areas where constructive proposals are in order. First, "human relations." We need by all means to continue to experiment and study. Whatever we call human relations, they are central to the problem of The Organization and the individual, and the more we find out about the effect of the one on the other the better we can find more living room for the individual. But it's not going to be done if many of those who propagate the doctrine cling to self-proving assumptions about the overriding importance of equilibrium, integration, and adjustment. The side of the coin they have been staring at so intently is a perfectly good one, but there is another side and it should not be too heretical at least to have a peek at it. Thousands of studies and case histories have dwelled on fitting the individual to the group, but what about fitting the group to the person? What about *individual* dynamics? The tyranny of the happy work team? The adverse effects of high morale?

One does not have to be in favor of unhappiness to explore such hypotheses, and now, encouragingly, a few whose good will is unquestionable are showing more disposition to do so. The Harvard Business School, which almost grew old with human relations, has been using the word *administrator* less, the word *leader* more, and lately its best research seems directed at the matter of individual initiative more than of group happiness. Rensis Likert, the leader of the "group dynamics" school, has announced that recent studies of organization are leading him and his colleagues to question their earlier conclusions that good morale necessarily produces high productivity. They still

believe that the work group should be supervised as a group rather than on a man-to-man basis, but they do warn that the supervisor who concentrates on making the group happy may produce belongingness but not very much else.

Another fruitful approach would be a drastic re-examination of the now orthodox view that the individual should be given less of the complete task, the team more of it. For a century we have been breaking down tasks into the components and sub-components, each to be performed by a different cell member, and this assembly-line mentality has affected almost everything that men do for a living, including the arts. We can grant that to a degree the benefits of compartmentalized work have surpassed the disadvantages. But do we have to grant that progress demands more of same? That the monotony, the sacrifice of individual accomplishment are inevitable? On the assembly line itself, where specialization would seem most necessary, some companies have found that a reversal of emphasis can actually lead to more productivity. Instead of trying to offset the monotony of a task with externals, such as bowling alleys and "economic education," they have enlarged the task itself. By giving the worker more of the total job to do—asking him to wire the whole set, for example, instead of just one relay—they have given him that wonderful thing that is challenge, and he has responded with more effort, more skill, more *self-respect.*

Is there not a moral here for all organization life? If we truly believe the individual is more creative than the group, just in day-to-day routine there is something eminently practical we can do about it. Cut down the amount of time the individual has to spend in conferences and meetings and team play. This would be a somewhat mechanical approach to what is ultimately a philosophical problem, but if organization people would take a hard look at the different types of meetings inertia has accumulated for The Organization, they might find that the ostensibly negative act of cutting out many of them would lead to some very positive benefits over and above the time saved. Thrown more on their own resources, those who have nothing to offer but the skills of compromising other people's efforts might feel bereft, but for the others the climate might be invigorating. Of itself such a surface change in working conditions would not give them more freedom, but it would halt a bad momentum, it would force organization to distinguish between what are legitimate functions of the group and what are not, and even if it yielded only a few more hours, this would be no small blessing. Once enjoyed, room to move around in is sweet indeed, and men partially liberated might be tantalized into demanding more.

In fighting the incubus of team work, we need to look more understandingly at the frustrations of those involved. Let's go back a moment to the situation of the professional employee. Studies have now convinced organization people that engineers and scientists in industry make up its most disaffected group, and that something should be done about it. The diagnosis is valuable. But how does organization interpret it? Organization people have concluded that the trouble is that the professional tends to be career-oriented rather than company-oriented. What The Organization must do, they believe, is to direct its efforts at integrating him by giving him more company status, indoctrinating him more effectively in the "big picture," by making him, in short, a company man.

How futile, how destructive is this solution! Why should the scientist be company-oriented? Is he to be called maladjusted because he does not fit the administrator's Procrustean bed? And of what profit would be his integration? It is not to his self-interest, neither is it to that of The Organization. Leave him his other allegiance. It is his work that must be paramount, and efforts to divert him into contentment are the efforts best calculated to bridle the curiosity that makes him productive.

Is it so practical? There is a magnificent piece of evidence that it is anything but. In the great slough of mediocrity that is most corporation research, what two laboratories are conspicuous exceptions in the rate of discovery? They are General Electric's research department and Bell Labs: exactly the two laboratories most famous for their encouragement of individualism—the most tolerant of individual differences, the most patient with off-tangent ideas, the least given to the immediate, closely supervised team project. By all accounts, the scientists in them get along quite well, but they do not make a business of it, and neither do the people who run the labs. They care not a whit if scientists' eyes fail to grow moist at company anthems; it is enough that the scientists do superbly well what they want to do, for though the consequences of profit for The Organization are secondary to the scientist, eventually there are these consequences, and as long as the interests of the group and the individual touch at this vital point, such questions as belongingness are irrelevant. Hard-boiled? No, tough-minded—and what more moral basis, it can be asked, for people working together, scientists or others?

It is not just for the scientist, not just for the brilliant, that the moral should be drawn, and this brings us to what ultimately is the single greatest vehicle for constructive change—education. The many points against the social adjustment emphases now prevailing are being vigorously sounded, and it is right that they should be, but one point needs to be made much more emphatically. The case for a rigorously fundamental schooling can be made on the utilitarians' own grounds: social usefulness. There are better reasons for the development of the individual, but until this point is made more clearly we seem by default to leave the debate on the either/or grounds of "democratic education" versus a highly trained elite. This is false antithesis. The great bulk of people will face organization pressures as inhibiting for them as for the few, and they need, as much if not more, to have the best that is within them demanded early. Is it "democratic" to hold that the humanities can have no meaning for them? They do not have to be taught to shake hands with other people; society will attend to this lesson. They have to be taught to reach. All of them. Some will be outstanding, some not, but the few will never flourish where the values of the many are against them.

I have been speaking of measures organizations can take. But ultimately any real change will be up to the individual himself, and this is why his education is so central to the problem. For he must look to his discontents with different eye. It has been said that dominance of the group is the wave of the future and that, lament it or not, he might as well

accept it. But this is contemporaryism at its worst; things are not as they are because there is some good reason they are. Nor is the reverse true. It may one day prove true, as some prophets argue, that we are in a great and dismal tide of history that cannot be reversed, but if we accept the view we will only prove it.

Whatever kind of future suburbia may foreshadow, it will show that at least we have the choices to make. The organization man is not in the grip of vast social forces about which it is impossible for him to do anything; the options are there, and with wisdom and foresight he can turn the future away from the dehumanized collective that so haunts our thoughts. He may not. But he can.

He must *fight* The Organization. Not stupidly, or selfishly, for the defects of individual self-regard are no more to be venerated than the defects of co-operation. But fight he must, for the demands for his surrender are constant and powerful, and the more he has come to like the life of organization the more difficult does he find it to resist these demands, or even to recognize them. It is wretched, dispiriting advice to hold before him the dream that ideally there need be no conflict between him and society. There always is; there always must be. Ideology cannot wish it away; the peace of mind offered by organization remains a surrender, and no less so for being offered in benevolence. That is the problem.

29
Cosmopolitans and Locals: Toward an Analysis of Latent Social Roles
Alvin W. Gouldner

The problem that will be explored in the following analysis is whether there are latent identities and roles of general significance for the study of the modern complex organization. That is, can we discern latent identities and roles which are common to a number of different complex organizations? In this connection, we will explore the possibility that, as distinguished from and in addition to their manifest identities, members of formal organizations may have two latent social identities, here called "cosmopolitan" and "local."[1] Development of these concepts may enable organizational analysis to proceed without focusing solely on the relatively visible, culturally differentiated, manifest organizational identities and roles, but without confining analysis to an undifferentiated blob of "bureaucrats." There are of course other latent identities which

are of organizational significance, and, in Part II of this paper, we shall consider a more complex structure of latent identities.

CONCERNING COSMOPOLITANS AND LOCALS

A number of prior researches have identified certain role-playing patterns which appear convergent with each other and which, further, seem to be commonly based upon those latent identities which will be called "cosmopolitans."

In a study of a factory,[2] "The General Gypsum Company," I noted a type of company executive which I called the "expert." Experts tend to be staff men who never seem to win the complete confidence of the company's highest authorities and are kept removed from the highest reaches of power. Much like staff men in other companies, these experts can advise but cannot command. They are expected to "sell" management on their plans, but cannot order them put into effect. It is widely recognized

[1]These terms are taken from Robert K. Merton, "Patterns of Influence, Local and Cosmopolitan Influentials," in Merton, *op. cit.* Merton's terms are used with respect to types of roles within communities rather than in connection with formal organizations, as they are here. Moreover, Merton's focus is on the conjunction between influence and cosmopolitans-locals, whereas our analysis applies cosmopolitan and local orientations to role players apart from considerations of their influence. Note, also, the similarity between my own discussion of "latent" identities and roles and that of R. Linton, in T. N. Newcomb and E. L. Hartley, eds., *Readings in Sociology* (New York, 1947), p. 368.

[2]Alvin W. Gouldner, *Patterns of Industrial Bureaucracy* (Glencoe, Ill., 1954). It may be worth mentioning that the research published here represents an effort at deliberate continuity and development of some of the conceptions that emerged in the *Patterns* volume.

Source: From "Cosmopolitans and Locals: Toward an Analysis of Latent Social Roles–1" by Alvin W. Gouldner in *Administrative Science Quarterly*, 2, 3 (December 1957), pp. 287–303. Reprinted by permission of Administrative Science Quarterly.

that these experts are not given the "real promotions." The expert is under pressure to forego the active pursuit of his specialty if he wishes to ascend in the company hierarchy. Among the reasons for the experts' subordination may be the fact that they are less frequently identified as "company men" than others in the executive group. The "company man," a pervasive category for the informal classification of industrial personnel, is one who is regarded as having totally committed his career aspirations to his employing company and as having indicated that he wishes to remain with it indefinitely. In effect, then, company personnel were using a criterion of "loyalty to the company" in assigning social identities to members of their organization. A company man is one who is identified as "loyal."

Experts are less likely to be identified in this manner in part because their relatively complex, seemingly mysterious skills, derived from long formal training, lead them to make a more basic commitment to their job than to the organization in which they work. Furthermore, because of their intensive technical training, experts have greater opportunities for horizontal job mobility and can fill jobs in many different organizations. As E. C. Hughes would say, they are more likely to be "itinerants." Consequently, experts are less likely to be committed to their employing organization than to their specialty.

The expert's skills are continually being refined and developed by professional peers outside of his employing organization. Moreover, his continued standing as a competent professional often cannot be validated by members of his own organization, since they are not knowledgeable enough about it. For these reasons, the expert is more likely than others to esteem the good opinion of professional peers elsewhere; he is

disposed to seek recognition and acceptance from "outsiders." We can say that he is more likely to be oriented to a reference group composed of others not a part of his employing organization, that is, an "outer reference group."

Leonard Reissman's study of the role conceptions of government bureaucrats provides another case in point.[3] Among these is the "functional bureaucrat" who is found to be oriented toward groups outside of his employing bureaucracy and is especially concerned with securing recognition from his professional peers elsewhere. If he is an economist, for example, he wants other economists to think well of him, whether or not they are his organizational associates. The functional bureaucrats are also more likely to associate with their professional peers than with their bureaucratic colleagues. They are less likely than other types of bureaucrats to have sentiments of loyalty to their employing bureaucracy. Finally, more than other bureaucrats their satisfaction with their job depends upon the degree to which their work conforms with professional standards, and they seem to be more deeply committed to their professional skills. In short, Reissman's "functional bureaucrat" is much the same as our "expert," insofar as both tend to manifest lesser organizational loyalty, deeper job commitment, and an outer reference group orientation, as compared with their colleagues.

A third study, by Vernon J. Bentz,[4] of a city college faculty, again indicates the interrelationship of these variables and suggests their relevance in another organizational setting. Bentz divided

[3]Leonard Reissman, A Study of Role Conceptions in Bureaucracy, *Social Forces*, 27 (1949), 305–310.

[4]Vernon J. Bentz, "A Study of Leadership in a Liberal Arts College" (Columbus, O.: Ohio State University, 1950; mimeo.).

the college faculty into two groups, those who publish much and those publishing little or nothing. Publication as such is not of course theoretically interesting, but it becomes so if taken as an index of something else. The difficulty is that it is an ambiguous index. Within limits, it seems reasonable to treat it as an index of the degree of commitment to professional skills. However, "high" publication might also indicate a desire to communicate with other, like professionals in different organizations. The high publisher must also take cognizance of the publications which others elsewhere are producing. Thus high publication may also be an index of an outer reference group orientation. High publishers also tend to deemphasize the importance which their own college department had to them and to express the feeling that it had comparatively little control over them. This might be taken to imply a lower degree of commitment or loyalty to that particular group.

Although Bentz's research findings are less direct than the others examined, they do seem to point in the same direction, indicating similarities between the high publisher, the functional bureaucrat, and the expert. They were also particularly useful to my own later study of a college by suggesting indices for some of the significant variables.

These three cases suggested the importance of three variables for analyzing latent identities in organizations: (1) loyalty to the employing organization, (2) commitment to specialized or professional skills, and (3) reference group orientations. Considerations of space do not permit this to be developed here, but each of these studies also found role-playing patterns polar to those discussed. This led us to hypothesize that *two* latent organizational identities could be found. These were:

1. *Cosmopolitans:* those low on loyalty to the employing organization, high on commitment to specialized role skills, and likely to use an outer reference group orientation.

2. *Locals:* those high on loyalty to the employing organization, low on commitment to specialized role skills, and likely to use an inner reference group orientation.

Cosmopolitans and locals are regarded as *latent* identities because they involve criteria which are not fully institutionalized as bases for classifying people in the modern organization, though they are in fact often used as such. For example, "loyalty" usually tends to be taken for granted and is, under normal circumstances, a latent social identity in a rational bureaucracy. For example, it may be preferred, but it is not usually prescribed, that one should be a "company man." While loyalty criteria do become activated at irregular intervals, as, for example, at occasional "testimonial dinners" or during outbursts of organizational conflict and crisis, other criteria for identifying personnel are routinely regarded as more fully legitimate and relevant. For example, skill and competence or training and experience are usually the publicly utilized standards in terms of which performances are judged and performers identified.

While organizations are in fact concerned with the loyalty of their personnel, as indicated by the ritual awarding of gold watches for lengthy years of "faithful service," the dominant organizational orientation toward rationality imposes a ban of pathos on the use of loyalty criteria. Organizational concern with the skill and competence of its personnel exerts pressure against evaluating them in terms of loyalty. Indeed, one of the major dilemmas of the modern organization is the tension between promotions based on skill versus promotions based on seniority, the latter often being an informal index of loyalty. Despite the devotion to rational criteria in the modern organization, however, considerations of loyalty can never be entirely excluded and loyalty criteria frequently serve as a basis for assigning latent identities. In some measure, loyalty to the organization often implies the other two criteria, (1) a willingness to limit or relinquish the commitment to a specialized professional task and (2) a dominant career orientation to the employing organization as a reference group. This linking of organizational criteria is only barely understood by the group members. Thus cosmopolitans and locals are also latent identities because the *conjunction* of criteria involved is not normatively prescribed by the organization.

Each of the other two criteria involved may, however, become an independent basis for assigning organizational identities. For example, in the modern organization people tend to be distinguished in terms of their commitment to their work as well as to their employing organization. A distinction is commonly made between the "cynics" and "clock watchers" or those who are just "doing time," on the one hand, and those who "believe in" or are "fired up" by their task.[5] This distinction is based on the common, if not entirely documented, assumption that the latter are likely to be superior role performers.

It is, however, relatively difficult to know how a person feels about his job; it is easier, and is therefore frequently regarded as more important, to know how he *does* it. Performance rather than belief more commonly becomes the formal criterion for assigning organizational identity. Nonetheless, belief is never totally neglected or discarded but tends, instead, to become a basis on which more latent identities are assigned.

While the significance of reference group orientation varies from one type of organization to another, it remains a common-place if somewhat subtle criterion for assigning latent identities. In colleges, groups distinguish between "insiders" and "outsiders," sometimes using such informal indices as whether or not individuals orient themselves to certain "schools of thought" or people, share familiarity with a prestigious literature, or utilize certain styles of research. In trade unions, different identities may be assigned to those who orient themselves to political movements or to professional peers in other types of organizations and to those who are primarily oriented to the more limited goals of the union—the "union men." Such identities are not fully institutionalized or legitimated, although they may obliquely impinge on promotions, election to office, and evaluation of performance.

COSMOPOLITANS AND LOCALS IN "CO-OP COLLEGE"

A new research was undertaken within the framework of the above considerations. Like Bentz's research this one was also in a college setting. But whereas Bentz's had been a large municipal col-

[5]For a broader discussion of this problem, see Howard S. Becker and Blanche Geer, "The Fate of Idealism in Medical School" (unpublished paper, available from authors at Community Studies, Inc., Kansas City, Mo.).

lege in a metropolitan area, this one was a small, private liberal arts college, with about 1,000 students and 130 faculty situated in a town with a population of less than 5,000. I shall refer to it as "Co-op College" because it was conducted on a "cooperative plan," under which students had alternating periods of regular academic instruction and of work experience away from the campus.

The statistical paraphernalia that follow should not be allowed to obscure the fact that our principal objective was that of concept construction. Our aims were to develop the concepts of cosmopolitan and local latent identities with the use of data and not merely by logical refinement, to provide some warrant that these concepts were useful in organizational analysis, and to show that they were of value in organizational research.

Pursuing the implications of our reexamination of the above studies, we wanted to determine whether organizational personnel did, in fact, manifest the combination of characteristics implied by the notions of cosmopolitan and local. It was therefore assumed that the following variables would be positively correlated: high organizational loyalty, low commitment to specialized skills, and the use of an inner reference group orientation. The finding of such a correlation would be taken to indicate the "locals." The opposite combination, low organizational loyalty, high commitment to specialized skills, and use of an outer reference group orientation, would be taken to indicate the "cosmopolitans." It would seem reasonable to expect that persons manifesting two such different combinations of variables would have differing self-conceptions and identities, as well as being differently perceived and identified by others in their group.

The sample was drawn from the names listed in the college catalogue of 1952–53, consisting of all those mentioned as teaching and administrative faculty, and was supplemented by a list of new faculty members who had joined the staff that year. All those listed in either roster, with the exception of those whose jobs were entirely clerical or secretarial, were to be interviewed. Five refused to be interviewed, four of these being department heads. The loss of such a homogeneous group could affect the representativeness of the sample. Nonetheless, we were unable to detect any way in which this could adversely affect the conditions required to test our specific hypotheses. One hundred and twenty-five interviews, with teaching, research, and administrative personnel, were secured, providing a nearly complete census of the faculty then on campus.

SOME INITIAL FINDINGS

In order to test the central hypotheses we first designed Guttman scales for each of the three key variables. Quasi-scales were constructed for inner-outer reference group orientation, for commitment to specific role skills, and for organizational loyalty. In order to secure adequate scales for each variable, we had to remove a number of questions which we had initially thought would be scalable. We then assigned Guttman scores for each of the three variables to each person and correlated them. The first three tables below indicate that the three key variables were related in the predicted direction.

As a further indication that the above three variables were interrelated in the predicted direction, a single Guttman scale was constructed out of the individual scores derived from the

TABLE 1 ● PEOPLE HIGHER ON ORGANIZATIONAL LOYALTY TENDED TO BE LOWER ON COMMITMENT TO SKILLS.

		Commitment to Skill		
		High	Low	N
		%	%	
Organizational loyalty	High	61	78	(88)
	Low	39	22	(37)
		100	100	
	N	57	68	125

TABLE 2 ● PEOPLE WITH AN "OUTER" REFERENCE GROUP ORIENTATION TENDED TO BE LOWER ON ORGANIZATIONAL LOYALTY.

		Organizational Loyalty		
		High	Low	N
		%	%	
Reference group orientation	Outer	35	57	(52)
	Inner	65	43	(73)
		100	100	
	N	88	37	125

TABLE 3 ● PEOPLE WITH AN "OUTER" REFERENCE GROUP TENDED TO BE HIGHER ON COMMITMENT TO SKILLS.*

		Commitment to Skill		
		High	Low	N
		%	%	
Reference group orientation	Outer	53	32	(52)
	Inner	47	68	(73)
		100	100	
	N	57	68	125

*All the foregoing tables (1–3) were significant on the Chi Square test at better than the .05 level.

TABLE 4

	Category	Number of People
Extreme cosmopolitans	1	29
	2	23
	3	30
Extreme locals	4	43
	N	125

three previous scales. This new "scale of scales" was constructed on the hypothesis that high skill commitment, low organizational loyalty, and an outer reference group orientation were positively correlated, as were low skill commitment, high organizational loyalty, and an inner reference group orientation. The resulting scale had a coefficient of reproducibility of 91.4 per cent and yielded four categories, as shown in Table 4.

The meanings of the concepts "cosmopolitan" and "loyal" as measured by this scale can perhaps best be indicated by comparing the mean scores of the two extremes on each of the items in the scale. The following statements present a composite picture. In the parenthesis following each statement, "Q." refers to the question number. The number in brackets indicates the level of significance of the difference of the mean scores between cosmopolitans and locals, that is, categories 1 and 4, as tested by Chi Square. ("Cosmopolitans" are called "cosmos" hereafter.)

DIFFERENCES BETWEEN COSMOPOLITANS AND LOCALS

1. Cosmos were more likely than locals to believe that faculty members should have their loads lightened to make more time available for private research, writing, or other work in their own fields. (Q. 39) [.001]

2. Cosmos were more likely than locals to maintain that if they saw no opportunity to do their own personal research at Co-op College they would find their jobs less satisfying. (Q. 42) [.001]

3. Cosmos were more likely to feel that there were very few people around the college with whom they could share their professional interests. (Q. 54) [.001]

4. Cosmos were more likely to have, or to be working on, their Ph.D.s, while locals were more likely to have, or to be working on, their M.A.s. (Q. 110) [.01–.001]

5. Cosmos had published more than locals. (Q. 111) [.01–.001]

6. Cosmos showed less organizational loyalty than locals in that they would more readily leave Co-op College for another. (Q. 69) [.01–.001]

7. Cosmos knew fewer faculty members at Co-op College than did locals. (Q. 77) [.01–.001]

8. Cosmos were less likely to regard the local chapter of the AAUP as an "outside" organization and on that ground subject to criticism. (Q. 24) [.05–.02]

9. Cosmos were more likely to get most of their intellectual stimulation from sources outside of the college than were locals. (Q. 73) [.05–.02]

10. Cosmos were more inclined than locals to believe that recent investigations of communism had affected the local campus adversely. (Q. 89A) [.17]

11. Cosmos were more likely to regard salaries at the college as unfortunately low. (Q. 55) [.22]

THE ORGANIZATIONAL RELEVANCE OF COSMOPOLITANS AND LOCALS

From the above analysis it seemed that we had succeeded in distinguishing two latent identities, cosmos and locals, and had begun to confirm empirically some of their predicted characteristics. At this point we wanted to know whether being a cosmo or a local made a difference in the organizationally relevant behavior of the person. For example, did cosmos have more or less influence than local in the group? Did they participate more or less in its activities? Which type was more inclined to use formal rules and regulations, to behave in a "red-tape" way, in the solution of group problems? If there were some empirical indication that cosmos and locals behaved differently in these respects, there would be reason to believe that these concepts could prove useful in organizational analysis.

A significant variable for organizational analysis is the degree of influence which different kinds of people have in the administration of the group. A measure of degree of influence was obtained in the following manner. Respondents were asked, "Which of the following policy decisions are you in on?" They were asked to check the items in the following list which they believed applied to them.

1. Deciding on the tenure of faculty members.
2. Making faculty and administrative appointments.
3. Deciding upon curriculum and organizational changes.
4. Deciding on student tenure; for example, dismissal or suspension.
5. Deciding upon the allocation of college funds.
6. Deciding who assembly speakers should be.
7. Deciding upon the selection of prospective students.
8. Deciding course and examination schedules.
9. Deciding "community-government" structure.
10. Deciding upon broad educational objectives.

The "influence score" of each faculty member was determined by adding together the total number of those items which he checked. No effort was made to assign different weights to participation in different decision-making areas. It was our impression that competent raters from within the college who might rank order the influence implied by different decisions would disagree considerably among themselves. In part, this was so because they were loath to make such distinctions, since Co-op College is strongly committed to a belief system which stresses the equality of different people and positions. The influence distribution was dichotomized and correlated with cosmos and locals, and Table 5 was produced.

Though the differences in Table 5 *lack* statistical significance, they do exhibit a tendency for influence to

TABLE 5

		Cosmos (1)	Intermediates (2)	(3)	Locals (4)	N
		%	%	%	%	
Degree of influence	High	55	65	67	53	74
	Low	45	35	33	47	51
		100	100	100	100	
	N	29	23	30	43	125

increase steadily as one moves from cosmos to locals—until, that is, the extreme locals (4), who manifest a sharp decline in influence. As will be noted in Part II, the above similarity in influence of the extreme locals and extreme cosmos may derive from two factors: (1) There is more than one type of cosmo, and one of these does *not* have low influence. (2) Extreme locals are decidedly older than the extreme cosmos, and the exigencies of advanced age may serve to reduce the influence of some locals. These considerations should also be borne in mind in interpreting the participation patterns of locals.

Where there is room for choice, the degree of participation which an individual manifests in a group is a significant item in organizational analysis. In order to determine whether participation varied among cosmos and locals, a "degree-of-participation" index was constructed in the following manner. The respondents answered the question: "Here is a list of community activities (councils, committees, etc.). Check those in which you participated during the year." Respondent was also to indicate whether this participation was "regular" or "occasional." Weightings were assigned by multiplying each "reg-

ular" activity checked by 3 and each "occasional" one by 1; the individual's total participation score was then added. In Table 6 "high" means that the respondent's participation score was six or more points, while "low" participation means five or fewer points.

One of the most interesting elements in organizational analysis is the degree to which the organization is administered in terms of formal rules and regulations and the degree to which members feel inclined to solve group problems using such formal rules. To test for a possible relation between cosmos and locals and such a disposition, a measure of "rule tropism" was constructed. The following Likert-type questions, which it will be noticed deal mainly with faculty orientation toward *student* behavior, were used to construct a Guttman scale of rule tropism. (A five-point check list ranging from "Strongly Agree" to "Strongly Disagree" was provided for each of these questions.)

1. By and large regulations at Co-op College are too lenient.

2. The behavior of the student body during the past few years suggests that hours for freshmen might be desirable.

TABLE 6 ● EXTREME LOCALS TEND TO PARTICIPATE MORE THAN
EXTREME COSMOS, THOUGH THE INTERMEDIATE PARTICIPATES
MORE THAN EITHER.*

			(1) Cosmos	(2,3) Inter- mediate	(4) Locals	N
			%	%	%	
Degree of participation	High		38	58	46	(62)
	Low		62	42	54	(63)
			100	100	100	
		N	29	53	43	125

*Chi Square: P < .05

TABLE 7 ● LOCALS TEND TO BE HIGHER ON RULE TROPISM
THAN COSMOS.*

			Cosmos	Inter- mediate	Locals	N
			%	%	%	
Rule tropism	High		32	50	56	(59)
	Low		68	50	44	(66)
			100	100	100	
		N	29	53	43	125

*Chi Square: P. 07

3. Looking at developments in the area of "community living" and at the widespread violations of the honor system, it would seem that we need more supervision of student behavior.

These questions were deliberately "biased" to facilitate answers which agreed with the desirability of using formal controls. Pretests had showed that, unless questions were formulated in this way, answers would tend to cluster around a tendency to disagree with the use of formal controls, since this was the official and strongly affirmed college ideology. The final scale had a reproducibility of 90.6 per cent. The individual's score on this rule-tropism scale was then correlated with his latent social role, as Table 7 shows.

A question arises as to whether it is cosmopolitanism-localism as such that accounts for rule tropism. Perhaps "influence," which may have a relation to cosmo-localism, determines rule tropism? How does the possession of influence in general relate to rule tropism? This can be seen from Table 8.

Table 8 suggests the possibility that

TABLE 8 • PEOPLE WITH LOW INFLUENCE ARE MORE LIKELY TO BE HIGH ON RULE TROPISM THAN THOSE WITH HIGH INFLUENCE.*

| | | Degree of Influence | | |
		Low	High	N
		%	%	
Rule tropism	High	61	38	(59)
	Low	39	62	(66)
		100	100	
	N	51	74	125

*Chi Square: P < .05

TABLE 9 • REGARDLESS OF THEIR DEGREE OF INFLUENCE, LOCALS TEND TO BE HIGHER ON RULE TROPISM THAN COSMOS.*

| | | Degree of Influence | | | | | | |
| | | | *Low* | | | *High* | | |
		Cos-mos	Inter-mediate	Lo-cals	Cos-mos	Inter-mediate	Lo-cals	N
		%	%	%	%	%	%	
Rule tropism	High	31	72	70	31	37	48	(66)
	Low	69	28	30	69	63	52	(59)
		100	100	100	100	100	100	
	N	13	18	20	16	35	23	125

*Chi Square: P < .05

being a cosmo or local may in no way affect the individual's propensity toward rule tropism and that the latter may be determined by the amount of his influence. This possibility can be examined in Table 9, in which the degree of influence is held constant and the latent identities are varied.

Table 9 suggests that even when the effects of varying degrees of influence are held constant, the import of Table 7 is still valid; that is, locals are still more prone to rule tropism than cosmos. It does not follow, however, that variations in influence considered in con-

junction with variations in latent social identities have *no* effect on the propensity toward rule tropism. This possibility may be explored by reversing the interpretation of Table 9; that is, by now holding constant the latent social identities and simultaneously varying the degree of influence possessed by people who have the same latent social identities. This can be done by comparing column one with column four in Table 9. It shows that cosmos who are low on influence have exactly the same degree of rule tropism as cosmos who are high on influence. Table 10 compares

TABLE 10 ● LOCALS.*

			Degree of Influence		
			Low	High	N
			%	%	
Rule tropism	High		70	48	(17)
	Low		30	52	(26)
			100	100	
		N	20	23	43

*Chi Square: P < .05

with each other *locals* having a low and a high degree of influence in respect to their rule tropism. Unlike the cosmos, there *is* a difference in the rule tropism of locals who are influential and those who are not.

In other words, Tables 9 and 10 indicate that differences in influence affect the rule tropism of cosmos and locals differently. Cosmos' rule tropism seems unaffected by variations in their influence, while differences in influence do seem to affect the rule tropism of locals. Locals with low influence are much more disposed to rule tropism than those with high influence. Put differently, it appears to make less difference to cosmos whether they have high or low influence within their employing organization.

The analysis thus far provides some basis for believing that cosmos and locals behave differently with respect to the formal organization of the group. The question then arose whether or not cosmo and local identities affected *informal* relations in the group. An effort was first made to approach this in the following manner. During the interview people had been presented with the names of a randomly selected list of twenty-six faculty members. They were asked to indicate how well they knew each by checking one of these four possibilities: (1) do not know him at all, (2) greet him occasionally in the hall or on campus, (3) drop into each other's offices occasionally, (4) are guests in each other's homes several times a month. Respondents checking categories (1) or (2) were classified as having a "low" degree of sociability with the particular faculty member, and those checking categories (3) and (4) as having a "high" degree of sociability.

Since we had interviewed the people on this list we could determine what their latent social identity was, that is, whether they were cosmos or locals. Similarly, we also knew whether the respondent doing the rating was a cosmo or a local. We were thus in a position to ascertain whether the latent social identity tended to influence patterns of sociability. Our hypothesis was that latent-identity homophily tended to increase sociable interaction; that is, people having the same latent identity were expected to be more sociable with each other than with those having a different latent identity.[6] In constructing Table 11 we sought to determine whether cosmos were more sociable with cosmos and locals more sociable

TABLE 11 ● LATENT IDENTITY HOMOPHILY.*

			C→C	C→L	L→C	L→L	N
			%	%	%	%	
Degree of sociability	High		30	29	34	38	(960)
	Low		70	71	66	62	(1935)
			100	100	100	100	
		N	603	610	847	835	2895

*Chi Square: P < .05

with locals. The arrow (→) indicates the direction of choice, going from chooser to chosen.

Some conclusions from Table 11 might be:

1. Locals are a little more likely to be homophilous than cosmos; that is, locals are more likely to have higher sociability with other locals than with cosmos.

2. In general, locals seem to have a slightly higher rate of sociability than do cosmos, regardless of whether their choices are homophilous or heterophilous.

3. Cosmos manifest little or no tendency to prefer homophilous to heterophilous sociability.

It is clear that Table 11 presents no conclusive evidence whatsoever of the significance of cosmos and locals for patterns of informal sociability. Nonetheless, there are slight trends in the predicted direction which indicate that the matter is worth pursuing. This, together with the findings presented in earlier tables which suggest that locals and cosmos have different degrees of influence, participation, and propensity toward rule tropism, indicated that cosmos and locals might be concepts useful in organizational analysis and that further efforts at refining them could be rewarding. The results of these efforts will be presented in the next issue of the *Quarterly*.

[6]For a discussion of homophily and heterophily and its bearing on friendship, see Paul F. Lazarsfeld and Robert K. Merton, "Friendship as Social Process: A Substantive and Methodological Analysis," in M. Berger, T. Abel, and C. Page, *Freedom and Control in Modern Society* (New York, 1954).

30

"Democracy" as Hierarchy and Alienation

Frederick C. Thayer

If the organizational revolution is to expand its frontiers and help show us the way to a meaningful future, we must sweep aside the conventional wisdom of politics and economics which contributes so much to the alienation the revolution seeks to remove. We are less accustomed to thinking of "democracy"* and hierarchy as unalterably wedded to each other, for we tend to see "democracy" as something which has liberated us from the oppressive rulers of the past. True enough, Henry VIII does not stalk the earth any more, but Hitler came to power in a "democratic" setting. Even at its best, "democracy" has tended only to *limit* the power of rulers, without changing the fundamental *relationship* between those who rule and those who are ruled. This is because all theories of "democracy" contain within them the pervasive assumption that hierarchy is inevitable, desirable, and necessary, the assumption that *no organization (family, church, corporation, public agency, nation-state) can achieve its social purposes other than through the interaction of those designated "superiors" and those labeled "subordinates."*

We have lost sight of this long-term association of "democracy" and hierarchy, in part because "democracy" developed as a reaction to more oppressive forms of government and in part because

cause most "democracies" began as limited governments—that is, most of the activities of individuals and groups took place outside the control of political leaders. These activities, however, were also based upon the assumption of hierarchy; and, as modern governments take on more and more of them, we feel increasingly alienated from those activities without understanding why.

This does not mean that alienation is *solely* a modern phenomenon; it is caused by hierarchy, and social hierarchies existed long before anyone began thinking of political "democracy." If alienation is traceable to hierarchy, as argued herein, the association of "democracy" with hierarchy means that the way we look at government now does not offer us an escape from alienation. Certainly the association exists, even if we do not emphasize it in our formal theories; we believe almost as a matter of course that we are better off if we have a "strong" President and that he can perform more effectively if he has a "mandate" (in the form of a huge majority vote) from the people, which enables him to exert his "authority."

It might have been useful to concentrate upon power instead of hierarchy; one new book calls for a dissolution of power and an end to its central position in our approaches to politics.[1] It also might have worked to focus upon authority—always important in studies of social behavior—and one author observes that it is time we recognized au-

---

*"Democracy" refers throughout to our conventional approach to government. It implies that we must transform ourselves if the quotation marks are to be removed.

Source: From the book, *An End to Hierarchy and Competition* by Frederick C. Thayer. Copyright © 1981. Reprinted by permission of the publisher, Franklin Watts.

thority as something "extraneous to democracy."[2] Power, however, is equally
meaningful in unstructured social interaction of minor concern here, and authority is closely related to modern theories of bureaucracy which cover only
part of our history.[3] Hierarchy gives us
a conceptual window upon a greater
range of our past: it spans both feudalism and postfeudalism, modern social
structures being an uncomfortable combination of both. To begin, then, we
must look at the historical connections
between hierarchy and alienation.

HIERARCHY AND ALIENATION: CAUSE AND EFFECT

Alienation, despite its widespread use
in describing social malaise, remains
unsatisfactorily defined. Most attempts
to do so begin with the admission that
most of us, perhaps all of us in modern
societies, have never experienced *un*-
alienation or *non*alienation. Alienation
and unalienation can be understood
only with reference to each other,
somewhat in the way we think of health
and disease. We only know what it is
like to have a particular disease because
we know what it is like not to have it;
without an experiential definition of
health, the symptoms of the disease
would appear normal.[4] Lacking any experience of unalienation, all we can do
is examine the plausibility of arguments
as to both the underlying causes and immediate symptoms of alienation. If we
are *all* alienated, some are unaware of
their illness, while others cannot comprehend its extent. If nobody can claim
to *know* exactly how to transform alienation into unalienation, it seems reasonable to dismiss the claims of those
who describe their Utopian communes
as unalienated. To define unalienation
as a state achieved by "dropping out" of
society is to glorify a separateness which

must itself be alienating. The analysis
here departs substantially from much of
the literature on the subject. It suggests
that the fundamental source of alienation is *hierarchy*, that this is not a phenomenon associated only with the modern age of industry and technology but
has existed for six thousand years or
more, and that "democratic" political
theory and "democratic" political systems, because they are based upon hierarchy, are inherently alienating. In
this sense, there is nothing to choose
between capitalist and socialist versions
of "democracy."

Because of the influence of Karl
Marx, or the influence of his interpret-
ers, we have tended to associate alienation with people who work in industry,
especially on assembly lines in plants
"owned" by capitalist entrepreneurs and
exploiters. Even though we have admit-
ted since the 1930's that the "managerial revolution" has transferred control
of corporations from owners to managers, many socialists still pronounce
ownership the most important factor.
To the contrary, we are beginning only
now to learn, more than a century after
we started to think about it, that a
change from "private" to "public" ownership does nothing to alleviate alienation.[5] We are learning that the individual worker cannot comprehend what it
would mean to own the plant in which
he works, and that he has no desire to
do so. This also holds for the pilot who
flies an airliner, the soldier who fires a
howitzer, and the government clerk
who uses a file cabinet.[6] The problem
has been and is hierarchy; though it exists in secular and postfeudal modern
Western societies, its roots are as old
as the shift from gathering and hunting
to agriculture and urbanism. In other
words, hierarchy and organization, well
established long before anyone thought
seriously about "democratic" govern-

ment, are hence imbedded in all theories of "democratic" government. The first analytical step, then, is to explore the *supposed* sources of alienation.

Conventionally, alienation is thought to exist when the world, society, or organization does not respond to the individual member, and subjects him to forces he can neither comprehend nor influence in a meaningful way. Usually the industrial worker is thought alienated because he cannot control his immediate work processes, develop a sense of purpose, feel himself a member of an integrated industrial community, and become involved in his work as a mode of self-expression. In extreme cases, the individual only reacts in unvaried fashion to the ceaseless rhythms of technology. He becomes a *thing*, simply the extension of a machine. Chained by the wrench in his hand to the ever-present assembly line, he has no alternative if he is to be paid and to survive. The image was provided many years ago by Charlie Chaplin, in *Modern Times*. The worker is separated from his work, for he plays no part in deciding what to do or how to do it. He is separated from his product, for he has no control over what he makes or what becomes of it. He is separated from his fellows; some of them are, as he is, just extensions of machines, while others (those who "own" what he makes) are his natural enemies. He is separated from himself, because he can view his work only as something which divides his present from his future; it is only a means to an end which he hopes to realize at some indeterminate future point. All the forces he can neither control nor influence end up controlling him and, in effect, "to keep from dying, the worker sells his life."[7]

French sociologist Jacques Ellul expands this view to take in the whole of modern technological society. He uses "technique" as his focus, and defines it as the entire range of methods human beings consciously and systematically have used to organize what they do.[8] While technique is involved in such a simple task as driving a nail with a hammer, it reaches fruition in the complex organizations of modern society. In every field of endeavor, whether the organizing of intellectual activity so as to discover and disseminate knowledge, or the designing of a government agency, we use a "rational division of labor" to spell out in detail the tasks of every individual. By the very size of the phenomena which embody it, technique produces self-perpetuating organizational monstrosities which totally dehumanize the individual. Even when we speak of adapting the machine or the organization to the individual, we forget that adaptation is inevitably reciprocal; hence the individual adapts to the organization, and it swallows him. Over time, so goes the Ellulian argument, the *means* (organization) consumes those for whom it was designed to achieve an *end*.

Ellul's counsel is almost totally one of despair, and critics have taken him to task for it.[9] His mistake, a serious one, lies in his insistence that alienation is traceable solely to the replacement, by modern organizations, of earlier traditional institutions (families, religious orders) which provided individuals with a sense of community on a scale recognizable to them. When these institutional ties were torn asunder by attacks made in the name of individual freedom, the human being was left fragmented and atomized, easy prey for the onrush of modern organization. The experts of technique were able to herd individuals together, as in industrial communities, and so create the modern monstrosities. Perhaps because he is a traditional Christian and thus assumes hierarchy desirable, Ellul takes pains to dissociate the rise of modern organization from Christianity. This leads him to minimize the evidence he presents that technique is not a modern invention. After all, the pyramids of Egypt and the Great Wall of China were assembled by complex organizations that long preceded large-scale undertakings in the West.

Some of the traditional structures to which Ellul gives so much credit may have given individuals a sense of belongingness and community, but living within the confines of a feudalistic system, they must still have been very alienated. While some organizations which dominated the life of the individual were smaller than what we are used to now, they assumed hierarchy to be sacred. Indeed, the dictionary still links hierarchy directly with religion. In feudal systems, true enough, superiors and subordinates (lords and serfs) regarded each other as *persons* and, despite the degrading nature of these social relationships, persons felt a mutual responsibility to each other (lords should help serfs in need of help).[10] These relationships, however, were hardly sufficient to define such social systems as unalienated, and it is nonsense for Ellul to so argue. Serfs knew they had no choice but to accept as permanent their personal submission to their masters, to accept without question the social norms handed down to them, and to look for salvation only in some ill-defined hereafter. For the serf, the "here-and-now" was miserable and alienating; that is why people in traditional societies today laugh when we suggest they should avoid modernization in order to keep from becoming alienated.

The distinguishing characteristic of modern postfeudal organization, of course, is that relationships between superiors and subordinates are *impersonal*.

The modern organization in a "democratic" society includes the premise that we are free and independent citizens; hence we glorify administration that is "neutral," "impartial," "dispassionate," "disinterested," and "objective." Yet it is the phrase "impersonal bureaucracy" which reflects our frustration when public agencies supposedly dedicated to helping us are separated, or alienated, from us. The fiction of freedom and independence, and the corollary objective of political equality, encourage us to believe that as *persons* we interact with each other in free and equal fashion. In organizations, we are *not* free and equal, so we describe ourselves not as persons, but as *roles;* we "act out" the norms prescribed by other roles. We interact, in other words, as *nonpersons*—a framework in which we are automatically alienated from one another and from ourselves. We are defined, and we define ourselves as husbands, wives, students, workers, managers, or inmates. As *roles*, we find ourselves on a treadmill; our rank, status, and accomplishments are attributed to our roles, *not* to our *selves*.

To deal with husbands, wives, and managers in the same context is to emphasize that we live today amid an uneasy combination of feudalism and postfeudalism, which prevails in virtually all social organizations:

1. The family remains basically a feudal organization, a superior-subordinate relationship of persons. In an attempt to escape the worst aspects of feudalism, we have impersonalized the family to some extent, but to regard marriage as the interaction of nonpersons, or roles, is inherently unsatisfying.[11]

2. The Mafia emphasizes close-knit feudalistic family structures, but its

leaders make postfeudalistic policy decisions to contract for the removal of individuals.[12]

3. Professional athletes are the feudalistic property of owners, who make postfeudalistic decisions to sell, trade, or otherwise dispose of them for "the good of the organization."

4. The corporation is, by custom and law, a fictious and artificial person; in this setting, superiors have no *personal* responsibility for subordinates. In the effort to modify this alienating atmosphere, we attempt to humanize the organization and transform it into a community; we can see this happening when we speak of a top manager as the "old man." These warming relationships are shattered when the superior, acting in his impersonal role, must fire the subordinate.[13] The combination of feudalism and postfeudalism is especially difficult for women who become the "bosses" of other executives. If the organization has attempted to humanize itself, it takes on the appearance of a matriarchal family, thus reversing the pattern of marriage. Whether women care to admit it or not, this becomes as disorienting to them as to men, for it suggests that women can be liberated only if they dominate men.

5. Intellectuals pride themselves on the "collegial" or "family" relationships they enjoy as supposedly self-actualized individuals. At the same time, they raise higher walls between academic disciplines, argue that "facts" can objectively be separated from values, insist that knowledge can be made certain, and retain the right, by virtue of their "knowledge," to impose their views upon students or junior colleagues seeking tenure—thereby acting out roles indistinguishable from those in other superior-subordinate relationships.[14]

6. The modern nation-state prides itself on being a government of laws instead of men, but the organizational structures of nation-states were initially designed by monarchs who looked upon their realms as private enterprises and upon themselves as agents of the Almighty (Louis XIV and Frederick the Great).[15] Present-day "democracies" retain much of the symbolism of the traditional past. The British monarch is crowned in church, and the "Speech From The Throne" is used to announce major policies. We look upon our President as both an impersonal *office* and a *person* who somehow stands above us. We insist he lay his hand upon the Bible as a condition of taking office, we scrutinize his attendance at religious services, and we have even changed our pledge to the flag to emphasize that as a nation-state we exist "under God."

The constant factor in our past and present, the one standing everywhere in the way, is hierarchy; it makes feudalism, postfeudalism, and any middle ground which combines them equally intolerable. Given our inclination to accept the inevitability of hierarchy in organizations, we ricochet back and forth between feudalism and postfeudalism in the search for a nonexistent compromise. Where large landowners and sharecroppers once constituted a feudal system, farm workers increasingly seek postfeudal unionization to deal with corporate farmers. Where industrial workers once lived in feudalistic "company towns," only to turn to postfeudal unionization, contemporary attempts to redesign industry will propel workers back toward feudalism unless hierarchy is eroded. More and more, university faculty members seek postfeudal unionization to offset what they perceive as the arbitrary decisions of quasi-feudal administrators, failing to note that the cycle cannot be broken within the confines of hierarchy. The formal, or officially acknowledged, interactions within any hierarchical structure are those of *ruling* and *being ruled, issuing commands* and *obeying them, repressing* and *being repressed.*

Those seeking to explain or escape alienation fail to recognize hierarchy as the historical cause of alienation, and thus miss the point. Ellul retains a wistful longing for the traditional priesthood of Christianity and for the presumed solace available in other traditional organizations, but that was a social design in which individuals directly repressed other individuals. Surely those whose place in life was decided upon by others must have been as alienated as anyone living today. Marx was dedicated to raising the class consciousness of workers to a level where the "dictatorship of the proletariat" would transform everyone else, perhaps the classic example of a *means* which, if implemented, would prevent the attainment of the end allegedly sought. The person defined solely as a worker is, even in Marxist terms, one whose identity is erased by his role. Where hierarchy is concerned, then, there is no choice between Ellul, Marx, and others. All of them accept hierarchy, and their proposed cures for alienation involve only more of the same. No "dictatorship" can help.*

NOTES

1. Silviu Brucan, *The Dissolution of Power: A Sociology of International Relations and Politics* (New York: Knopf, 1971), Ch. IX. A former Romanian diplomat, Brucan resur-

*This analysis bypasses the long-debated question of whether Marx's successors corrupted his theories. *Organizationally* speaking, he subverted himself.

rects the Marx-Engels notion of "self-administration of things and people" in a classless society, something requiring administration but not power. While this envisions the end of the nation-state, it is not at all clear that Brucan has in mind a nonhierarchical form of administration.

2. Holtan P. Odegard, *The Politics of Truth: Toward Reconstruction in Democracy* (University of Alabama Press, 1971), p. 288. The author's argument throughout, however, implies an authoritative role for relatively autonomous administrators.

3. Martin Albow, *Bureaucracy* (New York: Praeger, 1970), pp. 39–40.

4. Bertell Ollman, *Alienation: Marx's Conception of Man in Capitalist Society* (Cambridge: University Press, 1971), Ch. 18.

5. "It ought . . . to be plain that command depends not on ownership but on the division of labor in detail. . . . The command structure of a nationalized industry is, in essentials, no whit different from that of private industry, hedged about though it invariably is by the trappings of constitutionalism (joint consultation). It is at last plain to see that capitalism in industry is one thing, command in industry quite another." Graham Wootton, *Workers, Unions, and the State* (New York: Schocken Books, 1967), Ch. III. Wootton's view is that Engels grasped this point, Marx did not.

6. Robert Blauner, *Alienation and Freedom: The Factory Worker and His Industry* (University of Chicago Press, 1964), p. 17.

7. The quotation is from Ollman, *op. cit.*, p. 173. The outline of alienation is a composite of Blauner, *op. cit.*, Ch. 1, and Amitai Etzioni, *The Active Society: A Theory of Social and Political Processes* (New York: Free Press, 1968), Ch. 21, "Alienation, Inauthenticity, and Their Reduction."

8. Jacques Ellul, *The Technological Society* (New York: Vintage Books, 1964), Ch. 1.

9. ". . . He creates a despair so profound as to render resistance hopeless, leaving many who accept what he has to say with the conviction that the only dignified thing left to do is await the end." Victor C. Ferkiss, *Technological Man: The Myth and the Reality* (New York: Braziller, 1969), p. 87.

10. Ollman, *op. cit.*, p. 213.

11. "If I had to describe in one word the general mood and tenor of the relationship between husband and wife in this country at this moment, I would choose, unhappily and unoriginally, alienation." Natalie Gittelson, *The Erotic Life of the American Wife* (New York: Delacorte Press, 1969, 1972), p. xii.

12. In describing why he wanted to act the title role in *The Godfather*, Marlon Brando observed, "The picture itself made a useful commentary on corporate thinking in this country . . . because the Mafia patterned itself so closely on the corporation. . . . Whenever they wanted to kill somebody it was always a matter of policy. Before pulling the trigger, they told him: 'Just business. Nothing personal.'" *Life,* March 10, 1972.

13. "Of all the corporate chores performed by executives, the most painful is firing other executives. . . . It is principally because of the 'democratization' of American business that this process is becoming more traumatic every year . . . in the modern corporation, increasingly dominated by humanist values and a democratic ethic . . . it becomes harder all the time to view one's colleagues as just names on the table of organization—which means, among other things, that it becomes harder all the time to fire them." Judson Gooding, "The Art of Firing an Executive," *Fortune,* October 1972.

14. In recounting the debate over theories of prehistory and evolution, one author notes that defenders of the dominant theory successfully threatened textbook publishers with destruction of their university markets unless they removed from their book lists authors who did not conform. "The Galileos of today," he adds, "are not likely to be kneeling before cardinals and mumbling the truth under their breath; they will be kneeling before professors with tenure." William I. Thompson, *At the Edge of History* (New York: Harper and Row, 1970), pp. 128–32.

15. Dwight Waldo, "Some Thoughts on Alternatives, Dilemmas, and Paradoxes, in a Time of Turbulence," in his (ed.) *Public Administration in a Time of Turbulence* (Scranton, Pa.: Chandler Publishing, 1971), pp. 282–84. The conclusion came from Waldo's attempt to search out the longer history of public administration in the West.

CHAPTER V

Power and Influence

Power is the latent ability to influence others' actions, thoughts, or emotions. It is the potential to get people to do things the way you want them done—a social energy waiting to be used, to be transformed into influence or, as in the words of R.G.H. Siu, to be transformed from *potential power* into *kinetic power*. Power is influence over the beliefs, emotions, and behaviors of people and, according to Siu, "potential power is the capacity to do so, but kinetic power is the act of doing so. . . . One person exerts power over another to the degree that he is able to exact compliance as desired" (Siu, 1979, p. 31).

As we have seen throughout this book almost everything necessary for understanding organizational behavior is related to everything else, and *power* is no exception. The subject of power in organizations is inseparable from the topics and issues that have been the focuses of earlier chapters, most notably (but certainly not exclusively) *the organizational context* (including specialization, division of labor, and the functions of structure), *intergroup dynamics,* and *leadership.*

As a concept of organizational behavior, *power* is associated with several other organizational subjects which many people find distasteful. First, for most of us, power suggests an ability to overcome resistance. This "black side" of power is behind Rosabeth Moss Kanter's (1979, p. 65) observation: "Power is America's last dirty word. It is easier to talk about money—and much easier to talk about sex—than it is to talk about power. People who have it deny it; people who want it do not want to appear hungry for it; and people who engage in its machinations do so secretly." Second, power owes much of its existence to feelings of dependence. Power exists only when there is an unequal relationship between two people—where one of the two is dependent upon the other (Emerson, 1962).

THE ORGANIZATIONAL CONTEXT

Power starts with structural issues. Although individual skill determines the effectiveness of the use of power, power is not fundamentally an issue of person or personality. "Power is first and foremost a structural phenomenon, and should be understood as such" (Pfeffer, 1981, p. x). *Specialization* and *division of labor,* two related subjects that were discussed rather extensively in the *Introduction,* are the most fundamental causes of dependence among individuals and organizational units. With division of labor, people in organizations are dependent upon others

420

for all sorts of things that are needed to accomplish their tasks: They are dependent for timely completion of prior tasks, accurate information, materials and supplies, competent people, and political support.

Chapter IV asserts that "structure establishes how *roles, expectations,* and *resource allocations* are defined for people and groups in any given organization." Thus, the structural forces caused by specialization and division of labor are extended (by the vital importance of these three functions of structure) to the people and groups in organizations. The functions of structure in the establishment of organizational roles, expectations, and resource allocations make it very clear why power is first and foremost a structural phenomenon, and why effective use of power in organizations is crucial for success. Jeffrey Pfeffer emphasizes this point in his "Preface" to *Power in Organizations* (1981): "Those persons and those units that have the responsibility for performing the more critical tasks in the organization have a natural advantage in developing and exercising power in the organization" (p. x). Resource allocation decisions have enormous impacts on a person's (or group's) ability to do its job, to "shine" or "excel." Structure affects resource allocations. A primary reason for using power is to affect resource allocations, and resource allocations affect the balance of power in organizations: The variables are inseparable. Power cannot be understood independent of the structural context, and vice versa.

INTERGROUP DYNAMICS

Organizations are complex systems which often can be visualized most clearly as grids or spider webs of overlapping, interwoven, and competing *coalitions* of individuals, formal groups, and informal groups, each having its own interests, beliefs, values, preferences, perspectives, and perceptions. The coalitions compete with each other continuously for scarce organizational resources. Conflict is inevitable. Influence—and the power and political activities through which influence is acquired and maintained—is the primary "weapon" for use in competition and conflicts. Thus, power, politics, and influence are critically important and permanent facts of organizational life.

Returning for a moment to the subject of *organizational context,* power relations are permanent features of organizations primarily because specialization and the division of labor result in many interdependent organizational units with varying degrees of importance. The units compete with each other for scarce resources— as well as with the transitory coalitions. As James D. Thompson points out in *Organizations in Action* (1967), lack of balance in the interdependence among units sets the stage for the use of power relations.

LEADERSHIP

Leadership involves "an interpersonal process through which one individual influences the attitudes, beliefs, and especially the behavior of one or more other people" (see Chapter III). The parallels and overlappings among issues of *leadership* and of *power in organizations* are obvious, and this chapter attempts to emphasize the parallels and explain the overlappings.

Historically, power in organizations and authority were viewed as being essentially synonymous. Such "classical era" students of organization as Max Weber (1922) and Henri Fayol (1949, 1916) simply *assumed* that power and formal rules (promulgated and enforced by those in authority) flow downward through people who occupy offices to successively lower levels in hierarchical organizations. Even today, proponents of the "modern structural perspective of organization theory" (see Shafritz and Ott, 1987, Chapter III) tend to see authority as *the* source of power in organizations (or, at least the primary source). From this perspective, *leader, supervisor,* and *manager* mean the same thing: people who possess power by virtue of the authority inherent in the organizational position they occupy. Power is legitimized by virtue of a person being in such a position. In fact, the aptly descriptive phrases *legitimate power* and *legitimate authority* gained common usage and still are seen and heard occasionally in today's management literature.

In contrast, most organizational behavioralists see power in a very different light. For example, John Kotter (1985) argues that in today's organizational world, the gap is increasing between the power one needs to get the job done and the power that automatically comes with the job (authority). Most organizational behavioralists view authority as only one of many available sources of organizational power, and power is aimed in *all* directions—not just down through the hierarchy. For example, Robert W. Allen and Lyman W. Porter divide their 1983 book of readings on *Organizational Influence Processes* into three major parts: downward influence (authority), lateral influence, and upward influence.

Authority-based power is far from being the only form of power in organizations. In fact, other forms of power and influence often prevail over authority-based power. Several of this chapter's selections identify different sources of power in organizations (particularly the first reading, "The Bases of Social Power," by John R. P. French and Bertram Raven) so only a few are listed here as examples:

- *Control over scarce resources,* for example, office space, discretionary funds, current and accurate information, and time and skill to work on projects;
- *Easy access to others who are perceived as having power,* important customers or clients, members of the board of directors, or someone else with formal authority or who controls scarce resources;
- *A central place in a potent coalition;*
- *Ability to "work the organizational rules,"* such as knowing how to get things done or to prevent others from getting things done; and
- *Credibility,* for example, that one's word can be trusted.

The more that leadership issues in organizations are separated or differentiated from management issues, the more closely they become aligned with power issues— issues that extend beyond authority issues.

SELECTIONS IN THIS CHAPTER

The readings on power that comprise this chapter span thirty-five years and address a spectrum of issues associated with power and behavior in organizations. The first, Dorwin Cartwright's "Power: A Neglected Variable in Social Psychology" (1959), is adapted from an address he delivered to the Society for the Psychological Study of Social Issues in 1953. The article is not organization-specific. Rather, it provides a foundation for the readings that follow. It defines the historical place of power in the field of social psychology originating with "metaphysical era social psychologists" including Hobbes (1651) and Nietzsche (1912). However, "twentieth century social psychologists have been 'soft' on power" (p. 2), preferring to avoid it or to study it only in "safe or weak populations—witness the classical stature of research on pecking order among chickens and on dominance among children" (p. 2). Cartwright identifies leading social issues (phenomena which are social psychological in nature) that "cannot be adequately understood without the concept of power" (p. 3). They include leadership and social roles, public opinion, rumor, propaganda, prejudice, attitude change, morale, communications, race relations, and conflicts of value. Cartwright concludes that these phenomena raise questions about power in society which cannot be answered with our existing systems of knowledge.

"The Bases of Social Power," by John R. P. French and Bertram Raven (1959), reprinted here, accepts Dorwin Cartwright's challenge head on. In their often-cited analysis, French and Raven start from the premise that power and influence involve relations between at least two agents (they limit their definition of agents to individuals), and theorize that the reaction of the *recipient agent* is the more useful focus for explaining the phenomena of social influence and power. The core of French and Raven's piece, however, is their identification of five bases or sources of social power: reward power, the perception of coercive power, legitimate power (organizational authority), referent power (through association with others who possess power), and expert power (power of knowledge or ability).

French and Raven examine the effects of power derived from the five different bases on *attraction* (the recipient's sentiment toward the agent who uses power) and *resistance* to the use of power. Their investigations show that the use of power from the different bases has different consequences. For example, coercive power typically decreases attraction and causes high resistance, whereas reward power increases attraction and creates minimal levels of resistance. In what amounts to one of the earliest looks at ethical limits on the use of power, they conclude that "the more legitimate the coercion (is perceived to be) the less it will produce resistance and decreased attraction" (p. 165).

Like Dorwin Cartwright before him, Mason Haire begins "The Concept of Power and the Concept of Man" (1962), which is reprinted here, with a historical review of sources of organizational power. Haire, however, approaches the essence of power by asking: "Why do people in organizations do what they are told?" (Sennett, 1980). As the title implies, Haire's exploration causes him to focus on two related but separate issues: *(a)* the concept of power in organizations and changes in its bases over the course of organizational history, and *(b)* our changing concept of the nature of man.

Haire's article briefly reviews the history of *the state* as the philosophical and legal basis of *authority* and the source of organizational power during the days when the Roman Empire controlled the Mediterranean shores, and the British East India Company colonized and controlled much of southern Asia. "The ultimate authority of the manager of a business was grounded not in ownership but in the state" (p. 164). The Industrial Revolution was the point in time when *business ownership* replaced *the state* as the primary source of authority. Technological advances in machinery and the evolution of the factory system of production caused capital and property to become the crux of industrial strength and *authority* to remain as the basis of organizational power. Haire then examines how and why the basis of power in organizations moved from external ownership to internal management, and forecasts future moves of its bases to staff experts, work groups, and self-control. The shift to an internal basis of power reflects "a real shift in the ultimate source of authority . . . (to a socially-based) internalization of the ground on which it is based, and . . . the dynamics of social interaction and the process of management rather than property rights" (pp. 166–167). Haire concludes his analysis of power in organizations by predicting that "the final source of authority will be the authority of the work group. The final control will be self-control" (p. 169).

Haire justifies his conclusions about changes in the bases of power in organizations with what he perceives to be a changing societal concept of man from a "classical organization theory" concept to an organizational behavior perspective view: from a McGregor Theory X to Theory Y set of assumptions. In this way, Haire neatly links changes in the bases of organizational power to fundamental changes in our societal assumptions about the character of humans. Thus, our concepts of humans influence the forms of our organizations. As the basis of power continues its historical trek from state-based authority toward work groups and individual power, our institutionalized systems of organization and control will inexorably alter.

From Dorwin Cartwright, French and Raven, and Mason Haire, it is a fifteen-year leap to Gerald Salancik and Jeffrey Pfeffer's 1977 widely respected analysis, "Who Gets Power—And How They Hold on to It: A Strategic-Contingency Model of Power." This article also reflects the field of organizational behavior's tremendous strides during the 1970s in accepting power as a legitimate subject for serious investigation.

Salancik and Pfeffer see power as one of the few mechanisms available for aligning an organization with the realities of its environment. Their assertion rests on the premise that power is derived from being essential to an organization's functional needs. According to Salancik and Pfeffer's notion (which they label *strategic-contingency theory*), power accrues to individuals and subunits that handle an organization's most critical problems. Effective use of power allows those subunits that are engaged in critical activities to "place allies in key positions," "control scarce critical resources," and thereby enhance the probability of their survival and expansion. Subunits engaged in critical functions prosper, those engaged in non-critical functions wither, and the organization realigns itself. Because the most critical contingencies organizations face involve the environmental context, this power allocating process explains how organizations constantly readjust themselves with the needs of their external worlds.

Salancik and Pfeffer believe that power is shared in organizations "out of necessity more than out of concern for principles of organizational development or participatory democracy" (p. 7). It is shared out of structural-functional need. To repeat an earlier quotation: "Power is first and foremost a structural phenomenon, and should be understood as such" (Pfeffer, 1981, p. x).

Strategic-contingency theory has far-reaching consequences. If the use of power by subunits helps organizations align themselves with their critical needs, then suppression of the use of power, for example to reduce unwanted *politics* and *conflicts*, reduces organizational adaptability. Thus, in the current literature of organizational behavior, one seldom sees the phrase *conflict resolution* used. It has been almost totally replaced with the concept of *conflict management*—using conflict (and power struggles) constructively for the organization's benefit.

"Who Gets Power—And How They Hold on to It," contains a second very important contribution to the understanding of power in organizations. Salancik and Pfeffer identify three contextual conditions under which the use of power by members of subunits can be expected to determine how important decisions are decided. (For Salancik and Pfeffer, "important decisions" usually are resource allocation decisions.)

- The degree of resource scarcity,
- The criticalness of the resources to subunits' core activities, and
- The level of uncertainty existing about what or how an organization should do.

When these conditions are linked with Salancik and Pfeffer's identification of subunits that are most likely to get and hold on to power, it is possible to predict an organization's decision processes (under certain circumstances) by using a power perspective of organizational behavior. When clear-cut criteria do not exist, the use of power to control resource allocation decisions is likely to be most effective.

John P. Kotter's article, "Power, Dependence, and Effective Management" (1977), which is reprinted in this chapter, focuses on the inexorable relationship between power and dependence, and examines how an appreciation of this relationship permits effective managerial performance. Kotter's article attempts to answer three questions:

1. Why are the dynamics of power necessarily an important part of managerial processes?
2. How do effective managers acquire power?
3. How and for what purposes do effective managers use power?

Kotter's answer to his first question is found in the dependency consequences of "two organizational facts of life, division of labor and limited resources" (p. 126). Managers often are dependent on people over whom they have no control for information, resources, and the performance of activities. Kotter makes an argument which since has been popularized by Kanter (1979) and that is contrary to common wisdom: The more formal authority managers possess, the less powerful and the more vulnerable they are.

Kotter's answer to his second question is: Successful managers build their power by creating a sense of obligation in others, creating images of expertise and skill, "fostering others' unconscious identification with them or with ideas they 'stand for'" (p. 131), and feeding peoples' beliefs that they are dependent on the manager. Successful managers create perceptions of dependence by finding and acquiring important resources and, more importantly, by influencing *perceptions* of their ability to marshal resources.

Kotter answers his third question: "How and for what purposes do effective managers use power?", with a matrix-type analysis of the advantages and disadvantages of face-to-face and indirect influence processes for different types of purposes.

"Identifying and Using Political Resources," a chapter reprinted here from Douglas Yates, Jr.'s bestselling book, *The Politics of Management* (1985), is one of the most widely read books on organizational politics. *Organizational politics* and *organizational political behavior* are very difficult concepts to define. Many writers have tried (for example, Mayes & Allen, 1977; Robbins, 1976; and Tushman, 1977), and most disagree with each other. Porter, Allen & Angle (1981) have proposed perhaps the most comprehensive definition of *organizational political behavior*:

1. "Social influence attempts,
2. That are discretionary (i.e., that are outside the behavioral zones prescribed or prohibited by the formal organization),
3. That are intended (designed) to promote or protect the self-interests of individuals and groups (units),
4. And that threaten the self-interests of others (individuals, units)" (p. 409).

Yates avoids the definitional question in order to concentrate on his contingency-type action program of politics and power. Managers should find and employ resources and strategies to fit the particular conflicts they face. "In a particular management environment, any leader must decide which leadership resource or combination of resources is likely to be effective in transforming conflicts into positive forms of cooperation, conciliation, or consensus" (p. 91). The management of political conflict is the process of managing strategic conflict between actors who possess different forms of resources. In a particularly important point, Yates reminds managers that using power is costly because its use depletes one's reservoir of credible power.

Power and influence are integral aspects of organizational behavior. Their contributions to understanding the behavior of people in organizations can be understood only in relationship to leadership, group and intergroup dynamics, the organizational context, and motivational structures. In 1959, Dorwin Cartwright wrote about power as a neglected variable in social psychology. In 1979, Rosabeth Moss Kanter called power "America's last dirty word," a word and a concept that people in organizations (and elsewhere) try to avoid. But power is a subject that cannot and should not be avoided. The importance of power will become even more clear in Chapter VI, *Organizational Change and Development*.

REFERENCES

Allen, R. W., Madison, D. L., Porter, L. W., Renwick, P. A., & Mayes, B. T. (1979). Organizational politics: Tactics and characteristics of its actors. *California Management Review, 22,* 77–83.

Allen, R. W., & Porter, L. W. (Eds.) (1983). *Organizational influence processes.* Glenview, IL.: Scott, Foresman.

Cartwright, D. (1959). Power: A neglected variable in social psychology. In, D. Cartwright (Ed.), *Studies in social power* (pp. 1–14). Ann Arbor, MI: University of Michigan, Institute for Social Research.

Emerson, R. M. (1962). Power-dependence relations. *American Sociological Review, 27,* 31–40.

Fayol, H. (1949). *General and industrial management* (C. Storrs, Trans.) London: Pitman Publishing Co. (Original work published 1916).

French, J. R. P., & Raven, B. (1959). The bases of social power. In, D. Cartwright & A. Zander (Eds.), *Studies in social power* (pp. 150–167). Ann Arbor, MI: University of Michigan, Institute for Social Research.

Haire, M. (1962). The concept of power and the concept of man. In, G. B. Strother (Ed.), *Social science approaches to business behavior* (pp. 163–183). Homewood, IL: Richard D. Irwin.

Hobbes, T. (1651). *Leviathan.* Reprinted in 1904, Cambridge, UK: University Press.

Kanter, R. M. (July–August, 1979). Power failure in management circuits. *Harvard Business Review, 57,* 65–75.

Korda, M. (1975). *Power.* New York: Ballantine Books.

Kotter, J. P. (March–April, 1976). Power, success, and organizational effectiveness. *Organizational Dynamics,* 27–40.

Kotter, J. P. (July–August, 1977). Power, dependence, and effective management. *Organizational Dynamics,* 125–136.

Kotter, J. P. (1985). *Power and influence.* New York: Free Press.

March, J. G. (1962). The business firm as a political coalition. *Journal of Politics, 24,* 662–678.

Mayes, B. T., & Allen, R. W. (1977). Toward a definition of organizational politics. *Academy of Management Review, 2,* 672–678.

McClelland, D., & Burnham, D. (March–April, 1976). Power is the great motivator. *Harvard Business Review,* 100–110.

Mechanic, D. (December, 1962). Sources of power of lower participants in complex organizations. *Administrative Science Quarterly, 7*(3), 349–364.

Mintzberg, H. (1983). *Power in and around organizations.* Englewood Cliffs, NJ: Prentice-Hall.

Nietzsche, F. (1912). *Der Wille zur Macht.* Book 3, sec. 702. In, F. Nietzsche, *Werke* (Vol. 16). Leipzig: Alfred Kroner.

Perrow, C. (1970). Departmental power and perspectives in industrial firms. In, M. N. Zald (Ed.), *Power in organizations* (pp. 59–89). Nashville, TN: Vanderbilt University Press.

Pfeffer, J. (1981). *Power in organizations.* Marshfield, MA: Pitman Publishing Co.

Porter, L. W., Allen, R. W., & Angle, H. L. (1981). The politics of upward influence in organizations. In, L. L. Cummings & B. M. Staw (Eds.), *Research in organizational behavior* (Vol. 3) (pp. 408–422). Greenwich, CT: JAI Press.

Robbins, S. P. (1976). *The administrative process: Integrating theory and practice.* Englewood Cliffs, NJ: Prentice-Hall.

Salancik, G. R., & Pfeffer, J. (1977). Who gets power—and how they hold on to it: A strategic-contingency model of power. *Organizational Dynamics, 5,* 2–21.

Sennett, R. (1980). *Authority.* New York: Alfred A. Knopf, Inc.

Shafritz, J. M., & Ott, J. S. (1987). *Classics of organization theory* (2d ed.). Chicago: The Dorsey Press.

Siu, R. G. H. (1979). *The craft of power.* New York: John Wiley & Sons.

Thompson, J. D. (1967). *Organizations in action.* New York: McGraw-Hill.

Tushman, M. L. (April, 1977). A political approach to organizations: A review and rationale. *The Academy of Management Review, 2,* 206–216.

Weber, M. (1922). Bureaucracy. In, H. Gerth & C. W. Mills (Eds.), *Max Weber: Essays in sociology.* Oxford, U.K.: Oxford University Press.

Yates, D., Jr. (1985). *The politics of management.* San Francisco: Jossey-Bass.

31

Power: A Neglected Variable in Social Psychology[1]

Dorwin Cartwright

Twentieth century social psychology can be traced back to the earliest philosophers, but its complexion is largely determined by developments in this century. Prior to World War I social psychology had failed by and large to meet those requirements of an abstract, positive science which Comte had laid down about the middle of the nineteenth century. Today, in sharp contrast, the spirit of positivism holds sway, and the only problems deemed worthy of attention are those susceptible to objective observation and, preferably, quantification. But this gain has not been made without cost, for scientific status has been achieved by neglecting any phenomena which do not lend themselves readily to the operations of science.

In his review of the history of social psychology, Allport (2) points out that writers in its metaphysical epoch mapped out many of the phenomena which a developed scientific social psychology must handle. Advances in our present era will largely consist, then, in devising ways for treating by scientific techniques (empirical and conceptual) the many phenomena identified by the early theorists.

Power is such a phenomenon. This topic received considerable attention in

the metaphysical era of social psychology. The classic reference is Hobbes (14) who in 1651 analyzed the motivation for power and some of its social consequences. More recent discussions, still in the metaphysical era, are those of Nietzsche (27) and Adler (1). Many other philosophical and speculative treatments could, of course, be cited.

At the present time questions about power are more commonly raised by men of practical affairs than by social psychologists. How does one best organize a group so that the activities of its members are coordinated? Why do so many people react to leaders by displaying either dependence or defiance? Is it possible for groups to be effective without concentrating power in the hands of a very few people? How can one keep a group from destroying the individuality and personal freedom of its members? Must strong groups always exploit weaker ones? Questions of this sort are concerned with the influence exerted by some people over others, or, in short, with power.

Both early social psychology and modern society recognize the importance of power. If, however, we examine social psychology since the beginning of its scientific epoch, we search in vain for any concentrated attack on the problem. Surely this constitutes a

[1]This chapter is based on the presidential address delivered at the 1953 annual meeting of the Society for the Psychological Study of Social Issues.

Source: Dorwin Cartwright, "Power: A Neglected Variable in Social Psychology," in Studies in Social Power, edited by Dorwin Cartwright (Ann Arbor, MI: Institute for Social Research, The University of Michigan, 1959), pp. 1–14. Reprinted by permission of the publisher.

weakness of modern social psychology. We can only conclude that twentieth century social psychologists have been "soft" on power. Direct investigation has been evaded in many ways. One mode of evasion has been to study power in safe or weak populations—witness the classical stature of research on pecking order among chickens and on dominance among children. Another has been to convert the problem of power into one of attitudes, expectations, and perceptions. Thus, there is more interest in authoritarianism than authority; expectations are made the critical element in the notion of role rather than behavioral restrictions or compulsions; prestige is studied because it can be investigated apart from any specific situation of interpersonal interaction and influence.

It is not here suggested that social psychologists have been cowardly; the fact is that the softer aspects of power have been more accessible to investigation. Nor is it implied that these softer aspects are irrelevant or psychologically uninteresting. The complaint is, rather, that power is often seen as essentially not a psychological problem. When asked about power the social psychologist has typically referred the question to the political scientist, sociologist, or economist; or, worse, he has given answers based upon purely personal values. In any case, the social psychologist has not seen how the central body of his knowledge could be brought to bear on such problems. But surely inability to deal with power within traditional theories does not mean that the problem should be ignored in the future.

The point may be stated differently: it simply is not possible to deal adequately with data which are clearly social psychological without getting involved with matters of power.

SOME ILLUSTRATIVE PROBLEMS INVOLVING POWER

To document the point it is necessary to show how power is inevitably a part of the accepted phenomena of social psychology. This task is made difficult by the fact that there is considerable ambiguity concerning the boundaries of the field. Nevertheless, it is possible to identify certain phenomena (problem areas) as essentially social psychological in nature. Allport (2) has provided a list of these, not intended to be exhaustive, which contains the following: leadership, public opinion, rumor, propaganda, prejudice, attitude change, morale, communications, race relations, and conflicts of value. We shall attempt to show that phenomena of this sort cannot be adequately understood without the concept of power.

Leadership and Social Roles

Empirical research has progressively forced a restatement of the problem of leadership from that of identifying personal traits of the leader to one of determining the causes and consequences of leadership behavior. In this analysis concepts like "social situation," "position," "function," and "role" have come to the fore. As long as leadership was viewed only as a particular combination of personality traits, properties of the social system could easily be ignored. A major advance in the study of leadership therefore came with the abandonment of this narrow point of view, mistakenly labeled "psychological."

Some of the features of the new approach may be illustrated by brief reference to a study of the relation between supervisory practices and employee satisfaction. In this investigation, carried out by the University of Michigan Survey Research Center, Pelz (28) analyzed data from a large manufacturing company to determine whether employee satisfactions were related to certain supervisory practices which could be classified along a continuum from employee goal facilitation to hindrance. His results proved to be inconclusive until he separated the supervisors into two classes: those with high influence in their department at large and those with little influence. The results then formed a consistent pattern. Considering only high-influence supervisors and their subordinates, 19 of 28 correlations between supervisory practices and employee attitudes were positive (goal facilitative behavior of the supervisor being associated with employee satisfaction). For the low-influence supervisors, 20 out of the 28 correlations were zero or negative. The significance of these results is clear: a supervisor who is helpful in form only is not appreciated or even resented, and a spiteful supervisor who cannot carry out his malevolent designs offers no real threat.

The implications of such findings as these have been explored with regard to leadership training in an excellent study by Fleishman, Harris, and Burtt (12). Their careful evaluation of a foreman training program operated by a large industrial concern revealed that there is often a discrepancy between the behavior taught in the program and that expected by the foreman's supervisor. They conclude that "when what is taught in the School is at variance with what is practiced in the plant, the latter is generally the more powerful influence." (p. 58) They show, moreover, that trained foremen who are returned to a setting whose leadership climate is at odds with the style of leadership advocated by the School display signs of conflict.

The gradually accumulating evidence

from studies such as these fosters a dim view of supervisory training schemes which ignore the power structure of the organization; any theory of leadership which ignores power cannot be viewed more favorably.

If we turn our attention to the general theory of role, we are forced to conclude that here too power is inevitably involved. Since recent work on role, especially that of Newcomb (26), has broadened the scope of social psychology and increased its ability to deal with important phenomena in an integrated fashion, the significance of this conclusion is far-reaching.

Perhaps the best way to communicate the qualitative flavor of the phenomena of role is to quote some anthropological reports made by Campbell (8) from his participant-observing among the tribe Social-Researcher. Here is his account of the role of research administrator.

"The researcher who assumes the position of administrator is likely to be slower in recognizing his new role than are the people whom he directs. . . . The people who now report to him know immediately that he has become the 'gatekeeper' on a variety of critical decisions. They see him almost at once in his new role and they quickly develop expectations for appropriate administrative behaviors for him.

"This change of roles may be difficult for the new executive to accept. He has to learn to modify his behavior in many subtle ways. He has to guard against casual thoughtless remarks that might be interpreted as criticism and to be wary of hopeful observations that may be recalled later as promises. He must not indicate undue uncertainty about future appropriations or appointments for fear of setting disquieting rumors spreading through his staff. He learns not to make light of salary levels in his organization or of other perquisites which his staff may feel they deserve.

". . . He cannot escape the basic fact that as the director he has the ultimate word on many questions of great personal importance to his associates, and that he is universally seen by these people as having this power." (p. 225)

Certain features of this description deserve emphasis. (a) The occupant of the position of research administrator (and this may be generalized to other positions in society) can determine whether or not certain other people are able to satisfy their important needs. The occupant of this position also has a decisive voice in group action, so that when others engage in behavior relevant to the group they must relate their behavior to his. (b) The occupant of even a powerful position is not personally free to do certain things and not to do others. (c) If we consider the same person when he is located inside and outside a given position, we find that others behave toward him in drastically different ways under the two conditions. (d) Any communications originating from the occupant of a powerful position are likely to be highly authoritative, that is, have pronounced effects on others.

Strodtbeck (31, 32) has devised an ingenious experimental method for determining the relative influence of roles. He has used this method to study the roles of husband, wife, and son in different cultures. The procedure is to place members of a family in a situation where they will have a difference of opinion and then to record the ensuing events. He finds, for example, that among Navahos the wife wins 46 arguments to the husband's 34. But among Mormons it is husband 42 to 29! The son seldom wins except by forming coalitions. This research of Strodtbeck

and that of others makes it clear that even in groups having no formal table of organization the power of one person to influence another depends upon the role he occupies.

The program of investigations by Shartle, Stogdill, Hemphill and others in the Ohio State Leadership Studies (30) is providing important documentation for our theories of role. In their work the concept of responsibility is assuming fundamental importance; each member of an organization is responsible for the performance of certain activities and is responsible to certain other individuals. Positions in an organization can be described in terms of these two aspects of responsibility. What people in the organization do, with whom they interact, whom they like, from whom they receive recognition, and so forth—all these factors depend to a high degree upon the nature of the responsibility structure. Members of the organization may vary in the extent to which they accept this structure, but if a member does accept it, his behavior is then guided by certain other people and organizational requirements. Stated differently, the whole organizational structure acquires power over the member and consequently certain other people have power over him, the specific persons depending upon his position in the organization.

This raises the ancient sociological problem which Jaques (20) has analyzed in some detail and has referred to as the "sanctioning of authority." It seems that a group member cannot simply proclaim a new position of power with himself as the occupant. The authority of a position must be sanctioned by others if it is to possess power. In one of the earliest experiments upon the process of interpersonal influence, Frank (13) found that when students agreed to be subjects they automatically gave such authority to the role of experimenter that he could not get them to resist his efforts to have them perform very disagreeable tasks. He finally had to instruct them to resist before he could measure the relative effectiveness of his different techniques of pressure! In a study on changing mothers' behavior toward their children, Brim **(7)** found that mothers were more likely to try out advice given by a doctor the more they attributed high prestige to the role of doctor. Much of the research on the effects of prestige and credibility, it would seem, can best be interpreted in terms of the sanctioning of the authority of certain roles.

This line of theorizing raises an important question: what determines whether a person accepts the authority of a position occupied by others (or even by himself)? Although there is no research which answers this question directly, the work relating group cohesiveness to strength of group standards (discussed below) suggests that if the authority structure of a group is functionally equivalent to the standards of a group, then the more strongly members are attracted to the group the more will they accept its authority structure. This hypothesis could readily be tested.

The personality characteristics of individuals may also be expected to influence their readiness to sanction the authority of a role. Much of the work on authoritarianism can be interpreted as dealing with this problem. Another provocative approach is represented by the research of Jeanne and Jack Block **(6)** who, though not investigating directly the sanctioning of authority of a role, do show how the amount of influence exerted by a role on a person is related to certain of his personality characteristics. In this experiment they asked subjects to do a monotonous and repetitive task until satiated. When the sub-

jects stopped, the experimenter (assumed to be an authority figure) asked, "don't you want to do some more?" Subjects either continued or not. Certain personality variables of all subjects had previously been evaluated, and relations between these variables and compliance with the experimenter's request were examined. The results show compliance to be related to (a) a trichotomy on "ego control" into over-controllers, appropriate controllers, and under-controllers; (b) scores on the California test of ethnocentrism; and (c) speed of establishing norms in an experiment on autokinetic movement. The Blocks propose that conforming to a suggestion from an authority is the expression of a more general "structuring" approach to an unpredictable environment. This predisposition, in turn, may be viewed as part of a larger syndrome of ego control which they term "over-control." The results of this one study do not, of course, tell us whether these over-controllers tend to accept the authority of all roles which might claim authority or whether they are inclined to give sanction only to certain sorts of potentially authoritative roles.

An experiment by Hoffman **(15)** should also be mentioned in this connection. He, too, related behavior in an experimental setting to personality variables. In his study, subjects were dichotomized into conformers and nonconformers on the basis of conformity to an announced group average of judgments of perceived distance. His results show that the conformers scored significantly higher on such measures as parental dominance, inability to tolerate impulses, overconcern for the well-being of parents, and strict moralism. Whether submitting to an authority figure is psychodynamically the same as conforming to the norms of a group and how "ego control" relates to Hoffman's personality measures need to be known before the results of these two studies can be put together. In any case it appears that we may soon be able to isolate relatively enduring attributes which predispose people to give sanction to certain roles and to the norms of certain groups.

This brief overview of research on role raises doubt that such soft properties as expectations and perceptions adequately characterize the actual phenomena of role. The harder properties of power are inextricably a part of the phenomena referred to by the concept of role.

Communication

If we turn to research on communication, we find that power must be recognized here, too. In fact, it is the power aspect of communication which gives the concept such a central place in current social psychological theory. Communication is the mechanism by which interpersonal influence is exerted. Without communication there would be no group norms, group goals, or organized group action. Let us examine the evidence for these conclusions.

First, it is perfectly obvious as soon as one bothers to raise the question that all communications are not equally influential. This, of course, has been known for a long time, and there is a respectable literature on the effectiveness of different kinds of content in communications. We are not so well supplied, however, with findings concerning the way in which the relations between communicator and recipient influence the effectiveness of communication. The work of Hovland and Weiss (16) and Kelman and Hovland (23) on source credibility dramatizes the importance of treating separately the content of a communication and its source.

They have shown that the so-called "sleeper effect" depends upon the more rapid decay over time of the effects of the source than of the content. Future work in this productive program might well examine sources of communication more integrally related to the groups to which people belong to see whether the effectiveness of source decays over time when source and recipient maintain a concrete relationship.

A program of research conducted at the Research Center for Group Dynamics adds further insight into the nature of communication. First, Festinger, Schachter, and Back (11) and Back (4) show that a communication between people in a group to which they are strongly attracted is more effective than a similar communication between people in a less attractive group. To account for such findings, Festinger has developed the concept of the "internal power of a group." The upshot of this work supports the view outlined by Barnard (5) that all communications carry some degree of authoritativeness and that a person, role, or group capable of giving authority to communications possesses power. Thus, we start out to study communication but are soon asking questions about the determinants of power.

Second, the direction and content of the flow of communication in an organized group or community are not indifferent to the social position of the people involved. Orders, for example, seldom flow up a power hierarchy, but certain other types of communication are quite likely to do so. The studies by Hurwitz, Zander, and Hymovitch (18), Jackson (19), Kelley (22), and others are beginning to reveal how upward communication may serve an individual as a substitute for upward locomotion in a power hierarchy, how a person may use communication as a device for minimizing the dangers of hostile actions by those in higher positions, and how a person of superior power may tailor the content and direction of his communications to maintain the belief among others that his superior behavior justifies his position. Thus, we must specify the power relations among people to understand either the frequency and content of communications passing among them or the authority of such communications.

Third, even the study of rumor cannot safely ignore the power situation. This conclusion dramatically arose from the experience of an action-research project in a community where the project leaders unexpectedly became the target of a hostile rumor (10). As a result of the project's stimulation of several new community activities, such as a cooperative nursery school and a softball league, new leaders began to emerge to replace the old ones. Suddenly, when everything seemed to be moving along well, the new activities came to a halt. A rumor was sweeping the community that the project leaders and the new local leaders were taking orders from Moscow. If we try to understand what happened, it seems especially significant that the content of the rumor was about power (namely, who was controlling people's behavior), that it was initiated and spread by those losing power, and that it was credible to those who believed it because they did not in fact know why these new activities were being undertaken in their community. (In a desire not to contaminate the experiment the community had not been given this information.) A general hypothesis is suggested that rumors are especially likely to flourish among people who see that their fates are in other people's hands.

If communication is to be a basic concept of social psychology, so too is power.

Interpersonal and Intergroup Relations

Let us turn now from abstract concepts like role and communication to more concrete social problems. One such problem which has long interested social psychologists deals with the kinds of things referred to by the phrase "human relations." What are the causes of harmony and conflict among people? Although systematic theories have been slow to emerge from efforts to answer this question, a sizable body of empirical data has accumulated. From this wealth of material we cite only a few specific findings to illustrate the critical place of power in shaping human relations.

A few years ago the Research Center for Group Dynamics was asked by a group of junior high school teachers to help them understand better the sources of conflict and irritation in the relations among teachers, parents, and students. A project was organized by Jenkins and Lippitt (21) which included interviews with a sample of each of these populations. Respondents were asked to indicate what they believed were the things that each group did that each other group liked (for example, "What are the things that parents do that teachers like?"). They were also asked parallel questions to indicate disliked behavior.

Consider, first, the teacher-student relationship. Of all categories of teacher behavior, the one having most significance for students is that the teacher be fair. This seems to imply that the teacher is a sort of judge who hands down decisions of importance, thus making fairness a matter of real concern. When we examine the other side of the relationship and consider the responses of teachers, we get further confirmation of the teacher's power over students. Seventy-three percent of the teachers mention as important student behavior "being respectful" and "accepting the teacher as authority." Forty-two per cent mention "obedience."

The relations between parents and students turn out to be much the same, but with different realms of behavior coming under the control of parents. Complaints about parents consists of a long list of things "they won't let us do" and of other things "they make us do." Though parents tend not to mention the importance of obedience and respect as much as teachers, the students nonetheless report that parents do place major emphasis upon compliance to parental authority.

More subtle is the finding concerning teacher-parent relations. Here it is clear that teachers have strong needs for friendship with adults and for acceptance as members of the community. Parents chiefly control the fate of teachers in this respect; they can give or withhold gratification of these needs. This relation is, moreoover, one way; there is no indication that parents would feel deprived without the friendship, recognition, or acceptance of teachers. Knowledge of this asymmetrical power relation is essential for understanding the behavior, attitudes, and feelings of teachers and parents.

Experience with intergroup discrimination and prejudice points the same lesson. Can we really hope to explain these phenomena or to build programs of social action solely with such variables as authoritarianism, ethnocentrism, displaced aggression, and attitude? How do these concepts help to understand the substantial improvement of conditions for Negroes in the automobile industry following certain union policy-decisions or the presence of a nonsegregated dining room at Montgomery, Alabama—on the Air Force Base? Kurt Lewin (24) recognized the importance of power in intergroup

relations when he asserted that "discrimination against minorities will not be changed as long as forces are not changed which determine the decisions of the gatekeepers." (p. 186) With such a perspective social psychologists will take more than passing notice of such findings as that of Hunter (17) in his study of the power structure of Regional City—a medium sized city with a Negro population of nearly one-third the total. Through various devices he was able to construct a list of 40 people who could safely be called the city's most powerful; the approval of these people is required for the success of any community project. Those who wish to better intergroup relations in this city might be well advised to work with this group. They should know, however, that not a single Negro is on this list of influential people. (Only 3 could be considered even nominees on a list of 175.)

Whether one's objective is social action or understanding human behavior, one should examine the possibilities of reducing discrimination and prejudice through the *fait accompli*, legal action, and administrative order. It is interesting in this connection to note the conclusion reached by Deutsch and Collins (9) from their study of the effects upon interracial attitudes of different patterns of interracial public housing.

"We are, in effect, rejecting the notion that has characterized much of sociological thinking in the field of race relations: the notion, originating with William S. Summer, that 'stateways cannot change folksways.' The evidence of our study is that official policy, executed without equivocation, can result in large changes in beliefs and feelings despite initial resistance to the policy. Thus, it is clear from our data that although most of the white housewives in the integrated projects we studied did not, upon moving into the projects, like the idea of living in the same buildings with Negro families (and certainly the community as a whole did not favor it), a considerable change in attitudes and 'folkways' has taken place as a consequence of their experiences resulting from a 'stateway.'" (p. 127)

Unfortunately there is as yet insufficient systematic knowledge about the social psychology of power for us to specify with much conviction the conditions under which administrative orders and legal action will carry along attitudinal changes or will stimulate heightened resistance.

Social Determinants of Emotional Adjustment

The importance of the concept of power for social psychology may be illustrated with respect to one other social problem. What determines the mental health or illness of individuals? While it is clear that physiological determinants are important, it is now known that social situations differ significantly in their impact upon the emotional adjustment of all those involved in them. Perhaps one of the clearest demonstrations of such influences was provided by the experiment of Lewin, Lippitt, and White (25) on different styles of leadership. Here it was found that the aggressiveness of a given child depended upon the style of leadership provided by the adult in charge of the group. Although the different styles of leadership studied in this experiment differed from one another in a number of ways, it appears that the most critical aspects of leadership were the size of the space of free movement allowed the children and whether the leader's power was used to support or obstruct the behavior of the children. The leader's use of power basically affected the emotional climate of the group.

In any social situation, and especially in hierarchical ones, certain people have power to help or hinder the goal-directed behavior of others. Emotional security depends rather directly upon the magnitude of this power and upon the benevolence of its use.

Experiments by Arsenian (3) and Wright (33) have examined this conception in greater detail. They propose that a person's feeling of security is determined by the relative magnitude of two sets of factors which may be expressed as a ratio. The numerator is the person's perception of the magnitude of his own power plus all friendly or supportive power he can count upon from other sources; the denominator is the person's perception of the magnitude of all hostile power that may be mobilized against him. In the Arsenian experiment the emotionality of young children was measured when they were left alone in a strange room and when put there in the presence of a friendly (but passive) adult. Consistent with the formulation of the determinants of security proposed, Arsenian found less emotional disturbance when the supportive power of the adult was present. The experiment by Wright may be interpreted in similar terms. He compared the reactions to frustration of pairs of children varying in the strength of their friendship and found that strong friends displayed less reduction in constructiveness of play, less negative emotionality, more cooperation between themselves, and more aggression against the experimenter than did weak friends. The power of each of the strong friends was supportive to the other.

Consistent with this general conception of the relation between security and power are the findings of a rather different sort of experiment conducted by Pepitone (29). He placed boys in a situation where the achievement of an attractive object was under the control of a panel of three judges. After a standardized interaction between the boy and the panel, each boy was asked to rate the relative power and relative benevolence of each member of the panel. In this setting Pepitone found perceptual distortions designed, as it were, to minimize the threatening power of the panel members—if a member was rated as powerful, his benevolence was rated higher; and if he was rated as malevolent, his power was rated lower.

From the findings of research of the sort reported here it seems clear that the impact of social situations upon emotional adjustment will be adequately understood only if power is explicitly recognized.

SUMMARY

This brief overview of the field of social psychology leads to four conclusions:

1. A major deficiency of the theories of social psychology is that they have been soft on power.

2. The important social problems which demand our attention raise questions about power—questions which our systematic knowledge cannot answer.

3. Quite apart from any practical considerations, a social psychological theory without the concept of power (or its equivalent) is incomplete. Such concepts as communication, role, attitude, expectation, and norm cannot by themselves account realistically for the processes of influence to which they refer, nor can they deal effectively with social change and resistance to change.

4. A concerted attack on the problem of power should produce a major advance in the field of social psychology. Such an advance will consist of an improved understanding of the proper subject-matter of social psychology and a reorganization of its conceptual systems.

REFERENCES

1. Adler, A. A study of organ inferiority and its psychic compensations. *Trans. Nerv. ment. Dis. Monogr. Ser.*, 1917, **24**.

2. Allport, G. W. The historical background of modern social psychology. In G. Lindzey (Ed.), *Handbook of social psychology.* Cambridge: Addison-Wesley, 1954, 3–56.

3. Arsenian, J. M. Young children in an insecure situation. *J. abnorm. soc. Psychol.*, 1943, **38**, 225–249.

4. Back, K. W. Influence through social communication. *J. abnorm. soc. Psychol.*, 1951, **46**, 9–23.

5. Barnard, C. I. *The functions of the executive.* Cambridge: Harvard Univer. Press, 1938.

6. Block, J., & Block, J. An interpersonal experiment on reactions to authority. *Hum. Relat.*, 1952, **5**, 91–98.

7. Brim, O. G., Jr. The acceptance of new behavior in child-rearing. *Hum. Relat.*, 1954, **7**, 473–491.

8. Campbell, A. Administering research organizations. *Amer. Psychol.*, 1953, **8**, 225–230.

9. Deutsch, M., & Collins, M. E. *Interracial housing: A psychological evaluation of a social experiment.* Minneapolis: Univer. Minnesota Press, 1951.

10. Festinger, L., Cartwright, D., et al. A study of a rumor: Its origin and spread. *Hum. Relat.*, 1948, **1**, 464–486.

11. Festinger, L., Schachter, S., & Back, K. W. *Social pressures in informal groups.* New York: Harper, 1950.

12. Fleishman, E. A., Harris, E. F., & Burtt, H. E. *Leadership and supervision in industry: An evaluation of a supervisory training program.* Columbus: Ohio State University Bureau of Educational Research, 1955.

13. Frank, J. D. Experimental study of personal pressures and resistance: I. Experimental production of resistance. *J. gen. Psychol.*, 1944, **30**, 23–41.

14. Hobbes, T. *Leviathan*. Reprint of 1st (1651) Ed., Cambridge: Univer. Press, 1904.

15. Hoffman, M. L. Some psychodynamic factors in compulsive conformity. *J. abnorm. soc. Psychol.*, 1953, **48**, 383–393.

16. Hovland, C. I., & Weiss, W. The influence of source credibility on communication effectiveness. *Pub. Opin. Quart.*, 1952, **15**, 635–650.

17. Hunter, F. *Community power structure*. Chapel Hill: Univer. North Carolina Press, 1953.

18. Hurwitz, J. I., Zander, A. F., & Hymovitch, B. Some effects of power on the relations among group members. In D. Cartwright & A. Zander (Eds.), *Group dynamics: Research and theory*. Evanston: Row, Peterson, 1953, pp. 483–492.

19. Jackson, J. M. Analysis of interpersonal relations in a formal organization. Unpublished doctor's dissertation, Univer. Michigan, 1952.

20. Jaques, E. *The changing culture of a factory*. London: Tavistock, 1951.

21. Jenkins, D., & Lippitt, R. *Interpersonal perceptions of teachers, students and parents*. Washington: Nat. Train. Labor. Group Devel., 1951.

22. Kelley, H. H. Communication in experimentally created hierarchies. *Hum. Relat.*, 1951, **4**, 39–56.

23. Kelman, H. C., & Hovland, C. I. "Reinstatement" of the communicator in delayed measurement of opinion change. *J. abnorm. soc. Psychol.*, 1953, **48**, 327–335.

24. Lewin, K. *Field theory in social science*. New York: Harper, 1951.

25. Lewin, K., Lippitt, R., & White, R. K. Patterns of aggressive behavior in experimentally created "social climates." *J. soc. Psychol.*, 1939, **10**, 271–299.

26. Newcomb, T. *Social psychology*. New York: Dryden, 1950.

27. Nietzsche, F. *Der Wille zur Macht*. Book 3, sec. 702. In Nietzsche's complete *Werke*, vol. **16**. Leipzig: Alfred Kröner, 1912.

28. Pelz, D. C. Influence: A key to effective leadership in the first line supervisor. *Personnel*, 1952, **3**, 3–11.

29. Pepitone, A. Motivational effects in social perception. *Hum. Relat.*, 1950, **3**, 57–76.

30. Stogdill, R. M. Leadership, membership and organization. *Psychol. Bull.*, 1950, **47**, 1–14.

31. Strodtbeck, F. L. Husband-wife interaction over revealed differences. *Amer. sociol. Rev.*, 1951, **16**, 468–473.

32. Strodtbeck, F. L. The family as a three-person group. *Amer. sociol. Rev.*, 1954, **19**, 23–29.

33. Wright, M. E. The influence of frustration on the social relations of young children. *Charact. Pers.*, 1943, **12**, 111–122.

32
The Bases of Social Power
John R. P. French, Jr. & Bertram Raven

The processes of power are pervasive, complex, and often disguised in our society. Accordingly one finds in political science, in sociology, and in social psychology a variety of distinctions among different types of social power or among qualitatively different processes of social influence (1, 6, 14, 20, 23, 29, 30, 38, 41). Our main purpose is to identify the major types of power and to define them systematically so that we may compare them according to the changes which they produce and the other effects which accompany the use of power. The phenomena of power and influence involve a dyadic relation between two agents which may be viewed from two points of view: (a) What determines the behavior of the agent who exerts power? (b) What determines the reactions of the recipient of this behavior? We take this second point of view and formulate our theory in terms of the life space of P, the person upon whom the power is exerted. In this way we hope to define basic concepts of power which will be adequate to explain many of the phenomena of social influence, including some which have been described in other less genotypic terms.

Recent empirical work, especially on small groups, has demonstrated the necessity of distinguishing different types of power in order to account for the different effects found in studies of social influence. Yet there is no doubt that more empirical knowledge will be needed to make final decisions concerning the necessary differentiations, but this knowledge will be obtained only by research based on some preliminary theoretical distinctions. We present such preliminary concepts and some of the hypotheses they suggest.

POWER, INFLUENCE, AND CHANGE

Psychological Change

Since we shall define power in terms of influence, and influence in terms of psychological change, we begin with a discussion of change. We want to define change at a level of generality which includes changes in behavior, opinions, attitudes, goals, needs, values and all other aspects of the person's psychological field. We shall use the word "system" to refer to any such part of the life space.[1] Following Lewin (26, p. 305) the state of a system at time 1 will be noted $s_1(a)$.

Psychological change is defined as any alteration of the state of some system a over time. The amount of change is measured by the size of the difference between the states of the system a at time 1 and at time 2: $ch(a) = s_2(a) - s_1(a)$.

[1] The word "system" is here used to refer to a whole or to a part of the whole.

Source: John R. P. French, Jr., and Bertram Raven, "The Bases of Social Power," in *Studies in Social Power*, edited by Dorwin P. Cartwright (Ann Arbor, MI: Institute for Social Research, The University of Michigan, 1959), pp. 150–167. Reprinted by permission of the publisher.

Change in any psychological system may be conceptualized in terms of psychological forces. But it is important to note that the change must be coordinated to the resultant force of all the forces operating at the moment. Change in an opinion, for example, may be determined jointly by a driving force induced by another person, a restraining force corresponding to anchorage in a group opinion, and an own force stemming from the person's needs.

Social Influence

Our theory of social influence and power is limited to influence on the person, P, produced by a social agent, O, where O can be either another person, a role, a norm, a group or a part of a group. We do not consider social influence exerted on a group.

The influence of O on system *a* in the life space of P is defined as the resultant force on system *a* which has its source in an act of O. This resultant force induced by O consists of two components: a force to change the system in the direction induced by O and an opposing resistance set up by the same act of O.

By this definition the influence of O does not include P's own forces nor the forces induced by other social agents. Accordingly the "influence" of O must be clearly distinguished from O's "control" of P (Chapter 11). O may be able to induce strong forces on P to carry out an activity (i.e., O exerts strong influence on P); but if the opposing forces induced by another person or by P's own needs are stronger, then P will locomote in an opposite direction (i.e., O does not have control over P). Thus psychological change in P can be taken as an operational definition of the social influence of O on P only when the effects of other forces have been eliminated.

It is assumed that any system is interdependent with other parts of the life space so that a change in one may produce changes in others. However, this theory focuses on the primary changes in a system which are produced directly by social influence; it is less concerned with secondary changes which are indirectly effected in the other systems or with primary changes produced by nonsocial influences.

Commonly social influence takes place through an intentional act on the part of O. However, we do not want to limit our definition of "act" to such conscious behavior. Indeed, influence might result from the passive presence of O, with no evidence of speech or overt movement. A policeman's standing on a corner may be considered an act of an agent for the speeding motorist. Such acts of the inducing agent will vary in strength, for O may not always utilize all of his power. The policeman, for example, may merely stand and watch or act more strongly by blowing his whistle at the motorist.

The influence exerted by an act need not be in the direction intended by O. The direction of the resultant force on P will depend on the relative magnitude of the induced force set up by the act of O and the resisting force in the opposite direction which is generated by that same act. In cases where O intends to influence P in a given direction, a resultant force in the same direction may be termed positive influence whereas a resultant force in the opposite direction may be termed negative influence.

If O produces the intended change, he has exerted positive control; but if he produces a change in the opposite direction, as for example in the negativism of young children or in the phenomena of negative reference groups, he has exerted negative control.

Social Power

The strength of power of O/P in some system *a* is defined as the maximum potential ability of O to influence P in *a*.

By this definition influence is kinetic power, just as power is potential influence. It is assumed that O is capable of various acts which, because of some more or less enduring relation to P, are able to exert influence on P[2]. O's power is measured by his maximum possible influence, though he may often choose to exert less than his full power.

An equivalent definition of power may be stated in terms of the resultant of two forces set up by the act of O: one in the direction of O's influence attempt and another resisting force in the opposite direction. Power is the maximum resultant of these two forces:

$$\text{Power of } O/P(a) = (f_{a,x} - f_{\overline{a,x}})^{\max}$$

where the source of both forces is an act of O.

Thus the power of O with respect to system *a* of P is equal to the maximum resultant force of two forces set up by any possible act of O: (a) the force which O can set up on the system *a* to change in the direction x, (b) the resisting force,[3] in the opposite direction.

Whenever the first component force is greater than the second, positive power exists; but if the second component force is greater than the first, then O has negative power over P.

It is necessary to define power with respect to a specified system because the power of O/P may vary greatly from one system to another. O may have great power to control the behavior of P but little power to control his opinions. Of course a high power of O/P does not imply a low power of P/O; the two variables are conceptually independent (Chapter 11).

For certain purposes it is convenient to define the range of power as the set of all systems within which O has power of strength greater than zero. A husband may have a broad range of power over his wife, but a narrow range of power over his employer. We shall use the term "magnitude of power" to denote the summation of O's power over P in all systems of his range.

The Dependence of s(a) on O.

Several investigators have been concerned with differences between superficial conformity and "deeper" changes produced by social influence (1, 5, 6, 11, 12, 20, 21, 22, 23, 26, 36, 37). The kinds of systems which are changed and the stability of these changes have been handled by distinctions such as "public vs. private attitudes," "overt vs. covert behavior," "compliance vs. internalization," and "own vs. induced forces." Though stated as dichotomies, all of these distinctions suggest an underlying dimension of the degree of dependence of the state of a system on O.

---

[2] The concept of power has the conceptual property of *potentiality*; but it seems useful to restrict this potential influence to more or less enduring power relations between O and P by excluding from the definition of power those cases where the potential influence is so momentary or so changing that it cannot be predicted from the existing relationship. Power is a useful concept for describing social structure only if it has a certain stability over time; it is useless if every momentary social stimulus is viewed as actualizing social power.

[3] We define resistance to an attempted induction as a force in the opposite direction which is set up by the same act of O. It must be distinguished from opposition which is defined as existing opposing forces which do not have their source in the same act of O. For

example, a boy might resist his mother's order to eat spinach because of the manner of the induction attempt, and at the same time he might oppose it because he didn't like spinach.

We assume that any change in the state of a system is produced by a change in some factor upon which it is functionally dependent. The state of an opinion, for example, may change because of a change either in some internal factor such as a need or in some external factor such as the arguments of O. Likewise the maintenance of the same state of a system is produced by the stability or lack of change in the internal and external factors. In general, then, psychological change and stability can be conceptualized in terms of dynamic dependence. Our interest is focused on the special case of dependence on an external agent, O **(31).**

In many cases the initial state of the system has the character of a quasistationary equilibrium with a central force field around $s_1(a)$ (**26,** p. 106). In such cases we may derive a tendency toward retrogression to the original state as soon as the force induced by O is removed.[4] Let us suppose that O exerts influence producing a new state of the system, $s_2(a)$. Is $s_2(a)$ now dependent on the continued presence of O? In principle we could answer this question by removing any traces of O from the life space of P and by observing the consequent state of the system at time 3. If $s_3(a)$ retrogresses completely back to $s_1(a)$, then we may conclude that maintenance of $s_2(a)$ was completely dependent on O; but if $s_3(a)$ equals $s_2(a)$, this lack of change shows that $s_2(a)$ has become completely independent of O. In general the degree of dependence of $s_2(a)$ on O, following O's influence, may be defined as equal to the amount of retrogression following the removal of O from the life space of P:

Degree of dependence of $s_2(a)$ on $O = s_2(a) - s_3(a)$.

A given degree of dependence at time 2 may later change, for example, through the gradual weakening of O's influence. At this later time, the degree of dependence of $s_4(a)$ on O, would still be equal to the amount of retrogression toward the initial state of equilibrium $s_1(a)$. Operational measures of the degree of dependence on O will, of course, have to be taken under conditions where all other factors are held constant.

Consider the example of three separated employees who have been working at the same steady level of production despite normal, small fluctuations in the work environment. The supervisor orders each to increase his production, and the level of each goes up from 100 to 115 pieces per day. After a week of producing at the new rate of 115 pieces per day, the supervisor is removed for a week. The production of employee A immediately returns to 100 but B and C return to only 110 pieces per day. Other things being equal, we can infer that A's new rate was completely dependent on his supervisor whereas the new rate of B and C was dependent on the supervisor only to the extent of 5 pieces. Let us further assume that when the supervisor returned, the production of B and of C returned to 115 without further orders from the supervisor. Now another month goes by during which B and C maintain a steady 115 pieces per day. However, there is a difference between them: B's level of production still depends on O to the extent of 5 pieces whereas C has come to rely on his own sense of obligation to obey the order of his legitimate supervisor rather than on the supervisor's ex-

---

[4]Miller (**33**) assumes that all living systems have this character. However, it may be that some systems in the life space do not have this elasticity.

ternal pressure for the maintenance of his 115 pieces per day. Accordingly, the next time the supervisor departs, B's production again drops to 110 but C's remains at 115 pieces per day. In cases like employee B, the degree of dependence is contingent on the perceived probability that O will observe the state of the system and note P's conformity (5, 6, 11, 12, 23). The level of observability will in turn depend on both the nature of the system (e.g., the difference between a covert opinion and overt behavior) and on the environmental barriers to observation (e.g., O is too far away from P). In other cases, for example that of employee C, the new behavior pattern is highly dependent on his supervisor, but the degree of dependence of the new state will be related not to the level of observability but rather to factors inside P, in this case a sense of duty to perform an act legitimately prescribed by O. The internalization of social norms is a related process of decreasing degree of dependence of behavior on an external O and increasing dependence on an internal value; it is usually assumed that internalization is accompanied by a decrease in the effects of level of observability (37).

The concepts "dependence of a system on O" and "observability as a basis for dependence" will be useful in understanding the stability of conformity. In the next section we shall discuss various types of power and the types of conformity which they are likely to produce.

THE BASES OF POWER

By the basis of power we mean the relationship between O and P which is the source of that power. It is rare that we can say with certainty that a given empirical case of power is limited to one source. Normally, the relation between O and P will be characterized by several qualitatively different variables which are bases of power (30, Chapter 11). Although there are undoubtedly many possible bases of power which may be distinguished, we shall here define five which seem especially common and important. These five bases of O's power are: (1) reward power, based on P's perception that O has the ability to mediate rewards for him; (2) coercive power, based on P's perception that O has the ability to mediate punishments for him; (3) legitimate power, based on the perception by P that O has a legitimate right to prescribe behavior for him; (4) referent power, based on P's identification with O; (5) expert power, based on the perception that O has some special knowledge or expertness.

Our first concern is to define the bases which give rise to a given type of power. Next, we describe each type of power according to its strength, range, and the degree of dependence of the new state of the system which is most likely to occur with each type of power. We shall also examine the other effects which the exercise of a given type of power may have upon P and his relationship to O. Finally, we shall point out the interrelationships between different types of power, and the effects of use of one type of power by O upon other bases of power which he might have over P. Thus we shall both define a set of concepts and propose a series of hypotheses. Most of these hypotheses have not been systematically tested, although there is a good deal of evidence in favor of several. No attempt will be made to summarize that evidence here.

Reward Power

Reward power is defined as power whose basis is the ability to reward. The strength of the reward power of O/P increases with the magnitude of the rewards which P perceives that O can mediate for him. Reward power depends on O's ability to administer positive valences and to remove or decrease negative valences. The strength of reward power also depends upon the probability that O can mediate the reward, as perceived by P. A common example of reward power is the addition of a piecework rate in the factory as an incentive to increase production.

The new state of the system induced by a promise of reward (for example the factory worker's increased level of production) will be highly dependent on O. Since O mediates the reward, he controls the probability that P will receive it. Thus P's new rate of production will be dependent on his subjective probability that O will reward him for conformity minus his subjective probability that O will reward him even if he returns to his old level. Both probabilities will be greatly affected by the level of observability of P's behavior. Incidentally, a piece rate often seems to have more effect on production than a merit rating system because it yields a higher probability of reward for conformity and a much lower probability of reward for nonconformity.

The utilization of actual rewards (instead of promises) by O will tend over time to increase the attraction of P toward O and therefore the referent power of O over P. As we shall note later, such referent power will permit O to induce changes which are relatively independent. Neither rewards nor promises will arouse resistance in P, provided P considers it legitimate for O to offer rewards.

The range of reward power is specific to those regions within which O can reward P for conforming. The use of rewards to change systems within the range of reward power tends to increase

reward power by increasing the probability attached to future promises. However, unsuccessful attempts to exert reward power outside the range of power would tend to decrease the power; for example if O offers to reward P for performing an impossible act, this will reduce for P the probability of receiving future rewards promised by O.

Coercive Power

Coercive power is similar to reward power in that it also involves O's ability to manipulate the attainment of valences. Coercive power of O/P stems from the expectation on the part of P that he will be punished by O if he fails to conform to the influence attempt. Thus negative valences will exist in given regions of P's life space, corresponding to the threatened punishment by O. The strength of coercive power depends on the magnitude of the negative valence of the threatened punishment multiplied by the perceived probability that P can avoid the punishment by conformity, i.e., the probability of punishment for nonconformity minus the probability of punishment for conformity (11). Just as an offer of a piece-rate bonus in a factory can serve as a basis for reward power, so the ability to fire a worker if he falls below a given level of production will result in coercive power.

Coercive power leads to dependent change also; and the degree of dependence varies with the level of observability of P's conformity. An excellent illustration of coercive power leading to dependent change is provided by a clothes presser in a factory observed by Coch and French (3). As her efficiency rating climbed above average for the group the other workers began to "scapegoat" her. That the resulting plateau in her production was not independent of the group was evident once she was removed from the presence of the other workers. Her production immediately climbed to new heights.[5]

At times, there is some difficulty in distinguishing between reward power and coercive power. Is the withholding of a reward really equivalent to a punishment? Is the withdrawal of punishment equivalent to a reward? The answer must be a psychological one—it depends upon the situation as it exists for P. But ordinarily we would answer these questions in the affirmative; for P, receiving a reward is a positive valence as is the relief of suffering. There is some evidence that conformity to group norms in order to gain acceptance (reward power) should be distinguished from conformity as a means for forestalling rejection (coercive power) **(5)**.

The distinction between these two types of power is important because the dynamics are different. The concept of "sanctions" sometimes lumps the two together despite their opposite effects. While reward power may eventually result in an independent system, the effects of coercive power will continue to be dependent. Reward power will tend to increase the attraction of P toward O; coercive power will decrease this attraction **(11, 12)**. The valence of the region of behavior will become more negative, acquiring some negative valence from the threatened punishment. The negative valence of punishment would also spread to other regions of the life space. Lewin **(25)** has pointed out this distinction between the effects of rewards and

---

[5]Though the primary influence of coercive power is dependent, it often produces secondary changes which are independent. Brainwashing, for example, utilizes coercive power to produce many primary changes in the life space of the prisoner, but these dependent changes can lead to identification with the aggressor and hence to secondary changes in ideology which are independent.

punishment. In the case of threatened punishment, there will be a resultant force on P to leave the field entirely. Thus, to achieve conformity, O must not only place a strong negative valence in certain regions through threat of punishment, but O must also introduce restraining forces, or other strong valences, so as to prevent P from withdrawing completely from O's range of coercive power. Otherwise the probability of receiving the punishment, if P does not conform, will be too low to be effective.

Legitimate Power

Legitimate power is probably the most complex of those treated here, embodying notions from the structural sociologist, the group-norm and role oriented social psychologist, and the clinical psychologist.

There has been considerable investigation and speculation about socially prescribed behavior, particularly that which is specific to a given role or position. Linton **(29)** distinguishes group norms according to whether they are universals for everyone in the culture, alternatives (the individual having a choice as to whether or not to accept them), or specialties (specific to given positions). Whether we speak of internalized norms, role prescriptions and expectations **(34)**, or internalized pressures **(15)**, the fact remains that each individual sees certain regions toward which he should locomote, some regions toward which he should not locomote, and some regions toward which he may locomote if they are generally attractive for him. This applies to specific behaviors in which he may, should, or should not engage; it applies to certain attitudes or beliefs which he may, should, or should not hold. The feeling of "oughtness' may be an internalization from his parents, from his teachers, from his religion, or may have been logically developed from some idiosyncratic system of ethics. He will speak of such behaviors with expressions like "should," "ought to," or "has a right to." In many cases, the original source of the requirement is not recalled.

Though we have oversimplified such evaluations of behavior with a positive-neutral-negative trichotomy, the evaluation of behaviors by the person is really more one of degree. This dimension of evaluation, we shall call "legitimacy." Conceptually, we may think of legitimacy as a valence in a region which is induced by some internalized norm or value. This value has the same conceptual property as power, namely an ability to induce force fields (**26,** p. 40–41). It may or may not be correct that values (or the superego) are internalized parents, but at least they can set up force fields which have a phenomenal "oughtness" similar to a parent's prescription. Like a value, a need can also induce valences (i.e., force fields) in P's psychological environment, but these valences have more the phenomenal character of noxious or attractive properties of the object or activity. When a need induces a valence in P, for example, when a need makes an object attractive to P, this attraction applies to P but not to other persons. When a value induces a valence, on the other hand, it not only sets up forces on P to engage in the activity, but P may feel that all others ought to behave in the same way. Among other things, this evaluation applies to the legitimate right of some other individual or group to prescribe behavior or beliefs for a person even though the other cannot apply sanctions.

Legitimate power of O/P is here defined as that power which stems from internalized values in P which dictate that O has a legitimate right to influence P and that P has an obligation to accept this influence. We note that legitimate power is very similar to the notion of legitimacy of authority which has long been explored by sociologists, particularly by Weber (**42**), and more recently by Goldhammer and Shils (**14**). However, legitimate power is not always a role relation: P may accept an induction from O simply because he had previously promised to help O and he values his word too much to break the promise. In all cases, the notion of legitimacy involves some sort of code or standard, accepted by the individual, by virtue of which the external agent can assert his power. We shall attempt to describe a few of these values here.

Bases for legitimate power. Cultural values constitute one common basis for the legitimate power of one individual over another. O has characteristics which are specified by the culture as giving him the right to prescribe behavior for P, who may not have these characteristics. These bases, which Weber (**42**) has called the authority of the "eternal yesterday," include such things as age, intelligence, caste, and physical characteristics. In some cultures, the aged are granted the right to prescribe behavior for others in practically all behavior areas. In most cultures, there are certain areas of behavior in which a person of one sex is granted the right to prescribe behavior for the other sex.

Acceptance of the social structure is another basis for legitimate power. If P accepts as right the social structure of his group, organization, or society, especially the social structure involving a hierarchy of authority, P will accept the legitimate authority of O who occupies a superior office in the hierarchy. Thus legitimate power in a formal organization is largely a relationship between offices rather than between persons. And the acceptance of an office as *right* is a basis for legitimate power—a judge has a right to levy fines, a foreman should assign work, a priest is justified in prescribing religious beliefs, and it is the management's prerogative to make certain decisions (10). However, legitimate power also involves the perceived right of the person to hold the office.

Designation by a legitimizing agent is a third basis for legitimate power. An influencer O may be seen as legitimate in prescribing behavior for P because he has been granted such power by a legitimizing agent whom P accepts. Thus a department head may accept the authority of his vice-president in a certain area because that authority has been specifically delegated by the president. An election is perhaps the most common example of a group's serving to legitimize the authority of one individual or office for other individuals in the group. The success of such legitimizing depends upon the acceptance of the legitimizing agent and procedure. In this case it depends ultimately on certain democratic values concerning election procedures. The election process is one of legitimizing a person's right to an office which already has a legitimate range of power associated with it.

Range of legitimate power of O/P. The areas in which legitimate power may be exercised are generally specified along with the designation of that power. A job description, for example, usually specifies supervisory activities and also designates the person to whom the jobholder is responsible for the duties described. Some bases for legitimate authority carry with them a very broad range. Culturally derived bases for legitimate power are often especially broad. It is not uncommon to find cultures in which a member of a given caste can legitimately prescribe behavior for all members of lower castes in practically all regions. More common, however, are instances of legitimate power where the range is specifically and narrowly prescribed. A sergeant in the army is given a specific set of regions within which he can legitimately prescribe behavior for his men.

The attempted use of legitimate power which is outside of the range of legitimate power will decrease the legitimate power of the authority figure. Such use of power which is not legitimate will also decrease the attractiveness of O (11, 12, 36).

Legitimate power and influence. The new state of the system which results from legitimate power usually has high dependence on O though it may become independent. Here, however, the degree of dependence is not related to the level of observability. Since legitimate power is based on P's values, the source of the forces induced by O include both these internal values and O. O's induction serves to activate the values and to relate them to the system which is influenced, but thereafter the new state of the system may become directly dependent on the values with no mediation by O. Accordingly this new state will be relatively stable and consistent across varying environmental situations since P's values are more stable than his psychological environment.

We have used the term legitimate not only as a basis for the power of an agent, but also to describe the general behaviors of a person. Thus, the individual P may also consider the legitimacy of the attempts to use other types of power by O. In certain cases, P will consider that O has a legitimate right to threaten punishment for nonconformity; in other cases, such use of coercion would not be seen as legitimate. P might change in response to coercive power of O, but it will make a considerable difference in his attitude and conformity if O is not seen as having a legitimate right to use such coercion. In such cases, the attraction of P for O will be particularly diminished, and the influence attempt will arouse more resistance (11). Similarly the utilization of reward power may vary in legitimacy; the word "bribe," for example, denotes an illegitimate reward.

Referent Power

The referent power of O/P has its basis in the identification of P with O. By identification, we mean a feeling of oneness of P with O, or a desire for such an identity. If O is a person toward whom P is highly attracted, P will have a feeling of membership or a desire to join. If P is already closely associated with O he will want to maintain this relationship (39, 41). P's identification with O can be established or maintained if P behaves, believes, and perceives as O does. Accordingly O has the ability to influence P, even though P may be unaware of this referent power. A verbalization of such power by P might be, "I am like O, and therefore I shall behave or believe as O does," or "I want to be like O, and I will be more like O if I behave or believe as O does." The stronger the identification of P with O the greater the referent power of O/P.

Similar types of power have already been investigated under a number of different formulations. Festinger (7) points out that in an ambiguous situation, the individual seeks some sort of "social reality" and may adopt the cognitive structure of the individual or group with which he identifies. In such a case, the lack of clear structure may be threatening to the individual and the agreement of his beliefs with those of a reference group will both satisfy his need for structure and give him added

security through increased identification with his group (16, 19).

We must try to distinguish between referent power and other types of power which might be operative at the same time. If a member is attracted to a group and he conforms to its norms only because he fears ridicule or expulsion from the group for nonconformity, we would call this coercive power. On the other hand if he conforms in order to obtain praise for conformity, it is a case of reward power. The basic criterion for distinguishing referent power from both coercive and reward power is the mediation of the punishment and the reward by O: to the extent that O mediates the sanctions (i.e., has means control over P) we are dealing with coercive and reward power; but to the extent that P avoids discomfort or gains satisfaction by conformity based on identification, regardless of O's responses, we are dealing with referent power. Conformity with majority opinion is sometimes based on a respect for the collective wisdom of the group, in which case it is expert power. It is important to distinguish these phenomena, all grouped together elsewhere as "pressures toward uniformity," since the type of change which occurs will be different for different bases of power.

The concepts of "reference group" (40) and "prestige suggestion" may be treated as instances of referent power. In this case, O, the prestigeful person or group, is valued by P; because P desires to be associated or identified with O, he will assume attitudes or beliefs held by O. Similarly a negative reference group which O dislikes and evaluates negatively may exert negative influence on P as a result of negative referent power.

It has been demonstrated that the power which we designate as referent power is especially great when P is attracted to O (2, 7, 8, 9, 13, 23, 30). In our terms, this would mean that the greater the attraction, the greater the identification, and consequently the greater the referent power. In some cases, attraction or prestige may have a specific basis, and the range of referent power will be limited accordingly: a group of campers may have great referent power over a member regarding campcraft, but considerably less effect on other regions (30). However, we hypothesize that the greater the attraction of P toward O, the broader the range of referent power of O/P.

The new state of a system produced by referent power may be dependent on or independent of O; but the degree of dependence is not affected by the level of observability to O (6, 23). In fact, P is often not consciously aware of the referent power which O exerts over him. There is probably a tendency for some of these dependent changes to become independent of O quite rapidly.

Expert Power

The strength of the expert power of O/P varies with the extent of the knowledge or perception which P attributes to O within a given area. Probably P evaluates O's expertness in relation to his own knowledge as well as against an absolute standard. In any case expert power results in primary social influence on P's cognitive structure and probably not on other types of systems. Of course changes in the cognitive structure can change the direction of forces and hence of locomotion, but such a change of behavior is secondary social influence. Expert power has been demonstrated experimentally (8, 33). Accepting an attorney's advice in legal matters is a common example of expert influence; but there are many instances based on much less knowledge, such as the acceptance by a stranger of directions given by a native villager.

Expert power, where O need not be a member of P's group, is called "informational power" by Deutsch and Gerard (4). This type of expert power must be distinguished from influence based on the content of communication as described by Hovland et al. (17, 18, 23, 24). The influence of the content of a communication upon an opinion is presumably a secondary influence produced after the *primary* influence (i.e., the acceptance of the information). Since power is here defined in terms of the primary changes, the influence of the content on a related opinion is not a case of expert power as we have defined it, but the initial acceptance of the validity of the content does seem to be based on expert power or referent power. In other cases, however, so-called facts may be accepted as self-evident because they fit into P's cognitive structure; if this impersonal acceptance of the truth of the fact is independent of the more or less enduring relationship between O and P, then P's acceptance of the fact is not an actualization of expert power. Thus we distinguish between expert power based on the credibility of O and informational influence which is based on characteristics of the stimulus such as the logic of the argument or the "self-evident facts."

Wherever expert influence occurs it seems to be necessary both for P to think that O knows and for P to trust that O is telling the truth (rather than trying to deceive him).

Expert power will produce a new cognitive structure which is initially relatively dependent on O, but informational influence will produce a more independent structure. The former is likely to become more independent with the passage of time. In both cases the degree of dependence on O is not affected by the level of observability. The "sleeper effect" (18, 24) is an interesting case of a change in the degree of dependence of an opinion on O. An unreliable O (who probably had negative referent power but some positive expert power) presented "facts" which were accepted by the subjects and which would normally produce secondary influence on their opinions and beliefs. However, the negative referent power aroused resistance and resulted in negative social influence on their beliefs (i.e., set up a force in the direction opposite to the influence attempt), so that there was little change in the subjects' opinions. With the passage of time, however, the subjects tended to forget the identity of the negative communicator faster than they forgot the contents of his communication, so there was a weakening of the negative referent influence and a consequent delayed positive change in the subjects' beliefs in the direction of the influence attempt ("sleeper effect"). Later, when the identity of the negative communicator was experimentally reinstated, these resisting forces were reinstated, and there was another negative change in belief in a direction opposite to the influence attempt **(24).**

The range of expert power, we assume, is more delimited than that of referent power. Not only is it restricted to cognitive systems but the expert is seen as having superior knowledge or ability in very specific areas, and his power will be limited to these areas, though some "halo effect" might occur. Recently, some of our renowned physical scientists have found quite painfully that their expert power in physical sciences does not extend to regions involving international politics. Indeed, there is some evidence that the attempted exertion of expert power outside of the range of expert power will reduce that expert power. An undermining of confidence seems to take place.

SUMMARY

We have distinguished five types of power: referent power, expert power, reward power, coercive power, and legitimate power. These distinctions led to the following hypotheses.

1. For all five types, the stronger the basis of power the greater the power.

2. For any type of power the size of the range may vary greatly, but in general referent power will have the broadest range.

3. Any attempt to utilize power outside the range of power will tend to reduce the power.

4. A new state of a system produced by reward power or coercive power will be highly dependent on O, and the more observable P's conformity the more dependent the state. For the other three types of power, the new state is usually dependent, at least in the beginning, but in any case the level of observability has no effect on the degree of dependence.

5. Coercion results in decreased attraction of P toward O and high resistance; reward power results in increased attraction and low resistance.

6. The more legitimate the coercion the less it will produce resistance and decreased attraction.

REFERENCES

1. Asch, S. E. *Social psychology.* New York: Prentice-Hall, 1952.

2. Back, K. W. Influence through social communication. *J. abnorm. soc. Psychol.*, 1951, **46**, 9–23.

3. Coch, L., & French, J. R. P., Jr. Overcoming resistance to change. *Hum. Relat.*, 1948, **1**, 512–32.

4. Deutsch, M., & Gerard, H. B. A study of normative and informational influences upon individual judgment. *J. abnorm. soc. Psychol.*, 1955, **51**, 629–36.

5. Dittes, J. E., & Kelley, H. H. Effects of different conditions of acceptance upon conformity to group norms. *J. abnorm. soc. Psychol.*, 1956, **53**, 100–107.

6. Festinger, L. An analysis of compliant behavior. In Sherif, M., & Wilson, M. O., (Eds.). *Group relations at the crossroads.* New York: Harper, 1953, 232–56.

7. Festinger, L. Informal social communication. *Psychol. Rev.*, 1950, **57**, 271–82.

8. Festinger, L., Gerard, H. B., Hymovitch, B., Kelley, H. H., & Raven, B. H. The influence process in the presence of extreme deviates. *Hum. Relat.*, 1952, **5**, 327–346.

9. Festinger, L., Schachter, S., & Back, K. The operation of group standards. In Cartwright, D., & Zander, A. *Group dynamics: research and theory.* Evanston: Row, Peterson, 1953, 204–23.

10. French, J. R. P., Jr., Israel, Joachim & Ås, Dagfinn. "Arbeidernes medvirkning i industribedriften. En eksperimentell undersøkelse." Institute for Social Research, Oslo, Norway, 1957.

11. French, J. R. P., Jr., Levinger, G., & Morrison, H. W. The legitimacy of coercive power. In preparation.

12. French, J. R. P., Jr., & Raven, B. H. An experiment in legitimate and coercive power. In preparation.

13. Gerard, H. B. The anchorage of opinions in face-to-face groups. *Hum. Relat.*, 1954, **7**, 313–325.

14. Goldhammer, H., & Shils, E. A. Types of power and status. *Amer. J. Sociol.*, 1939, **45**, 171–178.

15. Herbst, P. G. Analysis and measurement of a situation. *Hum. Relat.*, 1953, **2**, 113–140.

16. Hochbaum, G. M. Self-confidence and reactions to group pressures. *Amer. soc. Rev.*, 1954, **19**, 678–687.

17. Hovland, C. I., Lumsdaine, A. A., & Sheffield, F. D. *Experiments on mass communication.* Princeton: Princeton Univer. Press, 1949.

18. Hovland, C. I., & Weiss, W. The influence of source credibility on communication effectiveness. *Publ. Opin. Quart.*, 1951, **15**, 635–650.

19. Jackson, J. M., & Saltzstein, H. D. The effect of person-group relationships on conformity processes. *J. abnorm. soc. Psychol.*, 1958, **57**, 17–24.

20. Jahoda, M. Psychological issues in civil liberties. *Amer. Psychologist*, 1956, **11**, 234–240.

21. Katz, D., & Schank, R. L. *Social psychology.* New York: Wiley, 1938.

22. Kelley, H. H., & Volkart, E. H. The resistance to change of group-anchored attitudes. *Amer. soc. Rev.*, 1952, **17**, 453–465.

23. Kelman, H. Three processes of acceptance of social influence: compliance, identification and internalization. Paper read at the meetings of the American Psychological Association, August 1956.

24. Kelman, H., & Hovland, C. I. "Reinstatement" of the communicator in delayed measurement of opinion change. *J. abnorm. soc. Psychol.*, 1953, **48**, 327–335.

25. Lewin, K. *Dynamic theory of personality.* New York: McGraw-Hill, 1935, 114–170.

26. Lewin, K. *Field theory in social science.* New York: Harper, 1951.

27. Lewin, K., Lippitt, R., & White, R. K. Patterns of aggressive behavior in experimentally created social climates. *J. soc. Psychol.*, 1939, **10**, 271–301.

28. Lasswell, H. D., & Kaplan, A. *Power and society: A framework for political inquiry.* New Haven: Yale Univer. Press, 1950.

29. Linton, R. *The cultural background of personality.* New York: Appleton-Century-Crofts, 1945.

30. Lippitt, R., Polansky, N., Redl, F., & Rosen, S. The dynamics of power. *Hum. Relat.*, 1952, **5**, 37–64.

31. March, J. G. An introduction to the theory and measurement of influence. *Amer. polit. Sci. Rev.*, 1955, **49**, 431–451.

32. Miller, J. G. Toward a general theory for the behavioral sciences. *Amer. Psychologist*, 1955, **10**, 513–531.

33. Moore, H. T. The comparative influence of majority and expert opinion. *Amer. J. Psychol.*, 1921, **32**, 16–20.

34. Newcomb, T. M. *Social psychology.* New York: Dryden, 1950.

35. Raven, B. H. The effect of group pressures on opinion, perception, and communication. Unpublished doctoral dissertation, University of Michigan, 1953.

36. Raven, B. H., & French, J. R. P., Jr. Group support, legitimate power, and social influence. *J. Person.*, 1958, **26,** 400–409.

37. Rommetveit, R. *Social norms and roles.* Minneapolis: Univer. Minnesota Press, 1953.

38. Russell, B. *Power: A new social analysis.* New York: Norton, 1938.

39. Stotland, E., Zander, A., Burnstein, E., Wolfe, D., & Natsoulas, T. Studies on the effects of identification. University of Michigan, Institute for Social Research. Forthcoming.

40. Swanson, G. E., Newcomb, T. M., & Hartley, E. L. *Readings in social psychology.* New York: Henry Holt, 1952.

41. Torrance, E. P., & Mason, R. Instructor effort to influence: an experimental evaluation of six approaches. Paper presented at USAF-NRC Symposium on Personnel, Training, and Human Engineering. Washington, D.C., 1956.

42. Weber, M. *The theory of social and economic organization.* Oxford: Oxford Univer. Press, 1947.

33
The Concept of Power and the Concept of Man
Mason Haire

It is a fad just now to have social scientists working on the problems of business. I will address myself to the question, "Why should this be so?" I suggest that it is *not* just because the Ford Foundation thinks it a good idea, although that makes it much easier. I think it is *not* simply because there is a growing interest both in studies of business and in the social sciences in some common problems like the structure of groups, communication, and the like, although these provide a fertile ground for the interaction. I think it is *not* because of the developing theory and method in the social sciences, although these two developments go a long way toward making the interaction possible. It seems to me that the reason for including the social sciences in the study of business is because the problems of the industrial organization and the setting in which they occur are changing. This change in the social context of business is making the social sciences an integral and necessary part of any considerations of business. I want to speak particularly about two of these changes—the changing concept of power and the changing concept of man. In these two broad areas it seems to me that society's view has changed—and changed in such a way that we can no longer look at business in the narrow sense that we once did. In speaking about these things, I shall deal primarily with organization theory

because it is a convenient framework for seeing the impact of these changes on the study of business. However, a variety of other specific aspects of the business problem would serve the purpose equally well.

THE CHANGING CONCEPT OF POWER

Where is authority ultimately grounded? Why do people do what they are told? It seems to me that the answer to these questions in the industrial organization shows a series of steps over a long historical period, all of them tied together as part of a progressive internalization of the seat of power. Let us ask the questions in "classical" organization theory. When I use "classical" in this sense, I mean the kind of theory of organization that we have been used to in the recent past (from, say, Chester Barnard's *Functions of the Executive*). In this kind of system the ultimate seat of authority is clearly outside the corporation. Authority, in the last analysis, is grounded in ownership. It is legitimatized and vested temporarily in the chief executive officer through the medium of the board of directors representing the stockholders. The answer to the question "Why do people do what they are told?" in this system is that they do it because the "or else" means essentially "get off my property."

Source: *Social Science Approaches to Business Behavior* by Chris Argyris, Robert Subin, Mason Haire, R. Duncan Luce, W. Lloyd Warner, William Foote Whyte, and George B. Strother, Editors, 1962. Homewood, Il.: The Dorsey Press, Inc. and Richard D. Irwin, Inc. Copyright © 1962 by Richard D. Irwin, Inc. Reprinted by permission.

FIGURE 1 • THE RISE AND FALL OF POWER IN INDUSTRIAL ORGANIZATIONS.

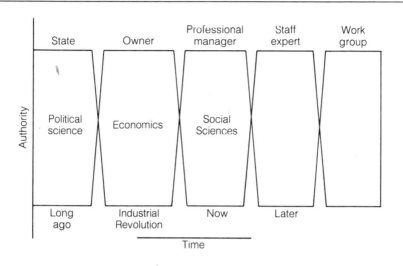

This position of the owners as the ultimate source of authority has not always been true in the past and is not likely to be true in the future. For a long historical period—we might roughly indicate the period from the Roman Empire to the Industrial Revolution—the ultimate authority of the manager of a business was grounded not in ownership but in the state. For example, Toynbee points out, in *Management's Mission in a New Society,* that the geographical conquests of the Roman armies faced the government with a real dilemma. With the rudimentary administrative machinery of a peasant state, Rome controlled almost all the shores of the Mediterranean. It solved this problem by turning over to private business enterprise every possible branch of public activity—the collection of customs duties, the operation of the farm economy in captured territories, the operation of confiscated mines, and the provisioning of Roman armies. The *authority* with which all this was carried out was still the authority of the state. The *authority*

for all the normal business functions—hiring and firing, and the setting of prices and fees, insuring against business risks—came from the state; the *operation* was in the hands of the businessman. This separation of the authority grounded well outside the business activity and the operation inside it is the important characteristic of this period.

It was not only in the Roman Empire that this kind of thing was true. The British East India Company is an outstanding example of the same sort of thing. The operation of privateers with letters patent from the American Revolution through the Civil War fits the same pattern. In some senses the subsidized growth of the railroads and communications industry in the United States continued the trend.

I place the change to the primacy of the owner roughly at the time of the Industrial Revolution. It may well be because the technological change at the time made property, plants, and machinery more and more important and made the formation of concentrated capital the crux of the problem. Before that time, in the simple, dispersed industrial operation, capital was not as important as the protection and approval of the state. At about the same time we see the rise of the rights of property both as a source of authority for the industrial manager and as a general source of value for the community. That well-known social philosopher, Alfred Doolittle, in *My Fair Lady* (and in George Bernard Shaw's *Pygmalion*), speaks of the rights of property as the ultimate prop of middle-class morality, and, indeed, this probably has been true for something over one hundred years as both a social principle and an industrial one.

Today it is reasonable to say that our society is shifting from a success-oriented culture to adjustment-oriented culture. We worry about the teen-ager's psyche and how he fits in with his fellows; he responds by not worrying about property rights, and vandalism is rife. When he breaks all the windows in a schoolhouse and throws paint on the walls, his parents and our schools and our courts do not worry so much about the property as they do about his adjustment. The physical damage is unfortunate, but in an affluent society this does not matter as much as the fact that he is mixed up.

In the industrial organization the parallel to this shift from success to adjustment as a characteristic of the culture (or from property rights to individual rights) is a shift from a conception of executive authority grounded in ownership to one of the same authority which is grounded inside the organization in the process of managing itself. We hear more and more phrases like "the imperatives of the science of management," "the logic of the situation," and "the principles of management." Now, much more than before, when we ask "Why do people do what they are told?" I think the answer is that they either see or have faith that what they are told to do is in fact the appropriate thing to do. This represents a real shift in the ultimate source of authority; in the first place, it is an internalization of the ground on which it is based, and, in the second place, it bases authority on the dynamics of social interaction and the process of management rather than property rights. The internalization has been a progressive thing: when the manager's authority derived from the prince, its ultimate basis was farthest from the corporation; as it shifted to the owner, it came closer to the corporation itself, although it was still outside it; the newer development marks the first time that the ultimate source of authority may be said to have moved inside the corporation itself.

A group of identifiable developments seems to me to have taken place that have made possible this change—from ownership to management—in the answer to the question "Why do people do what they are told?" One of them is the very nature of corporate ownership. The corporation has become very largely divorced from the stockholder-owner and from the financial control of the community in which it operates. The very much more widespread ownership of common stock has made the "owner" of a corporation more impersonal and unidentifiable than ever before. As far as the normal operations of management go, the stockholders' meetings or, indeed, the board of directors' meeting has very little to say. While it is a little extreme, it is perhaps not too much to say that there is no reason, in the operation of the modern corporation, to believe that equity entitles one to any voice in management. Most company presidents, while reluctant to avow this philosophy explicitly in public, operate on this basis in fact. The separation of the corporation from the financial control of the community is equally dramatic. It arises largely out of the growing tendency to finance expansion and diversification out of retained earnings and out of depreciation reserves. This development has cut the corporation loose from the traditional check of the community—from the idea that the corporation has to go to the money market, where the community can exercise its approval or disapproval by furnishing or withholding funds. Both these developments—cutting the corporation off from the owners and cutting the corporation off from the community—have served to internalize and make autonomous the values by which management operates and to divorce the corporation further from the traditional values that flow from property rights.

A second major development that contributes to this change is the growth of the professional manager. The professional manager is not an owner-manager. Management is once more separated from equity. More than that, the term "professional" means that he has a different orientation in seeking for approval. The professional tends to find approval for his activities among his professional colleagues, among the professional specialists of whom he feels himself to be a member. In this case, he tends to operate, not the way the owner thinks he ought to operate, but the way professional managers approve of operating. Not only is the process of management cut off from ownership, but the value and virtues inherent in the process of management itself are reinforced by the approval of a group of professional managers. A third thing that helped to contribute this change, I think, has been our experience with the tight labor market since the war. It was

easy, in prewar days, to think that a subordinate did what he was told because, if he did not, he would lose his job. After fifteen years during which subordinates felt that they could get another job just as good around the corner, the force of this "or else" behind a directive diminished sharply. Management began to look for and find other ways to enlist cooperation and direct activities.

I have pointed to three broad steps in the history of the grounding of industrial authority—the prince, the owner, and the professional manager. Now we come to the reason why we started this whole business: "Why should the social sciences be involved in the study of business?" Different academic disciplines seem clearly relevant to each of these three phases. In the first phase—the ascendancy of the state—the general discipline of political science is particularly appropriate. In the second phase—the era of ownership and property rights, where capital formation and the utilization of a somewhat casual labor market were particularly important—the discipline of economics is particularly relevant. In the third phase, where the seat of authority moves inside the organization itself and becomes grounded in the process of dealing with people in the organization, as well as the economic decisions, the disciplines of the social sciences are clearly demanded. Let me make it perfectly clear, at this time, that I do not mean any of these historical steps to be exclusive. That is, the power of the state never entirely disappeared; the role of the owner has not diminished to zero. Similarly, the relevance of the three disciplines is not an either-or proposition. Political science still has a role to play in the study of business, and no amount of emphasis on the social sciences eliminates the consideration of the corporation as an economic unit.

However, looking at the other side of the coin, the changes in the context of the business operation do seem to force a consideration of the problems of the social sciences in a way in which they were never demanded in an earlier social economy.

The purpose of this historical description has been to document an argument for the necessity of considering the social sciences in the study of business. While we have the model before us, we may use it, also, for a bit of forecasting. It seems to me that the tendency to internalize the ultimate seat of authority will go on in the corporation and that it will shift farther and farther inside. I suggest that it will be shifted from being grounded in the professional manager and the process of management until it is ultimately grounded in the work group itself. The final source of authority will be the authority of the work group. The final control will be self-control; the self-control will come from the individual's commitment to the organization, and the individual's commitment will come from his integration into the general goals and activities of the organization.[1] Let me point out that this prediction has no necessary political implications. It is not a prediction, in politico-economic terms, of the socialist development, because it carries with it no necessary implications of the actual ownership of the plant. In many countries this kind of development has gone on along with a political revolution and ended in some form of socialism. There seems to be no inherent necessity for the two to go together. It seems to me perfectly possible to maintain the kind of loose democratic form of political government that we have

and still have the authority in hierarchical organizations to move essentially to one that is grounded in the work group itself.

Even before this ultimate development of self-control occurs, another shift in the seat of authority may take place. Indeed, it seems to me that to some extent we are already seeing a shift in authority from the professional manager to the staff expert. In many cases the staff expert is getting to be able to couch the problems in such unintelligible esoterica that the manager cannot make a decision. He can hardly understand what the problem is after it gets restated. Once the computer expert has reprogrammed the problem for analysis, the kinds of outcome are all decided, and the degrees of freedom that are left to the manager are considerably reduced. A great deal of the decision making went by unnoticed in setting up the program. The same kind of thing has already happened in the restriction that the industrial relations department has put on the manager in terms of the kinds of things he can and cannot do. We may have here a fine coming-to-fruit of the biblical prediction "Blessed are the meek, for they shall inherit the earth," but it seems to me that the staff expert is in the process of usurping a great deal of the authority of the professional manager. Long before the utopian realization of the authority of self-control, the private language and professional mystery of the staff expert seem likely to come between the manager and the process he is managing.

THE CHANGING CONCEPT OF MAN

A second change is the changing concept of man. This is nowhere so clear as in the outline of the theory of industrial organization. Whenever we try to plan what an organization should be like, it

[1]On this point I am specifically indebted to D. M. McGregor, of the Massachusetts Institute of Technology. On many others I am equally, though less specifically, indebted to him.

is necessarily based on an implicit concept of man. If we look a little at the outline of a "classical" organization theory and some more modern alternatives, we begin to see the change in the concept of man.

It seems possible to outline the classical organization theory briefly in a series of points:

1. *Classical organization theory is built on a combination accounting and industrial engineering model.* It breaks the total job down "rationally" and assigns the parts neatly to a group of boxes spread about a family tree. It uses a balance system of authority and responsibility. In principle, a certain amount of authority is pumped into each one of the boxes, and along with this goes a responsibility to pump out a certain kind of productivity. This kind of double-entry system of input and output seems to be one of the first essentials.

   This neat balance of authority and responsibility has become a very important myth in writings on organization and perhaps deserves an extra word here. It is a principle that is stated in most of the textbooks and loudly avowed by most companies. I have never been able to understand why, or, indeed, to understand exactly what is meant by it. Let me list, briefly, some of my difficulties with it.

   a. In no other part of one's life is authority equivalent to responsibility. We all of us have responsibilities that far exceed our authority. A good check on this point is to consider one's responsibility as a parent. I have never seen a parent whose authority in bringing up

his children came anywhere near his responsibility. Similarly, our responsibility as citizens and in many other spheres goes well beyond any kind of authority we have. It is interesting to wonder why organization theorists felt that this should suddenly be changed for the industrial operation. I can only conclude that there was some feeling that it was neater to have the two balance out, whatever that means.

   b. A situation in which people's responsibilities are precisely and explicitly defined and limited seems to me potentially frightfully expensive. There is no more expensive operation than the situation in which everyone does exactly what he is told to do and no more. The ideal dodge of the system beater is to say "I did exactly what I was responsible for." We always expect people to do more and to assume more responsibility than their job description speaks of; there seems to be no possible way to give them authority commensurate with this.

   c. If we were to try to equalize authority and responsibility, it is a complete mystery to me how it would ever be done. What amount of authority is equal to what amount of responsibility? What kinds of units do we use to measure the two commodities? I can see the argument that if we give a person more responsibility, we ought to give him more authority; this kind of quantification makes sense on the surface. But how much authority is "more" authority? Surely, if we want to equate the two, we must be careful to be fairly precise about how much we mean, and yet the units are not at all clear. If a salesman is responsible for a given territory, the balance theory would presume that he had a given amount of authority. If transportation and communication facilities make it possible for him to cover twice the territory, he has a bigger responsibility. I am not sure that he has twice the responsibility; the geographical units or the dollar volume units may not be good measures of responsibility. But, with this increased responsibility, how do we estimate how much more authority to give him in order to keep the two equal? He has the authority to spend a little more on his expense account. But surely that is not the kind of authority or at least not the only kind of authority that we meant to keep equivalent to his responsibility. Alongside his responsibility, his expense account is a picayune authority. I simply do not understand how this calculus is to be made.

d. The myth of a balanced authority and responsibility seems to me to be in conflict with some other characteristic myths in the classical organization theory. We like to say that the line has the responsibility for producing and selling the product; the staff is there to advise and support and provide expert assistance to the line in this function. A line has the authority. The staff has no authority except within its own staff groups. But, if we maintain the balance of authority and responsibility, this would seem to mean that the staff, lacking authority, has no responsibility! What a comfortable position for the staff man! Can we really say at the same time that the authority is in the line and that authority and responsibility are equivalent?

2. A close second essential characteristic is that the classical *organization theory maximizes neatness and control.* This system of breaking up the job into little pieces and putting them into appropriate boxes at least gives the impression that one knows exactly what ought to be done everywhere, and the balance system of authority and responsibility means that we always have an overview of the output for which a box is responsible. This gives us something we can storm about all the way down through the organization whenever something goes wrong.

3. In line with this emphasis on neatness and control, *classical organization theory puts special emphasis on error* and particularly on the detection of error and its correction *after it has happened.* The standard organization is set up so that everyone has something he ought to do, and, as soon as he does not do it, we find out about it, give him hell, and see that it gets done. Described this way it sounds ideal; we might, in passing, consider the other possibility—that is, a system which made it less likely that the error would occur in the first place. This kind of detection and correction of er-

ror is closely associated with the emphasis on neatness and control. It gives us a kind of system where any boss can go home at the end of the day feeling, "Well, we got through another day without anything going seriously wrong, or at least I caught it as soon as it did." It is probably worth noticing in passing that this value in the organization system is one of the most important for the adjustment of the executive. It assuages his anxieties about his own adequacy and about the kind of job he is doing. He always has a check to be sure that, contrary to what he was afraid of, nothing has gone seriously wrong. It does not provide the symmetrical check as to whether anything serious has gone right.

4. *This approach to the organization is the classical embodiment of the "extra pair of hands" concept.* The total job is understood only at the top or at the level of the corporate staff. At that level it is clear that more than one man will have to be involved in doing it. Consequently, the pieces are broken up, and an extra pair of hands is recruited for each appropriate little piece and is given the appropriate responsibility and the authority with which to do it. He is not necessarily given much of anything else—that is, much information about why he ought to do it or much feedback about how it is going, unless it is going poorly.

5. In designing the job and in picking these "extra pairs of hands," *classical organization theory assumes man to be relatively homogeneous and relatively unmodifiable.* That

is, except for minor differences in abilities and training, which we will take advantage of in selection and assignment, we assume that all people are pretty much alike and that they are going to stay the way they are. Relatively little emphasis needs to be put on the growth and development of the individual.

6. As a matter of fact, very much growth or development in the individual will upset the system. He was put into a job that was an appropriate size for him. If he grows much bigger, he will either want to reach out and do more, which will upset the apple cart, or he will work only about half speed, which has deleterious effects upon his and others morale. Consequently, *another tenet of classical organization theory is that the stability of the employees is a goal.* This means stability not only in the sense of minimizing turnover but stability in the sense of minimizing change within the employees.

7. It is clear from these points that the *classical organization theory is, in its essential character, centralized.* This centralization is necessary for the original planning that parceled out the jobs for the extra pair of hands, is continuously necessary for the error control which runs through the entire system.

8. *The integration of the system is achieved through the authority and control of the central mechanism.*
   This last point about integration is a particularly important one, and I should like to digress for a moment from listing the characteristics of organization to discuss this. When we examine

an organization, we tend to ask what it is built to do, but we often overlook the most fundamental thing that it is built to do—it is built to hold the organization together. The strongest force that seems to threaten the continued existence of any organization is the persistent centrifugal force that is constantly tending to make it fly apart in all directions at once. This force arises from the fact that the organization is made up of a group of individuals. Whenever an individual joins a group, he gives up some of his individual freedoms, some of his individual goals, and some of his individual satisfactions. This seems to be an inevitable consequence of joining any sort of group, from the marriage partnership up to the largest and most complex corporation or, indeed, a national or international organization. The reason he is willing to do this, presumably, is that, in return for the freedoms and satisfactions that he gave up, he gets some satisfactions as a result of his membership in the group that he would not be able to get otherwise. This contract is always an uneasy one, however. He is still an individual, and he still has individual goals, and there is a constant tendency for him to follow his individual goals at the expense of the group goals. This means that there is a constant tendency for all the individuals in the organization to fly off in the directions determined by their own goals, rather than to move ahead with the singleness of purpose of the group goal. Consequently, one of the most important functions of the organization is to maintain

the integration that keeps the individuals together and keeps them (more or less) working toward the single goal of the group.

Two very important consequences flow from this: In the first place, one of the first characteristics of the organization's structure ought to be building it in such a way that it will be maximally resistant to this destructive centrifugal force—that is, that it will tend to hang together. In the second place, one of the primary responsibilities of the chief executive officer is simply to hold the group together. Indeed, most corporations will run pretty well for a long time without much direction. Their direction is pretty well laid down in the general nature of the business and in the things that they have been doing and the equipment they have to do them with. If nobody made any high-level policy, it probably would be quite a while before we noticed it. On the other hand, if nobody kept the parts from flying off in their own directions, we should probably notice it right away. This is the reason why such a large part of the executive's time is spent in running around and pasting the organization back together and tying up discordant and divergent parts in what seems on the surface to be an irrelevant activity but is in fact probably the most important one. As we look at this threat of disintegration, we should remember that the integration in a classical organization theory is primarily achieved through the centralized processes of authority and control. We shall come back to them later in more detail.

Here, then, is a group of characteristics that seem to me to describe the traditional approach to organization. Already we have seen some of the implicit assumptions about the nature of man. Let us look at them in a little more detail. What kind of man would fit well in this system? What kind of assumptions can we safely make about the large body of the labor force from which we must draw all the people to go into the organization, from the lowest hourly paid levels up to, but not including, our own? That is, what are people like? Other people than ourselves, that is.

I think this approach to organization theory is based on the notion that other people (but not I) are, unfortunately, lazy. That is, they will not do anything unless they have to, and consequently we had better build a system that sees to it that they have to do it. This assumption that people are lazy is one of the most crucial and one of the most universal assumptions underlying organization theory. It is the assumption that people will not do anything unless they have to, that they really do not like to work, and that passivity is the essential nature of man. It is from this notion that the idea arises that the system must be thoroughly equipped both with the carrot and the prod. We must design a system with an incentive to hang just before the person's nose and a goad to stimulate him to action whenever he stops. Both of these—the carrot and the prod—are operated from outside the person. The system leaves little room for initiative arising inside the person. The assumption leaves little room for any idea of self-starting. It is often dignified with the elaborate phrase of "The Law of Least Effort." It takes no account of the considerable effort expended in the do-it-yourself movement. A serious question seems to me to be proposed by the man who does exactly what he is told on the job and no more and then goes home and sweats blood building a boat in a bottle or putting a new patio on the side of his house.

Further than that, and equally unfortunately, people are shortsighted. Not only will they not do anything unless they have to, but they will not see that it ought to be done. We better add that to the system—build in a mechanism that will make sure that they know from moment to moment what ought to be done. There is no real need to let them know beyond the moment to moment; that would only confuse them.

This is partly because it is, also unfortunately, generally true that people are not interested in the company when they are on the job. (We must keep remembering that this is people other than ourselves.) Not only are they lazy and shortsighted, but they are selfish. Consequently, we build a system in which they do what they are told, rather than rely on their seeing what ought to be done in the company's interest and doing it.

People are quite apt to make mistakes, and we had better build a system that will allow for that.

People (again other people, that is) have poor judgment, if any. Since this is unfortunately so, we had better build a system that gives them a minimum of judgmental discretion. Ideally, we shall need a program that tells them what to do all the time, since they do not know and cannot foresee the factors involved.

Finally, and so unfortunate that perhaps we ought not to mention it, there is sometimes a suspicion that people may even be a little dishonest basically.

These are the implicit assumptions about man which classical organization theory seems to me to be based: He is lazy, short-sighted, selfish, liable to make mistakes, has poor judgment, and may even be a little dishonest. With this kind of building material, it is no

TABLE 1 • ATTITUDES TOWARD OTHER'S SATISFACTIONS

What Subordinates Want in a Job Compared to Their Superiors' Estimates

	As Men: Rated Selves	As Foremen: Men Would Rate	Rated Selves	As General Foremen: Foremen Would Rate	Rated Selves
Economic Variables:					
Steady work-steady wages	61%	79%	62%	86%	52%
High wages	28	61	17	58	11
Pensions and security	13	17	12	29	15
Not to work too hard	13	30	4	25	2
Human Satisfaction Variables:					
Get along with people	36	17	39	22	43
Get along with superior ...	28	14	28	15	24
To do good quality work ..	16	11	18	13	27
To do interesting work	22	12	38	14	43
Chance for promotion	25	23	42	24	47
Good working conditions	21	19	18	4	11
Total	*	*	*	*	*
Number of Cases	2499	196	196	45	45

Source: Copyright © 1961 by McGraw-Hill Book Co., Inc. Used by permission of Rensis Likert and McGraw-Hill.

*Percentages total over 100 because they include three rankings for each person.

wonder that we do not come up with much in the way of organization.

Now let us try another view of the nature of man. Let us assume that he has the same basic drives as the next fellow. The trick is to build and operate an organization that will elicit and use them.

His shortsightedness may come from the fact that information has been withheld from him for one reason or another. Maybe we can overcome some of that.

He may well make mistakes—if so, many of them are probably part of a reaching-out for new behaviors, and, as such, we had better be careful not to sit on them too hard. Innovation and growth come from this; error will still have to be watched closely.

He needs more information to make better judgments. Further than that, his personal commitments to the organization and its objectives will greatly influence the goodness of his judgment.

Even his honesty (whether it is putting his hand directly in the till or soldiering on the job or padding his expense account) is probably largely a function of his integration into the organization and his commitment to it. Now we are making a quite different set of assumptions about the basic nature of people. There is a surprising tendency to consider other people as having quite different characteristics from oneself. Table 1 shows some interesting data presented by Likert in his recent book, *Organization Theory.* In this situation workers were asked to rate how important various things were to them on the job. Their foremen were then asked to make the same rating in the way they thought the men would make it and then to make the rating for themselves. Then the general foremen were asked to make the rating the way they thought the foremen would do it and then to make the rating for themselves. The foremen rated steady work and high wages as important variables for the men (79 per cent and 61 per cent). On the other hand, they thought that they were much less important for themselves (62 and 28 per cent). On the other hand, the general foremen thought that the foremen would rate these variables much higher (86 and 58 per cent). For themselves the general foremen only rated them 52 and 11 per cent. All the way across, each group thought these were very important for their subordinates but not for themselves. The same kind of pattern shows up in the variable "not working too hard." Each superior thought it important for his subordinate; each person thought it not very important for himself. The other side of the coin shows up in the value that is placed on getting along with other people and getting along with a superior. In each case the superiors thought that these were not very important to the subordinates; in each case everyone thought that these were important to themselves. When we think about the kinds of people for whom we have to build an organization, we tend to have a very pessimistic view for everyone except ourselves.

Some similar data appear in an unpublished study done by Professor Lyman Porter at the University of California. A random sample of the American Management Association was asked a series of questions, among them the question "How important is initiative in your job? In your superior's? In your sub-

ordinate's?" The data showed answers to these three questions at a variety of levels in the organization. In every case, no matter what the level of the respondent, his job and his superior's demanded initiative. His subordinate's did not. This was true all the way up and down the hierarchical ladder. The man had to have initiative to do his job; the person below him was better off without it.

Suppose we were to build an organization based on the radical assumption that the other people in the organization are not very different from ourselves.

Again, let me list in bare headings a set of the characteristics that seem to me to flow from an organization based on this kind of man.

1. Such an organization would look for not the "extra pair of hands" but for the initiative, innovation, and judgment of the individual.

2. It would be built not on an accounting model but on a group-structure model emphasizing the cohesion and integrity of each unit group and the linkage of each group to the groups above and below it and the groups around it. This "group-structure model" is illustrated in Figure 2. While this picture of an organization chart does not look very much different from the conventional one, it has markedly different implications. Likert uses this description to emphasize the "linking pin" function of the superior at every level. His primary responsibilities are to see that the people below him are indeed a closely knit group (indicated by the triangle), to see that he is a member of that group, and to be a member of the group formed by the people at his level and the person above him. In this sense he is a member of the group below and the group above, he is the "linking pin" between the two. This emphasis on the

FIGURE 2 • GROUP-STRUCTURE MODEL OF AN ORGANIZATION.

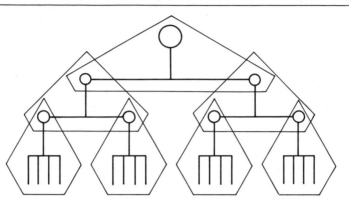

Source: Rensis Likert, "A Motivational Approach to a Modified Theory of Organization and Management," in Mason Haire (ed.), *Modern Organization Theory* (New York: John Wiley & Sons, Inc., 1959), p. 193.

group membership in two directions is important. It also means, with respect to authority and influence, that the superior's capacity to influence his subordinates depends on his capacity to influence his own superiors.

3. It would maximize participation.

4. In seeking initiative, it creates an atmosphere in which there is freedom to make mistakes. This does *not* maximize error. It is the situation we hope to create for a child growing up, in which he is free to try things, to learn, to grow, and to develop without someone looking over his shoulder all the time, expecting him to fail. I repeat that this does not involve a lower standard of quality or more error, but it does involve an atmosphere that places a real reliance on the other person. It is worth pointing out here that, just as the control of error in the classical system is a protection to the adjustment of the executive, this freedom to make mistakes may well be adjustmentally threatening to the executive. We need to ask, then, how much of the organization's drive we can afford to spend in order to protect the executive's adjustment.

5. Such an organization would assume man not only to have initiative but to be highly modifiable. Both training and leadership in general would encourage him to change, develop, and learn.

6. Integration in such a system is obtained through mutual confidence and trust, shared objectives, commitment, and both social and job skills appropriate to these structures and objectives of the organization.

7. This kind of organization is, in its essential nature, decentralized.

8. The growth and development of the employees is a primary goal of such an approach.

Now we have a very different kind of organization. What kinds of things will we have to do differently? Let me list just a few of the outstanding ones briefly:

1. Probably the first and most important thing will be giving up the use of financial data for punitive control. A typical system now is for an executive to have periodic financial reports on the

operations of the divisions under him. In general, he usually employs these reports to hit his subordinates over the head when things are not going well or to hold over their heads like a threatening club just in case they slip. We generally collect financial data on operations (budget data) and production data and forward them to higher levels of the organization which can use them as a means for tight control over their subordinate group. In principle, as far as management goes, these data should probably be reported at the level of the group which generates them. This group would then report them on up to the next level, where they could be discussed in terms of the degree in which they met the shared objectives which had originally been set, in terms of the problems encountered in accomplishing these objectives, and the like. When this is accomplished for the managerial process, it should still be possible to forward such data to higher levels for planning purposes. The purpose of the exercise is to avoid using this information for punitive control.

2. The next big thing that would have to be changed would probably be the neat job descriptions. Such descriptions are typically set up to tell a man exactly what he should do and exactly where his bailiwick ends. They are designed to eliminate conflict in the system. An alternative approach to the organization might well be to permit overlapping and conflict in areas of responsibility, hoping to encourage the initiative and to utilize the conflict rather than to smother it.

3. The next big thing that would be challenged would be the concept of "information appropriate to the level." All three of these tie together—the broad job description and total responsibility, using operating information for shared

objectives rather than punitive controls, and the sharing of information. Typically, we have hoarded information to protect the status of each level from those beneath it. The approach I speak of would suggest that the information appropriate to any level is all the information. Current technological developments in the communication process present a real alternative in this dimension. As electronic data processing develops, we have the clear alternative of using the greater speed either to centralize more information or to collect information so rapidly that it can be decentralized efficiently. Which choice we take seems to be of crucial importance to the concept of organization and the concept of management. A good example of the extreme use of technological advance in the centralization of the managerial process was reported in the newspapers at the time of the Little Rock integration crisis. When National Guard troops were sent in, a closed-circuit television and radio system connected the Pentagon directly with the field. This made it possible for the commanding general to look over his subordinate's shoulder even at the range of a thousand miles, to second-guess every decision, and to say, "Now do this— Oops! you did it wrong—now do the other thing." The kind of subordinate leadership that this kind of operation is apt to develop is appalling.

4. In order to make this concept of organization work, some very creative rethinking of compensation is necessary. It is not perfectly clear how it would work, but two lines of approach seem to me apparent: Our present approach, from the philosophy of job evaluation, is to state exactly what a person is supposed to do, assess its difficulty, its danger, its arduousness, its skill, and the like, and then pay him in return for

these things. The pay, to the person, is an asset balancing the liabilities of the work. A very different spirit is entailed when we consider the possibility of paying a person, not in return for the unpleasant thing he has just done, but in order to make it possible for him to do all he can. I might suggest that that seems to be the model on which university compensation is based. Research workers tend to be paid, not on a piecework basis, but in order to make it possible for them to work creatively. A second influence in the compensation philosophy comes from rewarding specific work accomplished and not from the function of making it possible to accomplish it. Let me cite an example from another sphere. Our basketball coach at the University of California was noted for building teams rather than prima donnas (and very successful teams, too!). One of the things he insisted on was a change in the system for awarding letters. Traditionally, in order to get a letter, a man had to play sixty minutes during the season. The coach insisted that a Senior who had been working with the team through his college career, had kept himself in condition, in practice, and ready to play deserved a letter. The reward, he insisted, should go not for making baskets but for making it possible to make baskets. The shift in emphasis from the reward for individual accomplishment to the reward for contributing to team potential is an important one. We often overlook the same kinds of reward in industry. For example, we usually insist that one of the functions of the supervisor is to train people to assume leadership positions, and yet there are very few cases in which this kind of effort on the part of the supervisor is rewarded. We tend to reward or punish in terms of the number of widgets produced. They are so much easier to measure. It does not

matter that their ultimate production may rest on subtler criteria. Our compensation scheme typically overlooks the constructive variables and pays off for individual accomplishment.

Here we see a little bit of the influence of concepts of man on the forms of organization. When we look at the problem of organization, we seem to be answering the question, "What is the best way to organize?" In fact, we are answering the question, "Given the way I believe people to be, what is the best way to organize?" We usually do not question the first part of that—"What I believe people to be." It is clear that there are very widely different answers to the question of organization, depending on the implicit assumptions about the nature of human nature. I have the strong feeling that assumptions about human nature are in the process of shifting from the former to the latter these days and that, with this shift in the assumptions, the shape of the organization is also changing. I think that the change in our thinking has gone further with respect to the concept of man than it has with respect to the philosophy of organization, although that is following, too. It seems to me that one sees little bits and pieces of changes in organization that are flowing unwittingly from changes in the concept of man and that the wave of the future is going to be this kind of organization. While we anticipate this change in the organization of the future, it is worth pointing out that it is quite apt to have a tremendous competitive advantage attached to it. Operating with an outmoded organization—or with an organization that implies a concept of man which employees are unwilling to accept for themselves—may well put a firm at a decided disadvantage vis-à-vis a competitor whose thinking is more in tune with the kinds of things that the members of his organization are ready to accept.

One might ask "is this 'nothing but' human relations warmed over?" I think not. In its pure form the human relations movement seems to ask for increased satisfactions for members of the work force because they were a good thing in themselves—that is, that one *ought* to provide more satisfactions for people. This approach suggests:

1. That there is more impetus and initiative to be derived in an organization based on a concept of man that is clearly different from the fundament of classical organization theory.

2. That there is a competitive advantage in a concept of man that is acceptable to the society and the labor force from which organization members are drawn.

3. That a concept of authority that is acceptable to the society is closely related to the forms of organization and the conception of man and, importantly, to the continued existence of corporate entities in the sense that we know them.

34

Who Gets Power—And How They Hold on to It: A Strategic-Contingency Model of Power

Gerald R. Salancik & Jeffrey Pfeffer

Power is held by many people to be a dirty word or, as Warren Bennis has said, "It is the organization's last dirty secret."

This article will argue that traditional "political" power, far from being a dirty business, is, in its most naked form, one of the few mechanisms available for aligning an organization with its own reality. However, institutionalized forms of power—what we prefer to call the cleaner forms of power: authority, legitimization, centralized control, regulations, and the more modern "management information systems"—tend to buffer the organization from reality and obscure the demands of its environment. Most great states and institutions declined, not because they played politics, but because they failed to accommodate to the political realities they faced. Political processes, rather than being mechanisms for unfair and unjust allocations and appointments, tend toward the realistic resolution of conflicts among interests. And power, while it eludes definition, is easy enough to recognize by its consequences—the ability of those who possess power to bring about the outcomes they desire.

The model of power we advance is an elaboration of what has been called strategic-contingency theory, a view that sees power as something that accrues to organizational subunits (individuals, departments) that cope with critical organizational problems. Power is used by subunits, indeed, used by all who have it, to enhance their own survival through control of scarce critical resources, through the placement of allies in key positions, and through the definition of organizational problems and policies. Because of the processes by which power develops and is used, organizations become both more aligned and more misaligned with their environments. This contradiction is the most interesting aspect of organizational power, and one that makes administration one of the most precarious of occupations.

WHAT IS ORGANIZATIONAL POWER?

You can walk into most organizations and ask without fear of being misunderstood, "Which are the powerful groups or people in this organization?" Although many organizational informants may be *unwilling* to tell you, it is unlikely they will be *unable* to tell you. Most people do not require explicit definitions to know what power is.

Power is simply the ability to get things done the way one wants them to be done. For a manager who wants an increased budget to launch a project that he thinks is important, his power is measured by his ability to get that budget. For an executive vice-president who wants to be chairman, his power is evidenced by his advancement toward his goal.

People in organizations not only know what you are talking about when you ask who is influential but they are likely to agree with one another to an amazing extent. Recently, we had a chance to observe this in a regional office of an insurance company. The office had 21 department managers; we asked ten of these managers to rank all 21 according to the influence each one had in the organization. Despite the fact that ranking 21 things is a difficult task, the managers sat down and began arranging the names of their colleagues and themselves in a column. Only one person bothered to ask, "What do you mean by influence?" When told "power," he responded, "Oh," and went on. We compared the rankings of all ten managers and found virtually no disagreement among them in the managers ranked among the top five or the bottom five. Differences in the rankings came from department heads claiming more influence for themselves than their colleagues attributed to them.

Such agreement on those who have influence, and those who do not, was not unique to this insurance company. So far we have studied over 20 very different organizations—universities, research firms, factories, banks, retailers, to name a few. In each one we found individuals able to rate themselves and their peers on a scale of influence or power. We have done this both for specific decisions and for general impact on organizational policies. Their agreement was unusually high, which suggests that distributions of influence exist

well enough in everyone's mind to be referred to with ease—and we assume with accuracy.

WHERE DOES ORGANIZATIONAL POWER COME FROM?

Earlier we stated that power helps organizations become aligned with their realities. This hopeful prospect follows from what we have dubbed the strategic-contingencies theory of organizational power. Briefly, those subunits most able to cope with the organization's critical problems and uncertainties acquire power. In its simplest form, the strategic-contingencies theory implies that when an organization faces a number of lawsuits that threaten its existence, the legal department will gain power and influence over organizational decisions. Somehow other organizational interest groups will recognize its critical importance and confer upon it a status and power never before enjoyed. This influence may extend beyond handling legal matters and into decisions about product design, advertising production, and so on. Such extensions undoubtedly would be accompanied by appropriate, or acceptable, verbal justifications. In time, the head of the legal department may become the head of the corporation, just as in times past the vice-president for marketing had become the president when market shares were a worrisome problem and, before him, the chief engineer, who had made the production line run as smooth as silk.

Stated in this way, the strategic-contingencies theory of power paints an appealing picture of power. To the extent that power is determined by the critical uncertainties and problems facing the organization and, in turn, influences decisions in the organization, the organization is aligned with the realities it faces. In short, power facilitates the organization's adaptation to its environment—or its problems.

We can cite many illustrations of how influence derives from a subunits's ability to deal with critical contingencies. Michael Crozier described a French cigarette factory in which the maintenance engineers had a considerable say in the plantwide operation. After some probing he discovered that the group possessed the solution to one of the major problems faced by the company, that of troubleshooting the elaborate, expensive, and irrascible automated machines that kept breaking down and dumbfounding everyone else. It was the one problem that the plant manager could in no way control.

The production workers, while troublesome from time to time, created no insurmountable problems; the manager could reasonably predict their absenteeism or replace them when necessary. Production scheduling was something he could deal with since, by watching inventories and sales, the demand for cigarettes was known long in advance. Changes in demand could be accommodated by slowing down or speeding up the line. Supplies of tobacco and paper were also easily dealt with through stockpiles and advance orders.

The one thing that management could neither control nor accommodate to, however, was the seemingly happenstance breakdowns. And the foremen couldn't instruct the workers what to do when emergencies developed since the maintenance department kept its records of problems and solutions locked up in a cabinet or in its members' heads. The breakdowns were, in truth, a critical source of uncertainty for the organization, and the mainte-nance engineers were the only ones who could cope with the problem.

The engineers' strategic role in coping with breakdowns afforded them a considerable say on plant decisions. Schedules and production quotas were set in consultation with them. And the plant manager, while formally their boss, accepted their decisions about personnel in their operation. His submission was to his credit, for without their cooperation he would have had an even more difficult time in running the plant.

Ignoring Critical Consequences

In this cigarette factory, sharing influence with the maintenance workers reflected the plant manager's awareness of the critical contingencies. However, when organizational members are not aware of the critical contingencies they face, and do not share influence accordingly, the failure to do so can create havoc. In one case, an insurance company's regional office was having problems with the performance of one of its departments, the coding department. From the outside, the department looked like a disaster area. The clerks who worked in it were somewhat dissatisfied; their supervisor paid little attention to them, and they resented the hard work. Several other departments were critical of this manager, claiming that she was inconsistent in meeting deadlines. The person most critical was the claims manager. He resented having to wait for work that was handled by her department, claiming that it held up his claims adjusters. Having heard the rumors about dissatisfaction among her subordinates, he attributed the situation to poor supervision. He was second in command in the office and therefore took up the issue with her immediate boss, the head of administrative services. They consulted with the personnel manager and the three of them concluded that the manager needed leadership training to improve her relations with her subordinates. The coding manager objected, saying it was a waste of time, but agreed to go along with the training and also agreed to give more priority to the claims department's work. Within a week after the training, the results showed that her workers were happier but that the performance of her department had decreased, save for the people serving the claims department.

About this time, we began, quite independently, a study of influence in this organization. We asked the administrative services director to draw up flow charts of how the work of one department moved on to the next department. In the course of the interview, we noticed that the coding department began or interceded in the work flow of most of the other departments and casually mentioned to him, "The coding manager must be very influential." He said "No, not really. Why would you think so?" Before we could reply he recounted the story of her leadership training and the fact that things were worse. We then told him that it seemed obvious that the coding department would be influential from the fact that all the other departments depended on it. It was also clear why productivity had fallen. The coding manager took the training seriously and began spending more time raising her workers' spirits than she did worrying about the problems of all the departments that depended on her. Giving priority to the claims area only exaggerated the problem, for their work was getting done at the expense of the work of the other departments. Eventually the company hired a few more clerks to relieve the pressure in the coding department and

performance returned to a more satisfactory level.

Originally we got involved with this insurance company to examine how the influence of each manager evolved from his or her department's handling of critical organizational contingencies. We reasoned that one of the most important contingencies faced by all profit-making organizations was that of generating income. Thus we expected managers would be influential to the extent to which they contributed to this function. Such was the case. The underwriting managers, who wrote the policies that committed the premiums, were the most influential; the claims managers, who kept a lid on the funds flowing out, were a close second. Least influential were the managers of functions unrelated to revenue, such as mailroom and payroll managers. And contrary to what the administrative services manager believed, the third most powerful department head (out of 21) was the woman in charge of the coding function, which consisted of rating, recording, and keeping track of the codes of all policy applications and contracts. Her peers attributed more influence to her than could have been inferred from her place on the organization chart. And it was not surprising, since they all depended on her department. The coding department's records, their accuracy and the speed with which they could be retrieved, affected virtually every other operating department in the insurance office. The underwriters depended on them in getting the contracts straight; the typing department depended on them in preparing the formal contract document; the claims department depended on them in adjusting claims; and accounting depended on them for billing. Unfortunately, the "bosses" were not aware of these dependences, for unlike the cigarette factory, there were no massive breakdowns that made them obvious, while the coding manager, who was a hard-working but quiet person, did little to announce her importance.

The cases of this plant and office illustrate nicely a basic point about the source of power in organizations. The basis for power in an organization derives from the ability of a person or subunit to take or not take actions that are desired by others. The coding manager was seen as influential by those who depended on her department, but not by the people at the top. The engineers were influential because of their role in keeping the plant operating. The two cases differ in these respects: The coding supervisor's source of power was not as widely recognized as that of the maintenance engineers, and she did not use her source of power to influence decisions; the maintenance engineers did. Whether power is used to influence anything is a separate issue. We should not confuse this issue with the fact that power derives from a social situation in which one person has a capacity to do something and another person does not, but wants it done.

POWER SHARING IN ORGANIZATIONS

Power is shared in organizations; and it is shared out of necessity more than out of concern for principles of organizational development or participatory democracy. Power is shared because no one person controls all the desired activities in the organization. While the factory owner may hire people to operate his noisy machines, once hired they have some control over the use of the machinery. And thus they have power over him in the same way he has power over them. Who has more power over

whom is a mooter point than that of recognizing the inherent nature of organizing as a sharing of power.

Let's expand on the concept that power derives from the activities desired in an organization. A major way of managing influence in organizations is through the designation of activities. In a bank we studied, we saw this principle in action. This bank was planning to install a computer system for routine credit evaluation. The bank, rather progressive-minded, was concerned that the change would have adverse effects on employees and therefore surveyed their attitudes.

The principal opposition to the new system came, interestingly, not from the employees who performed the routine credit checks, some of whom would be relocated because of the change, but from the manager of the credit department. His reason was quite simple. The manager's primary function was to give official approval to the applications, catch any employee mistakes before giving approval, and arbitrate any difficulties the clerks had in deciding what to do. As a consequence of his role, others in the organization, including his superiors, subordinates, and colleagues, attributed considerable importance to him. He, in turn, for example, could point to the low proportion of credit approvals, compared with other financial institutions, that resulted in bad debts. Now, to his mind, a wretched machine threatened to transfer his role to a computer programmer, a man who knew nothing of finance and who, in addition, had ten years less seniority. The credit manager eventually quit for a position at a smaller firm with lower pay, but one in which he would have more influence than his redefined job would have left him with.

Because power derives from activities rather than individuals, an individual's or subgroup's power is never absolute and derives ultimately from the context of the situation. The amount of power an individual has at any one time depends, not only on the activities he or she controls, but also on the existence of other persons or means by which the activities can be achieved and on those who determine what ends are desired and, hence, on what activities are desired and critical for the organization. One's own power always depends on other people for these two reasons. Other people, or groups or organizations, can determine the definition of what is a critical contingency for the organization and can also undercut the uniqueness of the individual's personal contribution to the critical contingencies of the organization.

Perhaps one can best appreciate how situationally dependent power is by examining how it is distributed. In most societies, power organizes around scarce and critical resources. Rarely does power organize around abundant resources. In the United States, a person doesn't become powerful because he or she can drive a car. There are simply too many others who can drive with equal facility. In certain villages in Mexico, on the other hand, a person with a car is accredited with enormous social status and plays a key role in the community. In addition to scarcity, power is also limited by the need for one's capacities in a social system. While a racer's ability to drive a car around a 90° turn at 80 mph may be sparsely distributed in a society, it is not likely to lend the driver much power in the society. The ability simply does not play a central role in the activities of the society.

The fact that power revolves around scarce and critical activities, of course, makes the control and organization of those activities a major battleground

in struggles for power. Even relatively abundant or trivial resources can become the bases for power if one can organize and control their allocation and the definition of what is critical. Many occupational and professional groups attempt to do just this in modern economies. Lawyers organize themselves into associations, regulate the entrance requirements for novitiates, and then get laws passed specifying situations that require the services of an attorney. Workers had little power in the conduct of industrial affairs until they organized themselves into closed and controlled systems. In recent years, women and blacks have tried to define themselves as important and critical to the social system, using law to reify their status.

In organizations there are obviously opportunities for defining certain activities as more critical than others. Indeed, the growth of managerial thinking to include defining organizational objectives and goals has done much to foster these opportunities. One sure way to liquidate the power of groups in the organization is to define the need for their services out of existence. David Halberstam presents a description of how just such a thing happened to the group of correspondents that evolved around Edward R. Murrow, the brilliant journalist, interviewer, and war correspondent of CBS News. A close friend of CBS chairman and controlling stockholder William S. Paley, Murrow, and the news department he directed, were endowed with freedom to do what they felt was right. He used it to create some of the best documentaries and commentaries ever seen on television. Unfortunately, television became too large, too powerful, and too suspect in the eyes of the federal government that licensed it. It thus became, or at least the top executives believed it had become, too dangerous to have in-depth, probing commentary on the news. Crisp, dry, uneditorializing headliners were considered safer. Murrow was out and Walter Cronkite was in.

The power to define what is critical in an organization is no small power. Moreover, it is the key to understanding why organizations are either aligned with their environments or misaligned. If an organization defines certain activities as critical when in fact they are not critical, given the flow of resources coming into the organization, it is not likely to survive, at least in its present form.

Most organizations manage to evolve a distribution of power and influence that is aligned with the critical realities they face in the environment. The environment, in turn, includes both the internal environment, the shifting situational contexts in which particular decisions get made, and the external environment that it can hope to influence but is unlikely to control.

THE CRITICAL CONTINGENCIES

The critical contingencies facing most organizations derive from the environmental context within which they operate. This determines the available needed resources and thus determines the problems to be dealt with. That power organizes around handling these problems suggests an important mechanism by which organizations keep in tune with their external environments. The strategic-contingencies model implies that subunits that contribute to the critical resources of the organization will gain influence in the organization. Their influence presumably is then used to bend the organization's activities to the contingencies that determine its resources. This idea may strike one as obvious. But its obviousness in no way diminishes its importance. Indeed, despite its obviousness, it escapes the notice of many organizational analysts and managers, who all too frequently think of the organization in terms of a descending pyramid, in which all the departments in one tier hold equal power and status. This presumption denies the reality that departments differ in the contributions they are believed to make to the overall organization's resources, as well as to the fact that some are more equal than others.

Because of the importance of this idea to organizational effectiveness, we decided to examine it carefully in a large midwestern university. A university offers an excellent site for studying power. It is composed of departments with nominally equal power and is administered by a central executive structure much like other bureaucracies. However, at the same time it is a situation in which the departments have clearly defined identities and face diverse external environments. Each department has its own bodies of knowledge, its own institutions, its own sources of prestige and resources. Because the departments operate in different external environments, they are likely to contribute differentially to the resources of the overall organization. Thus a physics department with close ties to NASA may contribute substantially to the funds of the university; and a history department with a renowned historian in residence may contribute to the intellectual credibility or prestige of the whole university. Such variations permit one to examine how these various contributions lead to obtaining power within the university.

We analyzed the influence of 29 university departments throughout an 18-month period in their history. Our chief interest was to determine whether departments that brought more critical resources to the university would be more powerful than departments that contributed fewer or less critical resources.

To identify the critical resources each department contributed, the heads of all departments were interviewed about the importance of seven different resources to the university's success. The seven included undergraduate students (the factor determining size of the state allocations by the university), national prestige, administrative expertise, and so on. The most critical resource was found to be contract and grant monies received by a department's faculty for research or consulting services. At this university, contract and grants contributed somewhat less than 50 percent of the overall budget, with the remainder primarily coming from state appropriations. The importance attributed to contract and grant monies, and the rather minor importance of undergraduate students, was not surprising for this particular university. The university was a major center for graduate education; many of its departments ranked in the top ten of their respective fields. Grant and contract monies were the primary source of discretionary funding available for maintaining these programs of graduate education, and hence for maintaining the university's prestige. The prestige of the university itself was critical both in recruiting able students and attracting top-notch faculty.

From university records it was determined what relative contributions each of the 29 departments made to the various needs of the university (national prestige, outside grants, teaching). Thus, for instance, one department may have contributed to the university by teaching 7 percent of the instructional units, bringing in 2 percent of the outside contracts and grants, and having a national ranking of 20. Another department, on the other hand, may have taught one percent of the instructional units, contributed 12 percent to the grants, and be ranked the third best department in its field within the country.

The question was: Do these different contributions determine the relative power of the departments within the university? Power was measured in several ways; but regardless of how measured, the answer was "yes." Those three resources together accounted for about 70 percent of the variance in subunit power in the university.

But the most important predictor of departmental power was the department's contribution to the contracts and grants of the university. Sixty percent of the variance in power was due to this one factor, suggesting that the power of departments derived primarily from the dollars they provided for graduate education, the activity believed to be the most important for the organization.

THE IMPACT OF ORGANIZATIONAL POWER ON DECISION MAKING

The measure of power we used in studying this university was an analysis of the responses of the department heads we interviewed. While such perceptions of power might be of interest in their own right, they contribute little to our understanding of how the distribution of power might serve to align an organization with its critical realities. For this we must look to how power actually influences the decisions and policies of organizations.

While it is perhaps not absolutely valid, we can generally gauge the relative importance of a department of an organization by the size of the budget allocated to it relative to other departments. Clearly it is of importance to the administrators of those departments whether they get squeezed in a budget crunch or are given more funds to strike out after new opportunities. And it should also be clear that when those decisions are made and one department can go ahead and try new approaches while another must cut back on the old, then the deployment of the resources of the organization in meeting its problems is most directly affected.

Thus our study of the university led us to ask the following question: Does power lead to influence in the organization? To answer this question, we found it useful first to ask another one, namely: Why should department heads try to influence organizational decisions to favor their own departments to the exclusion of other departments? While this second question may seem a bit naive to anyone who has witnessed the political realities of organizations, we posed it in a context of research on organizations that sees power as an illegitimate threat to the neater rational authority of modern bureaucracies. In this context, decisions are not believed to be made because of the dirty business of politics but because of the overall goals and purposes of the organization. In a university, one reasonable basis for decision making is the teaching workload of departments and the demands that follow from that workload. We would expect, therefore, that departments with heavy student demands for courses would be able to obtain funds for teaching. Another reasonable basis for decision making is quality. We would expect, for that reason, that departments with esteemed reputations would be able to obtain funds both because their quality suggests they might use such funds effectively and because such funds would allow them to maintain their quality. A rational model of bureaucracy intimates, then, that the

organizational decisions taken would favor those who perform the stated purposes of the organization—teaching undergraduates and training professional and scientific talent—well.

The problem with rational models of decision making, however, is that what is rational to one person may strike another as irrational. For most departments, resources are a question of survival. While teaching undergraduates may seem to be a major goal for some members of the university, developing knowledge may seem so to others; and to still others, advising governments and other institutions about policies may seem to be the crucial business. Everyone has his own idea of the proper priorities in a just world. Thus goals rather than being clearly defined and universally agreed upon are blurred and contested throughout the organization. If such is the case, then the decisions taken on behalf of the organization as a whole are likely to reflect the goals of those who prevail in political contests, namely, those with power in the organization.

Will organizational decisions always reflect the distribution of power in the organization? Probably not. Using power for influence requires a certain expenditure of effort, time, and resources. Prudent and judicious persons are not likely to use their power needlessly or wastefully. And it is likely that power will be used to influence organizational decisions primarily under circumstances that both require and favor its use. We have examined three conditions that are likely to affect the use of power in organizations: scarcity, criticality, and uncertainty. The first suggests that subunits will try to exert influence when the resources of the organization are scarce. If there is an abundance of resources, then a particular department or a particular individual has little need to attempt influence. With little effort, he can get all he wants anyway.

The second condition, criticality, suggests that a subunit will attempt to influence decisions to obtain resources that are critical to its own survival and activities. Criticality implies that one would not waste effort, or risk being labeled obstinate, by fighting over trivial decisions affecting one's operations.

An office manager would probably balk less about a threatened cutback in copying machine usage than about a reduction in typing staff. An advertising department head would probably worry less about losing his lettering artist than his illustrator. Criticality is difficult to define because what is critical depends on people's beliefs about what is critical. Such beliefs may or may not be based on experience and knowledge and may or may not be agreed upon by all. Scarcity, for instance, may itself affect conceptions of criticality. When slack resources drop off, cutbacks have to be made—those "hard decisions," as congressmen and resplendent administrators like to call them. Managers then find themselves scrapping projects they once held dear.

The third condition that we believe affects the use of power is uncertainty: When individuals do not agree about what the organization should do or how to do it, power and other social processes will affect decisions. The reason for this is simply that, if there are no clear-cut criteria available for resolving conflicts of interest, then the only means for resolution is some form of social process, including power, status, social ties, or some arbitrary process like flipping a coin or drawing straws. Under conditions of uncertainty, the powerful manager can argue his case on any grounds and usually win it. Since there is no real consensus, other contestants

are not likely to develop counter arguments or amass sufficient opposition. Moreover, because of his power and their need for access to the resources he controls, they are more likely to defer to his arguments.

Although the evidence is slight, we have found that power will influence the allocations of scarce and critical resources. In the analysis of power in the university, for instance, one of the most critical resources needed by departments is the general budget. First granted by the state legislature, the general budget is later allocated to individual departments by the university administration in response to requests from the department heads. Our analysis of the factors that contribute to a department getting more or less of this budget indicated that subunit power was the major predictor, overriding such factors as student demand for courses, national reputations of departments, or even the size of a department's faculty. Moreover, other research has shown that when the general budget has been cut back or held below previous uninflated levels, leading to monies becoming more scarce, budget allocations mirror departmental powers even more closely.

Student enrollment and faculty size, of course, do themselves relate to budget allocations, as we would expect since they determine a department's need for resources, or at least offer visible testimony of needs. But departments are not always able to get what they need by the mere fact of needing them. In one analysis it was found that high-power departments were able to obtain budget without regard to their teaching loads and, in some cases, actually in inverse relation to their teaching loads. In contrast, low-power departments could get increases in budget only when they could justify the increases by a recent growth in teaching load, and then only when it was far in excess of norms for other departments.

General budget is only one form of resource that is allocated to departments. There are others such as special grants for student fellowships or faculty research. These are critical to departments because they affect the ability to attract other resources, such as outstanding faculty or students. We examined how power influenced the allocations of four resources department heads had described as critical and scarce.

When the four resources were arrayed from the most to the least critical and scarce, we found that departmental power best predicted the allocations of the most critical and scarce resources. In other words, the analysis of how power influences organizational allocations leads to this conclusion: Those subunits most likely to survive in times of strife are those that are more critical to the organization. Their importance to the organization gives them power to influence resource allocations that enhance their own survival.

HOW EXTERNAL ENVIRONMENT IMPACTS EXECUTIVE SELECTION

Power not only influences the survival of key groups in an organization, it also influences the selection of individuals to key leadership positions, and by such a process further aligns the organization with its environmental context.

We can illustrate this with a recent study of the selection and tenure of chief administrators in 57 hospitals in Illinois. We assumed that since the critical problems facing the organization would enhance the power of certain groups at the expense of others, then the leaders to emerge should be those most relevant to the context of the hospitals. To assess this we asked each

chief administrator about his professional background and how long he had been in office. The replies were then related to the hospitals' funding, ownership, and competitive conditions for patients and staff.

One aspect of a hospital's context is the source of its budget. Some hospitals, for instance, are run much like other businesses. They sell bed space, patient care, and treatment services. They charge fees sufficient both to cover their costs and to provide capital for expansion. The main source of both their operating and capital funds is patient billings. Increasingly, patient billings are paid for, not by patients, but by private insurance companies. Insurers like Blue Cross dominate and represent a potent interest group outside a hospital's control but critical to its income. The insurance companies, in order to limit their own costs, attempt to hold down the fees allowable to hospitals, which they do effectively from their positions on state rate boards. The squeeze on hospitals that results from fees increasing slowly while costs climb rapidly more and more demands the talents of cost accountants or people trained in the technical expertise of hospital administration.

By contrast, other hospitals operate more like social service institutions, either as government healthcare units (Bellevue Hospital in New York City and Cook County Hospital in Chicago, for example) or as charitable institutions. These hospitals obtain a large proportion of their operating and capital funds, not from privately insured patients, but from government subsidies or private donations. Such institutions rather than requiring the talents of a technically efficient administrator are likely to require the savvy of someone who is well integrated into the social and political power structure of the community.

Not surprisingly, the characteristics of administrators predictably reflect the funding context of the hospitals with which they are associated. Those hospitals with larger proportions of their budget obtained from private insurance companies were most likely to have administrators with backgrounds in accounting and least likely to have administrators whose professions were business or medicine. In contrast, those hospitals with larger proportions of their budget derived from private donations and local governments were most likely to have administrators with business or professional backgrounds and least likely to have accountants. The same held for formal training in hospital management. Professional hospital administrators could easily be found in hospitals drawing their incomes from private insurance and rarely in hospitals dependent on donations or legislative appropriations.

As with the selection of administrators, the context of organizations has also been found to affect the removal of executives. The environment, as a source of organizational problems, can make it more or less difficult for executives to demonstrate their value to the organization. In the hospitals we studied, long-term administrators came from hospitals with few problems. They enjoyed amicable and stable relations with their local business and social communities and suffered little competition for funding and staff. The small city hospital director who attended civic and Elks meetings while running the only hospital within a 100-mile radius, for example, had little difficulty holding on to his job. Turnover was highest in hospitals with the most problems, a phenomenon similar to that observed in a study of industrial organizations in which turnover was highest among executives in industries with competitive environments and unstable market con-

ditions. The interesting thing is that instability characterized the industries rather than the individual firms in them. The troublesome conditions in the individual firms were attributed, or rather misattributed, to the executives themselves.

It takes more than problems, however, to terminate a manager's leadership. The problems themselves must be relevant and critical. This is clear from the way in which an administrator's tenure is affected by the status of the hospital's operating budget. Naively we might assume that all administrators would need to show a surplus. Not necessarily so. Again, we must distinguish between those hospitals that depend on private donations for funds and those that do not. Whether an endowed budget shows a surplus or deficit is less important than the hospital's relations with benefactors. On the other hand, with a budget dependent on patient billing, a surplus is almost essential; monies for new equipment or expansion must be drawn from it, and without them quality care becomes more difficult and patients scarcer. An administrator's tenure reflected just these considerations. For those hospitals dependent upon private donations, the length of an administrator's term depended not at all on the status of the operating budget but was fairly predictable from the hospital's relations with the business community. On the other hand, in hospitals dependent on the operating budget for capital financing, the greater the deficit the shorter was the tenure of the hospital's principal administrators.

CHANGING CONTINGENCIES AND ERODING POWER BASES

The critical contingencies facing the organization may change. When they do, it is reasonable to expect that the power of individuals and subgroups will change in turn. At times the shift can be swift and shattering, as it was recently for powerholders in New York City. A few years ago it was believed that David Rockefeller was one of the ten most powerful people in the city, as tallied by *New York* magazine, which annually sniffs out power for the delectation of its readers. But that was before it was revealed that the city was in financial trouble, before Rockefeller's Chase Manhattan Bank lost some of its own financial luster, and before brother Nelson lost some of his political influence in Washington. Obviously David Rockefeller was no longer as well positioned to help bail the city out. Another loser was an attorney with considerable personal connections to the political and religious leaders of the city. His talents were no longer in much demand. The persons with more influence were the bankers and union pension fund executors who fed money to the city; community leaders who represent blacks and Spanish-Americans, in contrast, witnessed the erosion of their power bases.

One implication of the idea that power shifts with changes in organizational environments is that the dominant coalition will tend to be that group that is most appropriate for the organization's environment, as also will the leaders of an organization. One can observe this historically in the top executives of industrial firms in the United States. Up until the early 1950s, many top corporations were headed by former production line managers or engineers who gained prominence because of their abilities to cope with the problems of production. Their success, however, only spelled their demise. As production became routinized and mechanized, the problem of most firms became one of selling all those goods they so efficiently produced. Marketing executives were more frequently found in

corporate boardrooms. Success outdid itself again, for keeping markets and production steady and stable requires the kind of control that can only come from acquiring competitors and suppliers or the invention of more and more appealing products—ventures that typically require enormous amounts of capital. During the 1960s, financial executives assumed the seats of power. And they, too, will give way to others. Edging over the horizon are legal experts, as regulation and antitrust suits are becoming more and more frequent in the 1970s, suits that had their beginnings in the success of the expansion generated by prior executives. The more distant future, which is likely to be dominated by multinational corporations, may see former secretaries of state and their minions increasingly serving as corporate figureheads.

THE NONADAPTIVE CONSEQUENCES OF ADAPTATION

From what we have said thus far about power aligning the organization with its own realities, an intelligent person might react with a resounding ho-hum, for it all seems too obvious: Those with the ability to get the job done are given the job to do.

However, there are two aspects of power that make it more useful for understanding organizations and their effectiveness. First, the "job" to be done has a way of expanding itself until it becomes less and less clear what the job is. Napoleon began by doing a job for France in the war with Austria and ended up Emperor, convincing many that only he could keep the peace. Hitler began by promising an end to Germany's troubling postwar depression and ended up convincing more people than is comfortable to remember that he was destined to be the savior of the world. In short, power is a capacity for influence that extends far beyond the original bases that created it. Second, power tends to take on institutionalized forms that enable it to endure well beyond its usefulness to an organization.

There is an important contradiction in what we have observed about organizational power. On the one hand we have said that power derives from the contingencies facing an organization and that when those contingencies change so do the bases for power. On the other hand we have asserted that subunits will tend to use their power to influence organizational decisions in their own favor, particularly when their own survival is threatened by the scarcity of critical resources. The first statement implies that an organization will tend to be aligned with its environment since power will tend to bring to key positions those with capabilities relevant to the context. The second implies that those in power will not give up their positions so easily; they will pursue policies that guarantee their continued domination. In short, change and stability operate through the same mechanism, and, as a result, the organization will never be completely in phase with its environment or its needs.

The study of hospital administrators illustrates how leadership can be out of phase with reality. We argued that privately funded hospitals needed trained technical administrators more so than did hospitals funded by donations. The need as we perceived it was matched in most hospitals, but by no means in all. Some organizations did not conform with our predictions. These deviations imply that some administrators were able to maintain their positions independent of their suitability for those positions. By dividing administrators into those with long and short terms of office one finds that the characteristics of

longer termed administrators were virtually unrelated to the hospital's context. The shorter termed chiefs on the other hand had characteristics more appropriate for the hospital's problems. For a hospital to have a recently appointed head implies that the previous administrator had been unable to endure by institutionalizing himself.

One obvious feature of hospitals that allowed some administrators to enjoy a long tenure was a hospital's ownership. Administrators were less entrenched when their hospitals were affiliated with and dependent upon larger organizations, such as governments or churches. Private hospitals offered more secure positions for administrators. Like private corporations, they tend to have more diffused ownership, leaving the administrator unopposed as he institutionalizes his reign. Thus he endures, sometimes at the expense of the performance of the organization. Other research has demonstrated that corporations with diffuse ownership have poorer earnings than those in which the control of the manager is checked by a dominant shareholder. Firms that overload their boardrooms with more insiders than are appropriate for their context have also been found to be less profitable.

A word of caution is required about our judgment of "appropriateness." When we argue some capabilities are more appropriate for one context than another, we do so from the perspective of an outsider and on the basis of reasonable assumptions as to the problems the organization will face and the capabilities they will need. The fact that we have been able to predict the distribution of influence and the characteristics of leaders suggests that our reasoning is not incorrect. However, we do not think that all organizations follow the same pattern. The fact that we have not been able to predict outcomes with 100 percent accuracy indicates they do not.

MISTAKING CRITICAL CONTINGENCIES

One thing that allows subunits to retain their power is their ability to name their functions as critical to the organization when they may not be. Consider again our discussion of power in the university. One might wonder why the most critical tasks were defined as graduate education and scholarly research, the effect of which was to lend power to those who brought in grants and contracts. Why not something else? The reason is that the more powerful departments argued for those criteria and won their case, partly because they were more powerful.

In another analysis of this university, we found that all departments advocate self-serving criteria for budget allocation. Thus a department with large undergraduate enrollments argued that enrollments should determine budget allocations, a department with a strong national reputation saw prestige as the most reasonable basis for distributing funds, and so on. We further found that advocating such self-serving criteria actually benefited a department's budget allotments but, also, it paid off more for departments that were already powerful.

Organizational needs are consistent with a current distribution of power also because of a human tendency to categorize problems in familiar ways. An accountant sees problems with organizational performance as cost accountancy problems or inventory flow problems. A sales manager sees them as problems with markets, promotional strategies, or just unaggressive salespeople. But what is the truth? Since it does not automatically announce itself, it is likely that those with prior credibility, or those with power, will be favored as the en-

lightened. This bias, while not intentionally self-serving, further concentrates power among those who already possess it, independent of changes in the organization's context.

INSTITUTIONALIZING POWER

A third reason for expecting organizational contingencies to be defined in familiar ways is that the current holders of power can structure the organization in ways that institutionalize themselves. By institutionalization we mean the establishment of relatively permanent structures and policies that favor the influence of a particular subunit. While in power, a dominant coalition has the ability to institute constitutions, rules, procedures, and information systems that limit the potential power of others while continuing their own.

The key to institutionalizing power always is to create a device that legitimates one's own authority and diminishes the legitimacy of others. When the "Divine Right of Kings" was envisioned centuries ago it was to provide an unquestionable foundation for the supremacy of royal authority. There is generally a need to root the exercise of authority in some higher power. Modern leaders are no less affected by this need. Richard Nixon, with the aid of John Dean, reified the concept of executive privilege, which meant in effect that what the President wished not to be discussed need not be discussed.

In its simpler form, institutionalization is achieved by designating positions or roles for organizational activities. The creation of a new post legitimizes a function and forces organization members to orient to it. By designating how this new post relates to older, more established posts, moreover, one can structure an organization to enhance the importance of the function in the organization. Equally, one can diminish the importance of traditional functions. This is what happened in the end with the insurance company we mentioned that was having trouble with its coding department. As the situation unfolded, the claims director continued to feel dissatisfied about the dependency of his functions on the coding manager. Thus he instituted a reorganization that resulted in two coding departments. In so doing, of course, he placed activities that affected his department under his direct control, presumably to make the operation more effective. Similarly, consumer-product firms enhance the power of marketing by setting up a coordinating role to interface production and marketing functions and then appoint a marketing manager to fill the role.

The structures created by dominant powers sooner or later become fixed and unquestioned features of the organization. Eventually, this can be devastating. It is said that the battle of Jena in 1806 was lost by Frederick the Great, who died in 1786. Though the great Prussian leader had no direct hand in the disaster, his imprint on the army was so thorough, so embedded in its skeletal underpinnings, that the organization was inappropriate for others to lead in different times.

Another important source of institutionalized power lies in the ability to structure information systems. Setting up committees to investigate particular organizational issues and having them report only to particular individuals or groups, facilitates their awareness of problems by members of those groups while limiting the awareness of problems by the members of other groups. Obviously, those who have information are in a better position to interpret the problems of an organization, regardless of how realistically they may, in fact, do so.

Still another way to institutionalize

power is to distribute rewards and resources. The dominant group may quiet competing interest groups with small favors and rewards. The credit for this artful form of cooperation belongs to Louis XIV. To avoid usurpation of his power by the nobles of France and the Fronde that had so troubled his father's reign, he built the palace at Versailles to occupy them with hunting and gossip. Awed, the courtiers basked in the reflected glories of the "Sun King" and the overwhelming setting he had created for his court.

At this point, we have not systematically studied the institutionalization of power. But we suspect it is an important condition that mediates between the environment of the organization and the capabilities of the organization for dealing with that environment. The more institutionalized power is within an organization, the more likely an organization will be out of phase with the realities it faces. President Richard Nixon's structuring of his White House is one of the better documented illustrations. If we go back to newspaper and magazine descriptions of how he organized his office from the beginning in 1968, most of what occurred subsequently follows almost as an afterthought. Decisions flowed through virtually only the small White House staff; rewards, small presidential favors of recognition, and perquisites were distributed by this staff to the loyal; and information from the outside world—the press, Congress, the people on the streets—was filtered by the staff and passed along only if initialed "bh." Thus it was not surprising that when Nixon met war protestors in the early dawn, the only thing he could think to talk about was the latest football game, so insulated had he become from their grief and anger.

One of the more interesting implications of institutionalized power is that executive turnover among the executives who have structured the organization is likely to be a rare event that occurs only under the most pressing crisis. If a dominant coalition is able to structure the organization and interpret the meaning of ambiguous events like declining sales and profits or lawsuits, then the "real" problems to emerge will easily be incorporated into traditional molds of thinking and acting. If opposition is designed out of the organization, the interpretations will go unquestioned. Conditions will remain stable until a crisis develops, so overwhelming and visible that even the most adroit rhetorician would be silenced.

IMPLICATIONS FOR THE MANAGEMENT OF POWER IN ORGANIZATIONS

While we could derive numerous implications from this discussion of power, our selection would have to depend largely on whether one wanted to increase one's power, decrease the power of others, or merely maintain one's position. More important, the real implications depend on the particulars of an organizational situation. To understand power in an organization one must begin by looking outside it—into the environment—for those groups that mediate the organization's outcomes but are not themselves within its control.

Instead of ending with homilies, we will end with a reversal of where we began. Power, rather than being the dirty business it is often made out to be, is probably one of the few mechanisms for reality testing in organizations. And the cleaner forms of power, the institutional forms, rather than having the virtues they are often credited with, can lead the organization to become out of

touch. The real trick to managing power in organizations is to ensure somehow that leaders cannot be unaware of the realities of their environments and cannot avoid changing to deal with those realities. That, however, would be like designing the "self-liquidating organization," an unlikely event since anyone capable of designing such an instrument would be obviously in control of the liquidations.

Management would do well to devote more attention to determining the critical contingencies of their environments. For if you conclude, as we do, that the environment sets most of the structure influencing organizational outcomes and problems, and that power derives from the organization's activities that deal with those contingencies, then it is the environment that needs managing, not power. The first step is to construct an accurate model of the environment, a process that is quite difficult for most organizations. We have recently started a project to aid administrators in systematically understanding their environments. From this experience, we have learned that the most critical blockage to perceiving an organization's reality accurately is a failure to incorporate those with the relevant expertise into the process. Most organizations have the requisite experts on hand but they are positioned so that they can be comfortably ignored.

One conclusion you can, and probably should, derive from our discussion is that power—because of the way it develops and the way it is used—will always result in the organization suboptimizing its performance. However, to this grim absolute, we add a comforting caveat: If any criteria other than power were the basis for determining an organization's decisions, the results would be even worse.

35

Power, Dependence, and Effective Management

John P. Kotter

Americans, as a rule, are not very comfortable with power or with its dynamics. We often distrust and question the motives of people who we think actively seek power. We have a certain fear of being manipulated. Even those people who think the dynamics of power are inevitable and needed often feel somewhat guilty when they themselves mobilize and use power. Simply put, the overall attitude and feeling toward power, which can easily be traced to the nation's very birth, is negative. In his enormously popular *Greening of America*, Charles Reich reflects the views of many when he writes, "It is not the misuse of power that is evil; the very existence of power is evil."[1]

One of the many consequences of this attitude is that power as a topic for rational study and dialogue has not received much attention, even in managerial circles. If the reader doubts this, all he or she need do is flip through some textbooks, journals, or advanced management course descriptions. The word *power* rarely appears.

This lack of attention to the subject of

power merely adds to the already enormous confusion and misunderstanding surrounding the topic of power and management. And this misunderstanding is becoming increasingly burdensome because in today's large and complex organizations the effective performance of most managerial jobs requires one to be skilled at the acquisition and use of power.

From my own observations, I suspect that a large number of managers—especially the young, well-educated ones—perform significantly below their potential because they do not understand the dynamics of power and because they have not nurtured and developed the instincts needed to effectively acquire and use power.

In this article I hope to clear up some of the confusion regarding power and managerial work by providing tentative answers to three questions:

1. Why are the dynamics of power necessarily an important part of managerial processes?

2. How do effective managers acquire power?

3. How and for what purposes do effective managers use power?

I will not address questions related to the misuse of power, but not because I

[1]Charles A. Reich, *The Greening of America: How the Youth Revolution Is Trying to Make America Liveable* (New York: Random House, 1970).

Author's note: This article is based on data from a clinical study of a highly diverse group of 26 organizations including large and small, public and private, manufacturing and service organizations. The study was funded by the Division of Research at the Harvard Business School. As part of the study process, the author interviewed about 250 managers.

think they are unimportant. The fact that some managers, some of the time, acquire and use power mostly for their own aggrandizement is obviously a very important issue that deserves attention and careful study. But that is a complex topic unto itself and one that has already received more attention than the subject of this article.

RECOGNIZING DEPENDENCE IN THE MANAGER'S JOB

One of the distinguishing characteristics of a typical manager is how dependent he is on the activities of a variety of other people to perform his job effectively.[2] Unlike doctors and mathematicians, whose performance is more directly dependent on their own talents and efforts, a manager can be dependent in varying degrees on superiors, subordinates, peers in other parts of the organization, the subordinates of peers, outside suppliers, customers, competitors, unions, regulating agencies, and many others.

These dependency relationships are an inherent part of managerial jobs because of two organizational facts of life: division of labor and limited resources. Because the work in organizations is divided into specialized divisions, departments, and jobs, managers are made directly or indirectly dependent on many others for information, staff services, and cooperation in general. Because of their organization's limited resources, managers are also dependent on their external environments for support. Without some minimal cooperation from suppliers, competitors,

unions, regulatory agencies, and customers, managers cannot help their organizations survive and achieve their objectives.

Dealing with these dependencies and the manager's subsequent vulnerability is an important and difficult part of a manager's job because, while it is theoretically possible that all of these people and organizations would automatically act in just the manner that a manager wants and needs, such is almost never the case in reality. All the people on whom a manager is dependent have limited time, energy, and talent, for which there are competing demands.

Some people may be uncooperative because they are too busy elsewhere, and some because they are not really capable of helping. Others may well have goals, values, and beliefs that are quite different and in conflict with the manager's and may therefore have no desire whatsoever to help or cooperate. This is obviously true of a competing company and sometimes of a union, but it can also apply to a boss who is feeling threatened by a manager's career progress or to a peer whose objectives clash with the manager's.

Indeed, managers often find themselves dependent on many people (and things) whom they do not directly control and who are not "cooperating." This is the key to one of the biggest frustrations managers feel in their jobs, even in the top ones, which the following example illustrates:

> After nearly a year of rumors, it was finally announced in May 1974 that the president of ABC Corporation had been elected chairman of the board and that Jim Franklin, the vice president of finance, would replace him as president. While everyone at ABC was aware that a shift would take place soon, it was not at all clear before the announcement who would be the next president. Most people

[2]See Leonard R. Sayles, *Managerial Behavior: Administration in Complex Organization* (New York: McGraw-Hill, 1964) as well as Rosemary Stewart, *Managers and Their Jobs* (London: Macmillan, 1967) and *Contrasts in Management* (London: McGraw-Hill, 1976).

had guessed it would be Phil Cook, the marketing vice president.

Nine months into his job as chief executive officer, Franklin found that Phil Cook (still the marketing vice president) seemed to be fighting him in small and subtle ways. There was never anything blatant, but Cook just did not cooperate with Franklin as the other vice presidents did. Shortly after being elected, Franklin had tried to bypass what he saw as a potential conflict with Cook by telling him that he would understand if Cook would prefer to move somewhere else where he could be a CEO also. Franklin said that it would be a big loss to the company but that he would be willing to help Cook in a number of ways if he wanted to look for a presidential opportunity elsewhere. Cook had thanked him but had said that family and community commitments would prevent him from relocating and all CEO opportunities were bound to be in a different city.

Since the situation did not improve after the tenth and eleventh months, Franklin seriously considered forcing Cook out. When he thought about the consequences of such a move, Franklin became more and more aware of just how dependent he was on Cook. Marketing and sales were generally the keys to success in their industry, and the company's sales force was one of the best, if not the best, in the industry. Cook had been with the company for 25 years. He had built a strong personal relationship with many of the people in the sales force and was universally popular. A mass exodus just might occur if Cook were fired. The loss of a large number of salesmen, or even a lot of turmoil in the department, could have a serious effect on the company's performance.

After one year as chief executive officer, Franklin found that the situation between Cook and himself had not improved and had become a constant source of frustration.

As a person gains more formal authority in an organization, the areas in which he or she is vulnerable increase and become more complex rather than the reverse. As the previous example suggests, it is not at all unusual for the president of an organization to be in a highly dependent position, a fact often not apparent to either the outsider or to the lower level manager who covets the president's job.

A considerable amount of the behavior of highly successful managers that seems inexplicable in light of what management texts usually tell us managers do becomes understandable when one considers a manager's need for, and efforts at, managing his or her relationships with others.[3] To be able to plan, organize, budget, staff, control, and evaluate, managers need some control over the many people on whom they are dependent. Trying to control others solely by directing them and on the basis of the power associated with one's position simply will not work—first, because managers are always dependent on some people over whom they have no formal authority, and second, because virtually no one in modern organizations will passively accept and completely obey a constant stream of orders from someone just because he or she is the "boss."

Trying to influence others by means of persuasion alone will not work either. Although it is very powerful and possibly the single most important method of influence, persuasion has some serious drawbacks too. To make it work requires time (often lots of it), skill, and information on the part of the persuader. And persuasion can fail simply because the other person chooses not to listen or does not listen carefully.

This is not to say that directing peo-

---

[3] I am talking about the type of inexplicable differences that Henry Mintzberg has found; see his article "The Manager's Job: Folklore and Fact," *HBR* July–August 1975, p. 49.

ple on the basis of the formal power of one's position and persuasion are not important means by which successful managers cope. They obviously are. But, even taken together, they are not usually enough.

Successful managers cope with their dependence on others by being sensitive to it, by eliminating or avoiding unnecessary dependence, and by establishing power over those others. Good managers then use that power to help them plan, organize, staff, budget, evaluate, and so on. *In other words, it is primarily because of the dependence inherent in managerial jobs that the dynamics of power necessarily form an important part of a manager's processes.*

An argument that took place during a middle management training seminar I participated in a few years ago helps illustrate further this important relationship between a manager's need for power and the degree of his or her dependence on others:

> Two participants, both managers in their thirties, got into a heated disagreement regarding the acquisition and use of power by managers. One took the position that power was absolutely central to managerial work, while the other argued that it was virtually irrelevant. In support of their positions, each described a very "successful" manager with whom he worked. In one of these examples, the manager seemed to be constantly developing and using power, while in the other, such behavior was rare. Subsequently, both seminar participants were asked to describe their successful manager's jobs in terms of the dependence *inherent* in those jobs.
>
> The young manager who felt power was unimportant described a staff vice president in a small company who was dependent only on his immediate subordinates, his peers, and his boss. This person, Joe Phillips, had to depend on his subordinates to do their jobs appropri-

ately, but, if necessary, he could fill in for any of them or secure replacement for them rather easily. He also had considerable formal authority over them; that is, he could give them raises and new assignments, recommend promotions, and fire them. He was moderately dependent on the other four vice presidents in the company for information and cooperation. They were likewise dependent on him. The president had considerable formal authority over Phillips but was also moderately dependent on him for help, expert advice, the service his staff performed, other information, and general cooperation.

The second young manager—the one who felt power was very important—described a service department manager, Sam Weller, in a large, complex, and growing company who was in quite a different position. Weller was dependent not only on his boss for rewards and information, but also on 30 other individuals who made up the divisional and corporate top management. And while his boss, like Phillips's, was moderately dependent on him too, most of the top managers were not. Because Weller's subordinates, unlike Phillips's, had people reporting to them, Weller was dependent not only on his subordinates but also on his subordinates' subordinates. Because he could not himself easily replace or do most of their technical jobs, unlike Phillips, he was very dependent on all these people.

In addition, for critical supplies, Weller was dependent on two other department managers in the division. Without their timely help, it was impossible for his department to do its job. These departments, however, did not have similar needs for Weller's help and cooperation. Weller was also dependent on local labor union officials and on a federal agency that regulated the division's industry. Both could shut his division down if they wanted.

Finally, Weller was dependent on two outside suppliers of key materials. Because of the volume of his department's purchase relative to the size of these two companies, he had little power over them.

Under these circumstances, it is hardly surprising that Sam Weller had to spend considerable time and effort acquiring and using power to manage his many dependencies, while Joe Phillips did not.

As this example also illustrates, not all management jobs require an incumbent to be able to provide the same amount of successful power-oriented behavior. But most management jobs today are more like Weller's than Phillips's. And, perhaps more important, the trend over the past two or three decades is away from jobs like Phillips's and toward jobs like Weller's. So long as our technologies continue to become more complex, the average organization continues to grow larger, and the average industry continues to become more competitive and regulated, that trend will continue; as it does so, the effective acquisition and use of power by managers will become even more important.

ESTABLISHING POWER IN RELATIONSHIPS

To help cope with the dependency relationships inherent in their jobs, effective managers create, increase, or maintain four different types of power over others.[4] Having power based in these areas puts the manager in a position both to influence those people on whom

[4]These categories closely resemble the five developed by John R. P. French and Bertram Raven; see "The Base of Social Power" in *Group Dynamics: Research and Theory*, Dorwin Cartwright and Alvin Zandler, eds. (New York: Harper & Row, 1968), Chapter 20. Three of the categories are similar to the types of "authority"-based power described by Max Weber in *The Theory of Social and Economic Organization* (New York: Free Press, 1947).

he or she is dependent when necessary and to avoid being hurt by any of them.

Sense of Obligation

One of the ways that successful managers generate power in their relationships with others is to create a sense of obligation in those others. When the manager is successful, the others feel that they should—rightly—allow the manager to influence them within certain limits.

Successful managers often go out of their way to do favors for people who they expect will feel an obligation to return those favors. As can be seen in the following description of a manager by one of his subordinates, some people are very skilled at identifying opportunities for doing favors that cost them very little but that others appreciate very much:

> "Most of the people here would walk over hot coals in their bare feet if my boss asked them to. He has an incredible capacity to do little things that mean a lot to people. Today, for example, in his junk mail he came across an advertisement for something that one of my subordinates had in passing once mentioned that he was shopping for. So my boss routed it to him. That probably took 15 seconds of his time, and yet my subordinate really appreciated it. To give you another example, two weeks ago he somehow learned that the purchasing manager's mother had died. On his way home that night, he stopped off at the funeral parlor. Our purchasing manager was, of course, there at the time. I bet he'll remember that brief visit for quite a while."

Recognizing that most people believe that friendship carries with it certain obligations ("A friend in need. . . ."), successful managers often try to develop true friendships with those on whom they are dependent. They will also make formal and informal deals in which they give something up in exchange for certain future obligations.

Belief in a Manager's Expertise

A second way successful managers gain power is by building reputations as "experts" in certain matters. Believing in the manager's expertise, others will often defer to the manager on those matters. Managers usually establish this type of power through visible achievement. The larger the achievement and the more visible it is, the more power the manager tends to develop.

One of the reasons that managers display concern about their "professional reputations" and their "track records" is that they have an impact on others' beliefs about their expertise. These factors become particularly important in large settings, where most people have only secondhand information about most other people's professional competence, as the following shows:

Herb Randley and Bert Kline were both 35-year-old vice presidents in a large research and development organization. According to their closest associates, they were equally bright and competent in their technical fields and as managers. Yet Randley had a much stronger professional reputation in most parts of the company, and his ideas generally carried much more weight. Close friends and associates claim the reason that Randley is so much more powerful is related to a number of tactics that he has used more than Kline has.

Randley has published more scientific papers and managerial articles than Kline. Randley has been more selective in the assignments he has worked on, choosing those that are visible and that require his strong suits. He has given more speeches and presentations on projects that are his own achievements. And in meetings in general, he is alleg-edly forceful in areas where he has expertise and silent in those where he does not.

Identification with a Manager

A third method by which managers gain power is by fostering others' unconscious identification with them or with ideas they "stand for." Sigmund Freud was the first to describe this phenomenon, which is most clearly seen in the way people look up to "charismatic" leaders. Generally, the more a person finds a manager both consciously and (more important) unconsciously an ideal person, the more he or she will defer to that manager.

Managers develop power based on others' idealized views of them in a number of ways. They try to look and behave in ways that others respect. They go out of their way to be visible to their employees and to give speeches about their organizational goals, values, and ideals. They even consider, while making hiring and promotion decisions, whether they will be able to develop this type of power over the candidates:

One vice president of sales in a moderate-size manufacturing company was reputed to be so much in control of his sales force that he could get them to respond to new and different marketing programs in a third of the time taken by the company's best competitors. His power over his employees was based primarily on their strong identification with him and what he stood for. Emigrating to the United States at age 17, this person worked his way up "from nothing." When made a sales manager in 1965, he begin recruiting other young immigrants and sons of immigrants from his former country. When made vice president of sales in 1970, he continued to do so. In 1975, 85% of his sales force was made up of people whom he hired directly or who were hired by others he brought in.

Perceived Dependence on a Manager

The final way that an effective manager often gains power is by feeding others' beliefs that they are dependent on the manager either for help or for not being hurt. The more they perceive they are dependent, the more most people will be inclined to cooperate with such a manager.

There are two methods that successful managers often use to create perceived dependence.

Finding & Acquiring Resources. In the first, the manager identifies and secures (if necessary) resources that another person requires to perform his job, that he does not possess, and that are not readily available elsewhere. These resources include such things as authority to make certain decisions; control of money, equipment, and office space; access to important people; information and control of information channels; and subordinates. Then the manager takes action so that the other person correctly perceives that the manager has such resources and is willing and ready to use them to help (or hinder) the other person. Consider the following extreme—but true—example.

When young Tim Babcock was put in charge of a division of a large manufacturing company and told to "turn it around," he spent the first few weeks studying it from afar. He decided that the division was in disastrous shape and that he would need to take many large steps quickly to save it. To be able to do that, he realized he needed to develop considerable power fast over most of the division's management and staff. He did the following:

- He gave the division's management two hours' notice of his arrival.
- He arrived in a limousine with six assistants.

- He immediately called a meeting of the 40 top managers.
- He outlined briefly his assessment of the situation, his commitment to turn things around, and the basic direction he wanted things to move in.
- He then fired the four top managers in the room and told them that they had to be out of the building in two hours.
- He then said he would personally dedicate himself to sabotaging the career of anyone who tried to block his efforts to save the division.
- He ended the 60-minute meeting by announcing that his assistants would set up appointments for him with each of them starting at 7:00 A.M. the next morning.

Throughout the critical six-month period that followed, those who remained at the division generally cooperated energetically with Mr. Babcock.

Affecting Perceptions of Resources. A second way effective managers gain these types of power is by influencing other persons' perceptions of the manager's resources.[5] In settings where many people are involved and where the manager does not interact continuously with those he or she is dependent on, those people will seldom possess "hard facts" regarding what relevant resources the manager commends directly or indirectly (through others), what resources he will command in the future, or how prepared he is to use those resources to help or hinder them. They will be forced to make their own judgments.

Insofar as a manager can influence people's judgments, he can generate much more power than one would generally ascribe to him in light of the reality of his resources.

[5]For an excellent discussion of this method, see Richard E. Neustadt, *Presidential Power* (New York: John Wiley, 1960).

In trying to influence people's judgments, managers pay considerable attention to the "trappings" of power and to their own reputations and images. Among other actions, they sometimes carefully select, decorate, and arrange their offices in ways that give signs of power. They associate with people or organizations that are known to be powerful or that others perceive as powerful. Managers selectively foster rumors concerning their own power. Indeed, those who are particularly skilled at creating power in this way tend to be very sensitive to the impressions that all their actions might have on others.

Formal Authority

Before discussing how managers use their power to influence others, it is useful to see how formal authority relates to power. By *formal authority*, I mean those elements that automatically come with a managerial job—perhaps a title, an office, a budget, the right to make certain decisions, a set of subordinates, a reporting relationship, and so on.

Effective managers use the elements of formal authority as resources to help them develop any or all of the four types of power previously discussed, just as they use other resources (such as their education). Two managers with the same formal authority can have very different amounts of power entirely because of the way they have used that authority. For example:

- By sitting down with employees who are new or with people who are starting new projects and clearly specifying who has the formal authority to do what, one manager creates a strong sense of obligation in others to defer to his authority later.
- By selectively withholding or giving the high-quality service his department can provide other departments,

one manager makes other managers clearly perceive that they are dependent on him.

On its own, then, formal authority does not guarantee a certain amount of power; it is only a resource that managers can use to generate power in their relationships.

EXERCISING POWER TO INFLUENCE OTHERS

Successful managers use the power they develop in their relationships, along with persuasion, to influence people on whom they are dependent to behave in ways that make it possible for the managers to get their jobs done effectively. They use their power to influence others directly, face to face, and in more indirect ways.

Face-to-face Influence

The chief advantage of influencing others directly by exercising any of the types of power is speed. If the power exists and the manager correctly understands the nature and strength of it, he can influence the other person with nothing more than a brief request or command:

> Jones thinks Smith feels obliged to him for past favors. Furthermore, Jones thinks that his request to speed up a project by two days probably falls within a zone that Smith would consider legitimate in light of his own definition of his obligation to Jones. So Jones simply calls Smith and makes his request. Smith pauses for only a second and says yes, he'll do it.
>
> Manager Johnson has some power based on perceived dependence over manager Baker. When Johnson tells Baker that he wants a report done in 24 hours, Baker grudgingly considers the costs of compliance, of noncompliance, and of complaining to higher authorities. He decides that doing the report is the

EXHIBIT • METHODS OF INFLUENCE

Face-to-face methods	What they can influence	Advantages	Drawbacks
Exercise obligation-based power.	Behavior within zone that the other perceives as legitimate in light of the obligation.	Quick. Requires no outlay of tangible resources.	If the request is outside the acceptable zone, it will fail; if it is too far outside, others might see it as illegitimate.
Exercise power based on perceived expertise.	Attitudes and behavior within the zone of perceived expertise.	Quick. Requires no outlay of tangible resources.	If the request is outside the acceptable zone, it will fail; if it is too far outside, others might see it as illegitimate.
Exercise power based on identification with a manager.	Attitudes and behavior that are not in conflict with the ideals that underlie the identification.	Quick. Requires no expenditure of limited resources.	Restricted to influence attempts that are not in conflict with the ideals that underlie the identification.
Exercise power based on perceived dependence.	Wide range of behavior that can be monitored.	Quick. Can often succeed when other methods fail.	Repeated influence attempts encourage the other to gain power over the influencer.
Coercively exercise power based on perceived dependence.	Wide range of behavior that can be easily monitored.	Quick. Can often succeed when other methods fail.	Invites retaliation. Very risky.
Use persuasion.	Very wide range of attitudes and behavior.	Can produce internalized motivation that does not require monitoring. Requires no power or outlay of scarce material resources.	Can be very time-consuming. Requires other person to listen.
Combine these methods.	Depends on the exact combination.	Can be more potent and less risky than using a single method.	More costly than using a single method.

(continued)

EXHIBIT • METHODS OF INFLUENCE (continued)

Indirect methods	What they can influence	Advantages	Drawbacks
Manipulate the other's environment by using any or all of the face-to-face methods.	Wide range of behavior and attitudes.	Can succeed when face-to-face methods fail.	Can be time-consuming. Is complex to implement. Is very risky, especially if used frequently.
Change the forces that continuously act on the individual: Formal organizational arrangements. Informal social arrangements. Technology. Resources available. Statement of organizational goals.	Wide range of behavior and attitudes on a continuous basis.	Has continuous influence, not just a one-shot effect. Can have a very powerful impact.	Often requires a considerable power outlay to achieve.

least costly action and tells Johnson he will do it.

Young Porter identifies strongly with Marquette, an older manager who is not his boss. Porter thinks Marquette is the epitome of a great manager and tries to model himself after him. When Marquette asks Porter to work on a special project "that could be very valuable in improving the company's ability to meet new competitive products," Porter agrees without hesitation and works 15 hours per week above and beyond his normal hours to get the project done and done well.

When used to influence others, each of the four types of power has different advantages and drawbacks. For example, power based on perceived expertise or on identification with a manager can often be used to influence attitudes as well as someone's immediate behavior and thus can have a lasting impact. It is very difficult to influence attitudes by using power based on perceived dependence, but if it can be done, it usually has the advantage of being able to influence a much broader range of behavior than the other methods do. When exercising power based on perceived expertise, for example, one can only influence attitudes and behavior within that narrow zone defined by the "expertise."

The drawbacks associated with the use of power based on perceived dependence are particularly important to recognize. A person who feels dependent on a manager for rewards (or lack of punishments) might quickly agree to a request from the manager but then not follow through—especially if the manager cannot easily find out if the person has obeyed or not. Repeated influence attempts based on perceived dependence also seem to encourage the other person to try to gain some power to balance the manager's. And perhaps most important, using power based on perceived dependence in a coercive way is very risky. Coercion invites retaliation.

For instance, in the example in which Tim Babcock took such extreme steps to save the division he was assigned to "turn around," his development and use of power based on perceived dependence could have led to mass resignation and the collapse of the division. Babcock fully recognized this risk, however, and behaved as he did because he felt there was simply *no other way* that he could gain the very large amount of quick cooperation needed to save the division.

Effective managers will often draw on more than one form of power to influence someone, or they will combine power with persuasion. In general, they do so because a combination can be more potent and less risky than any single method as the following description shows:

> "One of the best managers we have in the company has lots of power based on one thing or another over most people. But he seldom if ever just tells or asks someone to do something. He almost always takes a few minutes to try to persuade them. The power he has over people generally induces them to listen carefully and certainly disposes them to be influenced. That, of course, makes the persuasion process go quickly and easily. And he never risks getting the other person mad or upset by making what that person thinks is an unfair request or command."

It is also common for managers not to coercively exercise power based on perceived dependence by itself, but to combine it with other methods to reduce the risk of retaliation. In this way, managers are able to have a large impact without leaving the bitter aftertaste of punishment alone.

Indirect Influence Methods

Effective managers also rely on two types of less direct methods to influence those on whom they are dependent. In the first way, they use any or all of the face-to-face methods to influence other people, who in turn have some specific impact on a desired person.

Product manager Stein needed plant manager Billings to "sign off" on a new product idea (Product X) which Billings thought was terrible. Stein decided that there was no way he could logically persuade Billings because Billings just would not listen to him. With time, Stein felt, he could have broken through that barrier. But he did not have that time. Stein also realized that Billings would never, just because of some deal or favor, sign off on a product he did not believe in. Stein also felt it not worth the risk of trying to force Billings to sign off, so here is what he did:

> On Monday, Stein got Reynolds, a person Billings respected, to send Billings two market research studies that were very favorable to Product X, with a note attached saying, "Have you seen this? I found them rather surprising. I am not sure if I entirely believe them, but still. . . ."
>
> On Tuesday, Stein got a representative of one of the company's biggest customers to mention casually to Billings on the phone that he had heard a rumor about Product X being introduced soon and was "glad to see you guys are on your toes as usual."
>
> On Wednesday, Stein had two industrial engineers stand about three feet away from Billings as they were waiting for a meeting to begin and talk about the favorable test results on Product X.
>
> On Thursday, Stein set up a meeting to talk about Product X with Billings and invited only people whom Billings liked or respected and who also felt favorably about Product X.
>
> On Friday, Stein went to see Billings and asked him if he was willing to sign off on Product X. He was.

This type of manipulation of the environments of others can influence both behavior and attitudes and can often succeed when other influence methods fail. But it has a number of serious drawbacks. It takes considerable time and energy, and it is quite risky. Many people think it is wrong to try to influence others in this way, even people who, without consciously recognizing it, use this technique themselves. If they think someone is trying, or has tried, to manipulate them, they may retaliate. Furthermore, people who gain the reputation of being manipulators seriously undermine their own capacities for developing power and for influencing others. Almost no one, for example, will want to identify with a manipulator. And virtually no one accepts, at face value, a manipulator's sincere attempts at persuasion. In extreme cases, a reputation as a manipulator can completely ruin a manager's career.

A second way in which managers indirectly influence others is by making permanent changes in an individual's or a group's environment. They change job descriptions, the formal systems that measure performance, the extrinsic incentives available, the tools, people, and other resources that the people or groups work with, the architecture, the norms or values of work groups, and so on. If the manager is successful in making the changes, and the changes have the desired effect on the individual or group, that effect will be sustained over time.

Effective managers recognize that changes in the forces that surround a person can have great impact on that person's behavior. Unlike many of the other influence methods, this one doesn't require a large expenditure of limited resources or effort on the part of the manager on an ongoing basis. Once such a change has been successfully made, it works independently of the manager.

This method of influence is used by all managers to some degree. Many, however, use it sparingly simply because

they do not have the power to change the forces acting on the person they wish to influence. In many organizations, only the top managers have the power to change the formal measurement systems, the extrinsic incentives available, the architecture, and so on.

GENERATING & USING POWER SUCCESSFULLY

Managers who are successful at acquiring considerable power and using it to manage their dependence on others tend to share a number of common characteristics:

1. They are sensitive to what others consider to be legitimate behavior in acquiring and using power. They recognize that the four types of power carry with them certain "obligations" regarding their acquisition and use. A person who gains a considerable amount of power based on his perceived expertise is generally expected to be an expert in certain areas. If it ever becomes publicly known that the person is clearly not an expert in those areas, such a person will probably be labeled a "fraud" and will not only lose his power but will suffer other reprimands too.

A person with whom a number of people identify is expected to act like an ideal leader. If he clearly lets people down, he will not only lose that power, he will also suffer the righteous anger of his ex-followers. Many managers who have created or used power based on perceived dependence in ways that their employees have felt unfair, such as in requesting overtime work, have ended up with unions.

2. They have good intuitive understanding of the various types of power and methods of influence. They are sensitive to what types of power are easiest to develop with different types of people. They recognize, for example, that

professionals tend to be more influenced by perceived expertise than by other forms of power. They also have a grasp of all the various methods of influence and what each can accomplish, at what costs, and with what risks. (See the *Exhibit* on pages 495 and 496.) They are good at recognizing the specific conditions in any situation and then at selecting an influence method that is compatible with those conditions.

3. They tend to develop all the types of power, to some degree, and they use all the influence methods mentioned in the exhibit. Unlike managers who are not very good at influencing people, effective managers usually do not think that only some of the methods are useful or that only some of the methods are moral. They recognize that any of the methods, used under the right circumstances, can help contribute to organizational effectiveness with few dysfunctional consequences. At the same time, they generally try to avoid those methods that are more risky than others and those that may have dysfunctional consequences. For example, they manipulate the environment of others only when absolutely necessary.

4. They establish career goals and seek out managerial positions that allow them to successfully develop and use power. They look for jobs, for example, that use their backgrounds and skills to control or manage some critically important problem or environmental contingency that an organization faces. They recognize that success in that type of job makes others dependent on them and increases their own perceived expertise. They also seek jobs that do not demand a type or a volume of power that is inconsistent with their own skills.

5. They use all of their resources, formal authority, and power to develop still more power. To borrow Edward

Banfield's metaphor, they actually look for ways to "invest" their power where they might secure a high positive return.[6] For example, by asking a person to do him two important favors, a manager might be able to finish his construction program one day ahead of schedule. That request may cost him most of the obligation-based power he has over that person, but in return he may significantly increase his perceived expertise as a manager of construction projects in the eyes of everyone in his organization.

Just as in investing money, there is always some risk involved in using power this way; it is possible to get a zero return for a sizable investment, even for the most powerful manager. Effective managers do not try to avoid risks. Instead, they look for prudent risks, just as they do when investing capital.

6. Effective managers engage in power-oriented behavior in ways that are tempered by maturity and self-control.[7] They seldom, if ever, develop and use power in impulsive ways or for their own aggrandizement.

7. Finally, they also recognize and accept as legitimate that, in using these methods, they clearly influence other people's behavior and lives. Unlike many less effective managers, they are reasonably comfortable in using power to influence people. They recognize, often only intuitively, what this article is all about—that their attempts to establish power and use it are an absolutely necessary part of the successful fulfillment of their difficult managerial role.

[6]See Edward C. Banfield, *Political Influence* (New York: Free Press, 1965), Chapter II.

[7]See David C. McClelland and David H. Burnham, "Power Is the Great Motivator," HBR March-April 1976, p. 100.

36
Identifying and Using Political Resources
Douglas Yates, Jr.

Any leader is constantly in the business of managing political conflict—the pervasive conflicts of personal and bureaucratic interests. But there is a lot more to the job of managing political conflict than meets the eye. Here again, we expect that the manager of political conflict will be more effective if his or her responses and strategies fit the problems in his or her environment.

Managers used to beating down an aggressive Type A bureaucracy will find that their political approach to organizational problems will probably have very different results if they have to deal with the problem of how to piece together fragments, mediate free-for-alls, and try to establish methods of coordinated policy making in a Type B bureaucracy. These clues to the nature of political conflict management flow directly from an understanding of the implications of fragmentation, dominance, professionalism, hierarchy, technology, and operating procedures. This is not to say that appropriate strategies of conflict management can be mechanically derived from the structure of the problems. The manager's task is to fit resources and strategies to the particular conflict he or she faces.

POLITICAL RESOURCES

Managers possess a range of resources: authority, force, persuasion, symbolic rewards, personal style, bargaining tech-

niques, negotiating and mediating skills, coalition-building approaches, and allocations of benefits and other material rewards and punishments. In a particular management environment, any leader must decide which leadership resource or combination of resources is likely to be effective in transforming conflicts into positive forms of cooperation, conciliation, or consensus. A more specific argument about the role of a leader as manager of political conflict can assist in making this point more concrete. That is, the leader must pay attention to the benefits and costs inherent in the nature of the resources available in conflict management. For example, force is a powerful weapon, but it is costly. To apply it widely over a large number of people or organizations and for a substantial period of time entails the investment of large political resources. (Police states and army-backed juntas are foreign examples where close surveillance is a labor-intensive activity.) Authority is also widely believed to be a potent resource (for example, "The president wants . . .," "The treasurer would like you to do X"), but again the widespread application of authority is likely to strain the manager's claim of authority. Further, it is hard to exercise authority downward through multiple levels of bureaucracy: a third-level authority claim has less force than a second-level one, and the leader still always needs to know whether his or her

Source: From "Identifying and Using Political Resources" by Douglas Yates, Jr., in *The Politics of Management* (1985), pp. 90–104. Copyright © 1985 Jossey-Bass Inc., Publishers and Jossey-Bass Limited. Reprinted by permission.

orders have been carried out. (The good soldier Schweik, who always said "yes sir" and then did nothing, is not merely a curiosity of the Czechoslovakian Army.)

Bargaining strategies sound more democratic and benign, but they, too, are costly if there are many contestants and few benefits to disperse. Persuasion, as Richard Neustadt (1980) has shown, it is a widely deployed resource in a political system; but unless the leader possesses Lyndon Johnson's virtuoso skills at employing "The Treatment," the task of persuading X to do Y may require a long courtship that does not always lead to marriage. It depends on what you are trying to persuade someone to do (matters of problem context arise again). Coalition building is also a favorite leadership strategy in a democratic political system, but the design and maintenance of coalitions are tricky business. One does not want to build too large a coalition; William Riker (1962) says it is best to build the smallest possible winning coalition. Moreover, coalitions may easily become unstable or unravel in the face of changing problems or evolving interests. If a leader has constructed multiple coalitions for different purposes, the costs in time and energy of keeping them intact are likely to be high.

Negotiation and mediation are especially benign-sounding political resources, but anyone who has engaged in the painstaking art of being an honest broker or labor negotiator knows well how consuming an experience it is to ride the emotional roller coaster of trying to bring two opposing sides together.

The use of symbols is also an appealing resource for political leaders. Symbols can generate strong emotional attachments; they can reassure. But, as in the case of New York Mayor Koch's symbolic appeals to the middle class or Mr. Reagan's symbolic appeals to conservatives, it turns out that a leader can both develop overly high expectations among followers and also antagonize others through the use of symbolic politics. In addition, the more symbolic positions a leader takes, the more likely the symbols are to become either confused or conflicting.

We see in this analysis a glimmer of what I wish to call the political economy of leadership. That is, each resource has its strengths and weaknesses, benefits and costs, given its basic character. That is the simple point. If political economy is understood as the allocation of scarce resources, the more widely a given resource is deployed, the greater the costs become in time and energy. A manager can easily exercise authority over one subordinate. Exercising it over twenty, fifty, or a hundred people becomes progressively more difficult. Also, the more often a given resource is used, the less effective it is likely to become (this is a feature of diminishing marginal utility). If a worker receives an occasional order from the boss, he is likely to take it quite seriously. If he receives orders by the score, he is certain to take them less seriously, if only because he wonders about what the boss really wants. A worker is also likely to become skeptical of orders if they are too numerous. So a resource may have not only diminishing utility but also a negative effect. Following are two examples of negative effects: (1) If a manager is devoting a large amount of time to patient negotiation, organizational observers may easily come to conclude that the boss isn't getting anything done; he just meets with people all the time. And their negative reaction can be: "My God, another meeting on that subject. Can't we get anything resolved around here?" (2)

The tactic of firing a person can be used only on occasion and not as a regular instrument of control. If it becomes a strategy, the effect on organizational morale is disastrous, and the organizational instability caused by the perceived existence of a "reign of terror" is hardly apt to create a management environment inducing work. This applies to U.S. presidents, college presidents, baseball owners, bank presidents, and mayors. There were similarly vicious organizational climates in Lyndon Johnson's White House, at Boston University, and on George Steinbrenner's baseball team.

A final point should be made about the character and deployment of political resources when they are viewed as "weapons" independent of context. Not only are resources scarce, subject to depletion over time, and likely to diminish in utility with successive applications, but also there are inherent tradeoffs and constraints in their use. If a leader invests his or her time, energy, and style in asserting authority, he or she will not have equivalent resources for bargaining techniques, mediation skills, or force. Franklin Roosevelt has been described in favorable terms as "the lion and the fox" (Burns, 1956), but this ability to combine very different approaches to leadership and management certainly had sharp limits. If he chose to emphasize force or authority, it was hard for him to be a bargainer or mediator, and vice versa. Even when he was able to shift at will and at high speed from the use of force toward authority, bargaining, and coalition building, he had the problem of timing. The lion at breakfast and the fox at dinner will create a confused and confusing impact on an organization. Indeed, several decades later, one of Carter's problems as president was that he shifted his public stance—whether consciously or not—from that of a moralist to an engineer to a populist, and then back again, erratically.

The nature of a particular problem (including especially the politics of its definition) and the character of a particular management environment powerfully shape the choice of what management resource to deploy. The relationship between problem environment, on the one hand, and the choice of a management strategy, on the other, is akin to, though not as strictly delimited as, the choice of a medical technique to treat a disease. If a patient has a broken leg, it would be odd to recommend psychiatric counseling. If a patient complains of chest pains, it would be unlikely that a nurse would call in an orthopedic surgeon. These are, of course, easy cases of mismatched problems and responses. Presumably, medicine becomes more interesting—at least for the doctor—when the diagnosis is more puzzling and where there are multiple or interacting medical problems. Still, the basic point stands that we view doctors as *skillful,* good at diagnosis, if they apply the appropriate treatment to a given health problem, once its elements have been understood as fully as possible. And so it is regarding our manager of political conflict. Further, particular conflict situations strongly *indicate,* in the medical sense, the deployment of particular leadership resources and strategies. Elements of this analysis have already cropped up in the discussion of the implications for management of different aspects of the basic structural features of bureaucracy as well as of institutional differences. It is now time to reinforce the central line of argument by demonstrating the importance of organizational and environmental structure for the manager of political conflict.

Consider a bureaucratic conflict in which a leader is faced with a dominant bureaucracy with strong political resources that adamantly opposes a proposed change in policy. In surveying his or her own choice of political resources, the leader will doubtless view the use of mediation or persuasion or coalition building as inappropriate responses. The bureaucracy is hunkered down in the middle of the road and does not want to budge. A leader who did not conclude that he or she would have to turn to the use of force or authority would be misreading the problem. For the structure of the problem is that of a zero-sum game.

Consider a very different case. Imagine that a manager is faced with a conflict between two relatively equal bureaucratic powers who are stalemated in trying to reach a decision. Here, the structure of political conflict is very different, primarily because the leader in this script is not a direct combatant. Here, we would expect a leader to turn to bargaining, persuasion, and mediation resources *precisely* because these are the resources that address the conflict structure at hand. As a last resort, the leader might lock the two opposed parties in a room and not let them out until someone had won or until some kind of agreement had been struck. But it should be easy to see that this use of force is a risky and potentially costly move, for the leader has given up any hope of shaping the outcome according to his or her own preferences and cannot be at all certain whether the locked door will produce a best-case or worst-case result. If the latter, it will appear to bureaucratic observers that the leader has been unable to manage conflict successfully, and that impression itself will be very costly.

Consider a third conflict structure, in which there are a sizable number of contestants, with varying political resources, who are competing to receive the benefits of a government grant-in-aid program. Here, the natural response

for a leader is to employ bargaining techniques and try to structure a process of checks and balances in decision making so that the various interests are given strong procedural opportunities to argue their positions. The leader could, of course, try to impose by force or authority his or her own distribution decisions, but substantial social research indicates that the various contestants in the bargaining process will resent being excluded from participation in shaping the outcome (Mosher, 1967). If we alter one fact in this conflict situation, we can see how strongly variations in conflict structure affect the viability of possible management strategies.

Assume now that we have multiple competitors but no benefits to allocate. Rather, the problem is to reduce spending levels. In this case, a central decision to impose equal cuts across the board may be the least costly and most acceptable solution for all involved. For here, if multilateral bargaining techniques are chosen, the result is likely to be a fierce survival fight among the bureaucratic players determined to "save" their programs. This notably is the conflict situation that David Stockman faced in trying to reduce bureaucratic spending in the first Reagan administration.

Another case is a conflict structure of severe fragmentation in which the different organizational contestants are used to operating on their own and have avoided competition by establishing well-defined bureaucratic turfs and boundaries. Here, decentralized bargaining seems a feeble response, for the contestants have no experience of or inclination for bargaining out their differences. In this case, the appropriate leadership response would seem to be one of (1) using authority to force the fragmented bureaucracies to come together in the same room and (2) designing a *competitive policy dialogue* in which arguments over conflicting interests and policy positions can be joined openly. Indeed, to the extent that this kind of fragmentation and bureaucratic insularity is pervasive, competing policy dialogue may prove to be particularly prominent and valuable.

Finally, consider a conflict structure in which one strong bureaucratic power is pitted against two weak ones in ways that make an alliance of the two weak parties unviable as a countervailing force in bargaining. Here again, a straight bargaining process will send the old winner home again. The task of a leader—who is outside the process so far—might well be either to alter the rules of the bargaining process (which is why we often find proportional-representation rather than majority-rule voting systems) or to enter the bargaining process directly as an advocate of the minority interests. In all these cases, we see clearly that a leader cannot begin to manage until the structure of the conflict has been identified. Even sophisticated game theory has shown this (Shubik, 1982).

Having traveled this far in linking conflict structures to the use of management resources and strategies, we can go one step further by viewing the management of political conflict as managing a strategic conflict between individual players with different kinds of resources. (Here we are drawing on the analysis of distinctive bureaucratic resources and strategic moves discussed earlier. This step constitutes a move from a *macro* approach to conflict structures to a distinct *micro* analysis of the strategies employed by contestants in the conflict.) A leader needs to think carefully about whether he or she is equipped to marshal his or her own resources or make his or her own strategic moves against a bureaucratic subunit. Some concrete cases can be drawn from defense secretaries before Robert McNamara's time.

They were used to finding themselves at a strategic disadvantage in debates over weapons development, because the armed services largely controlled the information and technical knowledge involved in decision making. McNamara's counter to his strategic disadvantage was to deploy a corps of systems analysts to give him an independent and countervailing base of historical and technical information (Enthoven and Smith, 1971). It is also significant that the introduction of systems analysis as a mode of policy analysis greatly changed the language of debate. The military services suddenly found that they were at a strategic disadvantage against the Defense Department's "Whiz Kids" under Charles Hitch, and, indeed, they lost a number of important battles over weapons development.

Similarly, we can view the rise and increased centrality of the Office of Management and Budget in policy making as a deliberate attempt by presidents to offset the bureaucracy's natural strategic advantage in knowledge, program history, and operational details (Berman, 1979). The same logic of strategic competition—trying to counter the political resources of the bureaucracy—applies to the development of the National Security Council, the Domestic Council, and perhaps even the Council of Economic Advisors. This conception of strategic competition need not always point to the conclusion that a central policy maker must develop precisely the same set of resources as are possessed by other bureaucratic contestants. Indeed, if a central manager attempted to do this, as Richard Nixon has been viewed as doing in developing what Richard Nathan (1975) has called an "administrative presidency," the strong likelihood is that the White House, or any other "corporate headquarters," would become overloaded and bogged down in detail. Rather, a central manager will discover that there are a variety of resources that may be used to counter the particular resource of a bureaucracy. If, for example, a bureaucracy's political advantage lies in the establishment of an "iron triangle" with an interest group and a congressional committee, the president's best strategic move may be to build an alternative coalition by using the media to attack the iron triangle. An appeal of a president over the heads of powerful groups can occasionally be effective in rallying popular support.

A final example of how a leader used a different kind of resource to counter his bureaucratic subunit's own strategic resources is Elliot Richardson's discovery that the withholding of information, launching of end runs, and sabotaging of other subunits' policy positions were powerful organizational resources in bureaucratic infighting. He chose not to use the same tactics and thus escalate the confrontations. So he used an authority resource, his ability to structure a different decision-making process, to counter the "moves" that he believed were tearing his bureaucracy apart (Peters, 1974). He created an "Executive Secretariat" designed explicitly to force bureaucratic combatants to come together in the same room and argue out their differences openly. It worked, and he gained some secondary effects. Different policy recommendations and background information were made available to all contestants for inspection, comment, and debate.

THE POLITICS OF PROBLEM DEFINITION

We can bring our analysis of the management of political conflict full circle if we add in one further element that affects the character of the conflict structure. That is the nature of the problem itself—in terms of both its objective characteristics and the politics of problem definition surrounding it. Even a discussion of a small number of significant variables in the structure of policy problems as they affect management shows the importance of this last element. For one thing, some problems have a dichotomous quality: they involve go-no-go decisions, such as that to launch the Bay of Pigs invasion or end the grain embargo against the Soviet Union or build a new line of compact cars. Here the possibility of bargaining out competing points of view is limited, although possible, because bargained policy adjustment may remain in such decisions. (A go-no-go decision can be postponed or made subject to last-minute recall, as in the case of the Iran raid.) Still, a leader faced with this kind of problem must almost always rely heavily on authority resources and less on patient negotiation, persuasion, or bargaining tactics.

Some policy problems involve the distribution of benefits to broad classes of recipients. In such instances, a resort to participatory bargaining tactics will usually seem natural and appropriate. A policy issue with a *zero-sum* quality will pose a quite different problem for conflict management. For example, there is no way that the Secretary of the Department of Health, Education, and Welfare was going to agree happily to the creation of an independent Department of Education. The president, faced with this dilemma, recognized that bargaining and mediation resources were not useful. The problem required a decision based on the authority of the "boss" to reorganize or not reorganize his government.

Finally, differences in the underlying political structure of problem definition will greatly affect the nature of conflict management. Here, three cases where the political dimension of problem definition varies greatly can be discussed. First is the Bay of Pigs, which is distinctive because all the political actors in the decision had come to an agreement on problem definition and on a resulting course of action and had substantial historical investment in getting their policy implemented. This is a "train on the tracks" situation, and the problem for the leader is how to inject some conflict or multiple advocacy into the decision to "go or not go." In the past, this kind of problem context has been widely discussed in terms of the dangers of "groupthink" (Janis, 1972), the impact of having a devil's advocate, and so forth. The critical problem for the leader is the recognition of the fact that the existing problem definition (with its surrounding political structure) has created enormous momentum; it will require strong and costly measures to try to reverse the policy as it rolls down the track.

A second case is the Skybolt decision, where there were at least two arguable definitions of the problem: one based on cost-effectiveness analysis, yielding a conclusion to cancel the project, the other drawn from politics and a concern for the Anglo-American alliance and saying go ahead. The obvious pitfall for a leader is to adopt one definition and ignore the other. Here, the conflict manager's task is to recognize the competing claims about the problem, examine the trade-offs, and attempt to get the opposing problem definers to argue and connect their positions openly.

In a third case, we have a problem such as the formulation of the War on Poverty or, more recently, arms-control policy. Here, the central policy maker faces a highly fragmented political structure concerning problem definition. And here, too, we encounter a

conflict situation that requires the airing and comparison of numerous different definitions, symbols, and policy language—all in a context of high uncertainty about the probable consequences of accepting any given problem definition. This kind of conflict seems to call most naturally for the kind of competitive policy debate that Richardson sought to establish through his Executive Secretariat.

In sum, the nature of a problem and the politics of its definition clearly add another dimension to the job of managing political conflict. It is a dimension that, if ignored, can lead a decision maker into severe political and administrative traps.

POLITICAL CONFLICT IN BUSINESS

The political analysis of business management has been hampered and even ignored by a tendency to depict the private firm in idealized terms. In this idealized portrait, propagated by many journalistic treatments and business school cases, the chairperson of Company X gazes out the window and thinks about whether to close down a plant or reorganize the firm's divisions. The image is of a decisive, rational manager, a guiding bottom line, hiring and firing power, and a strong internal hierarchy—the denizens of which obey promptly when "the decision" is made. If we push this image a little further, we encounter a cartoon figure of the business decision maker as Attila the Hun running a wondrous business-efficiency machine. In this management environment, the internal decision-making process is a black box, and the external world is largely ignored. In such a world, there is obviously little use for political analysis—it would seem both undignified and beside the point. Why confuse our rational decision machine with thoughts of group conflict, differences in management environments, the nature of available leadership resources, and so forth? At the least, such thoughts would divert attention from the "real" task of making a sound business decision on the merits of the case.

It should take no particular genius to see that this idealized portrait or cartoon of the private firm *cannot* be right. For if it were, then all businesses would succeed in what they were trying to do: make impressive profits, experience satisfying increases in the value of their common stock, and so forth. One has only to read recent accounts of business leaderhsip to generate, at the extreme, our countercartoon: the business manager as Wizard of Oz. In this depiction, the leader, for all his imagined analytical and organizational resources, experiences great difficulty getting things to happen in his firm. Of course, he is afraid to let anyone know that he is *not* living in the idealized world of the executive suite. Hence, the defensive, worried reality of the Wizard of Oz. A more balanced depiction of the world of the corporate executive is that he or she shares many of the problems encountered by other leaders of large organizations. Goals are uncertain, alternative solutions highly arguable, group conflict pervasive, fragmentation an inexorable reality, conflict management an inevitability, implementation a constant headache, and external forces—be they other firms or government agencies—a persistent threat.

If these intimations about the real world of business leadership are correct—and we do not need to find a "Deep Throat" to confirm that they are more realistic than the standard idealized version—then it should become

obvious that a private leader lives in a highly political world in which group conflict over scarce resources is pervasive. Therefore, the ability to function as a skilled political detective and manager of political conflict is an absolutely central element in the repertoire of leadership. This is not to say that, after the serious business of financial, marketing, and other forms of "rational" analysis is done, it is well to factor in the political dimension of management. My claim is stronger than that. It is not only that a lack of a subtle understanding of the political dimension is critical in its own right but also that a failure of such understanding is likely to disturb if not subvert *other* forms of analysis.

If this is so, our advice is that the private leader should perform the same kind of step-by-step political analysis suggested for the public leader as a cornerstone of management problem solving and strategy development: (1) defining the problem (and its politics); (2) mapping the management environment; (3) analyzing the particular resources of competing bureaucratic actors; (4) examining the political economy of the resources he or she has to employ; (5) appraising alternative strategies of conflict leadership; and (6) squaring the circle by trying to fit resources and conflict management approaches to the nature of particular problems, organizational environments, and bureaucratic resources.

Of course, it should not be assumed or asserted that almost all private leaders fail to understand the importance of the political dimension in their roles. Rather, it is probably more true that, even as many public leaders operate with only a vague notion of the importance of bureaucratic politics, so private leaders operate with only a vague notion of corporate politics. The aim of this book is to present a more systematic way of analyzing the political dimension of management through the presentation of the fragmentation and competition tests, the identification of institutional differences, and the careful analysis of the costs and benefits of deploying different leadership resources.

The politics of private management is a particularly fertile and tricky dimension of leadership precisely because business decision making is idealized. To even perceive the centrality of the political dimension, one must first smash the *Business Week* cartoon of the chop-chop efficient business leader, strip the bottom line of some of its aura, question assumptions about hierarchy and authority, and recognize subtle (and not-so-subtle) political elements of competing problem definitions. Moreover, private organizations that want to ignore the political dimension of management are almost certain to lack the kinds of policymaking processes and conflict management strategies that are usefully employed in the public sector. In the public domain, the political dimension can hardly be ignored—except by heroically stubborn efficiency experts and an occasional president such as Jimmy Carter, who adopted the stance of a "Great Engineer." In contrast, where the political dimension in business is suppressed or viewed as a subject on the same order as sex and bribery, fundamental conflicts are almost certain to be perceived as office politics and to be treated as an annoying manifestation of the dark side of human nature.

In this light, it did come as a surprise to me to find that an insightful commentary on decision making within Exxon yielded a picture of decision making and conflict management that bears an almost eerie resemblance to the Founding Fathers' design for a pluralist system of checks and balances. As one journalist observer has written: "All through the Exxon system, checks and balances are built in. Each fall, the presidents of the 13 affiliates take their plans for the coming year and beyond to New York for a review at a meeting with the management committee and the staff vice presidents" ("Inside Exxon," 1980).

Thus, a decision-making process in business, as in government, is characterized by a continual competitive policy debate both between different layers of authority and between different horizontal jurisdictions. James Madison would doubtless be impressed by the degree of multiple advocacy, countervailing powers, and "cross talk" in the policy-making process found in Exxon. When a Madisonian system of checks and balances is put into place in bureaucracies, as was done by Elliott Richardson in his day, or with Exxon in its recent history, a similar set of "political" processes evolved. This decision-making process has been called, somewhat grandly, a Cooperative Agency Management System (Lynn and Seidl, 1977), but the same basic Madisonian principles apply. The striking point is that, having recognized the central need to manage political conflict, Madison, the chairperson of Exxon, and a cabinet secretary all wound up designing the same kind of organizational decision-making system. When we can learn to say James Madison, Exxon, and Health, Education, and Welfare in the same breath, we can begin to do a serious analysis of the politics of management.

REFERENCES

Berman, L. *The Office of Management and Budget and the Presidency.* Princeton, N.J.: Princeton University Press, 1979.

Burns, J. M. *Roosevelt: The Lion and the Fox.* New York: Harcourt Brace Jovanovich, 1956.

Enthoven, A. C., and Smith, K. W. *How Much Is Enough?* New York: Harper & Row, 1971.

"Inside Exxon." *New York Times Magazine,* Aug. 3, 1980, pp. 18–23.

Janis, I. *Victims of Groupthink.* Boston: Houghton Mifflin, 1972.

Lynn, L. E., Jr., and Seidl, J. "Bottom Line Management for Public Agencies." *Harvard Business Review,* 1977, 55 (1), 144–153.

Mosher, F. C. (ed.). *Governmental Reorganizations: Cases and Commentary.* Indianapolis. Ind.: Bobbs-Merrill, 1967.

Nathan, R. *The Plot That Failed: Nixon and the Administrative Presidency.* New York: Wiley, 1975.

Neustadt, R. *Alliance Politics.* New York: Columbia University Press, 1970.

Neustadt, R. *Presidential Power: The Politics of Leadership.* (2nd ed.) New York: Wiley, 1976.

Peters, C. "How to Take Over the Government." *Washington Monthly,* Sept. 1974, pp. 19–21.

Riker, W. *The Theory of Political Coalitions.* New Haven, Conn.: Yale University Press, 1962.

Shubik, M. *Game Theory in the Social Sciences: Concepts and Solutions.* Cambridge, Mass.: MIT Press, 1982.

CHAPTER VI

Organizational Change and Development

Organizational change requires the application of all of the other topics that have been addressed in this book. In order to confront organizational change in theory or in practice, one must tie together and use knowledge about human motivation, leadership, group and intergroup behavior, the relationship between people and their organizational contexts, and power and influence—all from the organizational behavior perspective. Thus, in examining the historical foundations and current practice of organizational change, this chapter incorporates contributions from:

*   The Hawthorne experiments, as described by Fritz Roethlisberger (included in Chapter I, *Motivation*);
*   Transformative leadership, as explained in the 1984 article by Noel Tichy and David Ulrich (reprinted in Chapter IV, *Leadership*);
*   The socio-technical systems-oriented group at the Tavistock Institute, as represented by Eric Trist and Kenneth Bamforth's article in Chapter III, *People in Organizations: The Context*;
*   Survey research and feedback techniques, that draw extensively from work done by Kurt Lewin and his associates (another piece by Lewin, on a different topic, "Group Decision and Social Change," appears in this chapter); and
*   The development of sensitivity training (or T-groups), a phenomenon which in itself incorporates theory, research, and practice on leadership, group development and behavior, intergroup behavior, motivation, power and influence, and individual-organizational context impacts.

ORGANIZATIONAL CHANGE FROM THE ORGANIZATIONAL BEHAVIOR PERSPECTIVE

The subject of organizational change has been receiving wide attention in the most recent literature on organizational behavior and organizational theory. Like the Hugo Münsterberg (1913) and Henry Gantt (1908) work on behavior in organizations that preceded the development of the organizational behavior perspective, much of the new writing about change in organizations is not based on familiar humanistic-type assumptions. Change is perhaps the most visible and heated current battleground between proponents of the organizational behavior perspective (and its assumptions, values, and methods) and the advocates of change through manipulation of power and/or perceptions. (For more on this subject, see Shafritz & Ott, 1987, Chapters V and VI.) So, the subject of organizational change provides a fitting, integrative subject with which to close this collection of classic readings in organizational behavior.

For almost thirty years (since about 1960), the organizational behavior perspective's interest in change has been riveted on *planned change*. The organizational behavior/planned change perspective assumptions have constituted the mainstream of organizational behavior literature and practice for so long that it sometimes is hard to think about any other. Thus, it is instructive to first take a brief glance at one of the new viewpoints on organizational change. A comparison between the 1960s-style "planned change" and the 1980s-style "transformational change," makes it easy to understand and appreciate the uniqueness of the planned organizational change assumptions.

FOR COMPARISON: A DIFFERENT VIEW OF ORGANIZATIONAL CHANGE—TRANSFORMATION

The 1984 article by Noel Tichy and David Ulrich, "The Leadership Challenge—A Call for the Transformational Leader" provides an excellent example of the transformational view of organizational change (earlier reprinted in Chapter III, *Leadership*). Tichy and Ulrich call for leaders who are able to manage *planned revolutionary organizational change* ("organizational transformations"). Transformational leaders (or as some authors call them, transformative leaders [Bennis, 1984; Bennis & Nanus, 1985]) are expected to accomplish different magnitudes of organizational change (qualitative and quantitative), using strategies and methods that are not compatible with the mores of the human relations/planned change perspective. Transformative leaders use *transformative power* (Bennis, 1984) or *transforming leadership* (Adams, 1986) literally to transform organizations and their cultures—to alter organizational norms, realities, beliefs, values and assumptions (Allaire & Firsirotu, 1985; Gemmill & Smith, 1985; Kilmann & Covin, 1988). In essence, transformative change is accomplished by violating organizational norms: by creating a new vision of the organization often through conscious manipulation of symbols, and then "selling" the new vision to important stakeholders. The best known model of a transformative leader who accomplished transformative change is Lee Iacocca (Iacocca, 1984).

ASSUMPTIONS ABOUT CHANGE FROM THE ORGANIZATIONAL BEHAVIOR/PLANNED CHANGE PERSPECTIVE

Before transformational leadership and radical change started to attract attention (during the two decades from about 1960 to the early 1980s), the literature and practice of people-oriented organizational change had been dominated by the assumptions, beliefs, and tactics of the organizational behavior perspective. These assumptions, which provided the technological and normative direction for at least two decades of change-oriented organizational behavior theory and practice, were articulated most clearly by Chris Argyris in the first chapter of his seminal 1970 book, *Intervention Theory and Methods,* excerpts from which are reprinted here. Although Argyris's words are descriptive, his tone and his message are very prescriptive.

> Valid information, free choice, and internal commitment are considered integral parts of any intervention activity, no matter what the substantive objectives are (for a change). These three processes are called the primary intervention tasks (p. 17).

As Argyris lists his three primary intervention tasks, his normative assumptions become unmistakably evident:

1. Without valid, usable information (including knowledge of the consequences of alternatives), there can be no free informed choice.
2. Without free informed choice, there can be no personal responsibility for decisions.
3. Without personal responsibility for decisions there can be no internalized commitment to the success of a decision (no *psychological ownership*).

The organizational behavior perspective also embraces strong beliefs about what constitutes organizational effectiveness. These beliefs have further steered the pursuit of organizational improvement away from the manipulation of extrinsic variables such as systems of rewards and punishments. Under this line of reasoning, organizational effectiveness is not defined as *outcomes* but rather as *ongoing process states.* Warren Bennis uses the analogy of *health* or *healthy organization* to communicate his widely accepted concept of organizational process effectiveness. Bennis's criteria for assessing organizational health (or effectiveness) are (in Schein, 1980, p. 232):

1. *Adaptability:* The ability to solve problems and to react with flexibility to changing environmental demands.
2. A *sense of identity:* Knowledge and insight on the part of the organization of what it is, what its goals are, and what it is to do. . . .
3. *Capacity to test reality:* The ability to search out, accurately perceive, and correctly interpret the real properties of the environment, particularly those which have relevance for the functioning of the organization.
4. *Integration:* A fourth, often-cited criterion that in effect underlies the others is a state of "integration" among the subparts of the total organization, such that the parts are not working at cross-purposes.

In a philosophically consistent vein, Schein (1980) identifies the organizational coping processes that are necessary conditions for maintaining or increasing organizational effectiveness (health):

1. The ability to take in and communicate information reliably and validly.
2. . . . internal flexibility and creativity to make changes which are demanded by the information obtained.
3. . . . integration of and commitment to the multiple goals of the organization, from which comes the willingness to change when necessary.
4. . . . an internal climate of support and freedom from threat, since being threatened undermines good communications, reduces flexibility, and stimulates self-protection rather than concern for the total system.
5. . . . the ability to continuously redesign the organization's structure to be congruent with its goal and tasks (pg. 249).

By comparing Bennis's and Schein's necessary conditions for organizational health/effectiveness with those of Hugo Münsterberg (1913) or Frederick Winslow Taylor (1911) (they are summarized in the *Introduction*), the vastness of the differences between these organizational perspectives becomes very evident. The organizational behavior perspective defines organizational effectiveness as a process state—not as it has been defined traditionally in terms of organizational outcomes such as market penetration, profitability, or quantity and/or quality levels of output.

ORGANIZATION DEVELOPMENT

The most dynamic and energetic manifestation of organizational behavior-based change has been the subfield of *organization development* or simply *O.D.* O.D. is a particular form of planned organizational change (or development) that embodies the full set of premises, assumptions, values, and strategies of the organizational behavior perspective. Although all authors' definitions of organization development vary in emphasis, most are quite consistent in substance. For example:

> Organization development is an effort (1) *planned* (2) *organization-wide*, and (3) *managed* from the *top*, to (4) *increase organization effectiveness* and *health* through (5) *planned intervention* in the organization's "processes," using *behavioral-science* knowledge (Beckhard, 1969). (Emphasis in original text.)

and

> Organization development is a long-range effort to improve an organization's problem-solving and renewal processes, particularly through a more effective and collaborative management of organizational culture . . . with the assistance of a change agent, or catalyst, and the use of the theory and technology of applied behavioral science, including action research (French and Bell, 1984).

Organization development is about planned organizational change as a process or strategy. O.D. is as concerned about *how* planned change is implemented as it is about specifically *where* change will lead an organization. Typically, the product or result of O.D. activities is an ongoing set of processes for organizational renewal that are *in-and-of-themselves defined as criteria of organizational effectiveness.* O.D.

assumes that change is purposeful and dynamic, is accomplished through application of behavioral science knowledge, and is accomplished according to carefully prescribed ground rules that are derived from the assumptions of the organizational behavior perspective. Thus, for example, revolutionary and evolutionary change generally are not considered to be within the purview of O.D.

O.D. is concerned with deep, long-lasting, organization-wide change or improvement—not in superficial changes in isolated organizational pockets. This concern for the broad-based and long-term led O.D. practitioners to an interest in the concept of organizational culture long before it became a fashionable management topic in the early 1980s (Ott, 1989).

O.D. practitioners have developed numerous strategies and techniques for improving organizations: Most of them utilize *interventions* facilitated by outsiders (often called *change agents*). Some of the most common strategies include organizational diagnosis, process consultation, team building (in many forms), action research, data feedback, job enlargement, job enrichment, and conflict management. But each author has his or her own preferred tactics. For example, in one of the best known such lists, Schmuck and Miles (1971) include: training and education, process consultation or coaching, confrontation meetings, data feedback, problem solving, goal setting, O.D. task force establishment, and techno-structural activity. Thus, organization development represents a very notable effort to apply an impressive array of research-based social science knowledge within a prescriptive value framework, to ongoing organizational improvement.

The origins of organization development can be traced to several events and movements that started in the 1930s and 1940s:

1. *The Hawthorne studies;*
2. *The sensitivity training* (or "T-group") *movement,* which originated in the late 1940s at the National Training Laboratories, under the leadership of such luminaries as Leland Bradford;
3. *Developments in survey research and feedback techniques,* particularly through the work of Kurt Lewin (1952), which presaged creation of the basic *action research* model of organizational change; and
4. *The socio-technical "school" of research and analysis,* pioneered at the Tavistock Institute by such pioneers as Eric Trist, Kenneth Bamforth, A. K. Rice, and Elliott Jaques.

The *Hawthorne studies* and their importance to understanding organizational behavior-oriented change processes, are discussed extensively in the *Introduction* and in Chapter III, *Leadership.* So, other than referring the reader to Fritz Roethlisberger's "The Hawthorne Experiments" (in Chapter I), we will move on to the remaining three historical trends and events that opened the way for organization development.

The *sensitivity training (or "T-group") movement* had its start in 1946 when Kurt Lewin, Leland Bradford, Ronald Lippitt, and Kenneth Benne collaboratively conducted a training workshop to help improve racial relations and community leadership in New Britain, Connecticut (Bradford, Gibb & Benne, 1964). During their evening staff meetings, they discussed the behavior of workshop participants and the dynamics of events. Several workshop participants asked to join the night discussions, and the results of the process eventually led to the initiation and institutionalization of *T-group technology*. Although the early T-groups focused primarily on individual growth and development, they quickly were adapted for organizational application. T-groups became the method by which organizational members learned how to communicate honestly and directly about facts and feelings (Argyris, 1962). (From the human relations perspective, *feelings are facts.*) Thus, T-groups became a keystone strategy for increasing organizational effectiveness by improving interpersonal communications (e.g., feedback), reducing defensiveness (and thus rigidity), and otherwise helping organizations achieve Bennis's criteria for organizational effectiveness—adaptability, sense of identity, capacity to test reality, and integration—through the development of coping processes that are necessary conditions for maintaining or increasing organizational effectiveness:

1. The ability to take in and communicate information reliably and validly;
2. The internal flexibility and creativity to make changes which are demanded by the information obtained;
3. The integration of and commitment to the multiple goals of the organization, from which comes the willingness to change when necessary;
4. An internal climate of support and freedom from threat; and
5. The ability to continuously redesign the organization's structure to be congruent with its goal and tasks (Schein, 1980, pg. 249).

Without sensitivity training groups (T-groups) there probably would never have been a subfield of organization development.

Survey research and feedback techniques, particularly the work initiated by Kurt Lewin and his associates at the Research Center for Group Dynamics first at M.I.T. and, after his death, at the University of Michigan. Survey research methodology, when combined with feedback/communication techniques, and applied to planned organizational change, resulted in the development of the *action research* model of organizational change—another mainstay of O.D. practitioners and theorists. The action research model is a prescribed process for identifying needs for organizational improvement and creating improvement strategies that utilizes external consultation but creates psychological ownership of problems and solutions by organizational members. Briefly, action research involves:

- Collecting organizational diagnostic-type data, usually either by questionnaire or through consultant interviews;
- Systematically feeding back information to groups of people (organization members) who provided input;
- Discussing what the information means to members and its implications for the organization in order to be certain the "diagnosis" is accurate and to generate psychological ownership of the need for improvement actions;

- Jointly developing action-improvement plans, using the knowledge and skills of the consultant and the insider perspective of members; and generating psychological ownership of the improvement action plan.

The action research model is diagrammed in Figure 1.

The socio-technical approach to research and analysis made its appearance in the late 1940s and early 1950s through a group of organizational researchers at the Tavistock Institute in London who identified a tight link between human and technological factors in the workplace. (See the article by Trist and Bamforth in Chapter IV.) They conclude that neither people nor work/technology takes precedence over the other. Once again, as was true with the Hawthorne studies, the socio-technical group does not assume that the task is to increase productivity by fitting people to the work. Eric Trist and Kenneth Bamforth found that changing the coal-mining technology from small group production to a physically spaced *long-wall* method, disrupts the social structure of the miners and in turn production. By modifying the work (technical) system to allow the social structure to reform, workers returned to helping each other, productivity and morale increased, and accidents and absenteeism decreased. (See "Some Social and Psychological Consequences of the Longwall Method of Coal-Getting" in Chapter IV.)

INTRODUCTION TO THE ARTICLES IN THIS CHAPTER

This chapter's first selection is one of the best known and most frequently quoted experiments on the introduction of organizational change, Lester Coch and John R. P. French's 1948 *Human Relations* article, "Overcoming Resistance to Change." Coch and French studied the relationship between worker participation in design decisions leading to the introduction of changes in work process, and their resistance to changes. The authors used a research design complete with experimental and control groups of pajama folders, pressers, and examiners at the Harwood Manufacturing Corporation in Marion, Virginia. Using Kurt Lewin's concepts of quasi-stationary equilibriums and change force fields, Coch and French conclude that group participation in planning reduces workers' resistance to changes, decreases turnover during and following changes, and accelerates worker re-learning curves (the rapidity with which workers return to full-speed production following process changes).

Whether it is 1948 or 1989, whenever organizational change is discussed, Kurt Lewin heads everyone's list of people who have made invaluable and lasting contributions to our understanding of change processes and dynamics. His 1952 article that is reprinted here, "Group Decision and Social Change," is a condensed restatement of ideas Lewin put forth in one of his best known works, "Frontiers in Group Dynamics: Concept, Method and Reality in Social Science; Social Equilibria and Social Change" (1947). Lewin describes social organizations as resting in a state of stable quasi-stationary equilibrium. In order to effect social change, one must begin with an "analysis of the conditions for 'no change,' that is, for the state of equilibrium." Quite obviously, the now-familiar technique of *force field analysis* evolved

FIGURE 1 ● THE ORGANIZATION DEVELOPMENT ACTION RESEARCH MODEL

Initial Diagnostic and Planning Phase

Preliminary conceptualization of organizational problems by management and consultant
↓
Consultant gathers diagnostic data through, for example, questionnaires, interviews, and observations
↓
Consultant prepares the data for feedback to organization members
↓
Consultant feeds back diagnostic data to organization members
↓
Joint interpretation of the meaning and implications of the data, by organization members and the consultant
↓
Joint action planning by organization members and consultant
↓
Implementation Phase 1 ←

Organization members implement action plans with assistance from consultant as desired or needed
↓
Consultant collects data on progress and effectiveness of action plan implementation
↓
Consultant feeds back data to organization members
↓
Joint interpretation of the meaning and implications of the data by organization members and the consultant
↓
Joint action planning by organization members and consultant
↓
Implementation Phase n

Organization members implement new action plans with assistance from consultant as desired or needed
↓
Repeat steps in Implementation Phase 1

from this concept, in which there are but two basic approaches for accomplishing change: "Adding forces in the desired direction, or by diminishing opposing forces." Lewin argues that the latter approach is less preferable because it tends to be accompanied by a "high state of tension" which in turn causes anger, aggressiveness and a lower propensity to be constructive. In this piece, Lewin articulates his well-known assertion that social change must be viewed as a three-step process of unfreezing, change, and refreezing. If one focuses only on the change process per se, change will be short-lived at best.

From Kurt Lewin's seminal piece, the articles in this chapter jump ahead seventeen years to Harold J. Leavitt's 1965 state-of-the-art overview of organizational change, "Applied Organizational Change in Industry: Structural, Technological and Humanistic Approaches." As the title of the article implies, Leavitt provides a descriptive and explanatory overview of three diverse perspectives of organizational change that received wide attention in the 1960s, and attempts to integrate them. The article concentrates on one of the three, the *humanistic approach* or, as he calls it, *the people approach*. The people approach actually consists of two sub-approaches: *manipulative people approaches*, as epitomized by Dale Carnegie's *How to Win Friends and Influence People*—which Leavitt brushes aside quickly in order to address his true object of attention in this article, the *power-equalization approaches*. (Leavitt credits Carl Rogers's client-centered therapy, T-groups, and the Scanlon plan equity sharing/motivational movements as the geneses of power-equalization approaches.) Leavitt concludes that the power-equalization approaches are "mostly right and mostly insufficient." It seems as though even today, most serious writing about organizational change arrives at a similar conclusion.

In Chapter III, Warren Bennis was described as one who always seems to be on the leading edge of organizational behavior. His 1966 chapter "Applying Behavioral Sciences to Planned Organizational Change," from *Changing Organizations*, is a prime example. Bennis describes organizational change from an organization development slant, as "a crucial link between theory and practice, between knowledge and action," and a "deliberate and collaborative process involving a change-agent and a client-system which are brought together to solve a problem." Bennis explains the differences between the assumptions of planned change and those of operations research (O.R.) that result in widely divergent change purposes, targets, methodologies, and change-agent/client relationships.

Chris Argyris's impact on organizational behavior started about the same time as Warren Bennis's, and the two pursued similar lines of theoretical and research interests for many years. Argyris's 1970 book, *Intervention Theory and Methods* is one of the most comprehensive, widely cited, and enduring works on organizational consulting for change written from an organizational behavior/organization development perspective. A portion of the first chapter from *Intervention Theory and Methods* is reprinted here. The book has remained central to the field because Argyris unambiguously lays out the fundamental tenets that undergird the organizational behavior perspective of change. (Argyris calls the tenets "the three primary intervention tasks." They are listed earlier in this chapter and in Article 43, so they are not repeated here.) These tenets define such fundamentals as the nature of the change-agent/client relationship, the necessity for valid and usable information, and necessary preconditions for organization members to internalize change.

Whereas the articles by Warren Bennis and Chris Argyris are about change processes in general, Herbert Kelman and Donald Warwick's (1978) "The Ethics of Social Intervention: Goals, Means, and Consequences" (which is reprinted here) analyzes one important organizational change issue: the ethics of intervening in ongoing social systems. The authors subsume Bennis's (and others') concepts of planned organizational change under the expanded topic of *social interventions*. Kelman and Warwick concentrate on four steps in any intervention in a social system that are likely to raise important ethical issues:

1. The choice of the change goal,
2. Definition of the change target,
3. Selection of intervention means, and
4. The assessment of the consequences of intervening in ongoing social systems.

Ethical issues inevitably arise during these steps because each involves questions about which competing values will take priority over others.

Rosabeth Moss Kanter has been among the most widely cited observers of organizational phenomena during the last decade. The concluding piece in this chapter (and the book) is from her 1983 bestselling book, *The Change Masters*, which she titled "The Architecture of Culture and Strategy Change." The core of Kanter's *architecture of change* is a set of five *building blocks of change* that permit change to progress beyond innovation to institutionalization (Kanter also sometimes refers to these building blocks as *forces*):

1. Departures from tradition,
2. A crisis or galvanizing event,
3. Strategic decisions,
4. Individual "prime movers," and
5. Action vehicles.

Kanter concludes that the "tools of change masters are creative and interactive; they have an intellectual, a conceptual, and a cultural aspect." Change masters are the right people (people with ideas), in the right place (integrative environments that support innovation), at the right time. According to Kanter, *right times* are:

> Those moments in the flow of organizational history when it is possible to reconstruct reality on the basis of accumulated innovations to shape a more productive and successful future (pg. 306).

REFERENCES

Adams, J. D. (Ed.). (1986). *Transforming leadership: From vision to results.* Alexandria, VA: Miles River Press.

Allaire, Y., & Firsirotu, M. (Spring, 1985). How to implement radical strategies in large organizations. *Sloan Management Review, 26*(3), 19–34.

Argyris, C. (1962). *Interpersonal competence and organizational effectiveness.* Homewood, IL: The Dorsey Press and Richard D. Irwin.

Argyris, C. (1970). *Intervention theory and methods.* Reading, MA: Addison-Wesley.

Beckhard, R. (1969). *Organization development: Strategies and models.* Reading, MA: Addison-Wesley Publishing Company.

Beckhard, R., & Harris, R. T. (1977). *Organizational transitions: Managing complex change.* Reading, MA: Addison-Wesley Publishing Co.

Bennis, W. G. (1966). Applying behavioral sciences to planned organizational change. In, W. G. Bennis, *Changing organizations* (pp. 81–94). New York: McGraw-Hill Book Company.

Bennis, W. G. (1969). *Organization development: Its nature, origins and prospects.* Reading, MA: Addison-Wesley Publishing Company.

Bennis, W. G. (1984). Transformative power and leadership. In, T. J. Sergiovanni & J. E. Corbally (Eds.), *Leadership and organizational culture* (pp. 64–71). Urbana, IL: University of Illinois Press.

Bennis, W. G., Benne, K. D., and Chin, R. (1961). *The planning of change.* New York: Holt, Rinehart & Winston.

Bennis, W. G., & Nanus, B. (1985). *Leaders.* New York: Harper & Row Publishers.

Bradford, L., Gibb, J. R., & Benne, K. D. (Eds.). (1964). *T-group theory and laboratory method; innovation in re-education.* New York: Wiley.

Coch, L., & French, J. R. P., Jr. (August, 1948). Overcoming resistance to change. *Human Relations,* 512–532.

Dyer, W. G. (1983). *Contemporary issues in management and organization development.* Reading, MA: Addison-Wesley Publishing Co.

Dyer, W. G. (1984). *Strategies for managing change.* Reading, MA: Addison-Wesley Publishing Co.

French, W. L., & Bell, C. H., Jr. (1984). *Organization development* (3rd ed.). Englewood Cliffs, NJ: Prentice-Hall.

French, W. L., Bell, C. H., Jr., & Zawacki, R. A. (Eds.). (1983). *Organization development: Theory, practice, and research* (rev. ed.). Plano, TX: Business Publications, Inc.

Gantt, H. L. (1908). Training workmen in habits of industry and cooperation. Paper presented to the American Society of Mechanical Engineers.

Gemmill, G., & Smith, C. (1985). A dissipative structure model of organization transformation. *Human Relations, 38,* 751–766.

Iacocca, L. (1984). *Iacocca, an autobiography.* Toronto: Bantam Books.

Jaffee, D. T., Scott, C. D., & Orioli, E. M. (1986). Visionary leadership: Moving a company from burnout to inspired performance. In, J. D. Adams (Ed.), *Transforming leadership: From vision to results.* Alexandria, VA: Miles River Press.

Jaques, E. (1951). *The changing culture of a factory.* London, UK: Tavistock Publications.

Kanter, R. M. (1983). *The change masters.* New York: Simon & Schuster.

Kelman, H. C., & Warwick, D. (1978). The ethics of social intervention: Goals, means, and consequences. In H. C. Bermant, H. C. Kelman, & D. P. Warwick, (Eds.), *The ethics of social intervention* (pp. 3–27). New York: Hemisphere Publishing Company.

Kilmann, R. H., & Covin, T. J. (Eds.). (1988). *Corporate transformation.* San Francisco: Jossey-Bass.

Kozmetsky, G. (1985). *Transformational management.* Cambridge, MA: Ballinger Publishing Company.

Leavitt, H. J. (1965). Applied organizational change in industry: Structural, technological, and humanistic approaches. In, J. G. March (Ed.), *Handbook of organizations* (pp. 1144–1170). Chicago: Rand McNally.

Lewin, K. (June, 1947). Frontiers in group dynamics: Concept, method and reality in social science; Social equilibria and social change. *Human Relations, 1*(1).

Lewin, K. (1952). Quasi-stationary social equilibria and the problem of permanent change. In, G. E. Swanson, T. N. Newcomb, & E. L. Hartley (Eds.), *Readings in social psychology* (rev. ed.) (pp. 207–211). New York: Holt, Rinehart & Winston.

Münsterberg, H. (1913). *Psychology and industrial efficiency.* Boston: Houghton Mifflin Company.

Ott, J. S. (1989). *The organizational culture perspective.* Chicago: The Dorsey Press.

Rice, A. K. (1953). Productivity and social organization in an Indian weaving shed: An examination of some aspects of the socio-technical system of an experimental automatic loom shed. *Human Relations, 6,* 297–329.

Schein, E. H. (1969). *Process consultation: Its role in organization development.* Reading, MA: Addison-Wesley Publishing Co.

Schein, E. H. (1980). *Organizational psychology* (3rd ed.). Englewood Cliffs, NJ: Prentice-Hall, Inc.

Schmuck, R. A., & Miles, M. B. (Eds.). (1971). *Organization development in schools.* Palo Alto, CA: National Press Books.

Shafritz, J. M., & Ott, J. S. (1987). *Classics of organization theory* (2d ed. rev. and expanded). Chicago: The Dorsey Press.

Taylor, F. W. (1911). *The principles of scientific management.* New York: W. W. Norton.

Tichy, N. M., & Ulrich, D. O. (Fall, 1984). The leadership challenge—A call for the transformational leader. *Sloan Management Review, 26*(1), 59–68.

Trist, E., & Bamforth, K. W. (1951). Some social and psychological consequences of the longwall method of coal-getting. *Human Relations, 4,* 3–38.

Varney, G. H. (1977). *Organization development for managers.* Reading, MA: Addison-Wesley Publishing Co.

37

Overcoming Resistance to Change[1]

Lester Coch & John R. P. French, Jr.

INTRODUCTION

It has always been characteristic of American industry to change products and methods of doing jobs as often as competitive conditions or engineering progress dictates. This makes frequent changes in an individual's work necessary. In addition, the markedly greater turnover and absenteeism of recent years result in unbalanced production lines which again makes for frequent shifting of individuals from one job to another. One of the most serious production problems faced at the Harwood Manufacturing Corporation has been the resistance of production workers to the necessary changes in methods and jobs. This resistance expressed itself in several ways, such as grievances about the piece rates that went with the new methods, high turnover, very low efficiency, restriction of output, and marked aggression against management. Despite these undesirable effects, it was

necessary that changes in methods and jobs continue.

Efforts were made to solve this serious problem by the use of a special monetary allowance for transfers, by trying to enlist the cooperation and aid of the union, by making necessary layoffs on the basis of efficiency, etc. In all cases, these actions did little or nothing to overcome the resistance to change. On the basis of these data, it was felt that the pressing problem of resistance to change demanded further research for its solution. From the point of view of factory management, there were two purposes to the research: (1) Why do people resist change so strongly? and (2) What can be done to overcome this resistance?

Starting with a series of observations about the behavior of changed groups, the first step in the overall program was to devise a preliminary theory to account for the resistance to change. Then on the basis of the theory, a real life action experiment was devised and conducted within the context of the factory situation. Finally, the results of the experiment were interpreted in the light of the preliminary theory and the new data.

BACKGROUND

The main plant of the Harwood Manufacturing Corporation, where the present research was done, is located in the

[1]Grateful acknowledgements are made by the authors to Dr. Alfred J. Marrow, president of the Harwood Manufacturing Corporation, and to the entire Harwood staff for their valuable aid and suggestions in this study.

The authors have drawn repeatedly from the works and concepts of Kurt Lewin for both the action and theoretical phases of this study.

Many of the leadership techniques used in the experimental group meetings were techniques developed at the first National Training Laboratory for Group Development held at Bethel, Maine, in the summer of 1947. Both authors attended this laboratory.

Source: From "Overcoming Resistance to Change" by Lester Coch and John R. P. French, Jr., in *Human Relations* (1948), pp. 512–532. Reprinted by permission of Plenum Publishing Corporation.

small town of Marion, Virginia. The plant produces pajamas and, like most sewing plants, employs mostly women. The plant's population is about 500 women and 100 men. The workers are recruited from the rural, mountainous areas surrounding the town, and are usually employed without previous industrial experience. The average age of the workers is 23; the average education is eight years of grammar school.

The policies of the company in regard to labor relations are liberal and progressive. A high value has been placed on fair and open dealing with the employees and they are encouraged to take up any problems or grievances with the management at any time. Every effort is made to help foremen find effective solutions to their problems in human relations, using conferences and role-playing methods. Carefully planned orientation, designed to help overcome the discouragement and frustrations attending entrance upon the new and unfamiliar situation, is used. Plant-wide votes are conducted where possible to resolve problems affecting the whole working population. The company has invested both time and money in employee services such as industrial music, health services, lunchroom, and recreation programs. In the same spirit, the management has been conscious of the importance of public relations in the local community; they have supported both financially and otherwise any activity which would build up good will for the company. As a result of these policies, the company has enjoyed good labor relations since the day it commenced operations.

Harwood employees work on an individual incentive system. Piece rates are set by time study and are expressed in terms of units. One unit is equal to one minute of standard work: 60 units per hour equal the standard efficiency rating. Thus, if on a particular operation the piece rate for one dozen is 10 units, the operator would have to produce 6 dozen per hour to achieve the standard efficiency rating of 60 units per hour. The skill required to reach 60 units per hour is great. On some jobs, an average trainee may take 34 weeks to reach the skill level necessary to perform at 60 units per hour. Her first few weeks of work may be on an efficiency level of 5 to 20 units per hour.

The amount of pay received is directly proportional to the weekly average efficiency rating achieved. Thus, an operator with an average efficiency rating of 75 units per hour (25 per cent more than standard) would receive 25 per cent more than base pay. However, there are two minimum wages below which no operator may fall. The first is the plantwide minimum, the hiring-in wage; the second is a minimum wage based on six months' employment and is 22 per cent higher than the plantwide minimum wage. Both minima are smaller than the base pay for 60 units per hour efficiency rating.

The rating of every piece worker is computed every day and the results are published in a daily record of production which is shown to every operator. This daily record of production for each production line carries the names of all the operators on that line arranged in rank order of efficiency rating, with the highest rating girl at the top of the list. The supervisors speak to each operator each day about her unit ratings. Because of the above procedures, many operators do not claim credit for all the work done in a given day. Instead, they save a few of the piece rate tickets as a "cushion" against a rainy day when they may not feel well or may have a great amount of machine trouble.

When it is necessary to change an operator from one type of work to another, a transfer bonus is given. This bonus is so designed that the changed operator who relearns at an average rate will suffer no loss in earnings after change. Despite this allowance, the general attitudes toward job changes in the factory are markedly negative. Such expressions as, "When you make your units (standard production), they change your job," are all too frequent. Many operators refuse to change, preferring to quit.

THE TRANSFER LEARNING CURVE

An analysis of the after-change relearning curve of several hundred experienced operators rating standard or better prior to change showed that 38 per cent of the changed operators recovered to the standard unit rating of 60 units per hour. The other 62 per cent either became chronically sub-standard operators or quit during the relearning period.

The average relearning curve for those who recover to standard production on the simplest type job in the plant (Figure I) is eight weeks long, and, when smoothed, provides the basis for the transfer bonus. The bonus is the percent difference between this expected efficiency rating and the standard of 60 units per hour. Progress is slow for the first two or three weeks, as the relearning curve shows, and then accelerates markedly to about 50 units per hour with an increase of 15 units in two weeks. Another slow progress area is encountered at 50 units per hour, the operator improving only 3 units in two weeks. The curve ends in a spurt of 10 units progress in one week, a marked goal gradient behavior. The individual curves, of course, vary widely in length according to the simplicity or difficulty

of the job to be relearned; but in general, the successful curves are consistent with the average curve in form.

It is interesting to note in Figure I that the relearning period for an experienced operator is longer than the learning period for a new operator. This is true despite the fact that the majority of transfers—the failures who never recover to standard—are omitted from the curve. However, changed operators rarely complain of "wanting to do it the old way," etc., after the first week or two of change; and time and motion studies show few false moves after the first week of change. From this evidence it is deduced that proactive inhibition or the interference of previous habits in learning the new skill is either non-existent or very slight after the first two weeks of change.

Figure II, which presents the relearning curves for 41 experienced operators who were changed to very difficult jobs, gives a comparison between the recovery rates for operators making standard or better prior to change, and those below standard prior to change. Both classes of operators dropped to a little below 30 units per hour and recovered at a very slow but similar rate. These curves show a general (though by no means universal) phenomenon; that the efficiency rating prior to change does not indicate a faster or slower recovery rate after change.

A PRELIMINARY THEORY OF RESISTANCE TO CHANGE

The fact that relearning after transfer to a new job is so often slower than initial learning on first entering the factory would indicate, on the face of it, that the resistance to change and the slow relearning is primarily a motivational problem. The similar recovery rates

FIGURE I • A COMPARISON OF THE LEARNING CURVE FOR NEW, INEXPERIENCED EMPLOYEES WITH THE RELEARNING CURVE FOR ONLY THOSE TRANSFERS (38 PER CENT) WHO EVENTUALLY RECOVER TO STANDARD PRODUCTION.

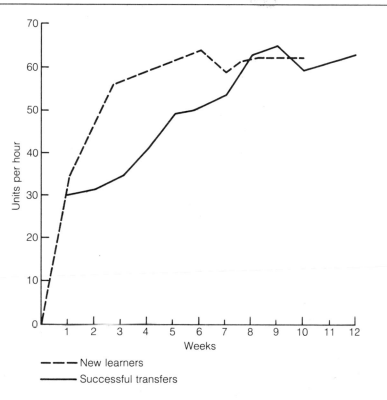

of the skilled and unskilled operators shown in Figure II tend to confirm the hypothesis that skill is a minor factor and motivation is the major determinant of the rate of recovery. Earlier experiments at Harwood by Alex Bavelas demonstrated this point conclusively. He found that the use of group decision techniques on operators who had just been transferred resulted in very marked increases in the rate of relearning, even though no skill training was given and there were no other changes in working conditions (2).

Interviews with operators who have been transferred to a new job reveal a common pattern of feelings and attitudes which are distinctly different from those of successful non-transfers. In addition to resentment against the management for transferring them, the employees typically show feelings of frustration, loss of hope of ever regaining their former level of production and status in the factory, feelings of failure, and a very low level of aspiration. In this respect these transferred operators are similar to the chronically slow workers studied previously.

Earlier unpublished research at Har-

FIGURE II • THE DROP IN PRODUCTION AND THE RATE OF RECOVERY AFTER TRANSFER FOR SKILLFUL AND FOR SUB-STANDARD OPERATORS.

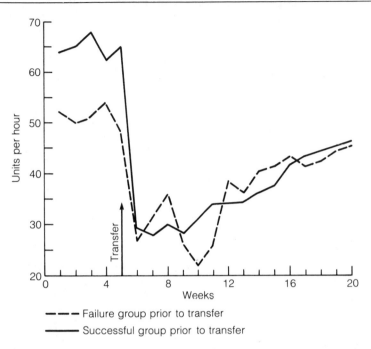

– – – Failure group prior to transfer

——— Successful group prior to transfer

wood has shown that the non-transferred employees generally have an explicit goal of reaching and maintaining an efficiency rating of 60 units per hour. A questionnaire administered to several groups of operators indicated that a large majority of them accept as their goal the management's quota of 60 units per hour. This standard of production is the level of aspiration according to which the operators measure their own success or failure; and those who fall below standard lose status in the eyes of their fellow employees. Relatively few operators set a goal appreciably above 60 units per hour.

The actual production records confirm the effectiveness of this goal of standard production. The distribution of the total population of operators in accordance with their production levels is by no means a normal curve. Instead there is a very large number of operators who rate 60 to 63 units per hour and relatively few operators who rate just above or just below this range. Thus we may conclude that:

1. There is a force acting on the operator in the direction of achieving a production level of 60 units per hour or more. It is assumed that the strength of this driving force (acting on an operator below standard) increases as she gets nearer the goal—a typical goal gradient (see Figure I).

On the other hand restraining forces operate to hinder or prevent her from reaching this goal. These restraining forces consist among other things of the difficulty of the job in relation to the operator's level of skill. Other things being equal, the faster an operator is sewing the more difficult it is to increase her speed by a given amount. Thus we may conclude that:

2. The strength of the restraining force hindering higher production increases with increasing level of production.

In line with previous studies, it is assumed that the conflict of these two opposing forces—the driving force corresponding to the goal of reaching 60 and the restraining force of the difficulty of the job—produces frustration. In such a conflict situation, the strength of frustration will depend on the strength of these forces. If the restraining force against increasing production is weak, then the frustration will be weak. But if the driving force toward higher production (i.e., the motivation) is weak, then the frustration will also be weak. Probably both of the conflicting forces must be above a certain minimum strength before any frustration is produced; for all goal-directed activity involves some degree of conflict of this type, yet a person is not usually frustrated so long as he is making satisfactory progress toward his goal. Consequently we assume that:

3. The strength of frustration is a function of the weaker of these two opposing forces, provided that the weaker force is stronger than a certain minimum necessary to produce frustration (1).

An analysis of the effects of such frustration in the factory showed that it resulted, among other things, in high turnover and absenteeism. The rate of turnover for successful operators with efficiency ratings above standard was much lower than for unsuccessful operators. Likewise, operators on the more difficult jobs quit more frequently than those on the easier jobs. Presumably the effect of being transferred is a severe frustration which should result in similar attempts to escape from the field.

In line with this theory of frustration, and the finding that job turnover is one resultant of frustration, an analysis was made of the turnover rate of transferred operators as compared with the rate among operators who had not been transferred recently. For the year September, 1946, to September, 1947, there were one hundred and ninety-eight operators who had not been transferred recently, that is, within the thirty-four week period allowed for relearning after transfer. There was a second group of eighty-five operators who had been transferred recently, that is, within the time allowed for relearning the new job. Each of these two groups was divided into seven classifications according to their unit rating at the time of quitting. For each classification the per cent turnover per month, based on the total number of employees in that classification, was computed.

The results are given in Figure III. Both the levels of turnover and the form of the curves are strikingly different for the two groups. Among operators who have not been transferred recently the average turnover per month is about 4½ per cent; among recent transfers the monthly turnover is nearly 12 per cent. Consistent with the previous studies, both groups show a very marked drop in the turnover curve after an operator becomes a success by reaching 60 units per hour or standard production. However, the form of the curves at lower unit ratings is markedly different for the two groups. The non-transferred operators show a gradually increasing rate of turnover up to a rating of 55 to 59 units per hour. The transferred operators, on the other hand,

FIGURE III • THE RATE OF TURNOVER AT VARIOUS LEVELS OF PRODUCTION FOR TRANSFERS AS COMPARED WITH NON-TRANSFERS.

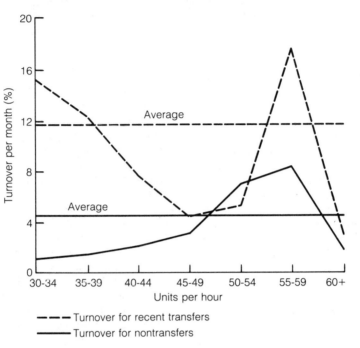

- - - Turnover for recent transfers
——— Turnover for nontransfers

show a high peak at the lowest unit rating of 30 to 34 units per hour, decreasing sharply to a low point at 45 to 49 units per hour. Since most changed operators drop to a unit rating of around 30 units per hour when changed and then drop no further, it is obvious that the rate of turnover was highest for these operators just after they were changed and again much later just before they reached standard. Why?

It is assumed that the strength of frustration for an operator who has *not* been transferred gradually increases because both the driving force towards the goal of reaching 60 and the restraining force of the difficulty of the job increase with increasing unit rating. This is in line with hypotheses (1), (2) and (3) above.

For the transferred operator on the other hand the frustration is greatest immediately after transfer when the contrast of her present status with her former status is most evident. At this point the strength of the restraining forces is at a maximum because the difficulty is unusually great due to proactive inhibition. Then as she overcomes the interference effects between the two jobs and learns the new job, the difficulty and the frustration gradually decrease and the rate of turnover declines until the operator reaches 45–49 units per hour. Then at higher levels of production the difficulty starts to increase again and the transferred operator shows the same peak in frustration and turnover at 55–59 units per hour.

FIGURE IV • THE EFFECTS OF PARTICIPATION THROUGH
REPRESENTATION (GROUP 1) AND OF TOTAL PARTICIPATION
(GROUPS 2 AND 3) ON RECOVERY AFTER AN EASY TRANSFER.

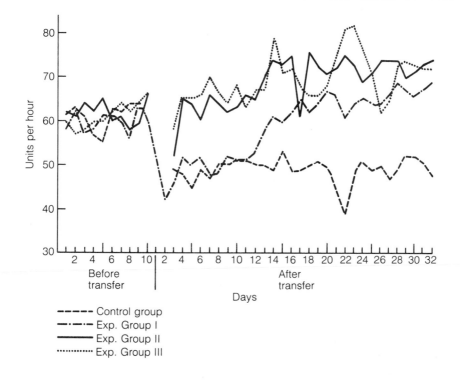

Though our theory of frustration explains the forms of the two turnover curves in Figure IV, it hardly seems adequate to account for the markedly higher level of turnover for transfers as compared to non-transfers. On the basis of the difficulty of the job, it is especially difficult to explain the higher rate of turnover at 55–59 units per hour for transfers. Evidently additional forces are operating.

Another factor which seems to affect recovery rates of changed operators is the amount of we-feeling. Observations seem to indicate that a strong psychological sub-group with negative attitudes toward management will display the strongest resistance to change. On the other hand, changed groups with high we-feeling and positive cooperative attitudes are the best relearners. Collections of individuals with little or no we-feeling display some resistance to change but not so strongly as the groups with high we-feeling and negative attitudes toward management. However, turnover for the individual transfers is much higher than in the latter groups. This phenomenon of the relationship between we-feeling and resistance to change is so overt that for years the general policy of the management of the plant was never to change a group as a group but rather to scatter the individuals in different areas throughout the factory.

An analysis of turnover records for changed operators with high we-feeling showed a 4 per cent turnover rate per month at 30 to 34 units per hour, not significantly higher than in unchanged operators but significantly lower than in changed operators with little or no we-feeling. However, the acts of aggression are far more numerous among operators with high we-feeling than among operators with little we-feeling. Since both types of operators experience the same frustration as individuals but react to it so differently, it is assumed that the effect of the in-group feeling is to set up a restraining force against leaving the group and perhaps even to set up driving forces toward staying in the group. In these circumstances, one would expect some alternative reaction to frustration rather than escape from the field. This alternative is aggression. Strong we-feeling provides strength so that members dare to express aggression which would otherwise be suppressed.

One common result in a sub-group with strong we-feeling is the setting of a group standard concerning production. Where the attitudes toward management are antagonistic, this group standard may take the form of a definite restriction of production to a given level. This phenomenon of restriction is particularly likely to happen in a group that has been transferred to a job where a new piece rate has been set; for they have some hope that if production never approaches the standard, the management may change the piece rate in their favor.

A group standard can exert extremely strong forces on an individual member of a small sub-group. That these forces can have a powerful effect on production is indicated in the production record of one presser during a period of forty days.

In the Group	
Days	Production per Day
1–3	46
4–6	52
7–9	53
10–12	56
Scapegoating begins	
13–16	55
17–20	48
Becomes a single worker	
21–24	83
25–28	92
29–32	92
33–36	91
37–40	92

For the first twenty days she was working in a group of other pressers who were producing at the rate of about 50 units per hour. Starting on the thirteenth day, when she reached standard production and exceeded the production of the other members, she became a scapegoat of the group. During this time her production decreased toward the level of the remaining members of the group. After twenty days the group had to be broken up and all the other members were transferred to other jobs leaving only the scapegoat operator. With the removal of the group, the group standard was no longer operative; and the production of the one remaining operator shot up from the level of about 45 to 96 units per hour in a period of four days. Her production stabilized at a level of about 92 and stayed there for the remainder of the twenty days. Thus it is clear that the motivational forces induced in the individual by a strong sub-group may be more powerful than those induced by management.

THE EXPERIMENT

On the basis of the preliminary theory that resistance to change is a combination of an individual reaction to frustration with strong group-induced forces it seemed that the most appropriate methods for overcoming the resistance to change would be group methods. Consequently an experiment was designed employing two variations of democratic procedure in handling groups to be transferred. The first variation involved participation through representation of the workers in designing the changes to be made in the jobs. The second variation consisted of total participation by all members of the group in designing the changes. A third control group was also used. Two experimental groups received the total participation treatment. The three experimental groups and the control group were roughly matched with respect to: (1) the efficiency ratings of the groups before transfer; (2) the degree of change involved in the transfer; (3) the amount of we-feeling observed in the groups.

In no case was more than a minor change in the work routines and time allowances made. The control group, the eighteen hand pressers, had formerly stacked their work in one-half dozen lots on a flat piece of cardboard the size of the finished product. The new job called for stacking their work in one half dozen lots in a box the size of the finished product. The box was located in the same place the cardboard had been. An additional two minutes per dozen was allowed (by the time study) for this new part of the job. This represented a total job change of 8.8 per cent.

Experimental group I, the thirteen pajama folders, had formerly folded coats with pre-folded pants. The new job called for the folding of coats with unfolded pants. An additional 1.8 minutes per dozen was allowed (by time study) for this new part of the job. This represented a total job change of 9.4 per cent.

Experimental groups 2 and 3, consisting of eight and seven pajama examiners respectively, had formerly clipped threads from the entire garment and examined every seam. The new job called for pulling only certain threads off and examining every seam. An average of 1.2 minutes per dozen was subtracted (by time study) from the total time on these two jobs. This represented a total job change of 8 per cent.

The control group of hand pressers went through the usual factory routine when they were changed. The production department modified the job, and a new piece rate was set. A group meeting was then held in which the control group was told that the change was necessary because of competitive conditions, and that a new piece rate had been set. The new piece rate was thoroughly explained by the time study man, questions were answered, and the meeting dismissed.

Experimental group 1 was changed in a different manner. Before any changes took place, a group meeting was held with all the operators to be changed. The need for the change was presented as dramatically as possible, showing two identical garments produced in the factory; one was produced in 1946 and had sold for 100 per cent more than its fellow in 1947. The group was asked to identify the cheaper one and could not do it. This demonstration effectively shared with the group the entire problem of the necessity of cost reduction. A general agreement was reached that a savings could be effected by removing the "frills" and "fancy" work from the garment without affecting the folders' opportunity to achieve a high efficiency rating. Management then presented a plan to set the new job and piece rate:

1. Make a check study of the job as it was being done.
2. Eliminate all unnecessary work.
3. Train several operators in the correct methods.
4. Set the piece rate by time studies on these specially trained operators.
5. Explain the new job rate to all the operators.
6. Train all operators in the new method so they can reach a high rate of production within a short time.

The group approved this plan (though no formal group decision was reached), and chose the operators to be specially trained. A sub-meeting with the "special" operators was held immediately following the meeting with the entire group. They displayed a cooperative and interested attitude and immediately presented many good suggestions. This attitude carried over into the working out of the details of the new job; and when the new job and piece rates were set, the "special" operators referred to the resultants as "our job," "our rate," etc. The new job and piece rates were presented at a second group meeting to all the operators involved. The "special" operators served to train the other operators on the new job.

Experimental groups 2 and 3 went through much the same kind of change meetings. The groups were smaller than experimental group 1, and a more intimate atmosphere was established. The need for a change was once again made dramatically clear; the same general plan was presented by management. However, since the groups were small, all operators were chosen as "special"

operators; that is, all operators were to participate directly in the designing of the new jobs, and all operators would be studied by the time study man. It is interesting to note that in the meetings with these two groups, suggestions were immediately made in such quantity that the stenographer had great difficulty in recording them. The group approved of the plans, but again no formal group decision was reached.

Results

The results of the experiment are summarized in graphic form in Figure IV. The gaps in the production curves occur because these groups were paid on a time-work basis for a day or two. The control group improved little beyond their early efficiency ratings. Resistance developed almost immediately after the change occurred. Marked expressions of aggression against management occurred, such as conflict with the methods engineer, expression of hostility against the supervisor, deliberate restriction of production, and lack of cooperation with the supervisor. There were 17 per cent quits in the first forty days. Grievances were filed about the piece rate, but when the rate was checked, it was found to be a little "loose."

Experimental group 1 showed an unusually good relearning curve. At the end of fourteen days, the group averaged 61 units per hour. During the fourteen days, the attitude was co-operative and permissive. They worked well with the methods engineer, the training staff, and the supervisor. (The supervisor was the same person in the cases of the control group and experimental group 1). There were no quits in this group in the first forty days. This group might have presented a better learning record if work had not been scarce during the first seven days. There was one act of aggression against the supervisor recorded in the first forty days. It is interesting to note that the three special representative operators in experimental group 1 recovered at about the same rate as the rest of their group.

Experimental groups 2 and 3 recovered faster than experimental group 1. After a slight drop on the first day of change, the efficiency ratings returned to a pre-change level and showed sustained progress thereafter to a level about 14 per cent higher than the pre-change level. No additional training was provided them after the second day. They worked well with their supervisors and no indications of aggression were observed from these groups. There were no quits in either of these groups in the first forty days.

A fourth experimental group, composed of only two sewing operators, was transferred by the total participation technique. Their new job was one of the most difficult jobs in the factory, in contrast to the easy jobs for the control group and the other three experimental groups. As expected, the total participation technique again resulted in an unusually fast recovery rate and a final level of production well above the level before transfer. Because of the difficulty of the new job, however, the rate of recovery was slower than for experimental groups 2 and 3, but faster than for experimental group 1.

In the first experiment, the control group made no progress after transfer for a period of 32 days. At the end of this period the group was broken up and the individuals were reassigned to new jobs scattered throughout the factory. Two and a half months after their dispersal, the thirteen remaining members of the original control group were again brought together as a group for a second experiment.

This second experiment consisted of transferring the control group to a new job, using the total participation technique in meetings which were similar to those held with experimental groups 2 and 3. The new job was a pressing job of comparable difficulty to the new job in the first experiment. On the average it involved about the same degree of change. In the meetings no reference was made to the previous behavior of the group on being transferred.

The results of the second experiment were in sharp contrast to the first (see Figure V). With the total participation technique, the same control group now recovered rapidly to their previous efficiency rating, and, like the other groups under this treatment, continued on beyond it to a new high level of production. There was no aggression or turnover in the group for 19 days after change, a marked modification of their previous behavior after transfer. Some anxiety concerning their seniority status was expressed, but this was resolved in a meeting of their elected delegate, the union business agent, and a management representative. It should be noted in Figure V that the pre-change level on the second experiment is just above 60 units per hour; thus the individual transfers had progressed to just above standard during the two and a half months between the two experiments.

INTERPRETATION

The purpose of this section is to explain the drop in production resulting from transfer, the differential recovery rates of the control and the experimental groups, the increases beyond their former levels of production by the experimental groups, and the differential rates of turnover and aggression.

The first experiment showed that the rate of recovery is directly proportional to the amount of participation, and that

FIGURE V • A COMPARISON OF THE EFFECT OF THE CONTROL
PROCEDURE WITH THE TOTAL PARTICIPATION PROCEDURE ON
THE SAME GROUP.

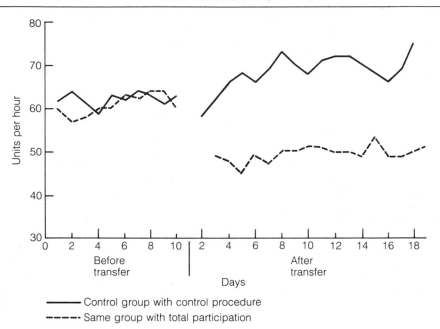

———— Control group with control procedure
– – – – · Same group with total participation

the rates of turnover and aggression are inversely proportional to the amount of participation. The second experiment demonstrated more conclusively that the results obtained depended on the experimental treatment rather than on personality factors like skill or aggressiveness, for identical individuals yielded markedly different results in the control treatment as contrasted with the total participation treatment.

Apparently total participation has the same type of effect as participation through representation, but the former has a stronger influence. In regard to recovery rates, this difference is not unequivocal because the experiment was unfortunately confounded. Right after transfer, experimental group number 1 had insufficient material to work on for a period of seven days. Hence their slower recovery during this period is at least in part due to insufficient work. In succeeding days, however, there was an adequate supply of work and the differential recovery rate still persisted. Therefore we are inclined to believe that participation through representation results in slower recovery than does total participation.

Before discussing the details of why participation produces high morale, we will consider the nature of production levels. In examining the production records of hundreds of individuals and groups in this factory, one is struck by the constancy of the level of production. Though differences among individuals in efficiency rating are very large, nearly every experienced operator maintains a fairly steady level of production given constant physical conditions.

Frequently the given level will be maintained despite rather large changes in technical working conditions.

As Lewin has pointed out, this type of production can be viewed as a quasistationary process—in the on-going work the operator is forever sewing new garments, yet the level of the process remains relatively stationary. Thus there are constant characteristics of the production process permitting the establishment of general laws.

In studying production as a quasi-stationary equilibrium, we are concerned with two types of forces: (1) forces on production in a downward direction, (2) forces on production in an upward direction. In this situation we are dealing with a variety of both upward forces tending to increase the level of production and downward forces tending to decrease the level of production. However, in the present experiment we have no method of measuring independently all of the component forces either downward or upward. These various component forces upward are combined into one resultant force upward. Likewise the several downward component forces combine into one resultant force downward. We can infer a good deal about the relative strengths of these resultant forces.

Where we are dealing with a quasistationary equilibrium, the resultant forces upward and the forces downward are opposite in direction and equal in strength at the equilibrium level. Of course either resultant forces may fluctuate over a short period of time, so that the forces may not be equally balanced at a given moment. However, over a longer period of time and on the average the forces balance out. Fluctuations from the average occur but there is a tendency to return to the average level.

Just before being transferred, all of the groups in both experiments had reached a stable equilibrium level at just above the standard production of 60 units per hour. This level was equal to the average efficiency rating for the entire factory during the period of the experiments. Since this production level remained constant, neither increasing nor decreasing, we may be sure that the strength of the resultant force upward was equal to the strength of the resultant force downward. This equilibrium of forces was maintained over the period of time when production was stationary at this level. But the forces changed markedly after transfer, and these new constellations of forces were distinctly different for the control and the experimental groups.

For the control group the period after transfer is a quasi-stationary equilibrium at a lower level, and the forces do not change during the period of thirty days. The resultant force upward remains equal to the resultant force downward and the level of production remains constant. The force field for this group is represented schematically in Figure VI. Only the resultant forces are shown. The length of the vector represents the strength of the force; and the point of the arrow represents the point of application of the force, that is, the production level and the time at which the force applies. Thus the forces are equal and opposite only at the level of 50 units per hour. At higher levels of production the forces downward are greater than the forces upward; and at lower levels of production the forces upward are stronger than the forces downward. Thus there is a tendency for the equilibrium to be maintained at an efficiency rating of 50.

The situation for the experimental groups after transfer can be viewed as a quasi-stationary equilibrium of a different type. Figure VII gives a schematic

**FIGURE VI • A SCHEMATIC DIAGRAM OF THE QUASI-STATIONARY
EQUILIBRIUM FOR THE CONTROL GROUP AFTER TRANSFER.**

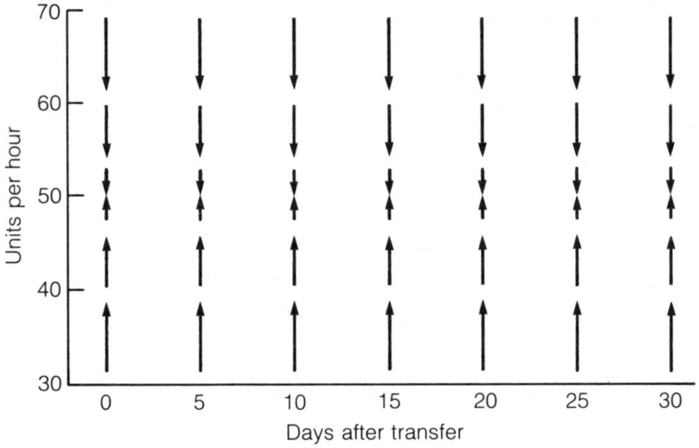

diagram of the resultant forces for the experimental groups. At any given level of production, such as 50 units per hour or 60 units per hour, both the resultant forces upward and the resultant forces downward change over the period of thirty days. During this time the point of equilibrium, which starts at 50 units per hour, gradually rises until it reaches a level of over 70 units per hour after thirty days. Yet here again the equilibrium level has the character of a "central force field" where at any point in the total field the resultant of the upward and the downward forces is in the direction of the equilibrium level.

To understand how the difference between the experimental and the control treatments produced the differences in force fields represented in Figures VI and VII, it is not sufficient to consider only the resultant forces. We must also look at the component forces for each resultant force.

There are three main component forces influencing production in a downward direction: (1) the difficulty of the job; (2) a force corresponding to avoidance of strain; (3) a force corresponding to a group standard to restrict production to a given level. The resultant force upward in the direction of greater production is composed of three additional component forces; (1) the force corresponding to the goal of standard production; (2) a force corresponding to pressures induced by the management through supervision; (3) a force corresponding to a group standard of competition. Let us examine each of these six component forces.

1. Job Difficulty. For all operators the difficulty of the job is one of the forces downward on production. The difficulty of the job, of course, is relative to the skill of the operator. The given job may be very difficult for an unskilled operator but relatively easy for a highly skilled one. In the case of a transfer a new element of difficulty enters. For some time the new job is much more difficult, for the operator is unskilled at that particular job. In addition to the difficulty experienced by any

FIGURE VII • A SCHEMATIC DIAGRAM OF THE QUASI-
STATIONARY EQUILIBRIUM FOR THE EXPERIMENTAL GROUPS
AFTER TRANSFER.

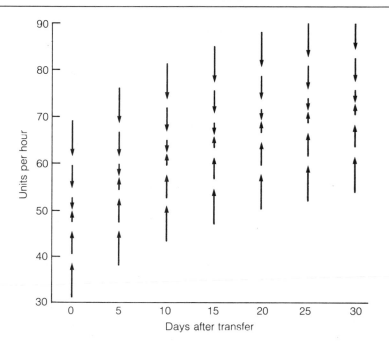

learner, the transfer often encounters the added difficulty of proactive inhibition. Where the new job is similar to the old job there will be a period of interference between the two similar but different skills required. For this reason a very efficient operator whose skills have become almost unconscious may suffer just as great a drop as a much less efficient operator (see Figure II). Except for group 4, the difficulty of these easy jobs does not explain the differential recovery rates because both the initial difficulty and the amount of change were equated for these groups. The two operators in group 4 probably dropped further and recovered more slowly than any of the other three groups under total participation because of the greater difficulty of the job.

2. Strain Avoidance. The force toward lower production corresponding to the difficulty of the job (or the lack of skill of the person) has the character of a restraining force—that is, it acts to prevent locomotion rather than as a driving force causing locomotion. However, in all production there is a closely related driving force towards lower production, namely "strain avoidance." We assume that working too hard and working too fast is an unpleasant strain; and corresponding to this negative valence there is a driving force in the opposite direction, namely towards taking it easy or working slower. The higher the level of production the greater will be the strain and, other things being equal, the stronger will be the downward force of strain avoidance. Likewise, the greater the difficulty of the job the stronger will be the force corresponding to strain avoidance. But the greater the operator's skill the smaller will be the strain and the strength of the force of strain avoidance. Therefore:

(4) The strength of the force of strain avoidance =

$$\frac{job \ difficulty \ \times \ production \ level}{skill \ of \ operator}$$

The differential recovery rates of the control group in both experiments and the three experimental groups in Experiment I cannot be explained by strain avoidance because job difficulty, production level, and operator skill were matched at the time immediately following transfer. Later, however, when the experimental treatments had produced a much higher level of production, these groups were subjected to an increased downward force of strain avoidance which was stronger than in the control group in Experiment I. Evidently other forces were strong enough to overcome this force of strain avoidance.

3. *The Goal of Standard Production.* In considering the negative attitudes toward transfer and the resistance to being transferred, there are several important aspects of the complex goal of reaching and maintaining a level of 60 units per hour. For an operator producing below standard, this goal is attractive because it means success, high status in the eyes of her fellow employees, better pay, and job security. On the other hand, there is a strong force against remaining below standard because this lower level means failure, low status, low pay, and the danger of being fired. Thus it is clear that the upward force corresponding to the goal of standard production will indeed be strong for the transfer who has dropped below standard.

It is equally clear why any operator, who accepts the sterotype about transfer, shows such strong resistance to being changed. She sees herself as becoming a failure and losing status, pay, and perhaps the job itself. The result is a lowered level of aspiration and a weakened force toward the goal of standard production.

Just such a weakening of the force toward 60 units per hour seems to have occurred in the control group in Experiment I. The participation treatments, on the other hand, seem to have involved the operators in designing the new job and setting the new piece rates in such a way that they did not lose hope of regaining the goal of standard production. Thus the participation resulted in a stronger force toward higher production. However, this force alone can hardly account for the large differences in recovery rate between the control group and the experimental groups; certainly it does not explain why the latter increased to a level so high above standard.

4. *Management Pressure.* On all operators below standard the management exerts a pressure for higher production. This pressure is no harsh and autocratic treatment involving threats. Rather it takes the form of persuasion and encouragement by the supervisors. They attempt to induce the low rating operator to improve her performance and to attain standard production.

Such an attempt to induce a psychological force on another person may have several results. In the first place the person may ignore the attempt of the inducing agent, in which case there is no induced force acting on the person. On the other hand, the attempt may succeed so that an induced force on the person exists. Other things being equal, whenever there is an induced force acting on a person, the person will locomote in the direction of the force.

An induced force, which depends on the power field of an inducing agent—some other individual or group—will cease to exist when the inducing power field is withdrawn. In this report it is different from an "own" force which stems from a person's own needs and goals.

The reaction of a person to an effective induced force will vary depending, among other things, on the person's relation to the inducing agent. A force induced by a friend may be accepted in such a way that it acts more like an own force. An effective force induced by an enemy may be resisted and rejected so that the person complies unwillingly and shows signs of conflict and tension. Thus in addition to what might be called a "neutral" induced force, we also distinguish an *accepted* induced force and a *rejected* induced force. Naturally the acceptance and the rejection of an induced force can vary in degree from zero (i.e., a neutral induced force) to very strong acceptance or rejection. To account for the difference in character between the acceptance and the rejection of an induced force, we make the following assumptions:

(5) The acceptance of an induced force sets up additional own forces in the same direction.

(6) The rejection of an induced force sets up additional own forces in the opposite direction.

The grievances, aggression, and tension in the control group in Experiment I indicate that they rejected the force toward higher production induced by the management. The group accepted the stereotype that transfer is a calamity, but the control procedure did not convince them that the change was necessary and they viewed the new job and the new piece rates set by management as arbitrary and unreasonable.

The experimental groups, on the contrary, participated in designing the changes and setting the piece rates so that they spoke of the new job as "our job" and the new piece rates as "our rates." Thus they accepted the new situation and accepted the management induced force toward higher production.

From the acceptance by the experimental groups and the rejection by the control group of the management induced forces, we may derive (by (5) and (6) above) that the former had additional own forces toward higher production whereas the latter had additional own forces toward lower production. This difference helps to explain the better recovery rate of the experimental groups.

5. Group Standards. Probably the most important force affecting the recovery under the control procedure was a group standard, set by the group, restricting the level of production to 50 units per hour. Evidently this explicit agreement to restrict production is related to the group's rejection of the change and of the new job as arbitrary and unreasonable. Perhaps they had faint hopes of demonstrating that standard production could not be attained and thereby obtain a more favorable piece rate. In any case there was a definite group phenomenon which affected all the members of the group. We have already noted the striking example of the presser whose production was restricted in the group situation to about half the level she attained as an individual. In the control group, too, we would expect the group to induce strong forces on the members. The more a member deviates above the standard the stronger would be the group-induced force to conform to the standard, for such deviations both negate any possibility of management's increasing the piece rate and at the same time expose the other members to increased pressure from management. Thus individual differences in levels of production should be sharply curtailed in the control group after transfer.

An analysis was made for all groups of the individual differences within the group in levels of production. In Experiment I the 40 days before change were compared with the 30 days after change; in Experiment II the 10 days before change were compared to the 17 days after change. As a measure of variability, the standard deviation was calculated each day for each group. The average daily standard deviations *before* and *after* change were as follows:

The table of variability also shows that the experimental treatments markedly reduced variability in the other four groups after transfer. In experimental group 1 (participation by representation) this smallest reduction of variability was produced by a group standard of individual competition. Competition among members of the group was reported by the supervisor soon after transfer. This competition was a force toward higher production which resulted in good recovery to standard and continued progress beyond standard.

Experimental groups 2 and 3 showed a greater reduction in variability following transfer. These two groups under to-

Group	Variability		
Experiment I	Before Change		After Change
Control group	9.8	. . .	1.9
Experimental 1	9.7	. . .	3.8
Experimental 2	10.3	. . .	2.7
Experimental 3	9.9	. . .	2.4
Experiment II			
Control group	12.7	. . .	2.9

There is indeed a marked decrease in individual differences within the control group after their first transfer. In fact the restriction of production resulted in a lower variability than in any other group. Thus we may conclude that the group standard at 50 units per hour set up strong group-induced forces which were important components in the central force field shown in Figure VI. It is now evident that for the control group the quasi-stationary equilibrium after transfer has a steep gradient around the equilibrium level of 50 units per hour—the strength of the forces increase rapidly above and below this level. It is also clear that the group standard to restrict production is a major reason for the lack of recovery in the control group.

tal participation were transferred on the same day. Group competition developed between the two groups. This group competition, which evidently resulted in stronger forces on the members than did the individual competition, was an effective group standard. The standard gradually moved to higher and higher levels of production with the result that the groups not only reached but far exceeded their previous levels of production.

Turnover and Aggression

Returning now to our preliminary theory of frustration, we can see several revisions. The difficulty of the job and its relation to skill and strain avoidance has been clarified in proposition (4). It is now clear that the driving force toward 60 is a complex affair; it is partly a negative driving force corresponding to the negative valence of low pay, low status, failure, and job insecurity. Turnover results not only from the frustration produced by the conflict of these two forces, but also as a direct attempt to escape from the region of these negative valences. For the members of the control group, the group standard to restrict production prevented escape by increasing production, so that quitting their jobs was the only remaining escape. In the participation groups, on the contrary, both the group standards and the additional own forces resulting from the acceptance of management-induced forces combined to make increasing production the distinguished path of escape from this region of negative valence.

In considering turnover as a form of escape from the field, it is not enough to look only at the psychological present; one must also consider the psychological future. The employee's decision to quit the job is rarely made exclusively on the basis of a momentary frustration or an undesirable present situation; she usually quits when she also sees the future as equally hopeless. The operator transferred by the usual factory procedure (including the control group) has in fact a realistic view of the probability of continued failure because, as we have already noted, 62 per cent of transfers do in fact fail to recover to standard production. Thus the higher rate of quitting for transfers as compared to nontransfers results from a more pessimistic view of the future.

The control procedure had the effect for the members of setting up management as a hostile power field. They rejected the forces induced by this hostile power field, and group standards to restrict production developed within the group in opposition to management. In this conflict between the power field of management and the power field of the group, the control group attempted to reduce the strength of the hostile power field relative to the strength of their own power field. This change was accomplished in three ways: (1) the group increased its own power by developing a more cohesive and well-disciplined group, (2) they secured "allies" by getting the backing of the union in filing a formal grievance about the new piece rate, (3) they attacked the hostile power field directly in the form of aggression against the supervisor, the time study engineer, and the higher management. Thus the aggression was derived not only from individual frustration but also from the conflict between two groups. Furthermore, this situation of group conflict both helped to define management as the frustrating agent and gave the members strength to express any aggressive impulses produced by frustration.

CONCLUSIONS

It is possible for management to modify greatly or to remove completely group resistance to changes in methods of work and the ensuing piece rates. This change can be accomplished by the use of group meetings in which management effectively communicates the need for change and stimulates group participation in planning the changes.

For Harwood's management, and presumably for managements of other industries using an incentive system, this experiment has important implications in the field of labor relations. A majority of all grievances presented at Harwood have always stemmed from a change situation. By preventing or greatly modifying group resistance to change, this concomitant to change may well be greatly reduced. The reduction of such costly phenomena as turnover and slow relearning rates presents another distinct advantage.

Harwood's management has long felt that action research such as the present experiment is the only key to better labor-management relations. It is only by discovering the basic principles and applying them to the true causes of conflict that an intelligent, effective effort can be made to correct the undesirable effects of the conflict.

REFERENCES

1. French, John R. P., Jr. The Behaviour of Organized and Unorganized Groups under Conditions of Frustration and Fear, Studies in Topological and Vector Psychology, III, *University of Iowa Studies in Child Welfare*, 1944, Vol. XX, pp. 229–308.

2. Lewin, Kurt. Frontiers in Group Dynamics, *Human Relations*, Vol. I, No. 1, 1947, pp. 5–41.

38
Group Decision and Social Change
Kurt Lewin

QUASI-STATIONARY SOCIAL EQUILIBRIA AND THE PROBLEM OF PERMANENT CHANGE

1. The Objective of Change. The objective of social change might concern the nutritional standard of consumption, the economic standard of living, the type of group relation, the output of a factory, the productivity of an educational team. It is important that a social standard to be changed does not have the nature of a "thing" but of a "process." A certain standard of consumption, for instance, means that a certain action—such as making certain decisions, buying, preparing, and canning certain food in a family—occurs with a certain frequency within a given period. Similarly, a certain type of group relations means that within a given period certain friendly and hostile actions and reactions of a certain degree of severity occur between the members of two groups. Changing group relations or changing consumption means changing the level at which these multitude of events proceed. In other words, the "level" of consumption, of friendliness, or of productivity is to be characterized as the aspect of an ongoing social process.

Any planned social change will have to consider a multitude of factors characteristic for the particular case. The change may require a more or less unique combination of educational and organizational measures; it may depend upon quite different treatments or ideology, expectation and organization. Still, certain general formal principles always have to be considered.

2. The Conditions of a Stable Quasi-stationary Equilibrium. The study of the conditions for change begins appropriately with an analysis of the conditions for "no change," that is, for the state of equilibrium.

From what has been just discussed, it is clear that by a state of "no social change" we do not refer to a stationary but to a quasi-stationary equilibrium; that is, to a state comparable to that of a river which flows with a given velocity in a given direction during a certain time interval. A social change is comparable to a change in the velocity or direction of that river.

A number of statements can be made in regard to the conditions of quasi-stationary equilibrium. (These conditions are treated more elaborately elsewhere.[1])

A. The strength of forces which tend to lower that standard of social life should be equal and opposite to the strength of forces which tend to raise its level. The resultant of forces on the line of

[1] K. Lewin, "Frontiers in Group Dynamics: Concept, Method and Reality in Social Science; Social Equilibria and Social Change," *Human Relations*, I, 1, June, 1947, pp. 5–42.

FIGURE 1 • GRADIENTS OF RESULTANT FORCES (f*).

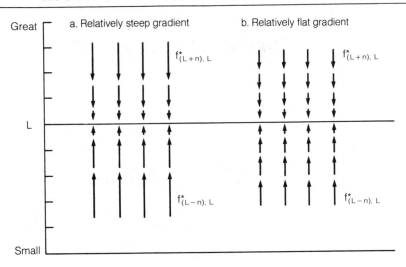

equilibrium should therefore be zero.

B. Since we have to assume that the strength of social forces always shows variations, a quasi-stationary equilibrium presupposes that the forces against raising the standard increase with the amount of raising and that the forces against lowering increase (or remain constant) with the amount of lowering. This type of gradient which is characteristic for a "positive central force field"[2] has to hold at least in the neighborhood of the present level (Fig. 1).

C. It is possible to change the strength of the opposing forces without changing the level of social conduct. In this case the tension (degree of conflict) increases.

3. *Two Basic Methods of Changing Levels of Conduct.* For any type of social management, it is of great practical importance that levels of quasi-stationary equilibria can be changed in either of two ways: by adding forces in the desired direction, or by diminishing opposing forces. If a change from the level L_1 to L_2 is brought about by increasing the forces toward L_2, the secondary effects should be different from the case where the same change of level is brought about by diminishing the opposing forces.

In both cases the equilibrium might change to the same new level. The secondary effect should, however, be quite different. In the first case, the process on the new level would be accompanied by a state of relatively high tension; in the second case, by a state of relatively low tension. Since increase of tension above a certain degree is likely to be paralleled by higher aggressiveness, higher emotionality, and lower constructiveness, it is clear that as a rule the second method will be preferable to the high pressure method.

The group decision procedure which

[2]*Ibid.*

is used here attempts to avoid high pressure methods and is sensitive to resistance to change. In the experiment by Bavelas on changing production in factory work (as noted below), for instance, no attempt was made to set the new production goal by majority vote because a majority vote forces some group members to produce more than they consider appropriate. These individuals are likely to have some inner resistance. Instead a procedure was followed by which a goal was chosen on which everyone could agree fully.

It is possible that the success of group decision and particularly the permanency of the effect is, in part, due to the attempt to bring about a favorable decision by removing counterforces within the individuals rather than by applying outside pressure.

The surprising increase from the second to the fourth week in the number of mothers giving cod liver oil and orange juice to the baby can probably be explained by such a decrease of counterforces. Mothers are likely to handle their first baby during the first weeks of life somewhat cautiously and become more ready for action as the child grows stronger.

4. Social Habits and Group Standards. Viewing a social stationary process as the result of a quasi-stationary equilibrium, one may expect that any added force will change the level of the process. The idea of "social habit" seems to imply that, in spite of the application of a force, the level of the social process will not change because of some type of "inner resistance" to change. To overcome this inner resistance, an additional force seems to be required, a force sufficient to "break the habit," to "unfreeze" the custom.

Many social habits are anchored in the relation between the individuals and certain group standards. An individual P may differ in his personal level of conduct (L_P) from the level which represents group standards (L_{Gr}) by a certain amount. If the individual should try to diverge "too much" from group standards, he would find himself in increasing difficulties. He would be ridiculed, treated severely and finally ousted from the group. Most individuals, therefore, stay pretty close to the standard of the groups they belong to or wish to belong to. In other words, the group level itself acquires value. It becomes a positive valence corresponding to a central force field with the force $f_{P,L}$ keeping the individual in line with the standards of the group.

5. Individual Procedures and Group Procedures of Changing Social Conduct. If the resistance to change depends partly on the value which the group standard has for the individual, the resistance to change should diminish if one diminishes the strength of the value of the group standard or changes the level perceived by the individual as having social value.

This second point is one of the reasons for the effectiveness of "group carried" changes[3] resulting from procedures which approach the individuals as part of face-to-face groups. Perhaps one might expect single individuals to be more pliable than groups of like-minded individuals. However, experience in leadership training, in changing of food habits, work production, criminality, alcoholism, prejudices, all indicate that it is usually easier to change individuals formed into a group than to change any one of them separately.[4] As long as group standards are unchanged, the individual will resist changes more strongly the farther he is to depart from

[3] N. R. F. Maier, *Psychology in Industry* (Boston: Houghton Mifflin Co., 1946).

[4] K. Lewin and P. Grabbe (eds.) *op. cit.*

FIGURE 2 ● EFFECT OF GROUP DECISION ON SEWING-MACHINE OPERATORS.

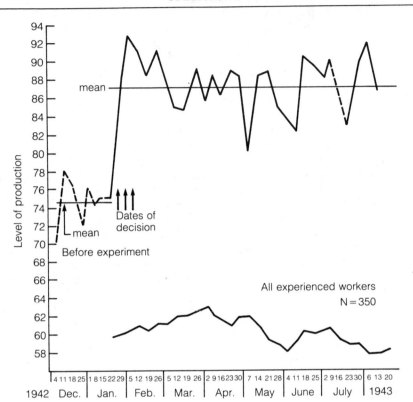

group standards. If the group standard itself is changed, the resistance which is due to the relation between individual and group standard is eliminated.

6. *Changing as a Three-step Procedure: Unfreezing, Moving, and Freezing of a Level.* A change toward a higher level of group performance is frequently short lived: after a "shot in the arm," group life soon returns to the previous level. This indicates that it does not suffice to define the objective of a planned change in group performance as the reaching of a different level. Permanency of the new level, or permanency for a desired period, should be included in the objective. A successful change in-

cludes therefore three aspects: unfreezing (if necessary) the present level L_1, moving to the new level L_2, and freezing group life on the new level. Since any level is determined by a force field, permanency implies that the new force field is made relatively secure against change.

The "unfreezing" of the present level may involve quite different problems in different cases. Allport[5] has described the "catharsis" which seems to be necessary before prejudices can be removed.

[5]G. W. Allport, "Catharsis and the Reduction of Prejudice" in K. Lewin and P. Grabbe (eds.), *op. cit.*, 3–10.

FIGURE 3 • RELATION BETWEEN OWN FOOD PREFERENCES AND EAGERNESS TO SUCCEED.

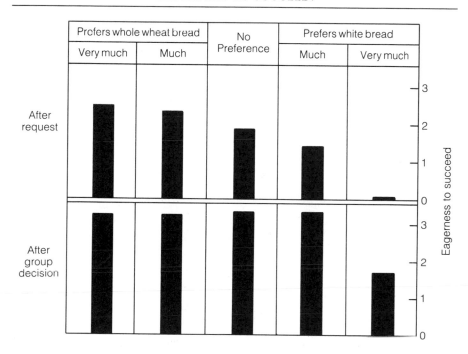

To break open the shell of complacency and self-righteousness, it is sometimes necessary to bring about deliberately an emotional stir-up.

Figure 2 presents an example of the effect of three group decisions of a team in a factory reported by Bavelas[6] which illustrates an unusually good case of permanency of change measured over nine months.

The experiments on group decision reported here cover but a few of the necessary variations. Although in some cases the procedure is relatively easily executed, in others it requires skill and presupposes certain general conditions. Managers rushing into a factory to raise production by group decisions are likely to encounter failure. In social manage-ment as in medicine there are no patent medicines and each case demands careful diagnosis.

One reason why group decision facilitates change is illustrated by Willerman.[7] Figure 3 shows the degree of eagerness to have the members of a students' eating cooperative change from the consumption of white bread to whole wheat. When the change was simply requested the degree of eagerness varied greatly with the degree of personal preference for whole wheat. In case of group decision the eagerness seems to be relatively independent of personal preference; the individual seems to act mainly as a "group member."

[6]N. R. F. Maier, *op. cit.*

[7]K. Lewin "Forces behind Food Habits . . .," *op. cit.*

SUMMARY

Group decision is a process of social management or self management of groups. It is related to social channels, gates and gatekeepers; to the problem of social perception and planning; and to the relation between motivation and action, and between the individual and the group.

Experiments are reported in which certain methods of group decision prove to be superior to lecturing and individual treatment as means of changing social conduct.

The effect of group decision can probably be best understood by relating it to a theory of quasi-stationary social equilibria, to social habits and resistance to change, and to the various problems of unfreezing, changing and freezing social levels.

39

Applied Organizational Change in Industry: Structural, Technological and Humanistic Approaches

Harold J. Leavitt

This chapter is divided into two parts. The first attempts to survey and interrelate several distinct sets of approaches to organizational change. The second part dissects one of these sets—the one here called the people approaches—in much more detail. The people approaches deserve this more intensive analysis because they are currently in wide and increasing use in industry, and because they remain, after 20 or more years of development, highly controversial issues even within the social-scientific community.

APPROACHES TO ORGANIZATIONAL CHANGE

One can view industrial organizations as complex systems in which at least four interacting variables loom especially large; task variables, structural variables, technological variables, and human variables. If one takes such a view, he can go on to categorize major applied approaches to organizational change by using three of the same variables: *structural* approaches to change, *technological* approaches, and *people* approaches.

Before reviewing these three classes of efforts to effect change, it will be use-

ful to elaborate a little on this four-variable conception of organizations.

Task in Fig. I refers, of course, to industrial organizations' *raisons d'être:* the production of goods and services, including the large numbers of different but operationally meaningful subtasks that may exist in complex organizations.

Actors refers chiefly to people, but with the qualification that acts executed by people at some time or place need not remain exclusively in the human domain.

Technology refers to direct problemsolving inventions like work-measurement techniques or computers or drill presses. Note that both machines and programs may be included in this category.

Finally, *structure* means systems of communication, systems of authority (or other roles), and systems of work flow.

These four are highly interdependent, as indicated by the arrowheads, so that change in any one usually results in compensatory (or retaliatory) change in others. In discussing organizational change, this chapter assumes that it is one or more of these variables which are to be changed. Sometimes, the aim may

Source: From "Applied Organizational Change in Industry: Structural, Technological, and Humanistic Approaches," by Harold J. Leavitt, in James G. March (Ed.), *Handbook of Organizations* (Chicago: Rand McNally, 1965), pp. 1144–1170. Reprinted by permission of James G. March, Editor.

FIGURE 1 ●

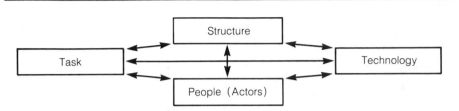

be to change one as an end in itself, sometimes as a mechanism for effecting changes in one or more of the others. Usually, but not necessarily, efforts to effect change are ultimately designed to influence the task variable.

Thus, structural change toward, say, decentralization should change the performance of certain organizational tasks (indeed, even the selection of tasks). But decentralization will also probably change the technology that is brought to bear (e.g., changes in accounting procedures or varieties and sizes of machines) and the nature, numbers, and/or motivation and attitudes of people in the organization. Any of these changes could presumably be consciously intended, or they could occur as unforeseen and often costly outcomes of efforts to change only one or two of the variables.

Similarly, the introduction of new technological tools computers, for example—may cause changes in structure (e.g., in the communication system or decision map of the organization), changes in actors (their numbers, skills, attitudes, and activities), and changes in performance or even definition of task, since some tasks may now become feasible of accomplishment for the first time, and others may become unnecessary.

Changes in the people and task variable could, comparably, branch out through the system to cause similar changes in other variables.

Interactions Among Several Approaches to Change

The discussion can now turn to the central focus of this chapter, a categorization and evaluation of several approaches to organizational change—approaches that differ markedly in their degree of emphasis and their ordering of these four variables.

Clearly, most efforts to effect change whether they begin with people, technology, structure, or task, soon must deal with the others. Students of human relations must cope with the intrusions of technological innovations. They must evaluate alternative structures, classing some as consonant and some as dissonant with their views of the world. Structuralists must take stands on the kinds of human interaction that are supportive of their position and the kinds that threaten to undermine it.

So, although structural approaches are here differentiated from technical and from humanistic approaches, the differentiation is in (a) points of entry into the organization, (b) relative weightings, and (c) underlying values, not in the exclusion of all other variables.

This categorization must be further complicated by the fact that the objectives of the several approaches to organizational change are not uniform. All of them are normative sharing an expressed interest in improving organizational behavior through improved performance of tasks. But although improved performance serves as a common goal for all of these approaches, the definition of "performance" varies considerably from one group to the next. Some students equate performance with the quality of decisions made, others with the way decisions are implemented. Some of the early structural approaches were almost as concerned with maintaining managerial prerogatives as with improving productivity. Some of the technological approaches appear as wedded to the aesthetic elegance as to the feasibility of their solutions. And some of the current people approaches are at least as interested in the fulfillment of the personal needs of the organization's members as they are in efficacious operations.

The several approaches are still further complicated by variations in the causal chains by which they are supposed to bring about their intended changes. Some of the structural approaches, for example, are not aimed directly at task but at people as mediating, intervening variables. In these approaches, one changes structure to change people to improve task performance (Chapple & Sayles, 1961). Similarly, some of the people approaches (Argyris, 1957; Likert, 1961) seek to change people to change structure and tools to change task performance and also to make life more fulfilling for people.

Despite all these complications, the three sets of approaches seem to this writer to be operationally real. Given, for example, the same statement of a problem by a client firm, one group of practitioners will try to solve it first by modifying structure ("What you need to do is decentralize"), another by changing technology ("Let's computerize"), or a third by changing people ("We'll set up a sensitivity training program").

The next sections discuss the several varieties of approaches, dealing relatively briefly with the structural and technical approaches, which are described more fully elsewhere in this Handbook, and in more detail with the people approaches.

Structural Approaches

Applied efforts to change organizations by changing structure can be categorized into four classes:

First, structural change has been the major mechanism of the "classical" organization theorist (Harrison, 1957). Out of the deductive, rational, largely military-based thinking of early nonempirical organization theory, there evolved the whole set of now-familiar "principles" for optimizing organizational performance by optimizing structure. These were deductive methods, carrying out their analyses from task backwards to appropriate divisions of labor and systems of authority. These early structural approaches almost always mediated their activities through people to task. One improves performance of tasks by clarifying and defining the jobs of people and setting up clearly defined relationships among those jobs, with authority, responsibility, and coordination mechanisms spelled out. Operationally, one worries about modifying spans of control, defining nonoverlapping areas of responsibility and authority, and logically defining necessary functions (Brown, 1947; Holden, Fish, & Smith, 1951; Urwick, 1956).

In retrospect, most students think of these early approaches as abstractions, formal and legalistic, and poorly anchored in empirical data. Some, but by no means all, were almost incredibly naive in their assumptions about human behavior (Follett [Metcalf & Urwick, 1942] is a clear exception; Brown [1947] is a case in point). In some cases, almost the only assumptions that were made were legalistic and ethical ones: that people, having contracted to work, would willingly carry out all the terms of their contract; that people assigned responsibility would necessarily accept it; that people when informed of the organization's goals would strive wholeheartedly to achieve them. The emphasis of such approaches is on internal consistency, orderliness, and hierarchical coordination.

Thus, Brown (1947) listed among his "principles of organization" such items as these:

Each responsibility implies a duty of performance in conformity to the requirements of other responsibility (p. 5).

No member may assume to perform any part of the responsibility of another (p. 5).

It is the duty of a delegant to provide for the harmonious performance of responsibilities delegated by him (p. 3).

The values underlying these classical approaches were those associated with order, discipline, system, and acceptance of authority. One objective, of course, was optimal task performance, but only within the constraints imposed by the hierarchy of authority, and no conflict was seen between the two.

In one variant or another, in one degree of sophistication or another, such structural approaches are still widely applied. It is still a commonplace for consultants or organization planning departments to try to solve organizational problems by redefining areas of responsibility and authority or by redesigning the approved set of organizational "channels." And debates on the validity of one or another of the classical structural concepts, like span of control, continue to pop up (Urwick, 1956).

A second widespread approach to structural change is perhaps more properly a subclass of the first, but it is

treated separately, since it is somewhat more sophisticated than its predecessors, albeit somewhat narrower in its scope. It is the mechanism of *decentralization.* The idea of changing organizations by decentralizing profit centers was probably more an invention of the accounting profession than of anyone else,[1] although it has been widely endorsed by structuralists, economists, and by human relators, too. Curiously, almost nobody is against it.

For the classicists, decentralization reduces the cost of coordination and increases controllability over subunits. But decentralization also affects the performance of tasks, partially through its intervening effects on people. By creating local profit centers, one presumably increases the motivation and goal-oriented behavior of local managers. One also automatically creates smaller decision centers, power centers, and information centers. And one also adds flexibility so that variations in technology appropriate to the different tasks of different decentralized units become more possible. So do subvariations in structure and local variations in the use of people. Decentralization can also be thought of as a mechanism for opening organizations to further change by increasing local autonomy. Thus, within limits, decentralized units may further change themselves through the use of any one of the many alternatives available. Perhaps because it has thus left room for variation, no group has questioned it—at least until the last few years (Leavitt & Whisler, 1958; Shultz & Whisler, 1960).

Recently, other structural approaches have shown up, but they have not yet reached a widespread level of applica-

---

[1]Dale (1956) ascribed the origins of decentralization to Henry V. Poor in his proposals to reorganize the railroads in the 1850s.

tion. A third is what Gouldner (1956) has called an "engineering" approach. The work of Chapple and Sayles (1961) is a good example. Theirs is a form of social engineering aimed at task, but via people. They seek to modify the behavior of people in order to improve task performance, but they do it by modifying structure, in this case the structural property of flow of work. Out of the tradition of applied anthropology, they argue that planning of work flows and groupings of specialties directly affects the morale, behavior, and output of employees. One of the failings of earlier structural models, in their view, is that the design of work was almost entirely determined by task and technical variables and failed to take account of human and social variables. Chapple and Sayles have provided illustrative cases to show that appropriate redesigning of work, in a social engineering sense, affects both human attitudes and output. Significantly, the book is subtitled "Designing Organizations for Human Effectiveness."

The work of Holmberg and his associates (1960) deserves special mention here. They have indeed effected change in a real organization, completely reorganizing the social structure of a hacienda; thereby radically affecting task and human variables.

One cannot overlook, in this discussion of structure, the implications of the research on communication networks and other recent related work (Glanzer & Glaser, 1961). *Direct* applications of this laboratory research to the real world are scarce, although it has had some significant indirect influence on structural planning. In that research, variations in communication nets affect both routine and novel task performance rather significantly. The results suggest that appropriate communication structures might vary considerably

within a complex organization depending upon the type of task that any subunit of the organization undertakes.

Thus, for programmed repetitive tasks, centralized communication structures seem to operate most efficiently, but with some human costs. For more novel, ill-structured tasks, more wide-open communication nets with larger numbers of channels and less differentiation among members seem to work more effectively.

The extrapolation of this work to air defense systems at the RAND Corporation can be considered an application to a set of real-life organizations (Chapman et al., 1959). In that case, research on a major communication problem led, by a rather complex route, to major change in the structure of certain air defense systems, and in effect to the development of a new structure, the Systems Development Corporation.

Technological Approaches to Organizational Change

Many observers have pointed out the critical role of technology in effecting organizational change (Meier, 1956; Mumford, 1934; Walker, 1962). In one instance after another, organizations have remolded themselves, not in direct response to great ideas, but in response to the development of intervening technology that stimulates implementation of those ideas. Information theory did not significantly change organizations until the development of computers and programming could serve as carriers of operational change. Scientific Management sprang into operation on the shoulders of techniques—the techniques of work measurement. Personnel management, too, had to wait for techniques to become operational—the techniques of testing, attitude-surveying, and job-evaluating.

Historically, the first major entry

into this technological category was Taylor's Scientific Management (1911). Its technique was empirical work measurement; it bore none of the abstract introspective flavor of the structural approaches. And from the classic programming of the labors of Schmidt, the immigrant pig-iron handler, on to the more sophisticated forms of work measurement and analysis of succeeding decades, Taylorism has constituted a significant force for change in American organizations since the turn of the century.

Scientific Management, almost from its inception, took a position outside the task, not of it. Out of Taylorism emerged a new set of technical skills, industrial engineering, and a new class of specialized agents of change, the industrial engineers. Theirs were generalized skills, planning and measuring skills, not specific to a task. They were the organizers and designers of work, not the doers.

Like the early structural approaches, Scientific Management was thus to a great extent ahuman, even, it has been argued, inhuman. For in creating the separate planning specialist, it removed planning from its old location, the head of the doer of work, leaving him only the physical labor. Many observers, both contemporary and subsequent (Mann & Hoffman, 1960; Sinclair, 1911), saw this phase of Scientific Management as demeaning mankind. And Taylor put his foot deeply into his mouth by taking positions like this one: "Now one of the very first requirements for a man who is fit to handle pig iron . . . is that he shall be so stupid and so phlegmatic that he more nearly resembles . . . the ox than any other type. . . . He must consequently be trained by a man more intelligent than himself" (1911, p. 59).

But despite the flurry of congressional inquiry and active counterattack by Taylor's contemporaries, Scientific Management grew and prospered and radically changed structure, people, and the ways that jobs got done. Indeed, it spread and flourished until no self-respecting manufacturing firm was without the paraphernalia of Scientific Management: time-study men, methods engineers, work standards, piece rates, job-classification schemes, and more.

The range of Scientific Management was limited by its relatively simple tools. It concentrated necessarily on the programming of eye-hand and muscle jobs. Although Taylor and his fellows were ready to generalize their methods to almost any organizational problem, the methods themselves fell short when applied to judgmental and informational tasks. One could program the work of pig-iron handling with a stop watch, but it was more difficult to program the work of a researcher.

If one asks why Scientific Management flourished, several reasonable answers appear. The environment of the day, despite the counterattacks, was probably supportive. It was an environment of growth, expansiveness, and muscle-flexing. Work in associated disciplines was supportive, too. Newly developing applied psychology, for example, was individually oriented (Moore, 1962), concerned with individual differences in physiological response and anxious to be treated as a science. Hence it, too, was measurement-happy. Finger-dexterity tests meshed neatly with Taylor's motion study.

Consider, for example, Bendix's (1956) account of the early enthusiasm of industrial psychologists. He quoted from Munsterberg's *Psychology and Industrial Efficiency*, published in 1913, appraising the promise of industrial psychology:

> . . . still more important than the valued commercial profit on both sides is the

cultural gain which will come to the total economic life of the nation, as soon as everyone can be brought to the place where his best energies may be unfolded and his greatest personal satisfaction secured. The economic experimental psychology offers no more inspiring idea than this adjustment of work and psyche by which mental dissatisfaction with the work, mental depression and discouragement, may be replaced in our social community by overflowing joy and perfect inner harmony (p. 275).

But most of all, Taylorism, like many other ideas, seemed to be carried by its own operational technics; by its cheap, workable, easily taught industrial engineering methods; and by its almost directly visible effectiveness.

Scientific Management receded into a relatively stable and undramatic background in the late thirties and forties, leaving some doubts and concerns among its practitioners. But technological approaches as a class were by no means dead. The development of the techniques of operations research out of World War II and the more or less contemporaneous invention of computers have more than revived them.

Operations-research and human-engineering methods for changing organizational problem-solving can be reasonably placed in the same category with Scientific Management. Each has developed a body of technical methods for solving work problems. Both are usually external in their approach, essentially separating the planning of problem-solving programs from the routine acting out of solutions. Operations research, too, is quickly developing a new class of staff specialists, in many ways analogous to the earlier staff efficiency man. The development of the Operations Research Society also parallels in many ways the development of the old Taylor Society, now the Society of the Advancement of Management. What is

clearly different, of course, is the nature of the techniques.

The operations-research and information-processing techniques appear to be, if not more general, at least applicable to large classes of tasks that Scientific Management could not encompass (Charnes & Cooper, 1961). Now armed with linear-programming methods, the operations researchers can approach tasks like media selection in an advertising agency or inventory control in a large firm (Cooper, 1961), although it would have been nonsense to approach such tasks armed only with time-study tools.

The over-all similarity between the two is, nevertheless, striking: Change the setting from Bethlehem, Pa., to Madison Avenue, the time from 1910 to 1962, the costuming from overalls to gray flannels, and the tasks from simple muscular labor to complex scheduling decisions. Recast worried laborer Schmidt with worried media executive Jones. Then replace time and motion study with linear programming or PERT, and replace the stop watch with the computer. The story line can remain intact.

A distinction needs to be drawn between operations research and some other computer-based information-processing techniques, although they are often closely allied. Organizations are also being changed (or are on the verge of it) by simulation techniques (Shultz & Whisler, 1960) and by heuristic problem-solving methods (Newell & Simon, 1961; Tonge, 1961). Their impact has not yet been felt in anything like full force, but it is already clear that these task-directed efforts are significantly affecting the variables of structure and people in many organizations.

Thus, heuristic methods for balancing assembly lines (Tonge, 1961) and even heuristic simulations of trust officers' and retail-store buyers' decisions

(Cyert & March, 1962) portend eventual effects on both structural and actor aspects of future organizations.

The development of consulting firms, is, of course, always a cue to directions of change. The industrial-engineering firm was followed by the psychological-servicing firm and then by the operations-research firm. And now several firms exist to apply simulation techniques to organizational problems.

Without delving further into the substance of these more recent technological approaches, it may be worth pointing up one value they share with many of their predecessors: a faith in the ultimate victory of their version of *better* (cheaper or more rational or more elegant) problem solutions over *worse* ones. This faith is sometimes perceived by people-oriented change agents as sheer naiveté about the nature of man. They may ascribe it to a pre-Freudian failure to realize that human acceptance of ideas is the "real" carrier of change and that emotional human resistance is the "real" road block. And they can point both to experimental evidence (Coch & French, 1948) and to a long list of cases in which technological innovations, or methods changes, or operations-research techniques have fallen short because they ignored the human factor (Lawrence, 1958; Mann & Hoffman, 1960; W. F. Whyte, 1955). It is not the logically better solutions that get adopted, this argument runs, but the more humanly acceptable, more feasible ones. And unless the new technologist learns that fact, he may end up a social isolate like his predecessor, the industrial engineer.

Without evaluating the belief that operations-research people can be incredibly naive in their insensitivity to human feelings, one can nevertheless argue that the OR technologists have simply taken a more macroscopic, longer view of the world than their humanistic brethren. This counterargument runs as follows: Better solutions do get accepted in the long run, because deeper, largely competitive forces in the economy press them upon the individual organization (Mansfield, 1961; Simon, 1960). Macroscopically, these ahuman or people-last approaches may encounter bumps and grinds in the microcosmos of the individual firm; but in the aggregate and over time, human resistance will be allayed or displaced or overcome, and the steam drill must inevitably defeat John Henry.

The technological approaches thus assume some communication among firms and between firms and the world, and, implicitly or explicitly, count on these forces eventually to carry them to victory. As the writer tries to show in the next part of this chapter, the people approaches, on the other hand, generally use the firm as the boundary of the world.

The technological approaches not only predict the victory of cleaner, more logical, and more parsimonious solutions but *value* them. Failure of human beings to search for or use more efficient solutions is a sign, from this perspective, of human weakness and inadequacy. People must be teased or educated into greater logic, greater rationality (Goode, 1962; Marschak, 1962). Resistance to better solutions is proof only of the poverty of our education; certainly it is not an indication that "optimal" solutions are less than optimal.

THE PEOPLE APPROACHES

The remainder of this chapter is devoted to the large set of efforts to effect organizational change by effecting changes in people. The people approaches try to change organizations by first changing the behavior of the organization's members. By changing human behavior, it is argued, one can cause the creative invention of new tools, or one can cause modifications in structure (especially power structure). By either or both of these means, changing human behavior will cause changes in task solutions and task performance and also cause changes toward human growth and fulfillment, usually highly valued in these approaches.

In surveying the people approaches, one is immediately struck by the fact that the recent literature dealing directly with organizational change is heavily people-oriented. In the last 15 years, for example, several volumes specifically concerned with human aspects of organizational change have been published. They include, among others, Lippitt, Watson, and Westley's *The Dynamics of Planned Change* (1958); Lawrence's *The Changing of Organizational Behavior Patterns* (1958); Guest's *Organizational Change* (1962); Ginzberg and Reilly's *Effecting Change in Large Organizations* (1957) (a special case emphasizing the top manager-consultant relationship, and accepting the power structure); and Bennis, Benne, and Chin's *The Planning of Change* (1961).

From across the Atlantic has come another set of works in the same category, but more clinically and therapeutically oriented; Sofer's *The Organization from Within* (1961) and Jacques's *The Changing Culture of a Factory* (1951) are good examples.

This micro-focus on the process of change itself constitutes one of the major distinguishing features of the people approaches. Technological and structural approaches, in contrast, focus chiefly on problem-solving mechanisms, sliding past the internal operations of the organization, and the processes by which new problem-solving means are generated and adopted into the organization.

Manipulative People Approaches

Historically, the people approaches have moved through at least two phases. The first was essentially manipulative, responsive to the primitive and seductive question, How can we get people to do what we want them to do?

Although most people identify such questions with scholars of questionable professional legitimacy, like Dale Carnegie, much of the early work (immediately after World War II) by social scientists on "overcoming resistance to change" dealt with the same issues. And much earlier thought also aimed at that recurring question.

Carnegie's *How to Win Friends and Influence People* was first published in 1936, a few years ahead of most of what is now regarded as psychological work in the same area. And, like those of the social scientists who followed, Carnegie's model for change focused on the relationship between changer and changee, pointing out that changes in feelings and attitudes were prerequisites to voluntary changes in overt behavior. Carnegie proposed that one change others first by developing a relationship valuable to the other person and then by using that relationship as a lever for bringing about the change sought. One does not attack with logic and criticism and advice. A offers B support, approval, a permissive atmosphere; having thus established warm, affective bonds (invariably "sincere" bonds, too), A then asks B to change in the way A wishes, while A holds the relationship as collateral.

Although social scientists have tended to reject it out of hand, current research on influence processes (Festinger, 1957) suggests that the Carnegie model is not technically foolish at all. Moreover, it has some current social-scientific parallels. Thus, Martin and Sims (1959) directly attacked the issue of how to be a successful power politician in industrial organizations. They argued that dramatic skill, readiness to withhold certain kinds of information, the appearance of decisiveness, limited loyalty, and a variety of other calculatedly strategic behaviors are effective in influencing behavior in organizational hierarchies. Strauss (1962), in a descriptive research article, has recently examined the tactics used by purchasing agents from the same perspective, a perspective also stimulated by recent research in bargaining behavior (Seigel & Fouraker, 1960; Joseph, 1961). In fact, Carnegie-like interest in face-to-face influence has finally become a respectable area of social-scientific research. For example, work by Hovland, Janis, and Kelley (1953) on influence and persuasion provides experimental support for the efficacy of certain behavioral techniques (e.g., primacy) of influence over others.

Moreover, much of the early work on "overcoming resistance to change" was still responsive to the same manipulative question. Consider, for example, the now classic work by Lewin (1952) and his associates on changing food habits, or the later industrial work by Coch and French (1948). In both cases, A set out to bring about a predetermined change in the behavior of B. Lewin set out to cause housewives to purchase and consume more variety meats—a selling problem. Coch and French set out to gain acceptance of a preplanned methods change by hourly workers in a factory. In both cases, the methodology included large elements of indirection, with less than full information available to the changees.

But while Carnegie had built warm personal relationships and then bargained with them, neither Lewin nor Coch and French were centrally concerned about intimate relationships between changer and changee. Their concern was much more with opening and warming the interrelationships among changees.

Thus, 32 per cent of Lewin's test housewives exposed to a group decision method served new variety meats, as against only 3 per cent of the women exposed to lectures. Lewin accounted for these results by calling upon two concepts, involvement and group pressure. Lectures leave their audiences passive and unpressed by the group, while discussions are both active and pressing. Similarly, Coch and French, causing the girls in a pajama factory to accept a methods change, emphasized *group* methods, seeing resistance to change as partially a function of individual frustration, and partially of strong group-generated forces. Their methodology, therefore, was to provide opportunities for need satisfaction and to corner the group forces and redirect them toward the desired change.

But this slight thread of stealth was the soft spot (both ethically and methodologically) of these early people approaches to change and the reason that they are here classified as manipulative. Surely no bright student has ever read the Coch and French piece without wondering about what would have happened if the change being urged by management just did not seem like a good idea to the "smaller—more intimate" work groups of Coch and French's "total participation" condition.

One might say that these early studies wrestled rather effectively with questions of affect and involvement but avoided a key variable, power. Coch and French modified behavior by manipulating participation, while trying to hold power constant. The boss remained the same boss he was before. Thus, the artistry of the discussion leader operated as an important but only vaguely controlled variable, causing difficulties in replicating results and generating widespread discomfort among other social scientists.

Other contemporary and subsequent people approaches also avoided the power problem and encountered similar soft spots. The Western Electric counseling program that emerged out of the Hawthorne researches (Roethlisberger & Dickson, 1939) sought for change through catharsis, with a specific prohibition against any follow-up action by counselors—a "power-free" but eminently human approach. Later, users of morale and attitude surveys sought to effect change, as described later in this chapter, by feeding back anonymous aggregate data so that the power groups might then modify their own behavior. But the very anonymity of the process represented an acceptance of the power *status quo.*

It was to be expected, then, that the next moves in the development of people approaches would be toward working out the power variable. And it was obvious, too, that the direction would be toward equalization rather than toward differentiation of power. The theoretical underpinnings, the prevalent values, and the initial research results all pointed that way.

The Power-Equalization Approaches

But, although this is what happened, it happened, as Cartwright (1959) has pointed out, in a complicated and largely implicit way. Most of the push has come from work on individuals and small groups and has then been extrapolated to organizations, and sometimes the extrapolations have been naive, at best. Client-centered therapy (Rogers, 1951) and applied group dynamics (Miles, 1959) have been prime movers. In both cases, theory and technique

were explicitly aimed at allocating at least equal power to the changee(s), a fact of considerable importance in later development of dicta for organizational change. Both of these approaches implicitly or explicitly shared the view that one changes the world by changing people; and, additionally, the view that one changes people either by helping them to change themselves or by developing some collaborative effort between changer and changee. Thus, Rogerian client-centered counseling contrasted with then-current psychiatric views of directive therapy (Rogers, 1942), with Rogers emphasizing the permissive, even supportive, but nondirective role of the counselor. In Rogerian therapy, the counselor did not set the goal or the direction of change; instead, he provided a method by which the client could set these for himself. Obviously, in so doing, Rogerians sought much less control over the goals or the directions of change that the client might take than directive therapists thought they had.

In small-group research, the development of applied group dynamics and the early training experiments at Bethel, Maine (Bradford, Gibb, & Benne, 1964), moved very much in the same direction. T-group (T for training) leaders brought about changes in their groups by taking extremely permissive, nonauthoritarian, sometimes almost nonparticipative roles.

It is interesting that these directions of thinking about organizational change were not entirely independent of one another. Thus, Rogers eventually interacted with Roethlisberger and the Western Electric group, the two men publishing together (Rogers & Roethlisberger, 1952). The Bethel group in its early stages included the substance of Rogerian thinking and people trained in nondirective therapy. It also reached out to include people in education and in industrial organizations. McGregor helped to pave the way for the development of Lewin's Research Center for Group Dynamics at M.I.T. immediately after the war. He also brought practitioners like Scanlon out of the steelworkers and into Academia to extend the spread of the Scanlon Plan (Lesieur, 1958), a lively member of the same participative, collaborative family.

So it became clear to many practitioners and researchers through the forties and fifties that they shared points of view about methods and to an extent about values. They tended also to share some fundamental propositions about the nature of change in human beings and some techniques for effecting change.

Besides the belief that one changes people first, these power-equalization approaches also place major emphasis on other aspects of the human phenomena of organizations. They are, for example, centrally concerned with affect; with morale, sensitivity, psychological security. Secondly, they value evolutionary, internally generated change in individuals, groups, and organizations over externally planned or implemented-change. Thirdly, they place much value on human growth and fulfillment as well as upon task accomplishment; and they often have stretched the degree of causal connection between the two. Finally, of course, the power-equalization approaches, in their early stages at least, shared a normative belief that power in organizations should be more equally distributed than in most existent "authoritarian" hierarchies. Operationally, this belief was made manifest in a variety of ways: in encouraging independent decision-making, decentralization, more open communication, and participation.

The Development of the PE Models

Under the power-equalization approaches, then, are included ideas and operational techniques for changing individuals, like client-centered counseling; for changing groups, as described in Lippitt, Watson, and Westley's *The Dynamics of Planned Change* (1958) and Bennis, Benne, and Chin's *The Planning of Change* (1961); and for changing organizations, as exemplified best perhaps by the work on participative management by McGregor (1960) and Likert (1961) in industry.

Thus, Rogers early described his approach to the counseling of individuals:

> This newer approach differs from the older one in that it has a genuinely different goal. It aims directly toward the greater independence and integration of the individual rather than hoping that such results will accrue if the counselor assists in solving the problem. The individual and not the problem is the focus. The aim is not to solve one particular problem, but to assist the individual to grow (1942, pp. 28–29).

It was also Rogers, the writer believes, who introduced the phrase "helping role," currently used so widely in people-oriented discussions of organizational change. Rogers' therapist is not a powerful agent coercing or inducing his client to change, but a "helper," a resource.

At the group level, a comparable phenomenon was occurring: the development of "laboratory training" through the T-group (sensitivity training group, or development group) (National Training Laboratories, 1953). The T-group is the core tool of a particular and now wide-spread set of programs aimed at teaching individuals about themselves, other individuals, groups, and organizations. It has also become a core tool for effecting organizational change. Surprisingly, too, it is one of the few tools for organizational change clearly born of social science.

Operationally, T-group leaders try actively to bring about changes in their groups by behaving "passively"; by taking permissive, nonauthoritarian, sometimes almost completely nonparticipating roles. By refusing authority, the leader thus presumably encourages group members to define and solve their own problems. The T-group leader becomes, in the language of the occupation, a "resource person" seeking changes in group processes, rather than in any substantive beliefs or behaviors.

Although the T-group is a piece of technology, an invention,[2] this writer includes it among the people approaches, for it evolved out of them as a mechanism specifically designed for effecting change in people.

In contrast to earlier group-discussion tools, the T-group tries to deal with the power variable directly. Thus, Bennis and Shepard, representing one of many wings of T-group trainers, commented:

> The core of the theory of group development is that the principal obstacles to the development of valid communication are to be found in the orientations toward authority and intimacy that members bring to the group. Rebelliousness, submissiveness or withdrawal as the characteristic response to authority figures . . . prevent consensual validation of experience. The behaviors determined by these orientations are directed toward enslave-

ment of the other in the service of the self, enslavement of the self in the service of the other, or disintegration of the situation. Hence, they prevent the setting, clarification of, and movement toward, group shared goals (1961, p. 323).

This is not a wishy-washy position, whatever else may be said about it. It is a direct attack upon the power variable, earlier neglected. Its objective is to transfer more power to the client or the group. On the other hand, initially at least, T-group practitioners dealt with the power variable only in sanitary, cultural-island situations, where strangers collected, stayed together for a few weeks, and then disbanded. In that setting, as in the client-therapist relationship, one can deal more easily and more cheaply with the power variable than can change agents working in a complex organizational setting, constrained by time, work flow, specialization of knowledge and skill, and the fixed power hierarchy.

At the organizational level, accordingly, theory has been somewhat less clear and inventions more scarce. Although in nonindustrial settings, counselors and group developers were able to take brave positions for radical, almost all-out power equalization, people working in industry could not be so glib, and the limits of power equalization were not clearly defined.

For example, McGregor's (1960) exposition of participative theory "Y" to replace authoritarian theory "X" has been one important direction of work within the large organization. McGregor's whole development of theory "Y" very clearly implies a shift from an all-powerful superior dealing with impotent subordinates to something much more like a balance of power:

> People today are accustomed to being directed and manipulated and controlled in

---

[2]According to Miles, "mythology has it that the first human relations training group (T group) was invented by accident . . . as participants overheard research staff discussing their observations at previous group meetings. They stayed to listen in fascination; to listen and to argue, and the notion of group self-study as a basic mode of learning was born. This version has the heroic simplification common to most myths . . ." (1961).

industrial organizations and to finding satisfaction for their social, egoistic and self-fulfillment needs away from the job. This is true of much of management as well as of workers. Genuine "industrial citizenship" . . . is a remote and unrealistic idea, the meaning of which has not even been considered by most members of industrial organizations.

Another way of saying this is that Theory "X" places exclusive reliance upon external control of human behavior, while Theory "Y" [the theory McGregor exposits] relies heavily on self-control and self-direction. It is worth noting that this difference is the difference between treating people as children and treating them as mature adults (1961, p. 429).

But, although McGregor has argued for heavy reliance on self-control, he has not advocated junking the power structure. Nor has he very clearly specified an optimal position between the two.

Likert's development of his Interaction-Influence Theory (1961) came close on McGregor's heels and parallels McGregor's theory. Drawing heavily this time on the large amounts of empirical data gathered at Michigan's Survey Research Center, Likert used his "principle of supportive relationships" as an organizing theme. He defined the principle as follows:

> The leadership and other processes of the organization must be such as to ensure a maximum probability that in all interactions and all relationships with the organization each member will, in the light of his background, values, and expectations, view the experience as supportive and one which builds and maintains his sense of personal worth and importance (p. 103).

He then went on to define organizational units as overlapping sets of groups rather than individuals. From these and other central notions he developed an ideal, normative model of an organization characterized by, among other things, the following features:

Each member of the organization would be loyal to his own work group, to its leader, and to the organization as a whole.

The members of each work group would be skilled in their respective roles.

Every member of the organization would feel that the overlapping groups which link the organization together enable him satisfactorily to exert influence on all parts of the total organization.

Every member of the organization would feel that the values and goals of his work group amply reflect his own values and needs. He would also feel that the value and objectives of the entire organization adequately reflect the values and needs of all members.

Every member of the organization would be identified with the objectives of the organization and the goals of his work group and see the accomplishment of them as the best way to meet his own needs and personal goals.

Every member of the organization would be motivated to behave in ways best calculated to help the organization accomplish its objectives. Cooperative motivation would prevail throughout the organization. Members would press for excellent performance, efficient methods, and low waste.

Since the pressure for production would come from the members themselves in the form of both individual and group goals, the anxieties associated with pressure from a superior in a hierarchy would be absent.

All the members of the organization, especially the leaders, would have a high level of accurate sensitivity to the reactions and behavior of other members. This sensitivity would enable the members of the organization to be alert also to the reactions of persons outside the organization but important to it, such as shareholders, customers, and suppliers . . . (pp. 181–183).[3]

Likert emphasized that this was a description only of his theoretical ideal,

[3]From *New Patterns of Management* by R. Likert. Copyright 1961. McGraw-Hill Book Company. Used by permission.

not of any known real organization. Certainly, it is as people-oriented a picture as this writer can imagine, paying hardly even lip service to problems of structure or technology. But even as a people-oriented model it seems unrealistically static and conflict-free.

Much of Likert's case rests upon a now-famous study by Morse and Reimer (1956), which covered 500 clerical employees in four parallel divisions of a large company. Two of these divisions had historically been high producers and two low producers. One high producer and one low was assigned to each experimental treatment. In one pair (the Participative Program), "an attempt was made to change the supervision so that decision levels were pushed down. . . . In addition, the managers, assistant managers, supervisors and assistant supervisors of these two divisions were trained in group methods of leadership. . . . Liberal use was made of methods developed by the National Training Laboratories" (Likert, p. 63). In the other two divisions a "Hierarchically Controlled Program" was used. It "called for an increase in closeness of supervision and a movement upward in the level at which decisions were made" (p. 63).

The hierarchically controlled program showed a productivity increase of 25 per cent. "This was a result of the direct orders from the general manager to reduce staff by that amount" (p. 64). A 20 per cent increase occurred in the participative program: "In the participative program the clerks themselves took part in the decision to reduce the size of the work group" (p. 64). The lowest increase of the four divisions was about 15 per cent, from one of the two participative divisions.

Likert then went on to point out that while gross productivity differences were not large, the two programs yielded very different effects when measurements

were taken on some intervening variables. "The productivity increases in the hierarchically-controlled program were accompanied by shifts in an adverse direction in such factors as loyalty, attitudes, interest, and involvement in the work. Just the opposite was true in the participative program" (p. 65). Likert noted, too, that the experiment lasted only a year. Over a longer period, the researchers felt, the mounting costs of the adverse intervening effects would have reduced productivity. This is a gratuitous forecast, of course, assuming that no parallel self-corrective measures would have been introduced into the hierarchical group.

Argyris (1962) has represented a third wing of PE theory. He has focused more on the end of human fulfillment than his colleagues and related it to the issue of organizational efficiency. In one of his recent works (1962) he reported a study (using T-group methods) aimed at helping "an organization increase its administrative competence." In it, he aimed to reduce defensiveness by setting an atmosphere of "authentic" relationships, "those relationships in which an individual enhances his self- and other awareness and acceptance in such a way that others can do the same" (p. 21). Organizationally, the outcomes of greater authenticity, Argyris argued, are improvements in decisions and in performance of tasks. He specifically attacked the "organizational planners" for their assumption of perfect rationality and their suppression of affective elements. He also questioned their beliefs about traditional distributions of power and control. All of these he attacked chiefly on the grounds that they restrict human growth and the full use of human potentials in the organization. Laboratory (T-group) methods are Argyris' tools for changing organizations toward different (more egalitarian) distributions of power and control, for thus, the logic of his case runs, one moves toward authenticity in relationships, and hence toward interpersonal competence.

All of these PE positions can be treated as efforts to relate the two great horns of the dilemma to one another: to relate personal fulfillment to organizational problem-solving and productivity (Bennis, 1959). This issue more than any other, in this writer's opinion, has held up the progress of the power-equalization approaches in industry. Power equalization in counseling and in group training did not have to deal with this issue, but PE applied to organizations cannot escape it.

Here, too, the evolution of positions is quite clear. The Coch and French (1948) and other early studies implied a causal relationship between psychological well-being and productivity, or, more properly, a negative causal relationship between psychological ill-being and productivity. The reasoning was simple and clear. People will work to satisfy needs. When work can be set up so that it is a means to appropriate need satisfaction, it will be carried out willingly and well.

But the problem turned out to be more complex than that, so that some "resolutions" between human needs and the requirements of work have appeared to be compromises rather than resolutions. The redistribution of authority apparently entails unforeseen costs of its own, at least at the experimental stages.

Recently, leading PE practitioners who have been close to industrial organization have been reformulating the problem, so that one does not either try to create high morale in order to achieve high productivity, nor does one pull back on work requirements enough to keep people moderately happy. One searches instead for what Blake and Mouton (1964), in their "managerial grid," have called "integrated manage-

ment." What they mean is some jointly maximized concern for persons and for task requirements. Blake has argued, in effect, that his colleagues have tried to compromise along a nonexistent dichotomous continuum ranging from a human-centered to a task-centered end. He suggested that both ends can be maximized simultaneously because the two variables are independent; but for the moment, at least, it is not clear whether he has introduced evidence or simply changed a conceptual scheme from a unidimensional to a bidimensional form. Blake thus has spoken of "team management," as an integration of "concern for relationships" and "concern for production." He distinguished this integration from traditional authoritarian "task management," from happy, low-conflict "country club management," and from what he perceived as the compromising positions of some of his colleagues.

The same concern about relating human to organizational needs, and efforts to work it out, is reflected in Bennis' case report of a failure of such effort (1962), and in Tannenbaum's recent article (1962) urging a redistribution of control for people reasons, which argues that the whole "influence pie" can be increased in size. "Increasing and distributing the exercise of control more broadly in an organization helps to distribute an important sense of involvement in the organization" (p. 251).

It may well be that many problems will be resolved by this reorientation of the human satisfaction-productivity issue into a search for an integrated human-productive system, but the reorientation can also be viewed as a belated and as yet only partial recognition of the significance of nonhuman variables in organizational systems.

But whether concerned with organizations, groups, or individuals, the power-equalization concept is taking hold in the practice of social change. Bennis, Benne, and Chin in their reader, *The Planning of Change* (1961), are so enamored of it that they have quite specifically set out power equalization as one of the distinguishing features of the deliberate collaborative process they define as "planned change" in "organizations." A power distribution in which the client and change agent have equal, or almost equal, opportunities to influence" is part of their definition of "planned change."

Power equalization has thus become a key concept in several of the prevalent people theories, a first step in the theoretical causal chain leading toward organizational change. It has been constructed as an initial subgoal, a necessary predecessor to creative change in structure, technology, task-solving, and task implementation. Although the distances are unmarked, there is no obscurity about direction: a more egalitarian power distribution is better.

It is worth pointing out that the *techniques* of causing redistribution of power in these models are themselves power-equalization techniques: techniques like counseling and T-group training. Thus, both Lippitt and his associates (1958) and Bennis and his (1961) have laid great emphasis on the need for collaboration between changer and changee for change to take place. But it is understandable that neither of those writers, nor most other workers in power equalization (Schein, 1961, is an exception), have seriously investigated the ways in which power may be redistributed by unilateral or authoritative means, e.g., by the creation of profit centers in a large business firm or by coercion.

The Implementation of Power Equalization

The discussion turns now from the conceptual to the operational implementation of PE ideas at the organizational level. These, too, have passed through a moderately clear set of evolutionary steps.

The Western Electric counseling program (Roethlisberger & Dickson, 1939), referred to earlier, was a monumental early effort. But it avoided the whole issue of power equalization by remaining well outside the "action" side of the organization. Its function was to drain off tension and disturbance generated by the power structure, but not to act on that structure.

Another and surviving but changing effort is represented by the internal attitude or morale survey. It, too, moved toward power equalization but, initially at least, by the indirection of anonymity. The survey mechanism is considered in more detail in the section of this chapter on communication.

A third and highly viable invention was the Scanlon Plan (Lesieur, 1958), which was not a creation of social scientists, but of Joseph N. Scanlon, who had grown up inside the labor movement. It was nurtured by social scientists (specifically by McGregor and Knickerbocker), and Scanlon eventually moved to the M.I.T. staff.

The Scanlon Plan is a union-management cooperation plan, now being used in several small companies and a few larger ones. Its essentials are two: (a) money bonuses to all members of the firm, in proportion to their base rates, for all improvements in over-all company efficiency relative to some base period; and (b) a system of work-improvement committees that cross organizational levels. Where the plan has been introduced, its impact has often been very great, not only on efficiency, but on the nature of interpersonal relations between managers and workers and among workers themselves. In general, the direction of movement is toward greater acceptance of responsibility by lower levels and greater sharing of responsibility by higher with lower groups in the hierarchy.

A variety of other techniques for implementing power-equalization theory were developed, often by converting existing techniques into a form more consistent with PE theory. Efforts to convert merit-rating plans to collaborative goal-setting sessions are a case in point (McGregor, 1957); so are specific experiments in specific firms like those at Harwood Manufacturing Company (Marrow & French, 1945) and Ansul Chemical Company (Stryker, 1956).

But *training* has almost from the start been the mechanism of choice. For what one wants to change are the beliefs and skills of people. Originally, it was supervisory and foreman training in human relations; later, it became training for higher executives. In both cases, the emphasis was on changing the power structure from its then existing state to some vaguely more egalitarian form.

In the last decade, a more direct confrontation of power-equalization theory and organizational constraints has begun to take place with the invasion of the T-group into industry. For the group has increasingly become the primary tool of the power-equalization models, and the T-group, adapted from nonorganizational settings, has increasingly become the specific mechanism of choice.

There is now enough perspective on the T-group in industrial settings to be able to observe several stages of movement. The stages seem to this writer to be important, for they reflect the cautious, gradual confrontation of PE beliefs with organizational realities.

Stage 1 settled for sending individual members of firms to T-group laboratory sessions—away from the plant to groups composed of personnel from several plants. These individuals, relatively na-

ive even after training, then bore the burden of adapting their T-group experiences to the organizational hierarchy. Often they fell flat on their faces, being perceived by their fellows as missionaries for some odd mystique that they could neither communicate orally nor demonstrate in the organizational setting.

Stage 2 was more daring. The T-group is carried into the firm, so that members of the firm are trained together (Foundation for Research on Human Behavior, 1960). Initially, these tended to be veiled T-groups, more task-oriented than the original. They used case discussions as tasks and later included traditional survey data, and they drew their membership from horizontal strata of the organization.

Recently, even more radical steps have been taken—more direct attacks on the power variable. T-groups have been formed diagonally across hierarchical levels, and sometimes even direct vertical slices have been placed in groups. Disguises like the case discussion have been removed. Thus, in this later stage, the T-group is built into the firm, encouraging direct, intimate, and power-free intercommunication across several organizational levels, ordinarily from first-line foremen upward.

The T-group has become a central tool of PE, as demonstrated by other facts than its direct invasion of industrial training. It has also become a tool of management education at many business schools.[4] But perhaps more significant is its adoption by most of the major theorists of participative management. Thus, McGregor (1960) treated the T-group as a major mechanism for promulgating his participative "theory

[4]At M.I.T., Pittsburgh, U.C.L.A., and Harvard, for example, and for one year in Columbia's executive program.

Y." Likert (1961) described the use of T-group-based methods for implementing the participative portion of his group's field experiment on participation in "hierarchically controlled" management. Tannenbaum, Weschler, and Massarik (1962) and Argyris (1962) have also built very heavily around the mechanism of "laboratory" (T-group) training. Blake's (Blake & Mouton, 1958) work in organizations has also developed out of T-group training. Abroad, much of the Tavistock group (Sofer, 1961) has utilized laboratory training quite intensively. But this is evidence only of spread and acceptance; it is no more evidence of validity than any other appeal to authority. But more on validity in later pages.

Perhaps unfairly, we have labeled a large and viable class of efforts to effect change by their common position on one variable—the distribution of power. A more comprehensive picture of these approaches can now be gleaned by considering the way several other organizational variables are dealt with.

1. The determination of goals. The goals question, in the PE models, is treated largely as a "who" question: "Who shall set goals?" And the question is answered, of course, "We all shall!" Goal-setting should be *shared* by as many members of the organization as possible.

Indeed, in nondirective counseling, goal-setting is largely turned over to the changee. The counselor seeks only ways in which he can help the client to clarify his own goals. In the T-group, the trainer either turns over the goal-setting process entirely to the group, or operates collaboratively with his group (after the questions of dependency have been resolved) to set the goals appropriate both for him and for the group.

At the organizational level, the goal-setting issue becomes a little less clear,

because the power-distribution issue is less clear. In general, the direction is the same. In industrial organizations, there has been active movement toward joint goal-setting by superior and subordinate. There is a movement in this direction especially as a substitute for more classical merit-rating activities in which superiors evaluate the performance of subordinates.

McGregor (1957) has argued such a case. And, similarly, Likert wrote:

> In every healthy organization there is, consequently, an unending process of examining and modifying individual goals and organizational objectives as well as consideration of the methods for achieving them. The newer theory specifies that the objectives of the entire organization and of its component parts must be in satisfactory harmony with the relevant needs and desires of the great majority, if not all of the members of the organization, and of the persons served by it (1961, p. 116).

In general, however, the power-equalization approaches to organizational change, especially in the large organization, have been much more ambiguous about goal-setting than these two examples imply. There is some agreement that goal-setting should be a shared process, but considerable vagueness about what aspects of it belong where in the organization. There is general agreement that whatever goals there are should be shared *affectively* by all members of the organization, a position that seems highly questionable to this writer. Thus, Lawrence, in describing an ideal model (idealized models are frequent in this area), said, "Ideally we would want one sentiment to be dominant in all employees from top to bottom, namely a complete loyalty to the organizational purpose" (1958, p. 208).

There is general agreement, too, that loyalty to purpose can be achieved through participation; that people will "support what they help to create." But when these two ideas meet at the level of the large organization, a great deal of uncertainty occurs about the boundaries. Almost everybody agrees that all (not almost all) members of the organization should wish to achieve the organization's goals. Almost everybody agrees that participation helps people want to achieve goals. But everybody does not agree that everybody must or can participate in everything. On the face of it, the size and complexity of large organizations set limits on who can participate in setting what aspects of the organization's goals. One of the reasons that decentralization so often appeals to social scientists with a participative bent may be because it at least partially resolves this goal-setting dilemma. In small units, it is more reasonable for everybody to participate in setting unit goals. But besides decentralization, McGregor's joint-performance appraisal, and some early efforts at "bottoms up" management, it is hard to find other operational devices for solving the goal-setting problem.

Recently, some old questions about collaboration versus unilateral goal-setting have arisen in a new form. Stedry, for example, reported experimental research on budgeting which indicates higher achievement by B under certain conditions in which goals are set for him by A than when B sets his own goals, and A then considers them (1960). Whisler (1958) has also questioned some of McGregor's critique of "traditional" performance-appraisal methods, suggesting that McGregor's device requires major changes in organizational structure before it can be realistically implemented.

In general, then, and in keeping with the affective and interpersonal emphasis, the PE models largely ignore the issue of *what* goals, concentrating instead on increasing organization-wide collaboration in goal-setting.

2. Communication in the power-equalization models. Another important organizational variable has not been at all neglected in the theory and practice of organizational change.

Again, the general outlines of the position taken on communication are implied by the position taken on power. The key propositions can be stated this way, other things being equal: (a) Two-way communication produces more positive outcomes for organizations than one-way communication. (b) Change can take place more readily in two-way interaction situations than in one-way situations. (c) More communication channels are better than fewer communication channels in a structure, and, correspondingly, (d) effective change can be brought about more readily in systems with many communication channels than in systems with few. (e) More valid (unconstrained?) communication in an organization is better than less valid communication, and (f) valid change takes place more readily in interactions where there is valid communication than where there is not.

Note the duality of these statements. On the one hand, they are about organizational ideals—normative statements. On the other hand, they are statements about methods for inducing change. The major reason for this duality may be that the power-equalization models also set change itself as a yardstick of organizational quality. One, if not the major criterion for evaluating the quality of an organization, is, from this view, the organization's capacity to change itself. This is in contrast, say, to the industrial engineer's criteria of efficiency and controllability.

Shepard (1961) has treated valid (unconstrained, easy, expressive of feelings) communication as a key objective in the T-group training process. "The trainer's major responsibility is to help the group identify and overcome obstacles to valid communication." Similarly, Miles (1959) and other writers on group development lay great emphasis on the communication process. "Feedback" has become a key concept in group training. The word "feedback" is derived, of course, from the use of the term in servomechanism theory, wherein a control mechanism makes adjustments of its own behavior in response to signals returned to it about the effects of its own behavior. In T-group situations, feedback usually refers to the gradual removal of defensive barriers from communication channels so that information (mainly affective information) about X's behavior may be fed back to him by the recipients of that behavior, the other members of his group. Leaders of T-groups recognize that affective feedback is neither given nor received readily. A considerable period of softening up, lowering of defenses, and general permissiveness usually precedes the opening up of the feedback loop.

The three labels "valid communication," "two-way communication," and "feedback" are all overlapping characterizations of the same process. They become important because they are presumed to be catalytic to learning. Valid, rapid information about the effects of one's own behavior provides one with a directional map for changing his behavior, if he is interested in change.

It is at this point that some anti-groupthink issues arise. If the feedback loop carries consistent information to oneself about the affective reactions of the group on one's behavior, the "appropriate" direction for change is toward the group standard and not away from it. When the good thermostat learns

that the room is too cool, it signals its furnace to go; it does not insist on keeping it at Stop. If the good group member discovers that his current behavior is producing displeasing or disturbing effects, he may try to please. If the feedback system is very accurate and quick, he may learn when he is too cold even by a very small amount and may, therefore, oscillate less and less away from the standard the group has now set for him. On the other hand, group standards may be redefined so that, on many issues, behavior that is approved is independent behavior.

In any case, at the group level, the communication process becomes important largely as a mechanism for speeding up and directing the learning process. Insofar as it uses group standards as a base line from which individuals measure their oscillations, it is simply substituting the power of the group to change behavior for other sources of power. But since this feedback process occurs simultaneously among all members, the situation is extremely dynamic. It allows wide latitudes for variations in the stability and tightness of the group standards against which individuals may be pressed to measure themselves.

This same feedback notion has been extrapolated to the organizational realm. One technique especially prevalent a decade or so ago was the morale survey (Jacobsen et al., 1951), the results of which were, as a first step, fed back to management as a basis for reassessing its behavior toward employees. That technique had problems. For one thing, it did not open direct channels upward, it circumvented them through the anonymity of aggregate statistics. Moreover, there were real problems in converting this feedback into forms emotionally acceptable to top management, so that they would take "reasonable" actions instead of retaliatory ones. Sometimes these attitude surveys were formalized, so that data from different departments—indeed, from different firms—could be compared. More recently, surveys like this have been built into larger programs in organizational change (Shepard, 1960). Sometimes the data have been gathered and then followed by a series of meetings at several levels of the organization to discuss the data and draw conclusions from them (Jacobsen et al., 1951). Sometimes the data served as the jumping-off place for programs in group dynamics in which several levels of management have participated (Shepard, 1960). Still more recently, the survey has given way altogether to training programs which involved intercommunication across levels about just the sort of questions usually asked in a survey (Foundation for Research on Human Behavior, 1960). But this time, the discussions take place face to face in small development groups, so that the "survey" and evaluation of the data go on simultaneously.

In all cases, however, it seems fair to say that the power-equalization approaches seek to increase the number of communication channels and the amount of information flow over them, to widen the distribution of information, and to change its nature. On this last point, the power-equalization approaches encourage the communication of affective as well as task information. In this last respect, too, they contrast considerably with earlier approaches, which intentionally set up filters against the transmittal of task-irrelevant information.

This endorsement of more and more communication in organizations is becoming less and less tenable with the development of new techniques for measuring and processing information and therefore for treating it selectively.

Presumably, however, the power-equalization models can be considered self-organizing mechanisms, which will set their own limits on communication, but only where and when members deem it appropriate.

3. *Group pressure, group cohesiveness, and conformity in the power-equalization approaches.* Again, the direction is clear. Since Lewin's early studies on changing food habits (1952), there has been a strong tendency to use the authority of the group as an alternative to hierarchical authority. The group can serve both as a pressure device and as a mechanism for gaining commitment. Public expression of commitment to a decision is deemed an effective aid to the superego, once an individual leaves the group. Similarly, group cohesiveness is highly valued in the power-equalization approaches.

In part, it is valued as a mechanism for increasing loyalty (see Likert's, 1961, and Lawrence's, 1958, emphases on loyalty cited earlier) and in part as a mechanism for controlling deviant or otherwise recalcitrant members.

In larger part, cohesiveness is valued for its releasing and supporting qualities. Membership in a cohesive group provides the individual with an environment of trust and security, disinhibiting him and allowing him to behave more creatively.

The extent to which groups are indeed powerful instruments for exerting pressure on individuals and, conversely, for protecting individuals from influence has been nicely analyzed by Schein (1960) in his review of the techniques used by the Chinese Communists in dealing with military prisoners during the Korean war. In that situation, alienation of individuals from their original groups became a major device for increasing their susceptibility to influence. Conversely, the later restructuring of new groups then became an effective mechanism for reinfluencing prisoners in new directions. As Schein pointed out, comparable processes are observable in a variety of change situations in the Western world.

The power-equalization models, then, try to use group pressures to increase commitment and involvement, while avoiding the stultifying impact of tight pressures to conform to "irrelevant" standards. It is on this point, of course, that many of the most virulent attacks against "human relations" have been directed. Thus, W. H. Whyte (1956), McNair (1957), and Fromm (1957) have bewailed the extent to which group pressures may reduce creativity and individuality.

Group dynamicists characteristically respond to these attacks, as Likert (1961) did, with the argument that group standards can be of many varieties and group pressures can push in many directions. If groups set high standards for performance and quality and value individual creativity, at the same time maintaining loose standards as far as social conformity is concerned, then the best of all possible worlds will result.

Cartwright and Lippitt, writing from a more research-oriented point of view, have taken a more objective stand than their application-oriented colleagues.

> We have seen that the pressures to uniformity are stronger the more cohesive the group. Shall we conclude from this that strong, need-satisfying, cohesive groups must always produce uniformity on matters that are important to the group? We believe not. We cannot, however, cite much convincing evidence since research has focused to date primarily on the sources of pressures to uniformity and has ignored the conditions which produce heterogeneity (1961, p. 272).

Cartwright and Lippitt then went on to discuss group standards of uniformity, freedom to deviate, subgroup formation, position, and roles. In their discussion of these parameters, they pointed out ways in which heterogeneity may be achieved within highly cohesive groups.

4. Decision-making in the power-equalization models. Decision-making, from the perspective of power equalization, is viewed, not as a cognitive process, nor substantively, but as a normative issue of achieving agreement. The much-discussed questions are about consensus, unanimity, group commitment. Relatively little has been written about such questions as the effect of power equalization on the amount and kind of search that a problem-solving group undertakes. Instead, the central issue is Sullivan's idea of "consensual validation." "Validating" in this sense means gaining commitment.

To a large extent, decision-making in organizations is treated as a direct extrapolation of the problem of decision-making in small groups, especially T-groups. Within the T-group, in turn, decision-making becomes largely a problem of achieving, not the best from a hierarchy of alternatives, but valid consensus among members. One becomes concerned, for example, about the "health" of a group that is forced to take votes on issues and to live with minority decisions. The ideal from the PE perspective is a sufficiently open and valid communication system that, given time, consensus can be achieved.

In general, the power-equalization models work from these propositions to move groups toward consensual decision-making: (a) Involvement in decision-making yields commitment to the decision; and since most decisions become meaningless in their execution unless they are supported, commitment becomes a necessary condition for effective decision-making. (b) It is useful to lower decision points in an organization (the writer can find no case in which an argument is raised for raising decision points under any circumstances). (c) It is reasonable for groups to make decisions; it is not necessary that decisions be made only by individuals.

Bennis, in a general paper on leadership theory, commented as follows: "Group decision making and its variations appear to be one of the basic pillars of the human relations approach, in contradistinction to more traditional theory where all responsibility is channeled into one office" (1959, p. 293). Then, after summarizing the work on group pressures on the individual, he went on: "The decision maker, then, faced with no operable means for evaluating a decision—as is often the case—and with limited data, has no other recourse than to utilize a group, both as a security operation and a validity tester. This is not to say that this method is the most effective; quite the opposite. It may be the most expensive, involved and tedious. Nevertheless, psychologically, it is functional" (p. 294). Under such costly conditions, it could be predicted that decision-makers should search energetically for other alternatives than groups, and, upon finding one, they would be expected to be ready to abandon groups forthwith.

The Technics of Power Equalization

The power-equalization models rest heavily on the ideas of self-imposed and collaborative change. Self-imposed change solved the problem of commitment by avoiding the causes of resistance, and it solved the problem of the manipulative soft spot precisely because it was self-imposed.

The tools invented or borrowed to implement power-equalization could therefore be selected only from among those that would permit self-imposition. The tools of industrial engineering were thus not applicable, nor were the strategies offered by Machiavellis, past or present. Nor could more cognitive analytic tools like the techniques of operations research be used directly, although presumably a group once changed could (and would if they were useful) subsequently use any of these secondarily.

The tools needed to be essentially motivational. The techniques of client-centered counseling served this purpose, but they were hard to generalize to organizations, firmly based as they were in the two-person relationship. Survey methods proved insufficient. Personal consulting has never developed a clearly institutionalized and transferable technology. But an even more viable tool was the T-group. The T-group could deal with people 12 or 15 at once, and with some time and effort could thereby be extended to cover large numbers of people within an organization.

But note that the T-group is used primarily to train working members of organizations, not just future trainers. The T-group is for presidents as well as for foremen or hourly workers or volunteer workers in nonprofit organizations. And note, too, that although T-group training may have important effects on the people it touches directly, the outcomes do not spread easily from the trained to the untrained.

In general, practitioners would much prefer to set up long-range programs in which large proportions of an organization's members go through T-group training; for the seeding of a few trained people does not easily bear fruit, in part because the home environment is often not supportive of changes started in the group (Harrison, 1962).

So, in practice, the evocation of organizational change through sensitivity training has begun to take a rather distinct form. Usually, a series of laboratory training programs for some 30 to 50 members of the organizations are arranged. They are usually held away from the home base, at relatively isolated resorts. Those attending are divided into two or three T-groups. The programs may last from three days to three weeks. They are staffed by outside consultants as trainers. The more daring programs face up to the power problem from the start by making up T-groups from several levels of authority.

But data (except clinical data) about results remain very scarce indeed, although they are beginning to arrive (Foundation for Research on Human Behavior, 1960; Harrison, 1962), and those that are available are not clear.[5]

Power Equalization and the Future: An Evaluative Summary

It is this reviewer's opinion that the power-equalization models are mostly right and mostly insufficient. They are blessed with a few social inventions that make concrete application more feasible than is true of some other sets of ideas (although the power-equalization tools are far from ideal for accomplishing their own ends). It seems a safe bet, too, that equalization approaches will increasingly be modified or supplanted by other, often far less people-oriented, mechanisms for effecting organizational change.

The PE models seem insufficient in these senses: First they have been overgeneralized. Like most good ideas, their developers feel that they are applicable everywhere. The writer submits that there are and will remain large task areas in organizations in which the criteria of creativity, flexibility, and capacity to deal with novel unprogrammed prob-

[5]As this chapter goes to press, new work begins to appear. Blake et al. (1964) and Bunker (1963) present impressive material on organizational effects of laboratory training.

lems will remain critically important. In those areas, the PE models are a feasible present alternative. In other, more highly programmed, task areas, in more constrained environments, the criteria of effectiveness are often different. They may be speed, quantity of output, controllability. In these realms, the PE approaches have much less to offer, economically speaking, although no less in terms of the psychological fulfillment of workers.

They are also insufficiently supported by empirical data. The issue of validity remains a critical and difficult issue. When empirical studies have been undertaken to evaluate outcomes, the results have been equivocal at best (Foundation for Research on Human Behavior, 1960; Harrison, 1962; Morse & Reimer, 1956). Even several of the individual case analyses (Bendix, 1956; Bennis, 1962) have led to equivocal or negative results.

PE practices have been carried much more by their transferable operational techniques and by their impact on persons than by their demonstrated results. But it must be pointed out quickly that the structural and technological models are at least as short on measurement as the PE models, and, perhaps more important, that the PE models with their emphasis on open inquiry are demonstrating a commendable readiness to explore and examine failure as well as success.

It is this reviewer's guess that the PE approaches will continue to grow in the number and breadth of their applications, because they are relatively operational and transferable. But they will be used more and more frequently in the unprogrammed areas of management like research and development, both because they seem more appropriate and because alternatives are scarce.

Close behind PE, however, other potentially more general methods for effecting change are developing and gradually moving from laboratory into application. These methods, largely technological, may change the map of areas susceptible to the PE models. For by programming what is now unprogrammed, some problems now effectively handled only by the PE approaches may become ripe for other kinds of work; and, conversely, some sets of issues now handled structurally or technologically may need more people work.

REFERENCES

Argyris, C. *Personality and organization.* New York: Harper, 1957.

Argyris, C. *Interpersonal competence and organizational effectiveness.* Homewood, Ill.: Irwin, 1962.

Bendix, R. *Work and authority in industry.* New York: Wiley, 1956.

Bennis, W. G. Bureaucracy and social change: an anatomy of a failure. Boston: Massachusetts Institute of Technology, School of Industrial Management, 1962. (Multilithed.)

Bennis, W. G. Leadership theory and administrative behavior: the problem of authority. *Admin. sci. Quart.,* 1959, 4, 259–301.

Bennis, W. G., Benne, K. D., & Chin, R. *The planning of change.* New York: Holt, 1961.

Bennis, W. G., & Shepard, H. A. A theory of group development. In W. G. Bennis, K. D. Benne, & R. Chin, *The planning of change.* New York: Holt, 1961. Pp. 321–340.

Blake, R. R., & Mouton, J. S. *Training for decision making in groups.* Austin, Texas: Licensed to Standard Oil Company (N.J.), 1958.

Blake, R. R., & Mouton, J. S. *The managerial grid.* Houston, Texas: Gulf, 1964.

Blake, R. R., Mouton, J. S., Barnes, L. B., & Greiner, L. E. Breakthrough in organization development. *Harvard bus. Rev.,* 1964, 42, 135–138.

Bradford, L. P., Gibb, J. R., & Benne, K. D. *T-group theory and laboratory method.* New York: Wiley, 1964.

Brown, A. *Organizations of industry.* New York: Prentice-Hall, 1947.

Bunker, D. R. *The effect of laboratory education upon individual behavior.* Boston: Harvard Univer., Graduate School of Business Administration, 1963. (Dittoed.)

Carnegie, D. *How to win friends and influence people.* New York: Simon & Schuster, 1936.

Cartwright, D. Power: a neglected variable in social psychology. In D. Cartwright & A. Zander (Eds.), *Studies in social power.* Ann Arbor: Univer. of Michigan, Institute for Social Research, 1959. Pp. 1–14.

Cartwright, D., & Lippitt, R. Group dynamics and the individual. In W. G. Bennis, K. D. Benne, & R. Chin, *The planning of change.* New York: Holt, 1961. Pp. 264–277.

Chapman, R. L., Kennedy, J. L., Newell, A., & Bill, W. C. The Systems Research Laboratory's air defense experiments. *Mgmt. Sci.,* 1959, 5, 250–269.

Chapple, E. D., & Sayles, L. R. *The measure of management.* New York: Macmillan, 1961.

Coch, L., & French, J. R. P. Overcoming resistance to change. *Hum. Relat.,* 1948, 1, 512–533.

Charnes, A., & Cooper, W. W. *Management models and industrial applications of linear programming.* 2 vols. New York: Wiley, 1961.

Churchman, C. W., Ackoff, R. L., & Arnoff, E. L. *Introduction to operations research.* New York: Wiley, 1957.

Cooper, W. W. Some implications of the newer analytic approaches to management. *Calif. mgmt Rev.,* 1961, 4, 51–64.

Cyert, R. M., & March, J. G. *A behavioral theory of the firm.* Englewood Cliffs, N.J.: Prentice-Hall, 1962.

Dale, E. Centralization vs. decentralization. *Advanced Mgmt,* 1955, 20, 11–16.

Fayol, H. *General and industrial management.* New York: Pitman, 1949.

Festinger, L. *A theory of cognitive dissonance.* Evanston, Ill.: Row, Peterson, 1957.

Foundation for Research on Human Behavior. *An action research program for organizational improvement (in Esso Standard Oil Company).* Ann Arbor: Author, 1960.

Fromm, E. Man is not a thing. *Sat. Rev.,* 1957, 40, 9–11.

Ginzberg, E., & Reilly, E. *Effecting change in large organizations.* New York: Columbia Univer. Press, 1957.

Glanzer, M., & Glaser, R. Techniques for the study of group structure and behavior II. *Psychol. Bull.,* 1961, 58, 1–27.

Guest, R. H. *Organizational change: the effect of*

successful leadership. Homewood, Ill.: Irwin, 1962.

Goode, I. J. How rational should a manager be? *Mgmt Sci.*, 1962, 8, 383–393.

Gouldner, A. Exploration in organizational social science. *Soc. Probl.*, 1956, 3, 173–181.

Gulick, L. H., & Urwick, L. (Eds.) *Papers on the science of administration.* New York: Institute of Public Administration, 1937.

Harrison, R. Impact of the laboratory on perceptions of others by the experimental group. In C. Argyris, *Interpersonal competence and organizational effectiveness.* Homewood, Ill.: Irwin, 1962. Pp. 261–271.

Holden, P. E., Fish, L. S., & Smith, H. L. *Top management organization and control.* New York: McGraw-Hill, 1951.

Holmberg, A. R. The research and development approach to change: participant intervention in the field. In R. N. Adams & J. J. Preiss (Eds.), *Human organization research.* Homewood, Ill.: Dorsey, 1960. Pp. 76–89.

Hovland, C., Janis, I., & Kelley, H. *Communication and persuasion.* New Haven: Yale Univer. Press, 1953.

Jacobsen, E., Kahn, R., Mann, F., & Morse, Nancy (Eds.) Human relations research in large organizations. *J. soc. Issues*, 1951, 7 (3).

Jacques, E. *The changing culture of a factory.* London: Tavistock, 1951.

Joseph, M. L. An experimental approach to the study of collective bargaining. *Indust. Relat. Res. Ass. Proceedings*, 1961. Pp. 1–17.

Lawrence, P. *The changing of organizational behavior patterns.* Boston: Harvard Univer., Division of Research, 1958.

Lawrence, P. R., et al. *Organizational behavior and administration.* Homewood, Ill.: Irwin, 1961.

Leavitt, H. J. Unhuman organizations. *Harvard bus. Rev.*, 1962, 40, 90–98.

Leavitt, H. J., & Whisler, T. L. Management in the 1980's. *Harvard bus. Rev.*, 1958, 36, 41–48.

Lesieur, F. *The Scanlon Plan.* Cambridge: Technology Press of M.I.T., 1958.

Lewin, K. Group decision and social change. In G. E. Swanson, T. M. Newcomb, & E. L. Hartley (Eds.), *Readings in social psychology.* (2nd ed.) New York: Holt, 1952. Pp. 459–473.

Likert, R. *New patterns of management.* New York: McGraw-Hill, 1961.

Lippitt, R., Watson, Jeanne, & Westley, B.

The dynamics of planned change. New York: Harcourt, Brace, 1958.

McGregor, D. *The human side of enterprise.* In W. G. Bennis, K. D. Benne, & R. Chin, *The planning of change.* New York: Holt, 1961. Pp. 422–431.

McGregor, D. An uneasy look at performance appraisal. *Harvard bus. Rev.*, 1957, 35, 89–94.

McNair, M. What price human relations? *Harvard bus. Rev.*, 1957, 35, 15–30.

Malcolm, D. G., Rowe, A. J., & McConnell, L. F. (Eds.), *Management control systems.* New York: Wiley, 1960.

Mann, F. C., & Hoffman, L. R., *Automation and the worker.* New York: Holt, 1960.

Mansfield, E. Technical change and the rate of innovation. *Econometrica*, 1961, 29, 741–766.

Marrow, A. J., & French, J. R. P. Changing a stereotype in industry. *J. soc. Issues*, 1945, 21, 33–37.

Marschak, J. Paper read at Seminar on Social Science of Organizations, Pittsburgh, June 1962.

Martin, N., & Sims, J. R. The problem of power. In W. L. Warner & N. Martin (Eds.), *Industrial man.* New York: Harper, 1959. Pp. 514–522.

Meier, R. L. Communication and social change. *Behav. Sci.*, 1956, 1, 43–58.

Metcalf, H. C., & Urwick, L. (Eds.) *Dynamic administration: the collected works of Mary Parker Follett.* New York: Harper, 1942.

Miles, M. B. *Learning how to work in groups.* New York: Teachers College, Columbia Univer., 1959.

Miles, M. B. Human relations training: processes and outcomes. *J. couns. Psychol.*, 1960, 7, 301–306.

Miles, M. B. Human relations training: current status. Paper read at Ass. Appl. Psychol., Copenhagen, July, 1961.

Moore, B. V. Some beginnings of industrial psychology. In B. Von H. Gilmer (Ed.), *Walter Van Dyke Bingham.* Pittsburgh: Carnegie Press, 1962. Pp. 1–22.

Morse, Nancy, & Reimer, E. The experimental change of a major organizational variable. *J. abnorm. soc. Psychol.*, 1956, 52, 120–129.

Mumford, L. *Technics and civilization.* New York: Harcourt, Brace, 1934.

National Training Laboratories. *Explorations in human relations training.* Washington, D.C.: Author, 1953.

Newell, A., & Simon, H. A. Computer simulation of human thinking. *Sci.*, 1961, 134, 2011–2017.

Roethlisberger, F. J., & Dickson, W., *Management and the worker.* Cambridge: Harvard Univer. Press, 1939.

Rogers, C. R. *Counseling and psychotherapy.* Boston: Houghton Mifflin, 1942.

Rogers, C. R. *Client centered therapy.* Boston: Houghton Mifflin, 1951.

Rogers, C. R., & Roethlisberger, F. J. Barriers and gateways to communication. *Harvard bus. Rev.*, 1952, 30, 28–34.

Schein, E. H. Interpersonal communication, organizational solidarity and social influence. *Sociometry*, 1960, 23, 148–161.

Schein, E. H. Management development as a process of influence. *Indust. mgmt Rev.*, 1961, 2, 59–77.

Shepard, H. A. Three management programs and the theories behind them. In *An Action Research Program for Organization Improvement (in Esso Standard Oil Company).* Ann Arbor: Foundation for Research on Human Behavior, 1960. Pp. 1–6.

Shepard, H. A. The T-group as training in observant participation. In W. G. Bennis, K. D. Benne, & R. Chin, *The planning of change.* New York: Holt, 1961. Pp. 637–642.

Shultz, G. P., & Whisler, T. L. *Management organization and the computer.* Glencoe, Ill.: Free Press, 1960.

Siegel, S., & Fouraker, L. E. *Bargaining and group decision making.* New York: McGraw-Hill, 1960.

Simon, H. A. The corporation: will it be managed by machines? In M. Anshen & G. L. Bach (Eds.), *Management and corporations,* 1985. New York: McGraw-Hill, 1960. Pp. 17–55.

Simon, H. A., Guetzkow, H., Kozmetsky, G., & Tyndall, G. *Centralization vs. decentralization in organizing the controller's department.* New York: Controllership Foundation, 1954.

Sinclair, U. Principles of scientific management: a criticism. *Amer. Mag.*, June, 1911.

Sofer, C. *The organization from within.* London: Tavistock, 1961.

Stedry, A. *Budget control and cost behavior.* Englewood Cliffs, N.J.: Prentice-Hall, 1960.

Strauss, G. Tactics of lateral relationships. *Admin. sci. Quart.*, 1962, 7, 161–186.

Stryker, P. How participative can a company get? *Fortune*, 1956, 54 (3), 134–136 ff.

Tannenbaum, A. S. Control in organizations. *Admin. sci. Quart.*, 1962, 7, 236–257.

Tannenbaum, R., Weschler, I., & Massarik, F. *Leadership and organization.* New York: McGraw-Hill, 1961.

Taylor, F. W. *Scientific management.* New York: Harper, 1911.

Tonge, F. M. *A heuristic program for assembly line balancing.* Englewood Cliffs, N.J.: Prentice-Hall, 1961.

Urwick, L. The manager's span of control. *Harvard bus. Rev.*, 1956, 34, 39–47.

Walker, C. R. (Ed.) *Modern technology and civilization.* New York: McGraw-Hill, 1962.

Whisler, T. L. Performance appraisal and the organization man. *J. Bus.* 1958, 31, 19–27.

Whyte, W. F. *Money and motivation.* New York: Harper, 1955.

Whyte, W. H. *The organization man.* New York: Simon & Schuster, 1956.

40

Applying Behavioral Sciences to Planned Organizational Change

Warren G. Bennis

THE NOTATION OF PLANNED CHANGE

Planned change is a method which employs social technology to solve the problems of society. The method encompasses the application of systematic and appropriate knowledge to human affairs for the purpose of creating intelligent action and choices. Planned change aims to relate to the basic disciplines of the behavioral sciences as engineering does to the physical sciences or as medicine does to the biological disciplines.* Thus, planned change can be viewed as a crucial link between theory and practice, between knowledge and action. It plays this role by converting variables from the basic disciplines into strategic instrumentation and programs. In historical perspective, the development of planned change can be viewed as the result of two forces: complex problems of modern (organizational) society requiring expert help and the growth and viability of the empirical behavioral sciences. "Behavioral sciences" is a term coined in the period following World War II by the more empirically minded of the profession in order to "safeguard" the social disci-

*It falls far short of this aim as of today, partly because of the relatively less mature state of the behavioral sciences and even more because of the lack of tradition in the application of the behavioral sciences.

plines from the nonquantitative humanists and the depersonalized abstractions of the econometricists. Typically, the field is thought to contain six disciplines: psychology, sociology, anthropology, political science, history, and economics. Planned change, as the term is used here, relies most heavily on the sociological and psychological disciplines.*

The process of planned change involves a *change-agent,* who is typically a behavioral scientist brought in to help a *client-system,* which refers to the target of change.† The change-agent, in *collaboration* with the client-system, attempts to apply *valid knowledge* to the client's problems. These four elements in combination—change-agent, client-system, valid knowledge, and a deliberate and collaborative relationship—circumscribe the class of activities referred to as "planned change." The terms are imprecise and somewhat ambiguous, but it is hoped that their mean-

*For a recent inventory of scientific findings of the behavioral sciences, see Berelson and Steiner;[1] for the best single reference on the philosophical foundations of the behavioral sciences, see Kaplan.[2]

†These terms, "change-agent" and "client-system," are awkward, but substitutes which would satisfy aesthetic criteria do not come to mind. And these terms are coming into wider usage. See Lippitt et al.[3] for a fuller account of these terms. See also Bennis[i] et al.[4]

TABLE 1 • TYPOLOGY OF CHANGE PROCESSES

	Collaborative		Noncollaborative	
	Mutual Goal Setting		**Goals Set by Only One or Neither Side**	
Power ratio	Deliberate on the part of one or both sides of the relationship	Nondeliberate on the part of both sides	Deliberate on the part of one side of the relationship	Nondeliberate on the part of both sides
.5:.5	Planned	Interactional	Technocratic	Natural
1:0	Indoctrinational	Socialization	Coercive	Emulative

ing will be clarified through a discussion of concrete illustration.

These four elements also help distinguish planned change from other forms of change. Planned change differs from "technocracy" in that it attempts to implement research results and relies more heavily on the relationship between change-agent and client-system. Planned change differs from most "coercive" change programs in that the change-agent has no formal power over the client-system. Planned change differs from spontaneous and secondary innovations in that it is a conscious and deliberate induction process.

Table 1 presents a typology where eight species of change may be identified. Along the horizontal axis are shown two variables, dichotomized for convenience: mutual goal setting and deliberateness of change. Along the vertical axis, power distribution between the change-agent and client-system is shown: .5:.5 indicates a fairly equal distribution of power, and 1:0 indicates a tilted or unequal power distribution. (In other words, in a .5:.5 power ratio, each party has the capability of influencing the other; in a 1:0 ratio, only one party is susceptible to influence.) "Valid knowledge" is omitted from the paradigm since it is, for the present, subsumed under "mutual goal

setting." In a later section we shall return to the question of valid knowledge and its relevance to planned change.

Planned change entails mutual goal setting, an equal power ratio (eventually), and deliberateness on the part of both sides.

Indoctrination involves mutual goal setting and is deliberate, but it involves an imbalanced power ratio. Many schools, prisons, and mental hospitals or other "total institutions"[5] fall into this category.

Coercive change is characterized by nonmutual goal setting, an imbalanced power ratio, and only one-sided deliberateness. Coercive change, as we are using the term, may be exemplified by the thought-control and "brainwashing" practices of the Chinese.[6,*]

Technocratic change may be distin-

---

*The distinctions between indoctrinational and coercive changes are complex. When all is said and done, hospital administrators and prisoner-of-war commandants may employ similar processes and techniques. There are probably more similarities than would be expected between forms of "acceptable" social influences, such as psychotherapy or teaching, and "unacceptable" forms, such as brainwashing. This paradigm, like all others, creates an ideal and abstract model to which empirical occurrences do not neatly conform. See my typology of change process.[7]

guished from planned change by the nature of the goal setting. The use of technocratic means to bring about change relies solely on collecting and interpreting data. Technocratic change, then, follows primarily an "engineering" model: the client defines his difficulties as deriving from inadequate knowledge and assumes that this lack of knowledge is accidental or a matter of neglect—not something that is functional to the system itself. The technocrat colludes in this assumption and merely makes and reports his findings.[*]

Interactional change is characterized by mutual goal setting, a fairly equal power distribution, but no deliberateness on either side of the relationship. (*Unconsciously* either may be committed to changing the other in some direction.) Such changes can be observed among good friends and married couples and in various other nondeliberate transactions among people. Change does occur in such relationships, possibly with beneficial effects, but there is a lack of self-consciousness about it and thus a lack of any definite change-agent–client-system relationship.

Socialization change has a direct kinship with hierarchical controls. Parent-child relationships would be the most obvious example, although the counselor-camper and teacher-pupil relationships would also be instances.

Emulative change takes place for the most part in formal organizations where there is a clear-cut superior-subordinate relationship. Change is brought about through identification with, and emulation of, the "power figures" by the subordinates.

Natural change refers to that class of changes brought about with no apparent deliberateness and no goal setting

on the part of those involved in it. Primarily it is a residual category encompassing all accidents, "quirks of fate," unanticipated consequences, spontaneous innovations, etc.

This typology is crude: in nature we can rarely observe these change processes exemplified so neatly. In addition, the distinctions made in it are somewhat arbitrary and certainly not all-inclusive. In order to give the notion of planned change more meaning and substance, it might be useful to compare it with some characteristics of operations research.

PLANNED CHANGE COMPARED WITH OPERATIONS RESEARCH[*]

My knowledge of OR stems from three sources: lay articles on OR that one might see in popular periodicals such as *Scientific American* or in Schuchman[9]; more recently, and in preparation for this paper, the basic introductory books recommended by OR professionals; and most of all, the OR "pros" who occasionally sit at the dining table at MIT across from me and talk mysteriously and cheerfully about their work in such a way that I hesitate to ask even the most elementary questions, such as: What do you *really* do? And I ruefully sense a kinship, the mutual incapacity to explain to each other the basic nature of our work. But as I read over some of the literature recently, I was encouraged by certain similarities between OR and what I mean by planned change. It may be useful to discuss these now.

---

[*]See Gouldner[8] for a full discussion of the technocrat as a change-agent.

[*]This section was written especially for the OR personnel attending the conference for which this paper was written. I have decided to retain it as I think it puts the idea of planned change in better focus.

SOME SIMILARITIES BETWEEN OR AND PLANNED CHANGE

Both are relatively recent *developments.* Both were products of World War II. As I understand it, OR was "founded" just before World War II, developed its status during the war, and flourished thereafter. Planned change, as was true of almost all applied behavioral research, was begun in earnest following World War II and was facilitated and promoted by practitioners who learned during the war that science could be practical.* Later on, I will have more to say about the relationship between science and action, but I should stress at this point that while there have been in the past fruitful liaisons between the behavioral sciences and action in rural sociology, in applied economics, and in clinical psychology—to mention only a few— the quality and quantity of these linkages have taken a significant upturn since World War II. From a pastime, the application of knowledge became a profession.

Both OR and planned change are problem-centered, as contrasted to the basic disciplines, which emphasize *concept* or *method.* This is a matter of emphasis only, for OR and applied research, in general, have often provided significant inputs to the concepts and methods of their parent basic disciplines. This is not a one-way street.†

Both OR and planned change emphasize improvement and optimization of performance. To that extent, they are *normative* in their approach to problems; that is, they attempt to maximize goals under certain conditions.

Both OR and planned change rely heavily on *empirical science* as their main means of influence. Ellis Johnson points out that the ". . . majority of practitioners of operations research were trained in the basic sciences rather than in engineering or administration."[11] Similarly, practitioners of planned change were mostly trained in psychology, sociology, or anthropology. To both, the old maxim, "Knowledge is power," seems appropriate as a model of action.

Both OR and planned change rely on a relationship with clients based on *confidence* and *valid communication.*

Both OR and planned change emphasize a *systems* approach to problems, meaning essentially an awareness of the interdependencies within the internal parts of the system as well as boundary maintenance with its environment.

Finally, both OR and planned change appear to be most effective when working with *systems which are complex, rapidly changing, and probably science-based.* It will be useful to quote Johnson again on this point:

> In those large and complex organizations for whom once-reliable constants have now become "galloping variables" because of the impact of increasing complexity, trial and error must give way to planning, and acceptance of marginal improvement must give way to an organized search for opportunities to make major shifts in the means of achieving organizational objectives. Today, so many industrial and other organizations are so huge, and major operations are so expensive, that a single major "wrong" decision may be fatal; trial and error becomes "trial and catastrophe."[12]

These characteristics, then—newness, problem orientation, normative approach, basis in science, collaborative relationship with clients, systems approach, and effectiveness in rapidly

---

*Kurt Lewin, one of the leaders of this group, was fond of saying: "There is nothing so practical as a good theory."

†See Gouldner[10] for a brilliant exposition on the contributions of applied research to "pure" theory.

changing environments—show some of the points of common interest and approach of OR and planned change. Let us turn now to some of the differences.

SOME DIFFERENCES BETWEEN OR AND PLANNED CHANGE

Perhaps the most crucial difference between OR and planned change has to do with the *identification of strategic variables*, that is, with those factors which appear to make a difference in the performance of the system under study. The marked difference in the selection of variables must undoubtedly stem from a unique "frame of reference" which leads to divergent problem-definitions. Ackoff and Rivett, for example, classify OR problems in the following way:[13]

> Inventory
> Allocation
> Queuing
> Sequencing
> Routing
> Replacement
> Competition
> Search

A similar inventory of problems in the planned-change field would probably include the following:

> Identification of appropriate mission and values
> Human collaboration and conflict
> Control and leadership
> Coping with, and resistance to, change
> Utilization of human resources
> Communication between hierarchical ranks
> Rapid growth
> Management and career development

The divergence of problem-definition leads to the selection of different variables. OR practitioners tend to select economic or engineering variables—most certainly variables which are quantitative and measurable and which appear to be linked directly to the profit and efficiency of the system. Not so of the planned-change practitioners. While there are vigorous attempts to measure rigorously and to conduct evaluation studies, the variables selected tend to be less amenable to statistical treatment and mathematical formulation. Upon even a superficial perusal of some of the literature on planned change and OR, the difference is evident: a significantly lower ratio of tables and mathematical formulas in the former.

An interesting example of the difference in variable identification and selection can be seen if we compare an example of OR with an example of planned change. Ackoff and Rivett, in their introductory chapter, report a case where OR was called on to help a major commercial airline decide how often it should run a class for stewardesses and how large the class should be. This led to a study of the following factors: cost of running the school, forecasts for future requirements, forecasting procedures, expenses and salaries of all personnel, maximum possible average number of flying hours per stewardess that could be obtained, factors in stewardesses' job satisfaction, number of reserve stewardesses required at each air base, number of bases and where they should be located, how flights should be assigned, etc., etc. As Ackoff and Rivett conclude:

> What originally appeared to be a simple and isolated problem turned out to be interconnected with almost all other operating problems of the airline. With extension of the problem the solutions to

the parts could be interrelated to assure best overall performance. This avoided a "local" improvement which might result in overall loss of efficiency.[14]

Compare the airline's case with a report of C. Sofer, a sociologist who employs techniques of planned change in his role as a social consultant to a variety of organizations. A small firm called upon him to help in the selection of a senior manager.[*] This "presenting symptom" led to a series of disclosures and causal mechanisms which Sofer uncovered during a series of talks and meetings with the top management group. The case itself unraveled a complicated cat's cradle of factors including family relationships (among the top management group), fantasies and mistrust among members of the management group, management and career development, selection procedures, etc. Sofer helped the firm overcome these problems through counseling, through devising new organizational structures, through a training program, and through developing improved selection devices. The case was completed in about three years with follow-up consultations from time to time.

When we compare the two cases, what differences appear? First and foremost, as we said before, the problems identified as crucial for the success of the enterprise. In the case of OR, the problems identified appear to be more concrete, more measurable, and more obviously related (at least in the short run) to the success of the enterprise, i.e., profits and losses. Sofer identified problems and variables which were less measurable, more subjective in that they were *felt* as problems by the partic-

ipants, and less obviously linked to the firm's success.

But beyond this, there appear to be some equally marked differences in the two approaches to organizational change. In the example given by Sofer, he concerns himself directly with his relationship to the client, studies this very carefully, and attempts to "use" this relationship both as a diagnostic instrument and as a training device. Even apparently "trivial" decisions, such as whether or not to have lunch with his clients, come under scrutiny:

> My staying to lunch was consistent with what is now a not uncommon Institute [Tavistock] pattern of associating to a certain degree with "clients" outside the professional situation as strictly defined. Not to do so would seem unnatural to them and highly discrepant from the ordinary conventions of business relationships to which they are accustomed. There is also the more positive reason that through such association clients are more likely to remain reality-oriented in their perceptions of the social consultant and to regard him simply as another human being who brings a particular type of expertise to bear on their problems.[16]

So a second major difference between OR and planned organizational change has to do with the *perceived importance* of the *relationship with the client*. The development and maintenance of this relationship are crucial elements in all planned-change programs. And *not solely*, or even most importantly, for "good human relations." Instead, the quality and the nature of the relationship are used as indicators for the measure of progress and as valid sources of data and diagnosis. This is not to say that OR practitioners do not concern themselves with matters of this kind. Undoubtedly they do, and probably the most successful of them operate with great sensitivity toward their clients. But if one looks at what they *say*

[*]This example is taken from Sofer's *Organization from Within.*[15] We shall return to this book later on when we take up the strategy and theory of planned organizational change.

about their work, there is no question that practitioners of planned change are clearly more *self-conscious* and concerned with the human interactions between client and change-agent. *

A third major difference can now be identified. In the airline case, the OR practitioner devoted the majority of his time to *research,* to problem solving. In the case Sofer presents, while there was some research effort and data gathering, perhaps slightly more time was spent on *implementation through programs* of one kind or another: counseling, training programs, selection procedures, management development schemes, etc.

A fourth major difference has to do with the degree to which OR and planned-change practitioners take seriously the idea of a *system* in their approaches. Though I said earlier that both were systems-oriented, it seems that this is less stringently upheld in most cases of planned change. Sofer dealt almost exclusively with the top management group, and though the actions taken may have "percolated" down to lower echelons, there is a wide zone of uncertainty regarding the effects of this program on other parts of the system. In a case cited by Argyris[17] which will be discussed later on, we shall see how a particular change program in only one part of the system may create negative disturbances and unanticipated consequences in other parts of the system. †

Two other differences should be mentioned before going on. First, the idea of an interdisciplinary team, so central

to OR, does not seem to be a part of most planned-changed programs. Usually, only one or two men work on a program. It is true that these change-agents are themselves "generalists" and are capable of bridging disciplines. Yet it is a lack, compared with OR. Many times, for example, an economist or an engineer would add significantly to the change-agent's skills—particularly as they relate to the measurement of effectiveness and performance variables. *

One thing that emerges from a study of these two approaches to organizational change is a realization of the complexity of modern organization. Look through the kaleidoscope one way, and a configuration of the economic and technological factors appears; tilt it, and nothing appears except the pattern of external environment surrounding the firm. Tilt it again, and what emerges is a pattern of the internal human relations problems confronting the organization. The practitioners of planned organizational change more often than not tend to focus on these last-named human factors and their effects upon the performance of the system. †

*Another factor may be that there is a greater homogeneity of theory among OR practitioners. I do, however, mistrust this observation, no matter how valid it is. My mistrust is based on a fundamental law of social perception; i.e. the "others" always seem more alike to the "outsider" ("Well, they all look alike to me.").

†This is not the place to elaborate on some of the issues involved in the identification of variables *internal* to the system or *external* to the system. This has been one of the pivotal issues dividing economists from social psychologists and other so-called human relationists. It is not unlike the debate Arthur Koestler wrestles with in his distinction between the yogi and the commissar, between those who turn *inward* for insight, for therapy, and for Nirvana and those who turn *outward* to the external environment for the location of variables of promise. This distinction seems to have lost a good deal of its impact recently,

*It may be that the extent to which science and instrumentation can be used in effecting change is directly and inversely proportional to the use of personal elements of the relationship. We shall return to this speculation later on.

†See Bavelas and Strauss[18] for a classic case where positive change in one part of a system created such perturbations in adjacent parts of the system that the entire program was scrapped.

A FOCUS OF CONVENIENCE FOR PLANNED ORGANIZATIONAL CHANGE

So far, I have discussed planned change in its broadest context without carefully distinguishing it from applied or developmental research in general. Let us turn to that task now and develop what George Kelley refers to as a "focus of convenience" for planned organizational change. Earlier I defined planned change as a deliberate and collaborative process involving a change-agent and a client-system which are brought together to solve a problem or, more generally, to plan and attain an improved state of functioning in the client-system by utilizing and applying valid knowledge.* This is still a vague and general definition, and I will have to make two aspects of it clearer, particularly the notion of a "collaborative relationship" and that of "valid knowledge."

I have implied in the last section that the outcome of a planned-change effort depends to some extent on the relationship between the client and the change-agent. So let us turn, first, to that. Criteria for evaluating the nature and quality of this relationship can be based on the following questions: (1) How well is the relationship understood and veridically construed by both parties? (2) To what extent do both parties determine the course and fate of the planned-change program? (3) To what extent is the relationship open to examination and reconstruction by one or both parties? In other words, a deliber-

ate and collaborative relationship can be optimized in a planned-change induction only when the following exist:

1. A joint effort that involves mutual determination of goals.
2. A "spirit of inquiry"—a relationship that is governed by data, publicly shared.
3. A relationship growing out of the mutual interaction of the client and the change-agent.
4. A voluntary relationship between the change-agent and the client, with either free to terminate the relationship after joint consultation.
5. A relationship where each party has equal opportunities to influence the other.

Now, what is meant by "valid knowledge"? Generally speaking, the criteria for valid knowledge are based on the requirements for a viable applied behavioral science research, that is, an applied behavioral science that

1. Takes into consideration the behavior of persons operating within their specific institutional environments.
2. Is capable of accounting for the interrelated levels (person, group, role, and large organization) within the context of the social change.
3. Includes variables that the policy maker and practitioner can understand, manipulate, and evaluate.
4. Allows, in specific situations, selection of variables most appropriate to a specific planned change in terms of its own values, ethics, and moralities.
5. Accepts the premise that groups and organizations as units are as

---

almost primarily because of the work of Tavistock groups, particularly Emery and Trist,[19] as well as Wilson,[20] who have brought the *environment* and boundary maintenance back into the mainstream of organizational theory and research.

*For a fuller treatment of some of these ideas, see Bennis.[21]

amenable to empirical and analytical treatment as the individual.

6. Takes into account external social processes of change as well as the interpersonal aspects of the collaborative process.

7. Includes propositions susceptible to empirical test, focusing on the dynamics of change.

The definition and criteria for planned change presented here must be construed as an arbitrary goal and not as an existing reality. To my knowledge, there is no program which fulfills these requirements fully. This realization raises the final consideration in this focus of convenience: the arbitrary selection of those change-agents working on organizational dynamics. This particular class of change-agents was selected not only because of my greater familiarity with their work but for two other factors as well. First, they seem to fulfill the criteria outlined to a greater extent than other change-agents. * Second, equally important in the choice of emphasis is the belief that changes in the sphere of organizations—primarily *industrial*—in patterns of work and relationships, in structure, in technology,

*There are others, from an assortment of fields, who undoubtedly deserve discussion here but who have to be omitted primarily for space reasons. I am referring to the work of rural sociologists such as Loomis, Sower, and Moe (see Rogers[22] for a recent summary of this work); to community and hospital and psychiatric change-agents such as Caplan, Lindemann, S. Levine, L. Howe, B. Paul, D. Klein, the Cummingses, and the Rapoports; to applied anthropologists working on directed culture change such as Holmberg, Goodenough, Kimball, and Barnett; and to those change-oriented economists Hagen, Hoselitz, Rosenstein-Rodan, and Eckaus. Each of these branches implies a research and theoretical tradition which falls beyond the scope of this chapter but which will be touched on briefly in the next section.

and in administration promise to be some of the most significant changes in our society. *

NOTES

1. Berelson, B., and G. A. Steiner, *Human Behavior*, Harcourt, Brace & World, Inc., New York, 1964.

2. Kaplan, A., *The Conduct of Inquiry*, Chandler, San Francisco, Calif., 1964.

3. Lippitt, R., J. Watson, and B. Westley, *The Dynamics of Planned Change*, Harcourt, Brace & World, Inc., New York, 1958.

4. Bennis, W. G., K. D. Benne, and R. Chin (eds.), *The Planning of Change*, Holt, Rinehart and Winston, Inc., New York, 1961.

5. Goffman, E., *Asylums: Essays on Social Situations of Mental Patients and Other Inmates*, Anchor Books, Doubleday & Company, Inc., Garden City, N.Y., 1961.

6. Schein, E. H., I. Schneier, and C. H. Barker, *Coercive Persuasion: A Sociopsychological Analysis of the "Brainwashing" of American Civilian Prisoners by the Chinese Communists*, W. W. Norton & Company, Inc., New York, 1961.

7. Bennis et al., *op. cit.*, p. 154.

8. Gouldner, A. W., "Engineering and Clinical Approaches to Consulting," in *ibid.*, pp. 643–653.

9. Schuchman, A., *Scientific Decision Making in Business*, Holt, Rinehart and Winston, Inc., New York, 1963.

*I do not exclude socialist societies from this statement. As Parsons pointed out, the one common feature between so-called capitalist systems and socialist systems is the presence of bureaucracy. In the United States, it is my guess that industrial bureaucracies are the most radical, innovative, and adventurous in adapting new ways of organizing—far ahead, it seems to me, of the government, universities, and labor unions, who appear rigid and stodgy in the face of rapid change. Industrial bureaucracies, at least in the United States, are acting with a verve and imagination regarding rapid change which, I wager, not only will be copied but will be a model for future organizational change programs in other institutions. For an elaboration of this point, see Slater and Bennis.[23]

10. Gouldner, A. W., "Theoretical Requirements of the Applied Social Sciences," in Bennis et al., *op. cit.*, pp. 83–95.

11. Johnson, E. A., "Introduction," in McCloskey and Trefethen (eds.), *Operation Research for Management*, The Johns Hopkins Press, Baltimore, 1954, p. xii.

12. *Ibid.*, p. xix.

13. Ackoff, R. L., and P. Rivett, *A Manager's Guide to Operations Research*, John Wiley & Sons, Inc., New York, 1963, p. 34.

14. *Ibid.*, p. 17.

15. Sofer, C., *The Organization from Within*, Tavistock, London, 1961.

16. *Ibid.*, p. 8.

17. Argyris, C., *Interpersonal Competence and Organizational Effectiveness*, Dorsey Press, Homewood, Ill., 1962.

18. Bavelas, A., and G. Strauss, "Group Dynamics and Intergroup Relations," in Bennis et al., *op. cit.*, pp. 587–591.

19. Emery, F. E., and E. L. Trist, *The Causal Texture of Organizational Environments*, Tavistock Institute, London, 1963. (Mimeographed.)

20. Wilson, A. T. M., "The Manager and His World," paper presented at the Centennial Symposium on Executive Development, Alfred P. Sloan School of Management, Massachusetts Institute of Technology, Cambridge, Mass., April 27, 1961.

21. Bennis, W. G., "A New Role for the Behavioral Sciences: Effecting Organizational Change," *Administrative Science Quarterly*, vol. 8, pp. 125–165, 1963.

22. Rogers, E. M., *Diffusion of Innovations*, The Free Press of Glencoe, New York, 1962.

23. Slater, P. E., and W. G. Bennis, "Democracy Is Inevitable," *Harvard Business Review*, vol. 42, pp. 51–59, 1964.

41

Intervention Theory and Methods

Chris Argyris

A DEFINITION
OF INTERVENTION

To intervene is to enter into an ongoing system of relationship, to come between or among persons, groups, or objects for the purpose of helping them. There is an important implicit assumption in the definition that should be made explicit: the system exists independently of the intervenor. There are many reasons one might wish to intervene. These reasons may range from helping the clients make their own decisions about the kind of help they need to coercing the clients to do what the intervenor wishes them to do. Examples of the latter are modern black militants who intervene to demand that the city be changed in accordance with their wishes and choices (or white racists who prefer the same); executives who invite interventionists into their system to manipulate subordinates for them; trade union leaders who for years have resisted systematic research in their own bureaucratic functioning at the highest levels because they fear that valid information might lead to entrenched interests—especially at the top—being unfrozen.

The more one conceives of the intervenor in this sense, the more one implies that the client system should have little autonomy from the intervenor; that its boundaries are indistinguishable from those of the intervenor; that its health or effectiveness are best controlled by the intervenor.

In contrast, our view acknowledges interdependencies between the intervenor and the client system but focuses on how to maintain, or increase, the client system's autonomy; how to differentiate even more clearly the boundaries between the client system and the intervenor; and how to conceptualize and define the client system's health independently of the intervenor's. This view values the client system as an ongoing, self-responsible unity that has the obligation to be in control over its own destiny. An intervenor, in this view, assists a system to become more effective in problem solving, decision making, and decision implementation in such a way that the system can continue to be increasingly effective in these activities and have a decreasing need for the intervenor.

Another critical question the intervenor must ask is, how is he helping—management or employees, black militants or Negro moderates, white racists or white moderates? Several chapters of the book are concerned with this question. At this point, it is suggested that the intervenor must be concerned with the system as a whole even though his initial contact may be made with only a few people. He therefore focuses on those intervention activities that eventually (not necessarily immediately) will provide *all* the members' opportunities to enhance their competence and effectiveness. If any individual or subsystem

Source: Chris Argyris, *Intervention Theory and Methods,* © 1970, Addison-Wesley Publishing Co., Inc., Reading, Massachusetts, pp. 15–20. Reprinted with permission.

wishes help to prevent other individuals or subsystems from having these opportunities, then the intervenor may well have to question seriously his involvement in the project.[1]

BASIC REQUIREMENTS FOR INTERVENTION ACTIVITY

Are there any basic or necessary processes that must be fulfilled regardless of the substantive issues involved, if intervention activity is to be helpful with any level of client (individual, group, or organizational)? One condition that seems so basic as to be defined axiomatic is the generation of *valid information*. Without valid information, it would be difficult for the client to learn and for the interventionist to help.

A second condition almost as basic flows from our assumption that intervention activity, no matter what its substantive interests and objectives, should be so designed and executed that the client system maintains its discreteness and autonomy. Thus *free, informed choice* is also a necessary process in effective intervention activity.

Finally, if the client system is assumed to be ongoing (that is, existing over time), the clients require strengthening to maintain their autonomy not only vis-à-vis the interventionist but also vis-à-vis other systems. This means

that their commitment to learning and change has to be more than temporary. It has to be so strong that it can be transferred to relationships other than those with the interventionist and can do so (eventually) without the help of the interventionist. The third basic process for any intervention activity is therefore the client's *internal commitment* to the choices made.

In summary, valid information, free choice, and internal commitment are considered integral parts of any intervention activity, no matter what the substantive objectives are (for example, developing a management performance evaluation scheme, reducing intergroup rivalries, increasing the degree of trust among individuals, redesigning budgetary systems, or redesigning work). These three processes are called the primary intervention tasks.

PRIMARY TASKS OF AN INTERVENTIONIST

Why is it necessary to hypothesize that in order for an interventionist to behave effectively and in order that the integrity of the client system be maintained, the interventionist has to focus on three primary tasks, regardless of the substantive problems that the client system may be experiencing?

Valid and Useful Information

First, it has been accepted as axiomatic that valid and useful information is the foundation for effective intervention. Valid information is that which describes the factors, plus their interrelationships, that create the problem for the client system. There are several tests for checking the validity of the information. In increasing degrees of power they are public verifiability, valid prediction, and control over the phenom-

[1]There is an important function within the scope of responsibility of the interventionist that will not be discussed systematically in this volume. It is the public health function. There are many individuals who do not ask for help because they do not know they need help or that help could be available to them. The societal strategy for developing effective intervention activity must therefore include a function by which potential clients are educated about organizational health and illness as well as the present state of the art in effecting change. The writer hopes that this volume plays a role in facilitating this function.

ena. The first is having several independent diagnoses suggest the same picture. Second is generating predictions from the diagnosis that are subsequently confirmed (they occurred under the conditions that were specified). Third is altering the factors systematically and predicting the effects upon the system as a whole. All these tests, if they are to be valid, must be carried out in such a way that the participants cannot, at will, make them come true. This would be a self-fulfilling prophecy and not a confirmation of a prediction. The difficulty with a self-fulfilling prophecy is its indication of more about the degree of power an individual (or subset of individuals) can muster to alter the system than about the nature of the system when the participants are behaving without knowledge of the diagnosis. For example, if an executive learns that the interventionist predicts his subordinates will behave (a) if he behaves (b), he might alter (b) in order not to lead to (a). Such an alteration indicates the executive's power but does not test the validity of the diagnosis that if (a), then (b).

The tests for valid information have important implications for effective intervention activity. First, the interventionist's diagnoses must strive to represent the total client system and not the point of view of any subgroup or individual. Otherwise, the interventionist could not be seen only as being under the control of a particular individual or subgroup, but also his predictions would be based upon inaccurate information and thus might not be confirmed.

This does not mean that an interventionist may not begin with, or may not limit his relationship to, a subpart of the total system. It is totally possible, for example, for the interventionist to help management, blacks, trade union leaders, etc. With whatever subgroup he

works he simply should not agree to limit his diagnosis to its wishes.

It is conceivable that a client system may be helped even though valid information is not generated. Sometimes changes occur in a positive direction without the interventionist having played any important role. These changes, although helpful in that specific instance, lack the attribute of helping the organization to learn and to gain control over its problem-solving capability.

The importance of information that the clients can use to control their destiny points up the requirement that the information must not only be valid, it must be useful. Valid information that cannot be used by the clients to alter their system is equivalent to valid information about cancer that cannot be used to cure cancer eventually. An interventionist's diagnosis should include variables that are manipulable by the clients and are complete enough so that if they are manipulated effective changes will follow.

Free Choice

In order to have free choice, the client has to have a cognitive map of what he wishes to do. The objectives of his action are known at the moment of decision. Free choice implies voluntary as opposed to automatic; proactive rather than reactive. The act of selection is rarely accomplished by maximizing or optimizing. Free and informed choice entails what Simon has called "satisficing," that is, selecting the alternative with the highest probability of succeeding, given some specified cost constraints. Free choice places the locus of decision making in the client system. Free choice makes it possible for the clients to remain responsible for their destiny. Through free choice the clients can maintain the autonomy of their system.

It may be possible that clients prefer to give up their responsibility and their autonomy, especially if they are feeling a sense of failure. They may prefer, as we shall see in several examples, to turn over their free choice to the interventionist. They may insist that he make recommendations and tell them what to do. The interventionist resists these pressures because if he does not, the clients will lose their free choice and he will lose his own free choice also. He will be controlled by the anxieties of the clients.

The requirement of free choice is especially important for those helping activities where the processes of help are as important as the actual help. For example, a medical doctor does not require that a patient with a bullet wound participate in the process by defining the kind of help he needs. However, the same doctor may have to pay much more attention to the processes he uses to help patients when he is attempting to diagnose blood pressure or cure a high cholesterol. If the doctor behaves in ways that upset the patient, the latter's blood pressure may well be distorted. Or, the patient can develop a dependent relationship if the doctor cuts down his cholesterol—increasing habits only under constant pressure from the doctor—and the moment the relationship is broken off, the count goes up.

Effective intervention in the human and social spheres requires that the processes of help be congruent with the outcome desired. Free choice is important because there are so many unknowns, and the interventionist wants the client to have as much willingness and motivation as possible to work on the problem. With high client motivation and commitment, several different methods for change can succeed.

A choice is free to the extent the members can make their selection for a course of action with minimal internal defensiveness; can define the path (or paths) by which the intended consequence is to be achieved; can relate the choice to their central needs; and can build into their choices a realistic and challenging level of aspiration. Free choice therefore implies that the members are able to explore as many alternatives as they consider significant and select those that are central to their needs.

Why must the choice be related to the central needs and why must the level of aspiration be realistic and challenging? May people not choose freely unrealistic or unchallenging objectives? Yes, they may do so in the short run, but not for long if they still want to have free and informed choice. A freely chosen course of action means that the action must be based on an accurate analysis of the situation and not on the biases or defenses of the decision makers. We know, from the level of aspiration studies, that choices which are too high or too low, which are too difficult or not difficult enough will tend to lead to psychological failure. Psychological failure will lead to increased defensiveness, increased failure, and decreased self-acceptance on the part of the members experiencing the failure. These conditions, in turn, will tend to lead to distorted perceptions by the members making the choices. Moreover, the defensive members may unintentionally create a climate where the members of surrounding and interrelated systems will tend to provide carefully censored information. Choices made under these conditions are neither informed nor free.

Turning to the question of centrality of needs, a similar logic applies. The degree of commitment to the processes of generating valid information, scanning, and choosing may significantly vary according to the centrality of the choice to the needs of the clients. The more central the choice, the more the system will strive to do its best in developing valid information and making free and informed choices. If the research from perceptual psychology is valid, the very perception of the clients is altered by the needs involved. Individuals tend to scan more, ask for more information, and be more careful in their choices when they are making decisions that are central to them. High involvement may produce perceptual distortions, as does low involvement. The interventionist, however, may have a greater probability of helping the clients explore possible distortion when the choice they are making is a critical one.

INTERNAL COMMITMENT

Internal commitment means the course of action or choice that has been internalized by each member so that he ex- periences a high degree of ownership and has a feeling of responsibility about the choice and its implications. Internal commitment means that the individual has reached the point where he is acting on the choice because it fulfills his own needs and sense of responsibility, as well as those of the system.

The individual who is internally committed is acting primarily under the influence of his own forces and not induced forces. The individual (or any unity) feels a minimal degree of dependence upon others for the action. It implies that he has obtained and processed valid information and that he has made an informed and free choice. Under these conditions there is a high probability that the individual's commitment will remain strong over time (even with reduction of external rewards) or under stress, or when the course of action is challenged by others. It also implies that the individual is continually open to reexamination of his position because he believes in taking action based upon valid information.

42

The Ethics of Social Intervention: Goals, Means, and Consequences

Herbert C. Kelman & Donald P. Warwick

Social intervention is any act, planned or unplanned, that alters the characteristics of another individual or the pattern of relationships between individuals. The range of acts covered in this definition is intentionally broad. It includes such macro phenomena as national planning, military intervention in the affairs of other nations, population policy, and technical assistance. It also applies to psychotherapy, sensitivity training, neighborhood action programs, experiments done with human beings, and other micro changes.

Most of the literature in this area, utilizing the concept of planned change (e.g., Bennis, Benne, Chin, & Corey, 1976; Lippitt, Watson, & Westley, 1958), has confined itself to micro efforts such as organization development or community action programs. An organized attempt by a business corporation to improve communication, morale, and productivity in its U.S. plant is considered planned change, but a decision by the same company to build a new plant in Guatemala is not. In fact, the greater the scale and impact of social intervention, the less likely it is to be called planned change. One reason is that models of planned change place heavy emphasis on the role of the change agent, often a social science consultant. In many cases of macro change, it is extremely difficult to fit the facts of the situation into a paradigm involving change agents and client systems.

We prefer to subsume planned change efforts under a broader definition of social intervention that provides for the ethical evaluation of institutional structures and practices with critical social effects, as well as of situations with more readily identifiable change agents. We can thus explore the ethical implications of government policies or intellectual traditions, for example, even though these are not explicitly geared toward producing social change and are not associated with a single individual or agency. The major focus of this book, however, is on deliberate interventions. In this book, while keeping the broad definition in mind, we use social intervention more narrowly to refer to deliberate attempts by professionals to change the characteristics of individuals or groups, or to influence the pattern of relationships between individuals and/or groups. The last clause in this working definition is designed to cover such interventions as mediation, where the intent is not to change individuals and groups as such, but to shape the course of their relationships and interactions on a short-term or long-term basis.

Source: H. C. Bermant, H. C. Kelman, and D. P. Warwick (Eds.), *The Ethics of Social Intervention* (pp. 3–27). New York: Hemisphere Publishing Company.

VALUE PREFERENCES AND VALUE CONFLICTS

There are four aspects of any social intervention that are likely to raise major ethical issues: (1) the choice of goals to which the change effort is directed, (2) the definition of the target of the change, (3) the choice of means used to implement the intervention, and (4) the assessment of the consequences of the intervention. At each of these steps, the ethical issues that arise may involve conflicting values, that is, questions about what values are to be maximized at the expense of what other values. (We define *values* as individual or shared conceptions of the desirable—"goods" considered worth pursuing.)

Thus, values determine the choice of goals to which a change effort is directed. Clearly, an intervention is designed to maximize a particular set of values. But those setting the goals of the intervention are equally concerned with minimizing the loss of certain other values. These imperiled values thus serve as criteria of tolerable and intolerable costs in a given intervention. Under pressures of rapid demographic growth and limited resources, for example, a government might contemplate a set of coercive population control measures, such as involuntary sterilization. The benefit to be promoted by this program would be the common welfare or, in extreme cases, even the physical survival of the country. At the same time, the policy makers might be concerned about the effects of this program on two other values: freedom and justice. These values would be seen as social goods to be preserved—benefits that should not fall below some minimal threshold. Values may influence the choice of goals not only in such explicit, conscious ways, but also in a covert way. This may

happen, as we shall see, when a change program departs from a value-based but unquestioned definition of a problem.

The definition of the target of change is often based on just this kind of implicit, unexamined conception of where the problem lies. For example, a change effort designed to improve the conditions of an economically disadvantaged group—such as the black population in the United States—may be geared primarily toward changing institutional arrangements that have led to the systematic exclusion of this group from the economic life of the country, or toward reducing the educational, environmental, or psychological "deficiencies" of the disadvantaged group itself. The choice between these two primary targets of change may well depend on one's value perspective: A focus on removing systemic barriers is more reflective of the values of the disadvantaged group itself, while a focus on removing deficiencies suggests the values of the more established segments of the society.

Third, values play a central role in an ethical evaluation of the means chosen to implement a given intervention. Questions about the morality of coercion, manipulation, deception, persuasion, and other methods of inducing change typically involve a conflict between the values of individual freedom and self-determination, on the one hand, and the values of social welfare, economic progress, or equal opportunity, on the other. For example, to what extent and under what conditions is a government justified in imposing limits on the freedom to reproduce for the sake of presumed long-run improvements in the quality of life?

Finally, conflicting values enter into assessment of the consequences of a social intervention. One of the consequences of industrialization, for example, may be a weakening of traditional authority structures or family bonds. The extent to which we are willing to risk these consequences depends on whether we are more committed to traditional values or to those values that industrialization is designed to enhance. In other words, our assessment of the consequences of an intervention depends on what values we are willing or unwilling to sacrifice in the interest of social change.

Analysis of the ethical problems that may arise at each of these four points in the change process, and of the value conflicts from which they derive, presupposes consideration of some more general procedural issues that must be faced in any effort at applied ethics. These refer to the procedures to be followed in deriving the values that apply in a social intervention, in determining whose values should be given what weight, and in adjudicating value conflicts.[1]

First, an analysis of the ethics of social intervention presumes some notion of what values should apply and how they are to be derived. The problem is simplified, of course, if the analyst simply accepts the values held by the initiators of the change. Thus, if a government agency says that it undertook a population control program in order to promote the general welfare and that it also considered the costs of the program for individual freedom, an analyst might simply confine his or her attention to the values of freedom and welfare. Few students of ethics, however, would be content to let the individual or group initiating a change be the sole judge of the relevant values at stake. The human inclination toward selective perception

and self-deception, not to mention the protection of vested political interests, is simply too great to justify this approach. In this example, the concerned observer might also wish to examine the effects of the population program on other values, such as justice, dignity, or the self-esteem of minority groups. To leave the definition of the ethical situation to the sponsor of a program would be to abdicate one's moral judgment.

Thus, before ethical analysis can begin, analysts must lay out the content of the values that, according to their view, must be promoted and protected in a particular intervention effort. In addition to making these values explicit, the analysts must also indicate how these values were derived and why a particular set was adopted. The bases for choosing and applying values are varied and sometimes incompatible (Gustafson, 1970). They may include appeals to revelation, to natural law, to the capacity of human reason as a guide to moral truths, to social science theories of human nature and society, to empirically documented cultural universals, or to the cultural traditions and social institutions prevailing in a particular society. Fortunately, these approaches often yield similar or overlapping sets of values. Nevertheless, explicit attention must be given to the process by which these values are derived. There is no other way to reduce arbitrariness in selecting the ingredients for ethical analysis and to provide a framework for comparing and debating alternative criteria in the ethical evaluation of intervention efforts.

A second fundamental procedural question concerns the weights assigned to the different, and often competing, sets of values held by different groups. Discussions of national population policy within the United States, for example, have revealed the variations in

---

[1]These procedural issues are discussed in greater detail in Warwick and Kelman (1973). Much of the discussion in this chapter is derived from that earlier publication.

cultural values and perspectives that different ethnic, religious, class, and professional groups bring to the population problem (Population Task Force, 1971). Thus, at the national level, decisions about social intervention must weigh the claims and concerns of diverse groups within the society. The problem of "whose values" becomes even more complex in international programs of development or technical assistance. Such programs are often planned and carried out by individuals and agencies external to the society in which the changes are to be introduced. Therefore, there is a real possibility that the values of the change agents may deviate from those of the local population. The question of whose values determine the goals, targets, and means of change takes on special importance in such cases. The issue is not only whose interests are being served by the program, but whose conceptual framework generates the definition of the problem and the setting of goals. This issue persists even when representatives of the local society are fully involved in the planning and execution of the change program because these representatives, who are often trained abroad, may have adopted the conceptual framework of the external agency. Since the writings of social scientists often provide the conceptual frameworks for development programs, it is particularly important to scrutinize them in terms of whose values they reflect and to balance them by assuring that proper weight is given to competing points of view.

Third, deliberate attention to the content and derivation of values and to the different groups whose values are engaged by a given action often reveals value conflicts. Different values held within the same group and differences in value priorities set by different groups may present incompatible claims. For

example, advocates of a noninterventionist population policy typically stress the value of freedom, while those who favor strong measures of population control emphasize the values of welfare and survival of the human species. The critical question is not which of the two sets of values to pick, but what is the optimum balance between them. How much freedom, in other words, ought to be sacrificed in the interests of welfare and survival? Debates on national development often array advocates of cultural diversity, of the right of all peoples to determine their own destinies, and of the importance of traditional values as a matrix for the development of self-identity and self-esteem, against those who feel that traditional values are by definition obstacles to development and must, therefore, be changed as rapidly and efficiently as possible. Again the question concerns the most desirable trade-offs between conflicting values: How much traditional culture ought to be sacrificed for the sake of modernization?

Perhaps the most difficult challenge for ethical analysis is in providing some approximate guidelines for adjudicating such competing claims. Though no neat formulas or mechanistic answers are possible, one can try to establish a rough order of ethical priorities. For example, in the population field, one might start with the proposition that freedom of procreative behavior should be respected unless there are clearly demonstrated threats to human survival or welfare, and that even then the limitations placed on freedom should be proportional to the danger involved. By this rule, it would not be justified to introduce compulsory sterilization or forced abortions because of the mere possibility that human welfare will be endangered by demographic growth within the next century. It might be ethically justified, on the other hand, to remove incentives, such as family allowances, that encourage large families and to provide free family planning assistance. Similarly, modernization efforts might be guided by the proposition that traditional values should be disrupted only if—and only to the extent that—considerations of survival and social welfare necessitate such disruptions.

These analytical steps do not eliminate the need for value judgments, but they do make such judgments more conscious and deliberate. With these procedural issues in mind, we now turn to some of the specific ethical questions raised by the four aspects of social intervention: the choice of goals, the definition of the target, the choice of means, and the assessment of consequences.

CHOICE OF GOALS

Social scientists and others writing about social change continually make explicit or implicit assumptions about the nature and the end-points of the changes that are necessary and desirable. These assumptions are influenced not only by the values that individual writers bring to their research but also by the interests and orientations that surround the general issue of social change in their societies. The choice of goals for social intervention thus depends on the particular intellectual and political perspectives from which the change agents and their advisors view the situation. Biased views cannot be avoided, but they can be counteracted insofar as they are made explicit and confronted with analyses based on alternative perspectives.

The process of goal setting can be illustrated with a perspective on social change described by Kelman (1968, pp. 62–63). He places social change in the context of a worldwide revolution of human rights, which has set into motion powerful forces toward political independence, economic development, and social reform, both in the developing world and within industrialized countries. Given this perspective, one would start the process of delineating goals for social intervention by asking how the challenge posed by this revolution can best be met. What can be done to facilitate social change and to increase the likelihood that it will move in constructive directions? What kinds of institutional arrangements would improve the living conditions of the masses of the population, would be consistent with their needs for security and dignity, and would broaden the base of participation in social, political, and economic affairs? What conditions are conducive to a population's sense of political legitimacy, its feeling of national identity, and its readiness for involvement in citizenship responsibilities, economic enterprises, and social planning? What techniques of change would minimize the use of violence, the brutalization of the active and passive participants in the change process, and the predisposition to govern by coercion and repression? How can social intervention be introduced without destroying the existing culture patterns that provide meaning and stability to a people, while at the same time helping to build the new patterns and values that a changing society requires if it is to remain human?

This list of questions—and the goals for social intervention that it implies—is clearly based on certain value assumptions. It presupposes not only the desirability of social change, but also a preference for certain kinds of social change. For example, it assumes that social institutions must be judged in terms of their consistency with human needs, and it favors institutional arrangements that encourage participation, legitimacy, nonviolence, and respect for traditional values.

This statement implies a rough ordering of priorities. It suggests that, in choosing goals for intervention, a major criterion should be the concrete needs of individuals rather than some abstract notion of what is good for society. It clearly regards changes that involve violence, coercion, or the destruction of traditional values as unacceptable except under the most compelling circumstances. The application of these criteria to a specific situation, however, requires some difficult judgments. How does one determine which of various alternative policies is most consistent with the concrete needs of individuals, or what circumstances are sufficiently compelling to justify changes that involve varying degrees of violence, coercion, or destruction of traditional values? Different analysts may agree on these priorities, but may nonetheless disagree on how they should be specifically applied.

There are also likely to be disagreements with the implicit goals and priorities as delineated in the statement. We would like to believe that these goals are consistent with basic and universal human needs and that they are widely shared across different population groups and cultures. Yet we are also cognizant of the very real possibility that our ordering of priorities reflects, in some important ways, our own cultural and ideological biases and that—even when it deviates from the governing ideology of our society—it is influenced by our own relatively favored positions within the society and our society's favored position within the international system. Thus, before basing the choice

of goals for intervention on such a statement, one must recognize that it represents one perspective, which has to be confronted with those derived from other relevant points of view.

The first and frequently neglected step, then, in an ethical analysis of social intervention is the recognition that the choice of goals for intervention is determined by the value perspective of the chooser, which is not necessarily shared by all interested parties. The goals to be pursued in social change are by no means self-evident. They depend very much on what we consider a desirable outcome and what costs in terms of other values we are prepared to bear for the achievement of this outcome—a complex judgment about which there may be considerable disagreement.

The role of cultural and ideological biases in the choice of goals is often ignored because the change effort may have a hierarchy of values built into its very definition. These values may simply be taken for granted without questioning their source and their possibly controversial nature. A clear example of such covert ideological influence is seen in the definition of national development. The word "development," whether used in botany, psychology, or economics, implies an unfolding toward some terminal state. Typically this state, whether it be adulthood, maturity, or an ideal economic system, is also considered desirable. By implication, a more developed nation is seen as better in some sense than a less developed nation. In the 1950s, the dominant models of national development took as their implicit end-points the economic and political systems of the Western industrial nations. Within this teleological framework, primary emphasis was given to economic values. Works such as *The Stages of Economic Growth* (Rostow, 1960) argued, in effect, that the ultimate measure of political and social institutions was their contribution to economic growth. From an ethical standpoint, the most serious problem with these models was that value judgments were slipped into seemingly value-free definitions of historical processes. Statements about goals for change deemed desirable from a particular value perspective were often presented as empirical statements about the conditions necessary for a universal process of development. Such latent choices of goals are especially troublesome because they are masked by connotations of scientific rigor and historical inevitability.

In recognizing the role of their own value preference, change agents (or social scientists who conceptualize the process of social change) do not abandon their values or attempt to neutralize them. It is neither possible nor desirable to do so. But being aware of their own value perspectives can allow change agents to bring other perspectives to bear on the choice of goals, which reduces the likelihood that they will impose their own values on the population in whose lives they are intervening. This process of relating our own values to those of others in the choice of goals for intervention—without either abandoning or imposing our own values—can often be aided by a distinction between general goals and specific institutional arrangements designed to give expression to these goals. It may be possible to identify certain broad, basic end-points that are widely shared across different cultures and ideological systems—at least among groups and individuals operating within a broadly humanistic framework. These groups or individuals may at the same time disagree about the specific political, social, and economic institutions that they regard as most conducive to the realiza-

tion of these ends. Thus, one may be able to define the goals for intervention in more or less universal terms, while recognizing that these goals may be achieved through a variety of specific arrangements and that different cultures and ideologies may differ sharply in their preferences among these arrangements.

Ethical issues in the choice of goals for intervention revolve around the question of what values are to be served by the intervention and whether these are the right values for the target population. Since answers to these questions are likely to differ for different individuals—and to differ systematically for groups with different cultural backgrounds and positions in society—the question of *what* values inevitably brings up the question of *whose* values are to be served by the intervention.

Any society, community, or organization in which a change program is introduced contains different segments, with differing needs and interests that may be affected by the intervention. Thus, a key issue concerns the extent to which the values of these different population segments are reflected in the goals that govern the intervention and the extent to which they participate in the goal-setting process. The question of who decides on the goals often has implications for who ultimately benefits from the outcome of the intervention. Since the interests and values of different groups may, to varying degrees, be incompatible, the change program usually involves some compromise between competing preferences. Representation and participation in goal setting may thus have an important bearing on how the values of a given group are weighted in the final outcome.

The problem of competing interests and values in the goal-setting process is complicated by the fact that the change agents and those to whom the change effort is directed usually represent different segments of the population. In national programs, the government officials and social engineers who initiate and carry out the intervention and the policy makers and social scientists who provide the conceptual frameworks on which it is based usually come from the more established, affluent, and highly educated segments of the society. The target population, on the other hand, usually consists of poorer and less educated segments, minority groups, or groups that are for various reasons (such as age, health, addiction, or criminality) in a dependent status. In international programs, the leadership and conceptual framework (whether Western or Marxist) usually come from the more powerful, industrialized nations, while the change is directed at developing countries. Thus, in both cases, the change agents are in some sense outsiders to the target population in terms of social class, national affiliation, or both. Moreover, they are usually not disinterested outsiders: Social change programs may have important implications for the wealth, power, and status of their own groups. The problem is further exacerbated by the fact that the agents and the targets of change usually represent groups that differ along a power dimension. The change agents come from the more powerful classes and nations, the targets from the less powerful ones.

The change agents are in a strong position to influence the choice of goals for the intervention. Those who formulate and run the program clearly play a direct role in goal setting. Those who provide the conceptual frameworks may have a more subtle, yet highly pervasive, impact in that they establish the perspective from which the goal setting proceeds and thus the way in which the

problem is defined and the range of choices seen as available. It is therefore quite possible that the change agents will view the problem from the perspective of their own group and set goals that will, often unintentionally, accrue to the benefit of their group at the expense of the target population. Given the power differntial, their intervention may in fact strengthen the status quo and increase the impotence of those who are already disadvantaged. It is not surprising, therefore, that population control or educational programs sponsored by white middle-class agencies in black ghettoes, or by U.S. agencies in developing countries, are sometimes greeted with suspicion by the target populations. Whatever the merits of the specific case may be, there are sound structural bases for fearing that such programs may end up serving the purposes of the advantaged group at the expense of the disadvantaged.

The ethical problems created by the value and power differentials between change agents and target groups are not easily resolved. Clearly, the more the target group participates in the process of goal setting, the greater the likelihood that the change program will indeed reflect its values. But bringing in representatives of the target group or turning the program over to indigenous agents may not go very far in correcting power imbalances. We have already mentioned that representatives of developing societies who are brought in by outside agencies may themselves be Westernized and may therefore operate in terms of the perspectives of these agencies. Similarly, representatives of minority groups, particularly if they have professional training, do not necessarily share the perspective of the lower-class, less educated members of their own group. Turning over a project may create its own ethical ambiguities if, in the process, the outsiders arrogate to themselves the decision of who is the proper spokesperson for the target population. This may be true whether they turn over the project to the established government (which may not be representative) or to an opposition group. In either case, they are deciding which side to strengthen in what may be an internal conflict within the target population and are thus indirectly imposing goals of their own choice.

Despite the ambiguities that often remain when an outside, more powerful change agent involves representatives of the less powerful target population in the change effort, such involvement constitutes the best protection against the imposition of foreign values. Thus, in an ethical evaluation of a social intervention, one would want to consider such criteria as: To what extent do those who are affected by the intervention participate in the choice of goals? What efforts are being made to have their interests represented in the setting of priorities, and to bring their perspectives to bear on the definition of the problem and the range of choices entertained? To what extent does the process enhance the power of the target population and provide them with countervailing mechanisms of protection against arbitrary and self-serving uses of power by the change agents?

DEFINITION OF THE TARGET

Social intervention usually begins as an effort to solve a problem. A decision to undertake a program of organization development, for example, may spring from a concern about poor communication, intraorganizational conflicts, or underutilization of employee abilities. The adoption of population controls may be an effort to deal with the problem of scarce resources or an attempt to preserve the quality of life. In every case, identification of the problem represents, in large part, a value judgment. What we consider to be problematic— that is, what we see as falling short of some ideal state and requiring action— depends very much on our particular view of the ideal state. Moreover, identification of the problem depends on the perspective from which we make this evaluation. For example, in the face of demonstrations, riots, or other forms of social unrest, different groups are likely to cite different problems as requiring social intervention. Those who identify with the status quo are likely to see the problem as a breakdown of social order, while those who identify with the protesters are more likely to see the problem as a breakdown of social justice.

Identification of the problem has important ethical implications because it determines selection of the target to which change efforts are directed. Where we intervene depends on where we, with our personal value preferences and perspectives, perceive the problem to lie. Thus, those who see social unrest as a breakdown of social order are likely to define the protesters as the proper targets of change. They may use a variety of means, ranging from more stringent social controls, through persuasion and education, to efforts at placating the protesters and giving them a stake in the system. Whatever the means, this is the wrong target from the point of view of those who see the problem as a failure in social justice and who want to direct change efforts to the existing institutions and policies. In their view, interventions designed to reduce the protesters' ability or motivation to protest merely perpetuate injustices and serve the interests of the advantaged segments of the population at the expense of the disadvantaged. In short, who and what is being targeted for change may have important consequences for the competing interests of different groups and for the fate of such core values as justice and freedom.

The issues are well illustrated in debates on the population problem. The specific crises that constitute this problem are variously defined as famine or impediments to economic development, pollution or other ecological damage threatening the possibility and quality of life, exhaustion of physical resources or strains on the carrying capacity of the earth, and revolution or social disorder resulting from population pressures joined with high levels of aspiration. The scientific evidence on the probability of any of these crises is highly ambiguous. Thus, there is ample room for personal values to enter into the definition of the problem.

The definition of the problem, in turn, determines the selection of targets for change. Those who see the problem in terms of the danger of famine and economic stagnation may direct change efforts at increasing economic productivity, including food production. Those who are primarily concerned with pollution and ecological damage may favor interventions directed at reducing the rate of industrialization or at strengthening governmental controls over waste products and other sources of environmental pollution. On the other hand, those concerned with exhaustion of physical resources or with the revolutionary potential of population pressures may prefer interventions aimed at reducing or reversing the rate of population growth. How we define the problem and, thus, whether we then take national economic policy or the child-

bearing couple as our target of change, depends on our value preferences and perspectives. For example, groups placing a high value on the preservation of the existing political order are likely to be disturbed by rising population pressures and thus to favor population control. On the other hand, those who advocate revolutionary change may actually favor rapid population growth combined with urbanization as important contributors to political mobilization. These two views, of course, do not exhaust the possible positions on population control, but they illustrate the point that definition of the target of change has important consequences for the competing interests of different groups within a society.

Social scientists play a major role in identifying, or at least articulating, the problems to which change efforts are to be directed and thus in defining the targets for social intervention. A good example is provided by research on various forms of social deviance. Much of this research has focused on "the deviant behaviour itself and on the characteristics of the individuals and groups that manifest it and the families and neighbourhoods in which it is prevalent, rather than on the systemic processes out of which it emerges" (Kelman, 1970, p. 82). Many reasons for this emphasis can be cited. In part it grows out of the "social problems" tradition, which has fostered among social scientists a commitment to helping troubled individuals and groups. In part it reflects the problem definition of agencies whose mission includes the control of deviant behavior and who sponsor much of the research in this field. Research on the characteristics of deviant populations, though perfectly legitimate in its own right, raises ethical questions insofar as it provides the dominant framework for conceptualizing deviance as a social phenomenon and thus for setting social policy. "By focusing on the carriers of deviant behaviour, social research has reinforced the widespread tendency to explain such behaviour more often in terms of the pathology of the deviant individuals, families, and communities, than in terms of such properties of the larger social system as the distribution of power, resources, and opportunities" (Kelman, 1970, p. 83). Research has thus contributed to a focus on the characteristics of the deviant as the problem to which social policy must address itself. In keeping with this problem definition, the deviant individuals and communities, rather than the institutional arrangements and policies conducive to social deviance, have commonly been singled out as the targets for intervention. This particular way of identifying the problem and defining the target for change tends to reflect the concerns of the more established segments of the population and has potential consequences for the competing interests of different groups within the society.

This example illustrates some of the ethical implications of social science research. Far from being ethically neutral, the models with which social scientists work may play a major role in determining the problems and targets for social intervention. In defining their research problems, choosing their models, and communicating their findings, therefore, social scientists have a responsibility to consider the consequences for the populations affected. More broadly, they have the responsibility to ensure that all segments of the population have the opportunity to participate in the research enterprise, which influences the definition of the problems for intervention, and have access to the research findings, which influence the setting of policy.

CHOICE OF MEANS

The most difficult ethical choices in deliberate social intervention usually concern the selection of means. Is it ever morally justified, for example, to force individuals to accept a program under the threat of death, physical harm, or other severe deprivation? What ethical problems are posed by manipulating the environment so that people are more likely to choose one alternative over others? Should a change program make full use of group pressures for conformity, or attempt to tamper with basic attitudes and motives? These are real questions in most change programs, and there are no easy answers.

It is possible, however, to clarify some of the issues at stake by relating the various means to the value of freedom. Warwick (1971) has defined freedom as the capacity, the opportunity, and the incentive to make reflective choices and to act on these choices. Individuals are thus free when:

1. The structure of the environment provides them with options for choice.

2. They are not coerced by others or forced by circumstances to elect only certain possibilities among those of which they are aware.

3. They are, in fact, aware of the options in the environment and possess knowledge about the characteristics and consequences of each. Though such knowledge may be less than complete, there must be enough to permit rational deliberation.

4. They are psychologically able to weigh the alternatives and their

consequences. In practice this means not only possessing information but being able to use it in coming to a decision.

5. Having weighed the relative merits of the alternatives, they can choose among them. Rollo May (1969) has argued that one of the pathologies of modern existence is an inability to choose—a deficiency of will. A person who cannot pass from deliberation to choice must be considered less than free.

6. Having chosen an alternative, they are able to act on it. Among the conditions that may prevent them from doing so is a lack of knowledge about how to implement the choice, anxiety about acting at all, or a low level of confidence in their abilities, even when they have sufficient knowledge to act.

This discussion of freedom suggests a typology of means used in implementing social interventions. At the "least free" end is coercion, a situation in which people are forced to do something they do not want to do, or are prevented from doing something they do want to do. Next comes manipulation, then persuasion, and finally, at the "most free" end, facilitation.

Coercion

In simple terms, coercion takes place when one person or group uses the threat of severe deprivation to induce other people or groups either to carry out actions that they desire not to perform or normally would not perform, or to refrain from carrying out actions that they want to perform or, in the normal course of events, would perform. It is difficult to arrive at precise definitions of "threat" or "deprivation," but basically these refer to the loss of highly valued goods, such as one's life, means of livelihood, or the well-being of one's relatives. Coercion should be distinguished from compliance that occurs within the framework of legitimate authority. In a certain sense, tax laws may be coercive because they force people to do things that they would prefer not to do under the threat of penalties. However, insofar as people comply with the law out of a belief that it is right to do so, since they see the law as rooted in consensual processes, their behavior would not be coerced.

Coercion forms an integral part of many programs of social intervention. Some clear examples would be the nationalization of a foreign-owned petroleum refinery or the outright confiscation of land in agrarian reform programs. In both cases, the government's action is immediately backed by the use of physical force—those who do not comply may be evicted or jailed. The population's acceptance of the government's legitimate right to carry out such interventions would usually be minimal. Other examples hover at the borders of coercion, manipulation, and persuasion. It has been proposed, for instance, that governments try to limit population by levying higher taxes against families with more than two or three children, or by depriving such families of social benefits such as free education, welfare, or medical coverage. Such programs could be considered coercive if the threatened deprivation involved highly valued goods or the threat of great hardship, and if those affected would not accept the legal or moral legitimacy of the interventions. If the rewards and punishments at stake were relatively moderate, on the other hand, the means of intervention could be considered either manipulative or persuasive, according to the circumstances.

Is coercion ever ethically justified in social intervention and, if so, under what conditions? Two broad conditions are commonly invoked to defend coercive methods. The first is a grave threat to basic societal values. Thus, highly coercive population control programs are frequently recommended on the grounds that excessive fertility jeopardizes the continued survival of the human race or the material welfare of a nation's citizens. The second justification is the need for prompt and positive action to accomplish the goals of a change program, even when there is no threat to such values as physical survival. This argument is typical of revolutionary governments bent on executing major reforms in a short period of time. The two arguments are related in the sense that a failure to show swift results might create a drastic loss in basic political values such as the legitimacy or credibility of the government.

In the first case, an ethical justification of coercion requires the change agent to demonstrate, rather than assume, the threat to basic values. The population field is punctuated with dire predictions of disaster offered to the public with little supporting evidence. The legal concept of "clear and present danger" would seem to be an appropriate test of any proposal for coercion. Even then, however, coercion may not be justified. In the second case, the defense of coercion usually rests on personal evaluations of the system in question. In gross terms, those who favor a given regime will generally support its use of coercion to promote rapid change, while those who oppose it will reject its coercive methods.

Since the justification of coercive tactics often rests on the legitimacy of those who use them, determinations of legitimacy become an important part of ethical analysis. The legitimacy of a regime, in Western democratic tradition, is evidenced by the fact that its major officials have been duly elected, but there are other ways of establishing that a regime is representative of the population and governs with its consent. Even if the regime is seen as generally legitimate, some of its specific policies and programs may be considered illegitimate by various segments of the population because they exceed the regime's range of legitimate authority, because they are discriminatory, or because they violate certain basic values. Ethical evaluations become even more difficult when coercive interventions are introduced by revolutionary movements, whose claim to legitimacy has not yet been established. In such a case, observers would be more inclined to justify coercive tactics to the extent that they see the movement as representative of wide segments of the population and feel that their tactics are directed at power wielders who themselves are illegitimate and oppressive.

Environmental Manipulation

Individual freedom has two core components: the availability of options in the environment, and the person's capacity to know, weigh, choose, and act on those options. Manipulation is a deliberate act of changing either the structure of the alternatives in the environment (environmental manipulation) or personal qualities affecting choice without the knowledge of the individuals involved (psychic manipulation). The cardinal feature of this process is that it maintains the semblance of freedom while modifying the framework within which choices are made. No physical compulsion or threats of deprivation are applied, and the individuals may be no more than dimly aware that they or the environment have been changed. Somewhat different ethical considerations are raised by environmental and psychic manipulation.

The term *environmental manipulation*, though it carries sinister overtones, applies to a broad range of activities generally regarded as necessary and desirable. These include city planning; governmental intervention in the economy through means such as taxation and control of interest rates; the construction of roads, dams, or railroads; and the addition of new consumer goods to the market. In each case a deliberate attempt is made to alter the structure of opportunities available, whether through addition, subtraction, or other modifications. Few people challenge the ethics of these changes, though they may question their wisdom. Other forms of environmental control arouse greater moral concern. Limitations on the freedom of the news media are widely attacked as abhorrent to a democracy. Job discrimination, ethnic quotas in universities, and similar restrictions on the equality of opportunity are similarly condemned.

Clearly, people make distinctions between justifiable and unjustifiable control of opportunities. But what are the limits of justifiable manipulation and what ethical calculus should be used to establish these limits? Is it morally justified, for example, to attempt to shape an entire cultural environment in the interest of promoting happiness and survival, as Skinner (1971) has proposed? Perhaps the key question raised by Skinner's proposals is who decides on the shape of the new environment and the controls to be instituted. Other questions concern the priorities in values and the assumptions about human nature by which the controllers operate.

Related ethical issues arise in behavior therapies, which rely on environmental manipulation and use techniques similar to those suggested by Skinner for the design of cultures. Unlike insight therapies, which concentrate on changing motives, perceptions, and other psychic qualities, behavior therapy aims at treating symptoms. Its techniques are based on the principle of selective reinforcement, through which desired behaviors are rewarded and undesired behaviors ignored or punished. Thus, behavior therapies emphasize specific acts rather than global personality characteristics (cf. London, 1969). From an ethical standpoint the principal difference between Skinner's macromanipulation and behavior therapy lies in the degree to which the individuals affected may control the process. Though there are vague murmurings in Skinner's book about "participation by those affected," his basic model is one of total control by an elite of culture designers. By contrast, in behavior therapy, the patients seek help with a problem and are free to terminate the therapeutic relationship at any time. In other words, though the therapy process involves careful manipulation of their behavior, they usually know what is happening and can exercise a fair degree of control over the process.

Other proposals for environmental control fall somewhere between these poles. It has been suggested, for instance, that governments try to limit fertility by manipulating conditions known to have indirect effect on family size, such as education, job opportunities for women, and income. Specifically, Judith Blake (1969) has recommended that women be given more competitive roles, such as improved job opportunities, as a means of reducing fertility. Daniel Callahan (1971) has raised several questions about this form of environmental manipulation, pointing to the ironic possibility that people can be manipulated by increasing their freedom.

Similar questions arise in any strategy for social change that relies on creating new realities that make it more necessary—or at least more possible—for people to change their behavior. In the field of race relations, for example, observers have noted that an effective way of changing individual attitudes and practices is to introduce a fait accompli: If an antidiscrimination law or policy is established without too much ado, people will be confronted with a new social reality that, for both practical and normative reasons, they are more likely to accept than to resist. Such environmental manipulation can be justified more readily if it is part of a larger social policy process that itself has been carried on through legitimate channels and exposed to public debate. It is also more justifiable from an ethical point of view if its effect is to expand rather than restrict the range of opportunities.

In sum, if human freedom and dignity are taken as critical values, there is reason for concern about deliberate attempts to manipulate one person's environment to serve the needs of another. The value of freedom requires not only the availability of options for choice at a given point in time, but an awareness of major changes in the structure of these alternatives. Complete awareness of these changes and their causes, however, is obviously impossible. There is also the danger of a strong conservative bias in defending the environment of choice within which we happen to find ourselves. Most of us, after all, are not aware of the origins of our present options for choice. Why, then, should we have a right to know when they are being changed? In other words, how much awareness of the

structure of our present environment and of modifications in this environment is necessary for human freedom and dignity? And, assuming that this awareness will always be less than complete, who should have the right to tamper with the environment without our knowledge and what conditions should govern such intervention? Some thought has been given to criteria for an ethical evaluation of environmental manipulation. For example, manipulation would seem more acceptable to the extent that the people affected participate in the process, are free to enter and leave the program, and find their range of choices broadened rather than narrowed. Manipulation also seems more acceptable if the manipulators are not the primary beneficiaries of the manipulation, are reciprocally vulnerable in the situation, and are accountable to public agencies.

Psychic Manipulation

Even within a constant environment of choice, freedom can be affected through the manipulation of its psychological components: for example, knowledge of the alternatives and their consequences; motives; and the ability to reason, choose, and implement one's choices. Recent decades have seen dramatic developments in the techniques of psychic manipulation. These include insight therapies; the modification of brain functioning through surgery, chemicals, or electrical stimulation; hypnosis; sensitivity training; and programs of attitude change (cf. London, 1969). The emergence of behavior control technology raises fundamental questions about human nature and the baseline assumptions for ethical analysis.

The ethical questions raised by psychic manipulation are similar to those presented by environmental control, and the same criteria for ethical evaluation are applicable. In many interventions of this type, however, particular attention must be paid to moral problems of deception and incomplete knowledge of effects—conditions on which these programs often rely for their success. The use of deception in such programs is based on considerations similar to those used to justify deceptive methods in psychological experiments and other forms of social research. It is assumed that some of the phenomena that the investigator is trying to create or observe would be destroyed if people were aware of the precise nature of the experimental manipulation or of the behavior under study. The moral problems posed by the use of deception in social research have received increasing attention in recent years (cf. Kelman, 1968, 1972; Warwick, 1973, 1975). For example, with reference to social-psychological experiments, Kelman (1972) has written:

> Deception presents special problems when it is used in an experiment that is stressful, unpleasant, or potentially harmful to the subject, in the sense that it may create self-doubts, lower his self-esteem, reveal some of his weaknesses, or create temporary conflicts, frustration, or anxiety. By deceiving the subject about the nature of the experiment, the experimenter deprives him of the freedom to decide whether or not he wants to be exposed to these potentially disturbing experiences. . . . The use of deception presents ethical problems even when the experiment does not entail potential harm or discomfort for the subject. Deception violates the respect to which all fellow humans are entitled and the trust that is basic to all interpersonal relationships. Such violations are doubly disturbing since they contribute, in this age of mass society, to the already powerful tendencies to manufacture realities and manipulate populations. Furthermore, by undermining the basis of trust in the relationship between investigator and

subject, deception makes it increasingly difficult for social scientists to carry out their work in the future. (p. 997)

Similar issues arise in all efforts at psychic manipulation.

In some situations, the ethical problem is not outright deception, but the participant's incomplete or distorted knowledge of the effects of an intervention. For example, many individuals enter sensitivity training sessions (T-groups) to learn about group processes and about their impact on others in a group. Though such learning may well take place, some critics have argued that there may also be potentially harmful side-effects to which participants are not alerted. For example, participants may find that the group process releases violent impulses or even patholoical reactions in themselves and others. They may be subjected to harsh personal attacks for their feelings and idiosyncrasies or may engage in such attacks on others. Or, according to Gottschalk and Pattison (1969), by fostering "a concept that anything goes regardless of consequences," T-groups "may preclude effective communication. . . . Communication may not be seen as an interpersonal event but merely as the opportunity to express oneself" (p. 835). Of course, properly structured and well-supervised sensitivity training may also bring unexpected benefits. The basic ethical question, however, concerns the right of the participant to be informed, not only of probable benefits, but also of potential dangers resulting from psychic manipulation. This question applies to other forms of psychic manipulation, such as brain stimulation or drug experimentation, as much as it does to group experiences.

Often change agents are unaware that they are engaged in manipulative efforts or that these efforts have ethical implications. They may be convinced that all they are doing is conveying information or providing a setting in which self-generated change processes are allowed to emerge. They may thus fail to recognize the situational and structural factors that enhance their power over their clients and the subtle ways in which they communicate their expectations of them. Even if they are aware of their manipulative efforts, they may be so convinced that what they are doing is good for the clients that they fail to recognize the ethical ambiguity of the control they exercise (cf. Kelman, 1968, Chapter 1). Such dangerous blindspots on the part of change agents, which preclude their even raising the ethical questions, are particularly likely to arise in the more subtle forms of psychic manipulation.

Persuasion

The technique of persuasion is a form of interpersonal influence in which one person tries to change the attitudes or behavior of another by means of argument, reasoning, or, in certain cases, structured listening. In the laboratory, as well as in the mass media, persuasion is usually a one-way process. In interpersonal relations in natural settings, it is generally a mutual process, in which the various participants try to persuade one another. Persuasion is frequently used as a means of social intervention in the mass media and, at the one-to-one level, in insight therapies.

At first blush, persuasion seems highly consistent with the value of freedom—almost its exemplification, in fact. The communication process appears to be carried out in the open, all parties appear to be free to consider the arguments, apparently have free choice whether to reject or accept them, and no coercion is consciously practiced.

Quite clearly, when compared with outright coercion or the more gross forms of manipulation, persuasion emerges as a relatively free method of intervention. But at the same time, its seeming openness may sometimes mask covert and far-reaching efforts at personality change.

Insight therapies such as psychoanalysis would generally be regarded as persuasive means of attitude and behavior change. Through such therapy, individuals are led to a better understanding of the sources of their complaints—why they think, act, and feel as they do. The guiding assumption is that self-knowledge will take them a long way toward dealing with the problems. The techniques used to promote understanding are generally nondirective, and the client is urged to assume major responsibility for talking during the therapy sessions.

In principle, at least, insight therapy shows a high degree of respect for people's freedom. The patients do most of the talking, the therapist does not impose his or her personal values, and the process can be ended by the patient at any time. However, closer analysis reveals numerous opportunities for covert influence. Many patients, for example, report feelings of guilt over violations of sexual standards. Following the moral traditions of psychoanalysis, most forms of insight therapy view the guilt feelings, rather than the sexual behavior, as the problem to be solved. Under the guise of moral neutrality, the therapist encourages patients to understand why they feel guilty and to see that such feelings are irrational and therefore unjustified. Similarly, by deftly steering the conversation in certain directions through probes and nods of assent, the therapist can lead the patient toward desirable attitudes on moral questions or other matters. And, as Perry London

(1964) has observed, even the attitude of moral neutrality in psychotherapy is an ethical stance: "It is, from the therapists's side, a libertarian position, regardless of how the client sees it (indeed, in some ways he may justly see it as insidious)" (p. 13). It is hard to escape the conclusion that the therapist, like the confessor, is an active agent of moral suasion. The ethical problem posed by psychotherapy, however, is that the values guiding the influence process are hidden behind global notions such as mental health, self-actualization, and normality. The problem is mitigated to the extent that therapists recognize that they are bringing their own values into the relationship and label those values properly for their patients. "Among other things, such a recognition would allow the patient, to a limited extent, to 'talk back' to the therapist, to argue about the appropriateness of the values that the therapist is introducing" (Kelman, 1968, pp. 25–26).

When we move from persuasion in the one-to-one context to efforts at mass persuasion, the question of who has the opportunity and the capacity to mount a persuasion campaign takes on central importance. Since such opportunities and capacities are not equally distributed in any society, this question is fraught with ethical implications. It arises, for example, in the debate over the impact of modernization on traditional values, to which we alluded earlier. In this connection, after defending the need for cultural diversity, Denis Goulet (1971) has written:

> Development economists often ask what they should do about local customs which get in development's way. No sensitive change agent is blind to the traumatic effects of the "bull-in-the-china-closet" approach to local customs. Nevertheless, persuasive campaigns are sometimes necessary, even if they are unpopular. (p. 270)

The question is, who should be responsible for deciding when and where persuasive campaigns are necessary? Should the interested parties from a community be involved in the decision about whether a campaign should be launched, as well as in the later stages of the intervention? Furthermore, how can illiterate villagers argue on an equal plane with sophisticated national planners armed with charts, statistics, debating skills, and prestige? Those in power are usually in a much better position to launch a persuasion campaign and to carry it out effectively. Thus, even though persuasion itself may be more consistent than other means of intervention with the principles of democratic dialogue and popular participation, it often occurs in a context where some are more equal than others.

Facilitation

Some strategies of intervention may simply be designed to make it easier for individuals to implement their own choices or satisfy their own desires. An underlying assumption in these strategies is that people have some sense of what they want to do and lack only the means to do it. Though facilitation, like persuasion, seems highly consistent with freedom, it too can move close to the borders of manipulation.

An example from the field of family planning can illustrate the different degrees of manipulativeness that a facilitation effort might involve. At the least manipulative extreme, a program providing a regular supply of contraceptive pills to a woman who is highly informed about the possibilities of contraception and strongly motivated to limit her family size, and who knows that she wants to use the pill but simply lacks the means to obtain it, would be a case of almost pure facilitation. At the other extreme would be the case of a woman who vaguely feels that she has too many children, but is not strongly motivated to limit her family size, and who possesses no information on contraception. The clinic arranges for visits to her home with the purpose of increasing her level of motivation and, once the vague concern is translated into a concrete intention to practice contraception, provides her free transportation to a local family planning center. Though facilitation is clearly involved in the latter stages of this program, in its origins it is basically a form of either manipulation or persuasion. That is, it requires that motivation be channeled before actual facilitation can take place. Falling somewhere between these two extremes would be a program designed to assist a woman, already motivated to limit her family size and aware of the possibilities of contraception, in choosing the means most appropriate in her case and in implementing that choice; or a program designed to promote a particular method (such as the IUD) for women who are motivated to limit their family size but uninformed about the possibilities of contraception.

The ethical problems of intervention increase as one moves from more or less pure facilitation to cases in which facilitation occurs as the last stage of a manipulative or persuasive strategy. But ethical questions can be raised even about seemingly pure facilitation. The most vexing problem is that the selective reinforcement of an individual's desires, even when these are sharply focused and based on adequate information, can be carried out for someone else's purposes. Here we face a critical question about the ethics of planned change: It is right for party A to assist

party B in attaining B's own desires when the reason for this assistance is that B's actions will serve A's interests? In other words, does any kind of facilitation also involve elements of environmental manipulation through the principle of selective reinforcement? For example, survey data suggest that many poor blacks and Mexican-Americans in the United States are desirous of family planning services. But racist groups would also like to see these minorities reduce their fertility. If the government decides to provide voluntary family planning services to these and other poor families, is it serving the interests of racism or the freedom of the families in question? While it is sometimes possible to determine that a given intervention leans more one way than the other, it is often impossible to say whose interests are served most by a change program.

Some have tried to handle the charge of manipulation through facilitation by being completely honest and open. Consider the case of a church-related action group that approaches a neighborhood organization with an offer of assistance. In such a relationship, open dialogue about why each party might be interested in the other, joint setting of goals, and complete liberty on both sides to terminate the relationship would certainly represent ethically laudable policies, but they would not remove the possibility of manipulation. The fact remains that the church group is making its resources available to one organization rather than another. It thereby facilitates the attainment of the goals associated with that organization and may weaken the influence and bargaining position of competing groups. In cases where there are numerous organizations claiming to represent essentially the same constituency, as among

Puerto Ricans in the United States, the receipt of outside aid may give one contender for leadership considerable advantage over the others. Moreover, since the church group retains ultimate control of the resources provided, it can exercise great leverage in setting goals by the implicit threat of withdrawing its support. It is therefore essential to distinguish between honesty in the process by which an intervention is carried out and the underlying power relationships operating in the situation.

ASSESSMENT OF CONSEQUENCES

A final set of ethical concerns arises from the consequences of a change program—its products as well as its by-products. Questions that might be raised about a specific case include: Who benefits from the change, in both the short and the long run? Who suffers? How does the change affect the distribution of power in the society, for example, between elites and masses, or between competing social groups? What is its impact on the physical environment? Which social values does it enhance and which does it weaken? Does the program create a lasting dependency on the change agent or on some other sponsor? What will its short-term and long-term effects be on the personalities of those involved? Many of these questions can be grouped under the heading of *direct* and *indirect consequences*.

An ethical analysis of the direct consequences, which flow immediately from the substance or contents of the intervention, would relate them to the set of basic values used as criteria for assessing the intervention. This general procedure was followed by the Popula-

tion Task Force of the Institute for Society, Ethics, and the Life Sciences (1971) in its examination of specific proposals for population policy. The core values used in its report were freedom, justice, security/survival, and welfare. Among the specific proposals examined in the light of these values were voluntarist policies, such as providing free birth control information and materials, and penalty programs, including those that would withhold certain social benefits (education, welfare, maternity care) from families with more than a certain number of children.

In brief, the task force concluded that voluntarist policies had the great advantage of either enhancing or at least maintaining freedom and, in certain cases, of promoting the general welfare. At the same time, there was some concern that, under conditions of rapid population growth and preferences for large families, relying only on voluntarist policies might jeopardize the general welfare and possibly survival. Also, questions of justice could be raised if one group in the society was growing at a much faster rate than others. The major ethical drawback of penalty programs, on the other hand, was their possible injustice to those affected. The primary impact of measures such as the withdrawal of educational benefits would be precisely on those who needed them most—the poor. Considerations of justice would also arise if, as is likely, society or the family turned its wrath on the poor creature whose birth order happened to be one more than the stipulated number.

In addition to its direct consequences, almost any change program creates by-products or side effects in areas of society and personality beyond its immediate intentions or scope of influence. These indirect effects must form part of any serious ethical evaluation. Such an evaluation requires a guiding theory of change, of how one part of a system affects another. Unfortunately, many efforts at social intervention completely ignore these systems effects, or discover them too late. Among the most common unanticipated effects are the destruction or weakening of integrative values in the society, change in the balance between aspirations and achievement, and strengthening the power of one group at the expense of another.

One of the latent consequences of many programs of modernization is to undercut or challenge existing values and norms, particularly in rural areas. The introduction of a new road, building of an industrial plant, teaching literacy, or even selling transistor radios may expose isolated villagers to a variety of new stimuli that challenge their traditional world view. Though the direct effects of such programs often serve the values of welfare, justice, and freedom, the indirect effects may generate abundant confusion and a search for new alternatives. Similarly, quasi-coercive population policies, such as penalty programs, can affect societal values in subtle ways. Warwick (1971) points out that they might increase political corruption since some people "may find it more palatable to bribe local enforcement officials than to limit their procreative behavior"; or cynicism about government in general, "in cases where the moral or even political legitimacy of a program was seriously questioned by large segments of the population." Incentive programs that, in effect, bribe people not to have children, may also have undesirable long-term effects, such as "encouragement of the same commercial mentality in other spheres of life. . . . Before experimenting with fi-

nancial incentive programs, therefore, it would be prudent to ask if there are certain goods which we would rather not have bought and sold on the open market, such as one's body, one's vote, and one's personal liberty" (Warwick, 1971, pp. 20–21).

Another common side-effect of change involves a shift in the balance between individual aspirations and the opportunities for achieving them. The delicate ethical question in this case concerns the degree to which a change agent is justified in tampering with aspirations. The dilemma is often severe. On the one hand, to do nothing implies an endorsement of the status quo. On the other hand, in raising aspirations to stir up motivation for change, a program may overshoot its mark. The unintended result may be a rise in frustration. Questions of this type could be raised about the innovative method of literacy instruction developed by Paulo Freire (1971), which attempts to develop not only an ability to read, but also a heightened consciousness of one's position in society and the forces shaping one's destiny. One can certainly argue that this experience enhances the person's freedom. But a change in critical consciousness and political aspirations without a corresponding modification of the social environment may also be a source of profound frustration. Where collective action to change the system is impossible, either because of strong political repression or other barriers to organization, the net effect may be short-term enthusiasm followed by long-term depression. In fact, the experience of having been stimulated and then frustrated may lead to a lower probability of future action than existed before the intervention. One must then ask if it is morally justifiable to raise political aspirations without ensuring that there are opportunities for implementing those aspirations.

A program of social intervention may also have the unintended effect of strengthening the bargaining position of one group *vis-à-vis* another. This problem was well illustrated in a debate at Harvard University in 1969. The focus of the debate was the Cambridge Project, an interuniversity program aimed at developing and testing computer systems for use in the behavioral sciences. The major point of contention was the project's sponsorship by the U.S. Department of Defense. Though the project was not designed to carry out military research or provide other direct services to the sponsor, its connection with the Defense Department aroused considerable concern in the Harvard community. The strongest objection was that acceptance of funds from the Defense Department might increase its involvement in university affairs and broaden its constituency among social scientists. In this way, some felt, the project would reinforce the dominant role of the military in U.S. society and simultaneously weaken the university's capacity for critical analysis of that role. In other words, by accepting a major grant from the Defense Department, Harvard would be lending its institutional prestige to the sponsor, legitimizing the Defense Department's involvement in nonmilitary activities, and perhaps creating pressures within the university to refrain from political dissent. The opponents also argued that a heavy infusion of funds into the area of computer applications would change the ecological balance of social science research within the university. According to this line of reasoning, students and faculty would be drawn to computer-oriented research and away from areas lacking comparable support.

REFERENCES

Bennis, W. G., Benne, K. D., Chin, R., & Corey, K. E. (Eds.). *The planning of change* (3rd ed.). New York: Holt, Rinehart and Winston, 1976.

Blake, J. Population policy for Americans: Is the government being misled? *Science,* 1969, *164,* 522–529.

Callahan, D. Population limitation and manipulation of familial roles. Unpublished manuscript. Hastings-on-Hudson, N.Y.: Institute of Society, Ethics, and the Life Sciences, 1971.

Freire, P. *Pedagogy of the oppressed.* New York: Herder and Herder, 1971.

Gottschalk, L. A., & Pattison, E. M. Psychiatric perspectives on T-groups and the laboratory movement: An overview. *American Journal of Psychiatry,* 1969, *126,* 823–840.

Goulet, D. *The cruel choice.* New York: Atheneum, 1971.

Gustafson, J. M. Basic ethical issues in the bio-medical fields. *Soundings,* 1970, *53*(2), 151–180.

Kelman, H. C. *A time to speak: On human values and social research.* San Francisco: Jossey-Bass, 1968.

Kelman, H. C. The relevance of social research to social issues: Promises and pitfalls. In P. Halmos (Ed.), *The sociology of sociology* (The Sociological Review: Monograph No. 16). Keele: University of Keele, 1970.

Kelman, H. C. The rights of the subject in social research: An analysis in terms of relative power and legitimacy. *American Psychologist,* 1972, *27,* 989–1016.

Lippitt, R., Watson, J., & Westley, B. *The dynamics of planned change.* New York: Harcourt Brace Jovanovich, 1958.

London, P. *The modes and morals of psychotherapy.* New York: Holt, Rinehart and Winston, 1964.

London, P. *Behavior control.* New York: Harper & Row, 1969.

May, R. *Love and will.* New York: Norton, 1969.

Population Task Force of the Institute of Society, Ethics, and the Life Sciences. *Ethics, population, and the American tradition.* A study prepared for the Commission on Population Growth and the American Future. Hastings-on-Hudson, N.Y.: Institute of Society, Ethics, and the Life Sciences, 1971.

Rostow, W. W. *The stages of economic growth.*

New York: Cambridge University Press, 1960.

Skinner, B. F. *Beyond freedom and dignity.* New York: Knopf, 1971.

Warwick, D. P. Freedom and population policy. In Population Task Force, *Ethics, population, and the American tradition.* Hastings-on-Hudson, N.Y.: Institute of Society, Ethics, and the Life Sciences, 1971.

Warwick, D. P. Tearoom trade: Means and ends in social research. *Hastings Center Studies,* 1973, *1*(1), 27–38.

Warwick, D. P. Social scientists ought to stop lying. *Psychology Today,* 1975, 8(9), 38–40, 105–106.

Warwick, D. P., & Kelman, H. C. Ethical issues in social intervention. In G. Zaltman (Ed.), *Processes and phenomena of social change.* New York: Wiley, 1973.

43
The Architecture of Culture and Strategy Change
Rosabeth Moss Kanter

It is hard to imagine anything more frustrating to middle-level corporate entrepreneurs and their teams than doing everything right to develop an innovation, only to have it melt away because higher-level executives fumble their part in the change process—by failing to design and construct the new "platform" to support the innovation.

Corporate change—rebuilding, if you will—has parallels to the most ambitious and perhaps most noble of the plastic arts, architecture. The skill of corporate leaders, the ultimate change masters, lies in their ability to envision a new reality and aid in its translation into concrete terms. Creative visions combine with the building up of events, floor by floor, from foundation to completed construction. How productive change occurs is part artistic design, part management of construction.

All the pieces can be right—new product prototypes already test-marketed, new work methods measured and found effective, new systems and structures piloted in local areas—and still an organization can fail to incorporate them into new responses to changing demands. As General Electric's Vice-President of Corporate Research and Development remarked recently, it does not matter what kinds of highly promising new ideas the company develops in the laboratory: if the overall climate for innovation does not exist throughout the whole organization—a readiness to readjust in response to the changes that use of the innovation will require—it is highly unlikely that even the best ideas will reach the economic mainstream.

The ultimate skill for change mastery works on just that larger context surrounding the innovation process. It consists of the ability to conceive, construct, and convert into behavior a new view of organizational reality.

I find it interesting that organizational theorists have produced much more work, and work of greater depth and intellectual sophistication, on the recalcitrance of organizations and their people—how and why they resist change—than on the change process. Maybe the first is easier, because "change" is an elusive concept. Not only is it notoriously hard to measure accurately—so how do we know when we have one?—but it can connote an abrupt disjunction, a separation of one set of organizational events and activities from others, in a way that does not match reality.

Many kinds of activities or tendencies are present in an organization at any one time. Some of these cohere and are called "the" structure or "the" strategy or "the" culture. But there may be other activities which contradict this core or begin to depart from it. Thus, at another time we could simply reconceptualize what the pattern is, emphasizing some activities in place of others *which may still linger*, and decide that the or-

Source: From *The Change Masters* (pp. 278–306) by Rosabeth Moss Kanter, 1983, New York: Simon & Schuster, Inc. Copyright © 1983 by Rosabeth Moss Kanter. Reprinted by permission of Simon & Schuster, Inc.

ganization has "changed." Indeed, the act of making changes may involve merely reconceptualizing and repackaging coexisting organizational tendencies, as the balance tips from the dominance of one tendency to the dominance of another. The historian Barbara Tuchman once used the image of a kaleidoscope to describe this: when the cylinder is shaken, the same set of fragments form a new picture.

Acknowledging the elusiveness of "change," I use a modest definition of it here, one that stays close to the idea of innovation: Change involves the crystallization of new action possibilities (new policies, new behaviors, new patterns, new methodologies, new products, or new market ideas) based on reconceptualized patterns in the organization. The architecture of change involves the design and construction of new patterns, or the reconceptualization of old ones, to make new, and hopefully more productive, actions possible.[1]

It is important to remember that organizations change by a variety of methods, not all of them viewed as desirable by the people involved. The innovations implemented by entrepreneurial managers by participative methods or those designed and carried out by employee teams may reflect more *constructive* and *productive* methods of change, but they do not exhaust the possibilities, nor are they even typical in organizations with a high degree of segmentation and segmentalism. I catalogued earlier some of the authoritarian ways that segmented organizations introduce change: top-down announcements, rigidly controlled formal mechanisms, and the use of outsiders for whom some of the rules are suspended. Changes may also be brought about by internal political actions: for example, a *"coup d'état,"* in which officials plot to remove the chief executive; a rebellion, in which some members refuse to abide by the directives of the top and act according to their own rules; or a mass movement, in which grass-roots groups of activists mobilize to protest organizational policies or actions.[2]

The choice of methods—participative, authoritarian, or political—may be independent of the source of the pressure for change, although there is a strong likelihood that participative methods will be used when an organization's prime movers see the impetus for change as internally driven, based on choice and responsiveness, rather than externally imposed, based on coercion and resistance. In contrast, in a cascade-down effect, a change demand seen as imposed from without and not embraced by the organization's leaders may be handled in authoritarian or political fashion by the organization. (Both are segmentalist in nature.) To put it another way, organization leaders who are not sure they really want to change—whether in response to market pressures, government regulation, or the actions of competitors—may be more likely to restrict the chance for members to participate in shaping the kinds of changes that could occur, thus missing the opportunity to transfer potential threat into innovation.

The external world surrounding an organization and poking and prodding it in numerous ways is obviously important in stimulating change. But since the "environment" is itself made up of numerous organizations and groups—stakeholders and constituencies—pressing numerous claims, with varying degrees of power, and since a company is made up of numerous action possibilities not always expressed in official policy or strategy at any moment, any assumption of correspondence between what the environment "does" and what the company "does" has to be simple-minded and misleading, especially in the short run. If in the long run there appears to be adjustment by the company in predictable ways, that might be *mutual* adjustment—parties in the environment shifting in response to the organization's actions.[3]

But the fact that the environment is important—and its "discovery" represents one of the important developments for both real organizations and organization theory in the last two decades—does not mean that it "causes" change either automatically or directly.

This is a subtle point. Organizational change is stimulated not by *pressures* from the environment, resulting in a buildup of problems triggering an automatic response, but by the *perceptions* of that environment and those pressures held by key actors. Organizations may not respond to environments so much as "enact" them—create them by the choice to selectively define certain things as important. When an organization tries to "see" its environment, as Cornell social psychologist Karl Weick put it, what might it do to create the very displays it sees? And how might the environment change when it "knows" it is being "watched"?[4]

Clearly, decision makers, via their patterns of attention and inattention, intervene between a company and its environment. And this, of course, means that a company with a diverse group in the "dominant coalition" at the top—more fields and functions represented, more diversity in sex, race, and culture—is more likely to pick up on more external cues, as did the task forces at Honeywell or the management committees at J. C. Penney, than a company with a smaller, more homogeneous set of top decision makers or with a single function—whether finance, marketing, or any other—having disproportionate power to define the appropriate focuses of attention.

Furthermore, even if the "environment" looks objective and real in an industry, so that companies in it share *perceptions* of strategic issues, strategy does not automatically follow, and leaders may sometimes make strategic choices based on their own areas of competence and career payoff, rather than on what the best response might be to the anticipated character of the environment. A chief executive with a financial background might have more knowledge of balance sheets than operations and might get more credit in the press for acquiring and merging than for technical advances in manufacturing methods—and so long-term investment in productivity may be neglected.[5]

Innovation and change, I am suggesting, are bound up with the meanings attached to events and the action possibilities that flow from those meanings. But that very recognition—of the symbolic, conceptual, cultural side of change—makes it more difficult to see change as a mechanical process and extract the "formula" for producing it.

"TRUTH" IS IMPOSSIBLE— AND THEREIN LIES A "TRUTH": ACCOUNTS OF CORPORATE CHANGE

It is hard to tell the "truth" about organizational changes, and thus to learn what "really" makes them happen. I am not referring to something mundane and mechanical like the limits of participant perception and memory, but to rather more profound systematic forces built into the nature of organizational change itself. In understanding why change accounts are often distorted, we understand some important things about the architecture of change itself.

One limitation on the accuracy of models of change and even accounts of specific changes is shared by all historical analysis: the problem of when the clock starts running. In trying to reconstruct how a particular company got from state A to state B, we are also assuming there were a Time I and a Time II. But what is called Time I? Many current models of strategic planning or planned change begin at the point at which strategic decisions were made to seek an alternative course; recognizing a problem, leaders set out to mobilize the search for solutions or to move the organization in an envisioned direction. This, of course, reflects the rational-planning bias so nicely critiqued by business analyst James Brian Quinn on the basis of his examination of important strategic shifts at major companies like General Mills and Texas Instruments.[6] It also reflects a bias toward "official" history—the assumption that only leadership actions "count."

Generally, however, by the time high-level organizational odometers are set at zero to record change, a large number of other—perhaps less public—events have already occurred that set the stage for the "official" decision process, that indeed make it possible, like a successful experiment by a corporate entrepreneur. And still other events may have occurred that contradict the direction of change.

Thus, lack of awareness of this "prehistory" of change makes any conclusions about how a particular organization managed a change suspect, to say the least, and perhaps impossible to replicate elsewhere, a point to which I shall return. Most of us—and corporate actors are no exception—begin the recording of "history" at the moment at which we become conscious of our own strategic actions, neglecting the groundwork already laid before we became aware of it. What seems to us the "beginning" is, in another sense, a midpoint of a longer process, and not seeing this "prehistory" we may not understand the dynamism of the process already in motion, and we may be haunted later by some of its ghosts. Or we may try to repeat someone else's success based on his/her account of what he/she did "first," as I have seen many companies do, finding that little of it works, because the supposed "first step" was in reality preceded by a large number of other events that set the stage but go unreported because no "intelligent strategy" was involved.

In conceiving of a different future, change masters have to be historians as well. When innovators begin to define a project by reviewing the issues with people across areas, they are not only seeing what is possible, they may be learning more about the past; and one of the prime uses of the past is in the construction of a story that makes the future seem to grow naturally out of it in terms compatible with the organization's culture.

The architecture of change thus requires an *awareness of foundations*—the bases in "prehistory," perhaps below the surface, that make continued construction possible. And if the foundations will not support the weight of what is about to be built, then they must be shored up before any other actions can take place.

I see this repeatedly in the work of innovators and in my own involvement as consultant to change efforts. A new plant manager at Honeywell eager to move worker involvement into his plant, for example, tried to get the workers interested in quality circles or other forms of team participation, to no avail. When he stopped trying to "begin" and looked into the history of the plant, he found repeated instances of violations by management of promises to the workers to improve such comfort factors as the noise level and the intermittently broken air-conditioning system. Here the foundation was a negative one, and trust was low. So the manager had to reset his clock, give up on fast action, and go back; he fulfilled earlier promises, repaired the facilities, in order to build the trust to permit his innovation in worker involvement to take place.

But often the foundations enabling innovations to occur are positive ones: some experience with similar events that provides at least some skilled, knowledgeable people; a history of joint planning by the leaders who are going to have to act as a team to manage the innovation; preexisting relationships of cooperation and trust cross segments involved in the change. Changes really "start" there. If those foundations do not exist, they have to be constructed first, and if they do exist, they may need to become part of the story that is told about the change, because foundations not only make change possible, they also provide security and stability—"grounding"—in the midst of it.

The complicated question of "beginning" is only one issue that can distort change accounts. The other is more subtle and complex: the *rewriting of corporate history* is often part of the innovation-and-change process itself.

The actual events in a change sequence (as seen by a detached on-the-spot observer) may seem very different from how they are rendered in retrospective public accounts, especially "official" ones.[7] The reconstruction itself serves important organizational purposes. For example, if the changes are ones that require many people's support to implement, then we are likely to see these well-intentioned "distortions" in official accounts:

Individuals disappear into collectives. What was initiated and pushed by one person may be redefined, because the person was successful in involving others and getting them to take ownership, as the will and the act of the group.

For example, one of my high-level corporate informants was concerned that I not make him too central in one of the accomplishments I recount or give him too much credit as an individual, because he pushed new concepts through the system by working with others to make them feel they had initiated and owned the change—"planting seeds" and then letting the harvest be reaped collectively. For organizational purposes, the whole group had done it, and to assert otherwise would be destructive of the new reality that had been built together. There was another striking example of this in the development of Data General's important new computer by several teams of engineers under the leadership of Thomas West. Though West had put the project together virtually singlehanded, one of his chief lieutenants predicted: "When this is all over there are gonna be thirty inventors of the Eagle machine. . . . Tom's letting them believe that they invented it. It's cheaper than money."[8]

In American companies, this transformation smooths power relations. The use of "power" is made possible partly by the power user's tacit agreement to keep his or her power invisible once others have agreed to participate. Others' participation may be contingent on a feeling that they are involved out of commitment or conviction—not because power is being exercised over them. Successful innovators know this, and so they often downplay their own role in an accomplishment in official organizational communications in favor of credit's going to the whole team. Or they spend time "convincing" their subordinates and giving them a piece of the action even if they could in fact apply visible power.

Early events and people disappear into the background as later events and people come forward. I saw this repeatedly in the course of managerial innovations. The account of a change at any particular moment has to feature most prominently those actors whose actions are most immediately connected to the foundations of the next necessary development. And so the earlier people and events may appear to be forgotten—not because memory fades with time, but because there is little to be gained in terms of continuing the momentum of the change by remembering them.

A Polaroid product-testing manager who worked for many months laying the groundwork for persuading the company to replace the product it was to display at a prominent site allowed the marketing group to take the credit and let his own role recede because he knew that they were the ones who would be taking what he had done further; the story now had to feature them and their work. Similarly, after West's computer design team at Data General managed the remarkable achievement of a superior machine in record time, their long months of intensive effort were turned into just a few occasional words in accounts of the development of the product; once it existed, other groups—manufacturing, sales—needed to take up more room in the story. And as far as I can tell, West seemed comfortable with this, understood it as part of the nature of innovation and change.

Conflicts disappear into consensuses. Just as in the treaties after a war, "losers" may disappear into allies. Pain, suffering, trauma, and resistance may disappear into "necessary evils." What was highly contentious at the time eventually gets worked out, and the price of the final agreement is to forget that conflict had existed, as in political systems where the final vote has to be unanimous despite the acrimony of the debate. The organizational memory, at least, cannot afford grudges, especially in integrative systems; segmentalist ones seem to nurse old wounds longer. One gets cooperation by agreeing to save the face of those who were critical or opposed and not embarrass them by reminding them of it. And the survivors of pain and trauma may, in their turn, agree to forget in exchange for some of the benefits of the change.

Equally plausible alternatives disappear into obvious choices. To get commitment and support for a course of action may require that it appear essential—not as one of a number of possibilities. By the time a decision is announced, it may need to be presented as the *only* choice, even if there are many people aware of how much debate went into it or how many other options looked just as good.

The announcers—the champions of the idea—have to look unwaveringly convinced of the rightness of their choice to get other people to accept the change. Unambivalent and unequivocal communication—once a variety of alternatives have been explored—provides security. One CEO of my acquaintance is not particularly good at this; he presents decisions about new procedures tentatively, expressing ambivalence about the favored option in the light of plausible alternatives—and others say to themselves, "If *he* isn't convinced, then why should we do anything about this?" The consequence is that change is stalled; no one ever does seem to get around to using the new procedures.

Accidents, uncertainties, and muddle-

headed confusions disappear into clear-sighted strategies. There is a long philosophic tradition arguing that action precedes thought; a "reconstructed logic" helps us make sense out of events, and they always sound more strategic and less accidental or fortuitous later. Some analysts are even willing to go so far as to say that organizations formulate strategy *after* they implement it.[9]

But the importance of defining a clear direction, even if one is already almost at the destination, is to build commitment by reducing the plausibility of other directions, to reinforce the pride people take in the intelligence of the system, or to reward those leading the pack by crediting their vision, to remove any lingering doubts about what the direction is, and to signal to critics that the time for opposition is over. Thus, it may be organizationally important to present the image of strategy in the accounts that are constructed whether or not this rational model conveys the "truth." For the innovators to get the coalition to chip in with investments, for example, they have to feel that the entrepreneur knows what he or she is doing; strategic plans are one of those symbols which are highly reassuring to investors.[10]

Multiple events disappear into single thematic events. How a story about change is constructed also comes to reflect what the organization needs to symbolize, what images it wishes to create or preserve, what lessons it wants to draw to permit the changes to be reinforced or the next actions to be taken. Sometimes this reflects the preservation of power: e.g., creating the appearance that the leader did something that was really the result of a great deal of behind-the-scenes staff work, eliminating the messy events and focusing on the outstanding success, or telling about only the times when the leaders showed their commitment to quality of work life and ignoring the times they did not. Sometimes this simply reflects the human reality that too much complexity and detail cannot be grasped and remembered easily and thus interferes with a clear conception of what the situation now *is*. So a large number of things that might have occurred are reduced to just a few critical ones which tell a story that gives people a common image of what is now the right thing to do.

The fragility of changes (that exist alongside the residues of the old system) disappear into images of solidity and full actuality. Multiple organizational tendencies, including contradictory ones, often coexist, but these are ignored in favor of insistence that an innovation has taken hold simply because it exists at all. In some companies, this helps reward the innovators, builds commitment, and disarms the critics. But in others, where innovation is still threatening even when successful and productive, I suspect that this represents a kind of collective sigh of relief that "now we've done it; we don't have to think about change anymore"; some organizations are too ready to believe that all the hard work is over when *one* example is in place.

As if all these "distortions" were not enough, the organization's culture also influences the stories that must be constructed about change. Some prefer to submerge changes into continuity; others like to turn continuities into change. I have pointed out that segmented organizations may promote change-aversiveness and, thus, a preference for denying that major change has occurred. This makes it easy, of course, for the rest of the system to avoid adjusting in response; if the official story says that nothing much has happened any differently from what the system already knew, then no one has to move out of the safety of his or her segment.

On the other hand, change-embracing organizations like "Chipco" that pride themselves on entrepreneurship may do just the opposite: deny continuity and prefer to cast a large number of events—even those not particularly innovative—as "changes." At Chipco, credit went to originators, not to initiators; so people were pressed to claim "change" even when what they were doing was not greatly different, and people were consequently a little less able to build on one another's innovations than at other innovating companies.

There are tactical uses to these ways of constructing change, too. For example, announcing "change!" in one part of an organization's world to make clear the need for change in others is a stimulus to action in a way that stressing continuity is not. It is a power move, used well by leaders of social movements to rally the troops as well as by corporate staffs to influence the line organization. And younger people invoke change to show the older ones in power that their wisdom no longer fits, and they should step aside. In contrast, in "cultures of age," denial of change preserves the power of the establishment.

All of this tells us something important about the essence of the change process: *Organizational change consists in part of a series of emerging constructions of reality, including revision of the past, to correspond to the requisites of new players and new demands.* Organizational history *does* need to be rewritten to permit events to move on. (In a sense, change is partly the construction of such reconstructions.) To use a physical analogy: as each floor of a building is built, the supports need to be made invisible to

permit focusing on the important current thing—the *use* of the space. Similarly, as an innovator "sells" each member of her coalition on the worth of her project, the influence process and perhaps even the origin of the idea may have to be "forgotten" and not revealed outside the group to permit attention to go to the people whose role is critical now. Official histories of changes, reports about projects, and even the way organization members tell one another about what happened to move the system from A to B always serve a present function.

The art and architecture of change, then, also involves *designing reports about the past to elicit the present actions required for the future*—to extract the elements necessary for current action, to continue to construct and reconstruct participants' understanding of events so that the next phase of activity is possible. "Power" may need to remain less than fully visible; "prime movers" may need to make sure others are equally credited; room at center stage may need to be given over to those people and activities that are now necessary to go on from here—e.g., the marketing people instead of the product developers becoming the "heroes" of the account.

Change masters should understand these phenomena and work with them; they should know how to create and use myths and stories.[11] But we should not confuse the results—an official, retrospective account of organizational actions—with lessons about guiding organizational change. We need to understand what goes on behind and beyond official accounts, to create models that are closer to events-as-they-happened than to events-as-they-are-retold.

In short, those who master change know that they can never tell the "truth," but they also know what the "truth" is. In their actions they exhibit knowledge at both levels, recapturing those aspects of a change process which have faded or disappeared in official accounts and rational models. Thus:

- Where groups or organizations appear to "act," there are often strong individuals persistently pushing.
- Where recent events seem the most important in really bringing the change about, a number of less obvious early events were probably highly important.
- Where there is apparent consensus, there was often controversy, dissent, and bargaining.
- Where the ultimate choice seems the only logical one, unfolding naturally and inevitably from what preceded it, there were often a number of equally plausible alternatives that might have fitted too.
- Where clear-sighted strategies are formulated, there was often a period of uncertainty and confusion, of experiment and reaching for anyone with an answer, and there may have been some unplanned events or "accidents" that helped the strategy to emerge.
- Where single leaders or single occurrences appear to be the "cause" of the change, there were usually many actors or many events.
- Where an innovation appears to have taken hold, there may be contradictory tendencies in the organization that can destroy or replace it, unless other things have occurred to solidify—institutionalize—the change.
- And where there appears to be only continuity, there was probably also change. Where there appears to be only change, there was probably also continuity.

These realizations constitute part of the "architecture" of change. But there are also a set of building blocks that together constitute the structure behind the process of change.

THE BUILDING BLOCKS OF CHANGE: FROM INNOVATION TO INSTITUTIONALIZATION

It is important to see how micro-innovations and macro-changes come to be joined together, how major change is constructed out of the actions of numerous entrepreneurs and innovators as well as top decision makers.

"Breakthrough" changes that help a company attain a higher level of performance are likely to reflect the interplay of a number of smaller changes that together provide the building blocks for the new construction. Even when attributed to a single dramatic event or a single dramatic decision, major changes in large organizations are more likely to represent the accumulation of accomplishments and tendencies built up slowly over time and implemented cautiously. "Logical incrementalism," to use Quinn's term, may be a better term for describing the way major corporations change their strategy:

The most effective strategies of major enterprises tend to emerge step-by-step from an iterative process in which the organization probes the future, experiments, and learns from a series of partial (incremental) commitments rather than through global formulations of total strategies. Good managers are aware of this process, and they consciously intervene in it. They use it to improve the information available for decisions and to build the psychological identification essential to successful strategies. . . . Such logical incrementalism is not "muddling," as most people understand that word. . . . [It] honors and utilizes the global analyses inherent in formal strategy formulation models [and] embraces the central tenets of the political or power-behavioral approaches to such decision making.[12]

An organization's "total" strategy is defined by the interaction of major subsystem strategies, each reflecting the unique needs, capacities, and power requirements of local units. Even when it is impossible to fully guide the organization from the top—i.e., predict in advance how these units will evolve—the right kinds of integrative mechanisms, including communication between areas, can ensure the coordination among these substrategies and micro-innovations that ultimately results in a company's strategic posture. In short, effective organizations benefit from integrative structures and cultures that promote innovation below the top and learn from them.

This kind of analysis of change provides a link between micro-level and macro-level innovation: the actions of numerous managerial entrepreneurs and problem-solving teams, on one hand, and on the other the overall shift of a company's direction to better meet current challenges. The buildup of experiences from successful small-scale innovations—or even the breakthrough idea that an innovator's work produces, in the case of new products or new technological processes—can then be embraced by those guiding the organization as part of an important new strategy.

In short, action first, thought later; experience first, making a "strategy" out of it second. Strategy may not so much drive structure as exist in an interdependent relationship with it.[13] In many cases new structural possibilities out of experiments by middle-level innovators make possible the formulation of a new strategy to meet a sudden external challenge of which even the middle-level innovators might have been unaware. Then the new strategy, in effect, elevates the innovators' experiments to the level of policy.

I see a combination of five major building blocks present in productive

corporate changes, changes that increase the company's capacity to meet new challenges.

Force A. Departures from Tradition

First, activities occur, generally at the grass-roots level, that deviate from organizational expectations. Either these are driven by entrepreneurial innovators, or they "happen" to the organization in a more passive fashion.[14]

Some departures may be random or chance events reflecting "loose coupling" in the system—i.e., no one does everything entirely according to plan even if he or she intends to, and slight local variations on procedures may result in new ideas. They may be the result of "accidents"—i.e., events occur for which there is no contingency plan, or the organization's traditional sources are exhausted, so the company innovates by default, turning to a new idea or a new person just to fill a gap. Or a "hole" in the system may open up because another change is taking place: a changeover of bosses leaving a temporary gap, a new system being installed that does not yet work perfectly. All these constitute the "unplanned opportunities" that permit entrepreneurs to step forward even in highly segmented, noninnovating companies; they may work best at the periphery, in "zones of indifference" where no one else cares enough to prevent a little occasional deviance. The ideas or experiences resulting from deviant events then constitute "solutions looking for problems"[15]—models that can be applied elsewhere.

In innovating companies, in contrast to their less receptive counterparts, a high proportion of these departures from tradition are brought about through the actions of entrepreneurs who seek to move beyond the job-as-given. They may be stimulated by a plan, in the form of an assignment, but they may also be invented by the entrepreneur in response to cues he or she is getting that suggest there is a problem to be solved. As I have shown, there will be more such initiative-taking innovators in an organization with a large number of integrative mechanisms that provide incentives for initiative and make it easy to grab power. The presence of many integrative mechanisms also makes it more likely that the innovation will succeed, producing immediate payoff.

Departures from tradition provide the organization with a *foundation in experience* to use to solve new problems as they arise or to replace existing methods with more productive ones. This foundation in experience suggests the possibility of a new strategy—one that could not be developed as easily without the existence of organizational experiences. At the same time, those experiences condition the direction of any new strategies. In effect, it is hard to see where you want to go until you have a few options, but those options do not limit later choices.

One lesson is straightforward: an organization that wants to innovate to stay ahead of change should be just loosely enough controlled to promote local experiments, variations on a plan. It should make it easy for ambitious innovators to grab the power to experiment—within bounds, of course. It is those variations—sometimes more than the plan itself—which may be the keys to future successes. And there need to be enough experiments for organizational policymakers to have choices when it comes to reformulating strategies. This constitutes the internal equivalent of a "diversified portfolio" for turbulent times.

There is another important value

that successful experiments or small-scale innovations have for the change process: they prove the organization's capacity to take productive action. An unfortunate number of change efforts seem to begin with the negative rather than the positive: a catalogue of problems, a litany of woes. But identification of potential, description of strengths, seems to be a better—and faster—way to begin. In my own experience helping corporations develop new modes of operating, I have found it valuable to look for the already existing innovations that signal ability to make the shift, and then to use these as the organization's own foundation for solving its problems and designing a better system. Exemplars—positive innovations—are better to highlight than trouble spots when one is trying to move a whole system.

But deviant events do not by themselves produce major change. Large systems are capable of containing many contradictions, many departures from tradition that do not necessarily affect the organization's central tendency. As in the case of the Petrocorp Marketing Services Department, innovations can easily disappear.

"Deviant" events result in overall change only under one or more of these circumstances: Perhaps enough similar instances of the event or idea accumulate slowly over time so that at some point, definition of the organization's central tendency changes in response to the new reality—a very slow process. (But these are much more common in integrative than segmentalist organizations.) Or, as a second possibility, the organization has mechanisms for the transmission of positive innovations to other sectors which might take advantage of them—e.g., informal or formal communication mechanisms for cross-fertilization. Or, finally, impending crisis or obvious problems that cannot be solved by traditional means lead the organization to search for a solution to grab, and so the deviant idea is pushed forward. The first circumstance is too slow and leaves too much to chance for today's competitive business environment. The second circumstance is more characteristic of high-innovation organizations than of noninnovating ones. But the crisis factor is central to major changes at both ends of the spectrum.

Force B. Crisis or Galvanizing Event

The second set of forces in the change process involves "external" ones, changes elsewhere that appear to require a response. By external-in-quotes I mean that they do not necessarily come from outside the organization—e.g., a lawsuit, an abrupt market downturn, the oil embargo, a competitor's new-product introduction—but may also be events within an organization's borders that are outside current operating frameworks—e.g., a new demand from a higher-level official, a change of technology, a recognition of change in the work force. The change-stimulating-change chain is one reason it is so hard to develop an orderly model of the change process; overlapping events intrude on one another. What is "external" to any change sequence we are trying to describe—or *manage*—may be the A force (tradition departure) or C force (strategic decision) in some other change sequence.

The critical point for the people involved is that the event or crisis has a demand quality and seems to require a response. If the crisis is defined as insoluble by traditional means, or if traditional solutions quickly exhaust their value, or if the external parties pushing indicate that they will not be satisfied by the same old response—then a nontraditional solution may be pushed forward. One of the grass-roots experiments or local innovations may be grabbed.

I propose that organizations with segmentalist approaches to problems will be less "externally" responsive. A tendency to isolate problems—more accurately, pieces of problems—in segmented subunits, and a reluctance on the part of each subunit to admit to being unable to handle its piece adequately, will result in less ability to perceive earlier crises before they add up to full-blown disasters. The "seen it all before" syndrome in a culture of age may result in few things being seen as "crises." Danger signals may simply not be attended to as events requiring response. And even if one unit—perhaps assigned to scan a particular part of the environment—sees the signs, there may be few mechanisms for transmitting this information to other units, or for getting others to cooperate in a response. Thus, perception may be restricted, and so may action.

On the other hand, integrative approaches may mean that an organization "sees" more galvanizing events in general and "sees" them earlier. A tendency to tie problems to larger wholes is one aspect of this. Rather than writing off potential external problems, an organization characterized by this approach may instead see small crises as symptomatic of larger dangers and prepare earlier preventive responses. Since information flows more freely across integrative structures, and since the culture encourages identification with larger units and issues rather than smaller units and specialties, it is easier for the signals of "external" change seen by one part of the system to be added to those seen by others, helping to define a "crisis" demanding response. In addition, the culture of change we saw in innovating companies may promote in people the desire to define events as "crises" that can be used to mobilize others around the search for an innovative response.

While I have generally refrained in this book from making comparisons to Japanese management, there is one generalization worth mentioning. MIT sociologist Eleanor Westney has found that large-scale Japanese organizations are prone to identify crises with what seems to the Western observer to be almost hysterical rapidity. Despite a decade of rising circulation for the national press, for example, Japanese newspapers have been finding "indicators" in demographic developments of an impending "newspaper crisis" in Japan, and using it to galvanize marketing strategies.[16]

At the same time, effective response to crisis may depend on the tradition-departure factor. That is, the organization already has in hand the possibility for a response with which it has experience, and thus it can move much faster to make the changes the crisis seems to demand. Thus, random departures from tradition that had occurred almost by accident, it seemed, helped General Motors respond quickly and innovatively to a number of crises facing its industry in the 1970s, as we shall see in the next chapter.

But neither deviance nor crisis alone guarantees changes without the next two conditions in place: leadership for making strategic decisions in favor of change and creating an orderly plan, and individuals with enough power to act as "prime movers" pushing for the implementation of changes once the decision has been made.

Force C. Strategic Decisions

At last we get to the point in the process familiar in most of the "change management" or "strategic planning" literature. This is the point at which leaders enter, and strategies are devel-

oped that use Force A to solve the problems inherent in Force B. A new definition of the situation is formulated, a new set of plans, that lifts the experiments of innovators from the periphery to center stage, that reconceptualizes them *as* the emergent tradition rather than as departures from it.

The notion at Chipco that leaders *select* strategy in part from among solutions developed from grass-roots efforts, rather than defining it in total in advance and thus constraining innovation, is only a more explicit and consciously designed example of the way much positive change seems to take place. It is just that the prior existence of Force A and Force B often goes unacknowledged in official accounts of change or in technical models of planning.

While "strategic" is clearly an overused word, and many companies are dropping it as an automatic modifier to "planning," it does express an important idea for this part of the change process: deliberate and conscious articulation of a direction. Strong leaders articulate direction and save the organization from change via "drift." They create a vision of a possible future that allows themselves and others to see more clearly the steps to take, *building on present capacities and strengths, on the results of Force A and Force B,* to get there.[17]

If one can never get the leaders together to do that kind of strategy formulation, to build on a set of innovations, then it is likely that the innovations will drift away. Or that so many kinds of innovations will float by that none of them will even gain the momentum and force to take hold. But what makes the leaders ready to engage in this formulation is the experience the organization has already had.

It may be more accurate to speak of a series of smaller decisions made over time than a single dramatic strategic decision, but I am stressing the symbolic aspects of strategy after events are already in motion. Thus, there may be key meetings at which a critical piece of what later became "the" strategy was formulated, a plan or mission statement generated that articulated a commitment, or an important "go-ahead" directive issued. For example, though it is hard to identify a *single* strategic-decision point in the case of General Motors' decision to downsize its fleet of cars, there were clear turning-point events. One was the executive-committee decision in December 1973 to speed downsizing of the fleet, at both the high and low ends. At Chipco's "Chestnut Ridge" plant and in various Honeywell divisions with change programs, the key event was formulation of explicit strategy by the executive steering committee, thus legitimizing earlier actions and permitting new ones to take place at greater speed. Thus, leaders' articulation of what may have been only embryonic up to that point represents "change" to the organization. Such leader action is important to crystallize change potential once departures from tradition have given the organization some experience with the new way.

Not surprisingly, more integrative systems have an advantage here too. More entrepreneurs, pushing more innovations, create pressure to do something with them. More overlaps and communication channels and team mechanisms keep more ideas circulating. And the existence of teams at the top, drawing together many areas and exchanging ideas among them—as contrasted with segmented officials running fiefdoms—are in a better position to engage in forward planning to tie together external circumstances and grass-roots experience. The preexistence of coalitions and cooperative traditions makes it easier to get moving; precious time

does not have to be expended forming the coalitions that will make the strategic decisions.

Of course, as we saw earlier in the contrast between Chipco and General Electric Medical Systems, innovating organizations can sometimes try to keep so many possibilities alive that they avoid strategic decisions, avoid strong leadership that imposes focusing mechanisms to promote some actions over others. The key is to allow a continual creative tension between grass-roots innovation in a free-wheeling environment and periodic strategic decisions by strong central leaders.

So now new strategies are defined that build new methods, products, structures, into official plans. The crystallized plans serve many purposes other than the obvious, as Karl Weick has pointed out:

> Plans are important in organizations, but not for the reasons people think. . . . Plans are symbols, advertisements, games, and excuses for interactions. They are *symbols* in the sense that when an organization does not know how it is doing or knows that it is failing, it can signal a different message to observers. . . . Plans are *advertisements* in the sense that they are often used to attract investors to the firm. . . . Plans are *games* because they often are used to test how serious people are about the programs they advocate. . . . Finally, plans become *excuses for interaction* in the sense that they induce conversations among diverse populations about projects that may have been low priority items.[18]

In short, strategic decisions help set into motion the next two major forces in "change."

Force D. Individual "Prime Movers"

Any new strategy, no matter how brilliant or responsive, no matter how much agreement the formulators have about it, will stand a good chance of not being implemented fully—or sometimes, at all—without someone with power pushing it. We have all had the experience of going to a meeting where many excellent ideas are developed, everyone agrees to a plan, and then no one takes any responsibility for doing anything about it, and again the change opportunity drifts away. Even assigning accountabilities does not always guarantee implementation if there is not a powerful figure concerned about pushing the accountable party to live up to it. Hence the importance of the corporate entrepreneur who remains steadfast in his or her vision and keeps up the momentum of the action team even when its effort wanes, or of a powerful sponsor of "idea champion" for innovations that require a major push beyond the actions of the innovating team. Empowering champions is one way leaders solidify commitment to a new strategy.[19]

Prime movers push in part by repetition, by mentioning the new idea or the new practice on every possible occasion, in every speech, at every meeting. Perhaps there are catchphrases that become "slogans" for the new efforts; John De Butts, the former AT&T chairman, used to repeat "the system is the solution" and built it into Bell's advertising, and Tom Jones, the CEO of Northrup, liked to reiterate, "everybody at Northrup is in marketing."[20] At Honeywell, then-President (now Vice-Chairman) James Renier instituted the "Winning Edge Program," a remarkably long-lasting corporatewide motivation program, and the slogan "We are the Winning Edge" has found its way onto everything from memo pads to coffee mugs. It is currently fashionable to draft "corporate philosophies" or compile lists of seven or eight "management principles" which stimulate the executive team and sometimes employee groups, to discuss the key phrases that represent a shared vision, phrases that can then be tacked on every wall and woven into every speech.

What is important about such communications is certainly not that they rest on pat phrases but that they are part of unequivocal messages about the firm commitment of the prime movers to the changes. It is easy for the people in the company to make fun of the slogans if they are unrelated to other actions or not taken seriously by the leaders themselves. Prime movers pushing a new strategy have to make clear that they *believe* in it, that it is oriented toward getting something that they want, because it is good for the organization. They might, for example, visit local units, ask questions about implementation, praise efforts consistent with the thrusts. The personal tour by a top executive is an important tool of prime movers.

This is especially important for changes that begin with pressures in the environment and were not sought by the corporation—changes in response to regulatory pressures, shifts to counter a competitor's strategy. The drive for change must become internalized even if it originated externally, or prime movers cannot push with conviction, and the people around them can avoid wholehearted implementation. I have seen numerous instances of this around affirmative action, for example; those companies where prime movers found a way to see the changes as meeting *organizational* needs and convey an unwavering commitment have a better track record with respect to women and minorities than places with weak or equivocating leadership.

People in organizations are constantly trying to figure out what their leaders *really* mean—which statements or plans can be easily ignored and which have command value. Leaders say too many things, suggesting too many courses of action, for people to act on all of them. Thus, prime movers have to communicate strategic decisions forcefully enough, often enough, to make their intentions clear, or they can run into the problems that arise when zealous subordinates, trying to interpret vague statements from the top, take strong action in the *wrong* direction. I call this the *"Murder in the Cathedral* problem,"* after T. S. Eliot's play. The drama, set in 1170, describes the events that followed when King Henry II of England said idly, not clearly meaning it, that he wished someone could get rid of that "pesky priest." His aides promptly slaughtered Thomas à Becket in Canterbury Cathedral, and Henry spent the rest of his life doing penance. How many other unintended or even wrongful acts have occurred in organizations because leaders were unclear about what they really wanted—or didn't want?

A few clear signals, consistently supported, are what it takes to change an organization's culture and direction: signposts in the morass of organizational messages. The job of prime movers is not only to "talk up" the new strategy but also to manipulate those symbols which indicate commitment to it. The devices which can be used to signal that organizational attention is redirected include such mundane tools as: the kinds of reports required, what gets on the agenda at staff meetings, the places at which key events are held, or the reporting level of people responsibile for the new initiatives.[21] At one high-tech company the CEO shook his executives out of their customary modes of thought by staging an elaborate hoax. The annual executive conference began at the usual place with a rather long-winded recital of standard facts and figures by the CEO himself. His soporific speech was interrupted after an hour by the arrival of helicopters, which flew the whole group to another, more remote

place where the "real" meeting began— still punctuated by surprises like elephants on the beach—with the theme of creativity and change.

A few events can have symbolic value far beyond their statistical importance; General Motors' commitment to quality of work life in cooperation with the United Auto Workers, for example, was signaled by such events as the promotion of Alfred Warren, long associated with programs in furtherance of that commitment, to the vice-presidency of industrial relations and the presence of Irving Bluestone, a UAW leader, as a speaker at a major executive conference. At Honeywell, a set of embryonic innovation-producing practices such as employee problem-solving task teams picked up speed when the general manager, Richard Boyle, who had decided to personally chair the steering committee, rearranged a crowded calendar to be present at every meeting and hooked up a speakerphone so that an operations head at a remote level could also "attend" the meetings.

Prime movers push—but to complete the process they need ways to embody the change in action.

Force E. Action Vehicles

The last critical force for guiding productive change involves making sure there are mechanisms that allow the new action possibilities to be expressed. The actions implied by the changes cannot reside on the level of ideas, as abstractions, but must be concretized in actual procedures or structures or communication channels or appraisal measures or work methods or rewards.

"The map is not the territory," philosophers warn us—but we cannot even begin to find our way around the territory to the people with whom we must interact *without* a map. This is not quite an obvious point—or at least, not obvious to all managers. I have seen too many ideas adopted by organizations as matters of policy while members at lower levels scratch their heads wondering what this means they should *do*. Quality of work life and participative management themselves often suffer from this syndrome: official endorsement and prime movers pushing, but no new vehicles to support change. Sophisticated proponents of QWL often decry the reduction of the concept to its manifestations in particular programs ("QWL is more than just a quality circle, it is a principle"), but without the specific vehicles it may be impossible to realize the principle. Organizations always have to steer a course between the need for an identity to the change expressed in concrete actions and the danger of falling into faddism or isolation of the practice as "just another campaign that will pass in time."

The problem is not the association of an idea with a program, but rather the existence of *too few* programs expressing the idea. Changes take hold when they are reflected in multiple concrete manifestations throughout the organization. After all, people's behavior in organizations is shaped by their place in structures and by the patterns those structures imply. It is when the structures surrounding a change also change to support it that we say that a change is "institutionalized"—that it is now part of legitimate and ongoing practice, infused with value and supported by other aspects of the system.

"Institutionalization" requires other changes to support the central innovation, and thus it must touch, must be integrated with, other aspects of the organization.[22] If innovations are isolated, in segmentalist fashion, and not allowed to touch other parts of the organization's structure and culture, then it is likely that the innovation will never

take hold, fade into disuse, or produce a lower level of benefits than it potentially could.

The first step, of course, is that something has to work; premature diffusion of an innovation is a mistake some companies make—trying to solidify something before it has proved its value. The new practices implied by an innovation need to produce results and a success experience for the people using them. Then the new practices can become defined and known to people. They take on an identity and perhaps a name, balancing the dangers of faddism with the need for identity. People can see their presence, recognize their absence, attribute results to them, and evaluate their use.

A number of integrative actions can help weave the innovation into the fabric of the organization's expected operations. Changes in training and communication are important. People need to learn how to use or incorporate the new structure or method or opportunity. This is aided by training for any new skills required, help provided for people to make the transition—why companies with successful employee-involvement programs invest so much in consultants and training, as Chipco did at Chestnut Ridge. Then communication vehicles (e.g., conferences, networks, informal visits) spread information about them, help transfer experiences from earlier users to newer ones. At Honeywell a variety of conferences, floating resources (staff available from a Center), training tapes, brochures, and traveling road shows are spreading the idea of participative management.

Furthermore, it is important that rewards change to support the new practices. Successes in using them get publicity and recognition or maybe even formal rewards, like the way parallel-organization participation was written into job descriptions and appraisals at Chipco. This can mean the development of measures of their use and accountability for doing so—e.g., in performance appraisals. (At Nashua Corporation, for example, the CEO made participation in a quality program the criterion for 20 percent of the bonus in 1980 and 50 percent in 1981.) Leaders or prime movers have to demonstrate that they want the changes and continue to push for them even when it looks as if things might slide back. In successful change efforts there is a continuing series of reinforcing messages from leaders, both explicit and symbolic. And individuals find that using the new practices clearly creates benefits for them: more of something they have always wished they could have or do.[23]

Other structures and patterns also need to change to support the new practices: the flow of information, the division of responsibilities, what regular meetings are held and who comes to them, the composition of teams, and so forth. Furthermore, incorporation of innovations is further aided when people are encouraged to look for broader applications, so that the new practices move from being confined to a few "experimental" areas off to the side to being broadly relevant to tasks of all sorts.

All of these ways of embodying change in the structure create *momentum* and critical mass: more and more people use the new practices, their importance is repeated frequently and on multiple occasions. It becomes embarrassing, "out-of-sync," not to use them.

It is also possible to go even further to build strength into the change that has been constructed. For example, new practices can become "contractual": a written or implied guarantee to customers, a written or implied condition of work in the organization, etc. They

can become a basis for the selection of people for work in the organization: Can they use the new practices? Do they fit with the new posture? And there can be mechanisms for educating new people who enter the organization in the practices. By this time, the practices are no longer "new" but, rather, simply "the way we do things around here."

The "failure" of many organizational change efforts has more to do with the lack of these kinds of integrating, institutionalizing mechanisms than with inherent problems in an innovation itself.[24] We have seen that some very positive innovations, as in the case of the Petrocorp Marketing Services Department project, are never taken advantage of because of oversegmentation and hence, overisolation of the innovation. Some new product or technological process ideas are never developed, as in the small steel company that sold an ultimately important invention to the Japanese rather than exploiting it—to its later regret. And even in innovations embraced by the organization as important strategies, like the QWL effort at General Motors, neighboring systems may not change to support them, such as selection systems, reward systems, and extension to other kinds of tasks (salaried workers or middle managers).

In short, innovations are built into the structure of the organization when they are made to touch—and change— a variety of supporting systems. But the action vehicles also need to be derived from a good theory, in order to avoid the "roast pig" problem.

The "Roast Pig" Problem

Pervading the time of institutionalizing innovations, when leaders want to ensure that their benefits can be derived repeatedly, is the nagging question of defining accurately the practice or method or cluster of attributes that is desired. Out of all the events and elements making up an innovation, what is the core that needs to be preserved? What *is* the essence of the innovation? This is a problem of theory, an intellectual problem of understanding exactly *why* something works.

I call this the "Roast Pig" problem after Charles Lamb's classic 1822 essay "A Dissertation on Roast Pig," a satirical account of how the art of roasting was discovered in a Chinese village that did not cook its food. A mischievous child accidentally set fire to a house with a pig inside, and the villagers poking around in the embers discovered a new delicacy. This eventually led to a rash of house fires. The moral of the story is: when you do not understand how the pig gets cooked, you have to burn a whole house down every time you want a roast-pork dinner.

The "Roast Pig" problem can plague any kind of organization that lacks a solid understanding of itself. One striking example comes from a high-technology firm I'll call "Precision Scientific Corporation." Precision grew steadily and rapidly from its founding to a position of industry preeminence. To the founders, many of whom still manage it, this success is due to a strongly enterpreneurial environment and an equally strong aversion to formal bureaucratic structures. But recently, growth has slackened, margins are down, competition is up, and Precision is even beginning to contemplate cutting back the work force. Increasingly Precision's leaders have the feeling that something needs to be done, but cannot agree on what it should be.

One obvious issue at Precision is waste and duplication. For example, there are a dozen nearly identical model shops on the same small site, neighboring operating units have their own systems for labeling and categorizing parts, and purchases tend to be haphazard and uncoordinated. But although this is well known, and although a number of middle-level "entrepreneurs" surface from time to time with systems innovations to solve the problems, the leaders express considerable reluctance to change anything. So each wave of good ideas for operational improvements that washes up from the middle goes out again with the tide.

The reason is simple: Roast Pig. Precision senior executives have been part of a very successful history, but they do not seem to fully understand that history. They have no theory to guide them. They do not act as though they knew exactly which aspects of the culture and structure they have built are critical, and which could profitably and safely be modified. They are afraid that changing *anything* would begin to unravel *everything*, like a loosely knit sweater. In the absence of a strong theory, they feel compelled to keep burning down the houses, even though house costs are rising and other villages are reputed to have learned new and less expensive cooking methods.

In many companies, management practices are much more vulnerable to the Roast Pig problem than products, because the depth of understanding of technology and markets sometimes far exceeds the understanding of organizational behavior and organizational systems. So among a dozen failures to diffuse successful work innovations were a number that did not spread because of uncertainty or confusion about what the "it" was that was to be used elsewhere.[25] Or I see "superstitious behavior," the mindless repetition of unessential pieces of a new practice in the false belief that it will not work without them—e.g., in the case of quality circles which companies often burden with excessive and unnecessary formulas for their operation from which people become afraid to depart.

Beliefs may indeed help something work, but beliefs can also be modified by information and theory. The consequences of failing to perform this intellectual task are twofold: first, as one innovation gets locked rigidly into place, further experimentation may be discouraged—house burning may become so ritualistic that the search for other cooking methods is stifled; and perhaps more important, the company may waste an awful lot of houses.

The other extreme also poses problems, of course: reductionism, or the stripping down to apparent "essentials," thus missing some critical piece out of the cluster of elements that makes the innovation work. This fallacy of understanding also needs to be corrected by theory and analysis. As usual, the issue is balance between inclusion of unnecessary rituals and the elimination of key supports.

Thus, the task of conceptualization is as important at the "end" of a change sequence, when the time comes to institutionalize an innovation, as it was at the beginning. Behind every institutionalized practice is a theory about why things work as they do; the success and efficiency of the organization's use of the practice depend on the strength of that theory.

THE VISIONS AND BLUEPRINTS OF CHANGE MASTERS

It has become fashionable among organizational-behavior theorists to apply the word "art" to management practice, setting it up in opposition to the idea of "technique." Thus, Richard Pascale and Anthony Athos speak of the "art" of Japanese management, covering a range of human sensibilities and sensitivities quite different from the analytic skills taught in business schools. "Great companies make meaning," they said, showing us that leadership deals with values and superordinate goals and not merely with technical matters. Warren Bennis has made a similar point in his discussion of the "artform" of leadership; leadership involves creating larger visions and engaging people's imaginations in pursuit of them. Even discussions of corporate strategic planning are beginning to stress the intuitive side, the artful crafting of an image of possibilities out of the materials provided by organizational subunits—dealing in symbols, creating coalitions with shared understandings, building comfort levels. Indeed, among the most popular models of the policymaking process today are those which focus on "accident" of circumstance more than rationality or even intelligent intuition; decision makers are shown as "muddling through" instead of rationally calculating.[26]

Such discussions add an important dimension to our understanding of how to guide organizations to achieve higher levels of success. They clearly do not replace the need for rational, analytic techniques such as budgets; reporting and control systems; objective setting and reviews; financial, production, and related quantitative measures; market analyses and environmental scans; and other tools in the modern manager's bag. But the role of such tools has to be seen in perspective. They are part of the management of ongoing operations, keeping the organization on course. They may even suggest areas where changes or improvements are necessary, and they provide the data to back up the argument and get a change effort moving. But overused to guide organizations, they may also stifle innovation, reduce creativity, and prevent organizations from benefiting from the departures from plan that produce entirely new strategies.

The art and architecture of change works through a different medium than the management of the ongoing, routinized side of an organization's affairs. Most of the rational, analytic tools *measure what already is* (or make forecasts as a logical extrapolation from data on what is). But change efforts have to *mobilize people around what is not yet known*, not yet experienced. They require a leap of imagination that cannot be replaced by reference to all the "architect's sketches," "planner's blueprints" or examples of similar buildings that can be mustered. They require a leap of faith that cannot be eliminated by presentation of all the forecasts, figures, and advance guarantees that can be accumulated.

"Do the right thing," Chipco tells its people; but who ever really knows in advance what that is, if change is involved? A comment by Charles L. Brown, Chairman of the Board of AT&T, a company now facing a dramatically new environment, is revealing in this respect: "I think we can do the internal job [of changing] without fear of failure, once we're given some decent understanding of what is expected of us. But the complexity of trying to change ourselves, when we don't know what the future rules are going to be, injects a degree of uncertainty that creates a lot of anxiety."[27]

Blueprints and forecasts are important tools and should be provided as much and as frequently as possible. But they are only approximations, and they may be modified dramatically as events unfold. And they are fundamentally different from the emotional appeal—the appeal to human imagination, human faith, and sometimes human greed—that needs to be made to get people on board. And of course, to the extent that change efforts raise concerns about loss and displacement—the negatives that people can easily imagine—architects of change also have to take these issues into account. They have to manage the politics and the anxiety with inclusive visions that give everyone a sense of both the direction of action and their piece of it.[28]

Thus, it is not surprising that I find myself concentrating on the symbolic or conceptual aspects of the change process—on new understandings, on the communication of those, and then on the inevitable reformulations as events move forward. The architects of change have to operate on a symbolic as well as a practical level, choosing, out of all possible "truths" about what is happening, those "truths" needed at the moment to allow the next step to be taken. They have to operate integratively, bringing other people in, bridging multiple realities, and reconceptualizing activities to take account of this new, shared reality. I know exactly how managers feel who come into a meeting with an excellent plan reflecting long hours of toil, only to find it reshaped by their colleagues in small respects even when there are no major flaws; I have been disquieted when my "perfect" proposal for a participative team has been revised by that very team. Here's the paradox: there needs to be a plan, and the plan has to acknowledge that it will be departed from.

In short, the tools of change masters are creative and interactive; they have an intellectual, a conceptual, and a cultural aspect. Change masters deal in symbols and visions and shared understandings as well as the techniques and trappings of their own specialties.

Thus, those of us interested in promoting change should be wary of excessively logical "how-to" approaches, whether in the form of strategic-planning models or that of other one-two-three guides. Those kinds of models can be extremely useful as a discipline and a structure for discussions resulting in plans—I say this not as a throwaway line but out of my own experience running top-executive strategy sessions. But they fit only one piece of the change process and, by themselves, provide no guarantee that action will *fit* the plans. Many companies, even very sophisticated ones, are much better at generating impressive plans on paper than they are at getting "ownership" of the plans so that they actually guide operational activities. Instead of a formal model of change, then, or a step-by-step rational guide, an outline of patterns is more appropriate and realistic, a set of guiding principles that can help people understand not how it *should* be done but how to understand what might fit the situation they are in.

Perhaps a key to the use of others' experience with change—indeed, a key to the process of innovation itself—is to learn to ask questions rather than assume there are preexisting answers, to trust the process of operating in the realm of faith and hope and embryonic possibility. Repeating the past works fine for routine events in a static environment, but it runs counter to the ability to change. What an innovating organization does is open up action possibilities rather than restrict them and thus trusts to faith as well as formal plans. A well-managed innovating organization clearly has plans—mission, strategies, structure, central thrust, a preference for some activities/products/markets over others—but it also has a willingness to reconceptualize the details and even sometimes the overarching frameworks on the basis of a con-

tinual accumulation of new ideas—innovations—produced by its people, both as individuals and as members of participating teams.

Change masters are—literally—the right people in the right place at the right time. The *right people* are the ones with the ideas that move beyond the organization's established practice, ideas they can form into visions. The *right places* are the integrative environments that support innovation, encourage the building of coalitions and teams to support and implement visions. The *right times* are those moments in the flow of organizational history when it is possible to reconstruct reality on the basis of accumulated innovations to shape a more productive and successful future.

The concepts and visions that drive change must be both inspiring and realistic, based on an assessment of that particular corporation's strengths and traditions. Clearly there is no "organizational alchemy" capable of transmuting an auto company into an electronics firm; there is only the hard work of searching for those innovations which fit the life stage and thrust of each company. But all companies can create more of the internal conditions that empower their people to carry out the search for those appropriate innovations. And in that search might lie the hope of the American economic future.

NOTES

1. As the noted anthropologist Clifford Geertz commented, "What we call our data are really our own constructions of other people's constructions of what they or their compatriots are up to . . . Explanation often consists of substituting complex pictures for simple ones while striving somehow to retain the persuasive clarity that went with the simple ones." Geertz, *The Interpretation of Cultures*, New York: Oxford, 1975. For a similar perspective in a larger context see Peter Berger and Thomas Luckmann, *The Social Con-*

struction of Reality, Garden City, N.Y.: Anchor Books, 1967.

2. Mayer N. Zald and M. A. Berger, "Social Movements in Organizations," *American Journal of Sociology,* 83 (1978): 823–61.

3. William H. Starbuck, "Organizations and Their Environments," in M. D. Dunnette, ed., *Handbook of Industrial and Organizational Psychology,* Chicago: Rand McNally, 1976, pp. 1069–1123.

4. Karl Weick, *The Social Psychology of Organizing,* second edition, Reading, Mass.: Addison Wesley, 1979, especially page 178.

5. Robert J. Litschert and T. W. Bonham, "Strategic Responses to Different Perceived Strategic Challenges," *Journal of Management,* 5 (1979): 91–105. Robert H. Hayes and William J. Abernathy, "Managing Our Way to Economic Decline," *Harvard Business Review,* 58 (July–August 1980): 67–77.

6. James Brian Quinn, *Strategies for Change: Logical Incrementalism,* Homewood, Ill.: Richard D. Irwin, 1980.

7. Howard Aldrich called my attention to research by Baruch Fischoff on reinterpreting the past. He shows, through experiments, that people cannot disregard what they already know about something, when it comes to constructing an explanation about why something happened in the past. That is, once they know the outcome, people build stories which lead, inevitably, to that outcome. The researchers investigated this by altering historical outcomes, using cases most people don't know much about. They took real historical data, and simply changed the outcome of some series of events. When people were asked to estimate the probability with which they could have successfully predicted the outcome of the events, given knowledge only of the past, they constantly overestimated their ability to successfully predict. They also, in writing up stories about the justification of their prediction, were able to put together a very coherent and compelling story line. Of course, they were historically wrong! See Fischoff, "For Those Condemned to Study the Past . . ." in D. Kahneman, P. Slovic, and A. Tversky, eds., *Judgment Under Uncertainty,* New York: Cambridge University Press, 1982.

8. Tracy Kidder, *The Soul of a New Machine,* Boston: Atlantic–Little Brown, 1981.

9. Weick, *The Social Psychology of Organizing,* pp. 158, 165. The philosopher Abraham Kaplan is associated with this position.

10. For arguments about the symbolic functions of various aspects of organizational structure, see John W. Meyer and Brian Rowan, "Institutionalized Organizations: Formal Structure as Myth and Ceremony," *American Journal of Sociology,* 83 (July 1977): 340–63.

11. It has become fashionable to urge the management of organizational myths and stories. See Ian I. Mitroff and Ralph H. Kilmann, "Stories Managers Tell: A New Tool for Organizational Problem Solving," *Management Review,* July 1975; David M. Boje, Donald B. Fedor, and Kendrith M. Rowland, "Myth Making: A Qualitative Step in OD Interventions," *Journal of Applied Behavioral Science,* 18 (1982): 17–28.

12. Quinn, *Strategies,* p. 58.

13. Weick, *Social Psychology of Organizing.*

14. The idea of random or planned deviance setting a change cycle in motion is consistent with the idea that organizational, like human, evolution begins with "variations," as captured in what has become known as the "population ecology" model. This is well explicated in Howard Aldrich, *Organizations and Environments,* Englewood Cliffs, N.J.: Prentice-Hall, 1979. I am suggesting that the evolutionary view is useful but requires a cognitive model of conscious and directed human action to flesh it out.

15. Michael D. Cohen, James March, and Johan P. Olsen, "A Garbage Can Model of Organizational Choice," *Administrative Science Quarterly,* 17 (1972): 1–25.

16. Eleanor Westney, personal communication, based on her research for her forthcoming book, *Organization Development in Meiji Japan.*

17. For a similar idea see Richard D. Beckhard and Reuben Harris, *Organizational Transitions: Managing Complex Change,* Reading, Mass.: Addison-Wesley, 1977.

18. Weick, *Social Psychology of Organizing.*

19. See Modesto A. Mardique, "Entrepreneurs, Champions, and Technological Innovation," *Sloan Management Review,* 21 (Winter 1980). Edward Roberts of the Sloan School at MIT is one of the first innovation researchers to identify the im-

portance of champions; there is also a similar idea in Quinn, *Strategies*.

20. Thomas J. Peters, "Symbols, Patterns, and Settings: An Optmistic Case for Getting Things Done," in H. J. Leavitt, L. R. Pondy, and D. M. Boje, *Readings in Managerial Psychology*, 3rd ed., Chicago: University of Chicago Press, 1980.

21. See Peters, *ibid.*, for other examples.

22. For an account of one of the most elaborate attempts at institutionalizing a system for organizational strategy and change by tying it to every unit—Texas Instruments' OST system—see Mariann Jelinek, *Institutionalizing Innovation*, New York: Praeger, 1979.

23. In a recent study of a large number of employee-involvement programs, one of the strongest predictors of new-program adoption was the staff's expectation of benefits. Philip H. Mirvis, "Assessing Factors Influencing Success and Failure in Organizational Change Programs," in S. Seashore, E. Lawler, P. Mirvis, and C. Cammann, eds., *Observing and Measuring Organizational Change*, New York: Wiley, in press.

24. In evolutionary theory ("population ecology") this is a "failure of retention." See Aldrich, *Organizations and Environments*.

25. Richard Walton, "The Diffusion of New Work Structures: Explaining Why Success Didn't Take," *Organizational Dynamics*, 4 (Winter 1975): 3–21.

26. Richard Pascale and Anthony Athos, *The Art of Japanese Management*, New York: Simon and Schuster, 1980. Warren Bennis, *More Power to You*, New York: Doubleday, forthcoming. Quinn, *Strategies*. Charles E. Lindblom, "The Science of Muddling Through," *Public Administration Review*, 19 (1959): 78–88. Cohen, March, and Olsen, "Garbage Can Model."

27. "Conversation with Charles L. Brown," *Organizational Dynamics*, 11 (Summer 1982): 28–36.

28. David Nadler includes politics and anxiety as two of his three key tasks of change management. The third is control: ensuring ongoing organizational maintenance while change is still in process. His solution to politics is the use of teams and visionary leaders; to anxiety, a clear vision; and to control, breaking the change down into a series of smaller, shorter, and thus more manageable transitions. Nadler, "Managing Transitions to Uncertain Future States," *Organizational Dynamics*, 11 (Summer 1982): 37–45. Noel Tichy has provided a full picture of the political-management tasks in change efforts in his *Managing Strategic Change*, New York: Wiley, 1983.